TEST ITEM FILE

PRINCIPLES OF
MACROECONOMICS

TEST ITEM FILE

Timothy C. Duy
University of Oregon

FIFTH EDITION

PRINCIPLES OF
MACROECONOMICS

CASE & FAIR

Prentice Hall, Upper Saddle River, NJ 07458

Acquisitions Editor: *Rod Banister*
Associate Editor: *Gladys Soto*
Production Editor: *Joseph F. Tomasso*
Formatter: *BookMasters, Inc.*
Manufacturer: *Bawden Printing*

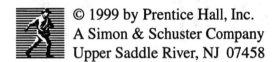

© 1999 by Prentice Hall, Inc.
A Simon & Schuster Company
Upper Saddle River, NJ 07458

Printed in the United States of America

10 9 8 7 6 5 4 3 2 1

ISBN 0-13-095739-9

Prentice-Hall International (UK) Limited, *London*
Prentice-Hall of Australia Pty. Limited, *Sydney*
Prentice-Hall Canada Inc., *Toronto*
Prentice-Hall Hispanoamericana, S.A., *Mexico*
Prentice-Hall of India Private Limited, *New Delhi*
Prentice-Hall of Japan, Inc., *Tokyo*
Simon & Schuster Asia Pte. Ltd., *Singapore*
Editora Prentice-Hall do Brasil, Ltda., *Rio de Janiero*

Contents

Preface

This test item file has been revised to accompany *Principles of Macroeconomics,* 5th edition by Karl Case and Ray Fair. The questions in the test item file were written to closely match the material as it is presented in the textbook. The same terminology, notation, and definitions that are used in the textbook are used in the test item file. Students will not be able to legitimately complain that the questions in the test item file bear no resemblance to the material they read in the text. Selected chapters, new to this edition, have been completely rewritten by Ken Parzych of Eastern Connecticut State University. The remaining chapters were carefully revised and rereferenced by Pamela Barter and Michele Fitzpatrick of O'Donnell & Associates.

Questions in the test item file allow an instructor to test his or her student's ability to define economic concepts, tie economic concepts to the real world, interpret graphs, analyze the effects of economic policies, and solve numerical problems. There are approximately 100 multiple choice, 10 true-false, and 10 short-answer essay questions for each chapter. The questions are page referenced and are presented in sequential order. There are enough questions available so that instructors can construct numerous exams over the same chapters without reusing questions over and over again.

Each question is coded for level of difficulty—easy, moderate, and challenging. Easy questions involve straightforward recall of information in the text. Moderate questions require some analysis on the student's part. Challenging questions usually entail more complex analysis and may require the student to go one step further than the material presented in the text.

Questions are also classified as Fact, Definition, Single, and Multi. A question labeled Fact tests the student's knowledge of factual information presented in the text. A Definition question asks the student to define an economic concept. A question classified as Single requires the student to use a single-step analytical process to answer the question. A question coded as Multi requires the student to use a multi-step analytical process to answer the question. For these questions the student needs to think through more than one relationship to answer the question.

This test item file contains numerous questions based on graphs. The test item file includes examples of all of the graphs that students have seen in the textbook. The questions ask the student to interpret the information that is presented in the graph. There are also many questions in the test item file that are not referenced to a graph, but which require students to sketch out a graph on their own to be able to answer the question. The test item file also includes tables and a series of questions asking students to solve for numerical values, such as profit or equilibrium output.

An instructor using this test item file will be able to test a student's knowledge of economic concepts on many different levels. An instructor can test students for their recall of economic concepts, as well as their ability to apply these economic concepts to real-world situations.

In addition to the bank of questions in the test item file, Real World Problem Sets are also offered with Case and Fair, *Principles of Macroeconomics,* 5th edition. This new ancillary features analytical problem sets that nicely complement the multiple choice, true-false, and short-answer essay questions found here. Numerous strong tests can be built that combine both ancillaries.

The Scope and Method of Economics

1.1: The income distribution is too skewed to the rich in the United States. This statement is best described as a

(a) positive statement.
(b) Marxist ideology.
(c) normative statement.
(d) descriptive economics statement.

Moderate
Application
Page: 8

Answer: (c)

1.2: High taxes have the effect of reducing the incentive of some individuals to work. This statement is best described as a

(a) positive statement.
(b) Marxist ideology.
(c) normative statement.
(d) descriptive economics statement.

Moderate
Application
Page: 8

Answer: (a)

1.3: The Commerce Department announced that economic growth rose by one half of a percentage point. This statement is best described as a

(a) positive statement.
(b) Marxist ideology.
(c) normative statement.
(d) descriptive economics statement.

Moderate
Application
Page: 8

Answer: (d)

1.4: Firms that are not concerned with the environment in the end only exploit their workers and the individuals who buy their products. This statement is best described as a

(a) positive statement.
(b) Marxist ideology.
(c) normative statement.
(d) descriptive economics statement.

Moderate
Application
Page: 8

Answer: (c)

1.5: The amount of education that one has is an important factor in the determination of his or her wage rate. This statement is best described as a

(a) positive statement.
(b) Marxist ideology.
(c) normative statement.
(d) descriptive economics statement.

Moderate
Application
Page: 8

Answer: (a)

Easy
Definition
Page: 14

1.6: The output of one large firm is compared to that of several smaller firms. Which of the following criteria should be used in each of the following situations?

(a) efficiency.
(b) equity.
(c) growth.
(d) stability.

Answer: (a)

Easy
Definition
Page: 14

1.7: In recent years, technological improvements in the United States have come less frequently than technological improvements in Japan. Which of the following criteria should be used in each of the following situations?

(a) efficiency.
(b) equity.
(c) growth.
(d) stability.

Answer: (c)

Easy
Definition
Page: 14

1.8: Rent control laws are imposed in a city because landlords have been exploiting tenants. Which of the following criteria should be used in each of the following situations?

(a) efficiency.
(b) equity.
(c) growth.
(d) stability.

Answer: (b)

Easy
Definition
Page: 14

1.9: High rates of unemployment in the 1970s gave workers a concern for their job security that was not present in the 1960s. Which of the following criteria should be used in each of the following situations?

(a) efficiency.
(b) equity.
(c) growth.
(d) stability.

Answer: (d)

Easy
Definition
Page: 14

1.10: A voluntary trade is made between two individuals that makes each one better off. Which of the following criteria should be used in each of the following situations?

(a) efficiency.
(b) equity.
(c) growth.
(d) stability.

Answer: (a)

1.11: Redistribution from the rich to the poor is achieved from a tax system that requires taxes to rise with income. Which of the following criteria should be used in each of the following situations?

Easy
Definition
Page: 14

(a) efficiency.
(b) equity.
(c) growth.
(d) stability.

Answer: (b)

1.12: Whenever the Democrats gain control of the Congress, spending on social programs increases; whenever Republicans gain control of the Congress, spending on defense increases. Hence, we know what the next party in control will do. This statement is an example of

Difficult
Application
Page: 12

(a) fallacy of inductive reasoning.
(b) post hoc, ergo propter hoc fallacy.
(c) fallacy of composition.
(d) ceteris paribus fallacy.

Answer: (b)

1.13: I have lived in a house on the ocean for many years and have never seen a hurricane. Therefore, there is no reason for anyone to buy flood insurance. This statement is an example of

Difficult
Application
Page: 12

(a) fallacy of composition.
(b) post hoc, ergo propter hoc fallacy.
(c) fallacy of inductive reasoning.
(d) ceteris paribus fallacy.

Answer: (a)

1.14: The economy had been expanding during all of the years that I was a student, but as soon as I graduated, the economy contracted. Therefore, the labor market was waiting to contract until I started looking for a job. This statement is an example of

Difficult
Application
Page: 12

(a) ceteris paribus fallacy.
(b) post hoc, ergo propter hoc fallacy.
(c) fallacy of composition.
(d) fallacy of inductive reasoning.

Answer: (b)

1.15: Experimental research in small cities suggests that mandating work for welfare recipients increases their income. Therefore, we should mandate work requirements for all welfare recipients. This statement is an example of

Difficult
Application
Page: 12

(a) fallacy of inductive reasoning.
(b) ceteris paribus fallacy.
(c) fallacy of composition.
(d) post hoc, ergo propter hoc fallacy.

Answer: (c)

Difficult
Application
Page: 12

1.16: The number of crimes is greater in large cities because there are more cars and, as a consequence, homeowners are away more often than those who live in small cities. This statement is an example of

(a) fallacy of division.
(b) ceteris paribus fallacy.
(c) fallacy of composition.
(d) post hoc, ergo propter hoc fallacy.

Answer: (d)

Easy
Definition
Page: 2

1.17: Which of the following is the best definition of economics?

(a) The study of how individuals and societies choose to use the scarce resources that nature and previous generations have provided.
(b) The study of how consumers spend their income.
(c) The study of how business firms decide what inputs to hire and what outputs to produce.
(d) The study of how the federal government allocates tax dollars.

Answer: (a)

Easy
Fact
Page: 2

1.18: Which of the following statements is INCORRECT?

(a) Economics is a behavioral science.
(b) In large measure, economics is the study of how people make choices.
(c) If poverty were eliminated there would be no reason to study economics.
(d) Economic analysis can be used to explain how both individuals and societies make decisions.

Answer: (c)

Moderate
Fact
Page: 2

1.19: The study of economics

(a) is a very narrow endeavor.
(b) is a way of analyzing decision-making processes caused by scarcity.
(c) is concerned with proving that capitalism is better than socialism.
(d) focuses on how a business should function.

Answer: (b)

Easy
Fact
Page: 2

1.20: Which of the following is a reason to study economics?

(a) to understand society
(b) to understand global affairs
(c) to be an informed voter
(d) all of the above

Answer: (d)

Challenging
Single
Page: 2

1.21: The concept of opportunity cost

(a) is relevant only for a capitalist economy like the United States.
(b) suggests all our wants can be achieved.
(c) would be irrelevant if we eliminated poverty.
(d) suggests a major increase in public health-care spending means an expansion in other areas will be harder to achieve.

Answer: (d)

1.22: Sunk costs are

(a) costs that cannot be avoided, because they have already been incurred.
(b) the costs of what we give up when we make a choice or a decision.
(c) the additional costs of producing an additional unit of a product.
(d) the additional costs of consuming an additional unit of a product.

Answer: (a)

Easy
Definition
Page: 3

1.23: You purchased a ticket to a concert for $30 a month ago. Last week someone invited you to a party on the same night as the concert. You would much rather go to the party than the concert. You have tried unsuccessfully to sell the concert ticket. Which of the following statements regarding this situation is correct?

(a) The $30 you paid for the concert ticket is relevant to the decision, since this represents the opportunity cost of attending the party.
(b) You should base your decision on whether or not the party will provide you with more than $30 in satisfaction.
(c) The $30 concert ticket should be irrelevant in your decision making, since it is a sunk cost.
(d) The $30 concert ticket should be irrelevant in your decision making, since it represents the marginal cost of attending the party.

Answer: (c)

Challenging
Single
Page: 3

1.24: You have decided that for Halloween you wanted to dress up as Batman. You estimated that it would cost $25 to purchase all the pieces of the costume. After spending $20 on the costume you realize that the additional pieces you need will cost you $15 more. The marginal cost of completing the costume is

(a) $5.
(b) $10.
(c) $15.
(d) $20.

Answer: (c)

Moderate
Single
Page: 3

1.25: The concept of opportunity cost

(a) is relevant only to economics.
(b) can be applied to the analysis of any decision-making process.
(c) applies to consumers but not to firms.
(d) refers only to actual payments and incomes.

Answer: (b)

Moderate
Fact
Page: 3

1.26: Opportunity cost is

(a) that which we forgo, or give up, when we make a choice or a decision.
(b) a cost that cannot be avoided, regardless of what is done in the future.
(c) the additional cost of producing an additional unit of output.
(d) the additional cost of buying an additional unit of a product.

Answer: (a)

Easy
Definition
Page: 3

Easy
Fact
Page: 3

1.27: The reason that opportunity costs arise is that

(a) an economy relies on money to facilitate exchange of goods and services.
(b) resources are scarce.
(c) there are no alternative decisions that could be made.
(d) people have unlimited wants.

Answer: (b)

Moderate
Single
Page: 3

1.28: A retired individual decides to spend the day golfing. The opportunity cost of this decision

(a) is zero, since the individual is retired and is not forgoing any income to spend the day golfing.
(b) is equal to cost of the golf outing.
(c) equals the cost of the golf outing plus the value of the individual's alternative use of time.
(d) is best measured by using the wage rate this individual earned prior to retirement.

Answer: (c)

Moderate
Single
Page: 3

1.29: Which of the following is NOT an opportunity cost of attending college?

(a) The tuition you pay.
(b) The income you could have earned if you didn't attend college.
(c) The alternative uses of the time you spend studying.
(d) The cost of the food that you consume while you are attending college.

Answer: (d)

Moderate
Single
Page: 3

1.30: If you own a building and you decide to use that building to open a restaurant,

(a) there is no opportunity cost of using this building for a restaurant because you own it.
(b) there is an opportunity cost of using this building for a restaurant because it could have been used in other ways.
(c) there are no sunk costs involved in this decision.
(d) the only cost relevant to this decision is the price you paid for the building.

Answer: (b)

Moderate
Single
Page: 3

1.31: You own a videotape of Beauty and the Beast. The opportunity cost of watching Beauty and the Beast for the second time

(a) is zero.
(b) is one-half the cost of the videotape, since this is the second time you have watched it.
(c) is the value of the alternative use of the time you spend watching the videotape.
(d) cannot be calculated.

Answer: (c)

1.32: A light rail system connecting two cities was originally thought to cost $20 million. After building part of the system at a cost of $15 million, the government realized that the total cost of the system would be $26 million, not $20 million. At this point, the MARGINAL cost of completing the light rail system is best estimated as

Challenging
Single
Page: 3

(a) $5 million.
(b) $6 million.
(c) $11 million.
(d) $26 million.

Answer: (c)

1.33: That which we forgo, or give up, when we make a choice or decision is called the _____ cost of that decision.

Moderate
Definition
Page: 3

(a) sunk
(b) marginal
(c) real
(d) opportunity

Answer: (d)

1.34: Costs that cannot be avoided, regardless of what is done in the future, because they have already been incurred are

Easy
Definition
Page: 3

(a) total costs.
(b) sunk costs.
(c) marginal costs.
(d) allocative costs.

Answer: (b)

1.35: The common expression which describes the efficient markets hypothesis is

Easy
Single
Page: 3

(a) no use crying over spilt milk.
(b) there's no such thing as a free lunch.
(c) sunk costs are sunk.
(d) correlation does not imply causation.

Answer: (b)

1.36: A market in which profit opportunities are eliminated almost instantaneously is

Easy
Definition
Page: 3

(a) a laissez-faire market.
(b) a capitalist market.
(c) a socialist market.
(d) an efficient market.

Answer: (d)

1.37: According to the efficient market hypothesis, as information becomes less costly and more easily available , this should

Moderate
Fact
Page: 3

(a) make markets more efficient.
(b) make markets less efficient.
(c) increase profit opportunities.
(d) increase the opportunity cost of acquiring more information.

Answer: (a)

**Challenging
Single
Page: 3**

1.38: Which of the following statements is most consistent with the efficient markets hypothesis?

(a) "It is not difficult to make money because profitable opportunities abound."
(b) "Hot tips from your stock broker should be acted on because the profit opportunities will be very long lasting."
(c) "Profit opportunities are rare because there are many people searching for such opportunities."
(d) "The bond market, but not the stock market, is very likely to be a source of profit opportunities."

Answer: (c)

**Easy
Definition
Page: 3**

1.39: An efficient market is a market

(a) that is always in equilibrium.
(b) in which profit opportunities are eliminated almost instantaneously.
(c) in which profits are always very high and persistent.
(d) in which opportunity costs are zero.

Answer: (b)

**Easy
Definition
Page: 7**

1.40: The branch of economics that examines the functioning of individual industries and the behavior of individual decision-making units is

(a) positive economics.
(b) normative economics.
(c) macroeconomics.
(d) microeconomics.

Answer: (d)

**Moderate
Single
Page: 7**

1.41: The study of why a person may decide to go to medical school instead of accepting a $30,000 a year job would be considered

(a) public finance.
(b) industrial organization.
(c) macroeconomics.
(d) microeconomics.

Answer: (d)

**Moderate
Single
Page: 7**

1.42: Studying how the management of US Steel, a large steel-producing company, decides how many tons of steel to produce and the price to charge for its steel would be considered

(a) descriptive economics.
(b) empirical economics.
(c) microeconomics.
(d) macroeconomics.

Answer: (c)

**Moderate
Single
Page: 7**

1.43: Studying how Mary allocates her time between work and leisure is an example of

(a) macroeconomics.
(b) microeconomics.
(c) industrial organization.
(d) descriptive economics.

Answer: (b)

1.44: The study of how wages are set for public-school teachers would be considered

(a) microeconomics.
(b) macroeconomics.
(c) descriptive economics.
(d) institutional economics.

Moderate
Single
Page: 7

Answer: (a)

1.45: Macroeconomics is the branch of economics that examines

(a) the economic behavior of aggregates - income, employment, and output - on a national scale.
(b) the functioning of individual industries and the behavior of individual decision-making units, that is, business firms and households.
(c) ways to understand behavior and the operation of systems without making judgments.
(d) outcomes of economic behavior, evaluates them as good or bad, and prescribes preferred courses of action.

Easy
Definition
Page: 7

Answer: (a)

1.46: A study of how increases in the corporate income tax rate will affect the national unemployment rate is an example of

(a) macroeconomics.
(b) descriptive economics.
(c) microeconomics.
(d) normative economics.

Moderate
Single
Page: 7

Answer: (a)

1.47: A study of whether or not employers discriminate against women by paying them lower wages and assigning them to lower-level positions than men would be in the area of

(a) industrial organization.
(b) microeconomics.
(c) law and economics.
(d) macroeconomics.

Moderate
Single
Page: 7

Answer: (b)

1.48: The branch of economics that examines the economic behavior of aggregates such as income and employment is

(a) positive economics.
(b) microeconomics.
(c) macroeconomics.
(d) normative economics.

Easy
Single
Page: 7

Answer: (c)

1.49: Inflation and unemployment

(a) are the focus of economic history.
(b) arc the focus of microeconomics
(c) are the focus of positive economics.
(d) are the focus of macroeconomics.

Moderate
Single
Page: 7

Answer: (d)

Moderate
Single
Page: 7

1.50: A study of the impact of an economic stimulus package on the number of jobs created in the economy would be considered

(a) microeconomics.
(b) macroeconomics.
(c) industrial organization.
(d) descriptive economics.

Answer: (b)

Challenging
Single
Page: 8

1.51: Which of the following is an example of a normative statement?

(a) People under six feet tall are the best stock brokers.
(b) There should be no unemployment in an advanced industrial society.
(c) Higher prices cause consumers to buy less.
(d) Equilibrium price implies that quantity demanded equals quantity supplied.

Answer: (b)

Easy
Definition
Page: 8

1.52: Positive economics is an approach to economics that

(a) seeks to understand behavior and the operation of systems without making judgments.
(b) analyzes outcomes of economic behavior, evaluates them as good or bad, and may prescribe preferred courses of action.
(c) applies statistical techniques and data to economic problems.
(d) examines the role of government in the economy.

Answer: (a)

Easy
Definition
Page: 8

1.53: Normative economics is an approach to economics that

(a) seeks to understand behavior and the operation of systems without making judgments.
(b) analyzes outcomes of economic behavior, evaluates them as good or bad, and may prescribe preferred courses of action.
(c) applies statistical techniques and data to economic problems.
(d) examines the role of government in the economy.

Answer: (b)

Moderate
Single
Page: 8

1.54: Which of the following is an example of a positive statement?

(a) The federal government should be required to have a balanced budget.
(b) Local governments ought to impose rent controls to allow people to afford housing.
(c) Studies indicate that the imposition of a minimum wage increases unemployment.
(d) The government should impose taxes on imported goods to protect the jobs of American workers.

Answer: (c)

Moderate
Single
Page: 8

1.55: Which of the following is a normative question?

(a) Should the government provide health insurance for any individual who cannot afford it?
(b) What will happen to the speed with which new drugs are developed if the government places price controls on prescription drugs?
(c) Why is the infant mortality rate higher in the United States than in most other developed countries?
(d) Will physicians' incomes increase or decrease if national health insurance is instituted in the United States?

Answer: (a)

1.56: Which of the following is a normative question?

(a) Why do gasoline prices increase before holiday weekends?
(b) What will happen to gasoline consumption if excise taxes on gasoline are increased?
(c) To reduce the regressivity of the gasoline excise tax, should a portion of the gasoline excise tax paid by low-income individuals be refunded to them?
(d) How will oil exploration be affected if the government imposes price controls on gasoline?

Answer: (c)

Moderate
Single
Page: 8

1.57: Which of the following is a positive question?

(a) Will the level of teenage unemployment increase if the minimum wage is increased?
(b) Should the minimum wage be set at one-half the average manufacturing wage to guarantee individuals a decent standard of living?
(c) Wouldn't it be more equitable if the minimum wage increased automatically with the cost of living?
(d) Wouldn't it be better to try to increase people's wages through job-training programs than by requiring employers to pay minimum wages?

Answer: (a)

Moderate
Single
Page: 8

1.58: Poverty should not exist in a nation as wealthy as the United States. This statement is best described as a

(a) positive statement.
(b) normative statement.
(c) descriptive economics statement.
(d) Marxist ideology.

Answer: (b)

Moderate
Single
Page: 8

1.59: There is great concern over the fact that millions of Americans do not have health insurance. A study of the costs of implementing a national health-insurance program is an example of

(a) descriptive economics.
(b) positive economics.
(c) labor economics.
(d) normative economics.

Answer: (b)

Moderate
Single
Page: 8

1.60: The difficulties that Third World nations face in achieving a high level of economic growth are most likely to be covered in a course in

(a) economic development.
(b) urban and regional economics.
(c) comparative economic systems.
(d) international trade.

Answer: (a)

Easy
Single
Page: 9

Moderate
Single
Page: 9

1.61: The study of why firms locate where they do is most likely to be covered in a course on

(a) labor economics.
(b) regional economics.
(c) international finance theory.
(d) economic development.

Answer: (b)

Easy
Single
Page: 8

1.62: Descriptive economics

(a) applies statistical techniques and data to economic problems.
(b) requires model building.
(c) looks at the outcomes of economic behavior and asks if they are good or bad.
(d) mainly involves the compilation of data that describe phenomena and facts.

Answer: (d)

Easy
Single
Page: 8

1.63: An example of descriptive economics is when an economist

(a) collects data on the wage rates and employment levels in the steel industry.
(b) tries to develop a model to explain the changes in employment and wages in the steel industry.
(c) tries to understand the relationship between the price of imported steel and the level of employment in the U.S. steel industry.
(d) tries to determine if there are any regular patterns in the employment levels in the steel industry and then makes generalizations from these patterns.

Answer: (a)

Moderate
Single
Page: 8

1.64: You work in a campus restaurant and you have observed that during finals week when the restaurant lowers the price of a cup of coffee, there is an increase in the number of customers buying coffee. From this information you generalize that as the price of coffee falls more cups of coffee will be purchased. This is an example of

(a) deductive reasoning.
(b) descriptive economics.
(c) inductive reasoning.
(d) Ockham's razor.

Answer: (c)

Moderate
Definition
Page: 8

1.65: The process of observing regular patterns from raw data and drawing generalizations from them is known as

(a) inductive reasoning.
(b) deductive reasoning.
(c) conductive reasoning.
(d) reductive reasoning.

Answer: (a)

Scenario 1 An economist wants to understand the relationship between minimum wages and the level of teenage unemployment. The economist collects data on the values of the minimum wage and the levels of teenage unemployment over time. The economist concludes that a 1% increase in the minimum wage causes a .2% increase in teenage unemployment. From this information he concludes that the minimum wage is harmful to teenagers and should be reduced or eliminated to increase employment among teenagers.

1.66: Refer to Scenario 1. The statement that a 1% increase in the minimum wage causes a .2% increase in teenage unemployment is an example of

Moderate
Single
Page: 8

(a) descriptive economics.
(b) normative economics.
(c) positive economics.
(d) Marxist economics.

Answer: (c)

1.67: Refer to Scenario 1. The statement that the minimum wage is harmful to teenagers and should be reduced or eliminated to increase employment among teenagers is an example of

Moderate
Single
Page: 8

(a) descriptive economics.
(b) normative economics.
(c) positive economics.
(d) Marxist economics.

Answer: (b)

1.68: Refer to Scenario 1. The process of collecting data on minimum wage and teenage unemployment levels is an example of

Moderate
Single
Page: 8

(a) law and economics.
(b) economic history.
(c) econometrics.
(d) descriptive economics.

Answer: (d)

1.69: Refer to Scenario 1. The process of generalizing that there is a direct relationship between the level of the minimum wage and teenage unemployment is an example of

Moderate
Single
Page: 8

(a) descriptive reasoning.
(b) economic theory.
(c) normative economics.
(d) inductive reasoning.

Answer: (d)

1.70: Refer to Scenario 1. The statement that a 1% increase in the minimum wage causes a .2% increase in the teenage unemployment is an example of

Moderate
Single
Page: 10

(a) an economic theory.
(b) inductive reasoning.
(c) descriptive economics.
(d) deductive reasoning.

Answer: (a)

Moderate
Single
Page: 10

1.71: Refer to Scenario 1. A graph of the value of the minimum wage on one axis and the level of teenage unemployment on the other axis is an example of

(a) an economic theory.
(b) a model.
(c) inductive reasoning.
(d) a variable theory.

Answer: (b)

Easy
Fact
Page: 11

1.72: To isolate the impact of one single factor, economists use the device of

(a) inductive reasoning.
(b) Ockham's razor.
(c) ceteris paribus.
(d) post hoc, ergo propter hoc.

Answer: (c)

Easy
Fact
Page: 10

1.73: The principle that irrelevant detail should be cut away is known as

(a) Say's Identity.
(b) ceteris paribus.
(c) Ockham's razor.
(d) Hobson's choice.

Answer: (c)

Easy
Fact
Page: 11

1.74: The phrase "ceteris paribus" is best expressed as

(a) "all else equal."
(b) "everything affects everything else."
(c) "scarcity is a fact of life."
(d) "there is no such thing as a free lunch."

Answer: (a)

Honors
Single
Page: 12

1.75: An economist in the nineteenth century noted a high correlation between economic prosperity and sunspots. Based on this observation he developed a "sunspot theory" of how the economy operates. This economist

(a) committed the fallacy of composition.
(b) has committed the ceteris paribus error.
(c) was too quick to conclude that correlation implies causation.
(d) showed good reasoning for the nineteenth but not the twentieth century.

Answer: (c)

Challenging
Single
Page: 12

1.76: You know that traffic gets very congested about 7:45. To avoid this congestion, you start leaving for work 15 minutes earlier every day. But many commuters make the same decision and now traffic becomes very congested at 7:30. This is an example of the

(a) post hoc, ergo propter hoc fallacy.
(b) ceteris paribus fallacy.
(c) fallacy of division.
(d) fallacy of composition.

Answer: (d)

1.77: You see better if you stand up at a football game. But if everyone stands up, your ability to see the game is no better than it was when you sat down to watch the game. This is an example of the

Challenging
Single
Page: 12

(a) post hoc, ergo propter hoc fallacy.
(b) ceteris paribus fallacy.
(c) fallacy of composition.
(d) fallacy of division.

Answer: (c)

1.78: It always rains about an hour after you finish washing your car. Concluding that washing your car caused it to rain is an example of the

Challenging
Single
Page: 12

(a) fallacy of composition.
(b) post hoc, ergo propter hoc fallacy.
(c) fallacy of inductive reasoning.
(d) ceteris paribus conditions.

Answer: (b)

1.79: You have observed that every time you eat scrambled eggs before taking an exam you get an A. You, therefore, conclude that to get an A on an exam, all you have to do is eat scrambled eggs before you take an exam. You have committed the

Challenging
Single
Page: 12

(a) fallacy of composition.
(b) fallacy of inductive reasoning.
(c) post hoc, ergo propter hoc fallacy.
(d) fallacy of division.

Answer: (c)

1.80: If you observe that Event A happens before Event B happens, and you conclude that Event A caused Event B, you would be guilty of an error called the

Moderate
Single
Page: 12

(a) fallacy of composition.
(b) fallacy of inductive reasoning.
(c) fallacy of ceteris paribus.
(d) post hoc, ergo propter hoc fallacy.

Answer: (d)

1.81: Two variables are said to be _____ if one variable changes when the other variable changes.

Easy
Definition
Page: 12

(a) causally related
(b) correlated
(c) statistically related
(d) dependent

Answer: (b)

1.82: The fallacy of composition is

Easy
Definition
Page: 12

(a) the belief that if Event A happens before Event B happens, then Event A causes Event B to occur.
(b) the belief that what is true for the whole is necessarily true of the parts.
(c) the belief that what is true for a part is necessarily true for the whole.
(d) the belief that it is impossible to draw generalizations about cause and effect.

Answer: (c)

Easy
Definition
Page: 13

1.83: The collection and use of data to test economic theories is

(a) empirical economics.
(b) descriptive economics.
(c) normative economics.
(d) positive economics.

Answer: (a)

Easy
Fact
Page: 14

1.84: A change is at least potentially efficient

(a) if the value of the resulting gains exceeds the value of the resulting losses.
(b) if the value of the resulting gains exactly equals the value of the resulting losses.
(c) only if no one is made worse off.
(d) if the value of the resulting gains is less than the value of the resulting losses.

Answer: (a)

Challenging
Single
Page: 14

1.85: Which of the following statements is FALSE?

(a) A voluntary exchange is efficient because it improves the well-being of the participants as they themselves define it.
(b) A change is at least potentially efficient if the value of the resulting gains exceeds the value of the resulting losses.
(c) Since it is impossible to define equity or fairness universally, public policy makers cannot judge the fairness of economic outcomes.
(d) When an economy grows, there is more of what people want and standards of living generally rise.

Answer: (c)

Easy
Definition
Page: 14

1.86: An efficient economy is an economy

(a) in which output is steady or growing and there is low inflation.
(b) that produces what people want and does so at least cost.
(c) that distributes output equally among all consumers.
(d) in which there is a fair distribution of wealth.

Answer: (b)

Easy
Fact
Page: 14

1.87: The four criteria that are frequently used in judging the outcome of economic policy are

(a) efficiency, equity, stability, and economic growth.
(b) efficiency, equality, stability, and economic growth.
(c) efficiency, equality, profitability, and stability.
(d) efficiency, equity, profitability, and stability.

Answer: (a)

Moderate
Fact
Page: 14

1.88: A change in the allocation of resources is potentially efficient if

(a) all individuals are made better off.
(b) it at least potentially makes some people better off without making others worse off.
(c) the number of people made better off is greater than the number of people made worse off.
(d) the value of the resulting gains equals the value of the resulting losses.

Answer: (b)

1.89: An equitable distribution of income would be accomplished if

(a) every household had the same income.
(b) every individual received an income based solely on what he or she contributed to society.
(c) the distribution of income was considered to be fair by society.
(d) total per capita output was rising.

Answer: (c)

Easy
Fact
Page: 14

1.90: You have noticed that there is an increase in the number of homeless people in your city. At the same time you observe there are also a number of vacant apartments. You believe that the government could reduce the number of homeless people if landlords were required to rent their apartments for less than they are currently charging. This policy recommendation would be motivated by concerns over

(a) efficiency.
(b) equity.
(c) economic growth.
(d) stability.

Answer: (b)

Moderate
Single
Page: 14

1.91: There is a possibility that a national sales tax will be implemented. Many economists argue that items such as food and clothing should be exempt from such a tax because low-income people spend a greater percentage of their income on these goods than high-income individuals. This argument is motivated by concerns over

(a) economic growth.
(b) economic stability.
(c) efficiency.
(d) equity.

Answer: (d)

Moderate
Single
Page: 14

1.92: An increase in total output per capita is

(a) economic growth.
(b) inflation.
(c) economic stability.
(d) an inflation .

Answer: (a)

Easy
Definition
Page: 14

1.93: A condition in which output is steady or growing, with low inflation and full employment of resources is

(a) equity.
(b) efficiency.
(c) stability.
(d) economic growth.

Answer: (c)

Easy
Definition
Page: 15

Easy
Definition
Page: 20

1.94: Refer to Figure 1.1. There is a
_____ relationship between the daily
temperature and the number of gallons of
ice cream purchased.

(a) a negative
(b) a positive
(c) either a negative or a positive
(d) an inverse

Answer: (b)

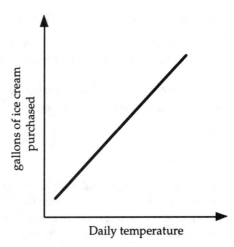

Figure 1.1

Moderate
Single
Page: 20

1.95: Refer to Figure 1.2. The slope of
the line between points A and B is

(a) .3.
(b) 2.3.
(c) 3.3.
(d) indeterminate from this information.

Answer: (a)

Moderate
Single
Page: 20

1.96: The slope of a straight line is -2. If
Y (the variable on the vertical axis)
increases by 4, then X (the variable on the
horizontal axis) will

(a) increase by 2.
(b) decrease by 2.
(c) increase by 8.
(d) decrease by 8.

Answer: (b)

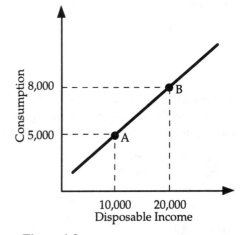

Figure 1.2

Moderate
Single
Page: 20

1.97: Refer to Figure 1.3. The slope of the line is

(a) positive.
(b) negative.
(c) increasing at an increasing rate.
(d) decreasing at an increasing rate.

Answer: (a)

Moderate
Single
Page: 20

1.98: Refer to Figure 1.3. The slope of the
line between points B and C is

(a) 5.
(b) -2.
(c) .5.
(d) 2.

Answer: (d)

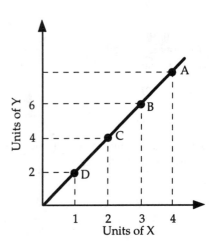

Figure 1.3

1.99: Refer to Figure 1.3. At point A, what is the value of Y ?

(a) 7.
(b) 8.
(c) 12.
(d) indeterminate from this information.

Answer: (b)

Challenging
Single
Page: 20

1.100: Refer to Figure 1.3. At point A the slope of the line is 2, so at point D the slope would be

(a) greater than 2.
(b) less than 2.
(c) equal to 2.
(d) indeterminate from this information.

Answer: (c)

Moderate
Single
Page: 20

1.101: Refer to Figure 1.4. Which of the curves or lines has a slope that is first positive and then negative?

(a) A
(b) B
(c) C
(d) D

Answer: (b)

Moderate
Single
Page: 22

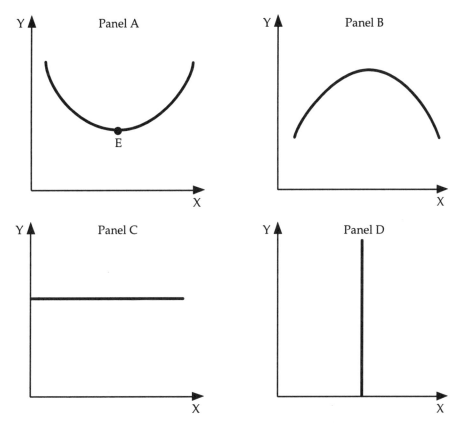

Figure 1.4

Moderate
Single
Page: 22

1.102: Refer to Figure 1.4. Which of the curves or lines has a slope that is negative and then positive?

(a) A
(b) B
(c) C
(d) D

Answer: (a)

Moderate
Single
Page: 22

1.103: Refer to Figure 1.4. Which of the following curves or lines has a zero slope throughout?

(a) A
(b) B
(c) C
(d) D

Answer: (c)

Moderate
Single
Page: 22

1.104: Refer to Figure 1.4. Which of the curves or lines has an infinite slope throughout?

(a) A
(b) B
(c) C
(d) D

Answer: (d)

Challenging
Single
Page: 22

1.105: Refer to Figure 1.4. At point E in panel A, the slope is

(a) zero.
(b) infinite.
(c) negative.
(d) indeterminate from this information.

Answer: (a)

Easy
Fact
Page: 21

1.106: The slope of a curve

(a) is always positive.
(b) must first increase then decrease.
(c) is continually changing.
(d) is constant.

Answer: (c)

Easy
Fact
Page: 21

1.107: The slope of a horizontal line is

(a) negative.
(b) zero.
(c) continually changing.
(d) infinite.

Answer: (b)

1.108: If the slope of a straight line is 5 and if X (the variable on the horizontal axis) increases by 10, then Y (the variable on the vertical axis) will

(a) decrease by .5.
(b) decrease by 50.
(c) increase by .5.
(d) incrcase by 50.

Answer: (d)

Easy
Single
Page: 20

1.109: If the slope of a straight line is 10 and if Y (the variable on the vertical axis) decreases by 20, then X (the variable on the horizontal axis)

(a) increases by 2.
(b) decreases by 2.
(c) increases by 200.
(d) decreases by 200.

Answer: (b)

Moderate
Single
Page: 20

1.110: A vertical line has _____ slope.

(a) a zero
(b) an infinite
(c) a continually changing
(d) a negative

Answer: (b)

Easy
Fact
Page: 21

1.111: Refer to Figure 1.5. Which of the curves has a slope that is positive and decreasing?

(a) A
(b) B
(c) C
(d) D

Answer: (b)

Easy
Single
Page: 22

1.112: Refer to Figure 1.5. Which of the curves has a slope that is positive and increasing?

(a) A
(b) B
(c) C
(d) D

Answer: (a)

Moderate
Single
Page: 22

1.113: Refer to Figure 1.5. Which of the curves has a slope that is negative and decreasing?

(a) A
(b) B
(c) C
(d) D

Answer: (c)

Moderate
Single
Page: 22

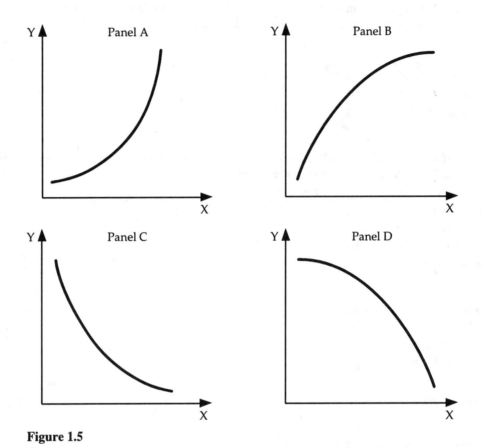

Figure 1.5

Moderate
Single
Page: 22

1.114: Refer to Figure 1.5. Which of the curves has a slope that is negative and increasing?

(a) A
(b) B
(c) C
(d) D

Answer: (d)

1.115: Refer to Figure 1.5. As income increases, consumption increases, but for each additional increase in income consumption increases by a smaller and smaller amount. If consumption is graphed on the vertical axis and income is graphed on the horizontal axis, the relationship between consumption and income would look like which of the following panels?

Challenging
Multi
Page: 22

(a) A
(b) B
(c) C
(d) D

Answer: (b)

1.116: Refer to Figure 1.5. In the clothing industry, as firms produce more units of output, average costs of production decline and for each additional unit of output produced average costs of production fall by a smaller and smaller amount. If output is graphed on the horizontal axis and average costs are graphed on the vertical axis, the relationship between average costs and output would be like which of the following panels?

Honors
Multi
Page: 24

(a) A
(b) B
(c) C
(d) D

Answer: (c)

TRUE/FALSE QUESTIONS

1.117: The value of the best forgone alternative is the opportunity cost of making a decision.

Answer: True

Easy
Definition
Page: 2

1.118: Scarcity is the reason that opportunity costs arise.

Answer: True

Easy
Fact
Page: 3

1.119: Positive economics attempts to understand the behavior and operation of economic systems without making judgments about whether the outcomes are good or bad.

Answer: True

Easy
Definition
Page: 8

1.120: Normative economics looks at outcomes of economic behavior and evaluates them as good or bad.

Answer: True

Easy
Definition
Page: 8

1.121: Positive economics is often divided into descriptive economics and economic theory.

Answer: True

Easy
Fact
Page: 8

1.122: Economic theory is a statement or series of statements about cause and effect, action and reaction.

Answer: True

Easy
Definition
Page: 10

1.123: The fallacy of division is the belief that what is true for a part must be true for the whole.

Answer: False

Easy
Definition
Page: 10

1.124: An efficient economy is one that produces what people want and does so at the least possible cost.

Answer: True

Easy
Definition
Page: 14

Easy
Definition
Page: 14

1.125: Efficiency refers to a situation of long-term economic growth.

Answer: False

Easy
Definition
Page: 15

1.126: Stability is a condition in which output is steady or growing, with low inflation and full employment of resources.

Answer: True

SHORT ANSWER QUESTIONS

Easy
Definition
Page: 3

1.127: Define marginalism and explain why it is useful to decision making. How does it relate to the notion of sunk costs?

Answer: Marginalism stresses the importance of incremental changes. It is useful in the decision-making process because only the additional costs or benefits resulting from the specific decision are being weighed. Sunk costs are not relevant to decision making as they do not change with the decision.

Easy
Definition
Page: 7

1.128: Carefully differentiate between microeconomics and macroeconomics.

Answer: Microeconomics is the study of individual decision makers or markets, while macroeconomics is the study of the entire economy.

Moderate
Definition
Page: 12

1.129: Carefully differentiate between the post hoc fallacy and the fallacy of composition.

Answer: The post hoc fallacy refers to a mistake about cause and effect, while the fallacy of composition states that what is true for a part is true for the whole.

For each of the following data sets, graph the relation. Place X on the horizontal axis and Y on the vertical axis.

Easy
Math
Page: 18

1.130:

X	Y
1	10
2	20
3	30
4	40
5	50

Answer:

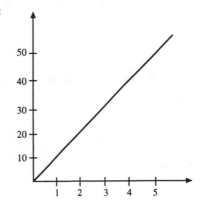

1.131:   X   Y
         1   100
         2   80
         3   60
         4   40
         5   20

Answer:

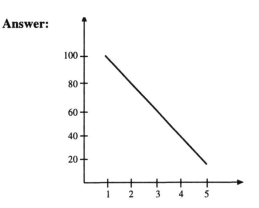

Easy
Fact
Page: 12

1.132:   X   Y
         1   1
         2   4
         3   9
         4   16
         5   25

Answer:

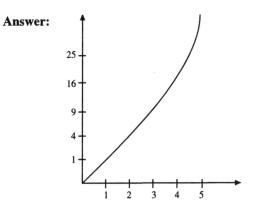

Easy
Math
Page: 18

1.133:   X   Y
         1   10
         2   10
         3   20
         4   30
         5   30

Answer:

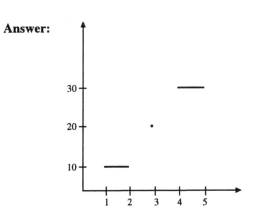

Moderate
Math
Page: 18

Graph each of the following relations.

Moderate
Math
Page: 18

1.134: P = 100 - 7 Qd , place Qd on horizontal axis.

Answer:

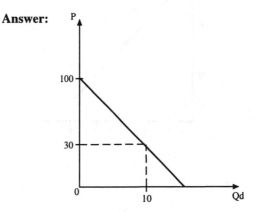

Moderate
Math
Page: 18

1.135: P = 50 - 4 Qd2 , place Qd on horizontal axis.

Answer:

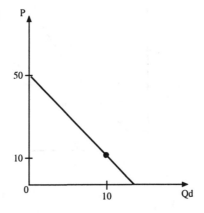

Moderate
Math
Page: 18

1.136: I = 400 - 30r , place r on vertical axis.

Answer:

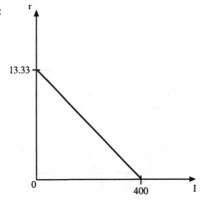

1.137: C = 50 + 30 Y, place Y on horizontal axis.

Answer:

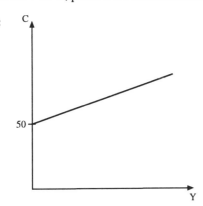

Moderate
Math
Page: 18

1.138: P = 60 + 8 Qd, place Qd on horizontal axis.

Answer:

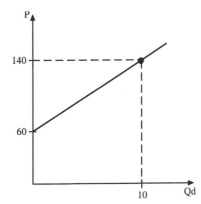

Moderate
Math
Page: 18

Scenario 2 Assume the following relation: P = 100 - 4 Q + 7 Y.

1.139: Refer to Scenario 2. Graph the relation between Q and P, place Q on the horizontal axis and assume Y = 50.

Moderate
Math
Page: 18

Answer:

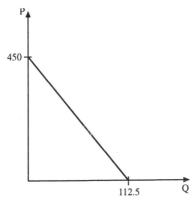

Moderate
Math
Page: 18

1.140: Refer to Scenario 2. Assume Y increases to 100 and graph the new relation between Q and P.

Answer:

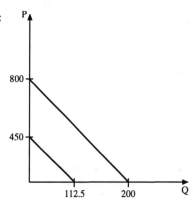

Moderate
Math
Page: 18

1.141: Refer to Scenario 2. Assume Q = 10 and graph the relation between P and Y, placing Y on the horizontal axis.

Answer:

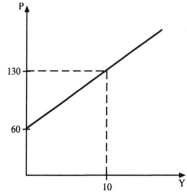

Moderate
Math
Page: 18

1.142: Refer to Scenario 2. Assume Q increases to 15 and graph the new relation between P and Y.

Answer:

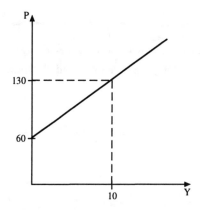

Difficult
Application
Page: 18

1.143: Refer to Scenario 2 and questions 40–43. Can you draw any generalizations from the above questions? If so, explain.

Answer: Yes, a change in a variable that is not explicitly on the graph causes a shift of the curve. This may be seen as a shift in item intercept.

Scenario 3 Assume that the demand for a product can be related to the product price by the following relation: Q = 70 - 3 P.

1.144: Refer to Scenario 3. Calculate the demand (Q) for a product at each of the following prices:
P = 1, 3, 5, 7, and 9.

Moderate
Math
Page: 18

Answer:

P	Q
1	67
3	61
5	55
7	49
9	43

1.145: Refer to Scenario 3. Graph the equation presented above, placing Q on the horizontal axis.

Easy
Math
Page: 18

Answer:

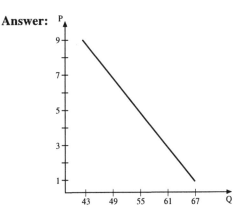

1.146: Refer to Scenario 3. Calculate the slope of the equation with Q on the horizontal axis.

Moderate
Math
Page: 18

Answer: Q = 70 - 3 P

   3P = 70 - Q

   P = 70/3 - 1/3(Q)

   DP/DQ = - 1/3

1.147: Refer to Scenario 3 and question 1.148. Now, graph the following equation alongside the one above and calculate the new slope: Q = 100 - 5 P.

Moderate
Math
Page: 18

Answer:

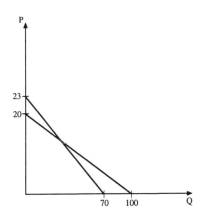

Moderate
Math
Page: 8

1.148: Refer to Scenario 3 and question 46–49. Compare the slopes and intercepts of the two relations between quantity and price.

Answer: The second equation, Q = 100 - 5 P, has a flatter slope and a larger intercept along the horizontal axis than the first equation, Q = 70 - 3 P.

Easy
Fact
Page: 2

1.149: List the four reasons for studying economics.

Answer: The four reasons for studying economics are: to learn a way of thinking, to understand society, to understand global affairs, and to be an informed voter.

Easy
Fact
Page: 2

1.150: Define opportunity cost. Explain the reason that opportunity costs arise.

Answer: Opportunity cost is that which we forgo, or give up, when we make a choice or decision. Opportunity costs arise because of scarcity.

Moderate
Single
Page: 14

1.151: Define an efficient market. Which of the following markets is more likely to be efficient: The fast-food market near your campus where there are no restrictions on who may enter the market, or the dormitory dining market where only one firm has the right to sell meals? Why?

Answer: An efficient market is a market in which profit opportunities are eliminated almost instantaneously. The fast-food market is likely to be more efficient than the dormitory dining market, because it is open to competition.

Easy
Single
Page: 8

1.152: Explain the difference between positive economics and normative economics.

Answer: Positive economics is an approach to economics that seeks to understand behavior and the operations of systems without making value judgments. Normative economics, however, does make value judgments because it is an approach to economics that analyzes outcomes of economic behavior and evaluates them as good or bad.

Moderate
Single
Page: 8

1.153: Give an example of a positive statement. Give an example of a normative statement.

Answer: Answers will vary.

Easy
Fact
Page: 11

1.154: Define ceteris paribus. Explain why the device of ceteris paribus is so important in economics.

Answer: Ceteris paribus means all else equal. It is important in economics because it allows economists to analyze the relationship between two variables while the values of other variables are held unchanged. It allows economists to isolate the effect of a single variable.

Easy
Definition
Page: 12

1.155: Define post hoc, ergo propter hoc. Give an example of this fallacy.

Answer: A common error made in thinking about causation: If event A happens before event B happens, it cannot be inferred that A caused B.

Easy
Fact
Page: 14

1.156: Explain the four criteria that are frequently used for judging the outcome of economic policy.

Answer: The four criteria for judging the outcome of economic policy are equity, efficiency, stability, and economic growth.

1.157: For every $100 increase in income, saving increases by $20. When income is zero saving, is also zero. Draw a graph that explains the relationship between saving and consumption; graphing income on the horizontal axis and saving on the vertical axis. What is the slope of this line?

Easy
Fact
Page: 20

Answer: The slope is .2.

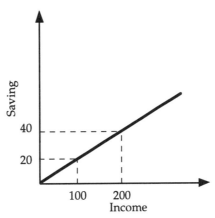

1.158: For every additional unit of labor hired total product increases, but at a decreasing rate (the slope gets smaller). Draw a graph of this situation. Place labor on the horizontal axis and total product on the vertical axis.

Moderate
Single
Page: 22

Answer: Graphs will vary.

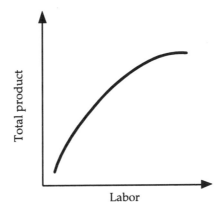

2 The Economic Problem: Scarcity and Choice

2.1: The process by which resources are transformed into useful forms is

(a) capitalization.
(b) consumption.
(c) production.
(d) allocation.

Answer: (c)

Easy
Definition
Page: 25

2.2: Which of the following is not a resource as the term is used by economists?

(a) land
(b) labor
(c) buildings
(d) money

Answer: (d)

Easy
Fact
Page: 25

2.3: Which of the following would an economist classify as capital?

(a) a deposit of silver
(b) a share of stock
(c) a public corporation's employees
(d) an automobile leased by an individual

Answer: (d)

Moderate
Single
Page: 25

2.4: Which of the following would an economist classify as capital?

(a) natural gas
(b) a typewriter
(c) a corporate bond
(d) a federal government employee

Answer: (b)

Moderate
Single
Page: 25

2.5: Capital, as economists use the term,

(a) is the money the firm spends to hire resources.
(b) is money the firm raises from selling stock.
(c) refers to the process by which resources are transformed into useful forms.
(d) refers to things that have already been produced that are in turn used to produce other goods and services.

Answer: (d)

Easy
Definition
Page: 25

2.6: The concept of opportunity cost is based upon the principle of

(a) need.
(b) consumption.
(c) scarcity.
(d) profit.

Answer: (c)

Easy
Fact
Page: 26

33

Moderate
Fact
Page: 27

2.7: The concept of choice would become irrelevant if

(a) we were dealing with a very simple, one-person economy.
(b) poverty were eliminated.
(c) scarcity were eliminated.
(d) capital were eliminated.

Answer: (c)

Moderate
Single
Page: 27

2.8: Suppose you have to decide whether to spend your tax refund on a new CD player or a new printer for your computer. You are dealing with the concept of

(a) diminishing marginal returns.
(b) comparative advantage.
(c) opportunity costs.
(d) the fallacy of composition.

Answer: (c)

Easy
Definition
Page: 28

2.9 According to the theory of comparative advantage, specialization and free trade will benefit

(a) all trading parties under any circumstances.
(b) all trading parties, even when some are absolutely more efficient producers than others.
(c) only that trading party that has an absolute advantage in the production of all goods.
(d) only that trading party that has a comparative advantage in the production of all goods.

Answer: (b)

Moderate
Single
Page: 28

2.10: Refer to Figure 2.1. For Matthew, the opportunity cost of vacuuming one rug is

(a) 1/5 of a window washed.
(b) 4 windows washed.
(c) 5 windows washed.
(d) 10 windows washed.

Answer: (c)

Moderate
Single
Page: 28

2.11: Refer to Figure 2.1. For Andrew, the opportunity cost of vacuuming one rug is

(a) 1/4 of a window washed.
(b) 2 windows washed.
(c) 4 windows washed.
(d) 8 windows washed.

Answer: (c)

	Matthew	**Andrew**
Windows washed	10	12
Rugs vacuumed	2	3

Figure 2.1

2.12: Refer to Figure 2.1. Which of the following statements is TRUE?

(a) Matthew has a comparative advantage in both washing windows and in vacuuming rugs.
(b) Andrew has a comparative advantage in both washing windows and in vacuuming rugs.
(c) Matthew has a comparative advantage in vacuuming rugs and Andrew has a comparative advantage in washing windows.
(d) Andrew has a comparative advantage in vacuuming rugs and Matthew has a comparative advantage in washing windows.

Moderate
Single
Page: 28

Answer: (d)

2.13: Refer to Figure 2.1. To maximize total production,

(a) Matthew should specialize in vacuuming rugs and Andrew should specialize in washing windows.
(b) Andrew should specialize in vacuuming rugs and Matthew should specialize in washing windows.
(c) Matthew and Andrew should both split their time between washing windows and vacuuming rugs.
(d) Matthew should wash windows and vacuum rugs, but Andrew should only wash windows.

Moderate
Single
Page: 28

Answer: (b)

2.14: Refer to Figure 2.1. For Andrew, the opportunity cost of vacuuming 4 rugs is _____ windows washed.

(a) 8
(b) 16
(c) 20
(d) an indeterminate number of

Easy
Single
Page: 28

Answer: (b)

2.15: Refer to Figure 2.1. For Matthew, the opportunity cost of vacuuming 3 rugs is _____ windows washed.

(a) 12
(b) 13
(c) 15
(d) 20

Moderate
Single
Page: 28

Answer: (c)

2.16: According to theory of comparative advantage, _____ raise(s) productivity by lowering opportunity costs.

(a) trade and specialization
(b) Investment in capital goods
(c) economic growth
(d) exchange and consumption

Easy
Fact
Page: 28

Answer: (a)

Moderate
Single
Page: 30

2.17: Which of the following does NOT constitute an act of "investment" as economists use the term?

(a) The city park commission authorizes the construction of a new swimming pool.
(b) An individual buys 100 shares of stock at $30 a share and then sells the stock at a profit for $35 a share.
(c) A corporate lawyer attends a seminar on changes in the federal tax code.
(d) A grocery store increases its inventory of potato chips and soda before the Memorial Day weekend.

Answer: (b)

Moderate
Single
Page: 30

2.18: Which of the following would an economist classify as an investment?

(a) Transferring your money from a non-interest-bearing checking account to an interest-bearing checking account.
(b) Buying a U.S. savings bond.
(c) Buying a share a stock.
(d) Building a vacation home.

Answer: (d)

Easy
Definition
Page: 30

2.19: In economics, investment always refers to

(a) the act of buying stocks or bonds.
(b) the creation of capital.
(c) improving the productivity of labor.
(d) an increase in per capita output.

Answer: (b)

Easy
Definition
Page: 30

2.20: The process of using resources to produce new capital is

(a) research and development.
(b) investment.
(c) consumption.
(d) economic growth.

Answer: (b)

Easy
Fact
Page: 29

2.21: An example of trading present for future benefits is

(a) production.
(b) saving.
(c) consumption.
(d) growth.

Answer: (b)

Easy
Fact
Page: 30

2.22: Because resources are scarce, the opportunity cost of investment in capital is

(a) zero.
(b) forgone future consumption.
(c) forgone present consumption.
(d) infinite.

Answer: (c)

2.23: The opportunity cost of investment in capital is forgone present consumption because

(a) capital takes a long time to produce.
(b) capital increases the productivity of labor.
(c) resources are scarce.
(d) capital is an intangible good.

Answer: (c)

Easy
Fact
Page: 30

2.24: If the unemployment rate decreases from 10 percent to 8 percent, the economy will

(a) move closer to the ppf.
(b) move away from the ppf toward the origin.
(c) remain on the ppf.
(d) remain on the origin.

Answer: (a)

Moderate
Single
Page: 31

2.25: Periods of less than full employment correspond to

(a) points outside the ppf.
(b) points inside the ppf.
(c) points on the ppf.
(d) either points inside or outside the ppf.

Answer: (b)

Easy
Fact
Page: 31

2.26: Refer to Figure 2.2. Macroland is currently operating at point A. The best explanation for this is that

(a) the economy has very poor technology.
(b) the economy's resources are being used inefficiently.
(c) the economy has very few resources.
(d) the economy is operated as a command economy.

Answer: (b)

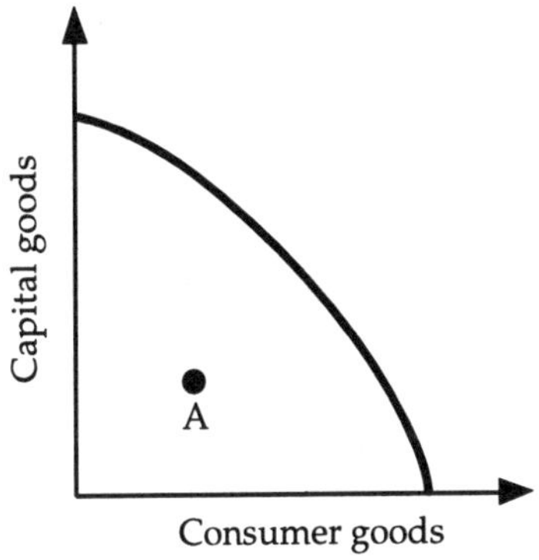

Figure 2.2
The production possibility
frontier for Macroland

Moderate
Single
Page: 31

2.27: The production possibility frontier is used to illustrate the concept of

(a) the laissez-faire economy.
(b) opportunity costs.
(c) equilibrium.
(d) aggregate demand.

Answer: (b)

Easy
Fact
Page: 31

2.28: A graph showing all the combinations of goods and services that can be produced if all of society's resources are used efficiently is the

(a) production possibility frontier.
(b) capital consumption frontier.
(c) Lorenz curve.
(d) circular-flow diagram.

Answer: (a)

Easy
Definition
Page: 31

Easy
Fact
Page: 31

2.29: Refer to Figure 2.3. A point like point B represents a situation of

(a) full employment but production inefficiency.
(b) less than full employment but production efficiency.
(c) both full resource to employment and production efficiency.
(d) less than full employment and production inefficiency.

Answer: (c)

Figure 2.3
The production possibility frontier for Microland

Moderate
Fact
Page: 31

2.30: Refer to Figure 2.3. Microland is currently operating at point B. You correctly deduce that

(a) in Microland all resources are fully employed and there are no production inefficiencies.
(b) Microland has achieved a position of inefficiency.
(c) Microland has recently experienced some type of technological breakthrough.
(d) Microland has overcome the problem of scarcity.

Answer: (a)

Easy
Definition
Page: 31

2.31: The production possibility frontier is a graph that shows

(a) all the combinations of goods and services that are consumed over time if all of society's resources are used efficiently.
(b) the amount of goods and services consumed at various average price levels.
(c) the rate at which an economy's output will grow over time if all resources are used efficiently.
(d) all the combinations of goods and services that can be produced if all of society's resources are used efficiently.

Answer: (d)

Moderate
Single
Page: 32

2.32: If the unemployment rate increases from 10% to 12%, the

(a) economy will move closer to the production possibility frontier.
(b) economy will move farther away from the production possibility frontier.
(c) economy will move up its production possibility frontier.
(d) economy's production possibility frontier will shift back and to the left.

Answer: (b)

Moderate
Fact
Page: 32

2.33: Production inefficiency can occur

(a) only when an economy is producing inside its production possibility frontier.
(b) only when an economy is producing at the wrong point on the production possibility frontier.
(c) either when an economy is producing inside the production possibility frontier or when an economy is producing at the wrong point on the production possibility frontier.
(d) only when the economy is producing outside the production possibility frontier.

Answer: (c)

2.34: An economy that is producing at the wrong point on its production possibility frontier is

Easy
Fact
Page: 32

(a) efficient, since it is on the production possibility frontier.
(b) inefficient, since the combination of goods and services produced is not what people want.
(c) efficient, since the economy is producing goods at the lowest possible cost.
(d) inefficient, since that combination of goods could be produced at a lower cost if more efficient technology were employed.

Answer: (b)

2.35: If resources are combined efficiently in production, then the society

Moderate
Fact
Page: 33

(a) is producing at the most desirable point on the production possibility frontier.
(b) is producing at a point on the production possibility frontier but not necessarily at the most desirable point.
(c) is producing at a point outside the production possibility frontier.
(d) is experiencing economic growth.

Answer: (b)

2.36: Suppose an economy produces television sets and computers in perfectly competitive industries. The economy is currently operating at a point on its ppf. If a firm gains monopoly control over the production of computers which of the following is most likely to happen?

Moderate
Multi
Page: 33

(a) The economy will move to a less desirable point on the ppf.
(b) The economy's ppf will shift inward.
(c) The economy will now be able to produce at a point outside its ppf.
(d) The economy's ppf will shift outward, but the maximum number of computers will remain the same.

Answer: (a)

2.37: The value of the slope of a society's production possibility frontier is called its

Easy
Fact
Page: 33

(a) marginal rate of substitution.
(b) inflation rate.
(c) unemployment rate.
(d) marginal rate of transformation.

Answer: (d)

2.38: Given the current state of technology it is possible to produce one more truck if two fewer cars are produced. But in Microland, to produce one more truck the production of cars must be reduced by three. This situation would be illustrated by Microland _____ its ppf for cars and trucks.

Challenging
Multi
Page: 32

(a) being on
(b) being inside
(c) being outside
(d) being at the origin of

Answer: (b)

Moderate
Single
Page: 33

2.39: Assume a society can produce either beef or chicken. If the marginal rate of transformation of beef into chicken is 5, then the opportunity cost of chicken is

(a) the two units of beef that must be forgone.
(b) the additional .5 unit of beef that can be produced.
(c) the .5 units of beef that must be forgone.
(d) the two units of chicken that must be forgone.

Answer: (c)

Easy
Definition
Page: 33

2.40: The marginal rate of transformation is the

(a) slope of the production possibility frontier.
(b) dollar value of the best forgone alternative.
(c) process of using resources to produce new capital.
(d) transformation of resources into a form that is useful to people.

Answer: (a)

Moderate
Single
Page: 33

2.41: Refer to Figure 2.4. Assume that in Microland the marginal rate of transformation of sweaters for blankets is constant and equal to -3. A graph of this society's production possibility frontier will be represented by

(a) A.
(b) B.
(c) C.
(d) D.

Answer: (c)

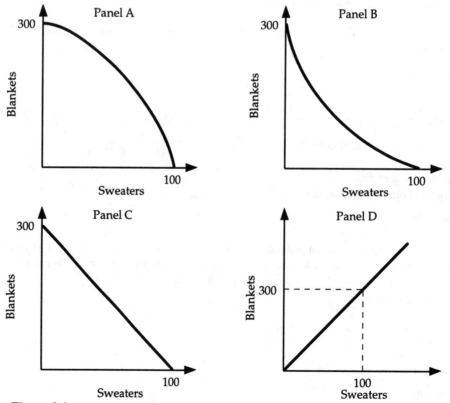

Figure 2.4

2.42: A society can produce two goods: bread and cookies. The society's production possibility frontier is negatively sloped and "bowed outward" from the origin. As this society moves down its production possibility frontier producing more and more units of cookies, the opportunity cost of producing cookies

Moderate
Single
Page: 33

(a) decreases.
(b) remains constant.
(c) increases.
(d) could decrease or increase depending on the technology.

Answer: (c)

2.43: According to Figure 2.5, the point where only cars are produced is

Easy
Single
Page: 31

(a) A.
(b) B.
(c) C.
(d) E.

Answer: (d)

2.44: According to Figure 2.5, the optimal point for the economy is

Moderate
Single
Page: 31

(a) A.
(b) B.
(c) F.
(d) indeterminate from the information given.

Answer: (d)

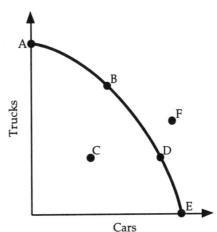

Figure 2.5

2.45: According to Figure 2.5, which point cannot be obtained with the current state of technology?

Moderate
Single
Page: 31

(a) A
(b) B
(c) C
(d) F

Answer: (d)

2.46: According to Figure 2.5, which point(s) may represent an inefficient use of resources?

Challenging
Single
Page: 31

(a) A
(b) B
(c) C
(d) all points except F

Answer: (d)

2.47: According to Figure 2.5, the point where only trucks are produced is

Easy
Single
Page: 31

(a) A.
(b) D.
(c) C.
(d) D.

Answer: (a)

Moderate
Single
Page: 31

2.48: According to Figure 2.5, a decrease in unemployment may be represented by the movement from

(a) F to A.
(b) B to D.
(c) C to D.
(d) A to C.

Answer: (c)

Moderate
Single
Page: 31

2.49: According to Figure 2.5, as the economy moves from point A to point D, the opportunity cost of cars, measured in terms of trucks,

(a) decreases.
(b) increases.
(c) remains constant.
(d) initially increases, then decreases.

Answer: (b)

Moderate
Single
Page: 31

2.50: According to Figure 2.5, as the economy moves from point D to point A, the opportunity cost of trucks, measured in terms of cars,

(a) increases.
(b) decreases.
(c) remains constant.
(d) initially increases, then decreases.

Answer: (a)

Moderate
Multi
Page: 31

2.51: Refer to Figure 2.5. The economy moves from point B to point D. This could be explained by

(a) a reduction in unemployment.
(b) an improvement in technology.
(c) an increase in economic growth.
(d) a change in society's preferences for cars versus trucks.

Answer: (d)

Moderate
Single
Page: 33

2.52: Refer to Figure 2.6. The economy is currently at point A. The opportunity cost of moving from point A to point B is

(a) the 60 bushels of soybeans that must be forgone to produce 10 additional bushels of wheat.
(b) the 20 bushels of soybeans that must be forgone to produce 30 additional bushels of wheat.
(c) the 80 bushels of soybeans that must be forgone to produce 20 additional bushels of wheat.
(d) the 20 bushels of soybeans that must be forgone to produce 10 additional bushels of wheat.

Answer: (d)

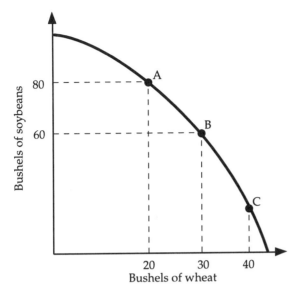

Figure 2.6

2.53: Refer to Figure 2.6. The marginal rate of transformation in moving from point A to point B is

Moderate
Single
Page: 33

(a) 5.
(b) -2.
(c) -2.8.
(d) -4.

Answer: (b)

2.54: Refer to Figure 2.6. For this economy to move from point B to point C so that an additional 10 bushels of wheat could be produced, production of soybeans would have to be reduced by

Moderate
Multi
Page: 33

(a) exactly 20 bushels.
(b) fewer than 20 bushels.
(c) more than 20 bushels.
(d) exactly 40 bushels.

Answer (c)

2.55: Refer to Figure 2.6. The best point for society would be

Challenging
Single
Page: 33

(a) point C since at this point there are approximately equal amounts of soybeans and wheat being produced.
(b) either point B or point C since the total amount being produced at either of these points is approximately the same.
(c) at any of the labeled points, since all of the points represent an efficient allocation of resources.
(d) indeterminate from this information, since we don't have any information about the society's wants.

Answer: (d)

Moderate
Fact
Page: 33

2.56: If the opportunity costs of producing a good increase as more of that good is produced, the economy's production possibility frontier will be

(a) negatively sloped and "bowed inward" toward the origin.
(b) negatively sloped and "bowed outward" from the origin.
(c) a negatively sloped straight line.
(d) a positively sloped straight line.

Answer: (b)

Moderate
Fact
Page: 33

2.57: As you move down the production possibility frontier, the absolute value of the marginal rate of transformation

(a) increases.
(b) decreases.
(c) initially increases, then decreases.
(d) initially decreases, then increases.

Answer: (a)

Challenging
Single
Page: 33

2.58: As more of a good, such as television sets, is produced the opportunity costs of producing it increases. This most likely occurs because

(a) as more of a good is produced the inputs used to produce that good will increase in price.
(b) consumers would be willing to pay higher prices for the good as more of the good is produced.
(c) resources are not equally well-suited to producing all goods and as more of a good is produced it is necessary to use resources less well-suited to the production of the good.
(d) as more of a good is produced the quality of the technology available to produce additional units of the good declines and therefore the costs of production increase.

Answer: (c)

Easy
Fact
Page: 34

2.59: Economic growth may occur when

(a) a society acquires new resources.
(b) a society learns to produce more using existing resources.
(c) the society begins to produce the combination of goods society wants most.
(d) both a and b.

Answer: (d)

Easy
Single
Page: 35

2.60: Refer to Figure 2.7. Economic growth is represented by a

(a) shift from ppf ^{2} to ppf ^{1}.
(b) shift from ppf ^{1} to ppf ^{2}
(c) movement from C to B along ppf ^{1}.
(d) movement from A to C.

Answer: (b)

Moderate
Multi
Page: 35

2.61: Refer to Figure 2.7. An improvement in technology may be represented by a

(a) shift from ppf ^{2} to ppf ^{1} .
(b) shift from ppf ^{1} to ppf ^{2}.
(c) movement from B to A.
(d) movement from C to B along ppf ^{1}.

Answer: (b)

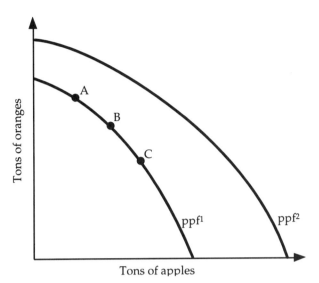

Figure 2.7

2.62: Refer to Figure 2.7. The economy's production possibility frontier shifted from ppf^1 to ppf^2. Which of the following statements best explains this movement?

(a) The economy's productivity has increased and the productivity increases were greater in the production of apples than oranges.
(b) The economy's productivity has increased and the productivity increases were greater in the production of oranges than apples.
(c) The economy's unemployment rate has decreased and the reduction in unemployment has been greater in the production of apples than in the production of oranges.
(d) The economy's unemployment rate has decreased and the reduction in unemployment has been greater in the production of oranges than in the production of apples.

Moderate
Multi
Page: 35

Answer: (a)

2.63: During the Persian Gulf War many of Kuwait's oil refineries were destroyed. This would best be represented by

(a) a movement down Kuwait's production possibility frontier.
(b) a movement off Kuwait's production possibility frontier to some point inside the frontier.
(c) a shift of Kuwait's production possibility frontier back and to the left.
(d) a movement up Kuwait's production possibility frontier.

Moderate
Multi
Page: 35

Answer: (c)

2.64: Refer to Figure 2.8. Which of the following will shift an economy's production possibility frontier from ppf^1 to ppf^2?

(a) a decrease in unemployment
(b) an increase in production efficiency
(c) a change in consumer's tastes
(d) an increase in the economy's capital stock

Moderate
Single
Page: 35

Answer: (d)

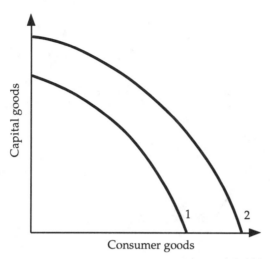

Figure 2.8

Easy
Multi
Page: 35

2.65: Refer to Figure 2.8. Which of the following will NOT cause the production possibility frontier to shift from ppf[1] to ppf[2]?

(a) the discovery of previously unknown oil fields
(b) an improvement in technology
(c) an increase in the stock of capital
(d) a decrease in the unemployment rate

Answer: (d)

Moderate
Single
Page: 35

2.66: Refer to Figure 2.8. Which of the following is most likely to shift the production possibility frontier from ppf[1] to ppf[2]?

(a) a change in consumer tastes
(b) the purchase of stocks on the New York Stock Exchange
(c) moving resources from capital to consumer goods
(d) an increase in the general educational level of the population

Answer: (d)

Challenging
Single
Page: 35

2.67: For an economy to produce at a point beyond its current ppf, the economy must

(a) waste less.
(b) be more efficient.
(c) reduce inputs.
(d) increase inputs.

Answer: (d)

Moderate
Single
Page: 35

2.68: In terms of the production possibility frontier, an increase in productivity attributable to new technology would best be shown by

(a) a movement along the frontier.
(b) the production possibility frontier shifting up and to the right.
(c) a movement from a point inside the frontier to a point on it.
(d) a movement toward the origin.

Answer: (b)

2.69: An improvement in technology will cause

(a) the production possibility frontier to shift up and to the right.
(b) the production possibility frontier to shift back and to the left.
(c) the economy to move down the production possibility frontier.
(d) the economy to move closer to its production possibility frontier.

Answer: (a)

Moderate
Single
Page: 35

2.70: Consider two countries, Germany and Sweden. Germany devotes a larger portion of its production to capital. Which of the following statements is most likely true?

(a) Germany is a poorer country than Sweden.
(b) Germany will move up its production possibility curve faster than Sweden.
(c) Sweden is producing inside its production possibility frontier, while Germany is producing at a point on its production possibility frontier.
(d) Germany's production possibility frontier will shift up and out farther and faster than Sweden's.

Answer: (d)

Moderate
Multi
Page: 35

2.71: The gap between rich and poor countries

(a) has decreased over time because poor countries can more easily devote resources to capital production.
(b) has increased over time because poor countries find it difficult to devote resources to capital production.
(c) has remained constant over time since technological advances can be easily shared among nations.
(d) has remained constant over time because the rate of capital production has remained constant in rich and poor nations.

Answer: (b)

Moderate
Fact
Page: 36

2.72: An economy produces capital goods and consumer goods. This economy is operating at a point on its production possibility frontier associated with a small amount of capital goods and a large amount of consumer goods. This is most likely to be a

(a) "poor" country because such a nation cannot devote many resources to the production of capital goods.
(b) "rich" country because such a nation can afford to sacrifice.
(c) country with a free market.
(d) country with a command economy.

Answer: (a)

Challenging
Single
Page: 36

2.73: The economic problem can best be stated as:

(a) How can the economy improve technology so as to shift the production possibility frontier up and to the right?
(b) Given scarce resources, how exactly do large, complex societies go about deciding what to produce, how to produce it, and who will get it?
(c) Given the fact that the economy is inefficient, how much and what type of government intervention should be used to improve the efficiency of the economy?
(d) What is the best rate of economic growth for a society?

Answer: (b)

Moderate
Fact
Page: 36

Easy
Definition
Page: 37

2.74: An economy in which a central authority draws up a plan that establishes what will be produced and when, sets production goals, and makes rules for distribution is

(a) a socialist economy.
(b) a laissez-faire economy.
(c) a public goods economy.
(d) a command economy.

Answer: (d)

Moderate
Single
Page: 37

2.75: Which of the following statements is FALSE?

(a) Planned economies have not fared very well in recent years, many of these economies have almost completely collapsed.
(b) In command economies there can never be an oversupply of a good.
(c) In command economies consumers still exercise choice.
(d) In a command economy the government answers the questions of what to produce, how to produce it and how to distribute it.

Answer: (b)

Moderate
Fact
Page: 37

2.76: Which of the following is an element of a command economy?

(a) The market decides distribution.
(b) The means of production are privately owned.
(c) Production decisions are centralized.
(d) The market decides what will be produced.

Answer: (c)

Easy
Fact
Page: 37

2.77: Which of the following statements is NOT true for a command economy?

(a) Consumers have some choices concerning what they buy.
(b) The government decides what is produced.
(c) The amount of a good supplied always equals the amount of the good demanded.
(d) The state decides how to distribute what is produced.

Answer: (c)

Easy
Fact
Page: 38

2.78: An economy in which individual people and firms pursue their own self-interest without any central direction or regulation is

(a) a command economy.
(b) a laissez-faire economy.
(c) an invisible-hand economy.
(d) a private sector economy.

Answer: (b)

Easy
Definition
Page: 38

2.79: In a laissez-faire economy _____ what gets produced, how it is produced, and who gets it.

(a) the behavior of buyers and sellers determines
(b) the central government authority determines
(c) firms but not consumers determine
(d) consumers but not firms determine

Answer: (a)

2.80: An institution through which buyers and sellers interact and engage in exchange is a

Easy
Definition
Page: 38

(a) central authority.
(b) laissez-faire.
(c) market.
(d) production frontier.

Answer: (c)

2.81: Which of the following is NOT true of a market economy?

Easy
Fact
Page: 38

(a) In its pure form, it is also known as a laissez-faire economy.
(b) Decisions are regulated by a central agency.
(c) The interaction between buyers and sellers answers the basic economic questions of what gets produced, how it gets produced, and who gets it.
(d) It relies upon millions of individual economic decisions to determine economic outcomes.

Answer: (b)

2.82: The shock therapy that Poland underwent refers to

Easy
Fact
Page: 39

(a) rapidly rising prices .
(b) a complete shift from a command economy to a laissez-faire economy.
(c) rapid decontrol of prices and privatization of government enterprises.
(d) a move from a policy of noninvolvement with the West to a policy of involvement with the West.

Answer: (c)

2.83: Consumer sovereignty

Easy
Definition
Page: 38

(a) is dependent upon profits.
(b) is the idea that consumers can buy whatever they want to.
(c) is the idea that consumers determine what is produced in the economy through their demands.
(d) is only possible in a monarchy.

Answer: (c)

2.-84: Shoe manufacturers reintroduced platform shoes for women, but nobody bought them and so shoe manufacturers stopped making them. This is an example of

Easy
Single
Page: 38

(a) consumer sovereignty.
(b) consumer surplus.
(c) let the buyer beware.
(d) a market.

Answer: (a)

2.85: The idea that consumers ultimately dictate what will be produced by choosing what to purchase is known as

Easy
Definition
Page: 38

(a) laissez-faire.
(b) the economic problem.
(c) centralized decision making.
(d) consumer sovereignty.

Answer: (d)

Easy
Definition
Page: 40

2.86: The amount that a household earns each year is

(a) savings.
(b) wealth.
(c) income.
(d) consumption.

Answer: (c)

Easy
Definition
Page: 40

2.87: The amount that households have accumulated out of past income through saving and inheritance is

(a) future income.
(b) wealth.
(c) consumption.
(d) past income.

Answer: (b)

Moderate
Single
Page: 40

2.88: Which of the following statements is FALSE?

(a) Income comes only from wages and salaries.
(b) Income is the amount a household earns during a year.
(c) Wealth is the amount that a household has accumulated through saving or inheritance.
(d) A painting that an individual owns is considered wealth and the fees the person earns by lending the painting to museums are considered income.

Answer: (a)

Easy
Fact
Page: 40

2.89: In a free market system, the amount of output that any one household gets depends upon its

(a) income.
(b) wealth.
(c) wage and interest income.
(d) income and wealth.

Answer: (d)

Moderate
Fact
Page: 40

2.90: Which of the following is NOT a problem associated with the free enterprise system?

(a) A market system does not always produce what people want at lowest cost.
(b) Income may be unevenly distributed and some groups will have very little ability to command goods and services.
(c) Within a free market economy there are no forces to guarantee that producers use efficient techniques of production.
(d) Periods of unemployment and inflation recur with some regularity.

Answer: (c)

Easy
Fact
Page: 40

2.91: Advocates of an unregulated market system argue that

(a) competition promotes efficiency.
(b) competition leads to innovation.
(c) competition leads to product variety and quality.
(d) all of the above.

Answer: (d)

2.92: The basic coordinating mechanism in a free market system is

(a) quantity.
(b) price.
(c) a central government authority.
(d) the corporation.

Easy
Fact
Page: 40

Answer: (b)

2.93: Which of the following statements is FALSE?

(a) In a free market system, the basic economic questions are answered without the help of a central government plan or directive.
(b) Individuals guided by their own-self interest will produce products and services that other people want.
(c) The basic coordinating mechanism in a free market system is quantity adjustments toward equilibrium.
(d) In a free market system, competition forces firms to adopt efficient production techniques.

Easy
Fact
Page: 40

Answer: (c)

2.94: The distinguishing characteristic of a public good is that

(a) once the good is produced, everyone gets to enjoy its benefits, whether they have paid for the good or not.
(b) private firms cannot produce public goods because they don't have access to the technology necessary to produce the good.
(c) the good is produced at a zero cost to the public sector.
(d) individuals do not benefit from consuming the good, but society as a whole benefits from its production.

Moderate
Fact
Page: 40

Answer: (a)

2.95: National defense

(a) will be provided by a free market system and private corporations.
(b) will be provided by a private corporation.
(c) will be paid for voluntarily by users.
(d) will not be efficiently provided by a completely free market system.

Easy
Single
Page: 40

Answer: (d)

2.96: The services provided by a public school system are

(a) a public good, since tax dollars pay for the services provided.
(b) not a true public good, because students could be prevented from receiving these services if they did not pay for them.
(c) a public good, because a free market would not produce educational services.
(d) not a public good, because the quality of educational services varies among school districts.

Challenging
Single
Page: 40

Answer: (b)

2.97: Which of the following is TRUE of a market economy?

(a) Private firms make a profit selling public goods.
(b) Monopolies can develop.
(c) Innovation and new production are discouraged.
(d) Inefficient producers have greater protection than in a command economy.

Challenging
Single
Page: 40

Answer: (b)

Moderate
Single
Page: 39

2.98: Which of the following is an INCORRECT statement about a free market economy?

(a) The forces of competition will drive out inefficient producers.
(b) Competition encourages innovation in both production techniques and products.
(c) Private firms in a free market economy would find it profitable to sell collective or public goods such as national defense, assuming the government would let them.
(d) Monopolies can develop even in a free market economy.

Answer: (c)

Moderate
Fact
Page: 40

2.99: The U.S. government would be engaging in a stabilization policy if it attempted to

(a) reduce the fluctuations in its tax revenues.
(b) increase its spending in an orderly manner.
(c) keep population growth at a constant rate.
(d) reduce the level of unemployment in the United States.

Answer: (d)

Easy
Fact
Page: 40

2.-100: Some economists would advocate government intervention in a market economy

(a) to produce collective goods and services.
(b) when resource costs for a private producer do not reflect the full cost to society.
(c) to stabilize the economy.
(d) all of the above.

Answer: (d)

TRUE/FALSE QUESTIONS

Easy
Fact
Page: 26

2.101: Resources are unlimited in the long run.

Answer: False

Easy
Fact
Page: 25

2.102: In economics, the term, capital, refers only to some form of money.

Answer: False

Easy
Fact
Page: 25

2.103: Things that have already been produced that are in turn used to produce other goods and services over time are called "capital."

Answer: True

Easy
Fact
Page: 32

2.104: The resulting unemployment from the recession of the early 90s corresponds to points outside our society's production possibility frontier.

Answer: False

Easy
Fact
Page: 35

2.105: Economic growth shifts a society's production possibility frontier up and to the right.

Answer: True

2.106: The "economic problem" is that given scarce resources, how do large societies go about answering the basic economic questions of what will be produced, how it will be produced, and who will get it?

Easy
Definition
Page: 36

Answer: True

2.107: A laissez-faire economy is one in which individual people and firms pursue their own self-interest without any central direction or regulation.

Easy
Fact
Page: 38

Answer: True

2.108: The notion that buyers determine what will be produced by choosing what they purchase is called consumer sovereignty.

Easy
Fact
Page: 38

Answer: True

2.109: In economics, income and wealth mean the same thing.

Easy
Fact
Page: 40

Answer: False

2.110: Public goods are those goods and services that are consumed by governmental bodies.

Easy
Definition
Page: 40

Answer: False

SHORT ANSWER QUESTIONS

2.111: Carefully define and differentiate between consumer goods and capital goods.

Easy
Definition
Page: 35

Answer: Consumer goods are goods for immediate consumption, usually within a year, while capital goods are goods that can produce other goods.

2.112: What are the implications for economic growth for countries specializing in consumer goods rather than capital goods?

Moderate
Application
Page: 35

Answer: All else equal, countries that specialize in consumer goods will likely grow less than those that specialize in capital goods, because specializing in capital goods will allow for more goods to be produced in the future.

2.113: What is unemployment and how may it be depicted in a production possibilities frontier?

Easy
Definition
Page: 32

Answer: Unemployment occurs when those willing to work cannot find a job. It may be depicted as a point inside a production possibilities frontier, because we can produce more output with the additional labor that is not employed.

2.114: Define the law of increasing opportunity costs.

Easy
Definition
Page: 33

Answer: The law of increasing opportunity costs suggests that equal increases in the production of one good will cause an increasing reduction in the maximum amount of the other good that is produced.

SCENARIO 1: Consider the following data for the harvest of crabs versus the harvest of fish off the coast of Virginia in answering the following questions.

Combination	Fish	Crabs
A	100	0
B	90	15
C	70	30
D	40	45
E	0	60

Easy
Math
Page: 31

2.115: Refer to Scenario 1 graph the production possibilities frontier.

Answer:

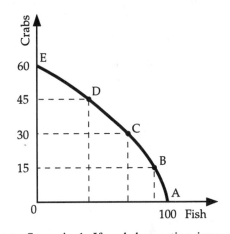

Moderate
Math
Page: 31

2.116: Refer to Scenario 1. If crab harvesting increases from 30 to 45, what is the opportunity cost?

Answer: The opportunity cost is 30 fish.

Moderate
Application
Page: 31

2.117: Refer to Scenario 1. What is the economic significance of 25 fish captured and 50 crabs captured?

Answer: The economic significance of capturing 25 fish and 50 crabs is that the harvest would be inside the production possibilities frontier, which suggests some resource unemployment.

Easy
Math
Page: 31

2.118: Refer to Scenario 1. Assuming an increase in fishing line technology improves the fish capture by 50 percent, graph the new production possibilities frontier.

Answer:

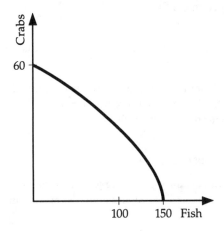

2.119: Refer to Scenario 1 and Question 118 what is the new opportunity cost for an increase in the production of crabs from 15 to 30?

Easy
Math
Page: 31

Answer: The opportunity cost is 30 fish.

SCENARIO 2: Assume that the production possibilities frontier for the production of corn and the production of wheat may be described by the following equation: $QC = 100 - 25 QW$ (where QC is the quantity of corn production and QW is the quantity of wheat production).

2.120: Graph the production possibilities frontier.

Moderate
Math
Page: 31

Answer:

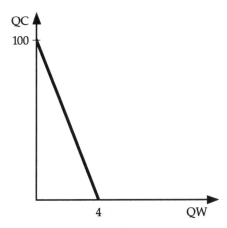

Moderate
Application
Page: 31

2.121: What is the opportunity cost of wheat production in terms of corn production?

Answer: The opportunity cost is one unit of wheat costs 25 units of corn.

2.122: Suppose technological change occurs which results in a production possibilities frontier of $QC = 150 - 40 QW$. Graph the new production possibilities frontier with the original and compare the two.

Moderate
Application
Page: 31

Answer:

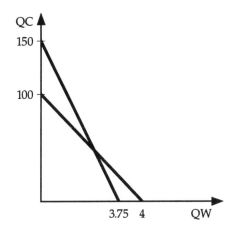

2.123: Refer to Scenario 2 and Question 122. Explain the economic significance of both the corn intercept and slope changes resulting from the technological change.

Moderate
Application
Page: 31

Answer: The intercept increase demonstrates the change in corn production if all resources are devoted to corn production. The slope change depicts a change in the opportunity cost of producing corn.

SCENARIO 3: Assume that two countries are the same in every way except that one allocates more of its resources to the production of capital goods as opposed to consumer goods.

Difficult
Math
Page: 35

2.124: Refer to Scenario 3. Graphically illustrate the production choices on a production possibilities frontier.

Answer:

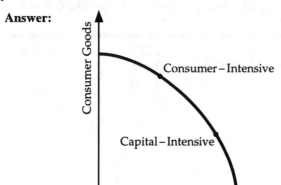

2.125: Refer to Scenario 3. Draw two separate sets of production possibilities frontiers to explain how economic growth may have different effects in the two countries.

Difficult
Math
Page: 35

Answer:

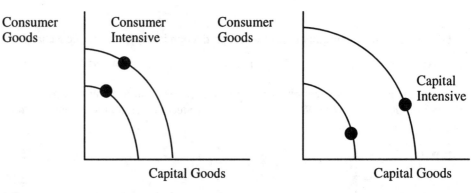

Difficult
Math
Page: 35

2.126: Refer to Scenario 3. Now assume that the countries are not alike, but that one is wealthier than the other in that it has more resources. Graphically illustrate this scenario using production possibilities frontiers.

Answer:

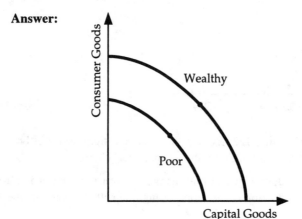

2.127: Refer to Scenario 3. What would be the impact of improvements in technology assuming that each country spends one-half of its resources on capital goods?

Difficult
Math
Page: 35

Answer: There should be a greater improvement in wealth for the wealthier country if each country continues to spend the same percentages.

2.128: Refer to Scenario 3. What happens to the relative income distribution between the two countries under the conditions in the previous question? Explain.

Difficult
Application
Page: 35

Answer: The relative income distributions, with income of the capital-good intensive country greater than the consumer-good intensive country, would be expected to widen as the growth is greater in the capital-good intensive country.

2.129: Would we expect the income distribution to be different in a mixed economy as opposed to a laissez-faire economy? Why or why not?

Moderate
Definition
Page: 38

Answer: Yes, in a mixed economy, we would expect a more equal distribution of income since, generally speaking, one of the functions of government is income redistribution.

2.130: Define consumer sovereignty and explain its role in a laissez-faire economy.

Moderate
Definition
Page: 38

Answer: Consumer sovereignty is the notion that consumer demand ultimately decides the answers to the economic questions. Because resources are allocated by firms maximizing profits to try to meet the consumer demand, it is the foundation of laissez-faire economies.

SCENARIO 4: Assume a desert island economy in which labor is the only scarce resource and labor can be used to gather food (coconuts) or to build huts. There are six equally productive individuals on the island. Each inhabitant can gather 25 coconuts in one day or build one hut in one day.

2.131: Refer to Scenario 4. Draw the production possibilities frontier the tradeoff between Coconuts and Huts.

Easy
Math
Page: 31

Answer:

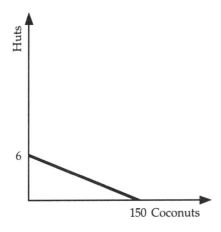

2.132: Refer to Scenario 4. Compute the opportunity cost of building two more huts in one day.

Moderate
Fact
Page: 31

Answer: The opportunity cost of building two more huts is 50 coconuts.

Moderate
Math
Page: 31

2.133: Refer to Scenario 4. If half of the workers build huts and half of the workers gather coconuts, what would be the production on the island?

Answer: In one day, the inhabitants would produce three huts and 75 coconuts.

Moderate
Math
Page: 31

2.134: Refer to Scenario 4. Assume that in one day, two huts were built and 75 coconuts were gathered. What does this situation depict?

Answer: The situation depicts the inefficient use of resources.

Moderate
Application
Page: 31

2.135: Refer to Scenario 4. What is the maximum potential increase in coconut production and maximum potential increase in hut production described in the previous question?

Answer: The maximum potential increase in production is either one more hut or 25 more coconuts.

Moderate
Application
Page: 31

2.136: Refer to Scenario 4. What would have to occur for three huts to be produced along with 100 coconuts?

Answer: Some form of economic growth or technological improvement would have to occur.

Honors
Application
Page: 31

2.137: Refer to Scenario 4. Provide possible explanations for the conditions described in the previous question to be achieved.

Answer: In order to exceed the maximum potential, perhaps the individuals could specialize according to their advantage or tools could be fashioned to improve production potentials.

SCENARIO 5: Suppose that a state needs to build both prisons and schools with a budget limited to ten million dollars. Schools cost $1 million each to build and prisons cost $2 million each to build.

Moderate
Math
Page: 31

2.138: Refer to Scenario 5. What is the maximum number of schools that can be built? The maximum number of prisons?

Answer: Ten is the maximum number of schools and five is the maximum number of prisons.

Easy
Math
Page: 31

2.139: Refer to Scenario 5. Draw the state's production possibilities frontier for the tradeoff between schools and prisons.

Answer:

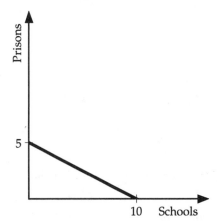

2.140: Refer to Scenario 5. What is the opportunity cost of building one more prison?

Moderate
Math
Page: 31

Answer: The opportunity cost of building one more prison is two schools.

2.141: Refer to Scenario 5. Assume that the price of prison production falls to $1.5 million each. Draw the new production possibilities frontier.

Moderate
Math
Page: 31

Answer:

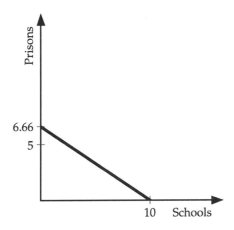

2.142: Refer to Scenario 5. What is the new opportunity cost of producing one more prison?

Moderate
Math
Page: 31

Answer: One more prison now costs one and one-half schools (10 / 6 2/3).

2.143: Refer to Scenario 5. Assume, after the prison price of production decreases, the price of school production rises to $2 million each. Draw the new production possibilities frontier.

Moderate
Math
Page: 31

Answer:

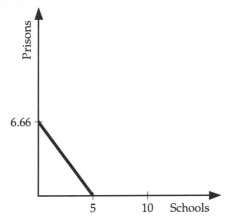

2.144: Refer to Scenario 5. What is the new opportunity cost of producing one more prison?

Moderate
Math
Page: 31

Answer: In the new situation, the opportunity cost of producing one more prison is two-thirds of a school.

2.145: Refer to Scenario 5. Assume that the state originally spent one-half of its budget on schools and one-half on prisons. What was the production of schools and prisons? Could the same number be achieved after the price of producing prisons falls to $1.5 million and the price of producing schools rises to $2 million? Explain.

Difficult
Application
Page: 31

Answer: Production is five schools and two and one-half prisons. No, the same number of schools and prisons could not be built after the price of production changes. If the state continues to divide its budget equally, production would be two and one-half schools and three and one-third prisons. If the budget were juggled, the maximum number of schools that could be built is five, but no prisons could be built. And, if two and one-half prisons were built, there would be enough left in the budget to build just over three schools.

Easy
Fact
Page: 26

2.146: Explain the three basic questions that each society must answer. Why must each society answer these questions?

Answer: The three basic questions are: What will be produced? How will it be produced? and Who will get what is produced? Each society must answer these questions because of resource scarcity.

Moderate
Single
Page: 27

2.147: Define opportunity cost. Given the definition of opportunity cost, explain what is meant by the statement "There is no such thing as a free lunch."

Answer: Opportunity cost is that which we give up, or forgo, when we make a choice. There is no such thing as a free lunch because everything involves a cost, even if it is just a time cost.

Moderate
Multi
Page: 28

2.148: Kathy and Amy paint pictures and do caricatures to sell to tourists. In one day, Kathy can either paint 2 pictures or do 4 caricatures. In one day, Amy can either paint 3 pictures or do 3 caricatures. For both Kathy and Amy, what is the opportunity cost of painting one picture? Who has the comparative advantage in painting pictures and who has the comparative advantage in doing caricatures? How might they be able to increase their total output?

Answer: Kathy's opportunity cost of painting a picture is 2 caricatures. Amy's opportunity cost of painting a picture is one caricature. Amy has a comparative advantage in painting and Kathy has a comparative advantage in doing caricatures. They could increase output by specializing in producing the goods for which they have a comparative advantage.

Easy
Definition
Page: 30

2.149: Explain how economists use the term "investment."

Answer: Investment is the process of using resources to produce new capital.

Moderate
Single
Page: 32

2.150: Use a production possibility frontier to illustrate an economy that is inefficient and an economy that has achieved efficiency. Explain the concept of efficiency.

Answer: An inefficient economy will either be inside the ppf or at the wrong point on the ppf. An efficient economy will be at a point on the ppf that represents the combination of goods most desired by society.

Answer:

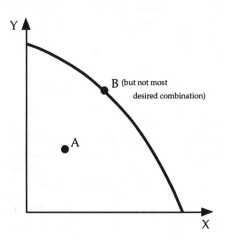

2.151: Define economic growth. Use a production possibility frontier to illustrate economic growth. Given this definition, explain why some people argue that an economy should not try to achieve economic growth.

Challenging
Multi
Page: 35

Answer: Economic growth is an increase in the total output of an economy. The ppf shifts up and outward as a result. Some people argue against growth because of the costs to the environment.

Answer: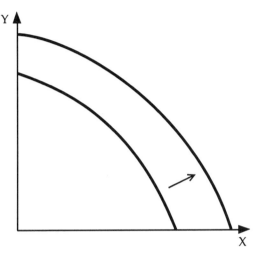

2.152: What is the economic problem? How does a command economy solve the economic problem?

Easy
Fact
Page: 37

Answer: The economic problem is that given scarce resources, how exactly do large, complex societies go about answering the basic economic questions? A command economy answers the questions through some centralized authority making decisions about what to produce, how to produce it, and how to distribute it.

2.153: Explain how a laissez-faire system answers three basic questions of what to produce, how to produce it, and how to distribute it.

Moderate
Fact
Page: 38

Answer: A laissez-faire system answers the three basic questions by allowing individuals to pursue their own self-interest without any central direction.

2.154: Explain three of the shortcomings of the free-enterprise system.

Moderate
Fact
Page: 38

Answer: The shortcomings of the free-enterprise system are: products may not always be produced at lowest cost, income may be unevenly distributed, and periods of inflation and unemployment may recur.

2.155: What is a public good? Why aren't public goods produced by the private sector? Give an example of a public good.

Easy
Fact
Page: 40

Answer: A public good is good whose benefits are social or collective. Public goods are not produced by the private sector because their benefits cannot be confined to those who paid for them. An example of a public good is national defense.

3 The Structure of the U.S. Economy: The Private, Public, and International Sectors

3.1: Which of the following would NOT be considered part of the private sector?

(a) a corporation whose stock is all held by one family
(b) a Catholic university
(c) the American Cancer Society, a charitable organization
(d) a public elementary school

Easy
Single
Page: 45

Answer: (d)

3.2: The public sector does NOT include which of the following?

(a) publicly-held corporations
(b) federal government employees
(c) civilian employees of the Defense Department
(d) public school teachers

Easy
Single
Page: 45

Answer: (a)

3.3: Jabot produces clothing sold both in the United States and England. Jabot is part of the

(a) private and public sectors.
(b) public and international sectors.
(c) private and international sectors.
(d) private and public sectors.

Moderate
Single
Page: 45

Answer: (c)

3.4: You need some extra money to pay for your living expenses and so you start a service to type resumes. You hire three people to type the resumes. This is an example of a

(a) proprietorship.
(b) partnership.
(c) corporation.
(d) not-for-profit firm.

Moderate
Single
Page: 46

Answer: (a)

3.5: The form of business organization that accounts for the largest percentage of total firms is the _____ and the form of business organization that accounts for the highest percentage of total sales is the _____.

(a) corporation; corporation
(b) corporation; partnership
(c) partnership; corporation
(d) proprietorship; corporation

Easy
Fact
Page: 46

Answer: (d)

63

Moderate
Single
Page: 46

3.6: After graduation, you start a management consulting firm with a gift of $5,000 from your parents. A year later, your consulting firm goes out of business with $50,000 of debt. Which of the following statements is true?

(a) You are liable only for the initial $5,000 that you invested in the business.
(b) You are liable for the $50,000 of debt.
(c) The assets you have in the firm must be liquidated to pay off the debt and if the value of the assets is less than $50,000, you are not liable for the difference.
(d) You are not liable for any of the debt.

Answer: (b)

Moderate
Single
Page: 46

3.6: After graduation, you start a restaurant with a gift of $5,000 from you uncle. A year later, your restaurant goes out of business with $70,000 of debt. Which of the following statements is true?

(a) You are liable for the $70,000 of debt.
(b) You are liable only for the initial $5,000 that you invested in the business.
(c) You are not liable for any of the debt.
(d) The assets you have in the restaurant must be liquidated to pay off the debt and if the value of the assets is less than $70,000, you are not liable for the difference.

Answer: (a)

Easy
Fact
Page: 46

3.7: In which form of business organization are the assets and liabilities of the firm the owner's assets and liabilities?

(a) proprietorship only
(b) partnership only
(c) proprietorship and partnership
(d) partnership and corporation.

Answer: (c)

Moderate
Fact
Page: 46

3.8: Which of the following would be considered a drawback of a proprietorship?

(a) A proprietorship can be started without any formal legal process.
(b) The proprietor alone is responsible for all the debt of the proprietorship.
(c) The proprietorship's income is taxed at the personal income tax rate rather than at the corporate income tax rate.
(d) both b and c.

Answer: (b)

Moderate
Fact
Page: 46

3.9: The primary disadvantage of a proprietorship is that

(a) there is a very complicated legal process involved in starting the proprietorship.
(b) there is no limit to the proprietor's liability.
(c) the profits of the proprietorship are doubly taxed.
(d) there is only one employee in the firm.

Answer: (b)

Challenging
Single
Page: 46

3.10: Ms. McLaughlin starts her restaurant as a proprietorship and is the sole owner. After a year of disastrous reviews, she has gone deeply into debt. Her liability is

(a) zero; she has already lost all her money.
(b) the amount of her original investment.
(c) limited to assets owned by the restaurant.
(d) unlimited; she may lose nearly all her personal belongings.

Answer: (d)

3.11: The most common and least complex form of business organization is the

(a) proprietorship.
(b) not-for-profit firm.
(c) partnership.
(d) corporation.

Answer: (a)

Easy
Fact
Page: 46

3.12: The type of business organization that accounts for the smallest percentage of total sales is the

(a) proprietorship.
(b) partnership.
(c) corporation.
(d) monopoly.

Answer: (b)

Easy
Fact
Page: 47

3.13: A partnership

(a) requires a charter from a state government in order to operate.
(b) is not taxed.
(c) has shared liability, since each partner can be held responsible only for his/her share of the debt.
(d) has no limit to liability. Either partner can be held responsible for the entire debt.

Answer: (d)

Easy
Definition
Page: 47

3.14: You form a partnership with two friends and you each invest $10,000. The partnership goes out of business with a debt of $60,000, and your partners cannot be located. You are liable for

(a) only the $10,000 of your initial investment.
(b) only $20,000, one-third of the partnership debt.
(c) $30,000, your initial investment plus one-third of the partnership debt.
(d) the entire $60,000 of debt.

Answer: (d)

Moderate
Single
Page: 47

13.14: You form a partnership with three very close friends and you each invest $15,000. The partnership goes out of business with a debt of $90,000, and your partners cannot be located. You are liable for

(a) only $22,500, one-fourth of the partnership debt.
(b) only the $15,000 of your initial investment.
(c) the enire $90,000 of debt.
(d) $27,500, your initial investment plus one-fourth of the partnership debt.

Answer: (c)

Moderate
Single
Page: 47

3.15: A corporation

(a) is owned by only one individual.
(b) is established by federal charter.
(c) is a legal entity separate from its owners.
(d) is like a partnership with many partners.

Answer: (c)

Moderate
Fact
Page: 47

Easy
Fact
Page: 47

3.16: A corporate charter is obtained from

(a) a local government.
(b) a state government.
(c) the federal government.
(d) a certified accounting firm.

Answer: (b)

Challenging
Single
Page: 47

3.17: Mr. Porter is the owner of a corporation and invests $60,000 in the business. Unfortunately, the firm goes out of business with debts totaling $100,000. The most Mr. Porter is liable for is

(a) $60,000, the amount of his investment.A
(b) $100,000, the amount of the corporation's debts.
(c) $60,000 plus whatever personal assets he has, up to the $100,000 of debt.
(d) $80,000, the average of his investment and what the firm owes.

Answer: (a)

Challenging
Single
Page: 47

3.17: Mr. Larson is the owner of a corporation and invests $40,000 in the business. Unfortunately, the firm goes out of business with debts totaling $120,000. The most Mr. Larson is liable for is

(a) $30,000, what the firm owes divided by the amount of his investment.
(b) $40,000, the amount of his investment.
(c) $40,000 plus whatever personal assets he has, up to the $120,000 of debt.
(d) $120,000, the amount of the corporation's debts.

Answer: (b)

Easy
Definition
Page: 47

3.18: A certificate of partial ownership of a corporation that entitles the holder to a portion of the corporation profit is a

(a) dividend.
(b) share of stock.
(c) corporate bond.
(d) mutual fund.

Answer: (b)

Easy
Single
Page: 47

3.19: You purchase a share of stock in the Nashbar Bicycle Corporation for $40. This year you received a payment of $5 from Nashbar Bicycle. Which of the following is TRUE?

(a) This has turned out to be a bad investment.
(b) You have received a 12.5% return of your investment.
(c) The corporation must have retained earning of $35 for every share of stock sold.
(d) This $5 represents income on which you don't pay taxes since the corporation already paid corporate profits taxes.

Answer: (b)

Easy
Single
Page: 47

3.19: You purchase a share of stock in the Enz of the World Corporation for $90. This year you received a payment of $15 from Enz of the World. Which of the following is TRUE?

(a) The corporation must have retained earnings of $75 for every share of stock sold.
(b) This has turned out to be a bad investment.
(c) This $15 represents income on which you don't pay taxes since the corporation already paid corporate profits taxes.
(d) You have received a 16.67% return on your investment.

Answer: (d)

3.20: In case of bankruptcy, corporate shareholders

(a) are liable up to the amount they have invested.
(b) are liable for a percentage of the corporation's debt corresponding to the percentage of stock they own.
(c) have unlimited liability.
(d) have no liability. If the corporation goes bankrupt, they must be repaid their original investment.

Answer: (a)

3.21: Which of the following is a legal entity that exists separately from its ownership?

(a) a proprietorship
(b) a partnership
(c) a corporation
(d) a monopoly

Answer: (c)

3.22: A disadvantage of the corporation is

(a) limited liability.
(b) state charters are difficult to get.
(c) "double" taxation of profits.
(d) the corporation is a separate legal entity.

Answer: (c)

3.23: A dividend is the

(a) profit that a corporation keeps, usually for the purchase of capital assets.
(b) certificate of partial ownership of a corporation that entitles the holder to a portion of the corporation's profits.
(c) portion of a corporation's profit that the firm pays out each period to the shareholders.
(d) payment made by a corporation to the corporation's bondholders.

Answer: (c)

3.24: Net income is another term for

(a) gross receipts.
(b) dividends.
(c) profits after taxes.
(d) profits.

Answer: (d)

3.25: A tax is paid twice on corporate income because

(a) corporate profits are taxed by both federal and state governments.
(b) the corporation pays the corporate income tax on its profits and shareholders pay personal income taxes on the dividends they receive.
(c) the corporation pays both the corporate income tax and the personal income tax on its profits.
(d) the corporation has to pay both a profits tax and social insurance taxes.

Answer: (b)

Easy
Fact
Page: 47

3.26: The federal corporate income tax is a tax on

(a) the net income of corporations.
(b) the total revenue earned by corporations
(c) the dividends paid by corporations
(d) the retained earnings of corporations.

Answer: (a)

Easy
Definition
Page: 48

3.27: The profits that a corporation keeps, usually for the purchase of capital assets, are

(a) retained earnings.
(b) dividends.
(c) net income.
(d) capital income.

Answer: (a)

Moderate
Single
Page: 48

3.28: The Nelson Bedding Corporation had a net income of $500,000 in 1993. Of this net income $250,000 was paid in taxes and $150,000 was retained to purchase capital assets. Therefore, the Nelson Bedding Corporation paid dividends of

(a) $50,000.
(b) $100,000.
(c) $150,000.
(d) an amount that can not be determined from this information.

Answer: (b)

Moderate
Single
Page: 48

3.28: The Shuey's Chewey Cookies Corporation had a net income of $650,000 in 1997. Of this net income $300,000 was paid in taxes and $100,000 was retained to purchase capital assets. Therefore, the Shuey's Chewey Cookies Corporation paid dividents of

(a) $250,000.
(b) $350,000.
(c) $550,000.
(d) an amount that can be determined from this information.

Answer: (a)

Easy
Definition
Page: 49

3.29: Market organization is the study of

(a) how to organize firms into industries.
(b) the way an industry pursues profits.
(c) the way an industry responds to government regulation.
(d) the way an industry is structured.

Answer: (d)

Moderate
Single
Page: 48

3.30: Which of the following would be considered an industry?

(a) all firms that are located in Santa Fe, New Mexico
(b) all the firms from which a steel company purchases its inputs
(c) all firms producing baby furniture
(d) all firms that are owned by a multinational conglomerate

Answer: (c)

3.31: An industry is a group of firms

(a) located in the same geographical area.
(b) producing similar products.
(c) that supply the various inputs needed to produce a final product.
(d) owned by a corporation.

Answer: (b)

Easy
Definition
Page: 48

3.32: You are conducting a study of whether or not the largest hospital in Cleveland, Ohio can control the salaries paid to nurses in that city. This would be included under the study of

(a) market performance.
(b) profitability analysis.
(c) competitiveness analysis.
(d) market organization.

Answer: (d)

Moderate
Single
Page: 48

3.33: You are studying whether or not competing firms can freely enter or leave the computer software industry. You are studying

(a) market organization.
(b) market performance.
(c) market conduct.
(d) competitiveness analysis.

Answer: (a)

Moderate
Single
Page: 49

3.34: Products in a perfectly competitive industry

(a) may be homogeneous or differentiated.
(b) are differentiated.
(c) are homogeneous.
(d) are actually homogeneous, but consumers perceive them as being differentiated.

Answer: (c)

Easy
Fact
Page: 49

3.35: Which of the following statements is FALSE?

(a) In perfect competition, no firm is large enough to have any control over price.
(b) In perfect competition, firms produce homogeneous products.
(c) In perfect competition, firms cannot freely enter and exit the market.
(d) In perfect competition, there are many firms each of which is small relative to the market.

Answer: (c)

Easy
Fact
Page: 49

3.36: In perfect competition

(a) there is a small number of firms.
(b) firms can freely enter and exit the market.
(c) firms produce differentiated products.
(d) firms are large enough to exert control over price.

Answer: (b)

Easy
Fact
Page: 53

3.37: An example of a perfectly competitive industry is the

(a) wheat industry.
(b) automobile industry.
(c) fast-food restaurant industry.
(d) United States post office.

Answer: (a)

Moderate
Single
Page: 54

Easy
Single
Page: 53

3.38: Which of the following statements is NOT true for perfect competition?

(a) There are many firms in the industry and each is small relative to the industry.
(b) Firms in the industry produce virtually identical products.
(c) No firm is large enough to have any control over price.
(d) New firms cannot freely enter and exit the market.

Answer: (d)

Easy
Fact
Page: 53

3.39: The industry structure characterized by a large number of firms producing virtually identical products is

(a) perfect competition.
(b) monopolistic competition.
(c) oligopoly.
(d) monopoly.

Answer: (a)

Moderate
Fact
Page: 53

3.40: In perfect competition

(a) each firm controls a relatively large share of the market.
(b) firms select the price at which they sell their product.
(c) advertising is likely to be effective.
(d) firms produce identical products.

Answer: (d)

Easy
Fact
Page: 53

3.41: In which market structure do firms have no price setting power?

(a) perfect competition
(b) monopolistic competition
(c) oligopoly
(d) monopoly

Answer: (a)

Challenging
Single
Page: 49

3.42: The market price for lead pencils is 25 cents. The Click Pencil Company tries to sell its lead pencils for 26 cents but finds that it cannot sell any lead pencils at that price. Firm A is in what type of industry?

(a) perfectly competitive.
(b) monopolistically competitive.
(c) oligopolistic
(d) monopolistic

Answer: (a)

Challenging
Single
Page: 49

3.42: The market price for erasers 75 cents. The Clear All Eraser Company tries to sell its erasers for 76 cents but finds that it cannot sell any erasers at that price. Firm A is in what type of industry?

(a) oligopolistic
(b) perfectly competitive.
(c) monopolistically competitive.
(d) monopolistic

Answer: (b)

3.43: Barriers to entry are the lowest in

(a) perfect competition.
(b) monopolistic competition.
(c) oligopoly.
(d) monopoly.

Answer: (a)

Easy
Fact
Page: 49

3.44: Which market structure has the most effective barriers to entry?

(a) monopoly
(b) oligopoly
(c) perfect competition
(d) monopolistic competition

Answer: (a)

Easy
Fact
Page: 50

3.45: A monopoly exists

(a) any time there is one seller of a product.
(b) any time there is one seller of a product with no close substitutes.
(c) any time entry into an industry is difficult.
(d) any time you own three or more pieces of the same color of real estate.

Answer: (b)

Moderate
Fact
Page: 50

3.46: Which of the following statements is NOT true of a monopoly?

(a) There is one firm in the industry.
(b) The product produced by the monopolist has many close substitutes.
(c) Monopolists can set prices but are subject to some market discipline.
(d) A monopolist is protected from competition by barriers to entry.

Answer: (b)

Easy
Fact
Page: 50

3.47: Ameritech® is the only supplier of local telephone service in Columbus. Ameritech represents an example of what market structure?

(a) perfect competition.
(b) monopolistic competition.
(c) oligopoly.
(d) monopoly.

Answer: (d)

Easy
Fact
Page: 50

3.48: In a monopolistically competitive industry, products are

(a) homogeneous.
(b) differentiated.
(c) produced by one firm, but sold by many.
(d) sold at a single price.

Answer: (b)

Moderate
Fact
Page: 51

3.49: The industry structure in which many firms compete by producing similar but slightly differentiated products is

(a) perfect competition.
(b) monopolistic competition.
(c) oligopoly
(d) monopoly

Answer: (b)

Easy
Fact
Page: 51

Moderate
Single
Page: 51

3.50: The difference between perfect competition and monopolistic competition is that in perfect competition _____, but in monopolistic competition _____.

(a) there is a large number of firms; there is a small number of firms
(b) firms produce identical products; firms produce similar but differentiated products
(c) firms have some control over price; firms have no control over price
(d) there is both price and quality competition; there is only quality competition

Answer: (b)

Moderate
Fact
Page: 51

3.51: Pizza Palace spends a large amount of money trying to differentiate its pizza from its competitors' pizza. This firm is most likely in

(a) a perfectly competitive industry.
(b) a perfectly competitive or monopolistically competitive industry.
(c) a monopolistically competitive or oligopolistic industry.
(d) an oligopolistic or monopolistic industry.

Answer: (c)

Moderate
Fact
Page: 51

3.52: The restaurant industry characterized by easy entry. The restaurant industry

(a) could be either perfectly competitive or monopolistically competitive.
(b) must be perfectly competitive.
(c) could be either monopolistically competitive or oligopolistic.
(d) could be either perfectly competitive, monopolistically competitive, or oligopolistic.

Answer: (a)

Moderate
Single
Page: 51

3.53: Which of the following is NOT true for monopolistically competitive industries?

(a) Firms in the industry produce differentiated products.
(b) There are a large number of relatively small firms in the industry.
(c) Firms in the industry have no control over price.
(d) Entry and exit from the industry are relatively easy.

Answer: (c)

Moderate
Single
Page: 51

3.54: Which of the following is MOST likely to be a firm in a monopolistically competitive industry?

(a) a Wisconsin dairy farmer
(b) IBM®
(c) Kodak®
(d) Sharyn's Hair Styling Salon

Answer: (d)

Moderate
Fact
Page: 51

3.55: Which of the following is NOT a characteristic of an oligopolistic industry?

(a) There are a few large firms in the industry.
(b) The firms in the industry always produce standardized products.
(c) The firms in the industry generally behave "strategically" with respect to one another.
(d) Entry of new firms is difficult but possible.

Answer: (b)

3.56: Which of the following statements is FALSE?

(a) Entry into an oligopolistic industry is relatively difficult.
(b) Firms in a monopolistically competitive industry can raise prices substantially without fear of losing many customers.
(c) Firms in a perfectly competitive industry have control over how much they sell but no control over price.
(d) In order for a monopoly to remain a monopoly there must be some type of barrier to entry.

Answer: (b)

Challenging
Single
Page: 51

3.57: US Air® is considering lowering its fares to increase its sales but is afraid of triggering a price war with its competitors. This firm is most likely in

(a) a perfectly competitive industry.
(b) a monopolistically competitive industry.
(c) a highly regulated industry.
(d) an oligopolistic industry.

Answer: (d)

Moderate
Single
Page: 51

3.58: An economist is studying the bicycle industry which is characterized by firms that behave somewhat unpredictably. The bicycle industry is likely to be

(a) perfectly competitive.
(b) oligopolistic.
(c) a monopoly.
(d) monopolistically competitive.

Answer: (b)

Challenging
Single
Page: 51

3.-59: An industry with a small number of firms is

(a) perfectly competitive.
(b) monopolistically competitive.
(c) oligopolistic.
(d) a corporation.

Answer: (c)

Easy
Fact
Page: 51

3.60: The industry structure which has the distinguishing characteristic of strategic behavior is

(a) perfect competition.
(b) monopoly.
(c) oligopoly
(d) monopolistic competition.

Answer: (c)

Easy
Fact
Page: 51

3.61: The industry structure that has the distinguishing characteristic of price competition only is

(a) perfect competition.
(b) monopoly.
(c) oligopoly.
(d) monopolistic competition.

Answer: (a)

Easy
Fact
Page: 49

Moderate
Single
Page: 51

3.62: The automobile industry is an example of

(a) perfect competition.
(b) monopolistic competition.
(c) monopoly.
(d) oligopoly.

Answer: (d)

Easy
Fact
Page: 52

3.63: The top four manufacturers of shampoo control 20% of the market. According to William G. Shepherd's classification scheme, the shampoo industry would be classified as

(a) a tight oligopoly.
(b) effectively competitive.
(c) perfectly competitive.
(d) a dominant firm industry.

Answer: (b)

Moderate
Fact
Page: 52

3.64: Which of the following statements is TRUE?

(a) The percentage of national income that is accounted for by monopolies has been increasing since 1939.
(b) In Shepherd's classification scheme, a firm is classified as a monopoly if its sales account for 90% or more of an industry's total sales.
(c) The percentage of national income that originates in the effectively competitive sector has been increasing since 1939.
(d) In Shepherd's classification scheme, a tight oligopoly is an industry in which the top eight firms account for 55 to 75% of total industry sales.

Answer: (c)

Easy
Fact
Page: 53

3.65: Which of the following is one of the factors that has caused the increased competitiveness of the U.S. economy over time?

(a) increased competition from exports
(b) reductions in the corporate profits tax
(c) deregulation of industries
(d) lax enforcement of antimonopoly laws

Answer: (c)

Moderate
Fact
Page: 53

3.66: According to Shepherd, the United States's economy

(a) was primarily monopolistic and still is.
(b) was primarily competitive but is now monopolistic.
(c) was primarily monopolistic but is now competitive.
(d) was effectively competitive and has become more so.

Answer: (d)

Easy
Fact
Page: 53

3.67: In 1990, the industry type that accounted for the largest share of national income was

(a) manufacturing.
(b) services.
(c) wholesale and retail trade.
(d) agriculture.

Answer: (b)

3.68: The fastest growing sector of the United States economy has been the

Easy
Fact
Page: 54

(a) government sector.
(b) manufacturing sector.
(c) service sector.
(d) agricultural sector.

Answer: (c)

3.69: Which of the following statements is FALSE?

Moderate
Fact
Page: 55

(a) Structural change in the United States can be viewed as a natural consequence of continued economic growth and progress.
(b) Resources are always shifting among sectors of the economy.
(c) Since 1970 the manufacturing sector has accounted for a decreasing share of national income.
(d) One of the major roles of the government in the U.S. economy has been to keep resources from shifting from one sector to another sector of the economy.

Answer: (d)

3.70: The total value of all goods and services produced in an economy in a given period of time is

Easy
Fact
Page: 55

(a) net national product.
(b) gross domestic product.
(c) gross private production.
(d) net public production.

Answer: (b)

3.71: Which category of government spending has almost doubled as a percentage of GDP from 1980 to 1990?

Challenging
Fact
Page: 56

(a) purchases of goods and services
(b) national defense
(c) transfer payments
(d) interest payments

Answer: (d)

3.72: Which of the following is NOT a category of government spending?

Easy
Fact
Page: 56

(a) purchases of goods and services
(b) taxes
(c) interest payments
(d) transfer payments

Answer: (b)

3.73: Which of the following statements is FALSE?

Moderate
Fact
Page: 56

(a) Government employment as a percentage of total employment in the economy has steadily increased since 1950.
(b) Taken together, transfer payments and interest payments account for nearly the entire increase in government expenditures between 1960 and 1980.
(c) During the 1980s, transfer payments stopped growing as a percentage of GDP.
(d) The increase in the size of the social security system accounts for much of the increase in transfer payments.

Answer: (a)

Easy
Fact
Page: 56

3.74: The wages and salaries paid for the services of government employees are included in what category of government spending?

(a) government transfer payments
(b) government interest payments
(c) government purchases of goods and services
(d) government subsidy payments

Answer: (c)

Easy
Fact
Page: 56

3.75: Interest payments in 1990 almost doubled as a percentage of GDP over the 1980 level. This is because of

(a) the huge deficits run up during the early 1980s.
(b) the huge increase in welfare payments made during the 1980s.
(c) rapidly rising interest rates during the 1980s.
(d) the huge increase in federal employment during the 1980s.

Answer: (a)

Moderate
Single
Page: 56

3.76: Which of the following is not a government transfer payment?

(a) Social security benefits paid to a disabled worker.
(b) Unemployment compensation paid to a worker who was laid off from his job.
(c) The interest paid to a government bond-holder.
(d) A housing subsidy granted to a low income family.

Answer: (c)

Easy
Fact
Page: 56

3.77: Which of the following statements is FALSE?

(a) In 1990 the federal government employed less than 3% of the total workforce.
(b) Federal employment as a percentage of total employment in the United States has fallen steadily since 1950.
(c) Since 1980 state and local government employment has grown steadily as a fraction of total employment.
(d) Total government employment in 1990 was less than 20% of total employment in the economy.

Answer: (c)

Moderate
Fact
Page: 57

3.78: The two largest categories in the federal budget are

(a) national defense and interest on the national debt.
(b) social security and interest on the national debt.
(c) national defense and social security.
(d) social security and health care.

Answer: (c)

Moderate
Fact
Page: 57

3.79: Which of the following statements is FALSE?

(a) Medicare and health-care expenditures taken together rose from 10% of the federal budget in 1982 to 15% of the federal budget in 1992.
(b) The percentage of federal expenditures accounted for by national defense has been shrinking with the end of the Cold War.
(c) The percentage of federal expenditures accounted for by interest payments has been decreasing since interest rates have dropped sharply since 1982.
(d) The percentage of federal expenditures accounted for by income security payments has decreased since 1982.

Answer: (c)

3.80: The single largest category of federal government spending is

(a) Social Security.
(b) interest payments.
(c) income security.
(d) education.

Answer: (a)

Easy
Fact
Page: 57

3.81: The largest state and local government expenditures are for

(a) education.
(b) welfare.
(c) highways.
(d) interest payments.

Answer: (a)

Easy
Fact
Page: 59

3.82: The biggest single source of revenue for the federal government is the

(a) corporate income tax.
(b) individual income tax.
(c) social insurance tax.
(d) property tax.

Answer: (b)

Easy
Fact
Page: 59

3.83: In 1994 the largest single source of federal receipts was

(a) property taxes.
(b) corporate income taxes.
(c) individual income taxes.
(d) social insurance taxes.

Answer: (c)

Easy
Fact
Page: 60

3.84: Taxes levied at a flat rate on wages and salaries are

(a) individual income taxes.
(b) work taxes.
(c) excise taxes.
(d) social insurance taxes.

Answer: (d)

Easy
Definition
Page: 60

3.85: Social insurance taxes on payrolls fund

(a) the social security system and the unemployment compensation system.
(b) the social security system and welfare programs.
(c) the unemployment compensation system and welfare.
(d) welfare programs and education.

Answer: (a)

Easy
Fact
Page: 60

3.86: Since 1980, payroll taxes _____ as a share of total tax revenue.

(a) have been decreasing
(b) have been increasing
(c) decreased and then increased
(d) increased and then decreased

Answer: (b)

Easy
Fact
Page: 60

Moderate
Fact
Page: 61

3.87: The largest source of state and local revenue is

(a) sales taxes.
(b) property taxes.
(c) personal income taxes.
(d) social insurance taxes.

Answer: (a)

Moderate
Fact
Page: 60

3.88: Profits from proprietorships and partnerships are

(a) subject to the corporate income tax.
(b) taxed as ordinary personal income of the owners.
(c) exempt from federal taxes.
(d) subject to double taxation.

Answer: (b)

Easy
Definition
Page: 60

3.89: A tax on a specific commodity is

(a) a general sales tax.
(b) an estate tax.
(c) an excise tax.
(d) a tariff.

Answer: (c)

Easy
Single
Page: 60

3.90: A federal tax levied on cigarettes is an example of

(a) a customs tax.
(b) an excise tax.
(c) a regulatory tax.
(d) a luxury tax.

Answer: (b)

Easy
Fact
Page: 61

3.91: The purpose of the North American Free Trade Agreement (NAFTA) is to

(a) reduce the United States's dependency on imported oil.
(b) reduce the amount the United States imports from Canada and Mexico.
(c) reduce trade barriers between the United States, Canada, and Mexico.
(d) speed up the transfer of technology among the United States, Canada and Mexico.

Answer: (c)

Easy
Fact
Page: 61

3.92: In 1992, imports were approximately _____ of GDP.

(a) 11%
(b) 12.9%
(c) 18%
(d) 25%

Answer: (a)

Easy
Fact
Page: 63

3.93 The largest category of U.S. exports is

(a) agricultural products.
(b) automobiles.
(c) consumer goods except automotive.
(d) capital goods, except automobiles.

Answer: (d)

3.94: The largest category of U.S. imports is

(a) automobiles, vehicles, parts and engines.
(b) capital goods except automotive.
(c) petroleum and petroleum products.
(d) industrial supplies and materials.

Easy
Fact
Page: 63

Answer: (b)

3.95: The volume of international trade in the United States increased significantly

(a) after the Great Depression.
(b) after the Second World War.
(c) beginning in 1960.
(d) beginning in 1970.

Easy
Fact
Page: 63

Answer: (d)

3.96: Which of the following statements is FALSE?

(a) In 1991 the United States imported more than it exported.
(b) The largest single category of imports in the United States is automobiles, vehicles, parts and engines.
(c) The largest single category of exports from the United States is capital goods except automotive.
(d) Imports have held steady at approximately 11% of GDP since 1987.

Moderate
Fact
Page: 63

Answer: (b)

3.97: Which of the following market structures would most likely define the market for home stereo equipment?

(a) perfect competition
(b) monopolistic competition
(c) oligopoly
(d) monopoly

Moderate
Application
Page: 51

Answer: (b)

3.98: Which of the following market structures would most likely define the market for cable television?

(a) perfect competition
(b) monopolistic competition
(c) oligopoly
(d) monopoly

Moderate
Application
Page: 50

Answer: (d)

3.99: Which of the following market structures would most likely define the marketplace for microbreweries?

(a) perfect competition
(b) monopolistic competition
(c) oligopoly
(d) monopoly

Moderate
Application
Page: 51

Answer: (b)

Challenging
Application
Page: 51

3.100: Which of the following market structures would most likely define the marketplace for textbook publishers?

(a) perfect competition
(b) monopolistic competition
(c) oligopoly
(d) monopoly

Answer: (c)

Challenging
Application
Page: 49

3.101: Which of the following market structures would most likely define the market for sea shells?

(a) perfect competition
(b) monopolistic competition
(c) oligopoly
(d) monopoly

Answer: (a)

Honors
Application
Page: 50

3.102: Which of the following market structures would most likely define the market for air travel in this situation?

(a) perfect competition
(b) monopolistic competition
(c) oligopoly
(d) monopoly

Answer: (d)

Honors
Application
Page: 51

3.103: Which of the following market structures would most likely define the market for dish washing soap?

(a) perfect competition
(b) monopolistic competition
(c) oligopoly
(d) monopoly

Answer: (c)

TRUE/FALSE QUESTIONS

Easy
Fact
Page: 47

3.104: In a partnership, the owners are jointly and separately liable for all the debts of the partnership.

Answer: True

Easy
Definition
Page: 47

3.105: A certificate of partial ownership of a corporation that entitles the holder to a portion of the corporation's profit is called a bond.

Answer: False

Easy
Fact
Page: 49

3.106: In a perfectly competitive industry, no single firm has any control over prices.

Answer: True

Easy
Fact
Page: 49

3.107: Firms in a perfectly competitive industry have control over how much they sell, but no control over price.

Answer: True

3.108: Most electric power companies and local telephone service companies are examples of government-protected monopolies.

Answer: True

Easy
Single
Page: 50

3.109: A monopoly is a one-firm industry that produces a product for which there are many close substitutes.

Answer: False

Easy
Definition
Page: 50

3.110: An oligopoly is an industry with a small number of producers and great ease of entry, and one in which no single company can affect price.

Answer: False

Easy
Definition
Page: 51

3.111: Recent empirical evidence indicates that the U.S. economy has become more competitive over the last 30 years.

Answer: True

Easy
Fact
Page: 52

3.112: The largest single category in the federal budget is national defense.

Answer: False

Easy
Fact
Page: 57

3.113: The largest single source of federal tax revenue is the corporate income tax.

Answer: False

Easy
Fact
Page: 59

3.114: each of the market structures, firms behave strategically with regard to each other.

Answer: False

Easy
Application
Page: 53

3.115: Monopolistically competitive markets are the only markets to exhibit product differentiation.

Answer: False

Moderate
Application
Page: 55

3.116: In perfectly competitive markets, firms have virtually no control over the product price.

Answer: True

Moderate
Application
Page: 51

3.117: Perhaps the key structural change in the shares of national income over the last twenty years is the growth of the manufacturing sector and the decline of the service sector.

Answer: False

Moderate
Application
Page: 49

3.118: Over the last fifty years, the percentage of the GDP devoted to government spending has remained relatively constant.

Answer: False

Easy
Application
Page: 57

SHORT ANSWER QUESTIONS

3.119: Define gross domestic product. What are its limitations?

Answer: Gross domestic product is the total value of all goods and services produced by a national economy over a period of time. GDP is not a measure of well-being because the distribution of income is not considered.

Easy
Definition
Page: 55

Moderate
Definition
Page: 60

3.120: Define the payroll tax and explain on whom the tax is levied.

Answer: The payroll tax is a flat-rate tax on earnings (FICA), and is paid equally by a worker and his or her firm. If a person is self-employed, however, the payroll tax is paid entirely by the worker, though at a lesser percentage.

Moderate
Definition
Page: 60

3.121: Define the corporate income tax and explain on whom the tax is levied.

Answer: The corporate income tax is a tax levied on net income of corporations and is paid by the corporations.

Moderate
Definition
Page: 60

3.122: Define excise taxes and explain on whom the taxes are levied.

Answer: Excise taxes are indirect business taxes on particular goods such as cigarettes, alcoholic beverages, and gasoline. These are paid by the firm selling the good.

Moderate
Fact
Page: 46

3.123: A business set up to make a profit may be organized in one of three basic legal forms. Explain each of the forms and one advantage and one disadvantage of each.

Answer: The three forms are: proprietorship, partnership, and corporation. A proprietorship is a form of business organization in which a person simply sets up to provide goods or services at a profit. An advantage of a proprietorship is that they are very easy to start up. A disadvantage of a proprietorship is that the owner of the firm has unlimited liability. A partnership is a form of business organization in which there is more than one proprietor. Advantages of a partnership include the fact that there is more than one person to share the responsibility for the firm and there is no formal legal process required to start the business. A disadvantage of a proprietorship is that the owners face unlimited liability. A corporation is a form of business organization resting on a legal charter that establishes the corporation as an entity separate from its owners. Advantages of the corporation are that funds can be raised through the sale of stock and shareholders are not liable for the debts of the corporation beyond what they have invested. A disadvantage of a corporation is that corporate profits face double taxation.

Easy
Single
Page: 51

3.124: Explain the similarities and differences between perfect competition and monopolistic competition.

Answer: Similarities: in both market structures there are a large number of firms with low barriers to entry. Differences: In perfect competition products are homogeneous and firms have no control over price, but in monopolistic competition products are differentiated and firms do exercise some price-setting power.

Moderate
Fact
Page: 50

3.125: A monopolist can set any price he wants to for his product because there are no close substitutes for what a monopolist produces. Do you agree with this statement? Why or why not?

Answer: No, a monopolist is still subject to discipline imposed by the market. The price a monopolist can charge will be constrained by the market demand for the product.

Moderate
Fact
Page: 51

3.126: Explain why oligopolies are characterized by a great deal of uncertainty.

Answer: Oligopolies are characterized by a great deal of uncertainty because one firm's action usually triggers another firm's reaction. The strategies and counterstrategies employed by firms in the industry determine which firms get the sales.

Easy
Fact
Page: 52

3.127: What are three reasons why the U.S. economy has become more competitive over time?

Answer: The United States economy has become more competitive over time because of increased competition from imports, deregulation of industries and enforcement of antitrust laws.

3.128: Briefly explain the major structural changes that have taken place in the U.S. economy since 1970.

Easy
Fact
Page: 53

Answer: The percentage of national income accounted for by the manufacturing sector has been declining. The fastest growing sector of the U.S. economy has been the service sector.

3.129: What are the two largest sources of revenue for the federal government?

Easy
Fact
Page: 60

Answer: Social insurance taxes and individual income taxes.

3.130: Explain why social insurance taxes now account for a much larger portion of federal revenues than they have in the past.

Moderate
Fact
Page: 60

Answer: Social insurance taxes account for a larger portion of federal revenues than they did in the past because of increasing tax rates. The tax rates have been increased because of concerns over future solvency of the social security system. Tax rates were increased to generate a surplus in the social security trust funds to prevent the collapse of the system in the future.

4 Demand, Supply, and Market Equilibrium

4.1: Michael Dell was the first individual who sold computers by mail order. The company founded by Dell is now one of the largest and most successful computer companies in the United States. Michael Dell would be classified as

Moderate
Single
Page: 68

(a) an entrepreneur.
(b) an opportunist.
(c) a monopolist.
(d) a socialist.

Answer: (a)

4.2: Economists consider households to be suppliers in which of the following markets?

Easy
Fact
Page: 68

(a) product and labor markets
(b) labor and capital markets
(c) product and capital markets
(d) product market only

Answer: (b)

4.3: The suppliers in the labor and capital markets are

Easy
Fact
Page: 68

(a) households.
(b) firms.
(c) government.
(d) the public sector.

Answer: (a)

4.4: Which of the following is held constant along the demand curve?

Moderate
Fact
Page: 70

(a) price of the good
(b) quantity
(c) income
(d) both a and b

Answer: (c)

4.5: Which of the following will NOT cause a shift in the demand curve for compact discs?

Moderate
Single
Page: 70

(a) a change in income
(b) a change in wealth
(c) a change in the price of prerecorded cassette tapes
(d) a change in the price of compact discs

Answer: (d)

85

Moderate
Fact
Page: 71

4.6: The "law of demand" implies that

(a) as prices fall, demand increases.
(b) as prices rise, demand decreases.
(c) as prices fall, quantity demanded increases.
(d) as prices rise, quantity demanded increases.

Answer: (c)

Moderate
Fact
Page: 71

4.7: According to the law of demand: As prices rise, *ceteris paribus*

(a) demand increases.
(b) demand decreases.
(c) quantity demanded decreases.
(d) quantity demanded increases.

Answer: (c)

Easy
Fact
Page: 71

4.8: According to the law of demand there is _____ relationship between price and quantity demanded.

(a) a positive
(b) a negative
(c) either a positive or negative
(d) a constantly changing

Answer: (b)

Easy
Fact
Page: 71

4.9: As an individual consumes more of a product within a given period of time, it is likely that each additional unit consumed will yield

(a) successively less satisfaction.
(b) successively more satisfaction.
(c) the same amount of satisfaction.
(d) less satisfaction for a while and then start to add more satisfaction.

Answer: (a)

Easy
Definition
Page: 74

4.10: When the price of a good falls and you buy the same quantity of that good, you have money left over and are better able to afford more of all goods. This is the

(a) income effect.
(b) substitution effect.
(c) measured effect
(d) output effect.

Answer: (a)

Easy
Fact
Page: 74

4.11: The price of hamburgers drops suddenly and you discover that you and your friends eat more hamburgers. This is due to the

(a) income and substitution effects.
(b) increase in hamburger quality.
(c) law of supply.
(d) increase in demand.

Answer: (a)

Easy
Definition
Page: 74

4.12: What effect is working when the price of a good falls and consumers tend to buy it instead of other goods?

(a) the income effect.
(b) the substitution effect.
(c) the diminishing marginal utility effect.
(d) *the ceteris paribus* effect.

Answer: (b)

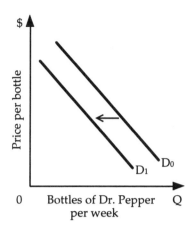

Figure 4.1

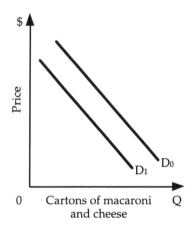

Figure 4.2

4.13: Refer to Figure 4.1. Which of the following would be most likely to cause the demand for Dr. Pepper to shift from D_0 to D_1?

(a) a decrease in income, assuming that Dr. Pepper is a normal good.
(b) an increase in the price of 7-UP, assuming 7-UP is a substitute for Dr. Pepper.
(c) a decrease in the price of Dr. Pepper.
(d) a reduction in the price of sugar used to make Dr. Pepper.

Answer: (a)

Moderate
Single
Page: 76

4.14: Refer to Figure 4.2. Which of the following would be most likely to cause the demand for Macaroni and Cheese to shift from D_1 to D_0?

(a) an increase in the price of Macaroni and Cheese.
(b) an increase in the price of flour used to make Macaroni and cheese.
(c) an increase in income, assuming Macaroni and Cheese is a normal good.
(d) an increase in the quantity demanded for Macaroni and Cheese.

Answer: (c)

Moderate
Single
Page: 76

4.15: The Setrite Corporation produces chairs. An economist working for the firm predicts that "if people's incomes rise next year, then the demand for our chairs will increase, *ceteris paribus*." The accuracy of the economist's prediction depends on whether the chairs Setrite produces

(a) have many complementary goods.
(b) have few substitutes.
(c) have few complementary goods.
(d) are normal goods.

Answer: (d)

Moderate
Single
Page: 74

4.16: If the demand for coffee decreases as income decreases, coffee is

(a) a normal good.
(b) an inferior good.
(c) a substitute good.
(d) a complementary good.

Answer: (a)

Easy
Single
Page: 74

4.17: If the demand for tortillas increases as income increases, tortillas are

(a) a normal good.
(b) an infereior good.
(c) a substitute good.
(d) a complementary good.

Answer: (a)

Easy
Single
Page: 74

Moderate
Multi
Page: 74

4.18: Refer to Figure 4.3. If consumer income falls, the demand for tuna fish sandwiches shifts from D_0 to D_1. This implies that tuna fish sandwiches are

(a) a normal good.
(b) an inferior good.
(c) a substitute good.
(d) a complementary good.

Answer: (b)

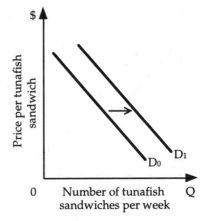

Figure 4.3

Moderate
Multi
Page: 74

4.19: Refer to Figure 4.4. If consumer income increases, the demand for bell peppers shifts from D1 to D0. This implies that bell peppers are

(a) a normal good.
(b) an inferior good.
(c) a substitute good.
(d) a complementary good.

Answer: (a)

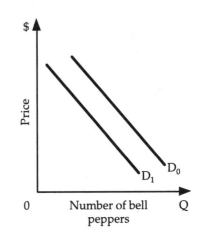

Figure 4.4

Easy
Fact
Page: 75

4.20: Suppose the demand for good Z goes up when the price of good Y goes down. We can say that goods Z and Y are

(a) complements.
(b) substitutes.
(c) unrelated goods.
(d) perfect substitutes.

Answer: (a)

Challenging
Multi
Page: 74

4.21: During an economic downturn when consumer income falls, the demand for ice cream increases and the demand for chocolate cake decreases. This implies that

(a) ice cream and chocolate cake are complements.
(b) ice cream is a normal good and chocolate cake is an inferior good.
(c) ice cream is an inferior good and chocolate cake is a normal good.
(d) ice cream is an economic bad and chocolate cake is an economic good.

Answer: (c)

Easy
Fact
Page: 74

4.22: A good whose demand is inversely related to income is

(a) a normal good.
(b) an inferior good.
(c) a regular good.
(d) a new good.

Answer: (b)

4.23: In college you practically existed on tuna fish, but now that you have a $45,000 a year job, you never want to see tuna fish again. We can safely conclude that you consider tuna fish to be

(a) a normal good.
(b) a complementary good.
(c) an inferior good.
(d) a luxury.

Answer: (c)

4.24: In college you practically existed on peanut butter, but now you have a $95, 000 a year job, you never want to see peanut butter again. We can safely conclude that you consider peanut butter to be

(a) a normal good.
(b) a complementary good.
(c) a luxury.
(d) an inferior good.

Answer: (d)

4.25: For inferior goods,

(a) an increase in income will cause the quantity demanded to fall.
(b) an increase in income will cause the demand to increase.
(c) an increase in income will cause the demand to fall.
(d) an increase in income will cause the quantity demanded to increase.

Answer: (c)

4.26: When the decrease in the price of one good causes the demand for another good to decrease, the goods are

(a) normal.
(b) inferior.
(c) substitutes.
(d) complements.

Answer: (c)

4.27: Demand for one item goes down when the price of another item goes up. These items are

(a) substitutes.
(b) complements.
(c) normal goods.
(d) inferior goods.

Answer: (b)

4.28: In response to news reports that taking aspirins daily can reduce an individual's risk of a heart attack, there will most likely be

(a) an increase in the supply of aspirins.
(b) a decrease in the supply of aspirins.
(c) an increase in the demand for aspirins.
(d) an increase in the quantity demanded of aspirins.

Answer: (c)

Moderate
Fact
Page: 74

4.29: Demand curves are derived while holding constant

(a) income, tastes, and the price of the good.
(b) income and tastes.
(c) income, tastes, and the price of other goods.
(d) tastes and the price of other goods.

Answer: (c)

Moderate
Single
Page: 76

4.30: The quantity demanded of Pepsi has decreased. The best explanation for this is that

(a) the price of Coca Cola has increased.
(b) Pepsi's advertising is not as effective as in the past.
(c) the price of Pepsi increased.
(d) Pepsi consumers had an increase in income.

Answer: (c)

Challenging
Multi
Page: 76

4.31: The Pizza World restaurant had to increase the price of its pizzas due to higher input costs, but found that the number of pizzas sold actually increased slightly. The likely explanation is:

(a) a violation of the law of supply.
(b) a violation of the law of demand.
(c) an outward shift in the demand curve for dinners.
(d) an elastic demand.

Answer: (c)

Easy
Multi
Page: 76

4.32: Refer to Figure 4.5. The number of videotapes Amy rents per week increases from 3 to 5. This would be caused by

(a) an increase in income if videotapes are a normal good.
(b) a decrease in the price of popcorn which is a complement to videotapes.
(c) a decrease in the rental price of videotapes.
(d) either a or b.

Answer: (c)

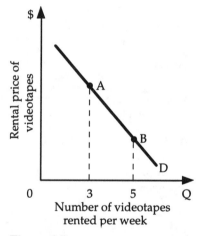

Figure 4.5

Easy
Multi
Page: 76

4.33: Refer to Figure 4.6. The number of videogames Rob rents per week decreases from 7 to 5. This would be caused by

(a) an increase in the rental price of videogames.
(b) an decrease in income if videogames are a normal good.
(c) a decrease in the price of popcorn which is a complement to videogames.
(d) either b or c.

Answer: (a)

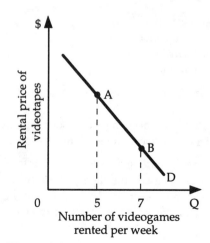

Figure 4.6

4.34: A change in the price of a good or service leads to a _____ which leads to a _____.

Easy
Single
Page: 76

(a) change in demand; movement along the demand curve
(b) change in quantity demanded; movement along the demand curve
(c) change in demand; shift in the demand curve
(d) change in quantity demanded; shift in the demand curve

Answer: (b)

4.35: A change in income, preferences, or prices of other goods or services leads to a _____ which leads to a _____.

Easy
Single
Page: 76

(a) change in demand; movement along the demand curve
(b) change in quantity demanded; movement along the demand curve
(c) change in demand; shift of the demand curve
(d) change in quantity demanded; shift of the demand curve

Answer: (c)

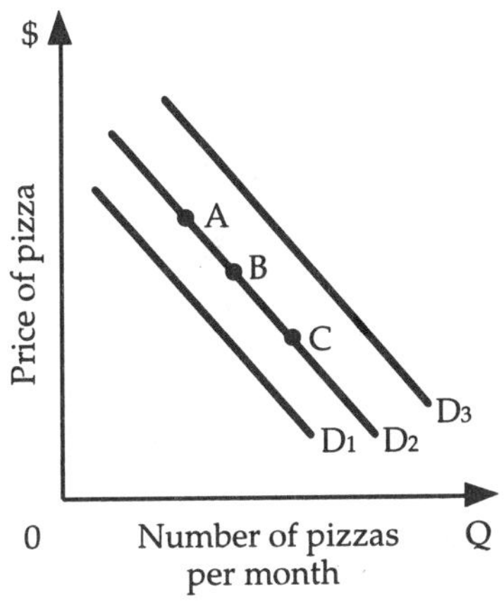

Figure 4.7

4.36: Refer to Figure 4.7. Assume the market is initially at point B and that pizza is a normal good. A decrease in income would cause the market to move from point B on demand curve to D_2 to

Easy
Single
Page: 76

(a) demand curve D_1 .
(b) demand curve D_3 .
(c) point A on demand curve D_2.
(d) point C on demand curve D_2 .

Answer: (a)

4.37: Refer to Figure 4.7. If pizza and beer are complements, a decrease in the price of beer will cause a movement from point B on demand curve to D_2 to

Moderate
Multi
Page: 76

(a) demand curve D_1 .
(b) demand curve D_3 .
(c) point A on demand curve D_2.
(d) point C on demand curve D_2 .

Answer: (b)

4.38: Refer to Figure 4.7. If pizza and hamburgers are substitutes, an increase in the price of hamburgers will cause a movement from point B on demand curve D_2 to

Moderate
Multi
Page: 76

(a) demand curve D_1 .
(b) demand curve D_3 .
(c) point A on demand curve D_2.
(d) point C on demand curve D_2 .

Answer: (b)\

4.39: Refer to Figure 4.7. A movement from point C to point B on demand curve D_2 would be caused by

Moderate
Multi
Page: 76

(a) an decrease in income, assuming pizza is a normal good.
(b) an decrease in the price of hamburgers, assuming that pizza and hamburgers are substitutes.
(c) a decrease in the price of pizza.
(d) an increase in the price of pizza sauce.

Answer: (d)

Easy
Single
Page: 76

4.40: Refer to Figure 4.7. A decrease in demand is represented by the movement

(a) from D_2 to D_1 .
(b) from D_2 to D_3.
(c) along D_2 from point B to point A.
(d) along D_2 from point B to point C.

Answer: (a)

Easy
Single
Page: 76

4.41: Refer to Figure 4.7. An increase in quantity demanded is represented by

(a) from D_2 to D_1 .
(b) from D_2 to D_3.
(c) along D_2 from point B to point A.
(d) along D_2 from point B to point C.

Answer: (d)

Easy
Single
Page: 76

4.42: Refer to Figure 4.8. Assume the market is initially at point B and that a cheeseburger is a normal good. An increase in income would cause the market to move from point C on demand curve D2 to

(a) demand curve D1.
(b) demand curve D3.
(c) point A on demand curve D2.
(d) point B on demand curve D2.

Answer: (b)

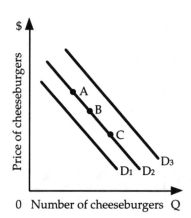

Figure 4.8

Easy
Single
Page: 76

4.43: Refer to Figure 4.8. If cheeseburgers and beer are complements, an increase in the price of beer will cause a movement from point B on demand curve D2 to

(a) demand curve D1.
(b) demand curve D3.
(c) point A on demand curve D2.
(d) point C on demand curve D2.

Answer: (a)

Easy
Single
Page: 76

4.44: Refer to Figure 4.8. If cheeseburgers and pizza are substitutes, a decrease in the price of pizza will cause a movement from point B on demand curve D2 to

(a) demand curve D1.
(b) demand curve D3.
(c) point A on demand curve D2.
(d) point C on demand curve D2.

Answer: (a)

Easy
Single
Page: 76

4.45: Refer to Figure 4.8. A movement from point A to point B on demand curve D2 would be caused by

(a) a decrease in the price of pizza, assuming that cheeseburgers and pizza are substitutes.
(b) a decrease in income, assuming a cheeseburger is a normal good.
(c) a decrease in the price of cheeseburger buns.
(d) an increase in the price of cheeseburgers.

Answer: (c)

4.46: Refer to Figure 4.8. An increase in demand is represented by the movement

(a) from D2 to D1.
(b) from D2 to D3.
(c) along D2 from point B to point A.
(d) along D2 from point B to point C.

Answer: (b)

Easy
Single
Page: 76

4.47: Refer to Figure 4.8. A decrease in quantity demanded is represented by the movement

(a) from D2 to D1.
(b) from D2 to D3.
(c) along D2 from point B to point A.
(d) along D2 from point B to point C.

Answer: (c)

Easy
Single
Page: 76

4.48: Refer to Figure 4.10. Assume that there are only two people in the market for movies: Person A and Person B. Along the market demand curve for movies, at a price of _____ quantity demanded would be _____.

(a) $10; 5
(b) $10; 7
(c) $8; 13
(d) $8; 16

Answer: (a)

Moderate
Multi
Page: 79

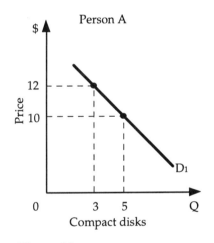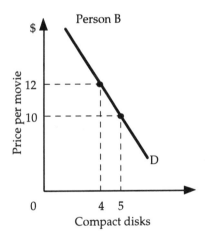

Figure 4.9

4.49: Refer to Figure 4.9. Assume that there are only two people in the market for compact discs: Person A and Person B. Along the market demand curve for compact disks, at a price of _____ quantity demanded would be _____.

(a) $12; 5
(b) $12; 7
(c) $10; 13
(d) $10; 16

Answer: (b)

Moderate
Multi
Page: 79

Moderate
Multi
Page: 79

4.50: Refer to Figure 4.10. Assume there are only two people in the market for movies: Person A and Person B. Along the market demand curve, at a price of _____ quantity demanded would be _____.

(a) $12; 5
(b) $12; 8
(c) $10; 10
(d) $10; 13

Answer: (c)

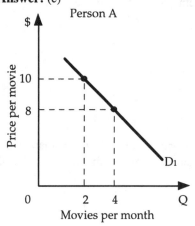 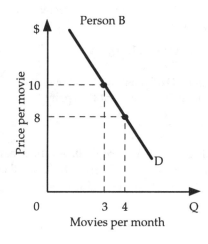

Figure 4.10

Moderate
Multi
Page: 79

4.51: Refer to Figure 4.10. Assume there are only two people in the market for movies: Person A and Person B. Along the market demand curve, at a price of _____ quantity demanded would be _____.

(a) $8; 5
(b) $8; 8
(c) $10; 7
(d) $10; 13

Answer: (b)

Easy
Definition
Page: 81

4.52: According to the law of supply, there is a

(a) negative relationship between price and the quantity of a good supplied.
(b) positive relationship between price and the quantity of a good supplied.
(c) negative relationship between price and the change in supply.
(d) positive relationship between price and the change in supply.

Answer: (b)

Easy
Fact
Page: 81

4.53: Refer to Figure 4.11. The number of pizzas this restaurant sells per week increases from 500 to 700. This could be caused by

(a) an improvement in technology that reduces the cost of making pizza.
(b) a decrease in the price of one of the ingredients used to make pizza.
(c) an increase in the price of pizza.
(d) a decrease in the demand for pizza.

Answer: (c)

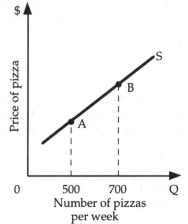

Figure 4.11

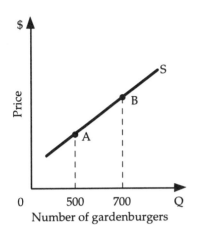

Figure 4.12

4.54: Refer to Figure 4.12. The number of Gardenburgers this restaurant sells per week decreases from 700 to 500. This could be caused by

(a) an improvement in technology that reduces the cost of making Gardenburgers.
(b) an increase in the price of one of the ingredients used to make Gardenburgers.
(c) a decrease in the price of Gardenburgers.
(d) an increase in the demand for Gardenburgers.

Answer: (c)

Easy
Fact
Page: 81

4.55: Which of the following is consistent with the law of supply?

(a) As the price of calculators rises, the supply of calculators increases, *ceteris paribus.*
(b) As the price of calculators falls, the supply of calculators increases, *ceteris paribus.*
(c) As the price of calculators rises, the quantity supplied of calculators increases, *ceteris paribus.*
(d) As the price of calculators rises, the quantity supplied of calculators decreases, *ceteris paribus.*

Answer: (c)

Moderate
Single
Page: 81

4.56: The price of computer chips used in the manufacture of personal computers has fallen. This will lead to _____ personal computers.

(a) an increase in the supply of
(b) a decrease in the supply of
(c) an increase in the quantity supplied of
(d) a decrease in the quantity supplied of

Answer: (a)

Moderate
Multi
Page: 82

4.57: If the price of pizza sauce increases, there will be _____ of pizza.

(a) an increase in the supply of
(b) a decrease in the supply of
(c) an increase in the quantity supplied of
(d) a decrease in the quantity supplied of

Answer: (b)

Moderate
Multi
Page: 82

4.58: A frozen food manufacturer can produce either pizzas or pepperoni rolls. As a result of an increase in the price of pepperoni rolls, the firm produces more pepperoni rolls and fewer pizzas. An economist would explain this by saying

(a) the supply of pepperoni rolls increased and the supply of pizzas decreased.
(b) there has been an increase in the quantity supplied of pepperoni rolls and a decrease in the quantity supplied of pizzas.
(c) there has been an increase in the quantity supplied of pepperoni rolls and a decrease in the supply of pizza.
(d) the supply of pepperoni rolls increased and the quantity supplied of pizza decreased.

Answer: (c)

Challenging
Multi
Page: 82

Easy
Single
Page: 83

4.59: Refer to Figure 4.13. A decrease in the wage rate of pizza makers will cause a movement from point B on supply curve S_2 to

(a) point A on supply curve S_2 .
(b) point B on supply curve S_2 .
(c) supply curve S_3 .
(d) supply curve S_1 .

Answer: (c)

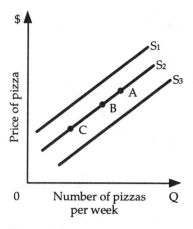

Figure 4.13

Easy
Single
Page: 83

4.60: Refer to Figure 4.13. An increase in supply is represented by the movement from

(a) S_2 to S_3 .
(b) S_2 to S_1 .
(c) point B to point A along supply curve S_2 .
(d) point B to point C along supply curve S_2 .

Answer: (a)

Easy
Single
Page: 83

4.61: Refer to Figure 4.13. A decrease in quantity supplied is represented by a movement from

(a) S_2 to S_3 .
(b) S_2 to S_1 .
(c) point B to point A along supply curve S_2 .
(d) point B to point C along supply curve S_2 .

Answer: (d)

Moderate
Single
Page: 83

4.62: Refer to Figure 4.13. An increase in the price of pizza sauce will cause a movement from point B on supply curve S_2 to

(a) supply curve S_3.
(b) supply curve S_1 .
(c) point A on supply curve S_2.
(d) point C on supply curve S_2 .

Answer: (b)

Challenging
Multi
Page: 83

4.63: Refer to Figure 4.13. A movement from point A to point B on supply curve S_2 would be caused by

(a) an increase in the price of pizza.
(b) a decrease in the demand for pizza.
(c) an increase in the price of pizza dough.
(d) an increase in the price of hamburgers, assuming hamburgers are a substitute for pizza.

Answer: (b)

Challenging
Multi
Page: 83

4.64: Refer to Figure 4.14. An increase n the wage rate of Gardenburger makers will cause a movement from point B on supply curve S2 to

(a) point A on supply curve S2.
(b) point B on supply curve S2.
(c) supply curve S3.
(d) supply curve S1.

Answer: (d)

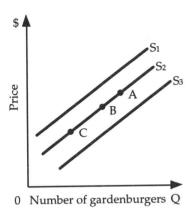

Figure 4.14

4.65: Refer to Figure 4.14. A decrease in supply is represented by the movement from

(a) S2 to S3.
(b) S2 to S1.
(c) point B to point A along supply curve S2.
(d) point B to point C along supply curve S2.

Answer: (b)

Challenging
Multi
Page: 83

4.66: Refer to Figure 4.14. An increase in quantity supplied is represented by a movement from

(a) S2 to S1.
(b) S2 to S3.
(c) point B to point A along supply curve S2.
(d) point B to point C along supply curve S2.

Answer: (c)

Challenging
Multi
Page: 83

4.67: Refer to Figure 4.14. A decrease in the price of mushrooms (an input for Gardenburgers) will cause a movement from point B on supply curve S2 to

(a) supply curve S3.
(b) supply curve S1.
(c) point A on supply curve S2.
(d) point C on supply curve S2.

Answer: (a)

Challenging
Multi
Page: 83

4.68: Refer to Figure 4.14. A movement from point C to point B on supply curve S would be caused by

(a) a decrease in the price of Gardenburgers.
(b) an increase in the demand for Gardenburgers.
(c) a decrease in the price of mushrooms.
(d) a decrease in the price of hamburgers, assuming hamburgers are a substitute for pizza.

Answer: (b)

Challenging
Multi
Page: 83

4.69: The change in the price of a good leads to a change in _____ which leads to a _____.

(a) quantity supplied; movement along a supply curve
(b) quantity supplied; shift of the supply curve
(c) supply; movement along a supply curve
(d) supply; shift of the supply curve

Answer: (a)

Moderate
Multi
Page: 83

4.70: Refer to Figure 4.15. The supply of curve of hula hoops shifts from S_0 to S_1. This could be caused by

(a) an decrease in the price of hula hoops.
(b) a decrease in the number of firms selling hula hoops.
(c) a decrease in the demand for hula hoops.
(d) either b or c.

Answer: (b)

Easy
Single
Page: 83

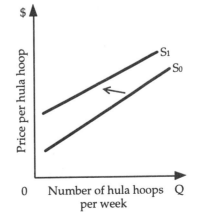

Figure 4.15

Moderate
Multi
Page: 86

4.71: Equilibrium is the condition that exists

(a) whenever there is no government intervention in the market.
(b) when the demand curve intersects the price axis.
(c) when quantity demanded equals quantity supplied.
(d) when the demand curve intersects the quantity axis.

Answer: (c)

Moderate
Single
Page: 86

4.72: Refer to Table 4.1. This market will be in equilibrium if the price per pizza is

(a) $6.
(b) $8.
(c) $10
(d) $12.

Answer: (b)

Table 4.1

Price per pizza	Quantity demanded (pizzas per month)	Quantity supplied (pizzas per month)
$4	1,000	700
$6	900	750
$8	800	800
$10	700	850
$12	600	900

Moderate
Multi
Page: 86

4.73: Refer to Table 4.1. If the price per pizza is $10, the price will

(a) remain constant because the market is in equilibrium.
(b) increase because there is an excess demand in the market.
(c) decrease because there is an excess demand in the market.
(d) decrease because there is an excess supply in the market.

Answer: (d)

Moderate
Multi
Page:86

4.74: Refer to Table 4.1. If the price per pizza is $12, there is

(a) a market equilibrium.
(b) an excess demand of 100 units.
(c) an excess demand of 750 units.
(d) an excess supply of 300 units.

Answer: (d)

Moderate
Multi
Page: 86

4.75: Refer to Table 4.1. If the price per pizza is $6, there is

(a) an excess demand of 150 pizzas.
(b) an excess demand of 50 pizzas.
(c) an excess supply of 200 pizzas.
(d) an excess supply of 50 pizzas.

Answer: (a)

4.76: Refer to Table 4.1. In this market there will be an excess demand of 150 pizzas at a price of

Moderate
Multi
Page: 86

(a) $6.
(b) $8.
(c) $10.
(d) $12.

Answer: (a)

4.77: Refer to Table 4.1. In this market there will be an excess supply of 150 pizzas at a price of

Moderate
Multi
Page: 86

(a) $6.
(b) $8.
(c) $10.
(d) $12.

Answer: (c)

4.78: Refer to Table 4.1. If the price per pizza is $12, the price will

Moderate
Multi
Page: 86

(a) remain constant because the market is in equilibrium.
(b) increase because there is an excess demand in the market.
(c) increase because there is an excess supply in the market.
(d) decrease because there is an excess supply in the market.

Answer: (d)

Table 4.2

Price per pizza	Quantity demanded (Gardenburgers per month)	Quantity supplied (Gardenburgers per month)
$6	1,000	650
$8	1,000	700
$10	900	750
$12	800	850
$14	700	850

4.79: Refer to Table 4.2. This market will be in equilibrium if the price per Gardenburger is

Moderate
Multi
Page: 86

(a) $6.
(b) $8.
(c) $10.
(d) $12.

Answer: (d)

4.80: Refer to Table 4.2. If the price per Gardenburger is $10, the price will

Moderate
Multi
Page: 86

(a) remain constant because the market is in equilibrium.
(b) decrease because there is an excess demand in the market.
(c) increase because there is an excess demand in the market.
(d) decrease because there is an excess supply in the market.

Answer: (c)

Moderate Multi Page: 86	**4.81: Refer to Table 4.2.** If the price per pizza is $14, there is (a) a market equilibrium. (b) an excess demand of 100 units. (c) an excess demand of 700 units. (d) an excess supply of 150 units. **Answer:** (d)
Moderate Multi Page: 86	**4.82: Refer to Table 4.2.** If the price per Gardenburgers is $6, there is (a) an excess demand of 150 Gardenburgers. (b) an excess supply of 50 Gardenburgers. (c) an excess demand of 450 Gardenburgers. (d) an excess supply of 150 Gardenburgers. **Answer:** (c)
Moderate Multi Page:86	**4.83: Refer to Table 4.2.** In this market there will be an excess demand of 150 Gardenburgers at a price of (a) $6. (b) $8. (c) $10. (d) $12. **Answer:** (c)
Moderate Multi Page: 86	**4.84: Refer to Table 4.2.** In this market there will be an excess supply of 150 Gardenburgers at a price of (a) $6. (b) $10. (c) $12. (d) $14. **Answer:** (d)
Moderate Multi Page: 86	**4.85: Refer to Table 4.2.** If the price per Gardenburgers is $12, the price will (a) remain constant because the market is in equilibrium. (b) increase because there is an excess demand in the market. (c) increase because there is an excess supply in the market. (d) decrease because there is an excess supply in the market. **Answer:** (a)
Easy Single Page: 88	**4.86:** When excess supply occurs in an unregulated market, there is a tendency for (a) price to rise. (b) price to decrease. (c) quantity supplied to increase. (d) quantity demanded to decrease. **Answer:** (b)

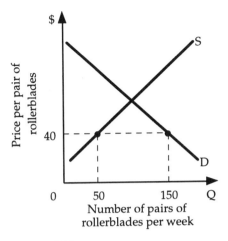

Figure 4.16

4.87: Refer to Figure 4.16. In the rollerblade market, you accurately predict that

(a) price will increase, the quantity demanded will fall, and the quantity supplied will rise.
(b) price will increase, the quantity demanded will rise, and the quantity supplied will fall.
(c) price will decrease, the quantity demanded will fall, and the quantity supplied will fall.
(d) price will decrease, the quantity demanded will rise, and the quantity supplied will fall.

Challenging
Multi
Page: 91

Answer: (a)

4.88: When the market operates without interference, price increases will distribute what is available to those who are willing and able to pay the most. This process is known as

Easy
Definition
Page: 87

(a) quantity adjustment.
(b) quantity setting.
(c) price rationing.
(d) price fixing.

Answer: (c)

4.89: Refer to Figure 4.17. Assume hamburgers are a normal good. An increase in income will cause a movement from

Moderate
Multi
Page: 91

(a) point A to point B.
(b) point G to point F.
(c) D_1 to D_2.
(d) S_1 to S_2.

Answer: (c)

4.90: Refer to Figure 4.17. Assume hamburgers and hot dogs are substitutes. A decrease in the price of hot dogs will cause a movement from

Moderate
Multi
Page: 91

(a) point A to point B.
(b) point F to point G.
(c) D_2 to D_1.
(d) D_1 to D_2.

Answer: (c)

4.91: Refer to Figure 4.17. Assume hamburgers and french fries are complements. A decrease in the price of french fries will cause a movement from

Moderate
Multi
Page: 91

(a) point A to point B.
(b) point G to point F.
(c) D_1 to D_2.
(d) S_2 to S_1.

Answer: (c)

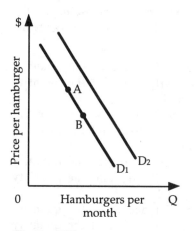 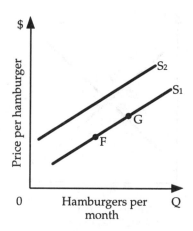

Figure 4.17

Challenging
Multi
Page: 91

4.92: Refer to Figure 4.17. A decrease in the number of cattle ranchers will cause a movement from

(a) point B to point A.
(b) point G to point F.
(c) D_2 to D_1.
(d) S_2 to S_1.

Answer: (a)

Easy
Single
Page: 86

4.93: Refer to Figure 4.18. The market for blue jeans is in equilibrium at a price of _____ and a quantity of _____ blue jeans.

(a) $20; 1,000
(b) $20; 200
(c) $30; 150
(d) $40; 100

Answer: (c)

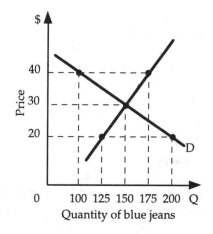

Figure 4.18

Moderate
Multi
Page: 86

4.94: Refer to Figure 4.18. At a price of $20, there is an

(a) excess demand of 75 blue jeans.
(b) excess demand of 50 blue jeans.
(c) excess demand of 25 blue jeans.
(d) excess supply of 50 blue jeans.

Answer: (a)

Moderate
Multi
Page: 86

4.95: Refer to Figure 4.18. If this market is unregulated and the price is currently $40, you would expect that

(a) the price of blue jeans would remain at $40, because firms would not want to reduce the price.
(b) the price of blue jeans would fall to $20, so the firm could sell its excess supply.
(c) the price would fall, but the new price is indeterminate from the information provided.
(d) the price would fall to $30, where quantity demanded equals quantity supplied.

Answer: (d)

4.96: Refer to Figure 4.18. At a price of $40, there is an

(a) excess demand of 50 blue jeans.
(b) an excess demand of 75 blue jeans.
(c) an excess supply of 50 blue jeans.
(d) an excess supply of 75 blue jeans.

Answer: (d)

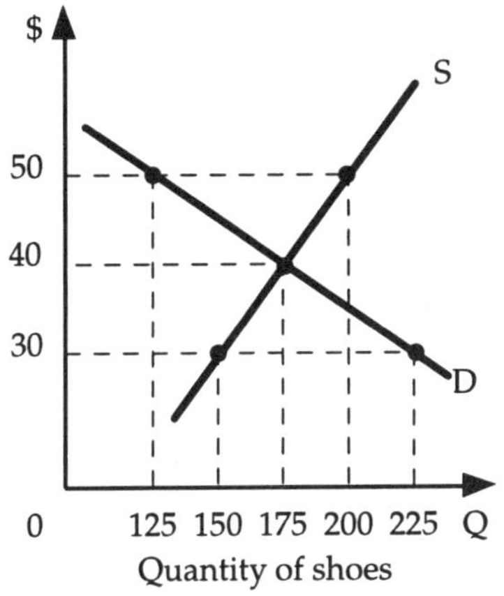

Moderate
Multi
Page: 86

Figure 4.19

4.97: Refer to Figure 4.19. The market for shoes is in equilibrium at a price of _____ and a quantity of _____ shoes.

(a) $40; 1,000
(b) $20; 200
(c) $30; 150
(d) $40; 175

Answer: (d)

Moderate
Multi
Page: 86

4.98: Refer to Figure 4.19. At a price of $30, there is an

(a) excess demand of 75 shoes.
(b) excess supply of 50 shoes.
(c) excess demand of 25 shoes.
(d) excess demand of 50 shoes.

Answer: (a)

Moderate
Multi
Page: 86

4.99: Refer to Figure 4.19. If this market is unregulated and the price is currently $50, you would expect that

(a) the price of shoes would remain at $50, because firms would not want to reduce the price.
(b) the price of blue shoes would fall to $30, so the firm could sell its excess supply.
(c) the price would fall to $40, where quantity demanded equals quantity supplied.
(d) the price would fall, but the new price is indeterminate form the information provided.

Answer: (c)

Moderate
Multi
Page: 86

4.100: Refer to Figure 4.19. At a price of $50, there is an

(a) excess demand of 50 shoes.
(b) excess supply of 75 shoes.
(c) excess demand of 75 shoes.
(d) excess supply of 50 shoes.

Answer: (b)

Moderate
Multi
Page: 86

4.101: When excess demand occurs in an unregulated market, there is a tendency for

(a) price to rise.
(b) price to fall.
(c) quantity demanded to increase.
(d) quantity supplied to decrease.

Answer: (a)

Easy
Single
Page: 86

Challenging
Multi
Page: 88

4.102: The market for tires is unregulated and is presently characterized by excess supply. You accurately predict that

(a) price will increase, the quantity demanded will fall, and the quantity supplied will rise.
(b) price will increase, the quantity demanded will rise, and the quantity supplied will fall.
(c) price will decrease, the quantity demanded will rise, and the quantity supplied will fall.
(d) price will decrease, the quantity demanded will fall, and the quantity supplied will rise.

Answer: (c)

Challenging
Multi
Page: 91

4.103: VCR's and videotapes are complements. An increase in the price of VCR's would cause which of the following in the market for videotapes?

(a) The equilibrium price and quantity of videotapes would increase.
(b) The equilibrium price and quantity of videotapes would decrease.
(c) The equilibrium price of videotapes would increase and the equilibrium quantity would decrease.
(d) The equilibrium price of videotapes would decrease and the equilibrium quantity would increase.

Answer: (b)

Challenging
Multi
Page: 91

4.104: Suppose that video game cartridges are a normal good. If the income of video game players increases, you predict that in the market for videotapes

(a) both equilibrium price and quantity will fall.
(b) both equilibrium price and quantity will increase.
(c) equilibrium price will increase and quantity will decrease.
(d) equilibrium price will fall but quantity will increase.

Answer: (b)

Challenging
Multi
Page: 88

4.105: Refer to Figure 4.20. The current price of a bag of pretzels is $1.10. You accurately predict that in this market

(a) price tends to remain constant and quantity supplied increases.
(b) price, quantity demanded, and quantity supplied decrease.
(c) price and quantity demanded increase and quantity supplied decreases.
(d) price and quantity supplied decrease and quantity demanded increases.

Answer: (d)

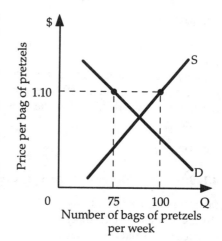

Figure 4.20

Moderate
Multi
Page: 91

4.106: When Hurricane Andrew passed through Louisiana in the summer of 1992, approximately a quarter of the sugar cane crop was destroyed. *Ceteris Paribus,*

(a) the supply of sugar has decreased and the price of sugar will increase.
(b) the supply of sugar has decreased and the price of sugar will decrease.
(c) the demand for sugar has increased and the price of sugar will increase.
(d) the demand for sugar has decreased and the price of sugar will decrease.

Answer: (a)

4.107: The price of pizza dough increases. In the market for pizza you would expect that

(a) the demand for pizza would increase and the price of pizza would increase.
(b) the demand for pizza would decrease and the price of pizza would fall.
(c) the supply of pizza would decrease and the price of pizza would increase.
(d) the supply of pizza would increase and the price of pizza would decrease.

Moderate
Multi
Page: 91

Answer: (c)

4.108: Improvements in technology have reduced the cost of producing personal computers. You accurately predict that in the market for personal computers, there will be

(a) an increase in the quantity supplied of personal computers, a reduction in the price and an increase in the quantity demanded.
(b) an increase in the supply of personal computers, a decrease in the price and an increase in the quantity demanded.
(c) an increase in the supply of personal computers, a reduction in the price and an increase in the demand.
(d) a decrease in the supply of personal computers, an increase in the price and a decrease in the demand.

Challenging
Multi
Page: 91

Answer: (b)

4.109: Which of the following will unambiguously occur when there is a simultaneous decrease in demand and a decrease in supply?

(a) an increase in equilibrium price
(b) a decrease in equilibrium price
(c) an increase in equilibrium quantity
(d) a decrease in equilibrium quantity

Honors
Multi
Page: 91

Answer: (d)

4.110: A movement along the demand curve to the left may be caused by

(a) a rise in income.
(b) a decrease in supply.
(c) a fall in the number of substitute goods.
(d) a rise in the price of inputs.

Moderate
Multi
Page: 91

Answer: (b)

4.111: Which of the following will unambiguously occur when there is a simultaneous increase in supply and decrease in demand?

(a) an increase in equilibrium price
(b) a decrease in equilibrium price
(c) an increase in equilibrium quantity
(d) a decrease in equilibrium quantity

Honors
Multi
Page: 91

Answer: (b)

4.112: Which of the following will unambiguously occur when there is a simultaneous increase in demand and a decrease in supply?

(a) an increase in equilibrium price
(b) a decrease in equilibrium price
(c) an increase in equilibrium quantity
(d) a decrease in equilibrium quantity

Honors
Multi
Page: 91

Answer: (a)

Challenging
Multi
Page: 91

4.113: An insect that is resistant to currently used pesticides has infested the cotton crop, and this year's crop is only half of what was produced last year. You accurately predict that this

(a) will shift the supply curve of cotton to the right, the equilibrium price of cotton will increase, and the demand for cotton will fall.
(b) will shift the supply curve of cotton to the right, the equilibrium price of cotton will increase, and the quantity demanded of cotton will decrease.
(c) will shift the supply curve of cotton to the left, the equilibrium price of cotton will increase, and the quantity demanded of cotton will decrease.
(d) will shift the supply curve of cotton to the left, the equilibrium price of cotton will increase, and the demand for cotton will fall.

Answer: (c)

Honors
Multi
Page: 91

4.114: Apples and oranges are substitute goods. A freeze in Florida destroyed a good portion of the orange crop. *Ceteris Paribus,*

(a) the price of both apples and oranges will increase.
(b) the price of both apples and oranges will fall.
(c) the price of oranges will increase and the price of apples will fall.
(d) the price of oranges will fall and the price of apples will increase.

Answer: (a)

Challenging
Multi
Page: 91

4.115: Assume upward-sloping supply curves and downward-sloping demand curves. You can unambiguously predict an increase in equilibrium quantity if

(a) demand and supply both increase.
(b) demand and supply both decrease.
(c) demand increases and supply decreases.
(d) demand decreases and supply increases.

Answer: (a)

Challenging
Multi
Page: 91

4.116: Refer to Figure 4.21. When the economy moves from point A to point B, there has been

(a) an increase in demand and an increase in supply.
(b) an increase in demand and an increase in quantity supplied.
(c) an increase in quantity demanded and an increase in quantity supplied.
(d) an increase in quantity demanded and an increase in supply.

Answer: (b)

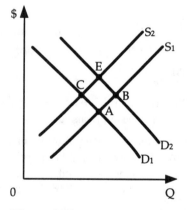

Figure 4.21

Challenging
Multi
Page: 91

4.117: Refer to Figure 4.21. When the economy moves from point A to point C, there has been

(a) a decrease in supply and a decrease in quantity demanded.
(b) a decrease in quantity supplied and a decrease in demand.
(c) a decrease in supply and an increase in quantity demanded.
(d) an increase in supply and a decrease in quantity demanded.

Answer: (a)

4.118: Refer to Figure 4.21. When the economy moves from point A to point E, there has been

(a) an increase in demand and an increase in supply.
(b) a decrease in demand and a decrease in supply.
(c) an increase in demand and a decrease in supply.
(d) an increase in quantity demanded and an increase in quantity supplied.

Challenging
Multi
Page: 91

Answer: (c)

4.119: Refer to Figure 4.21. When the economy moves from point E to Point B, there has been

(a) an increase in supply and an increase in quantity demanded.
(b) an increase in both supply and demand.
(c) a decrease in supply and an increase in demand.
(d) a decrease in supply and an increase in quantity demanded.

Challenging
Multi
Page: 91

Answer: (a)

4.120: An excess demand for a product serves as a signal that

(a) fewer resources should be allocated to producing this product.
(b) more resources should be allocated to producing this product.
(c) the government needs to intervene to correct the misallocation of resources.
(d) the supply of resources needed to produce this product are not abundant enough.

Moderate
Single
Page: 86

Answer: (b)

SITUATION 1: Lettuce and spinach are substitutes. Lettuce and tomatoes are complements. Lettuce is a normal good. During the winter of 1993, about 20% of the lettuce crop was destroyed by flooding in Arizona.

4.121: Refer to Situation 1. As a result of the flooding in Arizona during the winter of 1993, you would expect that

(a) the price of lettuce would increase, the supply of lettuce would increase and the quantity demanded of lettuce would decrease.
(b) the supply of lettuce decreased, the price of lettuce increased and the quantity demanded of lettuce decreased.
(c) the price of lettuce increased and both the quantity of lettuce supplied and the quantity of lettuce demanded increased.
(d) the supply of lettuce decreased, the price of lettuce increased and the demand for lettuce decreased.

Moderate
Multi
Page: 90

Answer: (b)

4.122: Refer to Situation 1. The floods that destroyed part of the lettuce crop would have caused the equilibrium price of spinach to _____ and the equilibrium quantity of spinach to _____.

(a) decrease; decrease
(b) decrease; increase
(c) increase; increase
(d) increase; decrease

Moderate
Multi
Page: 90

Answer: (c)

Challenging
Multi
Page: 90

4.123: Refer to Situation 1. The floods that destroyed part of the lettuce crop would have caused

(a) an increase in the demand for tomatoes.
(b) a decrease in the demand for tomatoes.
(c) an increase in the quantity demanded of tomatoes.
(d) a decrease in the quantity demanded of tomatoes.

Answer: (b)

Honors
Multi
Page: 90

4.124: Refer to Situation 1. At the same time that part of the lettuce crop was destroyed consumer income also decreased. *Ceteris Paribus,* in the market for lettuce this would have caused

(a) both the equilibrium price and quantity to decrease.
(b) the equilibrium price to increase and the equilibrium quantity to decrease.
(c) the equilibrium price to decrease. The equilibrium quantity could have increased, decreased or remained the same.
(d) the equilibrium price to either increase, decrease, or remain the same and the equilibrium quantity to decrease.

Answer: (d)

Moderate
Multi
Page: 86

4.125: Refer to Situation 1. The government wants to protect consumers from rising food prices. Therefore, price restrictions are imposed on lettuce growers prohibiting them from raising the price of lettuce. This will cause

(a) an excess supply of lettuce.
(b) an excess demand for lettuce.
(c) an increase in the demand for lettuce.
(d) a decrease in the supply of lettuce.

Answer: (b)

SITUATION 2: Rented videotapes and movies shown in theaters are substitutes. Rented videotapes and big screen TVs are complements. Big screen TVs and movies shown in theaters are normal goods. People watch rented videotapes more often in the winter than in the summer.

Honors
Multi
Page: 90

4.126: Refer to Situation 2. Most big screen TVs sold in the United States are imported from Japan. If the United States government reduces the number of big screen TVs that can be imported into the United States, *ceteris paribus*, what would happen?

(a) The price of big screen TVs and the rental price of videotapes would decrease.
(b) The price of big screen TVs would decrease and the rental price of videotapes would increase.
(c) The price of big screen TVs would increase and the rental price of videotapes would decrease.
(d) The price of big screen TVs and the rental price of videotapes would increase.

Answer: (c)

4.127: Refer to Situation 2. You have just read that the price of admission to a movie theater will be increased from $6.50 to $7.00. Which of the following could have led to this increase?

Challenging
Multi
Page: 90

(a) An increase in the cost of making videotapes.
(b) A decrease in consumer income.
(c) The licensing fee that theater owners pay to show first-run movies was reduced.
(d) There has been an increase in the number of theaters showing movies.

Answer: (a)

4.128: Refer to Situation 2. To raise additional revenues, the government imposes an entertainment tax on movie tickets, but there are no new additional taxes levied on rented videotapes. This would lead to

Honors
Multi
Page: 90

(a) an increase in the price of movie tickets, but no change in the rental price of videotapes.
(b) an increase in the price of movie tickets and the rental price of videotapes.
(c) an increase in the price of a movie ticket and a decrease in the rental price of videotapes.
(d) no change in the price of a movie ticket and an increase in the rental price of videotapes.

Answer: (b)

4.129: Refer to Situation 2. You observe that the rental price for videotapes is higher in the winter than in the summer. This would be explained by the fact that

Moderate
Multi
Page: 90

(a) demand for rented videotapes is higher in the winter than in the summer.
(b) the quantity demanded of rented videotapes is higher in the winter than in the summer.
(c) there are more videotapes released into the rental market in the winter than in the summer.
(d) consumer income tends to fall in the winter and increase in the summer.

Answer: (a)

4.130: Refer to Situation 2. If the number of stores renting videotapes is reduced by 25%, which of the following would occur?

Challenging
Multi
Page: 90

(a) The rental price of videotapes would increase and the price of big screen TVs and movie tickets would decrease.
(b) The rental price of videotapes would increase, but the price of big screen TVs and movie tickets would be unaffected.
(c) The rental price of videotapes and movie tickets would decrease, but the price of big screen TVs would increase.
(d) The rental price of videotapes and the price of movie tickets would increase, but the price of big screen TVs would decrease.

Answer: (d)

TRUE/FALSE QUESTIONS

Easy
Single
Page: 68

4.131: The Boston Symphony Orchestra would be classified as a firm by economists.

Answer: True

Easy
Fact
Page: 76

4.132: A change in demand occurs if the "*ceteris paribus*" assumption is violated.

Answer: True

Easy
Fact
Page: 76

4.133: On a demand curve, price is held constant.

Answer: False

Easy
Single
Page: 76

4.134: A change in demand is caused by an increase in the product's own price.

Answer: False

Easy
Single
Page: 76

4.135: The law of demand would be violated if, *ceteris paribus*, a firm raised its price and sold more than it did before.

Answer: True

Easy
Single
Page: 75

4.136: If cameras and film are complements, then a decrease in the price of cameras will result in a decrease in the demand for film.

Answer: False

Easy
Single
Page: 86

4.137: Excess demand in an unregulated market will cause price to rise.

Answer: True

Easy
Single
Page: 88

4.138: If the price of a product is kept above the equilibrium price, the market will be characterized by excess demand.

Answer: False

Easy
Multi
Page: 89

4.139: A decrease in demand for a product will cause the price of the product to fall and supply of the product to decrease.

Answer: False

Easy
Multi
Page: 89

4.140: A simultaneous increase in both the supply of and the demand for plaid flannel shirts would cause an increase in the equilibrium quantity of plaid flannel shirts.

Answer: True

SHORT ANSWER QUESTIONS

Easy
Math
Page: 85

4.141: Draw a typical supply and demand curve and show the market equilibrium. What does it mean to be in equilibrium?

Answer: Equilibrium occurs when quantity demanded equals quantity supplied.

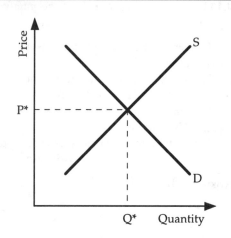

4.142: Graphically illustrate the existence of an excess demand. What will likely occur to equilibrate the market?

Moderate
Math
Page: 86

Answer: In a market exhibiting excess demand, prices will increase to equilibrate the market.

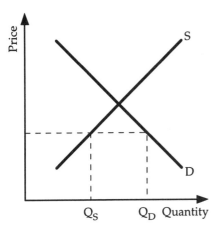

4.143: Graphically illustrate the existence of an excess supply. What will likely occur to equilibrate the market?

Moderate
Math
Page: 88

Answer: In a market exhibiting excess supply, prices will fall to equilibrate the market.

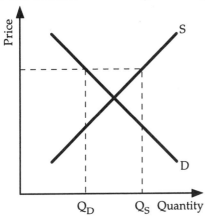

SCENARIO 1: Consider the market for generic light beer-a product that only has "Light Beer" on its label. We know that demand for generic light beer falls when income increases, demand rises when the price of other beer increases, and that demand rises when the price of potato chips falls.

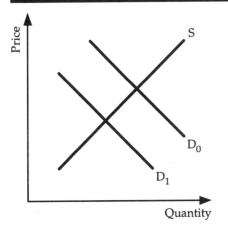

4.144: Refer to Scenario 1. Graph and explain the effect on equilibrium price and quantity of an increase in income. What type of good is "Light Beer"?

Moderate
Math
Page: 90

Answer: As income increases, demand for generic light beer falls and the equilibrium price and quantity both fall. Generic light beer is an inferior good.

Difficult
Math
Page: 90

4.145: Refer to Scenario 1. Graph and explain the effect on equilibrium price and quantity of an increase in the price of Coors beer. How are the goods related?

Answer: As the price for other beers, such as Coors, increases, the demand for generic light beer rises and the equilibrium price and quantity both rise. The goods are substitutes.

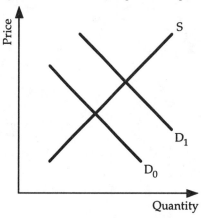

Difficult
Math
Page: 90

4.146: Refer to Scenario 1. Graph and explain the effect on equilibrium price and quantity of beer due to an increase in the price of potato chips. How are the goods related?

Answer: As the price of potato chips increases, the demand for generic light beer falls and the equilibrium price and quantity both fall. The goods are complements.

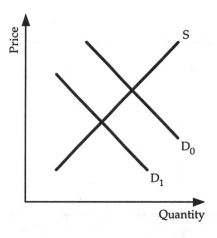

Difficult
Math
Page: 90

4.147: Refer to Scenario 1. Graph and explain the effect on equilibrium price and quantity if individuals become more concerned with their weight and change their tastes in favor of "Light Beer."

Answer: As individuals grow more concerned with weight, the demand for "Light Beer" rises and the equilibrium price and quantity both rise.

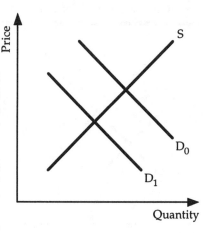

4.148: Refer to Scenario 1. Graph and explain the effect on equilibrium price and quantity if the number of consumers falls.

Difficult
Math
Page: 90

Answer: As the number of consumers falls, the demand for all beer, including generic light beer, falls and the equilibrium price and quantity both fall.

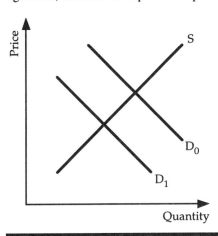

SCENARIO 2: Consider the market for plastic deck chairs. Production costs include labor costs, the cost of plastic, and electricity to operate machines.

4.149: Refer to Scenario 2. Graph and explain the effect on equilibrium price and quantity of an increase in the cost of plastic.

Easy
Math
Page: 90

Answer: Price increases and quantity decreases.

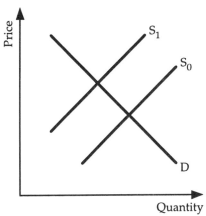

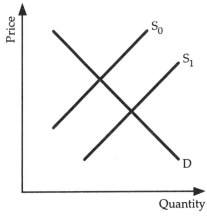

4.150: Refer to Scenario 2. Graph and explain the effect on equilibrium price and quantity of a decrease in the cost of electricity.

Easy
Math
Page: 90

Answer: Price decreases and quantity increases.

Easy
Math
Page: 90

4.151: Refer to Scenario 2. Graph and explain the effect on equilibrium price and quantity if technology improves the ability of workers to mold chairs faster.

Answer: Price decreases and quantity increases.

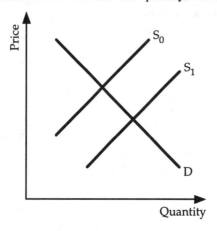

Difficult
Math
Page: 90

4.152: Refer to Scenario 2. Graph and explain the effect on equilibrium price and quantity if the price of plastic chairs for inside the home suddenly rises.

Answer: Price increases and quantity decreases.

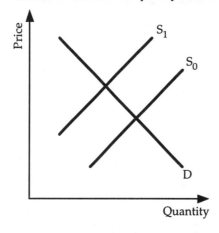

Difficult
Math
Page: 90

4.153: Refer to Scenario 2. Graph and explain the effect on equilibrium price and quantity if many families go on a "barbecue binge" and buy new barbecue grills to use outside with their deck chairs.

Answer: Price increases and quantity increases.

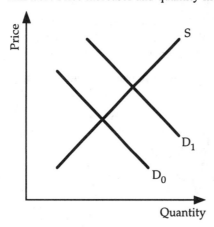

SCENARIO 3: Assume that the demand function for Sushi may be written QD = 180 - 3 P, where P is the price of a Sushi piece, and the supply may be written QS = 30 + 4 P.

4.154: Refer to Scenario 3. Graph the supply and demand curves for Sushi prices for the range P = 10, 15, 20, 25, 30.

Moderate
Math
Page: 90

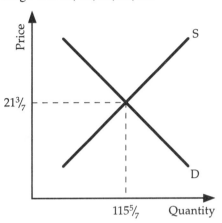

Answer:	P	QD	QS
	10	150	70
	15	135	90
	20	120	110
	25	105	130
	30	90	150

4.155: Refer to Scenario 3. Determine the equilibrium price and quantity exchanged.

Moderate
Math
Page: 90

Answer: To determine the equilibrium price, QS must equal QD, so:

$$180 - 3 P = 30 + 4 P$$
$$180 - 30 = 4 P + 3 P$$
$$150 = 7 P$$
$$P = 21\ 3/7$$

Then QS = 30 + 4(21 3/7)
QS = 30 + 600/7
QS = 115 5/7

4.156: Refer to Scenario 3. What occurs if the price is equal to 10? If the price is equal to 30?

Moderate
Math
Page: 90

Answer: At P = 10, QS = 70 and QD = 150. Since QD > QS, we have a shortage.
At P = 30, QS = 150 and QD = 90. Since QS > QD, we have a surplus.

Answer:

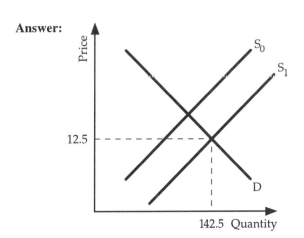

4.157: Refer to Scenario 3. Assume that an increase in the number of Japanese restaurants makes the Sushi supply curve become QS = 80 + 5 P. Graph the new supply and demand curves.

Moderate
Math
Page: 90

Challenging
Multi
Page: 90

4.158: Refer to Scenario 3. Calculate the new equilibrium price and quantity.

Answer: To determine the new equilibrium price, QS must equal QD, so:
$$180 - 3P = 80 + 5P$$
$$100 = 8P$$
$$P = 12.5$$

Then, QS = 80 + 5 (12.5)
QS = 80 + 62.5
QS = 142.5.

Moderate
Definition
Page: 90

4.159: Refer to Scenario 3. Provide an explanation for the change in price and quantity.

Answer: As new firms enter the market they must offer a lower price in order to entice consumers to buy their Sushi. Incumbent firms respond by also lowering their price.

SCENARIO 4: Graphically illustrate each of the following effects on the market for home fitness equipment with supply and demand curves. Consider each effect separately.

Moderate
Application
Page: 90

4.160: Refer to Scenario 4. Assume that the price of dues in local health clubs decreases.

Answer:

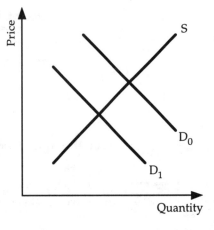

Moderate
Application
Page: 90

4.161: Refer to Scenario 4. "Infomercials" begin to run at night on Cable TV stations.

Answer:

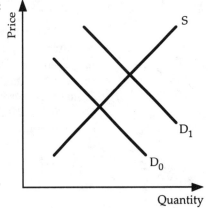

4.162: Refer to Scenario 4. The cost of steel used in the production of many of the exercise products increases.

Moderate
Application
Page: 90

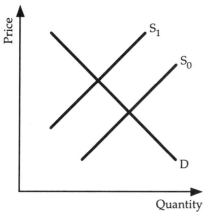

4.163: Refer to Scenario 4. Health clubs begin to offer extras to make going to health clubs easier, such as free parking and baby sitting to encourage family memberships.

Moderate
Application
Page: 90

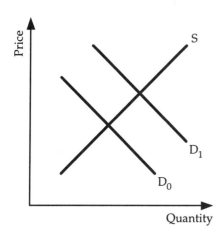

Answer:

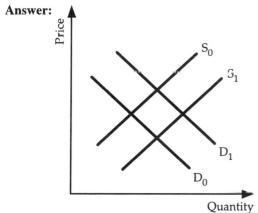

4.164: Refer to Scenario 4. The existence of a new health club craze occurs simultaneously as new home exercise products enter the market.

Difficult
Application
Page: 90

SCENARIO 5: Events prior to the 1995 Baseball Season, including a threatened "lock out" by owners if the players decided to end their strike, likely had a great effect on attendance at baseball games. Consider in this market attendance as a measure of quantity and ticket price the measure of price.

Easy
Math
Page: 71

4.165: Refer to Scenario 5. Draw the supply and demand curves and explain why they have the slope they do.

Answer: The demand curve slopes downward because as price falls, it is cheaper for individuals to attend games and attendance rises. The supply curve slopes upward because in order to allow for more attendance, there are greater costs on the owners.

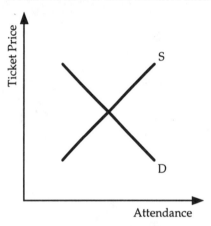

Easy
Math
Page: 90

4.166: Refer to Scenario 5. Graphically illustrate the effect of dissatisfaction with the teams by fans.

Answer:

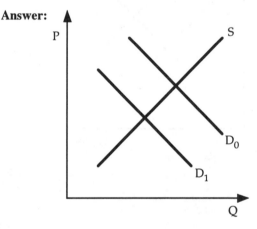

Moderate
Math
Page: 90

4.167: Refer to Scenario 5. Graphically illustrate the effect of a shortened season.

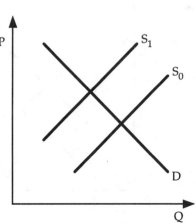

4.168: Refer to Scenario 5. Graphically illustrate the effect of both fan dissatisfaction and shorter seasons.

Moderate
Math
Page: 90

Answer:

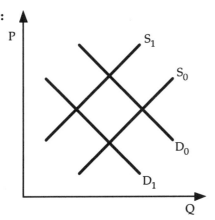

4.169: Refer to Scenario 5. Explain the effect of consumer dissatisfaction on the market for beer purchased at baseball games.

Moderate
Math
Page: 90

Answer: The lower demand for baseball games would have the effect of lowering the demand for beer purchases.

4.170: Using the concepts of income and substitution effects, explain why there is a negative relationship between price and quantity demanded.

Moderate
Math
Page: 90

Answer: According to the income effect, as the price of a good is reduced the consumer has more income available to purchase all goods, including the good whose price fell. According to the substitution effect, as the price of a good falls consumers will substitute toward this cheaper good and away from goods whose prices have not fallen. Therefore as price of a good falls, the quantity demanded of that good increases.

4.171: The law of demand is supported by the income effect. But for inferior goods as income increases the amount of the good purchased decreases. Why, then, do the demand curves for inferior goods still slope downward?

Honors
Multi
Page: 90

Answer: The substitution effect must be greater than the income effect.

4.172: Explain why demand curves always intersect the price axis and the quantity axis.

Challenging
Multi
Page: 90

Answer: The demand curve always intersects the price axis because there is a price above which no purchases will be made. The demand curve will intersect the quantity axis because demand for most goods is limited even at a zero price.

4.173: Explain three factors that could cause a change in the demand for a product.

Challenging
Multi
Page: 90

Answer: The factors that can change demand are: change in income, change in the prices of related goods, change in tastes and preferences, and expectations of the future.

4.174: Explain two factors that could cause a decrease in the supply of a product.

Challenging
Multi
Page: 90

Answer: The factors that could cause a decrease in the supply of a product are: increased costs, increased input prices, a reduction in the number of firms, and an increase in the price of another product that could be produced by the firm.

Challenging
Multi
Page: 90

4.175: Explain how excess supply is eliminated in an unregulated market.

Answer: Excess supply would be eliminated through raising prices, which would cause an increase in quantity supplied and a reduction in quantity demanded.

Challenging
Multi
Page: 90

4.176: At an urban college where most students commute to classes, there are 8,000 parking spaces for students. All students pay $20 a quarter for a pass that allows them to park in any one of those 8,000 spaces. Between 8 AM and 1 PM there are always students waiting in parking lots for spaces to open up. Students attending classes during this time are always complaining about how difficult it is to find a place to park. Between 5 PM and 9 PM there are always a large number of empty spaces in the parking lots. Students who attend classes at night never have a problem parking. Illustrate the parking situation for these two different times of day using supply and demand curves. Draw separate graphs for the day and night students. Are these markets in equilibrium? Explain. The Director of Parking Services has asked you to help him solve this problem. What would you suggest?

Answer: The supply curve of parking spaces is a vertical line in each case. For the day students there is excess demand at a price of $20 and for the night students there is an excess supply at $20. One suggestion would be to raise the parking fee for day students to eliminate the excess demand and reduce the fee for night students to eliminate the excess supply.

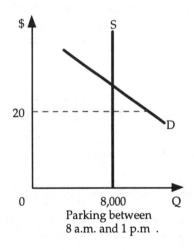

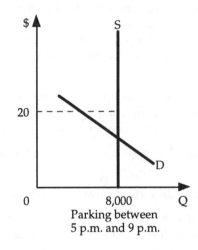

Challenging
Multi
Page: 90

4.177: After Hurricane Andrew inflicted millions of dollars of damage on Southern Florida, the prices of construction materials (such as plywood) doubled in price. In an effort to protect consumers, the government considered imposing price regulations that would require construction materials to be sold at the same prices that prevailed prior to the hurricane. Do you think this would have been a sound economic idea? Why or why not?

Answer: If price controls were imposed, there would have been excess demand for construction materials. The higher prices were necessary to encourage suppliers to sell more construction supplies in Southern Florida.

4.178: An unseasonably warm March is followed by an unseasonably cold April. This leads to a 30% reduction in the yield of apples. As a result, the price of peaches increases. Illustrate this situation with supply and demand curves (draw diagrams for both markets). Explain what will happen to equilibrium price and quantity in both markets.

Challenging
Multi
Page: 90

Answer: In the market for apples there was a decrease in supply that increased the price of apples and decreased the equilibrium quantity. The increase in the price of apples caused the demand for oranges to increase, which will increase the equilibrium price and quantity of apples.

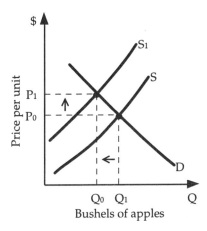
Bushels of apples

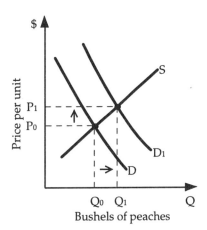
Bushels of peaches

4.179: Scientific reports have convinced people that it is better for their health to eat less beef and more chicken. Illustrate this situation with supply and demand curves (draw diagrams for both the market for beef and the market for chicken.) Explain what has happened to the equilibrium price and quantity in each of these markets.

Challenging
Multi
Page: 90

Answer: There will be a decrease in the demand for beef, which will decrease the equilibrium price and quantity of beef. There will be an increase in the demand for chicken, which will increase the equilibrium price and quantity of chicken.

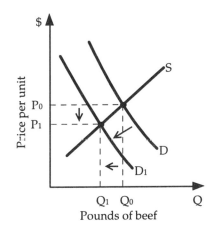
Pounds of beef

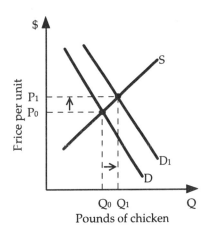
Pounds of chicken

5 SUPPLY, DEMAND, AND THE PRICE SYSTEM

5.1: Refer to Figure 5.1. The market is initially in equilibrium at point A. If demand shifts from D_1 to D_2 and the price of chicken remains constant at $3.00, there will be

(a) an excess supply of 150 million pounds of chicken.
(b) an excess demand of 150 million pounds of chicken.
(c) an excess supply of 50 million pounds of chicken.
(d) an excess demand of 100 million pounds of chicken.

Answer: (b)

Moderate
Single
Page: 98

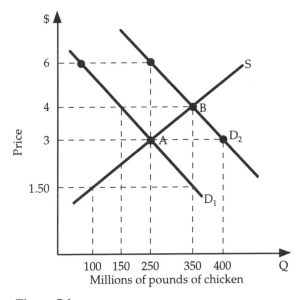

Figure 5.1

5.2: Refer to Figure 5.1. The market is initially in equilibrium at point B. If demand shifts from D_2 to D_1 and the price of chicken remains constant at $4.00, there will be

(a) an excess supply of 200 million pounds of chicken.
(b) an excess demand of 200 million pounds of chicken.
(c) an excess supply of 100 million pounds of chicken.
(d) an excess demand of 100 million pounds of chicken.

Answer: (a)

Moderate
Single
Page: 98

123

Moderate
Single
Page: 98

5.3: Refer to Figure 5.1. The market is initially in equilibrium at point A. If demand shifts from D_1 to D_2, the new equilibrium price will be _____ and the new equilibrium quantity will be _____.

(a) $3.00; 250
(b) $6.00; 250
(c) $4.00; 350
(d) $4.00; 150.

Answer: (c)

Moderate
Single
Page: 98

5.4: Refer to Figure 5.1. The market is initially in equilibrium at point B. If demand shifts from D_2 to D_1, the new equilibrium price will be _____ and the new equilibrium quantity will be _____.

(a) $4.00; 350
(b) $3.00; 250
(c) $3.00; 400
(d) $4.00; 150

Answer: (b)

Challenging
Multi
Page: 98

5.5: Refer to Figure 5.1. The market is initially in equilibrium at point A and demand shifts from D_1 to D_2. Which of the following statements is TRUE?

(a) There is no need for price to serve as a rationing device in this case since the new equilibrium quantity is higher than the original equilibrium quantity.
(b) Because demand increased instead of supply, decreasing quantity and not price will be the rationing device.
(c) The market cannot move to a new equilibrium until there is also a change in supply.
(d) Price will still serve as a rationing device causing quantity demanded to fall from 400 to 350 million pounds of chicken.

Answer: (d)

Moderate
Single
Page: 98

5.6. Refer to Figure 5.2. The market is initially in equilibrium at point A. If demand shifts from D1 to D2 and the price of beef remains constant at $1.00, there will be

(a) an excess supply of 50 million pounds of beef.
(b) an excess demand of 100 million pounds of beef.
(c) an excess supply of 25 million pounds of beef.
(d) an excess demand of 50 million pounds of beef.

Answer: (d)

Moderate
Single
Page: 98

5.7. Refer to Figure 5.2. The market is initially in equilibrium at point B. If demand shifts from D2 to D1 and the price of beef remains constant at $2.00, there will be

(a) an excess supply of 50 million pounds of beef.
(b) an excess demand of 100 million pounds of beef.
(c) an excess supply of 25 million pounds of beef.
(d) an excess demand of 50 million pounds of beef.

Answer: (a)

5.8 Refer to Figure 5.2. The market is initially in equilibrium at point A. If demand shifts from D1 to D2, the new equilibrium price will be _____ and the new equilibrium quantity will be _____.

(a) $1.00; 125
(b) $2.00; 50
(c) $2.00; 100
(d) $2.25; 75

Moderate
Single
Page: 98

Answer: (c)

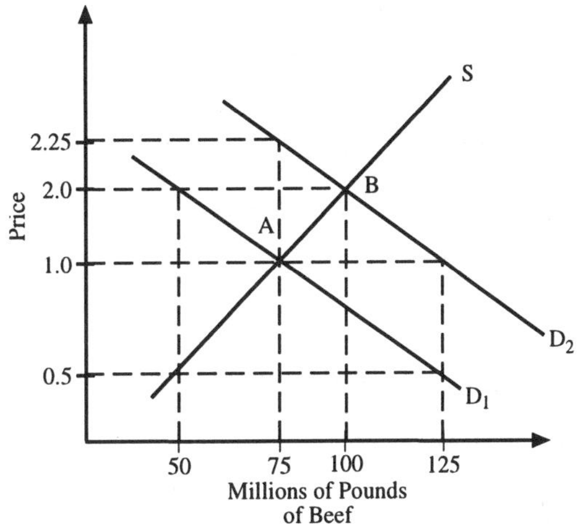

5.9. Refer to Figure 5.2. The market is initially in equilibrium at point B. If demand shifts from D2 to D1, the new equilibrium price will be _____ and the new equilibrium quantity will be _____.

Figure 5.2

Moderate
Single
Page: 98

(a) $1.00; 125
(b) $1.00; 75
(c) $2.00; 100
(d) $2.25; 75

Answer: (b)

5.10. Refer to Figure 5.2. The market is initially in equilibrium at point A and demand shifts from D1 to D2. Which of the following statements is TRUE?

Challenging
Multi
Page: 98

(a) There is no need for price to serve as a rationing device in this case since the new equilibrium quantity is higher than the original equilibrium quantity.
(b) Because demand increased instead of supply, decreasing quantity and not price will be the rationing device.
(c) The market cannot move to a new equilibrium until there is also a change in supply.
(d) Price will still serve as a rationing device causing quantity supplied to rise from 75 to 100 million pounds of beef.

Answer: (d)

5.11. Refer to Figure 5.3. The market is initially in equilibrium at point A. If demand shifts from D1 to D2 and the price of apples remains constant at $0.50, there will be

Moderate
Single
Page: 98

(a) an excess supply of 25 million apples.
(b) an excess demand of 20 million apples.
(c) an excess supply of 20 million apples.
(d) an excess demand of 15 million apples.

Answer: (b)

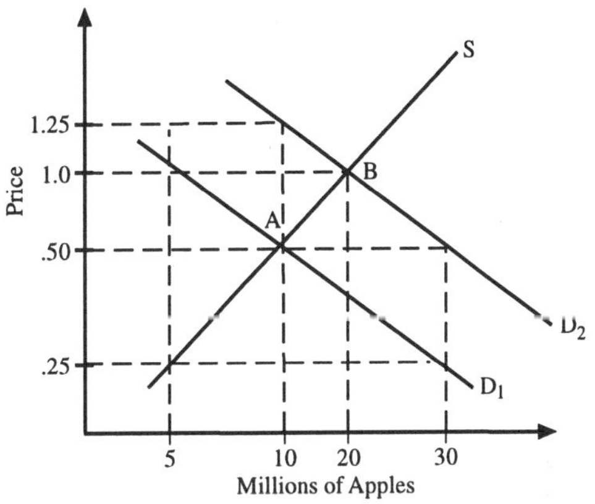

Figure 5.3

Moderate
Single
Page: 98

5.12. Refer to Figure 5.3. The market is initially in equilibrium at point B. If demand shifts from D2 to D1 and the price of apples remains constant at $1.00, there will be

(a) an excess supply of 20 million apples.
(b) an excess demand of 25 million apples.
(c) an excess supply of 15 million apples.
(d) an excess demand of 20 million apples.

Answer: (c)

Moderate
Single
Page: 98

5.13. Refer to Figure 5.3. The market is initially in equilibrium at point A. If demand shifts from D1 to D2, the new equilibrium price will be _____ and the new equilibrium quantity will be _____.

(a) $1.00; 20
(b) $0.25; 30
(c) $0.50; 10
(d) $1.25; 10

Answer: (a)

Moderate
Single
Page: 98

5.14 Refer to Figure 5.3. The market is initially in equilibrium at point B. If demand shifts from D2 to D1, the new equilibrium price will be _____ and the new equilibrium quantity will be _____.

(a) $1.00; 20
(b) $0.25; 30
(c) $0.50; 10
(d) $1.25; 10

Answer: (c)

Challenging
Multi
Page: 98

5.15. Refer to Figure 5.3. The market is initially in equilibrium at point A and demand shifts from D1 to D2. Which of the following statements is TRUE?

(a) Price will still serve as a rationing device causing quantity supplied to rise from 10 to 20 million apples.
(b) There is no need for price to serve as a rationing device in this case since the new equilibrium quantity is higher than the original equilibrium quantity.
(c) Price will still serve as a rationing device causing quantity demanded to fall from 20 to 10 million apples.
(d) The market cannot move to a new equilibrium until there is also a change in supply.

Answer: (a)

Moderate
Single
Page: 98

5.16. Refer to Figure 5.4. The market is initially in equilibrium at point A. If supply shifts from S1 to S2 and the price of pizzas remains constant at $7.00, there will be

(a) an excess supply of 5 thousand pizzas.
(b) an excess demand of 5 thousand pizzas.
(c) an excess supply of 2 thousand pizzas.
(d) an excess demand of 7 thousand pizzas.

Answer: (b)

5.17. Refer to Figure 5.4. The market is initially in equilibrium at point B. If supply shifts from S2 to S1 and the price of pizzas remains constant at $10.00, there will be

(a) an excess supply of 4 thousand pizzas.
(b) an excess demand of 5 thousand pizzas.
(c) an excess supply of 2 thousand pizzas.
(d) an excess demand of 7 thousand pizzas.

Moderate
Single
Page: 98

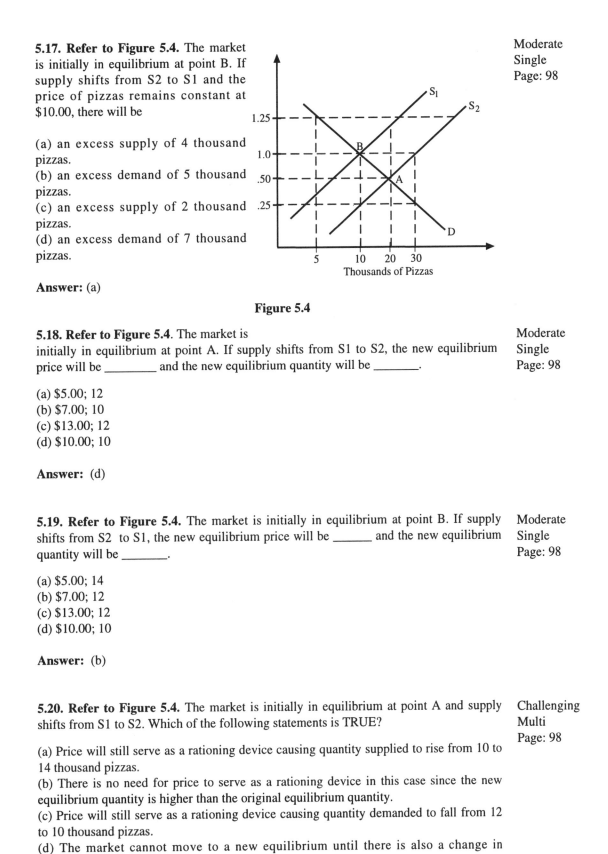

Answer: (a)

Figure 5.4

5.18. Refer to Figure 5.4. The market is initially in equilibrium at point A. If supply shifts from S1 to S2, the new equilibrium price will be _____ and the new equilibrium quantity will be _____.

Moderate
Single
Page: 98

(a) $5.00; 12
(b) $7.00; 10
(c) $13.00; 12
(d) $10.00; 10

Answer: (d)

5.19. Refer to Figure 5.4. The market is initially in equilibrium at point B. If supply shifts from S2 to S1, the new equilibrium price will be _____ and the new equilibrium quantity will be _____.

Moderate
Single
Page: 98

(a) $5.00; 14
(b) $7.00; 12
(c) $13.00; 12
(d) $10.00; 10

Answer: (b)

5.20. Refer to Figure 5.4. The market is initially in equilibrium at point A and supply shifts from S1 to S2. Which of the following statements is TRUE?

Challenging
Multi
Page: 98

(a) Price will still serve as a rationing device causing quantity supplied to rise from 10 to 14 thousand pizzas.
(b) There is no need for price to serve as a rationing device in this case since the new equilibrium quantity is higher than the original equilibrium quantity.
(c) Price will still serve as a rationing device causing quantity demanded to fall from 12 to 10 thousand pizzas.
(d) The market cannot move to a new equilibrium until there is also a change in supply.

Answer: (c)

Moderate
Single
Page: 98

5.21. Refer to Figure 5.5. The market is initially in equilibrium at point A. If supply shifts from S1 to S2 and the price of bicycles remains constant at $125, there will be

(a) an excess supply of 8 thousand bicycles.
(b) an excess demand of 2 thousand bicycles.
(c) an excess supply of 3 thousand bicycles.
(d) an excess demand of 5 thousand bicycles.

Answer: (d)

Moderate
Single
Page: 98

5.22. Refer to Figure 5.5. The market is initially in equilibrium at point B. If supply shifts from S2 to S1 and the price of bicycles remains constant at $175.00, there will be

(a) an excess supply of 5 thousand bicycles.
(b) an excess demand of 2 thousand bicycles.
(c) an excess supply of 3 thousand bicycles.
(d) an excess demand of 5 thousand bicycles.

Answer: (a)

Moderate
Single
Page: 98

5.23. Refer to Figure 5.5. The market is initially in equilibrium at point A. If supply shifts from S1 to S2, the new equilibrium price will be _____ and the new equilibrium quantity will be _____.

(a) $125; 8
(b) $125; 3
(c) $175; 6
(d) $100; 10

Answer: (c)

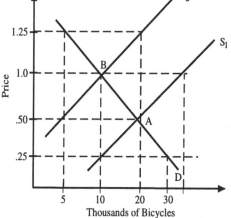

Moderate
Single
Page: 98

5.24. Refer to Figure 5.5. The market is initially in equilibrium at point B. If supply shifts from S2 to S1, the new equilibrium price will be _____ and the new equilibrium quantity will be _____.

(a) $125; 8
(b) $125; 3
(c) $175; 6
(d) $100; 10

Answer: (a)

Figure 5.5

Challenging
Multi
Page: 98

5.25. Refer to Figure 5.5. The market is initially in equilibrium at point A and supply shifts from S1 to S2. Which of the following statements is TRUE?

(a) Price will still serve as a rationing device causing quantity supplied to rise from 10 to 14 thousand bicycles.
(b) There is no need for price to serve as a rationing device in this case since the new equilibrium quantity is higher than the original equilibrium quantity.
(c) Price will still serve as a rationing device causing quantity demanded to fall from 8 to 6 thousand bicycles.
(d) The market cannot move to a new equilibrium until there is also a change in supply.

Answer: (c)

5.26. Refer to Figure 5.6. An example of a price ceiling would be the government setting the price of gasoline at

(a) $2.00.
(b) $1.75.
(c) $1.25.
(d) $1.00.

Easy
Single
Page: 101

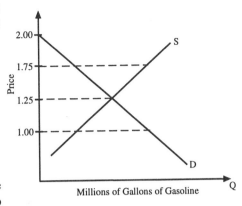

Answer: (d)

5.27. Refer to Figure 5.6. If the government will not allow oil companies to charge more than $1.00 per gallon of gasoline, which of the following will happen?

Moderate
Single
Page: 101

Figure 5.6

(a) Demand must eventually decrease so that the market will come into equilibrium at a price of $1.25.
(b) Supply must eventually increase so that the market will come into equilibrium at a price of $1.25.
(c) A nonprice rationing system such as ration coupons must be used to ration the available supply of gasoline.
(d) The market will be in equilibrium at a price of $1.00

Answer: (c)

5.28. Refer to Figure 5.7. An example of a price ceiling would be the government setting the price of rice at

(a) $2.00.
(b) $2.50.
(c) $1.00.
(d) $1.50.

Easy
Single
Page: 101

Answer: (c)

5.29. Refer to Figure 5.7. If the government will not allow rice farmers to charge more than $1.00 per pound of rice, which of the following will happen?

Moderate
Single
Page: 101

(a) Demand must eventually decrease so that the market will come into equilibrium at a price of $1.50.
(b) There will be a shortage of rice.
(c) Supply must eventually increase so that the market will come into equilibrium at a price of $1.50.
(d) The market will be in equilibrium at a price of $1.00

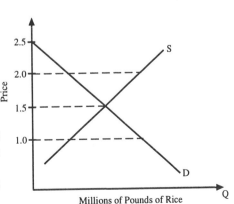

Answer: (b)

Figure 5.7

5.30: It is necessary to ration a good whenever _____ exists.

(a) excess demand
(b) excess supply
(c) a surplus
(d) a perfectly inelastic demand

Answer: (a)

5.31: Price rationing means that whenever there is a need to ration a good in a free market,

(a) the price of that good will fall until the market clears.
(b) the price of that good will rise until the market clears.
(c) price will remain constant but demand will decrease until the market clears.
(d) price will remain constant but supply will increase until the market clears.

Answer: (b)

5.32: The adjustment of _____ is the rationing mechanism in free markets.

(a) quantity
(b) price
(c) supply
(d) demand

Answer: (b)

Moderate
Fact
Page: 99

5.33: Price is determined solely by demand when

(a) demand is perfectly elastic.
(b) demand is perfectly inelastic.
(c) supply is perfectly inelastic.
(d) supply is perfectly elastic.

Answer: (c)

Moderate
Fact
Page: 99

5.34 When supply is perfectly inelastic,

(a) price is determined solely by supply.
(b) price is determined solely by demand.
(c) only the government can set the price.
(d) the price may be set by either supply or demand.

Answer: (b)

Challenging
Multi
Page: 99

5.35: In which of the following cases will price be demand determined?

(a) The number of seats in a stadium is fixed at 80,000 and the stadium is always sold out for events held there.
(b) There is only one consumer of kumquats and the supply curve of kumquats is upward sloping.
(c) The demand curve for corn is a horizontal line and the supply curve of corn is upward sloping.
(d) The demand for parking spaces at an apartment complex is fixed at 35 and the quantity of parking spaces supplied can be increased as people's willingness to pay for the fixed number of parking spaces increases.

Answer: (a)

5.36: A price ceiling is

Easy
Definition
Page: 101

(a) a minimum price usually set by government, that sellers must charge for a good.
(b) a maximum price usually set by government, that sellers may charge for a good.
(c) the difference between the initial equilibrium price and the equilibrium price after a decrease in supply.
(d) the minimum price that consumers are willing to pay for a good.

Answer: (b)

5.37. A maximum price, usually set by the government, that sellers may charge for a good is known as

Easy
Definition
Page: 101

(a) a price floor.
(b) a price rationing mechanism.
(c) a price ceiling.
(d) a subsidy.

Answer: (c)

5.38: Refer to Figure 5.8. An example of an effective price ceiling would be the government setting rental rates for apartments at

Easy
Single
Page: 101

(a) $400
(b) $500.
(c) $600.
(d) $700.

Answer: (a)

5.39: Refer to Figure 5.8. If the government will not allow landlords to charge more than $400 for an apartment, which of the following will happen?

Moderate
Single
Page: 101

(a) Demand must eventually decrease so that the market will come into equilibrium at a price of $400.
(b) Supply must eventually increase so that the market will come into equilibrium at a price of $400.
(c) A nonprice rationing system such as queuing must be used to ration the available supply of apartments.
(d) The market will be in equilibrium at a price of $400.

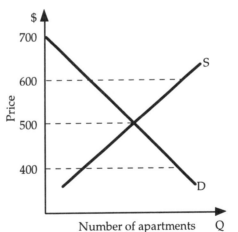

Figure 5.8

Answer: (c)

5.40: If the price ceiling is set below the equilibrium price,

Moderate
Fact
Page: 101

(a) quantity demanded will equal quantity supplied.
(b) quantity demanded will be less than quantity supplied.
(c) quantity demanded will be greater than quantity supplied.
(d) demand will be less than supply.

Answer: (c)

Moderate
Fact
Page: 101

5.41. If the price ceiling is set above the equilibrium price,

(a) quantity demanded will equal quantity supplied.
(b) quantity demanded will be less than quantity supplied.
(c) quantity demanded will be greater than quantity supplied.
(d) demand will be less than supply.

Answer: (a)

Challenging
Single
Page: 101

5.42: If the government imposes a maximum price that is above the equilibrium price,

(a) this maximum price will have no economic impact.
(b) quantity demanded will be less than quantity supplied.
(c) demand will be greater than supply.
(d) the available supply will have to be rationed with a nonprice rationing mechanism.

Answer: (a)

Challenging
Single
Page: 101

5.43. If the government imposes a maximum price that is below the equilibrium price,

(a) this maximum price will have no economic impact.
(b) quantity demanded will be less than quantity supplied.
(c) demand will be greater than supply.
(d) the available supply will have to be rationed with a nonprice rationing mechanism.

Answer: (d)

Challenging
Multi
Page: 101

5.44: The government imposes a maximum price on apartments that is BELOW the equilibrium price. You accurately predict that

(a) the law will have no economic impact.
(b) the law will create a surplus of apartments.
(c) renters will find that landlords start offering to furnish the apartments.
(d) landlords are less likely to do routine maintenance work in the apartments.

Answer: (d)

Challenging
Multi
Page: 101

5.45. The government imposes a maximum price on apartments that is ABOVE the equilibrium price. You accurately predict that

(a) the law will have no economic impact.
(b) the law will create a surplus of apartments.
(c) renters will find that landlords start offering to furnish the apartments.
(d) landlords are less likely to do routine maintenance work in the apartments.

Answer: (a)

Moderate
Single
Page: 101

5.46: The government imposes a price ceiling on gasoline that is below the market price. You are asked to suggest a rationing scheme which will minimize the misallocation of resources. You suggest

(a) using rationing coupons which can be resold.
(b) using rationing coupons which cannot be resold.
(c) using rationing on a first-come, first-served basis.
(d) using rationing only on weekdays.

Answer: (a)

5.47 The government imposes a price ceiling on sugar that is above the market price. You are asked to suggest a rationing scheme which will minimize the misallocation of resources. You suggest

(a) using rationing coupons which cannot be resold.
(b) using rationing on a first-come, first-served basis.
(c) using rationing coupons which can be resold.
(d) that no rationing system will be necessary.

Moderate
Single
Page: 101

Answer: (d)

5.48: You bought a ticket for a Madonna concert for $30. A friend who was unable to buy a ticket offers you $130 for your ticket. The real price of the ticket to you is

(a) $30.
(b) $100.
(c) $130.
(d) indeterminate from this information.

Challenging
Multi
Page: 102

Answer: (b)

5.49: People scalping tickets for a rock concert will be successful

(a) any time the rock group is popular.
(b) when the price set by the concert hall is less than the market equilibrium price.
(c) when prices are too high.
(d) only when there is excess supply.

Moderate
Single
Page: 102

Answer: (b)

5.50: Refer to Figure 5.9. At the world price of $10 per barrel of oil the United States imports _____ barrels of oil per day.

(a) 3
(b) 5
(c) 8
(d) 11.

Easy
Single
Page: 105

Answer: (b)

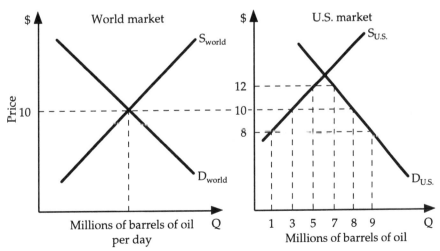

Figure 5.9

Moderate
Multi
Page: 105

5.51: Refer to Figure 5.9. If a $2 per barrel tax is levied on imported oil, the United States will

(a) import 2 million barrels of oil per day.
(b) import 5 million barrels of oil per day.
(c) import 8 million barrels of oil per day.
(d) export 8 million barrels of oil per day.

Answer: (a)

Moderate
Multi
Page: 105

5.-52: Refer to Figure 5.9. If the United States eliminates all taxes on imported oil, which of the following would occur?

(a) The price of oil in the United States would fall to $8 per barrel and the United States would import 8 million barrels of oil per day.
(b) The price of oil in the United States would be $10 per barrel and the United States would import 5 million barrels of oil per day.
(c) The price of oil in the United States would be $12 per barrel and the United States would import 2 million barrels of oil per day.
(d) The price of oil in the United States after the U.S. government eliminated all taxes on imported oil cannot be determined from this information.

Answer: (b)

Moderate
Multi
Page: 105

5.53: Refer to Figure 5.9. Assume that initially there is free trade. If the United States, then imposes a $2 tax per barrel of imported oil,

(a) the quantity demanded of oil will be reduced by 2 million barrels per day.
(b) the quantity of oil supplied by U.S. firms will increase by 5 million barrels per day.
(c) U.S. imports of oil will increase by 3 million barrels per day.
(d) the price of oil in the U.S. will increase to $12 per barrel.

Answer: (d)

Challenging
Multi
Page: 105

5.54: Refer to Figure 5.9. Assume that initially there is free trade. If the United States, then imposes a $2 tax per barrel of imported oil, the tax revenue generated will equal

(a) $4 million per day.
(b) $6 million per day.
(c) $10 million per day.
(d) $14 million per day.

Answer: (a)

Easy
Single
Page: 105

5.55. Refer to Figure 5.10. At the world price of 50 cents per bell pepper the United States imports _____ bell peppers per day.

(a) 3
(b) 2
(c) 1
(d) 4

Answer: (a)

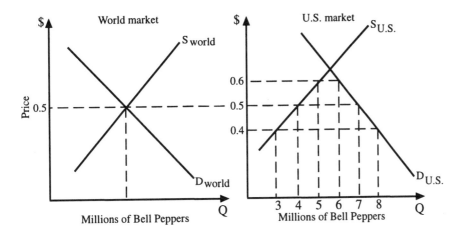

Figure 5.10

Moderate
Multi
Page: 105

5.56. Refer to Figure 5.10. If a 10 cent per bell pepper tax is levied on imported bell peppers, the United States will

(a) import 4 million bell peppers per day.
(b) import 3 million bell peppers per day.
(c) import 2 million bell peppers per day.
(d) import 1 million bell peppers per day.

Answer: (d)

Moderate
Multi
Page: 105

5.57. Refer to Figure 5.10. If the United States eliminates all taxes on bell peppers, which of the following would occur?

(a) The price of bell peppers in the United States would fall to 40 cents per bell pepper and the United States would import 5 million bell peppers per day.
(b) The price of bell peppers in the United States would be 60 cents per bell pepper and the United States would import 1 million bell peppers per day.
(c) The price of bell peppers in the United States would be 50 cents per bell pepper and the United States would import 3 million bell peppers per day.
(d) The price of bell peppers in the United States after the U.S. government eliminated all taxes on imported bell peppers cannot be determined from this information.

Answer: (c)

Moderate
Multi
Page: 105

5.58 Refer to Figure 5.10. Assume that initially there is free trade. If the United States then imposes a 10 cent tax per bell pepper,

(a) the quantity demanded of bell peppers will be reduced by 2 million bell peppers per day.
(b) the quantity of bell peppers supplied by U.S. firms will increase by 5 million bell peppers per day.
(c) the price of bell peppers in the U.S. will increase to 60 cents per bell pepper.
(d) U.S. imports of bell peppers will increase by 3 million per day.

Answer: (c)

Challenging
Multi
Page: 105

5.59. Refer to Figure 5.10. Assume that initially there is free trade. If the United States then imposes a 10 cent tax per bell pepper, the tax revenue generated will equal

(a) $400,000 per day.
(b) $600,000 per day.
(c) $100,000 per day.
(d) $1.4 million per day.

Answer: (c)

Easy
Single
Page: 105

5.60. Refer to Figure 5.11. At the world price of $100 per ton of steel, the United States imports _____ tons of steel.

(a) 8
(b) 15
(c) 7
(d) 10

Answer: (c)

Moderate
Multi
Page: 105

5.61. Refer to Figure 5.11. If a $25 per ton steel tax is levied on imported steel, the United States will

(a) import 1 ton of steel.
(b) import 7 tons of steel.
(c) import 5 tons of steel.
(d) import 12 tons of steel.

Answer: (a)

Moderate
Multi
Page: 105

5.62. Refer to Figure 5.11. If the United States eliminates all taxes on steel, which of the following would occur?

(a) The price of steel in the United States would fall to $125 per ton of steel and the United States would import 1 ton of steel.
(b) The price of steel in the United States would be $100 per ton of steel and the United States would import 7 tons of steel.
(c) The price of steel in the United States would be $75 per ton of steel and the United States would import 13 tons of steel.
(d) The price of steel in the United States after the U.S. government eliminated all taxes on imported steel cannot be determined from this information.

Answer: (b)

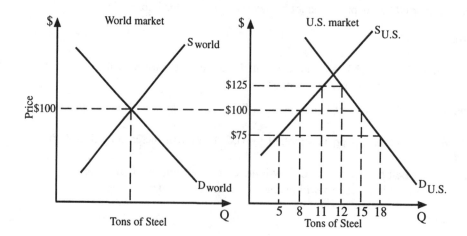

Figure 5.11

5.63. Refer to Figure 5.11. Assume that initially there is free trade. If the United States then imposes a $25 per ton steel tax,

Moderate
Multi
Page: 105

(a) the quantity demanded of steel will be reduced by 2 tons of steel.
(b) the quantity of steel supplied by U.S. firms will increase by 3 tons of steel.
(c) the price of steel in the U.S. will decrease to $75 per ton.
(d) U.S. imports of steel will increase by 3 million per day.

Answer: (b)

5.64. Refer to Figure 5.11. Assume that initially there is free trade. If the United States then imposes a $25 per ton steel tax, the tax revenue generated will equal

Challenging
Multi
Page: 105

(a) $25.
(b) $250.
(c) $175.
(d) $200.

Answer: (a)

5.67 Refer to Figure 5.12. At the world price of $2.00 per of mango, the United States imports _____ thousand mangos.

Easy
Single
Page: 105

(a) 1
(b) 2
(c) 3
(d) 5

Answer: (c)

5.68. Refer to Figure 5.12. If a $0.5 each mango tax is levied on imported mangos, the United States will

Moderate
Multi
Page: 105

(a) import 3 thousand mangos.
(b) import 1 thousand mangos.
(c) import 4 thousand mangos.
(d) import 5 thousand mangos.

Answer: (b)

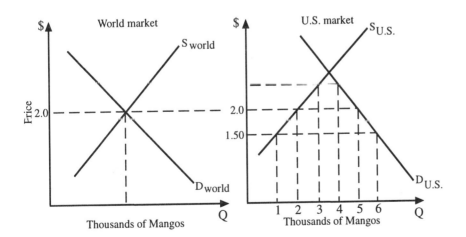

Figure 5.12.

Moderate
Multi
Page: 105

5.69. Refer to Figure 5.12. If the United States eliminates all taxes on mangos, which of the following would occur?

(a) The price of mangos in the United States would fall to $2.00 per mango and the United States would import 3 thousand mangos.
(b) The price of mangos in the United States would be $2.50 per mango and the United States would import 1 thousand mangos.
(c) The price of mangos in the United States would be $1.50 per mango and the United States would import 5 thousand mangos.
(d) The price of mangos in the United States after the U.S. government eliminated all taxes on imported mangos cannot be determined from this information.

Answer: (a)

Moderate
Multi
Page: 105

5.70 Refer to Figure 5.12. Assume that initially there is free trade. If the United States then imposes a $0.50 tax on imported mangos,

(a) the quantity demanded of mangos will be reduced by 2 thousand mangos.
(b) the quantity of mangos supplied by U.S. firms will decrease by 1 thousand mangos.
(c) the price of mangos in the U.S. will decrease to $1.50 per ton.
(d) U.S. imports of mangos will decrease by 2 thousand mangos.

Answer: (d)

Challenging
Multi
Page: 105

5.71. Refer to Figure 5.12. Assume that initially there is free trade. If the United States then imposes a $0.50 per mango tax on imported mangos, the tax revenue generated will equal

(a) $5500.
(b) $1500.
(c) $50.
(d) $500.

Answer: (d)

Easy
Single
Page: 105

5.72. Refer to Figure 5.13. At the world price of $20 per computer chip, the United States imports _____ million computer chips.

(a) 2
(b) 6
(c) 10
(d) 12

Answer: (b)

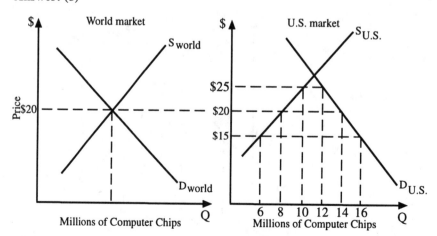

Figure 5.13.

5.73. Refer to Figure 5.13. If a $5.00 each computer chip tax is levied on imported computer chips, the United States will

Moderate
Multi
Page: 105

(a) import 6 million computer chips.
(b) import 10 million computer chips.
(c) import 4 million computer chips.
(d) import 2 million computer chips.

Answer: (d)

5.74. Refer to Figure 5.13. If the United States eliminates all taxes on computer chips, which of the following would occur?

Moderate
Multi
Page: 105

(a) The price of computer chips in the United States would be $15 per computer chip and the United States would import 10 million computer chips.
(b) The price of computer chips in the United States would be $25 per computer chip and the United States would import 2 million computer chips.
(c) The price of computer chips in the United States would be $20 per computer chip and the United States would import 6 million computer chips.
(d) The price of computer chips in the United States after the U.S. government eliminated all taxes on imported computer chips cannot be determined from this information.

Answer: (c)

5.75 Refer to Figure 5.13. Assume that initially there is free trade. If the United States then imposes a $5.00 tax on imported computer chips,

Moderate
Multi
Page: 105 .

(a) the quantity demanded of computer chips will be reduced by 4 million computer chips.
(b) the quantity of computer chips supplied by U.S. firms will increase by 2 millio computer chips.
(c) the price of computer chips in the U.S. will decrease to $15.
(d) U.S. imports of computer chips will increase by 1 millions of computer chips.

Answer: (b)

5.76 Refer to Figure 5.13. Assume that initially there is free trade. If the United States then imposes a $5.00 per computer chip tax on imported computer chips, the tax revenue generated will equal

Challenging
Multi
Page: 105

(a) $50 million.
(b) $10 million.
(c) $60 million.
(d) $75 million.

Answer: (b)

SHORT ANSWER QUESTIONS

SCENARIO 1 One issue in the recent health care reform debate was the attempt to entice new primary care physicians to provide their services in rural areas. Assume that the provision of care in rural areas is relatively less profitable to new physicians than working in urban areas because a greater population generates a greater demand. Answer each of the following:

Easy
Math
Page: 98

5.77: Refer to Scenario 1. Graphically illustrate with supply and demand curves why the physicians would prefer to work in urban areas.

Answer:

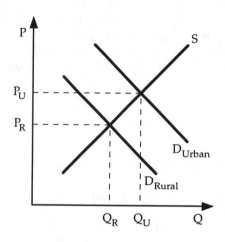

Easy
Math
Page: 98

5.78: Refer to Scenario 1. Graphically illustrate with supply and demand curves and explain how a subsidy would increase the supply in rural areas.

Answer:

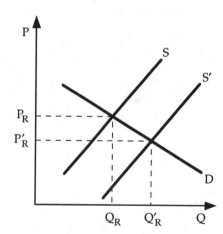

A subsidy would increase the supplyin rural areas, thus decreasing the price.

5.79: Refer to Scenario 1. Graphically illustrate with supply and demand curves how a tax on working in urban areas would increase the supply in rural areas.

Moderate
Math
Page: 98

Answer:

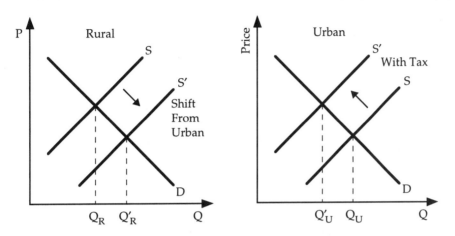

5.80: Refer to Scenario 1. Would an increase in migration out of urban areas into rural areas change the necessity for government involvement?

Moderate
Math
Page: 98

Answer: Migration out of urban areas may reduce the need for government regulation to force physicians into rural areas, because because demand will rise in rural areas, thus increasing prices.

Moderate
Math
Page: 98

5.81: Refer to Scenario 1. Graphically illustrate and explain the effects in both markets, rural and urban, of a set primary care physician salary that falls between the urban and rural salaries.

Answer:

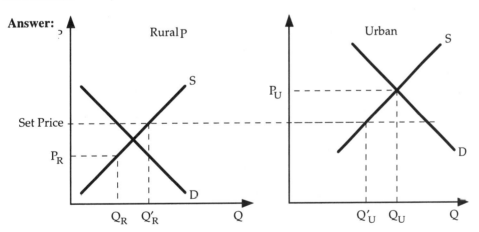

If a salary were to be set in both rural and urban markets, there would be an increase in quantity supplied in the rural areas and a decrease in quantity supplied in the urban areas. A shortage of medical would occur in urban areas, while rural areas will experiance a surplus of medical care.

SCENARIO 2 The following diagram represents the U.S. market for oil. Assume that OPEC can set the world price at any level it chooses to meet any difference between supply by U.S. firms and U.S. demand.

Answer:

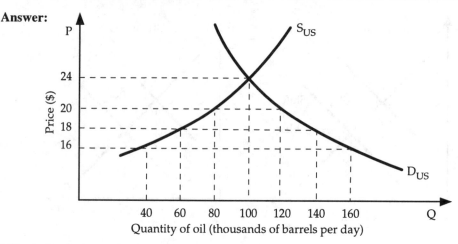

Quantity of oil (thousands of barrels per day)

Moderate
Math
Page: 106

5.82: Refer to Scenario 2. Use the total revenue test (on all oil sold) to determine elasticity of demand with a price drop from $18 to $16.

Answer: Revenue at P = $18, R = 18 * 140 = 2520
          Revenue at P = $16, R = 16 * 160 = 2560

As price falls from $18 to $16, revenue rises, hence demand is elastic.

Moderate
Math
Page: 106

5.83: Refer to Scenario 2. If the price is $18, how much is produced domestically and how much is imported from abroad?

Answer: If the price is $18, 60 units are produced domestically, 60 units are imported from abroad.

Moderate
Math
Page: 106

5.84: Refer to Scenario 2. If OPEC sets a price of $16 and the U.S. government sets an oil import fee of $2, explain what occurs in the market.

Answer: Combining the OPEC price and the oil import fee results in a price of $18. At this price, 40 units are imported.

Moderate
Math
Page: 106

5.85: Refer to Scenario 2. Calculate the tax revenue from the oil import fee proposed in the previous question.

Answer: Tax revenue = $2 * 40 = $80

Moderate
Definition
Page: 102

5.86 Compare and contrast the use of queuing, favored customers, and ration coupons as a way of rationing a good in excess demand.

Answer: In queuing, individuals wait in line; favored customers are those that get special treatment for a product; ration coupons give the right to purchase a good. All have the effect of rationing a limited supply. The difference between the rationing technique is which group of demanders receives the right to purchase the good.

Easy
Fact
Page: 102

5.87: Other than price, discuss two rationing devices that could be used to resolve a situation of excess demand.

Answer: Nonprice rationing techniques include: Favored customers (allowing some people to receive special treatment during shortages) and ration coupons (which entitle a person to purchase a certain amount of the product during a specified time).

5.88: The price that doctors are reimbursed for giving Medicare patients annual physicals is thought to be below the equilibrium price. Illustrate this situation on a graph. What evidence would you look for to determine if Medicare's reimbursement rate is below equilibrium?

Moderate
Fact
Page: 101

Answer: At the reimbursement rate there will be a shortage. Evidence may include such things as doctors' refusing to accept Medicare patients or Medicare patients' having to wait to see a physician.

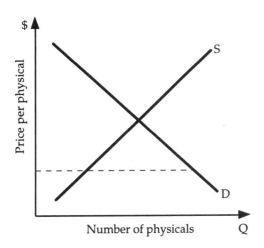

5.89: The price of water has been held below the market equilibrium price for many years. Explain two implications of allowing the price of water to reach the equilibrium price.

Moderate
Single
Page: 101

Answer: If the price reaches equilibrium, quantity demanded will decrease and quantity supplied will increase

6

Introduction to Macroeconomics

(Chapter 21 in Combined Text)

MULTIPLE CHOICE QUESTIONS

6.1: Macroeconomics is the branch of economics that deals with

(a) the economy as a whole.
(b) the functioning of individual industries and the behavior of individual decision-making units - business firms and households.
(c) imperfectly competitive markets.
(d) only the long run adjustments to equilibrium in the economy.

Answer: (a)

Easy
Definition
Page: 113
CT Page: 545

6.2: Prices that do not always adjust rapidly to maintain equality between quantity supplied and quantity demanded are

(a) sticky prices.
(b) fixed prices.
(c) regulatory prices.
(d) market prices.

Answer: (a)

Easy
Definition
Page: 113
CT Page: 546

6.3: The demand for lumber decreased in August. Supply of lumber has remained constant and five months later there still has been no change in lumber prices. This is an example of

(a) a price floor.
(b) a price control.
(c) a sticky price.
(d) a macroeconomic price.

Answer: (c)

Moderate
Single
Page: 113
CT Page: 546

6.4: The demand for nurses declined in the summer of 1993, but the starting wages paid to nurses was still the same at the end of 1993. This is an example of

(a) an equilibrium in the macroeconomy, but a disequilibrium in the microeconomy.
(b) a sticky price.
(c) a highly regulated market.
(d) a price control.

Answer: (b)

Moderate
Single
Page: 113
CT Page: 546

6.5: The key assumption behind the thinking of the Classical economists was that wages were

(a) flexible downward but not upward.
(b) flexible upward but not downward.
(c) flexible both upward and downward.
(d) not flexible either upward or downward.

Answer: (c)

Easy
Fact
Page: 114
CT Page: 547

Easy
Fact
Page: 114
CT Page: 547

6.6: According to the Classical model, unemployment

(a) could not persist because wages would fall to eliminate the excess supply of labor.
(b) could persist for long periods of time because wages are not flexible.
(c) could never exist.
(d) could be eliminated only through government intervention.

Answer: (a)

Moderate
Multi
Page: 114
CT Page: 547

6.7: Classical economists believe that if unemployment in the economy is high then

(a) wages will fall and both the quantity of labor demanded and supplied will decrease.
(b) wages will increase and both the quantity of labor supplied and demanded will increase.
(c) wages will increase and the quantity demanded of labor will fall and the quantity of labor supplied will increase.
(d) wages will fall and the quantity of labor demanded will increase and the quantity of labor supplied will decrease.

Answer: (d)

Easy
Fact
Page: 114
CT Page: 547

6.8: According to the Classical economists, the economy

(a) requires fine tuning to reach full employment.
(b) can never deviate from full employment.
(c) is self correcting.
(d) will never be at full employment.

Answer: (c)

Easy
Fact
Page: 114
CT Page: 547

6.9: Macroeconomic theory which emphasized the theories of Keynes and de-emphasized the Classical theory developed as the result of the failure of

(a) economic theory to explain the simultaneous increases in inflation and unemployment during the 1970s.
(b) fine tuning during the 1960s.
(c) the Classical model to explain the prolonged existence of high unemployment during the Great Depression.
(d) the economy to grow at a rapid rate during the 1950s.

Answer: (c)

Easy
Fact
Page: 115
CT Page: 547

6.10: According to Classical models, the level of employment is determined primarily by

(a) the level of aggregate demand for goods and services.
(b) prices and wages.
(c) government taxation.
(d) government spending.

Answer: (b)

Moderate
Single
Page: 115
CT Page: 547

6.11: According to Keynes, the level of employment is determined by

(a) the level of aggregate income.
(b) interest rates.
(c) price and wages.
(d) the level of aggregate demand for goods and services.

Answer: (d)

6.12: A group of Senators introduce legislation that would subsidize employers' hiring of recent high school graduates. This legislation is designed to stimulate the economy. This legislation is in line with

Easy
Fact
Page: 115
CT Page: 547

(a) Keynesian economics.
(b) Classical economics.
(c) the macrofoundations of microeconomics.
(d) supply-side economics.

Answer: (a)

6.13: The notion that the government can stabilize the macroeconomy is known as

Easy
Definition
Page: 115
CT Page: 547

(a) microeconomic foundations of macroeconomics.
(b) the Classical model.
(c) fine tuning.
(d) aggregate demand.

Answer: (c)

6.14: The government increases government spending to try to reduce unemployment. This is an example of

Moderate
Single
Page: 115
CT Page: 548

(a) the self-correcting nature of the economy.
(b) disequilibrium policies.
(c) laissez-faire.
(d) fine tuning.

Answer: (d)

6.15: Fine tuning refers to

Easy
Definition
Page: 115
CT Page: 548

(a) the government's role in regulating inflation and unemployment.
(b) the cyclical nature of aggregate output in the United States.
(c) price and wage adjustments that restore the economy to full employment.
(d) the process of aggregating individual decisions into macroeconomic variables.

Answer: (a)

6.16: Which of the following would be an example of fine tuning?

Moderate
Single
Page: 115
CT Page: 548

(a) There is an excess supply of labor, so firms reduce the starting salaries that they offer to workers.
(b) Firms' inventories are increasing, so firms reduce the prices of their products.
(c) The federal government enacts legislation to increase spending to try to stimulate the economy.
(d) The federal government passes legislation that would require that the government's budget always be balanced.

Answer: (c)

6.17: Rapid increases in the price level during periods of recession or high unemployment are known as

Easy
Definition
Page: 115
CT Page: 550

(a) stagnation.
(b) stagflation.
(c) fine tuning.
(d) inflation.

Answer: (b)

Easy
Definition
Page: 115
CT Page: 550

6.18: Stagflation occurs when

(a) the overall price level increases during an expansion in economic activity.
(b) the overall price level falls rapidly during periods of recession.
(c) the overall price level increases rapidly during periods of recession.
(d) both the overall price level and employment are stable.

Answer: (c)

Easy
Definition
Page: 117
CT Page: 551

6.19: The increase in the overall price level is known as

(a) stagnation.
(b) recession.
(c) inflation.
(d) stagflation.

Answer: (c)

Easy
Definition
Page: 117
CT Page: 551

6.20: Inflation is

(a) a decrease in the overall price level.
(b) a decrease in the overall level of economic activity.
(c) an increase in the overall price level.
(d) an increase in the overall level of economic activity.

Answer: (c)

Easy
Definition
Page: 117
CT Page: 551

6.21: A period of very rapid increases in the price level is

(a) recession.
(b) depression.
(c) inflation.
(d) hyperinflation.

Answer: (d)

Easy
Definition
Page: 117
CT Page: 551

6.22: Hyperinflation is

(a) a sustained increase in the overall price level.
(b) a period of rapid increases in the overall price level.
(c) a period of high prices and high unemployment.
(d) a period of declining aggregate output.

Answer: (b)

Easy
Definition
Page: 118
CT Page: 551

6.23: The term business cycle refers to the

(a) short-term ups and downs in the price level.
(b) long term trends in the price level.
(c) short-term ups and down in the economy.
(d) long-term trends in the level of economic activity.

Answer: (c)

6.24: A period during which aggregate output declines is known as

(a) a recession.
(b) an inflation.
(c) a hyperinflation.
(d) a boom.

Answer: (a)

Easy
Definition
Page: 118
CT Page: 552

6.25: A recession is

(a) a period of declining prices.
(b) a period during which aggregate output declines.
(c) a period of declining unemployment.
(d) a period of very rapidly declining prices.

Answer: (b)

Easy
Definition
Page: 118
CT Page: 552

6.26: It has become conventional to classify an economic downturn as a recession when aggregate output declines for

(a) two consecutive quarters.
(b) three consecutive quarters.
(c) a year.
(d) two years.

Answer: (a)

Easy
Definition
Page: 118
CT Page: 552

6.27: A prolonged and deep recession is called

(a) a business cycle.
(b) stagflation.
(c) a depression.
(d) hyperinflation.

Answer: (c)

Easy
Definition
Page: 118
CT Page: 552

6.28: A depression is

(a) a period of very rapid price declines.
(b) a prolonged and deep recession.
(c) a prolonged period of very rapidly falling unemployment.
(d) a period of rapidly increasing prices and unemployment.

Answer: (b)

Easy
Definition
Page: 118
CT Page: 552

6.29: Unemployment means that

(a) at the going wage rate, there are people who want to work but cannot find work.
(b) people are not willing to work at the going wage rate.
(c) there are some people who will not work at the going wage rate.
(d) there is excess demand in the labor market.

Answer: (a)

Moderate
Single
Page: 119
CT Page: 552

Moderate
Single
Page: 119
CT Page: 552

6.30: Unemployment implies that in the aggregate labor market

(a) there is an excess demand for labor.
(b) there is an excess supply of labor.
(c) there are too few workers for the jobs available.
(d) quantity demanded of labor exceeds quantity supplied.

Answer: (b)

Easy
Definition
Page: 119
CT Page: 552

6.31: The percentage of the labor force that is unemployed is the

(a) unemployment rate.
(b) labor force rate.
(c) unemployment population ratio.
(d) employment rate.

Answer: (a)

Easy
Definition
Page: 119
CT Page: 553

6.32: Government policies regarding taxes and expenditures are called

(a) monetary policy.
(b) income policies.
(c) supply-side policy.
(d) fiscal policy.

Answer: (d)

Moderate
Single
Page: 119
CT Page: 553

6.33: The government increases the amount of money budgeted for investment in social capital such as roads and bridges. This is an example of

(a) a monetary policy.
(b) an incomes policy.
(c) an inflationary policy.
(d) a fiscal policy.

Answer: (d)

Moderate
Single
Page: 119
CT Page: 553

6.34: The government reduces the personal income tax rates to encourage increased consumption spending. This is an example of

(a) an incomes policy.
(b) a monetary policy.
(c) a fiscal policy.
(d) a supply-side policy.

Answer: (c)

Moderate
Fact
Page: 119
CT Page: 553

6.35: To get the economy out of a slump, Keynes believed that the government should

(a) cut both taxes and government spending.
(b) increase both taxes and government spending.
(c) increase taxes and/or decrease government spending.
(d) decrease taxes and/or increase government spending.

Answer: (d)

6.36: To bring the economy out of an inflation, Keynes argued that the government should

(a) cut both taxes and government spending.
(b) increase both taxes and government spending.
(c) increase taxes and/or decrease government spending.
(d) decrease taxes and/or increase government spending.

Answer: (c)

Moderate
Fact
Page: 119
CT Page: 553

6.37: The government can affect the quantity of money in the economy through the

(a) Treasury Department.
(b) Congress.
(c) Federal Reserve.
(d) Banking Commission.

Answer: (c)

Easy
Fact
Page: 120
CT Page: 553

6.38: Direct attempts by the government to control prices and wages are known as

(a) fiscal policies.
(b) incomes policies.
(c) monetary policies.
(d) supply-side policies.

Answer: (b)

Easy
Definition
Page: 120
CT Page: 554

6.39: During World War II, the government imposed limits on the maximum amount by which prices and wages could increase. This is an example of

(a) an incomes policy.
(b) a fiscal policy.
(c) a monetary policy.
(d) a supply-side policy.

Answer: (a)

Moderate
Single
Page: 120
CT Page: 554

6.40: The Commission on Health Care Reform that was chaired by Hillary Clinton considered controlling the prices charged by pharmaceutical companies for drugs. If this policy were enacted, it would be an example of

(a) a fiscal policy.
(b) a monetary policy.
(c) a demand management policy.
(d) an incomes policy.

Answer: (d)

Moderate
Single
Page: 120
CT Page: 554

6.41: Incomes policies are government policies

(a) used to control the money supply.
(b) that directly attempt to control prices and wages.
(c) that focus on aggregate supply and increasing production.
(d) regarding taxes and expenditures.

Answer: (b)

Easy
Definition
Page: 120
CT Page: 554

Easy
Definition
Page: 120
CT Page: 554

6.42: Government policies that focus on increasing production rather than stimulating aggregate demand are known as

(a) incomes policies.
(b) fiscal policies.
(c) monetary policies.
(d) supply-side policies.

Answer: (d)

Easy
Definition
Page: 120
CT Page: 554

6.43: Supply-side policies are government policies

(a) regarding taxes and expenditures.
(b) that directly attempt to control prices and wages.
(c) that focus on aggregate supply and increasing production.
(d) used to control the money supply.

Answer: (c)

Moderate
Fact
Page: 120
CT Page: 554

6.44: The main instrument of supply-side policy has been the

(a) level of government expenditures.
(b) tax system.
(c) imposition of wage and price controls.
(d) monetary system.

Answer: (b)

Moderate
Single
Page: 120
CT Page: 554

6.45: A cut in the tax rate designed to encourage investment is an example of

(a) an inflation policy.
(b) a supply-side policy.
(c) a monetary policy.
(d) an incomes policy.

Answer: (b)

Moderate
Single
Page: 120
CT Page: 554

6.46: Some government regulations imposed on businesses have the impact of reducing productivity. The elimination of these regulations would be an example of

(a) a monetary policy.
(b) a fiscal policy.
(c) a supply-side policy.
(d) an incomes policy.

Answer: (c)

Easy
Definition
Page: 120
CT Page: 554

6.47: The federal budget deficit is

(a) the total amount of money owed by the federal government.
(b) the difference between the level of federal tax revenues and federal expenditures in a year.
(c) the ratio of federal tax revenues to federal expenditures in a year.
(d) the total amount of money owed by all levels of government.

Answer: (b)

6.48: After the tax cuts of 1981 and 1986,

(a) incentives to save and invest were increased, causing tax revenues
to increase by more than the increase in government spending and the federal deficit to
shrink.
(b) the economy expanded at a very fast rate.
(c) the federal deficit rose substantially.
(d) both tax revenues and government expenditures decreased.

Answer: (c)

Moderate
Fact
Page: 120
CT Page: 554

6.49: Proponents of supply-side policies argue that the best way to
increase the supply of goods and services is

(a) for the government to directly control prices and wages.
(b) to increase the supply of money in the economy.
(c) to increase government production so that public-sector
employment increases.
(d) to stimulate the supply of labor and capital and increase
investment.

Answer: (d)

Easy
Fact
Page: 120
CT Page: 554

6.50: The diagram that shows the income received and payments made by each sector of
the economy is the

(a) aggregate demand-aggregate supply diagram.
(b) income-price diagram.
(c) circular flow diagram.
(d) income-expenditures diagram.

Answer: (c)

Easy
Definition
Page: 120
CT Page: 554

6.51: Cash payments made by the government to people who do not supply goods,
services, or labor in exchange for these payments are
known as

(a) transfer payments.
(b) subsidy payments.
(c) relief payments.
(d) in-kind payments.

Answer: (a)

Easy
Definition
Page: 121
CT Page: 554

6.52: An example of a transfer payment is

(a) an interest payment on a government bond.
(b) the added value of stock from the time it was bought to the time
it was sold.
(c) a social security retirement benefit.
(d) the salary paid to a member of the armed forces.

Answer: (c)

Moderate
Single
Page: 121
CT Page: 554

Easy
Fact
Page: 121
CT Page: 555

6.53: A household that spends more than it receives in income during a given period is

(a) investing.
(b) dissaving.
(c) running a surplus.
(d) receiving transfer payments.

Answer: (b)

Easy
Fact
Page: 122
CT Page: 556

6.54: The major lesson of the circular flow diagram is that

(a) saving must always equal investment.
(b) taxes must equal government expenditures.
(c) one peron's expenditure is someone else's receipt.
(d) all of the above

Answer: (c)

Easy
Fact
Page: 123
CT Page: 556

6.55: The broadly defined market arenas in which households, firms, the government, and the rest of the world interact are

(a) the goods-and-services market and the money market.
(b) the goods-and-services market and the labor market.
(c) the goods-and-services market, the labor market, and the financial market.
(d) the goods-and-services market, the capital market, and the money market.

Answer: (c)

Easy
Fact
Page: 123
CT Page: 556

6.56: Consider the goods-and-services market. Firms

(a) only supply to this market.
(b) only demand from this market.
(c) both supply to and demand from this market.
(d) neither supply to nor demand from this market.

Answer: (c)

Easy
Fact
Page: 123
CT Page: 556

6.57: The demanders in the goods-and-services market are:

(a) households and business firms.
(b) households, the government, and the rest of the world.
(c) the government and business firms.
(d) households, the government, business firms, and the rest of the world.

Answer: (d)

Easy
Fact
Page: 123
CT Page: 557

6.58: In the labor market,

(a) households supply labor and only business firms demand labor.
(b) household supply labor and the government and business firms demand labor.
(c) the government and business firms supply labor and households demand labor.
(d) households supply labor and households demand labor.

Answer: (b)

6.59: Consider the labor market. The rest of the world can

(a) demand labor from this market and supply labor to this market.
(b) demand labor from this market but not supply labor to this market. (c) not demand labor from this market but can supply labor to this market.
(d) neither demand labor from this market nor supply labor to this market.

Easy
Fact
Page: 123
CT Page: 557

Answer: (a)

6.60: Promissory notes issued by the federal government when it borrows money are known as

(a) Treasury bonds.
(b) Treasury shares.
(c) Treasury stocks.
(d) all of the above.

Easy
Fact
Page: 124
CT Page: 557

Answer: (a)

6.61: A promissory note issued by a corporation when it borrows money is a

(a) share of stock.
(b) corporate bond.
(c) corporate dividend.
(d) capital gain.

Easy
Definition
Page: 124
CT Page: 557

Answer: (b)

6.62: The interest rate paid on a corporate bond

(a) is fixed.
(b) varies with the federal funds rate.
(c) depends on the profitability of the corporation.
(d) must equal the interest rate paid on Treasury notes.

Easy
Fact
Page: 124
CT Page: 557

Answer: (a)

6.63: A financial instrument that gives the holder a share in the ownership of a firm and, therefore, the right to share in the profits of the firm is a

(a) capital gain.
(b) dividend.
(c) corporate bond.
(d) share of stock.

Easy
Definition
Page: 124
CT Page: 557

Answer: (d)

6.64: A share of stock is

(a) a promissory note issued by a corporation when it borrows money.
(b) a promissory note issued by the federal government when it borrows money.
(c) a financial instrument that gives the holder a share in the ownership of a firm and therefore the right to share in the profits of the firm.
(d) a financial instrument given to the Federal Reserve from a commercial bank when the commercial bank borrows from the Federal Reserve.

Easy
Definition
Page: 124
CT Page: 557

Answer: (c)

Easy
Definition
Page: 124
CT Page: 557

6.65: A capital gain is

(a) a financial instrument that gives the holder a share in the ownership of a firm and therefore the right to share in the profits of the firm.
(b) the portion of a corporation's profits that the firm pays out each period to its shareholders.
(c) an increase in the value of an asset over the price initially paid for it.
(d) the difference between an individual's economic income and money income.

Answer: (c)

Easy
Definition
Page: 124
CT Page: 557

6.66: An increase in the value of an asset over the price initially paid for it is a

(a) dividend.
(b) share of stock.
(c) promissory note.
(d) capital gain.

Answer: (d)

Moderate
Multi
Page: 124
CT Page: 557

6.67. If Aaron purchases a share of stock for $50 and two years later sell it for $100, he will realize a

(a) dividend of $100.
(b) capital gain of $75.
(c) dividend of $25.
(d) capital gain of $50.

Answer: (d)

Moderate
Multi
Page: 124
CT Page: 557

6.68. If Aaron purchases a share of stock for $50 and two years later sell it for $100, he will realize a

(a) dividend of $100.
(b) capital gain of $75.
(c) dividend of $25.
(d) capital gain of $50.

Answer: (d)

Moderate
Multi
Page: 124
CT Page: 557

6.69: Bill purchased 100 autographed Jerry Rice football cards when he was 15 years old for a total cost of $100 and then sold those football cards ten years later for $1000.

(a) He earned a capital gain of $900.
(b) He earned a capital gain of $1000.
(c) He earned a dividend of $900.
(d) He earned a dividend of $1000.

Answer: (a)

Moderate
Multi
Page: 124
CT Page: 557

6.70. Bill purchased 100 autographed Jerry Rice football cards when he was 15 years old for a total cost of $100 and then sold those football cards ten years later for $1000.

(a) He earned a capital gain of $900.
(b) He earned a capital gain of $1000.
(c) He earned a dividend of $900.
(d) He earned a dividend of $1000.

Answer: (a)

6.71 You purchase 100 shares of stock for $25,000. A year later the stock is valued at $30,000. Instead of selling the stock you hold onto it for another year. Which of the following is TRUE?

(a) The $5000 increase in the value of the stock represents a capital gain.
(b) The $5000 increase in the value of the stock represents a dividend.
(c) To determine the capital gain it is first necessary to know the normal rate of return on capital.
(d) Because the stock has not been sold there can be no capital gain.

Moderate
Single
Page: 124
CT Page: 557

Answer: (a)

6.72. You purchase 100 shares of stock for $30,000. A year later the stock is valued at $35,000. Instead of selling the stock you hold onto it for another year. Which of the following is TRUE?

(a) The $5000 increase in the value of the stock represents a capital gain.
(b) The $5000 increase in the value of the stock represents a dividend.
(c) To determine the capital gain it is first necessary to know the normal rate of   return on capital.
(d) Because the stock has not been sold there can be no capital gain.

Moderate
Single
Page: 124
CT Page: 557

Answer: (a)

6.73: A dividend is

(a) a promissory note issued by corporations when they borrow money.
(b) an increase in the value of an asset over the purchase price initially paid for it.
(c) the difference between the interest rate a bank pays on deposits and the interest rate it charges for loans.
(d) the portion of a corporation's profits that the firm pays out each period to its shareholders.

Easy
Definition
Page: 124
CT Page: 557

Answer: (d)

6.74: The portion of a corporation's profits that a firm pays out each period to its shareholders is a

(a) capital gain.
(b) promissory note.
(c) dividend.
(d) corporate bond.

Moderate
Fact
Page: 124
CT Page: 559

Answer: (c)

6.75: The total demand for goods and services in an economy is known as

(a) gross national product.
(b) aggregate demand.
(c) economy-wide demand.
(d) national demand.

Moderate
Fact
Page: 125
CT Page: 559

Answer: (b)

Easy
Fact
Page: 125
CT Page: 559

6.76: Refer to Figure 6.1. The vertical axis should be labeled

(a) aggregate output.
(b) overall price level.
(c) percentage increase in the price level.
(d) average price index.

Answer: (b)

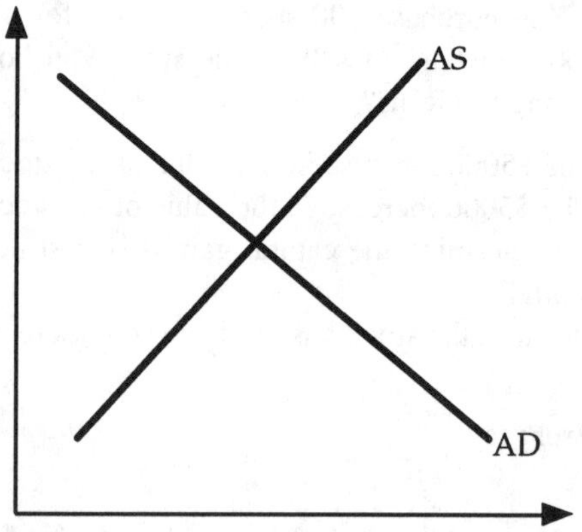

Figure 6.1

Moderate
Fact
Page: 125
CT Page: 559

6.77: Refer to Figure 6.1. The horizontal axis should be labeled

(a) overall price level.
(b) total industrial output.
(c) percentage change in output.
(d) aggregate output.

Answer: (d)

Moderate
Fact
Page: 125
CT Page: 559

6.78: Aggregate demand is the total demand for all goods and services in an economy from

(a) all sectors including the rest of the world.
(b) the household sector.
(c) the household and government sectors.
(d) all sectors except the rest of the world.

Answer: (a)

Easy
Fact
Page: 125
CT Page: 559

6.79: Aggregate supply is the total amount

(a) of labor supplied by all households.
(b) of products produced by a given industry.
(c) of goods and services produced in an economy.
(d) produced by the government.

Answer: (c)

Moderate
Fact
Page: 126
CT Page: 559

6.80: The downward slope of the aggregate demand curve is related to what goes on n the

(a) money market.
(b) labor market.
(c) goods market.
(d) capital market.

Answer: (a)

Easy
Fact
Page: 126
CT Page: 560

6.81: The aggregate demand curve

(a) is vertical.
(b) is horizontal.
(c) slopes downward to the right.
(d) slopes upward the right.

Answer: (c)

6.82: Which of the following statements is FALSE?

(a) The aggregate supply curve is based on the assumption of fixed prices.
(b) When analyzing the behavior of aggregate demand, the availability of substitutes is irrelevant.
(c) The downward slope of the aggregate demand curve is related to what goes on in the money (financial) market.
(d) The aggregate demand curve slopes downward and to the right.

Moderate
Fact
Page: 126
CT Page: 559

Answer: (a)

6.83: Macroeconomics is concerned with

(a) only long-run trends in economic activity.
(b) only short-run fluctuations in the business cycle.
(c) both long-run trends and short-term fluctuations in economic activity.
(d) only with changes in the overall price level.

Easy
Fact
Page: 127
CT Page: 560

Answer: (c)

6.84: Real output increased during the first four quarters of 1983. This is an example of

(a) an inflation.
(b) a slump.
(c) a peak.
(d) an expansion.

Easy
Single
Page: 127
CT Page: 561

Answer: (d)

6.85: The period in the business cycle from a peak to a trough is called

(a) a contraction, recession, or slump.
(b) an expansion or boom.
(c) a growth period.
(d) a depression.

Easy
Definition
Page: 127
CT Page: 561

Answer: (a)

6.86: If both output and employment are falling, the economy MUST be in

(a) a contraction.
(b) a boom.
(c) a depression.
(d) a hyperinflationary period.

Easy
Definition
Page: 127
CT Page: 561

Answer: (a)

6.87: The period in the business cycle from a trough up to a peak is

(a) a contraction or recession.
(b) a slowdown.
(c) an expansion or boom.
(d) a depression.

Easy
Fact
Page: 127
CT Page: 561

Answer: (c)

6.88: If both output and employment are rising, the economy must be in

(a) a hyperinflationary period.
(b) an expansion.
(c) a recession.
(d) a depression.

Easy
Fact
Page: 127
CT Page: 561

Answer: (b)

Easy
Fact
Page: 127
CT Page: 561

6.89: An expansion or boom is the period in the business cycle from a

(a) peak to a peak.
(b) trough to a trough.
(c) peak down to a trough.
(d) trough up to a peak.

Answer: (d)

Easy
Definition
Page: 127
CT Page: 561

6.90: A contraction or recession is the period in the business cycle from a

(a) peak to a peak.
(b) trough to a trough.
(c) peak down to a trough.
(d) trough up to a peak.

Answer: (c)

Easy
Fact
Page: 127
CT Page: 561

6.91: Whether an economy is expanding or contracting is judged by measuring

(a) the total level of economic activity.
(b) the rate of change in economic activity.
(c) the rate of change in the overall price level.
(d) the rate of change in economic activity relative to the overall price level.

Answer: (b)

Moderate
Single
Page: 127
CT Page: 561

6.92: If the rate of change in economic activity is negative

(a) then the economy is in the contractionary phase of the business cycle regardless of the overall level of economic activity.
(b) but the level of economic activity is high, then the economy is still in the expansionary phase of the business cycle.
(c) then the economy is in the expansionary phase of the business cycle regardless of the overall level of economic activity.
(d) but the level of economic activity is low, then the economy is entering the expansionary phase of the business cycle.

Answer: (a)

Moderate
Single
Page: 127
CT Page: 561

6.93: To measure where the economy is in the business cycle, it is necessary to know

(a) the level of economic activity.
(b) the rate of change in economic activity.
(c) both the level of economic activity and the rate of change in economic activity.
(d) the rate of change in the price level.

Answer: (b)

Easy
Fact
Page: 127
CT Page: 561

6.94: Which of the following statements is FALSE?

(a) The rate of change in economic activity is used to assess whether an economy is expanding or contracting.
(b) Short-term ups and downs in the economy are known as business cycles.
(c) During a recession, output and employment are falling.
(d) Business cycles are always symmetric - the length of an expansion is the same as the length of a contraction.

Answer: (d)

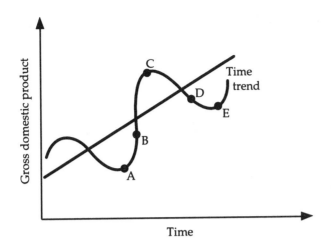

Figure 6.2

6.95: The length of a business cycle would be measured from

(a) peak to trough.
(b) trough to peak.
(c) peak to peak.
(d) the slump to the expansion.

Answer: (c)

Easy
Fact
Page: 127
CT Page: 561

6.96: Refer to Figure 6.2. The trough of the business cycle corresponds to point such as

(a) A.
(b) B.
(c) C.
(d) D.

Answer: (a)

Easy
Single
Page: 127
CT Page: 561

6.97: Refer to Figure 6.2. The expansionary phase of the business cycle corresponds to the region

(a) A - B.
(b) B - C.
(c) A - C.
(d) C -D.

Answer: (c)

Easy
Single
Page: 127
CT Page: 561

6.98: Refer to Figure 6.2. The peak of the business cycle is represented by a point such as

(a) A.
(b) B.
(c) C.
(d) D.

Answer: (c)

Easy
Single
Page: 127
CT Page: 561

Easy
Single
Page: 127
CT Page: 561

6.99: Refer to Figure 6.2. The recessionary phase of the business cycle corresponds to the region

(a) A - C.
(b) B - D.
(c) C - D.
(d) C - E.

Answer: (d)

Easy
Fact
Page: 127
CT Page: 561

6.100: Employment generally _____ during recessions and _____ during expansions.

(a) falls; rises
(b) falls; falls
(c) rises; falls
(d) rises; rises

Answer: (a)

Easy
Definition
Page: 130
CT Page: 564

6.101: One measure of the overall rate of inflation is

(a) the percentage change in the GDP deflator.
(b) the difference in the GDP deflator from year to year.
(c) the level of the GDP deflator.
(d) the GDP deflator minus 100.

Answer: (a)

Easy
Definition
Page: 130
CT Page: 564

6.102: An index of prices of all domestically produced goods in the economy is the

(a) Consumer Price Index.
(b) GDP deflator.
(c) Producer Price Index.
(d) Wholesale Price Index.

Answer: (b)

Easy
Definition
Page: 130
CT Page: 564

6.103: The GDP deflator is

(a) a measurement of the rate of change in an economy's output.
(b) an economy-wide output index.
(c) a measurement of the total amount of output produced in an economy in a year.
(d) an economy-wide price index.

Answer: (d)

Moderate
Application
Page: 120
CT Page: 553

6.104: The President bans wage and price increases. This is an example of a(n)

(a) Fiscal policy
(b) Supply-side policy
(c) Monetary policy
(d) Incomes policy

Answer: (d)

6.105: The central bank increases the money supply. This is an example of a(n)

(a) Fiscal policy
(b) Supply-side policy
(c) Monetary policy
(d) Incomes policy

Answer: (c)

Moderate
Application
Page: 120
CT Page: 553

6.106: Congress decreases government spending. This is an example of a(n)

(a) Fiscal policy
(b) Supply-side policy
(c) Monetary policy
(d) Incomes policy

Answer: (a)

Moderate
Application
Page: 119
CT Page: 553

6.107: Congress decreases taxes on business. This is an example of a(n)

(a) Fiscal policy
(b) Supply-side policy
(c) Monetary policy
(d) Incomes policy

Answer: (b)

Moderate
Application
Page: 119
CT Page: 553

TRUE/FALSE QUESTIONS

6.108: According to the Classical model, an excess supply of labor would drive down wages to a new equilibrium level and therefore unemployment would not persist.

Answer: True

Easy
Fact
Page: 114
CT Page: 547

6.109: According to Keynes, the level of employment is determined by wages and prices.

Answer: False

Easy
Fact
Page: 115
CT Page: 547

6.110: According to Keynes, the government's role during periods when private demand is low is to stimulate aggregate demand and, by so doing, lift the economy out of recession.

Answer: True

Easy
Fact
Page: 119
CT Page: 547

6.104: In the Classical model, the level of employment is determined by the level of aggregate demand.

Answer: False

Easy
Fact
Page: 115
CT Page: 547

6.111: Incomes policies generally take the form of regulations specifying the maximum amount by which the money supply can be changed.

Answer: False

Easy
Fact
Page: 120
CT Page: 554

Easy
Fact
Page: 120
CT Page: 554

6.112: Income policies are generally viewed with disfavor in the United States because they are believed to prevent the price system from generating as an efficient allocation of resources.

Answer: True

Easy
Fact
Page: 124
CT Page: 558

6.113 Macroeconomic behavior is the sum of all the microeconomic decisions made by individual households and firms.

Answer: True

Easy
Fact
Page: 126
CT Page: 559

6.114: The aggregate supply curve is the summation of all the individual firms' supply curves.

Answer: False

Easy
Fact
Page: 127
CT Page: 561

6.115: All business cycles are symmetric - the length of an expansion is the same as the length of a recession.

Answer: False

Easy
Fact
Page: 127
CT Page: 561

6.-116: If the economy is in an expansion, the level of economic activity must be high and the rate of change in economic activity must be positive.

Answer: False

SHORT ANSWER QUESTIONS

Easy
Definition
Page: 113
CT Page: 545

6.117: Identify the following topics as either predominantly macroeconomic or microeconomic.

    a.   Provision by firms of medical benefits for employees
    b.   The demand for coffee
    c.   Unemployment
    d.   The price of a government bond relative to the price of IBM stock
    e.   Unemployment among economics professors
    f.   The business cycle
    g.   Consumption spending by the household sector
    h.   Rent controls in New York
    i.   Inflation
    j.   The money supply

Answer: MIC: a, b, d, e, h.
            MAC: c, f, g, i, j.

Difficult
Application
Page: 113
CT Page: 547

6.118: How do microeconomists and macroeconomists differ in their perceptions of how well markets and prices function?

Answer: In general, microeconomists conclude that markets work well and that prices are flexible. Excess demand or supply is competed away. In contrast, macroeconomists observe that prices do not always adjust rapidly to maintain equality between quantity supplied and quantity demanded. Examining the labor market, for example, macroeconomists find sticky prices and persistent mismatches between the quantity of labor demanded and supplied.

Quarter	1996				1997				1998	
	I	II	III	IV	I	II	III	IV	I	II
Output	100	98	96	93	90	88	87	86	90	95

Table 6.1

6.119: Refer to Table 6.1 In terms of the business cycle, describe what is happening to this economy from 1996 to 1997. Using the table above, predict what is likely to be happening to the unemployment rate and the inflation rate during 1996 and 1997. If the government wished to restore the economy's production level to 100 using fiscal policy, should it use an expansionary fiscal policy or a contractionary fiscal policy? Explain.

Moderate
Application
Page: 127
CT Page: 552

Answer: There is a recession. In fact, since output has declined for at least two years, this may be classified as a depression. The unemployment rate will be increasing while the inflation rate will be decreasing. An expansionary policy would be called for. The government would wish aggregate output to expand.

6.120: In 1981, President Reagan cut tax rates for individuals and for businesses. Explain why this was an example of a supply-side policy.

Moderate
Application
Page: 120
CT Page: 554

Answer: This could have been classified as a fiscal policy, but fiscal policies, in fact, focus on adjusting aggregate demand. The tax rate changes, as noted in the text, were designed to stimulate aggregate supply by increasing worker and business effort.

6.121: Incomes policies control increases in wages and prices. Can you see any problems with the implementation of such a policy? What do you think might happen when the policy is terminated?

Moderate
Application
Page: 120
CT Page: 554

Answer: An incomes policy is unlikely to be enforced evenly throughout the economy. Government employees would be subject to control, but the private sector might find ways to increase wage incentives and/or increase prices. When the policy is terminated, all the workers and businesses who believe that they have fallen behind will immediately try to catch up-possibly triggering another round of wage and price increases.

6.122: In which of the three basic markets (goods-and-services, labor, financial) is each of the following items traded?

Easy
Definition
Page: 121
CT Page: 556

a. Pete Sampras' tennis skills
b. A pack of cigarettes
c. A government bond
d. A share of IBM stock
e. An IBM computer
f. The abilities of IBM's CEO

Answer: The items would be classified as follows:
   a. Labor market
   b. Goods-and-services market
   c. Financial market
   d. Financial market
   e. Goods-and-services market
   f. Labor market.

6.123: The circular flow diagram shows that a dollar spent is a dollar earned, i.e., everyone's expenditures go somewhere. If so, how can aggregate demand and aggregate supply differ?

Answer: The apparent paradox is caused by the circular flow diagram being a description of equilibrium. Aggregate demand and supply are derived independently and, there-fore, need not be in equilibrium.

6.124: Do you think that the entire economy ebbs and flows with equal intensity, as the business cycle seems to suggest? If not, which types of activity might be affected most vigorously by changing economic fortunes?

Answer: Components of the economy do not fluctuate in unison-luxuries, durable goods, and services tend to fluctuate more than, for example, consumption and production of basic foods.

6.125: What event provided the impetus for the development of modern macro-economics? Why did this event require a fundamental rethinking of how the macroeconomy operated?

Answer: The impetus for the development of macroeconomics was the Great Depression. The Classical model could not explain the Great Depression. According to the Classical model, the economy is self correcting and unemployment should not persist. During the Great Depression, very high levels of unemployment persisted for about 10 years. Because the classical model could not explain the Great Depression, the approach to macroeconomics had to be rethought.

6.126: Classical economists believed that recessions were self correcting. In their view, how did the economy self correct? Use a graph to illustrate your answer.

Answer: According to Classical economists, the economy adjusts because wages and prices are flexible. If there is unemployment, wages would fall and unemploy-ment would be reduced.

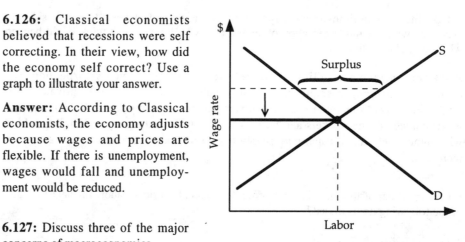

6.127: Discuss three of the major concerns of macroeconomics.

Answer: Four major concerns of macroeconomics are: the aggregate price level, aggregate output, and total employment

6.128: Explain the following statement: Almost all macroeconomic events are interrelated, and making progress on one front often means making conditions worse on another front.

Answer: There are trade-offs in attempting to manage the macroeconomy. For example, it may be possible to reduce inflation, but only at the cost of increasing unemployment.

6.129: If the inflation rate in the economy jumps from 3% in 1993 to 6% in 1994, does that mean that everyone is worse off in 1994 than they were in 1993? Explain.

Challenging
Multi
Page: 117
CT Page: 551

Answer: No, it does not necessarily imply that everyone is worse off. It will depend on how an individual's income is changing and also the composition of goods he or she buys and the price increases for those goods.

6.130: Explain the three different types of government policies that can be used to influence the macroeconomy.

Easy
Fact
Page: 119
CT Page: 551

Answer: The three different government policies are: fiscal policy, monetary policy, and growth or supply-side policies. Fiscal policy involves changing the level of government spending and taxes to either stimulate or contract the economy. Monetary policy involves changing the money supply. Growth or supply-side policies are policies that focus on the aggregate supply and increasing production.

6.131: Explain the three market arenas in which households, firms, the government, and the rest of the world interact.

Easy
Fact
Page: 121
CT Page: 556

Answer: The three market arenas are: the goods-and-services market, the labor market, and the money market.

6.132: Why do economists look to microeconomics to explain macroeconomic events.

Easy
Fact
Page: 124
CT Page: 558

Answer: Macroeconomic behavior is the sum of all the microeconomic decisions made by households and firms. The movement of macroeconomic aggregates reflect decisions being made by individual firms and households. To understand the aggregate measures it is necessary to understand the underlying individual decisions.

6.133: Draw a graph of a business cycle. Label and explain the phases of a business cycle.

Easy
Fact
Page: 127
CT Page: 561

Answer: During an expansion the level of economic activity is increasing. The peak is the highest level of economic activity. A contraction means that the level of economic activity is falling. A trough is the lowest level of economic activity.

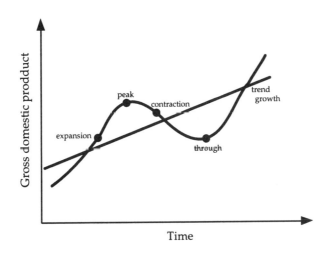

Moderate
Fact
Page: 127
CT Page: 558

6.134: The government releases GDP data on a quarterly basis. Explain why this would make it difficult for policy makers to determine at what point in the business cycle the economy is at currently.

Answer: You can not tell where we are in the business cycle until after the fact. You cannot tell if the economy has moved out of a recession until the data indicates that the level of economic activity has increased.

7 Measuring National Output and National Income

(Chapter 22 in Combined Text)

MULTIPLE CHOICE QUESTIONS

7.1: The total market value of all final goods and services produced within a given period by factors of production located within a country is

(a) gross national product.
(b) gross domestic product.
(c) net national product.
(d) net national income.

Answer: (b)

Easy
Definition
Page: 133
CT Page: 569

7.2: Gross domestic product is

(a) the total market value of all final goods and services produced within a given period by factors of production located within a country.
(b) the total market value of all final goods and services produced within a given period by factors of production owned by a country's citizens, regardless of where output is produced.
(c) a nation's total product minus what is required to maintain the value of its capital stock.
d) the total amount of income earned by the factors of production in the economy.

Answer: (a)

Easy
Definition
Page: 133
CT Page: 569

7.3: Which of the following is an example of a final good or service?

(a) Chocolate a bakery purchases to make cakes.
(b) Coffee beans that are purchased by a restaurant owner from a wholesale food distributor.
(c) An economics textbook you purchase with the intent of selling after your course is over.
(d) The lumber purchased by a construction company that will be used by the company to build a model house to show to its clients.

Answer: (c)

Moderate
Single
Page: 134
CT Page: 569

7.4: Which of the following is an example of an intermediate good?

(a) The wood you purchase to build yourself bookshelves in your room.
(b) The chocolate you buy to make yourself some cookies.
(c) The pizza sauce you purchase to make pizzas to sell for a fund-raiser for an organization you belong to.
(d) all of the above.

Answer: (c)

Moderate
Single
Page: 134
CT Page: 569

Easy
Fact
Page: 134
CT Page: 569

7.5: Double counting can be avoided by counting only

(a) the value of intermediate goods in production.
(b) the value of goods that a firm has in its inventory.
(c) the value added to a product by each firm in the production process
(d) the value of goods and services firms sell.

Answer: (c)

Easy
Fact
Page: 134
CT Page: 569

7.6: Which of the following would NOT be counted in 1997's GDP?

(a) The dividend check you receive in 1997 on stock you bought in 1997.
(b) The 1997 salary of a used car salesperson.
(c) The commissions earned by a real estate agent in selling houses built prior to 1997.
(d) The value of a computer manufactured in 1997 but not sold in 1997.

Answer: (a)

Moderate
Single
Page: 134
CT Page: 570

7.7: Which of the following would be counted in 1997's GDP?

(a) The value of the stock you purchased in 1997.
b) The value of a calculator that was produced in 1996 but not sold until 1997.
(c) The profit-sharing check that an employee receives in 1997.
(d) The value of a bond sold by the federal government.

Answer: (c)

Moderate
Single
Page: 135
CT Page: 570

7.8: Which of the following is NOT included in 1997's GDP?

(a) The value of a car produced in the United States and exported to England.
(b) The profit earned in 1994 from selling a stock that you purchased in 1990.
(c) The value of a computer chip that is used in the production of a personal computer.
(d) The commission earned by an employment counselor when she locates a job for a client.

Answer: (b)

Easy
Definition
Page: 135
CT Page: 570

7.9: Gross national product is

(a) the total market value of all final goods and services produced within a given period by factors of production located within a country.
(b) the total market value of all final goods and services produced within a given period by factors of production owned by a country's citizens, regardless of where output is produced.
(c) a nation's total product minus what is required to maintain the value of its capital stock.
(d) the total mount of income received by the factors of production in the economy.

Answer: (b)

Moderate
Fact
Page: 135
CT Page: 571

7.10: Which of the following statements is FALSE?

(a) The product produced by U.S. citizens, even when those citizens are working abroad for a foreign company, is counted in U.S. GNP.
(b) Profits earned abroad by U.S. companies are counted in U.S. GNP.
(c) The income of foreigners working in the United States is counted in the U.S. GNP as long as those foreigners work for U.S. company.
(d) Profits earned in the United States by foreign-owned companies are not counted in United States GNP.

Answer: (c)

7.11: Which of the following would be counted in the GNP of the United States, but not the GDP of the United States?

(a) Profits earned in the United States by foreign-owned companies.
(b) Wages paid to foreigners working in the United States for U.S.-owned companies.
(c) Dividends paid on stock in foreign-owned companies to U.S. citizens.
(d) Rent paid to an American who owns land in Ireland.

Challenging Multi
Page: 135
CT Page: 571

Answer: (d)

7.12: Which of the following is NOT counted in the GNP of the United States?

(a) The wage of a U.S. citizen who works in a foreign country for a foreign firm.
(b) The interest earned by a U.S. bank on loans to a business firm located in Brazil.
(c) The profit earned by a restaurant located in the United States but owned by a Mexican company.
(d) The value of services that are produced by state and local governments in the United States.

Moderate
Single
Page: 135
CT Page: 571

Answer: (c)

7.13: Gross national product measures the value of _____, while gross domestic product measures the value of _____.

(a) total production; only final goods produced
(b) output produced by domestically owned factors of production; output produced by the factors of production located in a country
(c) all production including government production; output produced in the private sector only
(d) all production including net exports; production excluding both imports and exports

Easy
Fact
Page: 135
CT Page: 571

Answer: (b)

7.14: Profits earned in the United States by foreign-owned companies are included in

(a) both GDP and GNP.
(b) neither GDP nor GNP.
(c) GNP but not GDP.
(d) GDP but not GNP.

Easy
Fact
Page: 135
CT Page: 571

Answer: (d)

7.15: GDP can be calculated from either the expenditure approach or the income approach because

(a) every payment by a buyer is at the same time a receipt for the seller. (b) only the expenditures on final goods and services are included in GDP.
(c) GDP includes the value of all final goods and services produced by a country's citizens regardless of where the goods and services are produced.
(d) GDP includes all income that is received by all individuals located in a country regardless of whether or not the income is a payment for current production.

Moderate
Fact
Page: 135
CT Page: 571

Answer: (a)

Easy
Fact
Page: 137
CT Page: 572

7.16: The equation for GNP using the expenditure approach is

(a) GNP = C + I + G + EX + IM.
(b) GNP = C + I + G + (IM - EX).
(c) GNP = C + I + G + (EX - IM).
(d) GNP = C + I + G - EX - IM.

Answer: (c)

Easy
Fact
Page: 137
CT Page: 572

7.17: The single largest expenditure component in GNP is

(a) consumption.
(b) investment.
(c) government purchases.
(d) net exports.

Answer: (a)

Moderate
Single
Page: 137
CT Page: 572

7.18: Refer to Figure 7.1. Personal consumption expenditures in billions of dollars are

(a) 650.
(b) 1150.
(c) 1300.
(d) 1450.

Answer: (b)

Moderate
Single
Page: 138
CT Page: 572

7.19: Refer to Figure 7.1. The value for gross private domestic investment in billions of dollars is

(a) 430.
(b) 450.
(c) 470.
(d) 680.

Answer: (a)

Moderate
Single
Page: 140
CT Page: 572

7.20: Refer to Figure 7.1. The value for net exports in billions of dollars is

(a) -150.
(b) 150.
(c) 300.
(d) 750.

Answer: (b)

Moderate
Multi
Page: 140
CT Page: 572

7.21: Refer to Figure 7.1. The value for gross domestic product in billions of dollars is

(a) 1855.
(b) 2105.
(c) 2405.
(d) 2445.

Answer: (c)

Moderate
Single
Page: 137
CT Page: 572

7.22. Refer to Figure 7.2. Personal consumption expenditures in billions of dollars are

(a) 1300.
(b) 1150.
(c) 1500.
(d) 1050.

Answer: (a)

	Billions of dollars
Durable goods	250
Nonresidential investment	350
Federal purchases of goods	275
Exports	450
State and local purchases of goods	400
Residential investment	100
Services	500
Imports	300
Change in business inventories	-20
Nondurable goods	400

Figure 7.1

	Billions of dollars
Durable goods	300
Nonresidential investment	450
Federal purchases of goods	375
Exports	350
State and local purchases of goods	500
Residential investment	200
Services	600
Imports	100
Change in business inventories	-20
Nondurable goods	400

Figure 7.2

Moderate
Single
Page: 138
CT Page: 572

7.23. Refer to Figure 7.2. The value for gross private domestic investment in billions of dollars is

(a) 830.
(b) 450.
(c) -20.
(d) 630.

Answer: (d)

Moderate
Single
Page: 140
CT Page: 572

7.24. Refer to Figure 7.2. The value for net exports in billions of dollars is

(a) -150.
(b) 250.
(c) 100.
(d) 350.

Answer: (b)

Moderate
Multi
Page: 140
CT Page: 572

7.25. Refer to Figure 7.2. The value for gross domestic product in billions of dollars is

(a) 3855.
(b) 2105.
(c) 3055.
(d) 4445.

Answer: (c)

Moderate
Single
Page: 138
CT Page: 573

7.26: A toy store adds bicycles to its inventory in 1994 in anticipation of an increased demand for bicycles. But the store is not able to sell the bicycles in 1994. The bicycles the toy store added to its inventory

(a) will not be counted in 1994 GDP, because they were not sold in 1994.
(b) will be counted in 1994 GDP as a durable consumption expenditure.
(c) will be counted in 1994 GDP as part of gross private domestic investment.
(d) will not be counted in 1994 GDP because they are intermediate goods.

Answer: (c)

Moderate
Single
Page: 138
CT Page: 573

7.27: A freelance graphic artist buys a color laser printer that she uses to produce pamphlets for her clients. This laser printer

(a) is included in GDP as a durable consumption good.
(b) is included in GDP as part of gross private investment.
(c) is included in GDP as a service.
(d) is not included in GDP because it is an intermediate good.

Answer: (b)

Easy
Fact
Page: 138
CT Page: 575

7.28: The change in business inventories is measured as

(a) final sales minus GDP.
(b) final sales plus GDP.
(c) GDP minus final sales.
(d) the ratio of final sales to GDP.

Answer: (c)

7.29 In 1994 final sales equal $120 billion and the change in business inventories is - $10 billion. GDP in 1994

(a) is $110 billion.
(b) is $120 billion.
(c) is $130 billion.
(d) cannot be determined from this information.

Answer: (a)

Moderate
Single
Page: 138
CT Page: 573

7.30. In 1997 final sales equal $350 billion and the change in business inventories is - $55 billion. GDP in 1994

(a) is $350 billion.
(b) is $405 billion.
(c) is $295 billion.
(d) cannot be determined from this information.

Answer: (c)

Moderate
Single
Page: 138
CT Page: 573

7.31: In 1994 the change in business inventories is -$20 billion and GDP is $190 billion. Final sales in 1994

(a) are $170 billion.
(b) are $190 billion.
(c) are $210 billion.
(d) cannot be determined from this information.

Answer: (c)

Moderate
Single
Page: 138
CT Page: 573

7.32. In 1997 the change in business inventories is -$10 billion and GDP is $500 billion. Final sales in 1994

(a) are $510 billion.
(b) are $490 billion.
(c) are $500 billion.
(d) cannot be determined from this information.

Answer: (a)

Moderate
Single
Page: 138
CT Page: 573

7.33: If the change in business inventories is zero, then final sales are

(a) zero.
(b) less than GDP.
(c) greater than GDP.
(d) equal to GDP.

Answer: (d)

Easy
Single
Page: 138
CT Page: 575

7.34: If in a year there is a negative inventory investment, then final sales

(a) exceed GDP.
(b) are less than GDP.
(c) equal GDP.
(d) are zero.

Answer: (a)

Easy
Fact
Page: 138
CT Page: 575

Easy
Definition
Page: 140
CT Page: 575

7.35: Gross investment minus depreciation is

(a) private investment.
(b) the change in business inventories.
(c) the capital consumption allowance.
(d) net investment.

Answer: (d)

Moderate
Fact
Page: 140
CT Page: 575

7.36: If net investment is zero, then

(a) gross investment is greater than depreciation.
(b) gross investment is less than depreciation.
(c) gross investment equals depreciation.
(d) depreciation is zero.

Answer: (c)

Moderate
Single
Page: 140
CT Page: 575

7.37: If gross investment is less than depreciation, then net investment

(a) is positive.
(b) is negative.
(c) is zero.
(d) could be positive or negative.

Answer: (b)

Easy
Definition
Page: 140
CT Page: 575

7.38: The total value of all capital goods newly produced in a given period is

(a) the change in business inventories.
(b) depreciation.
(c) net investment.
(d) gross investment.

Answer: (d)

Easy
Definition
Page: 140
CT Page: 575

7.39: The capital stock at the end of the period is equal to

(a) the ratio of the amount of the capital at the beginning of the period to the amount of depreciation.
(b) the amount of the capital stock at the beginning of the period plus depreciation.
(c) the amount of the capital at the beginning of the period plus net investment.
(d) the amount of the capital at the beginning of the period minus net investment.

Answer: (c)

Easy
Definition
Page: 140
CT Page: 575

7.40: Net investment is

(a) gross investment minus depreciation.
(b) gross investment plus depreciation.
(c) depreciation minus gross investment.
(d) GNP minus final sales.

Answer: (a)

7.41: The amount by which an asset's value falls in a given period is

(a) deflation.
(b) inflation.
(c) the net value.
(d) depreciation.

Answer: (d)

Easy
Definition
Page: 140
CT Page: 575

7.42: If net investment in 1994 is $200 billion and gross investment in 1994 is $300 billion, depreciation in 1994 is

(a) $.67 billion.
(b) $175 billion.
(c) $250 billion.
(d) $300 billion.

Answer: (b)

Moderate
Single
Page: 140
CT Page: 575

7.43. If net investment in 1997 is $300 billion and gross investment in 1994 is $475 billion, depreciation in 1994 is

(a) $.67 billion.
(b) $100 billion.
(c) $250 billion.
(d) $500 billion.

Answer: (b)

Moderate
Single
Page: 140
CT Page: 575

7.44: If gross investment in 1994 is $400 billion and depreciation in 1994 is $600 billion, net investment in 1994 is

(a)-$200 billion.
(b) $200 billion.
(c) -$1000 billion.
(d) none of the above.

Answer (a)

Moderate
Single
Page: 140
CT Page: 575

7.45. If gross investment in 1997 is $100 billion and depreciation in 1994 is $1000 billion, net investment in 1994 is

(a)-$1100 billion.
(b) $1000 billion.
(c) -$900 billion.
(d) none of the above.

Answer (c)

Moderate
Single
Page: 140
CT Page: 575

7.46: The value of net exports is

(a) the ratio of exports to imports.
(b) imports plus exports.
(c) imports minus exports.
(d) exports minus imports.

Answer: (d)

Easy
Definition
Page: 140
CT Page: 576

Easy
Fact
Page: 140
CT Page: 576

7.47: When calculating GDP, exports are _____ and imports are _____.

(a) added; added
(b) added; subtracted
(c) subtracted; added
(d) subtracted; subtracted

Answer: (b)

Easy
Definition
Page: 140
CT Page: 576

7.48: If the value of net exports is positive, then

(a) exports exceed imports.
(b) imports exceed exports.
(c) exports equal imports.
(d) imports are zero.

Answer: (a)

Moderate
Fact
Page: 141
CT Page: 576

7.49: The formula for calculating GDP from the income approach is

(a) GDP = National Income + Depreciation + (Indirect Taxes - Subsidies) + Net Factor Payments to the Rest of the World.
(b) GDP = National Income + Depreciation + (Subsidies - Indirect Taxes) - Net Factor Payments to the Rest of the World.
(c) GDP = National Income + Indirect Taxes - (Depreciation - Subsidies) + Net Factor Payments to the Rest of the World.
(d) GDP = National Income - Depreciation - (Indirect Taxes - Subsidies) - Net Factor Payments to the Rest of the World.

Answer: (a)

Easy
Fact
Page: 141
CT Page: 577

7.50: The largest income component of GDP is

(a) proprietors' income.
(b) compensation of employees.
(c) rental income.
(d) corporate profit.

Answer: (b)

Easy
Fact
Page: 141
CT Page: 577

7.51: The smallest income component of GDP is

(a) employee compensation.
(b) proprietors' income.
(c) rental income.
(d) corporate profit.

Answer: (c)

Easy
Definition
Page: 141
CT Page: 577

7.52: Proprietors' income is

(a) the income of unincorporated businesses.
(b) the income of all businesses - incorporated and unincorporated.
(c) the income of sole proprietorships.
(d) the income of partnerships.

Answer: (a)

7.53: Net interest is the interest on loans paid by

(a) businesses, households, and the government.
(b) businesses and households.
(c) businesses and the government.
(d) businesses.

Answer: (d)

Easy
Fact
Page: 141
CT Page: 577

7.54: Interest paid by households and by the government is

(a) counted in national income, but not in GDP.
(b) not counted in GDP because it is not assumed to flow from the production of goods and services.
(c) not counted in GDP but is counted in GNP because it is paid by U.S. citizens to people living in the United States.
(d) included in both GDP and GNP because it represents an expenditure by one group and a receipt of income by another group.

Answer: (b)

Easy
Fact
Page: 141
CT Page: 577

7.55: Depreciation is

(a) added to national income to calculate GDP using the income approach.
(b) included in investment when calculating GDP using the expenditure approach.
(c) included in GDP, but not GNP.
(d) both a and b.

Answer: (d)

Easy
Fact
Page: 141
CT Page: 577

7.56: Which of the following is an example of an indirect tax?

(a) Your landlord raises your rent because the property taxes he pays on the apartment building increased.
(b) You pay a tax on an imported car.
(c) Funds for unemployment compensation are raised through a payroll tax on employed workers.
(d) The federal government imposes an excise tax on the sale of gasoline.

Answer: (d)

Moderate
Single
Page: 141
CT Page: 577

7.57: Subsidies are

(a) subtracted from national income to get GDP.
(b) added to national income to get GDP.
(c) subtracted from GNP to get NNP.
(d) added to GNP to get NNP.

Answer: (a)

Easy
Fact
Page: 142
CT Page: 577

7.58: Refer to Figure 7.3. The value for National Income in billions of dollars is

(a) 380.
(b) 420.
(c) 430.
(d) 480.

Answer: (b)

Moderate
Single
Page: 141
CT Page: 576

	Billions of dollars
Compensation of employees	300
Proprietors' income	50
Corporate profits	25
Net interest	40
Rental income	5
Depreciation	60
Indirect taxes	30
Subsidies	10
Payments of factor income to the rest of the world	15
Receipts of factor income from the rest of the world	10

Figure 7.3

Moderate
Multi
Page: 141
CT Page: 576

7.59: Refer to Figure 7.3. The value for Gross Domestic Product in billions of dollars is

(a) 405.
(b) 485.
(c) 505.
(d) 525.

Answer: (c)

Moderate
Single
Page: 141
CT Page: 576

7.60. Refer to Figure 7.4. The value for National Income in billions of dollars is

(a) 480.
(b) 620.
(c) 530.
(d) 720.

Answer: (d)

Moderate
Multi
Page: 141
CT Page: 576

7.61. Refer to Figure 7.4. The value for Gross Domestic Product in billions of dollars is

(a) 755.
(b) 845.
(c) 705.
(d) 525.

Answer: (a)

	Billions of dollars
Compensation of employees	500
Proprietors' income	100
Corporate profits	25
Net interest	70
Rental income	25
Depreciation	60
Indirect taxes	10
Subsidies	30
Payments of factor income to the rest of the world	15
Receipts of factor income from the rest of the world	20

Figure 7.4

7.62: Net factor payments to the rest of the world are:

(a) payments of factor income to the rest of the world minus the receipt of factor income from the rest of the world.
(b) payments of factor income to the rest of the world plus the receipt of factor income from the rest of the world.
(c) the receipt of factor income from the rest of the world minus payments of factor income to the rest of the world.
(d) the payment for exports minus the payment for imports.

Easy
Definition
Page: 142
CT Page: 578

Answer: (a)

7.63: Refer to Figure 7.5. The value for GDP in billions of dollars is

(a) 495.
(b) 535.
(c) 555.
(d) 595.

Moderate
Multi
Page: 143
CT Page: 578

Answer: (b)

7.64: Refer to Figure 7.5. The value for GNP in billions of dollars is

(a) 530.
(b) 535.
(c) 550.
(d) 560.

Moderate
Multi
Page: 143
CT Page: 578

Answer: (a)

	Billions of dollars
Transfer payments	25
Subsidies	5
Social insurance payments	45
Depreciation	40
Receipts of factor income from the rest of the world	10
Government purchases	85
Imports	60
Payments of factor income to the rest of the word	15
Personal interest income	45
Indirect taxes	15
Exports	50
Net private domestic investment	120
Personal taxes	80
After-tax Corporate profits	60
Personal consumption expenditures	300
Dividends	10

Figure 7.5

Moderate
Multi
Page: 143
CT Page: 578

7.65: Refer to Figure 7.5. The value for NNP in billions of dollars is

(a) 455.
(b) 490.
(c) 495.
(d) 500.

Answer: (b)

Moderate
Multi
Page: 143
CT Page: 578

7.66: Refer to Figure 7.5. The value for National Income in billions of dollars is

(a) 445.
(b) 470.
(c) 480.
(d) 490.

Answer: (c)

7.67: Refer to Figure 7.5. The value for Personal Income in billions of dollars is

(a) 455.
(b) 465.
(c) 495.
(d) 550.

Answer: (a)

7.68: Refer to Figure 7.5. The value for Disposable Personal Income in billions of dollars is

(a) 375.
(b) 385.
(c) 415.
(d) 470.

Answer: (a)

7.69: If GDP is $500 billion, receipts of factor income from the rest of the world are $25 billion, and payments of factor income to the rest of the world are $10 billion, then GNP is

(a) $465billion.
(b) $485 billion.
(c) $515 billion.
(d) $535 billion.

Answer: (c)

7.70. If GDP is $200 billion, receipts of factor income from the rest of the world are $55 billion, and payments of factor income to the rest of the world are $20 billion, then GNP is

(a) $275 billion.
(b) $180 billion.
(c) $235 billion.
(d) $535 billion.

Answer: (c)

7.71: If GDP is $500 billion and depreciation is $50 billion, then Net National Product

(a) is $450 billion.
(b) is $500 billion.
(c) is $550 billion.
(d) cannot be determined from this information.

Answer: (d)

7.72 If GDP is $200 billion and depreciation is $100 billion, then Net National Product
(a) is $100 billion.
(b) is $400 billion.
(c) is $300 billion.
(d) cannot be determined from this information.

Answer: (d)

Moderate
Single
Page: 143
CT Page: 578

7.73: If GNP is $600 billion and depreciation is $40 billion, then Net National Product

(a) is $560 billion.
(b) is $600 billion.
(c) is $640 billion
(d) cannot be determined from this information.

Answer: (a)

Moderate
Single
Page: 143
CT Page: 578

7.74. If GNP is $750 billion and depreciation is $200 billion, then Net National Product

(a) is $950 billion.
(b) is $550 billion.
(c) is $640 billion
(d) cannot be determined from this information.

Answer: (b)

Moderate
Multi
Page: 143
CT Page: 578

7.75: If Net National Product is $650 billion, indirect taxes are $20 billion, and subsidies are $15 billion, then National Income is

(a) $167 billion.
(b) $645 billion.
(c) $655 billion.
(d) $685 billion.

Answer: (b)

Moderate
Multi
Page: 143
CT Page: 578

7.76. If Net National Product is $350 billion, indirect taxes are $40 billion, and subsidies are $5 billion, then National Income is

(a) $315 billion.
(b) $395 billion.
(c) $305 billion.
(d) $285 billion.

Answer: (a)

Easy
Definition
Page: 143
CT Page: 579

7.77: Net national product is

(a) GDP plus depreciation.
(b) GDP minus depreciation.
(c) GNP minus depreciation.
(d) GNP plus depreciation.

Answer: (c)

Moderate
Fact
Page: 143
CT Page: 579

7.78: Net national product

(a) is always less than GNP.
(b) is always greater than GNP.
(c) can be less than, greater than, or equal to GNP.
(d) can either be less or greater than but never equal to GNP.

Answer: (a)

7.79: A nation's total product minus what is required to maintain the value of its capital stock is

(a) gross national product.
(b) net national product.
(c) net domestic product.
(d) national income.

Answer: (b)

Easy
Definition
Page: 143
CT Page: 579

7.80: To calculate national income

(a) indirect taxes and subsidies are added to net national product.
(b) indirect taxes and subsidies are subtracted from net national product.
(c) indirect taxes are added to and subsidies are subtracted from net national product.
(d) indirect taxes are subtracted from and subsidies are added to net national product.

Answer: (d)

Easy
Fact
Page: 143
CT Page: 579

7.81: The total income of households is

(a) net national product.
(b) personal income.
(c) national income.
(d) production income.

Answer: (b)

Easy
Definition
Page: 143
CT Page: 579

7.82: Personal income is national income minus retained corporate earnings

(a) minus social insurance payments minus personal interest income received minus transfer payments.
(b) plus social insurance payments plus personal interest income received plus transfer payments.
(c) minus social insurance payments plus personal interest income received plus transfer payments.
(d) plus social insurance payments plus personal interest income received plus transfer payments.

Answer: (c)

Moderate
Fact
Page: 143
CT Page: 579

7.83: Disposable personal income is

(a) national income minus personal income taxes.
(b) national income minus social insurance payments.
(c) personal income plus transfer payments.
(d) personal income minus personal income taxes.

Answer: (d)

Easy
Definition
Page: 144
CT Page: 580

7.84: Transfer payments are

(a) included in both national income and personal income.
(b) excluded from both national income and personal income.
(c) included in national income but not in personal income.
(d) not included in national income but are included in personal income.

Answer: (d)

Easy
Fact
Page: 144
CT Page: 580

Moderate
Multi
Page: 144
CT Page: 579

7.85: Personal income

(a) is always less than national income.
(b) is always greater than national income.
(c) may be greater than or less than national income.
(d) will always equal national income.

Answer: (c)

Easy
Definition
Page: 144
CT Page: 579

7.86: The income received by households before paying personal income taxes but after paying social insurance contributions is

(a) national income.
(b) personal income.
(c) net personal income.
(d) disposable personal income.

Answer: (b)

Easy
Single
Page: 144
CT Page: 579

7.87: If personal income is $350 billion and personal income taxes are $30 billion, the value of disposable personal income

(a) is $320 billion
(b) is $350 billion.
(c) is $380 billion.
(d) cannot be determined from this information.

Answer: (a)

Easy
Fact
Page: 144
CT Page: 579

7.88: If total personal spending exceeds disposable personal income, then personal saving is

(a) zero.
(b) positive.
(c) negative.
(d) either positive or negative.

Answer: (c)

Easy
Fact
Page: 144
CT Page: 580

7.89: The personal saving rate is

(a) the difference between total personal spending and personal saving.
(b) the difference between personal income and personal disposable income.
(c) the ratio of personal income to personal saving.
(d) the percentage of personal disposable income that is saved.

Answer: (d)

Moderate
Multi
Page: 144
CT Page: 580

7.90: If disposable personal income is $400 billion and personal saving is $10 billion, the personal saving rate is

(a) .975%.
(b) 2.5%.
(c) 10%.
(d) 40%.

Answer: (b)

7.91: If the personal saving rate is 5% and personal saving is $10 billion, the value of personal disposable income

(a) is $50 billion.
(b) is $200 billion.
(c) is $500 billion.
(d) cannot be determined from this information.

Answer: (b)

Moderate
Multi
Page: 144
CT Page: 580

7.92: Saving rates tend to _____ during recessionary periods and _____ during boom times.

(a) rise; fall
(b) rise; rise
(c) fall; rise
(d) fall; fall

Answer: (a)

Easy
Fact
Page: 144
CT Page: 580

7.93: Gross domestic product measured in current dollars is

(a) real GDP.
(b) nominal GDP.
(c) current GDP.
(d) constant GDP.

Answer: (b)

Easy
Definition
Page: 145
CT Page: 581

7.94: Gross domestic product measured in terms of the prices of a fixed, or base, year is

(a) real GDP.
(b) nominal GDP.
(c) current GDP.
(d) base GDP.

Answer: (a)

Easy
Definition
Page: 145
CT Page: 581

7.95: Nominal GDP is gross domestic product measured

(a) in the prices of a base year.
(b) in current dollars.
(c) at a constant output level but at the base-year prices.
(d) as the difference between the current year's GDP and last year's GDP.

Answer: (b)

Easy
Definition
Page: 145
CT Page: 581

7.96: Real GDP is gross domestic product measured

(a) in the prices of a base year.
(b) in current dollars.
(c) at a constant output level but at current prices.
(d) as the difference between the current year's GDP and last year's GDP.

Answer: (a)

Easy
Definition
Page: 145
CT Page: 581

Easy
Fact
Page: 145
CT Page: 581

7.97: If real GDP decreased from 1993 to 1994, then

(a) only prices decreased from 1993 to 1994.
(b) output decreased from 1993 to 1994.
(c) it cannot be determined whether output or prices or both decreased from 1993 to 1994.
(d) output and prices both must have decreased from 1993 to 1994.

Answer: (b)

Easy
Fact
Page: 145
CT Page: 581

7.98: If nominal GDP increased from 1993 to 1994, then

(a) only prices increased from 1993 to 1994.
(b) only output increased from 1993 to 1994.
(c) it cannot be determined whether output or prices or both increased from 1993 to 1994.
(d) output definitely decreased from 1993 to 1994.

Answer: (c)

Moderate
Multi
Page: 146
CT Page: 581

7.99 Refer to Figure 7.6. Assume that this economy produces only two goods: Good X and Good Y. The value for this economy's nominal GDP in year 1

(a) is $110.
(b) is $150.
(c) is $240.
(d) cannot be determined from this information.

Answer: (a)

Moderate
Multi
Page: 146
CT Page: 581

7.100: Refer to Figure 7.6. Assume that this economy produces only two goods: Good X and Good Y. The value for this economy's nominal GDP in year 3

(a) is $178.
(b) is $230.
(c) is $250.
(d) cannot be determined from this information.

Answer: (c)

Moderate
Multi
Page: 146
CT Page: 581

7.101: Refer to Figure 7.6. Assume that this economy produces only two goods: Good X and Good Y. The value for this economy's nominal GDP in year 2 is

(a) $135.
(b) $150.
(c) $175.
(d) none of the above.

Answer: (b)

	Production			Price per unit		
	Year 1	Year 2	Year 3	Year 1	Year 2	Year 3
Good X	50	75	100	$1.00	$1.00	$1.20
Good Y	100	100	130	$ .60	$ .75	$1.00

Figure 7.6

7.102: Refer to Figure 7.6. Assume that this economy produces only two goods: Good X and Good Y. If year 1 is the base year, the value for this economy's real GDP in year 2 is

(a) $135.
(b) $150.
(c) $175.
(d) none of the above.

Moderate
Multi
Page: 146
CT Page: 581

Answer: (a)

7.103: Refer to Figure 7.6. Assume that this economy produces only two goods: Good X and Good Y. If year 1 is the base year, the value for this economy's GDP deflator in year 1 is

(a) 1.
(b) 100.
(c) 110.
(d) none of the above.

Easy
Fact
Page: 146
CT Page: 581

Answer: (b)

7.104: Refer to Figure 7.6. Assume that this economy produces only two goods: Good X and Good Y. If year 1 is the base year, the value for this economy's GDP deflator in year 2 is

(a) 11.
(b) 90.
(c) 111.
(d) 136.36.

Moderate
Multi
Page: 146
CT Page: 581

Answer: (c)

7.105: Refer to Figure 7.6. Assume that this economy produces only two goods: Good X and Good Y. If year 1 is the base year, the value for this economy's inflation rate between year 1 and year 2 is

(a) 9.9%.
(b) 11%.
(c) 100%.
(d) 111%.

Challenging
Multi
Page: 146
CT Page: 581

Answer: (b)

7.106: The GDP deflator is the

(a) difference between real GDP and nominal GDP multiplied by 100.
(b) difference between nominal GDP and real GDP multiplied by 100.
(c) ratio of nominal GDP to real GDP multiplied by 100.
(d) ratio of real GDP to nominal GDP multiplied by 100.

Easy
Definition
Page: 147
CT Page: 582

Answer: (c)

7.107: If nominal GDP is $4 trillion and real GDP is $2.5 trillion, the GDP deflator is

(a) 37.5.
(b) 62.5.
(c) 100.
(d) 160.

Moderate
Single
Page: 147
CT Page: 582

Answer: (d)

Moderate
Single
Page: 147
CT Page: 582

7.108: Nominal GDP is $5 trillion and the GDP deflator is 111.11, the value for real GDP is

(a) $2.22 trillion.
(b) $4.5 trillion.
(c) $5.6 trillion.
(d) none of the above.

Answer: (b)

Challenging
Multi
Page: 147
CT Page: 582

7.109: The GDP deflator in year 2 is 120 and the GDP deflator in year 3 is 125. The rate of inflation between years 2 and 3 is

(a)1.04%.
(b) 2.04%.
(c) 4%.
(d) 4.17%.

Answer: (d)

Moderate
Fact
Page: 145
CT Page: 581

7.110: Which of the following statements is FALSE?

(a) Nominal GNP generally grows faster than real GNP.
(b) If real GNP in a year is less than nominal GNP in that year, then prices have risen between the base year and the current year.
(c) Real GNP grows only from an increase in output.
(d) An increase in the GNP deflator means that all prices in the economy have risen.

Answer: (d)

Moderate
Single
Page: 149
CT Page: 583

7.111: Real GDP is not a perfect measure of social welfare because

(a) real GDP may be increasing only because of price increases, not increases in output.
(b) GDP accounting rules do not adjust for production that causes negative externalities.
(c) GDP includes output produced in both the market and in the home.
(d) GDP accounting rules lead to different weights being placed on goods produced in the government sector than in the private sector.

Answer: (b)

Easy
Fact
Page: 149
CT Page: 583

7.112: Which of the following statements is FALSE?

(a) GDP is adjusted to reflect losses or social ills.
(b) GDP says nothing about the distribution of output among individuals in a society.
(c) GDP cannot be used to measure the effects of policies that redistribute income from one group to another group.
(d) GDP is neutral about the kinds of goods that an economy produces - all goods get counted in the same way regardless of the different weights that society might attach to these items.

Answer: (a)

Easy
Definition
Page: 150
CT Page: 584

7.113: The part of the economy in which transactions take place and income is generated that is unreported and, therefore, not
counted in GDP is the

(a) illegitimate economy.
(b) barter economy.
(c) money economy.
(d) underground economy.

Answer: (d)

7.114: If real GDP is growing more slowly than the rate of population growth, then, ceteris paribus, the average standard of living is

Moderate
Single
Page: 150
CT Page: 584

(a) increasing.
(b) decreasing.
(c) either increasing or decreasing.
(d) remaining stable.

Answer: (b)

TRUE/FALSE QUESTIONS

7.115: GDP includes all transactions in which money or goods change hands.

Answer: False

Easy
Fact
Page: 133

7.116: The products produced by U.S. citizens when those citizens are working abroad for a foreign company are not counted in the U.S. GNP.

Answer: False

Easy
Fact
Page: 135
CT Page: 570

7.117: If we excluded inventories from GDP, we would be measuring sales, not production

Answer: True

Easy
Fact
Page: 138
CT Page: 575

7.118: If net investment is positive, then at the end of the period the capital stock has increased.

Answer: True

Easy
Fact
Page: 138
CT Page: 575

7.119: Because GDP does not take into account any depreciation of the capital stock that may have occurred, NNP is sometimes a better measure of how the economy is doing than is GDP.

Answer: True

Easy
Fact
Page: 143
CT Page: 579

7.120: Saving rates tend to rise during boom times and fall during recessionary periods.

Answer: False

Easy
Fact
Page: 145
CT Page: 580

7.121: Real GDP can increase either from an increase in output or from an increase in the price level, while nominal GDP increases only as a result of an increase in output.

Answer: False

Easy
Fact
Page: 145
CT Page: 581

7.122: Nominal GDP usually rises faster than real GDP because the price level tends to increase over time.

Answer: True

Easy
Fact
Page: 145
CT Page: 581

7.123: If in the same period output doubles and the price level doubles, real GDP will remains constant.

Answer: False

Easy
Single
Page: 145
CT Page: 581

Easy
Fact
Page: 145
CT Page: 581

7.124: To measure economic growth in an economy, the appropriate GDP measure to use is nominal GDP.

Answer: False

SHORT ANSWER QUESTIONS

Easy
Application
Page: 135
CT Page: 569

7.125: The small nation of Lesotho is entirely surrounded by the Republic of South Africa. A substantial percentage of Lesotho's workers cross the border and work in South Africa. Which will be larger, Lesotho's GDP or its gross national product (GNP)? Explain why.

Answer: Lesotho's GNP will exceed its GDP because GNP measures production by a nation's resources, regardless of location, while GDP measures output within the nation's boundaries. Much of Lesotho's productive activity takes place outside Lesotho.

Moderate
Application
Page: 135
CT Page: 569

7.126: Identify which of the following items would be included in U.S. GDP.

a. The salary of an American consultant hired by a British firm to go and analyze their European operations
b. The output of a U.S.-owned family farm in Kansas
c. Food stamp payments
d. Welfare checks
e. The wages of a field worker in Louisiana

Answer: The output of a U.S.-owned family farm in Kansas (b) and the wages of a field worker in Louisiana (e) would be included in U.S. GDP. Wages are counted because they represent a payment for the use of a productive resource. Transfers (e.g., food stamps and welfare checks) are not included because they do not represent the value of a productive resource. The consultant's services are excluded because they would be provided outside the United States.

Moderate
Math
Page: 143
CT Page: 573

7.127: Answer parts a through g using the information in Figure 7.7 describing the Macrovian economy. Quantities are given in millions of Macrovian dollars (M$).

a. Calculate gross private investment.
b. Calculate Macrovian GDP for 1996.
c. Calculate gross national product (GNP).
d. Calculate net national product (NNP).
e. Calculate national income.
f. Calculate personal income.
g. Calculate disposable personal income.

Answer: a. Gross private investment = Business investment in plant and equipment + Residential construction + Inventory investment = 586.1 + 453.7 + (-)30.9 = 1008.9.

b. GDP = C + I + G + (EX - IM) = 3514.8 + (586.1 + 453.7 - 30.9) + 1589.7 + (380.4 - 285.0) = 6208.8 (millions of Macrovian dollars)

c. GNP = GDP - Net factor payments to the rest of the world = 6208.8 - (-)17.3 = 6226.1.

d. NNP = GNP - Depreciation = 6226.1 - 643.5 = 5582.6.

e. National income = GNP - (Depreciation + Indirect business taxes minus subsidies) = 6226.1 - (643.5 + 489.6) = 5093.0.

Business investment in plant and equipment	586.1
Inventory investment	-30.9
Compensation of employees	5178.6
Corporate taxes	215.9
Macrovian exports of goods and services	380.4
Depreciation	643.5
Personal taxes	600.0
Personal consumption expenditures	3514.8
Government purchases of goods and services	1589.7
Indirect business taxes minus subsidies	489.6
Net factor payments to the rest of the world	-17.3
Residential construction	453.7
Business retained earnings	45.7
Government transfer payments and interest	337.1
Macrovian imports of goods and services	285.0
Payroll taxes	441.7

Figure 7.7

f. Personal income = National income + Government transfer payments and interest - (Payroll taxes + Corporate taxes + Business retained earnings) = 5093.0 + 337.1 - (441.7 + 215.9 + 45.7) = 4726.8.

g. Disposable personal income = Personal income - Personal taxes = 4726.8 - 600.0 = 4126.8.

7.128: Figure 7.8 contains the national income and product accounts data on the Freedonia economy. Quantities below are given in millions of Freedonian dollars (F$). Use this information to answer parts a ghrough g below.

Moderate
Math
Page: 143
CT Page: 573

a. Calculate Freedonian gross private investment.
b. Calculate Freedonian GDP.
c. Calculate Freedonian GNP.
d. Calculate net national product (NNP).
e. Calculate national income.
f. Calculate personal income.
g. Calculate disposable personal income.

Answer:

a. Gross private investment = Net private investment + Depreciation = 784.0 + 168.0 = 952.0.

b. GDP = Personal consumption expenditures + Gross private investment + Government purchases + Net exports = 2203.2 + 952.0 + 716.8 + (212.8 - 235.2) = 3849.6.

c. GNP = GDP + (Receipts of factor income from the rest of the world - Payments of factor income to the rest of the world) = 3849.6 + (35.2 - 68.8) = 3816.0.

d. NNP = GNP - Depreciation = 3816.0 - 168.0 = 3648.0.

e. National income = NNP - (Indirect taxes - Subsidies) = 3648.0 - (593.6 - 44.8) = 3099.2.

Depreciation	168.0
Compensation of employees	1407.7
Corporate profits	257.6
Dividends	78.4
Exports	212.8
Government purchases	716.8
Imports	235.2
Indirect taxes	593.6
Net interest income	182.2
Net private domestic investment	784.0
Personal consumption expenditures	2203.2
Personal interest income	112.0
Receipts of factor income from the rest of the world	35.2
Personal taxes	627.2
Proprietors' income	173.9
Payments of factor income to the rest of the world	68.8
Rental income	34.1
Social insurance payments	380.8
Subsidies	44.8
Transfer payments	504.0

Figure 7.8

f. Personal income = National income - (Corporate profits - Dividends) - Social insurance payments + Personal interest income + Transfer payments = 3099.2 - (257.6 - 78.4) - 380.8 + 112.0 + 504.0 = 3155.2.

g. Disposable personal income = Personal income - Personal taxes = 3155.2 - 627.2 = 2528.0.

7.129: Answer parts a and b below using the information contained in Figure 7.9. Assume this economy only produces corn and steel.

a. Refer to Figure 7.9. Calculate nominal GDP for Year 1 and Year 2.
b. Refer to Figure 7.9. Calculate real GDP for Year 1 and Year 2 (using fixed weights and Year 1 as base).

Answer: a. Nominal GDP for Year 1 = (2,000 x $1.00) + (100 x $6.00) = $2,600. Nominal GDP for Year 2 = (2,200 x $1.50) + (80 x $7.00) = $3,860.

b. Real GDP for Year 1 = (2,000 x $1.00) + (100 x $6.00) = $2,600.

7.130: Explain why each of the following items is excluded from GDP:

a. profits from the stock and bond market
b. transfer payments
c. sale of used goods
d. goods and services produced in the home.

	Corn		Steel	
	Quantity	Price	Quantity	Price
Year	12,000	$1.00	100	$6.00
Year	22,200	$1.50	80	$7.00

Figure 7.9

Easy
Math
Page: 155
CT Page: 581

Easy
Fact
Page: 135
CT Page: 571

Explain why the following items are included in GDP:

a. depreciation
b. change in business inventories
c. indirect taxes

Answer: Profits from the sale of stocks and bonds have nothing to do with current production so they are not included in GDP. Transfer payments are not included because they do not represent payments for current production. Used goods were counted in GDP in the year they were produced. They are not counted again when they are resold. Depreciation is included in GDP because GDP is a measure of all income, including the income that results from the replacement of existing plant and equipment. Change in business inventories is included because GDP is a measure of production, not sales. The change in inventories is necessary so that all current production is included even if it is not sold, and production from previous years that is finally sold is not included. Indirect taxes are included because they represent income to the government.

7.131: Explain the two approaches that can be used to compute GDP. Why do these two approaches lead to the same value for GDP?

Easy
Fact
Page: 136
CT Page: 571

Answer: The two approaches are the income approach and the expenditure approach. The income approach adds all sources of income and the expenditure approach adds all expenditures for goods and services. The two approaches yield the same result because every expenditure leads to an income flow for someone.

7.132: Explain the four main categories of expenditures used in calculating GDP.

Easy
Fact
Page: 137
CT Page: 572

Answer: The four main expenditure categories are consumption, investment, government spending and net exports.

7.133: Define GNP and GDP. Explain the difference between GNP and GDP. Why is the difference between GNP and GDP small for most countries?

Easy
Fact
Page: 135
CT Page: 579

Answer: GDP is the total market value of all final goods and services produced within a given period by factors of production located within a country. GNP is the total market value of all final goods and services produced within a given period by factors of production owned by a country's citizens, regardless of where the output is produced. For most countries the difference between GNP and GDP is small because the payments of factor income to the rest of the world is approximately the same value as the receipt of factor income from the rest of the world.

7.134: Explain the difference between GNP and NNP. Explain why NNP is sometimes a better measure of how the economy is doing than GNP is.

Moderate
Single
Page: 143
CT Page: 578

Answer: The difference between GNP and NNP is that NNP is GNP minus depreciation. NNP is a measure of total product minus what is required to maintain the value of the capital stock. NNP is sometimes a better measure of how the economy is doing because it accounts for the capital stock that is left over after depreciation has been accounted for.

7.135: Explain why economic growth must be measured using real GDP instead of nominal GDP.

Easy
Single
Page: 145
CT Page: 581

Answer: Real GDP must be used instead of nominal GDP to measure growth because real GDP adjusts for price- level changes. Thus any increase in real GDP results solely from an increase in output.

Moderate
Single
Page: 147
CT Page: 582

7.136: Explain now the GDP deflator is calculated. Why is the GDP deflator used instead of the CPI to calculate real GDP? If nominal GDP in 1994 is less than real GDP in 1994, then what can you conclude about the price level in 1994?

Answer: The GDP deflator is the ratio of nominal GDP to real GDP multiplied by 100. The GDP deflator is used instead of the CPI to calculate real GDP because it is a more inclusive measure of inflation. If nominal GDP is less than real GDP, then the price level has fallen.

Easy
Fact
Page: 149
CT Page: 583

7.137: Explain why GDP is not necessarily a good measure of social welfare.

Answer: GDP is not necessarily a good measure of social welfare because it doesn't adjust production for negative externalities, home production is not included, all activity produced in the underground economy is excluded, and it tells us nothing about how the output is distributed.

Challenging
Multi
Page: 149
CT Page: 583

7.138: How would you adjust GDP to make it a better measure of social welfare?

Answer: Answers here can vary. Students may discuss adjusting GDP for pollution, increases in crime, including an estimate of services produced in the home, and including an estimate of output produced in the underground economy

Challenging
Multi
Page: 149
CT Page: 583

7.139: Give an example of how real GDP could be increased even though no more output is produced.

Answer: Real GDP could be increased even though there is no more output produced if output that is currently produced in the home or in the underground economy is included. If activities that are currently illegal are declared legal, real GDP could increase.

8 Macroeconomic Problems: Unemployment and Inflation

(Chapter 23 in Combined Text)

MULTIPLE CHOICE QUESTIONS

8.1: A period in which real GDP declines for at least two consecutive quarters is

(a) a recession.
(b) a depression.
(c) an inflation.
(d) a hyperinflation.

Answer: (a)

Easy
Definition
Page: 156
CT Page: 590

8.2: A recession is marked by _____ output and _____ unemployment.

(a) falling; declining
(b) falling; rising
(c) rising; rising
(d) rising; declining

Answer: (b)

Easy
Fact
Page: 156
CT Page: 590

8.3: A prolonged and deep recession is a

(a) contraction.
(b) slowdown.
(c) depression.
(d) hyperinflation.

Answer: (c)

Easy
Definition
Page: 156
CT Page: 590

8.4: An individual who has a job but has been temporarily absent, with or without pay, is classified as

(a) employed.
(b) unemployed.
(c) a discouraged worker.
(d) not in the labor force.

Answer: (a)

Easy
Fact
Page: 157
CT Page: 592

8.5: Any person 16 years old or older who works without pay for 15 or more hours per week in a family enterprise is classified as

(a) not in the labor force.
(b) unemployed, because the person is not paid.
(c) employed.
(d) a discouraged worker.

Answer: (c)

Easy
Fact
Page: 157
CT Page: 592

Easy
Definition
Page: 157
CT Page: 592

8.6: An employed person is any person 16 years old or older

(a) who works for pay, either for someone else or in his or her own business for one or more hours per week.
(b) who works without pay for 15 or more hours per week in a family enterprise.
(c) who has a job but has been temporarily absent, with or without pay
(d) all of the above.

Answer: (d)

Moderate
Single
Page: 157
CT Page: 592

8.7: A 25-year-old steel worker has not worked for the past two months because her union is on strike against the company. During these past two months she has not been paid. She would be classified as

(a) not in the labor force.
(b) employed.
(c) unemployed.
(d) a discouraged worker.

Answer: (b)

Moderate
Single
Page: 158
CT Page: 592

8.8: A wife spends five hours a week sending bills to her husband's customers. She is not paid for her work. She spends the rest of her time as a full-time homemaker. She would be classified as

(a) not in the labor force.
(b) employed.
(c) unemployed.
(d) a discouraged worker.

Answer: (a)

Easy
Single
Page: 157
CT Page: 592

8.9: A 21-year-old college graduate wants to work full time but is unable to find a full-time job, so she accepts a part-time job. She is classified as

(a) unemployed.
(b) employed.
(c) a discouraged worker.
(d) frictionally employed.

Answer: (b)

Easy
Definition
Page: 157
CT Page: 592

8.10: To be classified as unemployed, an individual who is sixteen years of age or older

(a) must be receiving unemployment compensation.
(b) must be available for work and must have made specific efforts to find work during the previous four weeks, but was unable to do so.
(c) must not have turned down any job offers.
(d) must be available for work and must have made specific efforts to find work every day that he or she has not had a job.

Answer: (b)

Moderate
Single
Page: 158
CT Page: 592

8.11: Joe lost his job a year ago. He would take a job if one became available, but he hasn't looked for a job for the past three months. Joe would be classified as

(a) unemployed.
(b) a member of the labor force.
(c) not in the labor force.
(d) both a and b.

Answer: (c)

8.12: The labor force is the

(a) number of people employed minus the unemployed.
(b) number of people employed plus those unemployed.
(c) ratio of those employed to those unemployed.
(d) ratio of the population to those not in the labor force.

Answer: (b)

Easy
Definition
Page: 158
CT Page: 592

8.13: A retiree is considered to be

(a) employed.
(b) unemployed.
(c) not in the labor force.
(d) a discouraged worker.

Answer: (c)

Moderate
Fact
Page: 158
CT Page: 592

8.14: A full-time student who also works full time would be classified as

(a) employed but not in the labor force because the person is also a full-time student.
(b) neither employed nor unemployed and not in the labor force because the person is a full-time student.
(c) unemployed because the person is a full-time student.
(d) employed because the person meets the conditions necessary to be counted as employed.

Answer: (d)

Moderate
Single
Page: 158
CT Page: 592

8.15: Refer to Figure 8.1. The labor force

(a) equals 5,000.
(b) equals 5,500.
(c) equals 7,500.
(d) cannot be determined from this information.

Answer: (b)

Moderate
Single
Page: 158
CT Page: 592

8.16: Refer to Figure 8.1. The unemployment rate

(a) is 9.09%.
(b) is 10%.
(c) is 11%.
(d) cannot be determined from this information.

Answer: (a)

Moderate
Multi
Page: 158
CT Page: 592

Employed	5,000
Unemployed	500
Not in the labor force	2,000

Figure 8.1

Moderate
Multi
Page: 158
CT Page: 592

8.17: Refer to Figure 8.1. The labor-force participation rate is

(a) 71.43%.
(b) 73.33%.
(c) 90.91%.
(d) 136.36%.

Answer: (b)

Moderate
Multi
Page: 158
CT Page: 592

8.18: Refer to Figure 8.1. The number of individuals 16 years of age and older

(a) equals 5,000.
(b) equals 7,000.
(c) equals 7,500.
(d) cannot be determined from this information.

Answer: (c)

Moderate
Single
Page: 158
CT Page: 592

8.19. Refer to Figure 8.2. The labor force

(a) equals 1,000.
(b) equals 2,500.
(c) equals 3,000.
(d) cannot be determined from this information.

Answer: (c)

Moderate
Multi
Page: 158
CT Page: 592

8.20. Refer to Figure 8.2. The unemployment rate

(a) is 50%.
(b) is 33.33%.
(c) is 11%.
(d) cannot be determined from this information.

Answer: (b)

Moderate
Multi
Page: 158
CT Page: 592

8.21. Refer to Figure 8.2. The labor-force participation rate is

(a) 33.33%.
(b) 66.66%.
(c) 100%.
(d) 85.71%.

Answer: (d)

Moderate
Multi
Page: 158
CT Page: 592

8.22. Refer to Figure 8.2. The number of individuals 16 years of age and older

(a) equals 2,000.
(b) equals 1,000.
(c) equals 3,500.
(d) cannot be determined from this information.

Answer: (c)

Employed	2,000
Unemployed	1,000
Not in the labor force	500

Figure 8.2

8.23: The unemployment rate is

(a) the ratio of the number of unemployed to the total number of people in the labor force.
(b) the difference between the total number of people in the labor force and the number employed.
(c) the ratio of those unemployed to those employed.
(d) the ratio of the number of people unemployed to the total number in the population.

Easy
Definition
Page: 158
CT Page: 592

Answer: (a)

8.24: The number of people classified as employed is 250,000 and the number of people classified as unemployed is 50,000. The size of the labor force

(a) equals 200,000.
(b) equals 250,000.
(c) equals 300,000.
(d) cannot be determined from this information.

Moderate
Single
Page: 158
CT Page: 592

Answer: (c)

8.25. The number of people classified as employed is 550,000 and the number of people classified as unemployed is 150,000. The size of the labor force

(a) equals 700,000.
(b) equals 550,000.
(c) equals 400,000.
(d) cannot be determined from this information.

Moderate
Single
Page: 158
CT Page: 592

Answer: (a)

8.26: If the number of people classified as unemployed is 20,000 and the number of people classified as employed is 230,000, what is the unemployment rate?

(a) 8%
(b) 8.7%
(c) 9.2%
(d) 11.5%

Moderate
Single
Page: 158
CT Page: 592

Answer: (a)

8.27. If the number of people classified as unemployed is 70,000 and the number of people classified as employed is 530,000, what is the unemployment rate?
(a) 13.2%
(b) 11.6%
(c) 10%
(d) 12%

Moderate
Single
Page: 158
CT Page: 592

Answer: (b)

8.28: If the number of people employed is 120,000 and the labor force is 150,000, the unemployment rate

(a) is 8%.
(b) is 20%.
(c) is 25%.
(d) cannot be determined from this information.

Challenging
Multi
Page: 158
CT Page: 592

Answer: (b)

Challenging
Multi
Page: 158
CT Page: 592

8.29. If the number of people employed is 200,000 and the labor force is 750,000, the unemployment rate

(a) is 8%.
(b) is 26.66%.
(c) is 73.33%.
(d) cannot be determined from this information.

Answer: (c)

Easy
Definition
Page: 158
CT Page: 592

8.30: The ratio of the labor force to the total population 16 years old or older is the

(a) discouragement rate.
(b) unemployment rate.
(c) employment rate.
(d) labor-force participation rate.

Answer: (d)

Easy
Definition
Page: 158
CT Page: 592

8.31: If the labor force is 300,000 and the total population 16 years of age or older is 400,000, the labor-force participation rate is

(a) 25%.
(b) 43%.
(c) 75%.
(d) 133%.

Answer: (c)

Easy
Definition
Page: 158
CT Page: 592

8.32 If the labor force is 900,000 and the total population 16 years of age or older is 950,000, the labor-force participation rate is

(a) 5.3%.
(b) 43%.
(c) 75%.
(d) 94.7%.

Answer: (d)

Moderate
Multi
Page: 158
CT Page: 592

8.33: If the number of unemployed equals 10,000 and the number of employed equals 40,000 and the number not in the labor force is 30,000, the labor-force participation rate

(a) is 33.33%.
(b) is 62.5%.
(c) is 75%.
(d) cannot be determined from this information.

Answer: (b)

Moderate
Multi
Page: 158
CT Page: 592

8.34 If the number of unemployed equals 100,000 and the number of employed equals 240,000 and the number not in the labor force is 50,000, the labor-force participation rate

(a) is 87.18%.
(b) is 41.67%.
(c) is 25%.
(d) cannot be determined from this information.

Answer: (a)

8.35: The highest unemployment rate is for

Easy
Fact
Page: 159
CT Page: 593

(a) white women over 45.
(b) men over 55.
(c) African-American teenagers.
(d) African-American women over 25.

Answer: (c)

8.36: An individual who is not working and who has given up looking for work is classified as

Easy
Definition
Page: 160
CT Page: 595

(a) unemployed.
(b) a discouraged worker.
(c) unemployable.
(d) hard core unemployed.

Answer: (b)

8.37: The decline in the measured unemployment rate that results when people who want to work but cannot find work stop looking for jobs and then drop out of the ranks of the unemployed and the labor force is known as

Easy
Definition
Page: 160
CT Page: 595

(a) the discouraged worker effect.
(b) the hard core unemployed effect.
(c) the long-term unemployment effect.
(d) the temporary work effect.

Answer: (a)

8.38: The unemployment rate can drop even if the total number of people with and without jobs remains constant if

Easy
Fact
Page: 160
CT Page: 595

(a) people become discouraged about finding jobs and stop looking for work.
(b) people have been unemployed for so long that they no longer qualify for unemployment compensation.
(c) the size of the total population increases.
(d) the size of the total population decreases.

Answer: (a)

8.39. In June there are 20,000 people classified as unemployed and the size of the labor force is 500,000. The only change between June and July is that 5,000 people give up looking for work. Which of the following is true?

Challenging
Multi
Page: 160
CT Page: 595

(a) In June the unemployment rate was 4% and in July the unemployment rate was 3.03%.
(b) The unemployment rate in both June and July was 4%.
(c) In June the unemployment rate was 10.8% and in July the unemployment rate was 4%.
(d) In June the unemployment rate was 3.03% and in July the unemployment rate was 5%.

Answer: (a)

Easy
Fact
Page: 160
CT Page: 595

8.40: In June there are 5,000 people classified as unemployed and the size of the labor force is 100,000. The only change between June and July is that 1,000 people give up looking for work. Which of the following is true?

(a) In June the unemployment rate was 5% and in July the unemployment rate was 4%.
(b) The unemployment rate in both June and July was 5%.
(c) In June the unemployment rate was 4.8% and in July the unemployment rate was 4%.
(d) In June the unemployment rate was 5% and in July the unemployment rate was 4.04%.

Answer: (d)

Easy
Fact
Page: 160
CT Page: 595

8.41: Classifying discouraged workers as unemployed would

(a) increase the unemployment rate.
(b) decrease the unemployment rate.
(c) not change the unemployment rate.
(d) have an indeterminate impact on the unemployment rate.

Answer: (a)

Moderate
Single
Page: 160
CT Page: 595

8.42: In normal times the number of discouraged workers is approximately _____ of the labor force.

(a) .5%.
(b) 1%.
(c) 2%.
(d) 5%.

Answer: (b)

Moderate
Single
Page: 160
CT Page: 595

8.43: Which of the following statements is TRUE?

(a) An unemployment rate of 10% means that on average people have been unemployed for 10% of the year.
(b) An unemployment rate of 10% means that the unemployment rate in each sector of the economy is 10%.
(c) It is possible for the national unemployment rate to be 10% and a state to have an unemployment rate of only 5%.
(d) Both a and c.

Answer: (c)

Moderate
Single
Page: 160
CT Page: 595

8.44. Which of the following statements is TRUE?

(a) An unemployment rate of 25% means that on average people have been unemployed for 25% of the year.
(b) It is possible for the national unemployment rate to be 5% and a state to have an unemployment rate of 10%.
(c) An unemployment rate of 34% means that the unemployment rate in each sector of the economy is 34%.
(d) All of the above.

Answer: (b)

8.45: Which of the following statements is FALSE?

(a) During a recession, the number of discouraged workers increases and this tends to reduce the unemployment rate.
(b) A low national unemployment rate does not mean that the entire nation is growing and producing at the same rate.
(c) The national unemployment rate does not tell us how the burden of unemployment is distributed across the population.
(d) If the unemployment rate is 10%, this means that on average people have been unemployed for 10% of the year.

Moderate
Single
Page: 160
CT Page: 595

Answer: (d)

8.46: It is often true that as the economy begins to recover from a recession the unemployment rate rises. Which of the following statements would be the best explanation for this?

(a) The unemployment rate would rise because as the economy initially recovers from a recession the demand for goods and services falls, so the demand for workers falls.
(b) As the economy begins to recover from a recession, workers who were previously discouraged about their chances of finding a job begin to look for work again.
(c) The unemployment rate seems to rise as the economy begins to recover from a recession because of errors in the way the data are collected.
(d) As the economy initially recovers from a recession, firms do not immediately increase the number of workers they hire. Firms wait to hire more individuals until they are convinced that the recovery is strong.

Challenging
Multi
Page: 160
CT Page: 595

Answer: (b)

8.47: During recessions, the number of discouraged workers _____ and this _____ the unemployment rate.

(a) falls; reduces
(b) falls; increases
(c) increases; increases
(d) increases; reduces

Easy
Fact
Page: 160
CT Page: 596

Answer: (d)

8.48: The Humphrey-Hawkins Act formally established a specific unemployment target for the economy of

(a) 2%.
(b) 4%.
(c) 6%.
(d) 8%.

Easy
Fact
Page: 161
CT Page: 596

Answer: (b)

8.49: The portion of unemployment that is due to the short-run job/skill matching problems is called

(a) frictional unemployment.
(b) structural unemployment.
(c) cyclical unemployment.
(d) natural unemployment.

Easy
Definition
Page: 161
CT Page: 596

Answer: (a)

Easy
Definition
Page: 161
CT Page: 596

8.50: Frictional unemployment is the

(a) portion of unemployment that is due to changes in the structure of the economy that result in a significant loss of jobs in certain industries.
(b) unemployment that occurs during recessions and depressions.
(c) portion of unemployment that is due to the normal working of the labor market.
(d) unemployment that results when people become discouraged about their chances of finding a job so they stop looking for work.

Answer: (c)

Moderate
Single
Page: 161
CT Page: 596

8.51: A woman who retired becomes bored with retirement and begins to look for a job. During the time she is searching for work she would be classified as

(a) structurally unemployed.
(b) cyclically unemployed.
(c) frictionally unemployed.
(d) not in the labor force because she was not working before she started looking for a job.

Answer: (c)

Moderate
Single
Page: 161
CT Page: 596

8.52: A man is fired from his job because he was late for work too many times. While he is searching for another job he would be classified as

(a) not in the labor force because his employer had a legitimate reason for firing him.
(b) structurally unemployed.
(c) cyclically unemployed.
(d) frictionally unemployed.

Answer: (d)

Moderate
Single
Page: 161
CT Page: 596

8.53: A man who quits his job to search for a job that takes full advantage of his educational background represents an example of

(a) frictional unemployment.
(b) structural unemployment.
(c) cyclical unemployment.
(d) seasonal unemployment.

Answer: (a)

Easy
Definition
Page: 1621
CT Page: 597

8.54: The portion of unemployment that is due to changes in the shifts in the economy that result in a significant loss of jobs in certain industries is called

(a) frictional unemployment.
(b) structural unemployment.
(c) cyclical unemployment.
(d) natural unemployment.

Answer: (b)

Easy
Definition
Page: 162
CT Page: 597

8.55: Structural unemployment is the

(a) portion of unemployment that is due to changes in the structure of the economy that result in a significant loss of jobs in certain industries.
(b) unemployment that occurs during recessions and depressions.
(c) portion of unemployment that is due to the normal working of the labor market.
(d) unemployment that results when people become discouraged about their chances of finding a job so they stop looking for work.

Answer: (a)

8.56: An auto worker in Ohio who loses her job because the company relocated the plant represents an example of

(a) frictional unemployment.
(b) structural unemployment.
(c) cyclical unemployment.
(d) natural unemployment.

Moderate
Single
Page: 162
CT Page: 597

Answer: (b)

8.57: A textile firm closes a plant in Massachusetts and transfers production to a plant in South Carolina. The plant supervisor at the Massachusetts plant is given the opportunity to move to South Carolina as the plant supervisor at that plant. He turns down this opportunity because of family obligations. While he is searching for a new job he would be classified as

(a) structurally unemployed.
(b) cyclically unemployed.
(c) frictionally unemployed.
(d) not in the labor force because he turned down the opportunity to relocate.

Moderate
Single
Page: 162
CT Page: 597

Answer: (a)

8.58: An individual who cannot find a job because his or her job skills have become obsolete is an example of

(a) frictional unemployment.
(b) structural unemployment.
(c) cyclical unemployment.
(d) seasonal unemployment.

Easy
Fact
Page: 162
CT Page: 597

Answer: (b)

8.59: An individual worked for an airline that went out of business because the airline was unable to meet new federal safety standards. While the individual is unemployed, she will be classified as

(a) frictionally unemployed.
(b) naturally unemployed.
(c) cyclically unemployed.
(d) structurally unemployed.

Moderate
Single
Page: 162
CT Page: 597

Answer: (d)

8.60: The natural rate of unemployment is generally thought of as the

(a) ratio of the frictional unemployment rate to the cyclical unemployment rate.
(b) sum of structural unemployment and cyclical unemployment.
(c) sum of frictional unemployment and cyclical unemployment.
(d) sum of frictional unemployment and structural unemployment.

Easy
Definition
Page: 163
CT Page: 597

Answer: (d)

8.61: The sum of frictional and structural unemployment is thought of as the

(a) natural rate of unemployment.
(b) normal rate of unemployment.
(c) cyclical rate of unemployment.
(d) seasonal rate of unemployment.

Easy
Definition
Page: 163
CT Page: 597

Answer: (a)

Easy
Fact
Page: 163
CT Page: 597

8.62: Estimates for the natural rate of unemployment range from

(a) 2% to 4%.
(b) 4% to 5%.
(c) 4% to 7%.
(d) 5% to 8%.

Answer: (c)

Challenging
Multi
Page: 163
CT Page: 597

8.63: If the labor market becomes more efficient so that the unemployed are more quickly matched with jobs, this will

(a) increase the natural rate of unemployment.
(b) decrease the natural rate of unemployment.
(c) not affect the natural rate of unemployment.
(d) could either increase or decrease the natural rate of unemployment.

Answer: (b)

Challenging
Multi
Page: 163
CT Page: 597

8.64: During the early 1990s, companies started downsizing. One of the results of this downsizing was the permanent reduction in the number of middle management positions. This change in the way businesses operate would have

(a) increased the natural rate of unemployment.
(b) decreased the natural rate of unemployment.
(c) not affected the natural rate of unemployment.
(d) could have either increased or decreased the natural rate of unemployment.

Answer: (a)

Easy
Definition
Page: 163
CT Page: 597

8.65: The increase in unemployment that occurs during recessions and depressions is called

(a) frictional unemployment.
(b) structural unemployment.
(c) cyclical unemployment.
(d) normal unemployment.

Answer: (c)

Easy
Definition
Page: 163
CT Page: 597

8.66: Cyclical unemployment is the

(a) portion of unemployment that is due to changes in the structure of the economy that result in a significant loss of jobs in certain industries.
(b) unemployment that occurs during recessions and depressions.
(c) portion of unemployment that is due to the normal working of the labor market.
(d) unemployment that results when people become discouraged about their chances of finding a job so they stop looking for work.

Answer: (b)

Moderate
Single
Page: 1631
CT Page: 597

8.67: The demand for refrigerators falls when the economy enters a downturn. If a refrigerator manufacturer lays off workers during an economic downturn, this would be an example of

(a) frictional unemployment.
(b) natural unemployment.
(c) structural unemployment.
(d) cyclical unemployment.

Answer: (d)

8.68: The economy is in a recession and the housing market is in a slump. As a result of this, a real estate firm lays off half of its real estate agents. This is an example of

(a) frictional unemployment.
(b) structural unemployment.
(c) cyclical unemployment.
(d) natural unemployment.

Moderate
Single
Page: 163
CT Page: 597

Answer: (c)

8.69: During the severe recession of the early 1980s, cyclical unemployment increased as the recession continued. This increase in cyclical unemployment would have

(a) increased the natural rate of unemployment.
(b) decreased the natural rate of unemployment.
(c) had no effect on the natural of unemployment.
(d) either increased or decreased the natural rate of unemployment.

Challenging
Multi
Page: 163
CT Page: 597

Answer: (c)

8.70: During the Great Depression, real output fell by approximately

(a) 15%.
(b) 25%.
(c) 30%.
(d) 50%.

Easy
Fact
Page: 163
CT Page: 597

Answer: (c)

8.71: Recessions today may cause lost output in the future because during a recession

(a) consumption tends to fall.
(b) investment tends to fall.
(c) imports tend to fall.
(d) government spending tends to increase.

Easy
Fact
Page: 163
CT Page: 598

Answer: (b)

8.72: Which of the following is NOT a cost associated with recessions and unemployment?

(a) decreased real output
(b) the psychological harm done to the unemployed
(c) lost output in the future
(d) worsening of the nation's balance of payments

Moderate
Fact
Page: 163
CT Page: 598

Answer: (d)

8.73: Recessions tend to

(a) have no effect on the rate of inflation.
(b) increase the rate of inflation.
(c) slow down the rate of inflation.
(d) cause negative inflation rates.

Easy
Fact
Page: 163
CT Page: 599

Answer: (c)

Moderate
Fact
Page: 163
CT Page: 599

8.74: Which of the following statements is TRUE?

(a) The costs of recessions are distributed equally among all groups of the population.
(b) Recessions tend to increase the demand for imports and therefore improve the nation's balance of payments.
(c) Recessions may increase efficiency by driving the least efficient firms in the economy out of business.
(d) A recession may lead to an increase in the inflation rate.

Answer: (c)

Moderate
Fact
Page: 163
CT Page: 599

8.75: A recession tends to _____ the demand for imports, which _____ a nation's balance of payments.

(a) reduce; worsens
(b) reduce; improves
(c) increase; improves
(d) increase; worsens

Answer: (b)

Moderate
Single
Page: 165
CT Page: 599

8.76: The floods of 1993 caused the price of corn to increase. This is an example of

(a) inflation.
(b) deflation.
(c) a sustained inflation.
(d) the operations of supply and demand.

Answer: (d)

Moderate
Single
Page: 165
CT Page: 601

8.77: The decrease in the demand for mainframe computers caused manufacturers of mainframe computers to reduce prices by 20%. This is an example of

(a) inflation.
(b) deflation.
(c) a sustained inflation.
(d) the operations of supply and demand.

Answer: (d)

Easy
Definition
Page: 165
CT Page: 599

8.78: Inflation is an increase in

(a) the price of one item.
(b) the overall price level.
(c) the average income level.
(d) real gross national product.

Answer: (b)

Easy
Definition
Page: 165
CT Page: 599

8.79: An increase in the overall price level is

(a) inflation.
(b) deflation.
(c) a price index.
(d) a recession.

Answer: (a)

8.80: Deflation is a decrease in

(a) the price of one item.
(b) the overall price level.
(c) the average income level.
(d) real gross national product.

Answer: (b)

Challenging
Multi
Page: 165
CT Page: 601

8.81: An increase in the overall price level that continues over a significant period of time is a

(a) continuous inflation.
(b) sustained recovery.
(c) sustained inflation.
(d) super inflation.

Answer: (c)

Challenging
Multi
Page: 165
CT Page: 602

8.82: A price index is

(a) a measurement showing how the average price of a bundle of goods changes over time.
(b) a measurement showing the cost of a bundle of goods at a point in time.
(c) a sustained increase in the overall price level.
(d) a decrease in the overall price level.

Answer: (a)

Easy
Fact
Page: 165
CT Page: 602

8.83: Refer to Figure 8.3. The bundle price for the goods in period 1 is

(a) $20.
(b) $31.
(c) $62.
(d) $90.

Answer: (b)

Moderate
Single
Page: 165
CT Page: 602

8.84: Refer to Figure 8.3. If period 2 is the base period, the period 2 price index is

(a) 1.
(b) 41.
(c) 100.
(d) 132.26.

Answer: (c)

Moderate
Single
Page: 165
CT Page: 602

	Units consumed	Price Period 1	Price Period 2	Price Period 3
Good A	4	$1.00	$1.50	$2.00
Good B	10	$1.50	$2.00	$2.00
Good C	6	$2.00	$2.50	$3.00

Figure 8.3

Easy
Fact
Page: 166
CT Page: 603

8.85: Refer to Figure 8.3. If period 2 is the base period, the period 1 price index is

(a) 24.40.
(b) 32.26.
(c) 75.61.
(d) 132.26.

Answer: (c)

8.86: Refer to Figure 8.3 If period 2 is the base period, the period 3 price index is

(a) 10.9.
(b) 12.2.
(c) 89.13.
(d) 112.2.

Easy
Fact
Page: 165
CT Page: 603

Answer: (d)

8.87: Refer to Figure 8.3. If period 2 is the base period, the inflation rate between period 2 and period 3 is

(a) 1.12%.
(b) 8.9%.
(c) 12.2%.
(d) 112.2%.

Easy
Fact
Page: 165
CT Page: 603

Answer: (c)

8.88: Refer to Figure 8.3. If period 1 is the base period, the inflation rate between period 1 and period 3 is

(a) 16.13.
(b) 48.39.
(c) 67.39.
(d) 148.39.

Challenging
Multi
Page: 166
CT Page: 604

Answer: (b)

8.89: Refer to Figure 8.3. If period 1 is the base period, the inflation rate between period 2 and period 3 is approximately

(a) 10.88.
(b) 12.2.
(c) 16.14.
(d) 39.37.

Easy
Definition
Page: 168
CT Page: 606

Answer: (b)

8.90. Refer to Figure 8.4. The bundle price for the goods in period 1 is

(a) $100.
(b) $6.
(c) $34.
(d) $20.

Moderate
Single
Page: 168
CT Page: 606

Answer: (c)

	Units consumed	Price Period 1	Price Period 2	Price Period 3
Good A	6	$2.00	$3.50	$5.00
Good B	10	$1.00	$2.00	$3.00
Good C	4	$3.00	$3.50	$4.00

Figure 8.4

8.91 Refer to Figure 8.4. If period 2 is the base period, the period 2 price index is

(a) 34.
(b) 1.
(c) 100.
(d) 55.

Moderate
Single
Page: 168
CT Page: 606

Answer: (c)

8.92 Refer to Figure 8.4. If period 2 is the base period, the period 1 price index is

(a) 55.
(b) 61.81.
(c) 75.61.
(d) 34.

Easy
Fact
Page: 168
CT Page: 606

Answer: (b)

8.93 Refer to Figure 8.4. If period 2 is the base period, the period 3 price index is

(a) 76.
(b) 34.
(c) 138.18.
(d) 1.38.

Moderate
Fact
Page: 168
CT Page: 606

Answer: (c)

8.94. Refer to Figure 8.4. If period 2 is the base period, the inflation rate between period 2 and period 3 is

(a) 38.18%.
(b) 8.9%.
(c) 17.2%.
(d) 112.2%.

Moderate
Fact
Page: 168
CT Page: 607

Answer: (a)

8.95. Refer to Figure 8.4. If period 1 is the base period, the inflation rate between period 1 and period 3 is

(a) 16.13%.
(b) 223.53%.
(c) 167.39%.
(d) 348.39%.

Moderate
Single
Page: 168
CT Page: 607

Answer: (b)

8.96 Refer to Figure 8.4. If period 1 is the base period, the inflation rate between period 2 and period 3 is approximately

(a) 223%.
(b) 17%.
(c) 16%.
(d) 38%.

Moderate
Single
Page: 169
CT Page: 607

Answer: (d)

Moderate
Single
Page: 168
CT Page: 607

8.97: If period 1 is the base year and the bundle price of goods in period 1 is $150 and the bundle price of goods in period 2 is $225, the period 2 price index is

(a) 33.33.
(b) 50.
(c) 66.67.
(d) 150.

Answer: (d)

Moderate
Single
Page: 168
CT Page: 607

8.98 If 1997 is the base year and the bundle price of goods in 1997 is $500 and the bundle price of goods in 1998 is $775, the 1998 price index is

(a) 100.
(b) 155.
(c) 66.67.
(d) Cannot be determined from this information because the price year is not known.

Answer: (b)

Challenging
Multi
Page: 165
CT Page: 601

8.99: If the price index in period 3 is 125 and the price index in period 4 is 140, the rate of inflation between period 3 and period 4

(a) is 10.7%.
(b) is 12%.
(c) is 15%.
(d) cannot be determined from this information because the base year is not known.

Answer: (b)

Challenging
Multi
Page: 165
CT Page: 601

8.100. If the price index in 1999 is 195 and the price index in 2000 is 250, the rate of inflation between 1999 and 2000

(a) is 100%.
(b) is 55%.
(c) is 28.2%.
(d) None of the above.

Answer: (c)

Challenging
Multi
Page: 165
CT Page: 602

8.101: If the price index in period 3 is 125 and the price index in period 4 is 120, the rate of inflation between period 3 and period 4

(a) is -4%.
(b) is 4%.
(c) is 4.17%.
(d) cannot be determined from this information because the base year is not known.

Answer: (a)

Challenging
Multi
Page: 165
CT Page: 602

8.102. If the price index in 1998 is 115 and the price index in 1999 is 105, the rate of inflation between 1998 and 1999

(a) is 7%.
(b) is -8.6%.
(c) is 4.17%.
(d) cannot be determined from this information because the base year is not known.

Answer: (b)

8.103: The index used most often to measure inflation is the

(a) producer price index.
(b) GDP deflator.
(c) wholesale price index.
(d) consumer price index.

Answer: (d)

Easy
Fact
Page: 165
CT Page: 602

8.104: The CPI in 1991 was 136.2 and the CPI in 1992 was 140.1. The rate of inflation between 1991 and 1992

(a) was approximately 2.7%.
(b) was approximately 2.9%.
(c) was approximately 3.9%.
(d) cannot be determined from this information because the base year is unknown.

Answer: (b)

Moderate
Single
Page: 165
CT Page: 602

8.105 The CPI in 1994 was 125 and the CPI in 1995 was 140. The rate of inflation between 1994 and 1995

(a) was approximately 12%.
(b) was approximately 24.9%.
(c) was approximately 15%.
(d) cannot be determined from this information because the base year is unknown.

Answer: (a)

Moderate
Single
Page: 165
CT Page: 602

8.106: The CPI in period 1 is 150 and the CPI in period 2 is 200. The rate of inflation between period 1 and period 2 is

(a) 14.28%.
(b) 25%.
(c) 33.33%.
(d) 50%.

Answer: (c)

Moderate
Single
Page: 165
CT Page: 602

8.107. The CPI in period 1 is 250 and the CPI in period 2 is 100. The rate of inflation between period 1 and period 2 is

(a) 14.28%.
(b) -150%.
(c) 33.33%.
(d) -60%.

Answer: (d)

Moderate
Single
Page: 165
CT Page: 602

8.108: Which of the following statements is FALSE?

(a) One problem with any fixed-bundle index as a measure of the cost of living is that it does not account for substitutions that consumers might make in response to price changes.
(b) The Producer Price Index is considered to be a leading indicator of future inflation rates.
(c) The best overall indicator of inflationary pressures in the economy is the GNP deflator.
(d) The Consumer Price Index somewhat understates changes in the cost of living.

Answer: (d)

Moderate
Fact
Page: 165
CT Page: 603

Easy
Fact
Page: 165
CT Page: 603

8.109: An inflation rate that tends to be a leading indicator of future inflation rates is the

(a) Consumer Price Index.
(b) Producer Price Index.
(c) GDP deflator.
(d) Retail Price Index.

Answer: (b)

Easy
Fact
Page: 165
CT Page: 603

8.110: The broadest-based price index available is the

(a) Consumer Price Index.
(b) Producer Price Index.
(c) GDP deflator.
(d) Wholesale Price Index.

Answer: (c)

Easy
Fact
Page: 165
CT Page: 603

8.111: Most economists consider the best overall indicator of inflationary pressures in the economy to be the

(a) Consumer Price Index.
(b) Producer Price Index.
(c) Wholesale Price Index.
(d) GDP deflator.

Answer: (d)

Challenging
Multi
Page: 166
CT Page: 604

8.112: Which of the following statements is FALSE?

(a) An individual living on a fixed income is always made worse off as a result of inflation.
(b) Those individuals receiving welfare benefits have been harmed by inflation because increases in welfare payments have not kept pace with inflation.
(c) Inflation will have no effect on an individual whose income is indexed to the inflation rate.
(d) Some people in society benefit from inflation.

Answer: (c)

Easy
Definition
Page: 168
CT Page: 606

8.113: The difference between the interest rate on a loan and the inflation rate is the

(a) nominal interest rate.
(b) inflation premium.
(c) real interest rate.
(d) expected interest rate.

Answer: (c)

Moderate
Single
Page: 168
CT Page: 606

8.114: If you are paid an interest rate of 10% on your savings, but the inflation rate is 7%, the real interest rate is

(a) -3%.
(b) .7%.
(c) 3%.
(d) 4.3%.

Answer: (c)

8.115. If A. Jackson is paid an interest rate of 20% on his savings, but the inflation rate is 10%, the real interest rate is

(a) 10%.
(b) -20%.
(c) -10%.
(d) 20%.

Answer: (a)

Moderate
Single
Page: 168
CT Page: 606

8.116: You want to make a 4% real return on a loan that you are planning to make, and the expected inflation rate during the period of the loan is 5%. You should charge an interest rate of

(a) 1%.
(b) 4.5%.
(c) 5%.
(d) 9%.

Answer: (d)

Moderate
Single
Page: 168
CT Page: 606

8.117. Bridget wants to make a 8% real return on a loan that she is planning to make, and the expected inflation rate during the period of the loan is 10%. She should charge an interest rate of

(a) 8%.
(b) 18%.
(c) 5%.
(d) -2%.

Answer: (b)

Moderate
Single
Page: 168
CT Page: 606

8.118: If the inflation rate is greater than the interest rate, the real interest rate is

(a) positive.
(b) negative.
(c) zero.
(d) either positive or zero.

Answer: (b)

Easy
Fact
Page: 168
CT Page: 606

8.119: An unanticipated inflation will

(a) hurt debtors.
(b) hurt creditors.
(c) hurt debtors and creditors equally.
(d) have no effect on either creditors or debtors.

Answer: (b)

Moderate
Fact
Page: 168
CT Page: 606

8.120: An unanticipated inflation will

(a) make debtors better off.
(b) make creditors better off.
(c) make both debtors and creditors better off.
(d) have no effect on either creditors or debtors.

Answer: (a)

Moderate
Fact
Page: 168
CT Page: 607

Moderate
Single
Page: 168
CT Page: 607

8.121: Which of the following is a cost of anticipated inflation?

(a) Debtors are made worse off.
(b) Creditors are made worse off.
(c) The degree of risk associated with investments in the economy increases.
(d) If people are not fully informed about the price level changes, resources will be misallocated.

Answer: (d)

Moderate
Single
Page: 169
CT Page: 607

8.122: Stopping inflation

(a) can only benefit the economy, because the price level will be reduced.
(b) may be costly, if the inflation is stopped by inducing a recession.
(c) may be costly, but the benefits of stopping inflation will always outweigh the costs of such actions.
(d) will have no benefits or costs associated with it.

Answer: (b)

Moderate
Single
Page: 168
CT Page: 607

8.123: Which of the following statements is FALSE?

(a) Whether you gain or lose during a period of inflation depends on whether your income rises faster or slower than the prices of the things you buy.
(b) Inflation that is higher than expected benefits debtors, and inflation that is lower than expected benefits creditors.
(c) There are no costs or losses associated with anticipated inflation.
(d) When unanticipated inflation occurs regularly, the degree of risk associated with investments in the economy increases.

Answer: (c)

Easy
Fact
Page: 168
CT Page: 607

8.124: When unanticipated inflation occurs regularly, the degree of risk associated with investments in the economy

(a) increases.
(b) decreases.
(c) remains stable.
(d) falls to zero.

Answer: (a)

Moderate
Fact
Page: 169
CT Page: 607

8.125: Which of the following is TRUE?

(a) A recession will lead to reduced output in the future, but inflation has no effect on future output.
(b) Both recessions and inflations may reduce output in the future.
(c) A recession will lead to reduced output in the future, but inflation will lead to increased output in the future.
(d) A recession will lead to increased output in the future, but inflation will lead to decreased output in the future.

Answer: (b)

TRUE/FALSE QUESTIONS

8.126: The unemployment rate will fall if there is an increase in the number of discouraged workers.

Answer: True

Moderate
Definition
Page: 160
CT Page: 595

8.127: The labor force is comprised of the employed plus the unemployed plus discouraged workers.

Answer: False

Easy
Definition
Page: 158
CT Page: 595

8.128: An increase in search costs will decrease frictional unemployment.

Answer: True

Moderate
Definition
Page: 161
CT Page: 596

8.129: The natural rate of unemployment is the unemployment rate during a period of full employment.

Answer: True

Easy
Definition
Page: 163
CT Page: 597

8.130: Anyone 16 years of age or older who is not classified as employed is classified as unemployed.

Answer: False

Easy
Fact
Page: 157
CT Page: 592

8.131: If discouraged workers were counted as unemployed, the measured unemployment rate would increase.

Answer: True

Easy
Single
Page: 160
CT Page: 596

8.132: The unemployment rate is 10%, this means that the average worker has been unemployed for 10% of the year.

Answer: False

Easy
Single
Page: 160
CT Page: 596

8.133: If labor markets were perfectly efficient, the unemployment rate would fall to zero.

Answer: False

Easy
Single
Page: 161
CT Page: 596

8.134: Some unemployment is beneficial to the economy.

Answer: True

Easy
Single
Page: 161
CT Page: 596

8.135: The natural rate of unemployment is generally taken to be the sum of frictional and cyclical unemployment.

Answer: False

Easy
Fact
Page: 163
CT Page: 597

Easy
Fact
Page: 165
CT Page: 603

8.136: The CPI somewhat overstates changes in the cost of living because it does not allow for substitutions that consumers might make in response to price changes.

Answer: True

Easy
Fact
Page: 165
CT Page: 603

8.137: The Consumer Price Index is a fixed-bundle price index, but the GNP deflator is not.

Answer: True

Easy
Fact
Page: 168
CT Page: 607

8.138: An inflation that is lower than expected benefits creditors.

Answer: True

Easy
Fact
Page: 168
CT Page: 607

8.139: There are no costs associated with inflation if the inflation rate is perfectly anticipated.

Answer: False

SHORT ANSWER QUESTIONS

SCENARIO 1: The population of the nation of Arboc is 3,700,000, of which 1,600,000 are age 16 or older. Of this 1,600,000, 1,184,000 have jobs and 416,000 do not. There are 296,000 unemployed but actively seeking jobs, and there are 120,000 who have given up the job search in frustration.

Easy
Math
Page: 168
CT Page: 592

8.140: Refer to Scenario 1. Answer parts a through e using the information in scenario 1.

(a). Calculate the number of unemployed workers.
(b). Calculate the number of discouraged workers.
(c). Calculate the number of workers in the labor force.
(d). Calculate the unemployment rate.
(e). Calculate the labor-force participation rate.

Answer: (a). There are 296,000 unemployed workers.
(b). There are 120,000 discouraged workers.
(c). There are 1,480,000 workers in the labor force.
(d). Unemployment rate = unemployed/labor force = 296,000/1,480,000 = 20%.
(e). Labor-force participation rate = labor force/population = 1,480,000/3,700,000 = 40%.

SCENARIO 2: The nation of Arbez has a population of 2 million citizens. The labor-force participation rate is 70%. The number of Arbezanis with jobs is 1,246,000.

Moderate
Math
Page: 158
CT Page: 592

8.141: Refer to Scenario 2. Answer parts a through e using the information in scenario 2.

(a). Calculate the number in the labor force.
(b). Calculate the number of unemployed workers.

(c). Calculate the unemployment rate.

(d). Arbez has determined that the natural rate of unemployment is 6%. How many cyclically unemployed workers are there?

(e). The Arbezani economy moves out of a long recession, job openings increase, and 100,000 discouraged workers become "encouraged" and begin searching for a job. Calculate the new unemployment rate.

Answer: (a). Labor force = participation rate x population = .7 x 2,000,000 = 1,400,000.

(b). Unemployed = labor force - employed = 1,400,000 - 1,246,000 = 154,000.

(c). The unemployment rate = unemployed/labor force = 154,000/1,400,000 = 11%.

d). 70,000 or 5% of the labor force is cyclically unemployed.

(e). Initial unemployment rate = unemployed/labor force = 154,000/1,400,000 = .11 or 11%. When 100,000 new (unemployed) workers enter the labor force, the new unemployment rate = 254,000/1,500,000 = .1693 or 16.93%.

8.142: You are an employee of the Bureau of Labor Statistics involved in the monthly survey of households used to estimate the unemployment rate. In each of the following cases, classify the individual as employed, unemployed, or not in the labor force. Explain your classification.

Easy
Application
Page: 157
CT Page: 592

(a). During the entire week containing the twelfth of the month, Rosie the Riveter misses work simply because she didn't feel like going in to work.

(b). Jenny Wren is a volunteer 20 hours a week on a Rape Crisis telephone hotline. She feels she makes an important contribution to society and would not accept a paid job if one were offered to her.

(c). Cauley McCulkin is a hugely successful film star, age 12, who has earned over $5,000,000 each year for the past five years. Currently, Cauley is filming a new movie on location in Tenerife.

(d). Maxwell Edison, a full-time Ph.D. student, is involved in ground-breaking research in fiber optics. His dissertation advisor has already claimed that Maxwell's work will revolutionize telecommunications.

(e). Maggie Madd, 84, works 10 hours a week doing cleaning services for her son, Norman Neurotic. He pays her minimum wage.

Answer: (a). Rosie is employed. If Rosie is temporarily absent, with or without pay, she is considered employed.

(b). Jenny is not in the labor force. She is not seeking a job nor does she meet the criteria required to be classified as employed.

(c). Cauley is not in the labor force. He is less than 16 years old.

(d). Maxwell is not in the labor force. He is a full-time student.

(e). Maggie is paid and employed.

8.143: During a press conference, the Secretary of Employment notes that the unemployment rate is 7.0%. As a political opponent, how might you criticize this figure as an underestimate? In rebuttal, how might the Secretary argue that the reported rate is an overestimate of unemployment?

Difficult
Application
Page: 160
CT Page: 595

Answer: The unemployment rate given by the Secretary might be considered an underestimate because discouraged workers, who have given up the job search in frustration, are not counted as unemployed. In addition, full-time workers may have been forced to work part-time. In rebuttal, the Secretary might note that a portion of the unemployed have voluntarily left their jobs. Most workers are unemployed only briefly and leave the ranks of the unemployed by gaining better jobs than they had previously held.

Easy
Definition
Page: 157
CT Page: 597

8.144: You are an employee of the Bureau of Labor Statistics involved in the monthly survey of households used to estimate the unemployment rate. In each of the following cases, classify the individual as frictionally, structurally, or cyclically unemployed. Explain your classification.

(a). There has been a general economic slow down. Because of weak demand, Andy Capp has lost his portering job at the docks.
(b). Phil McCafferty, a newly-qualified dental school graduate, is looking for a place to set up practice.
(c). Coal miner Ned Ludd is thrown out of work by the introduction of a more mechanized production process.
(d). Latosha Hogan, a computer programmer with a large bank, quit her job two months ago in search of a better-paid programming position. She is still looking.

Answer: (a). Andy is cyclically unemployed. He has lost his job as a result of the general economic recession.
(b). Phil is frictionally unemployed. Job openings exist for him. It is merely a case of tracking down a position.
(c). Ned is structurally unemployed. Unemployment due to technological change in an industry is classified as structural.
(d). Latosha is frictionally unemployed. Job openings exist for her.

Moderate
Math
Page: 158
CT Page: 592

8.145: Answer parts a through e below using the following information.

Arboc has a population of 2,000,000. The labor-force participation rate is 90%. Assume that the citizens of Arboc, when trying to determine the inflation rate for the next twelve months, base their calculations solely on the current inflation rate. The following table provides information on the Consumer Price Index (CPI) and unemployment rate for Arboc over a five-year period.

Year	CPI	Unemployment Rate
1993	100.00	4.2%
1994	100.00	4.2
1995	110.00	6.7
1996	115.50	9.8
1997	117.81	12.3

(a). Based on the information above, calculate the number of workers in the labor force.
(b). Based on the information above, calculate the number of workers unemployed in 1994.
(c). Based on the information above, calculate the number of workers employed in 1996.
(d). Based on the information above, calculate the inflation rate for 1994, 1995, 1996, and 1997.
(e). In 1995, the market interest rate was 12%. Based on the information above, calculate the real interest rate.

Answer: (a). Labor force = population x participation rate = 2,000,000 x .9 = 1,800,000.

(b). Unemployed = labor force x unemployment rate = 1,800,000 x .042 = 75,600.

(c). Workers employed in 1996 = 1,800,000 x .902 = 1,623,600.

(d). The inflation rate = (change in CPI/initial CPI) x 100.
        1994-0%; 1995-10%; 1996-5%; 1997-2%.

(e). The market interest rate is based on the real interest rate plus the expected inflation rate. In 1995, the market interest rate was 12% and the expected inflation rate was 10%. The real interest rate was 2%.

8.146: Lenders and borrowers expect the inflation rate to equal the actual inflation rate. The consumer price index is 110 in Year 1 and 126.5 in Year 2. If the interest rate charged by Richie Rich in Year 2 is 40%, what is Rich's real interest rate?

Difficult
Application
Page: 168
CT Page: 605

Answer: Rich's real interest rate is 25%. The inflation rate in Year 2 is (change in CPI/initial CPI) x 100, or 15%. The real interest rate (25%) is the difference between the market interest rate (40%) and the expected inflation rate (15%).

8.147: How do the costs of unemployment differ in an economy with a large underground sector relative to one with a small underground sector?

Moderate
Application
Page: 161
CT Page: 597

Answer: The costs will be less in an economy with a large underground sector and output will be higher than officially recorded. Social costs such as low self-esteem, suicide, divorce rates, and so on will also be lower.

8.148: "If inflation is fully anticipated by all parties, the redistributional effects would be minimal. It's the fact that inflation surprises us that causes there to be winners and losers." Comment. Which costs still occur even with fully anticipated inflation?

Moderate
Application
Page: 168
CT Page: 606

Answer: It is true that unanticipated inflation can cause income redistribution. Individuals on fixed incomes may suffer greatly, for example, while workers in powerful unions may thrive. However, some costs are borne by society in general, even when inflation is fully anticipated. Administrative costs, hoarding of real goods, additional search costs, and so on reduce the welfare of society in general.

8.149: For each of the following, indicate if the person would be classified as employed, unemployed, or not in the labor force: (a) a 70-year-old man who left his job to help his daughter in her business for 10 hours a week; (b) a 20-year-old college student who is out of school for the summer and is looking for a job; (c) a 30-year-old woman with a Ph.D. in history who has not been able to find a teaching position and is driving a cab 30 hours a week; and (d) a 40-year-old steel worker who isn't working and has given up searching for a job.

Moderate
Single
Page: 157
CT Page: 592

Answer: These individuals would be classified: (a) not in the labor force, (b) unemployed, (c) employed, and (d) not in the labor force.

8.150: If the national unemployment rate is 7%, does every region in the country have a 7% unemployment rate? Explain.

Easy
Fact
Page: 159
CT Page: 593

Answer: No. Different regions of the country could have unemployment rates either above or below 7%, depending upon which sectors of the economy have been hardest hit by unemployment.

8.151: Explain why some economists argue that counting discouraged workers as unemployed gives a better picture of the unemployment situation. How would the magnitude of the unemployment rate change if discouraged workers were counted as unemployed?

Moderate
Single
Page: 160
CT Page: 595

Answer: Some argue that discouraged workers should be included because they would take jobs if a job became available. If discouraged workers were included, the unemployment rate would increase.

8.152: Explain why some unemployment is inevitable. How can unemployment actually benefit the economy?

Easy
Single
Page: 161
CT Page: 596

Answer: Some unemployment is inevitable because people switch jobs or need to search for a job after finishing school. The structure of the economy is always changing, so some people will find that their skills have become outdated and they no longer can find employment. Unemployment may benefit the economy if it leads to a better match between employee and employer.

Challenging
Multi
Page: 161
CT Page: 597

8.153: Explain the three different types of unemployment. Give an example of each type. Given what you have learned about the different types of unemployment, suggest three policies that could be used to reduce unemployment, one for each type of unemployment.

Answer: The three different types of unemployment are: frictional, structural, and cyclical. Frictional unemployment results from the normal workings of the labor market. An example of frictional unemployment is an individual looking for his or her first job after graduating from college. Structural unemployment is due to changes in the economy. An example of structural unemployment is a steel worker in Pittsburgh that lost his job because the steel plant he worked at shut down. Cyclical unemployment is the unemployment that occurs during recessions and depressions. An example of cyclical unemployment is a construction worker who loses his job because the demand for new office buildings has fallen. A policy that may reduce frictional unemployment is increasing the efficiency of the labor market by having information networks that provide information on jobs all across the country so the unemployed can more easily find jobs. Structural unemployment may be reduced through job relocation assistance or job retraining. Cyclical unemployment could be reduced through expansionary monetary and fiscal policies.

Easy
Fact
Page: 161
CT Page: 598

8.154: Explain the costs of unemployment. Be sure to include both the economic and noneconomic costs.

Answer: The costs of unemployment include the value of the output lost in the current time period and the value of the output lost in the future because unemployment leads to less investment. Unemployment also has social costs such, including increase in the crime rate, the divorce rate, and the suicide rate.

Easy
Fact
Page: 164
CT Page: 599

8.155: Explain the possible benefits of recessions.

Answer: Recessions will probably bring down the inflation rate. Recessions may also increase efficiency by forcing inefficient firms out of business. Recessions may also lead to an improvement in a nation's balance of payments

Challenging
Multi
Page: 165
CT Page: 602

8.156: The inflation rate measured by changes in the Consumer Price Index is 5%. Does this mean that every individual's cost of living has increased by 5%? Explain.

Answer: No. Everyone will not experience a 5% increase in the cost of living. It depends on the combination of goods and services consumers buy. If consumers spend a high percentage of their income on goods and services that have increased in price, then their cost of living may have risen by 5% or more. If consumers are able to substitute toward less expensive goods or if they don't purchase goods whose prices increased, then their cost of living would increase by less than 5%.

Challenging
Multi
Page: 165
CT Page: 602

8.157: If year 1 is the base year and the price index for year 2 is 105 and the price index for year 3 is 103, what is the inflation rate in years 2 and 3? Explain what has happened between years 1 and 2, years 2 and 3, and years 1 and 3 to the cost of living.

Answer: The inflation rate in year 2 is 5%. The inflation rate in year 3 is -1.9%. The cost of living increased between years 1 and 2 and years 1 and 3, but decreased between years 2 and 3.

8.158: Explain the costs associated with unanticipated inflation and the costs associated with anticipated inflation.

Easy
Fact
Page: 168
CT Page: 607

Answer: The costs associated with unanticipated inflation are: people's real income will fall if their income rises more slowly than the inflation rate; creditors are harmed, and the risk of investment rises. The costs of anticipated inflations are: the administrative costs associated with keeping up with the increasing inflation rates, the costs of additional financial transactions, and the misallocation of resources that may result if people are not fully informed about price changes.

9 Aggregate Expenditure and Equlibrium Output

(Chapter 24 in Combined Text)

9.1: Income increased by $100 which resulted in an increase of $75 in consumption spending. What is the MPC?

(a) .25.
(b) .75
(c) 4.
(d) 1.33.

Answer: (b)

Moderate
Math
Page: 180
CT Page: 619

9.2: Assume that the MPC is .9 and the consumption spending increased by $180. Calculate the amount by which income increased.

(a) $162.
(b) $800.
(c) $200
(d) $180

Answer: (c)

Difficult
Math
Page: 180
CT Page: 619

9.3: As income increased by $100, savings increased by $30. What is the MPS?

(a) .7.
(b) 3.33
(c) .3
(d) 1.43.

Answer: (c)

Moderate
Math
Page: 180
CT Page: 623

9.4: If the MPC is .8 and planned investment decreased by $10 billion, what would be the resulting impact upon the nation's income?

(a) .$62.5 billion.
(b) $50 billion
(c) $10 billion
(d) $8 billion

Answer: (b)

Difficult
Math
Page: 190
CT Page: 624

9.5: If the MPS is .25 and planned investment increased by $5 billion, what would be the resulting impact upon the nation's economy?

(a) .$20 billion.
(b) $1.25 billion
(c) $6.67 billion
(d) $5 billion

Answer: (a)

Difficult
Math
Page: 190
CT Page: 634

Easy
Definition
Page: 177
CT Page: 616

9.6: The total quantity of goods and services produced (or supplied) in an economy in a given period is

(a) aggregate output.
(b) aggregate demand.
(c) aggregate investment.
(d) aggregate expenditure.

Answer: (a)

Easy
Definition
Page: 177
CT Page: 616

9.7: Aggregate output is

(a) the total quantity of goods and services demanded in a given period.
(b) the total quantity of goods and services produced (or supplied) in an economy in a given period.
(c) the total amount spent on purchases of new capital and investment.
(d) the total amount spent on consumption and investment.

Answer: (b)

Easy
Fact
Page: 178
CT Page: 617

9.8: Savings is a _____ variable and saving is a _____ variable.

(a) flow; flow
(b) stock; stock
(c) flow; stock
(d) stock; flow

Answer: (d)

Easy
Single
Page: 178
CT Page: 617

9.9: Which of the following would NOT lead to an increase in consumption spending?

(a) a reduction in interest rates
(b) an increase in household income
(c) an increase in household wealth
(d) news reports that indicate the economy is moving into a downturn

Answer: (d)

Easy
Fact
Page: 178
CT Page: 618

9.10: Uncertainty about the future is likely to

(a) increase current spending.
(b) decrease current spending.
(c) have no impact on current spending.
(d) either increase or decrease current spending.

Answer: (b)

Moderate
Single
Page: 178
CT Page: 618

9.11: Lower interest rate are likely to

(a) have no effect on consumer spending or saving.
(b) increase both consumer spending and consumer saving.
(c) decrease both consumer spending and consumer saving.
(d) increase consumer spending and decrease consumer saving.

Answer: (d)

9.12: Consumption is

(a) positively related to household income and wealth, interest rates, and households' expectations about the future.
(b) negatively related to household income and wealth, interest rates, and households' expectations about the future.
(c) determined only by income.
(d) positively related to household income and wealth and households' expectations about the future, but negatively related to interest rates.

Moderate
Fact
Page: 178
CT Page: 618

Answer: (d)

9.13: If income is zero, consumption

(a) must be zero.
(b) is less than zero.
(c) is greater than zero.
(d) can be either greater than or less than zero.

Easy
Fact
Page: 178
CT Page: 618

Answer: (c)

9.14: In the equation C = a + bY, which describes the aggregate consumption function, "a" stands for

(a) the amount of consumption when income is zero.
(b) the amount of income when consumption is zero.
(c) the marginal propensity to consume.
(d) the average consumption level.

Easy
Definition
Page: 179
CT Page: 619

Answer: (a)

9.15: Refer to Figure 9.1. The MPC for this household is

(a) .36.
(b) .4.
(c) .8.
(d) 1.25.

Moderate
Single
Page: 179
CT Page: 619

Answer: (c)

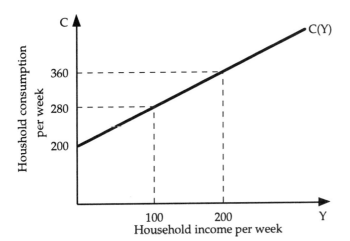

Figure 9.1

Challenging Multi Page: 180 CT Page: 619	**9.16: Refer to Figure 9.1.** The equation for this household's consumption function is (a) 200 + .8Y (b) 200 + Y. (c) 200 + .4Y. (d) 200 + 1.25Y. **Answer:** (a)
Challenging Multi Page: 180 CT Page: 619	**9.17: Refer to Figure 9.1.** This household's saving will be zero when income is (a) $400. (b) $800. (c) $1,000. (d) $1,800. **Answer:** (c)
Moderate Multi Page: 180 CT Page: 619	**9.-18: Refer to Figure 9.1.** This household's consumption will equal _____ when its income is $300. (a) $300 (b) $380 (c) $440 (d) $500 **Answer:** (c)
Moderate Multi Page: 180 CT Page: 619	**9.19: Refer to Figure 9.1.** This household's MPS is (a) 25. (b) .2. (c) .6. (d) .64. **Answer:** (b)
Honors Multi Page: 180 CT Page: 619	**9.20: Refer to Figure 9.1.** The equation for this household's saving function is (a) 200 + .2Y. (b) 200 + .25Y. (c) -200 25Y. (d) -200 + .2Y. **Answer:** (d)
Challenging Multi Page: 180 CT Page: 619	**9.21: Refer to Figure 9.1.** At an income level of $200, this household's <u>savings</u> (a) is -$160. (b) is -$80. (c) is $160. (d) cannot be determined from this information. **Answer:** (d)
Moderate Single Page: 180 CT Page: 619	**9.22: Refer to Figure 9.1.** If this household's income is $100, its saving is (a) -$180. (b) -$80. (c) $80. (d) $180. **Answer:** (a)

9.23: Refer to Figure 9.2. The MPC for
this household is

(a) .9.
(b) 1.0.
(c) .8.
(d) 1.55.

Answer: (a)

Moderate
Single
Page: 179
CT Page: 619

9.24; Refer to Figure 9.2. The equation
for this household's consumption
function is

(a) 500 + .8Y
(b) 500 - Y.
(c) 500 + 1.5Y.
(d) 500 + .9Y.

Figure 9.2.

Answer: (d)

Challenging
Multi
Page: 180
CT Page: 619

9.25: Refer to Figure 9.2. This household's saving will be zero when income is

(a) $0.
(b) $2,000.
(c) $1,000.
(d) $5000.

Answer: (d)

Challenging
Multi
Page: 180
CT Page: 619

9.26: Refer to Figure 9.2. This household's consumption will equal _____ when its
income is $300.

(a) $800
(b) $270
(c) $770
(d) $500

Answer: (c)

Moderate
Multi
Page: 180
CT Page: 619

9.27: Refer to Figure 9.2. This household's MPS is

(a) .9.
(b) .2.
(c) .1.
(d) 10.

Answer: (c)

Moderate
Multi
Page: 180
CT Page: 619

9.28: Refer to Figure 9.2. The equation for this household's saving function is

(a) -500 + .1Y.
(b) 500 + .1Y.
(c) -500 -.9Y.
(d) -500 + .2Y.

Answer: (a)

Honors
Multi
Page: 180
CT Page: 619

Challenging
Multi
Page: 180
CT Page: 619

9.29: Refer to Figure 9.2. At an income level of $200, this household's savings

(a) is $480.
(b) is $2000.
(c) is -$480.
(d) is -$250.

Answer: (c)

Moderate
Single
Page: 180
CT Page: 619

9.30: Refer to Figure 9.2. If this household's income is $10,000, its saving is

(a) -$500.
(b) $500.
(c) $50.
(d) $1,000.

Answer: (b)

Easy
Definition
Page: 180
CT Page: 619

9.31: The fraction of a change in income that is consumed or spent is called

(a) the marginal propensity of income.
(b) the marginal propensity to consume.
(c) the marginal propensity to save.
(d) average consumption.

Answer: (b)

Easy
Definition
Page: 180
CT Page: 619

9.32: The marginal propensity to consume is

(a) the ratio of consumption to income.
(b) the ratio of income to consumption.
(c) the ratio of the change in consumption to a change in income.
(d) the average amount of income that is consumed or spent.

Answer: (c)

Moderate
Single
Page: 180
CT Page: 619

9.33: If consumption is $25,000 when income is $21,000, and consumption increases to $25,900 when income increases to $22,000, the MPC is

(a) .59
(b) .84
(c) .9
(d) 1.11.

Answer: (c)

Moderate
Single
Page: 180
CT Page: 619

9.34:. If consumption is $5,000 when income is $10,000, and consumption increases to $10,000 when income increases to $25,000, the MPC is

(a) 1.0.
(b) .8.
(c) .9.
(d) .33.

Answer: (d)

Easy
Definition
Page: 180
CT Page: 620

9.35: The MPS is

(a) the ratio of saving to income.
(b) the ratio of income to saving.
(c) the average amount of income that is saved.
(d) the fraction of a change in income that is saved.

Answer: (d)

9.36: If consumption is $25,000 when income is $21,000, and consumption increases to $25,900 when income increases to $22,000, the MPS is

(a) 9.
(b) 1.
(c) .1.
(d) indeterminate from this information.

Answer: (c)

Moderate
Multi
Page: 180
CT Page: 602

937: If consumption is $2,000 when income is $2,500, and consumption increases to $2,500 when income increases to $3,200, the MPS is approximately

(a) -.29.
(b) .29.
(c) .1.
(d) 0.71.

Answer: (b)

Moderate
Multi
Page: 180
CT Page: 602

9.38: If the MPS is .4, the MPC is

(a) .4.
(b) .6.
(c) 1.4.
(d) 2.5.

Answer: (b)

Moderate
Single
Page: 180
CT Page: 620

9.39: If the MPS is .3, the MPC is

(a) .4.
(b) -.7.
(c) .7.
(d) 1.7.

Answer: (c)

Moderate
Single
Page: 180
CT Page: 620

9.40: If the MPC is .8, the MPS is

(a) .2.
(b) .8.
(c) 1.25.
(d) 1.8.

Answer: (a)

Moderate
Single
Page: 180
CT Page: 620

9.41:. If the MPC is 1, the MPS is

(a) -1.
(b) .9.
(c) 1.25.
(d) 0.

Answer: (d)

Moderate
Single
Page: 180
CT Page: 620

Moderate
Single
Page: 180
CT Page: 620

9.42: When Richard's income is $20,000 he saves $500 and when his income increases to $21,000 he saves $700. His MPS is

(a) .2.
(b) .25.
(c) .29.
(d) .33.

Answer: (a)

Moderate
Single
Page: 180
CT Page: 620

9.43: When Richard's income is $50,000 he saves $10,000 and when his income increases to $75,000 he saves $25,000. His MPS is

(a) .2.
(b) .6.
(c) -.6.
(d) .33.

Answer: (b)

Moderate
Multi
Page: 180
CT Page: 620

9.44: Refer to Figure 9.3. The equation for the aggregate consumption function is

(a) C = .6Y.
(b) C = 50 + .6Y.
(c) C = 60 + .4Y.
(d) C = 100 + .4Y.

Answer: (b)

Moderate
Single
Page: 180
CT Page: 620

9.45: Refer to Figure 9.3. Society's MPC is

(a) .4.
(b) .6.
(c) 1.67.
(d) 2.5.

Answer: (b)

Moderate
Single
Page: 180
CT Page: 620

9.46: Refer to Figure 9.3. Society's MPS is

(a) .4
(b) .6
(c) 1.67.
(d) 2.5.

Answer: (a)

Aggregate Income (billions of dollars)	Aggregate Consumption (billions of dollars)
0	50
100	110
200	170
300	230

Figure 9.3

9.47: Refer to Figure 9.3. At an aggregate income level of $300, aggregate saving would be

Easy
Single
Page: 180
CT Page: 620

(a)-$30.
(b) $30.
(c) $70.
(d) $120.

Answer: (c)

9.48: Refer to Figure 9.3. Assuming society's MPC is constant, aggregate consumption would be _____ at an aggregate income of $400.

Moderate
Single
Page: 181
CT Page: 620

(a) $240
(b) $280
(c) $290
(d) $368

Answer: (c)

9.49: Refer to Figure 9.4. The equation for the aggregate consumption function is

Moderate
Multi
Page: 180
CT Page: 620

(a) $C = .3Y$.
(b) $C = 300 + .3Y$.
(c) $C = 100 + .3Y$.
(d) $C = .6Y$.

Answer: (c)

9.50: Refer to Figure 9.4. Society's MPC is

Moderate
Single
Page: 180
CT Page: 620

(a) .3.
(b) .7.
(c) 1.4.
(d) .6.

Answer: (a)

9.51: Refer to Figure 9.4. Society's MPS is

Moderate
Single
Page: 180
CT Page: 620

(a) .3.
(b) .7.
(c) 1.4.
(d) .4.

Answer: (b)

Aggregate Income (billions of dollars)	Aggregate Consumption (billions of dollars)
0	100
100	130
200	160
300	190

Figure 9.4

Easy
Single
Page: 180
CT Page: 620

9.52: Refer to Figure 9.4. At an aggregate income level of $300, aggregate saving would be

(a) $90.
(b) $210.
(c) $110.
(d) -$110.

Answer: (c)

Moderate
Single
Page: 181
CT Page: 620

9.53: Refer to Figure 9.4. Assuming society's MPC is constant, aggregate consumption would be _____ at an aggregate income of $600.

(a) $240
(b) $280
(c) $290
(d) $368

Answer: (b)

Moderate
Single
Page: 180
CT Page: 621

9.54: Refer to Figure 9.5. The equation for the aggregate consumption function is

(a) 750Y.
(b) 150 + .9Y.
(c) 750 + .3Y.
(d) 150 + .8Y.

Answer: (d)

Honors
Multi
Page: 180
CT Page: 621

9.55:: Refer to Figure 9.5. The equation for the aggregate saving function is

(a) 250Y.
(b) -150 + .2Y.
(c) 150 - .8Y.
(d) indeterminate from this information.

Answer: (b)

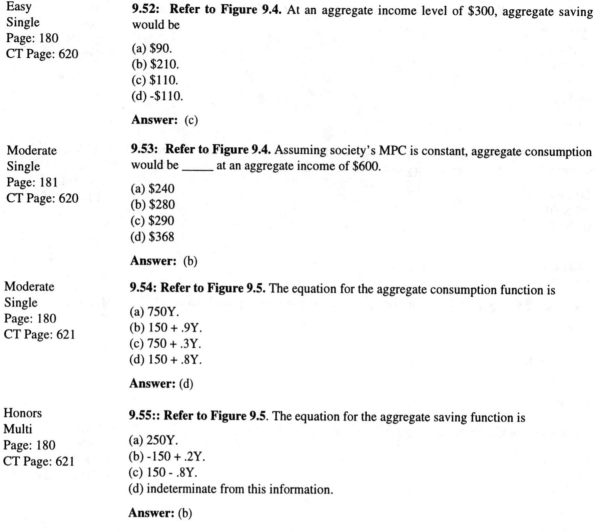

Figure 9.5

9.56: Refer to Figure 9.5. In this economy aggregate saving will be zero if income is

(a) $150 billion.
(b) $500 billion.
(c) $550 billion.
(d) $750 billion.

Moderate
Multi
Page: 181
CT Page: 622

Answer: (d)

9.57: Refer to Figure 9.5. For this society, aggregate saving is positive if aggregate income is

(a) above zero.
(b) between $0 and $750 billion.
(c) equal to $750 billion.
(d) above $750 billion.

Easy
Single
Page: 181
CT Page: 622

Answer: (d)

9.58: Refer to Figure 9.5. If aggregate income is $200 billion, then in this society aggregate saving is _____ billion.

(a) -$110
(b) -$80
(c) $0
(d) $50

Easy
Single
Page: 181
CT Page: 622

Answer: (a)

9.59: Refer to Figure 9.5. Which of the following statements is FALSE?

(a) Aggregate saving is negative for all income levels below $750 billion.
(b) For all aggregate income levels above $750 billion, aggregate consumption is less than aggregate income.
(c) If consumption is the only expenditure, this economy would be in equilibrium at an aggregate income level of $550 billion.
(d) If the level of aggregate income in this economy was $1 trillion, consumption would be $950 billion.

Easy
Single
Page: 181
CT Page: 622

Answer: (c)

9.60: Refer to Figure 9.6. The equation for the aggregate consumption function is

(a) .7Y.
(b) 300 + .7Y.
(c) 300 + .3Y.
(d) 300Y.

Moderate
Single
Page: 180
CT Page: 621

Answer: (b)

9.61: Refer to Figure 9.6. The equation for the aggregate saving function is

(a) -250Y.
(b) -150 + .2Y.
(c) -300 + .3Y.
(d) indeterminate from this information.

Honors
Multi
Page: 180
CT Page: 621

Answer: (c)

Figure 9.6

Moderate
Multi
Page: 181
CT Page: 622

9.62: Refer to Figure 9.6. In this economy aggregate saving will be zero if income is

(a) $1000 billion.
(b) $5000 billion.
(c) $300 billion.
(d) $750 billion.

Answer: (a)

Easy
Single
Page: 181
CT Page: 622

9.63: Refer to Figure 9.6. For this society, aggregate saving is positive if aggregate income is

(a) above $1000 billion.
(b) between $0 and $750 billion.
(c) equal to $750 billion.
(d) less than $0.

Answer: (a)

Easy
Single
Page: 181
CT Page: 622

9.64: Refer to Figure 9.6 If aggregate income is $200 billion, then in this society aggregate saving is _____ billion.

(a) $240
(b) -$240
(c) $60
(d) none of the above

Answer: (b)

Easy
Single
Page: 181
CT Page: 622

9.65: Refer to Figure 9.6. Which of the following statements is FALSE?

(a) If consumption is the only expenditure, this economy would be in equilibrium at an aggregate income level of $750 billion.
(b) Aggregate saving is negative for all income levels below $1000 billion.
(c) If the level of aggregate income in this economy was $750 billion, consumption would be $825 billion.
(d) For all aggregate income levels above $1000 billion, aggregate consumption is less than aggregate income.

Answer: (a)

9.66: If the consumption function is above the 45 degree line,

(a) consumption is less than income and saving is positive.
(b) consumption is less than income and saving is negative.
(c) consumption exceeds income and saving is positive.
(d) consumption exceeds income and saving is negative.

Answer: (d)

Easy
Single
Page: 183
CT Page: 620

9.67: Refer to Figure 9.7. The MPS for this saving function is

(a) 5.
(b) .25.
(c) .5.
(d) 4.

Answer: (b)

Easy
Single
Page: 183
CT Page: 622

9.68: Refer to Figure 9.7. If aggregate income is $400 billion, aggregate saving is _____ billion.

(a) -$300
(b) -$100
(c) $0
(d) $500

Answer: (b)

Moderate
Multi
Page: 183
CT Page: 622

9.69: Refer to Figure 9.7. If aggregate income is $900 billion, aggregate consumption

(a) is $25 billion.
(b) is $800 billion.
(c) is $875 billion.
(d) cannot be determined from this information.

Answer: (c)

Moderate
Multi
Page: 183
CT Page: 622

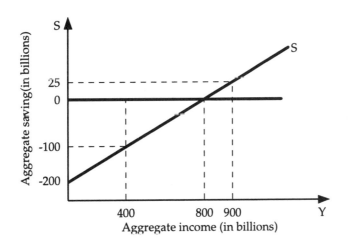

Figure 9.7

Moderate
Single
Page: 184
CT Page: 623

9.70: Refer to Figure 9.7. If aggregate consumption is the only expenditure in this society, the equilibrium level of income

(a) is $400 billion.
(b) is $800 billion.
(c) is $900 billion.
(d) cannot be determined from this information.

Answer: (b)

Easy
Single
Page: 183
CT Page: 622

9.71: Refer to Figure 9.8. The MPS for this saving function is

(a) -.5.
(b) .25.
(c) .5.
(d) 4.

Answer: (c)

Moderate
Multi
Page: 183
CT Page: 622

9.72: Refer to Figure 9.8. If aggregate income is $800 billion, aggregate saving is _____ billion.

(a) -$100
(b) -$300
(c) $100
(d) -$200

Answer: (a)

Moderate
Multi
Page: 183
CT Page: 622

9.73: Refer to Figure 9.8. If aggregate income is $1200 billion, aggregate consumption

(a) is $1100 billion.
(b) is $1200 billion.
(c) is $875 billion.
(d) cannot be determined from this information.

Answer: (a)

Figure 9.8

9.74: Refer to Figure 9.8. If aggregate consumption is the only expenditure in this society, the equilibrium level of income

(a) is $1200 billion.
(b) is $1000 billion.
(c) is $-200 billion.
(d) cannot be determined from this information.

Moderate
Single
Page: 184
CT Page: 623

Answer:(b)

9.75: The Tiny Tots Toy Company manufactures only sleds. In 1993 Tiny Tots manufactured 10,000 sleds, but sold only 9,000 sleds. In 1993 Tiny Tots' change in inventory was

(a) -1,000 sleds.
(b) 1,000 sleds.
(c) 9,000 sleds.
(d) 19,000 sleds.

Moderate
Single
Page: 184
CT Page: 623

Answer: (b)

9.76: The Jackson Tool Company manufactures only tools. In 1993 Jackson Tools manufactured 20,000 tools, but sold only 15,000 tools. In 1993 Jackson Tools' change in inventory was

(a) -5,000 tools.
(b) 1,000 tools.
(c) 5,000 tools.
(d) 15,000 tools.

Moderate
Single
Page: 184
CT Page: 623

Answer: (c)

9.77: In 1993 the Maiden Record Company planned to invest $540,000 by spending $500,000 to upgrade its recording facilities and by increasing inventories to $40,000 worth of CDs. But in 1993, the actual amount of investment made by Maiden Records was $600,000. Which of the following is the best explanation for how planned and actual investment by Maiden Records could have been different?

(a) The upgrade of its recording facilities cost less than the anticipated $500,000.
(b) Maiden Records was not able to upgrade its recording facilities because it could find no one willing to do the work. Therefore, it purchased $500,000 of government bonds and earned $40,000 interest on the bonds.
(c) The price level rose during 1993, so the value of its investment increased from $540,000 to $600,000.
(d) Sales of CDs were not as high as expected, so inventory accumulations equaled $100,000, not the $40,000 that Maiden Records had planned.

Moderate
Single
Page: 184
CT Page: 623

Answer: (d)

9.78: Over which component of investment do firms have the least amount of control?

(a) purchases of new equipment
(b) construction of new factories
(c) inventory adjustment
(d) the buying and selling of stock

Easy
Fact
Page: 184
CT Page: 624

Answer: (c)

Easy
Single
Page: 184
CT Page: 624

9.79: Assume that in Montega, planned investment is $40 billion but actual investment is $30 billion. Unplanned inventory investment is

(a) -$10 billion.
(b) $10 billion.
(c) $20 billion.
(d) $30 billion.

Answer: (a)

Easy
Single
Page: 184
CT Page: 624

9.80: Assume that in Smirnoff, planned investment is $60 billion but actual investment is $20 billion. Unplanned inventory investment is

(a) -$10 billion.
(b) -$20 billion.
(c) $30 billion.
(d) -$40 billion.

Answer: (d)

Moderate
Single
Page: 184
CT Page: 624

9.81: In 1993 Outland's planned investment was $50 billion and its actual investment was $70 billion. In 1993 Outland's unplanned inventory change was

(a) -$20 billion.
(b) $1.4 billion.
(c) $20 billion.
(d) $120 billion.

Answer: (c)

Moderate
Single
Page: 184
CT Page: 624

9.82:. In 1993 Golden State's planned investment was $100 billion and its actual investment was $170 billion. In 1993 Golden State's unplanned inventory change was

(a) -$70 billion.
(b) $70 billion.
(c) $170 billion.
(d) $120 billion.

Answer: (b)

Moderate
Fact
Page: 184
CT Page: 624

9.83: Inventory investment is higher than firms planned, therefore

(a) actual and planned investment are equal.
(b) actual investment is less than planned investment.
(c) actual investment is greater than planned investment.
(d) actual investment must be negative.

Answer: (c)

Easy
Single
Page: 185
CT Page: 624

9.84: Refer to Figure 9.9. In Azora planned investment does not vary with income. Azora's planned investment function is represented by

(a) Panel A.
(b) Panel B.
(c) Panel C.
(d) Panel D.

Answer: (b)

9.85: Refer to Figure 9.9. In Farley planned investment varies inversely with income. Farley's planned investment function is represented by

(a) Panel A.
(b) Panel B.
(c) Panel C.
(d) Panel D.

Easy
Single
Page: 185
CT Page: 624

Answer: (d)

9.86: Without the government or the foreign sector in the income- expenditure model, planned aggregate expenditure equals

(a) consumption plus actual investment.
(b) consumption plus inventory adjustment.
(c) consumption minus planned investment.
(d) consumption plus planned investment.

Easy
Fact
Page: 185
CT Page: 625

Answer: (d)

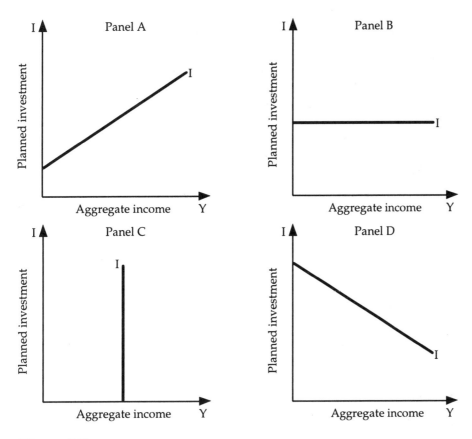

Figure 9.9

Easy
Fact
Page: 185
CT Page: 625

9.87: In macroeconomics, equilibrium is defined as that point at which

(a) saving equals consumption.
(b) planned aggregate expenditure equals consumption.
(c) planned aggregate expenditure equals aggregate output.
(d) aggregate output equals consumption minus investment.

Answer: (c)

Easy
Fact
Page: 185
CT Page: 625

9.88: The economy can be in equilibrium if, and only if,

(a) planned investment is zero.
(b) planned investment equals actual investment.
(c) planned investment is greater than actual investment.
(d) actual investment is zero.

Answer: (b)

Easy
Fact
Page: 185
CT Page: 625

9.89: If aggregate output is greater than planned spending, then

(a) unplanned inventory investment is positive.
(b) unplanned inventory investment is negative.
(c) unplanned inventory investment is zero.
(d) actual investment equals planned investment.

Answer: (a)

Easy
Fact
Page: 185
CT Page: 625

9.90: If unplanned inventory investment is negative, then

(a) planned investment must be zero.
(b) planned aggregate spending must be greater than aggregate output.
(c) planned aggregate spending must be less than aggregate output.
(d) planned aggregate spending must equal aggregate output.

Answer: (b)

Easy
Fact
Page: 185
CT Page: 625

9.91: If aggregate output equals planned aggregate expenditure, then

(a) unplanned inventory adjustment is positive.
(b) unplanned inventory adjustment is negative.
(c) unplanned inventory investment is zero.
(d) actual investment is greater than planned investment.

Answer: (c)

Moderate
Single
Page: 185
CT Page: 626

9.92: Refer to Figure 9.10. At an aggregate output level of $400 billion, planned expenditure equals

(a) $400 billion.
(b) $450 billion.
(c) $500 billion.
(d) $850 billion.

Answer: (c)

9.93: Refer to Figure 9.10. At an aggregate output level of $600 billion, aggregate saving

Easy
Single
Page: 185
CT Page: 626

(a) equals -$50 billion.
(b) equals $0.
(c) equals $50 billion.
(d) cannot be determined from this information.

Answer: (b)

9.94: Refer to Figure 9.10. At an aggregate output level of $200 billion, the unplanned inventory change is

Easy
Single
Page: 185
CT Page: 626

(a) -$150 billion.
(b) -$100 billion.
(c) -$50 billion.
(d) $100 billion.

Answer: (a)

9.95: Refer to Figure 9.10. At an aggregate output level of $600 billion, the unplanned inventory change is

Easy
Single
Page: 185
CT Page: 626

(a) -$100 billion.
(b) -$50 billion.
(c) $0.
 (d) $50 billion.

Answer: (b)

9.96: Refer to Figure 9.10. If aggregate output equals _____, there will be a $100 billion unplanned decrease in inventories.

Moderate
Single
Page: 185
CT Page: 626

(a) $200 billion
(b) $400 billion
(c) $600 billion
(d) $800 billion

Answer: (b)

(All figures in billions of dollars)		
Aggregate Output	**Aggregate Consumption**	**Planned Investment**
200	300	50
400	450	50
600	600	50
800	750	50
1,000	900	50

Figure 9.10

Moderate
Multi
Page: 185
CT Page: 626

9.97: Refer to Figure 9.10. The equilibrium level of aggregate output equals

(a) $400 billion.
(b) $600 billion.
(c) $800 billion.
(d) $1,000 billion.

Answer: (c)

Moderate
Single
Page: 185
CT Page: 626

9.98: Refer to Figure 9.10. Which of the following statements is FALSE?

(a) At output levels greater than $800 billion, there is a positive unplanned inventory change.
(b) If aggregate output equals $600 billion, then aggregate saving equals $0.
(c) The MPC for this economy is .75.
(d) At an output level of $400 billion, there is a $50 billion unplanned inventory decrease.

Answer: (d)

Moderate
Multi
Page: 185
CT Page: 627

9.99: Refer to Figure 9.10. Planned saving equals planned investment at an aggregate output level

(a) of $400 billion.
(b) of $600 billion.
(c) of $800 billion.
(d) that cannot be determined from this information.

Answer: (c)

Moderate
Multi
Page: 185
CT Page: 627

9.100: Refer to Figure 9.10. Planned investment equals actual investment at

(a) all income levels.
(b) at all income levels above $600 billion.
(c) all income levels below $600 billion.
(d) $800 billion.

Answer: (d)

Moderate
Single
Page: 185
CT Page: 626

9.101: Refer to Figure 9.11. At an aggregate output level of $400 billion, planned expenditure equals

(a) $600 billion.
(b) $800 billion.
(c) $200 billion.
(d) $400 billion.

Answer: (b)

Easy
Single
Page: 185
CT Page: 626

9.102: Refer to Figure 9.11. At an aggregate output level of $800 billion, aggregate saving

(a) equals -$50 billion.
(b) equals $0.
(c) equals -$200 billion.
(d) cannot be determined from this information.

Answer: (c)

(All figures in billions of dollars)		
Aggregate Output	Aggregate Consumption	Planned Investment
400	600	200
800	800	200
1,200	1000	200
1,600	1,200	200
2,000	1,400	200

Figure 9.11

9.103: Refer to Figure 9.11 At an aggregate output level of $1,200 billion, the unplanned inventory change is

(a) $1000 billion.
(b) -$200 billion.
(c) $200 billion.
(d) 0.

Answer: (d)

Easy
Single
Page: 185
CT Page: 626

9.104: Refer to Figure 9.11. At an aggregate output level of $2,000 billion, the unplanned inventory change is

(a) $400 billion.
(b) $200 billion.
(c) $0.
(d) $1300 billion.

Answer: (a)

Easy
Single
Page: 185
CT Page: 626

9.105: Refer to Figure 9.11. If aggregate output equals _____, there will be a $200 billion unplanned decrease in inventories.

(a) $400 billion
(b) $800 billion
(c) $1,200 billion
(d) $1,600 billion

Answer: (b)

Moderate
Single
Page: 185
CT Page: 626

9.106: Refer to Figure 9.11. The equilibrium level of aggregate output equals

(a) $400 billion.
(b) $800 billion.
(c) $1,600 billion.
(d) $1200 billion.

Answer: (d)

Moderate
Multi
Page: 185
CT Page: 626

Moderate
Single
Page: 185
CT Page: 626

9.107: Refer to Figure 9.11. Which of the following statements is FALSE?

(a) At output levels less than $1,200 billion, there is a positive unplanned inventory change.
(b) If aggregate output equals $1,200 billion, then aggregate saving equals $0.
(c) The MPC for this economy is .8.
(d) At an output level of $400 billion, there is a $400 billion unplanned inventory decrease.

Answer: (c)

Moderate
Multi
Page: 185
CT Page: 627

9.108: Refer to Figure 9.11. Planned saving equals planned investment at an aggregate output level

(a) of $400 billion.
(b) of $800 billion.
(c) of $1,200 billion.
(d) none of the above.

Answer: (c)

Moderate
Multi
Page: 185
CT Page: 627

9.109: Refer to Figure 9.11. Planned investment equals actual investment at

(a) all income levels.
(b) all income levels above $400 billion.
(c) all income levels below $2000 billion.
(d) income level $1,200 billion.

Answer: (d)

Challenging
Multi
Page: 188
CT Page: 626

9.110: If $C = 300 + .8Y$ and $I = 200$, then the equilibrium level of income is

(a) 625.
(b) 1,700.
(c) 2,500.
(d) 4,000.

Answer: (c)

Challenging
Multi
Page: 188
CT Page: 626

9.111: If $C = 500 + .5Y$ and $I = 400$, then the equilibrium level of income is

(a) 900.
(b) 1,800.
(c) 2,500.
(d) 4,000.

Answer: (b)

Challenging
Multi
Page: 188
CT Page: 626

9.112: If $C = 200 + .75Y$ and $I = 100$, then the equilibrium level of income is

(a) 300.
(b) 400.
(c) 900.
(d) 1,200.

Answer: (d)

9.113: If C = 700 + .25Y and I = 600, then the equilibrium level of income is approximately

Challenging
Multi
Page: 188
CT Page: 626

(a) 5200.
(b) 1300.
(c) 1733.
(d) 1,546.

Answer: (c)

9.114: Refer to Figure 9.12. The equilibrium level of income is

Easy
Single
Page: 187
CT Page: 626

(a) $200 billion.
(b) $250 billion.
(c) $400 billion.
(d) $600 billion.

Answer: (c)

9.115: Refer to Figure 9.12. At an aggregate output level of $200 billion, there is a

Moderate
Multi
Page: 187
CT Page: 627

(a) $125 billion unplanned decrease in inventories.
(b) $75 billion unplanned decrease in inventories.
(c) $0 change in unplanned inventories.
(d) $75 billion unplanned increase in inventories.

Answer: (a)

9.116: Refer to Figure 9.12. At aggregate output levels above $400 billion, there are

Moderate
Single
Page: 187
CT Page: 627

(a) unplanned increases in inventories and output increases.
(b) unplanned increases in inventories and output decreases.
(c) unplanned decreases in inventories and output increases.
(d) unplanned decreases in inventories and output decreases.

Answer: (b)

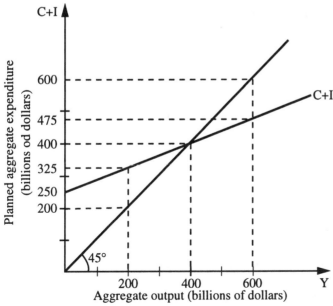

Figure 9.12

Moderate
Single
Page: 187
CT Page: 627

9.117: Refer to Figure 9.12. At aggregate output levels below $400 billion, there are

(a) unplanned increases in inventories and output increases.
(b) unplanned increases in inventories and output decreases.
(c) unplanned decreases in inventories and output increases.
(d) unplanned decreases in inventories and output decreases.

Answer: (c)

Challenging
Single
Page: 187
CT Page: 627

9.118: Refer to Figure 9.12. At aggregate output levels above $400 billion,

(a) leakages equal injections.
(b) leakages are greater than injections.
(c) leakages are less than injections.
(d) leakages are zero, but injections are positive.

Answer: (b)

Challenging
Single
Page: 187
CT Page: 627

9.119: Refer to Figure 9.12. At aggregate output levels below $400 billion,

(a) leakages equal injections.
(b) leakages are greater than injections.
(c) leakages are less than injections.
(d) leakages are positive, but injections are negative.

Answer: (c)

Easy
Single
Page: 187
CT Page: 626

9.120: Refer to Figure 9.13. The equilibrium level of income is

(a) $400 billion.
(b) $600 billion.
(c) $800 billion.
(d) $1,000 billion

Answer: (b).

Moderate
Multi
Page: 187
CT Page: 627

9.121: Refer to Figure 9.13. At an aggregate output level of $400 billion, there is a

(a) $150 billion unplanned increase in inventories.
(b) $75 billion unplanned decrease in inventories.
(c) $0 change in unplanned inventories.
(d) $150 billion unplanned decrease in inventories.

Answer: (d)

Moderate
Single
Page: 187
CT Page: 627

9.122: Refer to Figure 9.13. At aggregate output levels above $600 billion, there are

(a) unplanned increases in inventories and output decreases.
(b) unplanned decreases in inventories and output increases.
(c) unplanned decreases in inventories and output decreases.
(d) unplanned increases in inventories and output increases.

Answer: (a)

Moderate
Single
Page: 187
CT Page: 627

9.123: Refer to Figure 9.13. At aggregate output levels below $600 billion, there are

(a) unplanned decreases in inventories and output increases.
(b) unplanned increases in inventories and output increases.
(c) unplanned increases in inventories and output decreases.
(d) unplanned decreases in inventories and output decreases.

Answer: (a)

Figure 9.13

9.124: Refer to Figure 9.13. At aggregate output levels above $600 billion,

(a) leakages equal injections.
(b) leakages are less than injections.
(c) leakages are zero, but injections are positive.
(d) leakages are more than injections.

Answer: (d)

Challenging
Single
Page: 187
CT Page: 627

9.125: Refer to Figure 9.13. At aggregate output levels below $600 billion,

(a) leakages equal injections.
(b) leakages are less than injections.
(c) leakages are greater than injections.
(d) leakages are positive, but injections are negative.

Answer: (b)

Challenging
Single
Page: 187
CT Page: 627

9.126: Using the saving/investment approach to equilibrium, the equilibrium condition can be written as

(a) C + I = C + S.
(b) C = S + I.
(c) C - S = I.
(d) C + S = I.

Answer: (a)

Easy
Fact
Page: 188
CT Page: 628

9.127: Firms react to unplanned inventory reductions by

(a) reducing output.
(b) increasing output.
(c) reducing planned investment.
(d) increasing consumption.

Answer: (b)

Moderate
Fact
Page: 190
CT Page: 629

Moderate
Fact
Page: 190
CT Page: 629

9.128: Firms react to unplanned increases in inventories by

(a) reducing output.
(b) increasing output.
(c) increasing planned investment
(d) increasing consumption.

Answer: (a)

Easy
Single
Page: 190
CT Page: 629

9.129: Aggregate output will increase if there is

(a) an increase in saving.
(b) an unplanned rise in inventories.
(c) an unplanned fall in inventories.
(d) a decrease in consumption.

Answer: (c)

Easy
Fact
Page: 190
CT Page: 630

9.130: A decrease in planned investment causes

(a) output to increase.
(b) output to decrease but by a smaller amount than the decrease in investment.
(c) output to decrease but by a larger amount than the decrease in investment.
(d) output to decrease by an amount equal to the decrease in investment.

Answer: (c)

Easy
Definition
Page: 190
CT Page: 630

9.131: The ratio of the change in the equilibrium level of output to a change in some autonomous variable is the

(a) elasticity coefficient.
(b) multiplier.
(c) automatic stabilizer.
(d) marginal propensity of the autonomous variable.

Answer: (b)

Moderate
Single
Page: 192
CT Page: 631

9.132: Refer to Figure 9.14. If the aggregate expenditure function shifted from C + I to C + I', then

(a) autonomous consumption increased by $50 billion.
(b) planned investment increased by $50 billion.
(c) either autonomous consumption increased by $50 billion or planned investment increased by $50 billion.
(d) both autonomous consumption and planned investment increased by $50 billion.

Answer: (c)

Moderate
Single
Page: 192
CT Page: 631

9.133: Refer to Figure 9.14. After the aggregate expenditure functions shifts to C + I', then the new equilibrium level of aggregate output

(a) is $400 billion.
(b) is $500 billion.
(c) is $600 billion.
(d) cannot be determined from this information.

Answer: (c)

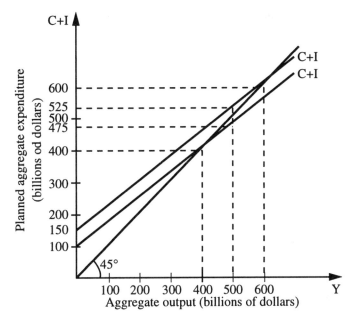

Figure 9.14

9.134: Refer to Figure 9.14. The value for the multiplier in this example

(a) is .25.
(b) is 4.
(c) is 16.
(d) cannot be determined from this example.

Answer: (b)

Moderate
Multi
Page: 192
CT Page: 631

9.135: Refer to Figure 9.14. The value for the MPC in this example

(a) is .25.
(b) is .75.
(c) is 4.
(d) cannot be determined from this information.

Answer: (b)

Moderate
Multi
Page: 193
CT Page: 631

9.136: As the slope of the aggregate expenditure function becomes steeper,

(a) the smaller the MPC becomes and the smaller the multiplier becomes.
(b) the smaller the MPC becomes and the larger the multiplier becomes.
(c) the larger the MPC becomes and the larger the multiplier becomes.
(d) the larger the MPC becomes and the smaller the multiplier becomes.

Answer: (c)

Moderate
Multi
Page: 193
CT Page: 632

9.137: Assuming no government or foreign sector, if the MPC is .8, the multiplier is

(a) .2.
(b) .8.
(c) 1.25.
(d) 5.

Answer: (d)

Moderate
Single
Page: 193
CT Page: 634

Easy
Fact
Page: 193
CT Page: 634

9.138: Assuming no government or foreign sector, the formula for the multiplier is

(a) 1/MPC.
(b) 1/MPS.
(c) 1/(1 + MPC).
(d) 1 - MPC.

Answer: (b)

Easy
Fact
Page: 193
CT Page: 634

9.139: Assuming there is no government or foreign sector, the formula for the multiplier is

(a) 1/(1 - MPC).
(b) 1/MPC.
(c) 1/(1 + MPC).
(d) 1 - MPC.

Answer: (a)

Challenging
Single
Page: 193
CT Page: 634

9.140: Assuming there is no government or foreign sector, if the multiplier is 2.5, the MPC is

(a) .25
(b) .4.
(c) .6.
(d) 2.5.

Answer: (c)

Moderate
Single
Page: 193
CT Page: 634

9.141 Assume there is no government or foreign sector. If the MPS is .1, the multiplier is

(a) .9.
(b) 1.11.
(c) 9.
(d) 10.

Answer: (d)

Moderate
Single
Page: 193
CT Page: 634

9.142: Assume there is no government or foreign sector. If the multiplier is 4, a $10 billion increase in planned investment will cause aggregate output to increase by

(a) $2.5 billion.
(b) $10 billion.
(c) $40 billion.
(d) $60 billion.

Answer: (c)

Moderate
Multi
Page: 193
CT Page: 634

9.143: Assume there is no government or foreign sector. If the MPC is .75, a $20 billion decrease in planned investment will cause aggregate output to decrease by

(a) $15 billion.
(b) $20 billion.
(c) $26.67 billion.
(d) $80 billion.

Answer: (d)

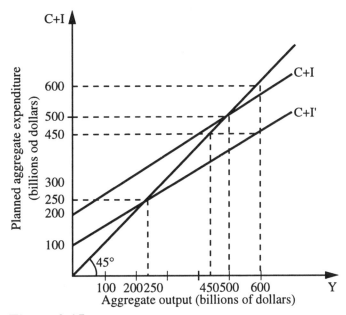

Figure 9.15

9.144: Assume there is no government or foreign sector. If the multiplier is 10, a $20 billion increase in investment will cause aggregate output to

(a) decrease by $2 billion.
(b) increase by $2 billion.
(c) increase by $20 billion.
(d) increase by $200 billion.

Moderate
Single
Page: 193
CT Page: 634

Answer: (d)

9.145: Assume there is no government or foreign sector in Outland. The MPC in Outland is .8. After planned investment was increased, the equilibrium level of output increased by $500 billion. Planned investment must have changed by

(a) $100 billion.
(b) $400 billion.
(c) $500 billion.
(d) an amount that cannot be determined from this information because the values for the equilibrium levels of output are not given.

Moderate
Multi
Page: 193
CT Page: 634

Answer: (a)

9.146: Refer to Figure 9.15. If the aggregate expenditure function is C + I, the equilibrium level of aggregate output is

(a) $250 billion.
(b) $450 billion.
(c) $500 billion.
(d) $600 billion.

Moderate
Single
Page: 192
CT Page: 632

Answer: (c)

Moderate
Multi
Page: 192
CT Page: 632

9.147: Refer to Figure 9.15. If the aggregate expenditure function shifts from C + I to C + I', the equilibrium level of aggregate output

(a) decreases by $350 billion.
(b) decreases by $250 billion.
(c) remains constant.
(d) increases by $50 billion.

Answer: (b)

Moderate
Multi
Page: 192
CT Page: 632

9.148 Refer to Figure 9.15. The value for the multiplier in this example is

(a) -2.5.
(b) 75
(c) .75.
(d) 2.5.

Answer: (d)

Moderate
Single
Page: 193
CT Page: 634

9.149: As the MPS increases, the multiplier will

(a) increase.
(b) decrease.
(c) remain constant.
(d) either increase or decrease depending on the size of the change in investment.

Answer: (b)

Challenging
Multi
Page: 193
CT Page: 634

9.150: Midwest State University in Nebraska is trying to convince Nebraska taxpayers that the tax dollars spent at Midwest State University are well spent. One of the university's arguments is that for every $1 spent by Midwest State University an additional $5 of expenditures are generated within Nebraska. Midwest State University is arguing that the multiplier for their expenditures is

(a) .2.
(b) 1.
(c) 4.
(d) 5.

Answer: (d)

Moderate
Multi
Page: 193
CT Page: 635

9.151: If autonomous consumption increases, the size of the multiplier would

(a) increase.
(b) decrease.
(c) remain constant.
(d) either increase or decrease depending on the size of the change in autonomous consumption.

Answer: (c)

Easy
Fact
Page: 195
CT Page: 635

9.152 In practice, the actual size of the multiplier is about

(a) 1.
(b) 1.4.
(c) 2.
(d) 4.

Answer: (b)

9.153: According to the "paradox of thrift," as individuals increase their saving,

(a) income in the economy increases because there is more money available for firms to invest.
(b) income in the economy increases because interest rates will fall and the economy will expand.
(c) income in the economy will remain constant because the change in consumption equals the change in saving.
(d) income in the economy will fall because the decreased consumption that results from increased saving causes the economy to contract.

Answer: (d)

Moderate
Fact
Page: 194
CT Page: 633

9.154: According to the "paradox of thrift," increased efforts to save will cause

(a) an increase in income and an increase in overall saving.
(b) an increase in income but no overall change in saving.
(c) a decrease in income and a overall decrease in saving.
(d) a decrease in income but an increase in saving.

Answer: (c)

Moderate
Single
Page: 194
CT Page: 633

TRUE/FALSE QUESTIONS

9.155: As interest rates fall, spending increases.

Answer: True

Easy
Fact
Page: 178
CT Page: 618

9.156: Uncertainty about the future is likely to increase current spending.

Answer: False

Easy
Fact
Page: 178
CT Page: 618

9.157: The marginal propensity to consume is the ratio of consumption to income.

Answer: False

Easy
Fact
Page: 180
CT Page: 619

9.158: If the marginal propensity to consume is .8, the marginal propensity to save is 8.

Answer: False

Easy
Fact
Page: 180
CT Page: 620

9.159: If actual inventory investment is less than that which firms planned, then actual investment is greater than planned investment.

Answer: False

Easy
Fact
Page: 184
CT Page: 623

9.160: Assuming there is no government or foreign sector, the economy will be in equilibrium if, and only if, planned investment equals actual investment.

Answer: True

Easy
Fact
Page: 186
CT Page: 628

Easy
Fact
Page: 190
CT Page: 629

9.161: Firms react to an unplanned inventory investment by reducing output.

Answer: True

Easy
Fact
Page: 190
CT Page: 629

9.162: If planned spending is less than output, there will be an unplanned decrease in inventories.

Answer: False

Easy
Fact
Page: 190
CT Page: 632

9.163: If planned investment increases, equilibrium will be restored only when saving has increased by exactly the amount of the initial increase in planned investment assuming there is no government or foreign sector.

Answer: True

Easy
Fact
Page: 193
CT Page: 634

9.164: The larger the MPC, the smaller the multiplier.

Answer: False

SHORT ANSWER QUESTIONS

Easy
Definition
Page: 177
CT Page: 616

9.165: What is aggregate output? What is aggregate income. Explain the relationship between aggregate output and income(Y).

Answer: Aggregate output represents the total quantity of goods and services produced within a nation's economy during a specified period of time. Aggregate income represents the total level of resource payments or income received by all factors of production during a specified period of time. There exists an equality between aggregate output or production and aggregate income during any specified period of time. Total income equals total product.

Easy
Definition
Page: 178
CT Page: 616

9.166: Explain the difference between savings and saving.

Answer: Savings represents the accumulated stock or amount of non-consumption of income. Saving is that portion of income that is not spent on the consumption of goods or services.

Moderate
Application
Page: 178
CT Page: 618

9.167: Explain how changes in interest rates influence spending.

Answer: Lower interest rates lessen the cost of borrowing which results in greater levels of borrowed income and spending. Higher rates increase the cost of borrowing and tend to lessen spending.

9.168: Define and graphically illustrate the consumption function. What does the slope of the consumption function measure?

Easy
Definition
Page: 179
CT Page: 618

Answer: The consumption function can be expressed as: C = a + bY. Consumption (C) is a function of, or depends upon, income (Y). The letter 'a' represents the   y-axis intercept and the letter 'b' is a measure of the slope of the line. The slope of the consumption function measures the change in consumption spending   that results from a change in income .

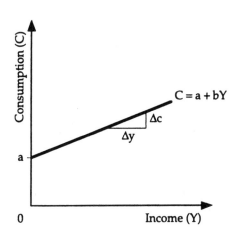

9.169: Using calculations, show the relationship among the MPC, MPS, and income changes.

Moderate
Application
Page: 180
CT Page: 625

Answer: Changes in income will result in changes in consumption and savings. Thus, $\Delta Y = \Delta C + \Delta S$ divide both sides of the equation by   and

$$1 = \frac{\Delta C}{\Delta Y} + \frac{\Delta S}{\Delta Y}$$
$$1 = MPC + MPS$$

9.170: Why doesn't equilibrium exist at aggregate output level Y0 in figure 9.10? Why doesn't equilibrium exist at aggregate output level Y1 in figure 9.10?

Honors
Math
Page: 197
CT Page: 623

Answer: At aggregate output level Y0, the level of aggregate expenditure exceeds the current level of output. This means that inventories are depleted and businesses will increase production and output which will increase income to the equilibrium level at YE. The level of aggregate expenditure is less than current income generated from aggregate output at Y1. This deficient level of spending represents an increase in unplanned business inventories and a resulting decrease in production and income back towards the equilibrium level at YE.

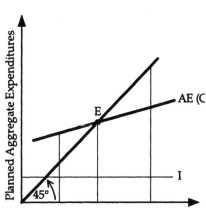

Figure 9.10

Easy
Fact
Page: 178
CT Page: 617

9.171: What are the four determinants of aggregate consumption? Explain how each of these determinants influences aggregate consumption.

Answer: The four determinants of aggregate consumption are: household income, household wealth, interest rates, and households' expectations about the future. As income and wealth increase, consumption increases. As interest rates fall, consumption increases. If households become more optimistic about the future, consumption increases.

Easy
Single
Page: 180
CT Page: 620

9.172: Explain why the MPC and the MPS must sum to one.

Answer: The MPS and the MPC must sum to zero because there are only two uses of income - consumption and saving. The portion of a household's income that is not consumed must be saved.

Easy
Single
Page: 186
CT Page: 623

9.173: Explain how a firm's actual investment can differ from planned investment. If actual investment is less than planned investment, what change will occur in the economy?

Answer: Actual investment is planned investment plus changes in inventory. A firm does not have complete control over its inventory changes. If demand is higher than anticipated, a firm's inventories will fall by more than expected and actual investment will be less than planned investment. If actual investment is less than planned investment, firms will increase production and aggregate output in the economy will rise.

Easy
Single
Page: 185
CT Page: 625

9.174: Define equilibrium as the term is used in macroeconomics. Draw a graph to show an economy that is in equilibrium if there is no government or foreign sector in the economy.

Answer: Equilibrium occurs when the level of planned expenditure equals aggregate output.

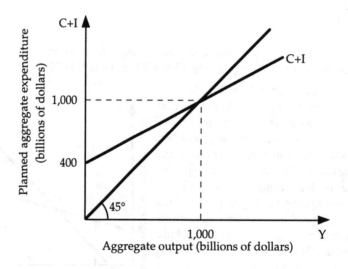

Moderate
Single
Page: 190
CT Page: 625

9.175: Planned aggregate expenditure is less than aggregate output. Explain the process by which the economy moves toward equilibrium.

Answer: If planned aggregate expenditure is less than aggregate output, there is unplanned inventory adjustment. Firms planned to sell more of their goods than they did, and the difference shows up as an unplanned increase in inventories. Firms will respond to this unplanned increase in inventories by reducing production. Production will continue to be reduced until planned expenditure equals aggregate output.

9.176: The consumption function for Outland is C = 300 + .6Y. Planned Investment in Outland is 100. (a.) Graph Outland's aggregate expenditure function. (b.) What is the equilibrium level of output in Outland? (c.) What is the value of the multiplier in Outland? (d.) If investment increases by $50, what is the new equilibrium level of output in Outland?

Challenging
Multi
Page: 192
CT Page: 628

Answer: (a.) See graph. (b.) The equilibrium level of output is $1,000. (c). The multiplier is 2.5. (d.) If investment increases by $50, the equilibrium level of output increases by $125.

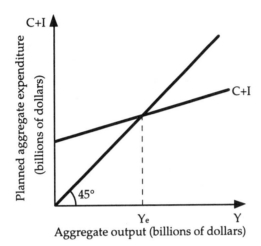

9.177: Explain the saving/investment approach to equilibrium. Use a graph to illustrate how equilibrium can be determined using the saving/investment approach.

Easy
Single
Page: 188
CT Page: 629

Answer: The equilibrium condition is C + I = C + S. Subtracting C from both sides leaves us with S = I. The economy will be in equilibrium only when saving equals investment.

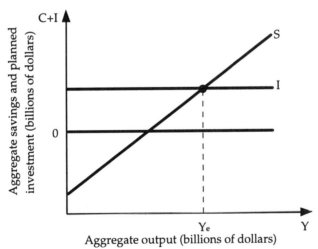

9.178: Explain how the multiplier process works. As the MPC increases, what happens to the size of the multiplier? Why?

Moderate
Single
Page: 190
CT Page: 630

Answer: The initial change in planned investment stimulates multiple spending increases. As the MPC increases, the multiplier increases. As the MPC increases, the more consumption increases as income increases. So for a given change in investment, the larger the MPC the larger the initial change in consumption. The more consumption changes, the more output has to change to achieve equilibrium. The larger the increase in output for a given change in investment, the larger the multiplier.

Moderate
Multi
Page: 178
CT Page: 632

9.179: For each of the following indicate if the change would lead to an increase or decrease in the equilibrium level of output. Explain each of your answers. (a.) Planned investment increases. (b.) Consumers become pessimistic about the future of the economy. (c.) Interest rates fall. (d.) Households begin to save a larger fraction of their income.

Answer: (a) If planned investment increases, the equilibrium level of aggregate output will increase. As investment increases, planned expenditure rises and the equilibrium level of aggregate output increases. (b.) If consumers become pessimistic about the future of the economy, the equilibrium level of aggregate output decreases. This will cause planned expenditure to fall. As planned expenditure falls, the equilibrium level of aggregate output decreases. (c.) As interest rates fall, the equilibrium level of aggregate output will increase. As interest rates fall, consumption increases and as consumption increases, the equilibrium level of aggregate output increases. (d.) As the proportion of income that is saved increases, the equilibrium level of output decreases. As saving increases, consumption decreases and the equilibrium level of aggregate output falls.

Easy
Fact
Page: 194
CT Page: 633

9.180: Explain the paradox of thrift.

Answer: An increase in planned saving causes consumption to fall and equilibrium output to decrease. At the new equilibrium level of income, saving is the same as it was at the initial equilibrium. Thus, increased efforts to save have caused equilibrium output to fall but no overall change in saving. If there is no increase in investment, saving has to return to its original level for the economy to return to equilibrium.

10 The Government and Fiscal Policy

(Chapter 25 in Combined Text)

MULTIPLE CHOICE QUESTIONS

10.1: Fiscal policy refers to

(a) the spending and taxing policies used by the government to influence the economy.
(b) the behavior of the nation's central bank, the Federal Reserve, regarding the nation's money supply.
(c) the techniques used by a business firm to reduce its tax liability.
(d) the government's ability to regulate a firm's behavior in the financial markets.

Answer: (a)

Easy
Definition
Page: 199
CT Page: 641

10.2: Net taxes are

(a) taxes paid by firms and households to the government minus thecost of collecting the taxes.
(b) taxes paid by firms and households to the government plus transfer payments made to firms and households.
(c) taxes paid by firms and households to the government minus the transfer payments made to firms and households.
(d) government expenditures minus government revenues.

Answer: (c)

Easy
Definition
Page: 200
CT Page: 642

10.3: Disposable income is

(a) total income plus transfer payments.
(b) total income minus saving.
(c) total income plus net taxes.
(d) total income minus net taxes.

Answer: (d)

Easy
Definition
Page: 200
CT Page: 642

10.4: Harry's total income is $50,000 and his net taxes are $15,000. Harry's disposable income is

(a) $33,333.
(b) $35,000.
(c) $50,000.
(d) $65,000.

Answer: (b)

Easy
Single
Page: 200
CT Page: 643

10.5. Pete's total income is $10,000 and his net taxes are $2,000. Pete's disposable income is

(a) $8,000.
(b) $10,000.
(c) $12,000.
(d) $2,000.

Answer: (a)

Easy
Single
Page: 200
CT Page: 643

Moderate
Single
Page: 200
CT Page: 643

10.6: Every family, regardless of income or family size, that lives in Mensa is assessed a $200 tax per year. The tax is used to maintain recreational facilities. This is an example of

(a) a net tax.
(b) a lump-sum tax.
(c) an ability-to-pay tax.
(d) a benefits-received tax.

Answer: (b)

Moderate
Single
Page: 200
CT Page: 643

10.7 Every family, regardless of income or family size, that lives in Cascadia is assessed a $500 tax per year. The tax is used to maintain basketball courts. This is an example of

(a) a lump-sum tax.
(b) an ability-to-pay tax.
(c) a net tax.
(d) a benefits-received tax.

Answer: (a)

Easy
Fact
Page: 201
CT Page: 643

10.8: When the government sector is included in the income-expenditures model, the equation for aggregate income is

(a) $C + S + T$.
(b) $C + S - T$.
(c) $C - S - T$.
(d) $C - I + G$.

Answer: (a)

Easy
Definition
Page: 202
CT Page: 643

10.9: The difference between what a government spends and what it collects in taxes in a year is

(a) net revenue.
(b) net taxes.
(c) the budget deficit.
(d) the government debt.

Answer: (c)

Easy
Single
Page: 202
CT Page: 643

10.10: In 1993, the city of Canfield collected $500,000 in taxes and spent $600,000. In 1993, the city of Canfield had a

(a) budget surplus of $100,000.
(b) budget surplus of 83%.
(c) budget deficit of $100,000.
(d) budget deficit of $1,100,000.

Answer: (c)

Easy
Single
Page: 202
CT Page: 643

10.11 In 1993, the city of Miketown collected $100,000 in taxes and spent $400,000. In 1993, the city of Miketown had a

(a) budget surplus of $300,000.
(b) budget surplus of 83%.
(c) budget deficit of $300,000.
(d) budget deficit of $400,000.

Answer: (c)

10.12: When the government sector is included in the income-expenditures model, planned aggregate expenditure is equal to

(a) C + S - T.
(b) C + I + G.
(c) C + I + S.
(d) C + G + T.

Answer: (b)

10.13: After government is added to the income-expenditures model, the formula for the aggregate consumption function is

(a) C = a - b(Y - T).
(b) C = a + b(Y - T).
(c) C = a + b(Y + T).
(d) C = a - b(T - Y).

Answer: (b)

10.14: The aggregate consumption function is C = 200 + .8Y$_d$. If income is $1,000 and net taxes are 100, consumption equals

(a) 900.
(b) 920.
(c) 1,000.
(d) 1,080.

Answer: (b)

10.15. The aggregate consumption function is C = 400 + .9Y$_d$. If income is $2,000 and net taxes are 500, consumption equals

(a) 2200.
(b) 1750.
(c) 1,300.
(d) -1,080.

Answer: (b)

10.16: The aggregate consumption function is C = 100 + .6Y$_d$. If income is $1,600 and net taxes are $100, consumption equals

(a) 900.
(b) 9600.
(c) 1,000.
(d) 1,120.

Answer: (c)

10.17. The aggregate consumption function is C = 300 + .3Y$_d$. If income is $3,600 and net taxes are $600, consumption equals

(a) 900.
(b) 9600.
(c) 1,380.
(d) 1,200.

Answer: (d)

Easy
Fact
Page: 203
CT Page: 644

10.18: If output exceeds planned aggregate expenditure, there will be

(a) an unplanned increase in inventories.
(b) an unplanned decrease in inventories.
(c) no change in inventories.
(d) a planned increase in inventories.

Answer: (a)

Moderate
Single
Page: 203
CT Page: 645

10.19: Refer to Figure 10.1. At an output level of $1,200 billion, the level of aggregate expenditure is _____ billion.

(a) $1,200
(b) $1,300
(c) $1,400
(d) $1,500

Answer: (b)

Moderate
Single
Page: 203
CT Page: 645

10.20: Refer to Figure 10.1. At an output level of $1,200 billion, there is an unplanned inventory

(a) decrease of $100 billion.
(b) change of $0.
(c) increase of $200 billion.
(d) increase of $300 billion.

Answer: (a)

Moderate
Single
Page: 203
CT Page: 645

10.21: Refer to Figure 10.1. At an output level of $2,200, the level of aggregate expenditure is _____ billion.

(a) $1,950
(b) $2,000
(c) $2,100
(d) $2,500

Answer: (c)

Moderate
Single
Page: 203
CT Page: 645

10.22 Refer to Figure 10.1. At an output level of $2,200, there is an unplanned inventory

(a) decrease of $300 billion.
(b) decrease of $100 billion.
(c) change of $0.
(d) increase of $100 billion.

Answer: (d)

Moderate
Single
Page: 203
CT Page: 645

10.23: Refer to Figure 10.1. The equilibrium level of output is _____ billion.

(a) $700
(b) $1,200
(c) $1,700
(d) $2,200

Answer: (c)

(All figures in billions of dollars)				
Output (Income)	Net Taxes	Consumption Spending	Planned Investment spending	Government Purchases
Y	T	C	I	G
700	200	600	150	150
1,200	200	1,000	150	150
1,700	200	1,400	150	150
2,200	200	1,800	150	150
2,700	200	2,200	150	150

Figure 10.1

10.24: Refer to Figure 10.1. At an output level of $1,200, disposable income

(a) is $1,000.
(b) is $1,200.
(c) is $1,400.
(d) cannot be determined from this information.

Answer: (a)

Easy
Single
Page: 203
CT Page: 645

10.25: Refer to Figure 10.1. At an output level of $2,700, the value for saving

(a) is $200.
(b) is $300.
(c) is $500.
(d) cannot be determined from this information.

Answer: (b)

Moderate
Multi
Page: 203
CT Page: 645

10.26: Refer to Figure 10.1. At the equilibrium level of income, leakages equal _____ billion.

(a) $0
(b) $100
(c) $200
(d) $300

Answer: (d)

Moderate
Single
Page: 204
CT Page: 645

10.27: Refer to Figure 10.1 At an output level of $2,700, there is a tendency for output

(a) to fall.
(b) to increase.
(c) to remain constant.
(d) to either increase or decrease.

Answer: (a)

Moderate
Single
Page: 203
CT Page: 645

Moderate
Single
Page: 203
CT Page: 645

10.28: Refer to Figure 10.2. At an output level of $1,500 billion, the level of aggregate expenditure is _____ billion.

(a) $1,300
(b) $1,400
(c) $1,500
(d) $1,600

Answer: (c)

Moderate
Single
Page: 203
CT Page: 645

10.29: Refer to Figure 10.2. At an output level of $1,500 billion, there is an unplanned inventory

(a) decrease of $200 billion.
(b) change of $0.
(c) increase of $300 billion.
(d) increase of $150 billion.

Answer: (b)

Moderate
Single
Page: 203
CT Page: 645

10.30: Refer to Figure 10.2. At an output level of $2,500, the level of aggregate expenditure is _____ billion.

(a) $1,500
(b) $2,000
(c) $2,300
(d) $2,400

Answer: (c)

Moderate
Single
Page: 203
CT Page: 645

10.31: Refer to Figure 10.2. At an output level of $2,500, there is an unplanned inventory

(a) decrease of $300 billion.
(b) decrease of $200 billion.
(c) change of $0.
(d) increase of $200 billion.

Answer: (d)

Moderate
Single
203
CT Page: 645

10.32: Refer to Figure 10.2. The equilibrium level of output is _____ billion.

(a) $1000
(b) $1,500
(c) $2,000
(d) $2,500

Answer: (b)

Easy
Single
Page: 203
CT Page: 645

10.33: Refer to Figure 10.2. At an output level of $1,500, disposable income

(a) is $1,000.
(b) is $1,200.
(c) is $1,400.
(d) cannot be determined from this information.

Answer: (c)

(All figures in billions of dollars)

Output (Income)	Net Taxes	Consumption Spending	Planned Investment spending	Government Purchases
Y	T	C	I	G
500	100	400	150	150
1,000	100	800	150	150
1,500	100	1,200	150	150
2,000	100	1,600	150	150
2,500	100	2,000	150	150

Figure 10.2

10.34: Refer to Figure 10.2. At an output level of $2,500, the level for saving

(a) is $300.
(b) is $400.
(c) is $500.
(d) cannot be determined from this information.

Answer: (b)

Moderate
Multi
Page: 203
CT Page: 645

10.35: Refer to Figure 10.2 At the equilibrium level of income, leakages equal _____ billion.

(a) $0
(b) $300
(c) $500
(d) $1,000

Answer: (b)

Moderate
Single
Page: 204
CT Page: 645

10.36: Refer to Figure 10.2. At an output level of $2,500, there is a tendency for output
(a) to increase.
(b) to remain constant.
(c) to either increase or decrease.
(d) to fall.

Answer: (d)

Moderate
Single
Page: 203
CT Page: 645

10.37: Refer to Figure 10.3. The equilibrium level of output for the Balkan economy is

(a) 3,000.
(b) 4,500.
(c) 4,800.
(d) 5,000.

Answer: (a)

Challenging
Multi
Page: 203
CT Page: 645

10.38: Refer to Figure 10.3. At the equilibrium level of output in Balka , leakages equal

(a) 400.
(b) 500.
(c) 700.
(d) 1,200.

Answer: (c)

Challenging
Multi
Page: 204
CT Page: 645

The Balkan economy can be characterized by the following equations:

$$C = 300 + .8Y_d$$
$$G = 600$$
$$T = 500$$
$$I = 100$$

Figure 10.3

Moderate
Multi
Page: 203
CT Page: 645

10.39: Refer to Figure 10.3. At the equilibrium level of output in Balka, consumption equals

(a) 2,200.
(b) 2,300.
(c) 2,400.
(d) 2,700.

Answer: (b)

Moderate
Multi
Page: 203
CT Page: 645

10.40: Refer to Figure 10.3. At the equilibrium level of output in Balka, saving equals

(a) 200
(b) 600.
(c) 700.
(d) 800.

Answer: (a)

Challenging
Multi
Page: 203
CT Page: 645

10.41: Refer to Figure 10.4. The equilibrium level of output for the French economy is

(a) 8,400.
(b) 8,500.
(c) 8,600.
(d) 8,700.

Answer: (d)

Challenging
Multi
Page: 204
CT Page: 645

10.42: Refer to Figure 10.4 At the equilibrium level of output in France, leakages equal

(a) 1,400.
(b) 2,000.
(c) 1,500.
(d) 1000.

Answer: (d)

The French economy can be characterized by the following equations:

$$C = 50 + .9Y_d$$
$$G = 900$$
$$T = 200$$
$$I = 100$$

Figure 10.4

10.43: Refer to Figure 10n.2. At the equilibrium level of output in France, consumption equals

(a) 200.
(b) 7,050.
(c) 7,700.
(d) 7,900.

Moderate
Single
Page: 203
CT Page: 645

Answer: (c)

10.44: Refer to Figure 10.4. At the equilibrium level of output in France, saving equals

(a) 330.
(b) 400.
(c) 500.
(d) 800.

Moderate
Multi
Page: 203
CT Page: 645

Answer: (d)

10.45: Assuming there is no foreign trade in the economy, the leakages/injections approach to equilibrium can be written as

(a) S + T + I = G.
(b) S - T = I + G.
(c) S + I = T + G.
(d) S + T = I + G.

Easy
Fact
Page: 204
CT Page: 646

Answer: (d)

10.46: Assuming there is no foreign trade in the economy, equilibrium is achieved when saving is exactly equal to planned investment

(a) minus the government deficit.
(b) plus the government deficit.
(c) minus government spending minus taxes.
(d) minus government spending plus taxes.

Easy
Fact
Page: 204
CT Page: 646

Answer: (b)

10.47: Refer to Figure 10.5. The equilibrium level of output is

(a) $400 billion.
(b) $600 billion. '
(c) $800 billion.
(d) $1,000 billion.

Moderate
Single
Page: 204
CT Page: 646

Answer: (d)

10.48: Refer to Figure 10.5. At the equilibrium level of output, injections

(a) are $200 billion.
(b) are $400 billion.
(c) are $600 billion.
(d) cannot be determined from this information.

Moderate
Multi
Page: 204
CT Page: 646

Answer: (a)

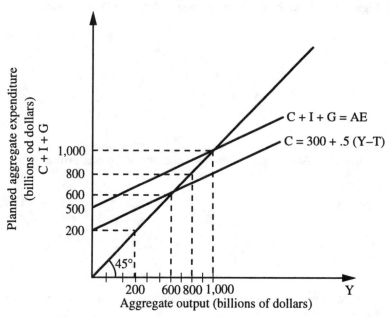

Figure 10.5

Moderate
Multi
Page: 204
CT Page: 646

10.49: Refer to Figure 10.5. Planned injections are

(a) $200 billion at the equilibrium level of output and greater than $200 billion at all other levels of output.
(b) $200 billion at the equilibrium level of output and less than $200 billion at all other levels of output.
(c) less than $200 billion at output levels below the equilibrium output, $200 billion at the equilibrium level of output, and greater than $200 billion at output levels above the equilibrium output level.
(d) $200 billion at all output levels.

Answer: (d)

Moderate
Multi
Page: 204
CT Page: 646

10.50: Refer to Figure 10.5. At the equilibrium level of output, leakages
(a) are $200 billion.
(b) are $400 billion.
(c) are $600 billion.
(d) cannot be determined from this information.

Answer: (a)

Moderate
Multi
Page: 204
CT Page: 646

10.51: Refer to Figure 10.5. At the equilibrium level of output, consumption

(a) is $600 billion.
(b) is $800 billion.
(c) is $1,000 billion.
(d) cannot be determined from this information.

Answer: (b)

Challenging
Multi
Page: 204
CT Page: 646

10.52: Refer to Figure 10.5. At the equilibrium level of output, taxes

(a) are $0.
(b) are $100 billion.
(c) are $200 billion.
(d) cannot be determined from this information.

Answer: (a)

10.53: Refer to Figure 10.5. At the equilibrium level of output, saving

(a) is $0.
(b) is $100 billion.
(c) is $200 billion.
(d) cannot be determined from this information.

Answer: (c)

10.54: Refer to Figure 10.6. The equilibrium level of output is
(a) $200 billion.
(b) $350 billion.
(c) $1,100 billion.
(d) none of the above.

Answer: (c)

10.55: Refer to Figure 10.6. At the equilibrium level of output, injections

(a) are $200 billion.
(b) are $300 billion.
(c) are $400 billion.
(d) cannot be determined from this information.

Answer: (b)

10.56: Refer to Figure 10.6. Planned injections are

(a) less than $300 billion at output levels below the equilibrium output, $300 billion at the equilibrium level of output, and greater than $300 billion at output levels above the equilibrium output level.
(b) $300 billion at the equilibrium level of output and less than $300 billion at all other levels of output.
(c) $300 billion at all output levels.
(d) $300 billion at the equilibrium level of output and greater than $300 billion at all other levels of output.

Answer: (c)

Challenging
Multi
Page: 204
CT Page: 646

Moderate
Single
Page: 204
CT Page: 646

Moderate
Multi
Page: 204
CT Page: 646

Moderate
Multi
Page: 204
CT Page: 646

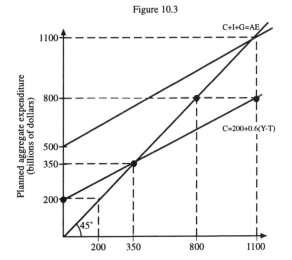

Figure 10.6.

Moderate
Multi
Page: 204
CT Page: 646

10.57: Refer to Figure 10.6 At the equilibrium level of output, leakages

(a) are $200 billion.
(b) are $300 billion.
(c) are $400 billion.
(d) cannot be determined from this information.

Answer: (b)

Moderate
Multi
Page: 204
CT Page: 646

10.58: Refer to Figure 10.6. At the equilibrium level of output, consumption

(a) is $600 billion.
(b) is $700 billion.
(c) is $1,200 billion.
(d) is $800 billion.

Answer: (d)

Challenging
Multi
Page: 204
CT Page: 646

10.59: Refer to Figure 10.6. At the equilibrium level of output, taxes

(a) are $100 billion.
(b) are $300 billion.
(c) are $0.
(d) none of the above.

Answer: (a)

Challenging
Multi
Page: 204
CT Page: 646

10.60: Refer to Figure 10.6. At the equilibrium level of output, saving

(a) is $150 million.
(b) is $100 million.
(c) is $200 million.
(d) $250 million.

Answer: (c)

Easy
Fact
Page: 204
CT Page: 646

10.61: If planned injections exceed leakages, output will

(a) decrease.
(b) increase.
(c) remain unchanged.
(d) either increase or decrease.

Answer: (b)

Easy
Single
Page: 204
CT Page: 646

10.62: If planned injections are less than leakages, output will

(a) decrease.
(b) increase.
(c) remain constant.
(d) either increase or decrease.

Answer: (a)

Easy
Fact
Page: 204
CT Page: 647

10.63: For the economy to be in equilibrium,

(a) government spending must equal tax revenue and saving must equal investment.
(b) government spending must equal the sum of tax revenue, saving and investment.
(c) investment plus tax revenue must equal government spending plus saving.
(d) government spending plus investment must equal saving plus tax revenue.

Answer: (d)

10.64: If the government wants to reduce unemployment, government spending should be _____ and/or taxes should be _____.

Easy
Fact
Page: 205
CT Page: 647

(a) increased; increased
(b) increased; decreased
(c) decreased; increased
(d) decreased; decreased

Answer: (b)

10.65: The President of Vulcan hires you as an economic consultant. He is concerned that the output level in Vulcan is too high and that this will cause prices to rise. He feels that it is necessary to reduce output by $50 billion. He tells you that the MPC in Vulcan is .8. Which of the following would be the best advice to give to the Vulcan President?

Moderate
Multi
Page: 205
CT Page: 648

(a) Reduce government spending in Vulcan by $50 billion.
(b) Increase taxes in Vulcan by $50 billion.
(c) Reduce government spending in Vulcan by $10 billion.
(d) Increase taxes in Vulcan by $10 billion.

Answer: (c)

10.66: The leader of Atlantis hires you as an economic consultant. He is concerned that the output level in Atlantis is too low and that this will cause prices to fall. He feels that it is necessary to increase output by $100 billion. He tells you that the MPC in Atlantis is .9. Which of the following would be the best advice to give to the Atlantin President?

Moderate
Multi
Page: 205
CT Page: 648

(a) Reduce government spending in Atlantis by $100 billion.
(b) Increase taxes in Atlantis by $10 billion.
(c) Reduce government spending in Atlantis by $10 billion.
(d) Increase government spending in Atlantis by $10 billion.

Answer: (c)

10.67: Refer to Figure 10.7. The equilibrium level of income is

Moderate
Multi
Page: 205
CT Page: 648

(a) $1,000 billion.
(b) $1,600 billion.
(c) $2,200 billion.
(d) $2,800 billion.

Answer: (b)

10.68: Refer to Figure 10.7. The MPS

Moderate
Multi
Page: 205
CT Page: 648

(a) is 8.
(b) is .2.
(c) is .8.
(d) cannot be determined from the available information.

Answer: (b)

10.69: Refer to Figure 10.7. The value of the government spending multiplier

Moderate
Multi
Page: 205
CT Page: 648

(a) is .2.
(b) is 1.10.
(c) is 5.
(d) cannot be determined from the available information.

Answer: (c)

Challenging
Multi
Page: 205
CT Page: 648

10.70: Refer to Figure 10.7. The economy is at the equilibrium level of output. If government spending increases to $440 billion, the new equilibrium level of output is

(a) $1,640 billion.
(b) $1,840 billion.
(c) $2,040 billion.
(d) $2,800 billion.

Answer: (d)

Challenging
Multi
Page: 205
CT Page: 648

10.71: Refer to Figure 10.7. The economy is at the equilibrium level of output. If government spending decreases by $50 billion, the new equilibrium level of output is

(a) $1,250 billion.
(b) $1,350 billion.
(c) $1,450 billion.
(d) $1,550 billion.

Answer: (b)

Challenging
Multi
Page: 205
CT Page: 650

10.72: Refer to Figure 10.7. If taxes are reduced from $100 billion to $50 billion, the new equilibrium level of output

(a) is $1,550 billion.
(b) is $1,600 billion.
(c) is $1,800 billion.
(d) cannot be determined from this information.

Answer: (c)

(All figures in billions of dollars)					
Output (Income)	Net Taxes	Consumption Spending $(C = 100 + .8Y_d)$	Saving	Planned Investment Spending	Government Purchases
600	100	500	0	100	200
1,000	100	820	80	100	200
1,600	100	1300	200	100	200
1,800	100	1460	240	100	200
2,200	100	1780	320	100	200
2,800	100	2260	440	100	200
3,400	100	2740	560	100	200

Figure 10.7

10.73: Refer to Figure 10.7. If taxes are reduced from $100 billion to $50 billion and government spending is reduced from $200 billion to $150 billion, the new equilibrium level of income

(a) is $1,400 billion.
(b) is $1,550 billion.
(c) is $1,650 billion.
(d) cannot be determined from this information.

Answer: (b)

Challenging
Multi
Page: 205
CT Page: 651

10.74: Refer to Figure 10.8. The equilibrium level of income is

(a) $800 billion.
(b) $1,600 billion.
(c) $2,000 billion.
(d) $3,600 billion.

Answer: (d)

Moderate
Multi
Page: 205
CT Page: 648

10.75: Refer to Figure 10.8. The MPS

(a) is .8.
(b) is .1.
(c) cannot be determined from the available information.
(d) none of the above.

Answer: (b)

Moderate
Multi
Page: 205
CT Page: 648

10.76: Refer to Figure 10.8. The value of the government spending multiplier
(a) is 10.
(b) is .9.
(c) is 5.
(d) cannot be determined from the available information.

Answer: (a)

Moderate
Multi
Page: 205
CT Page: 648

10.77: Refer to Figure 10.8. The economy is at the equilibrium level of output. If government spending increases to $500 billion, the new equilibrium level of output is

(a) $1,640 billion.
(b) $2,100 billion.
(c) $6,040 billion.
(d) $6,600 billion.

Answer: (d)

Challenging
Multi
Page: 205
CT Page: 648

10.78: Refer to Figure 10.8. The economy is at the equilibrium level of output. If government spending decreases by $50 billion, the new equilibrium level of output is

(a) $3,100 billion.
(b) $1,350 billion.
(c) $1,450 billion.
(d) $1,550 billion.

Answer: (a)

Challenging
Multi
Page: 205
CT Page: 648

Challenging
Multi
Page: 205
CT Page: 650

10.79: Refer to Figure 10.8. If taxes are reduced from $100 billion to $50 billion, the new equilibrium level of output

(a) is $4,050 billion.
(b) is $1,600 billion.
(c) is $1,800 billion.
(d) is $2,100 billion.

Answer: (a)

Challenging
Multi
Page: 205
CT Page: 651

10.80: Refer to Figure 10.8. If taxes are reduced from $100 billion to $50 billion and government spending is reduced from $200 billion to $150 billion, the new equilibrium level of income

(a) is $1,400 billion.
(b) is $3,550 billion.
(c) is $1,600 billion.
(d) cannot be determined from this information.

Answer: (b)

Easy
Definition
Page: 205
CT Page: 648

10.81: The government spending multiplier is

(a) the ratio of the change in the equilibrium level of output to a change in government spending.
(b) the ratio of the change in government spending to the change in the equilibrium level of output.
(c) the difference between the old equilibrium level of output and the new equilibrium level of output.
(d) the difference between the new and old levels of government spending.

Answer: (a)

Easy
Fact
Page: 205
CT Page: 648

10.82: The formula for the government spending multiplier is

(a) 1/(1 + MPC).
(b) 1/MPC.
(c) 1/MPS.
(d) 1/(1 + MPS).

Answer: (c)

(All figures in billions of dollars)

Output (Income)	Net Taxes (C = 100 + .9Yd)	Consumption Spending Spending	Saving Investment	Planned Purchases	Government
2,400	100	2170	150	150	200
2,800	100	2530	170	150	200
3,000	100	2710	190	150	200
3,200	100	2890	210	150	200
3,400	100	3070	230	150	200
3,600	100	3250	250	150	200
3,800	100	3300	270	150	200

Figure 10.8

10.83: If the MPS is .1, the government spending multiplier is

(a) .11.
(b) 1.11.
(c) 9.
(d) 10.

Answer: (d)

10.84: If the MPS is .5, the government spending multiplier is

(a) .11.
(b) 1.11.
(c) 5.
(d) 2.

Answer: (d)

10.85: If.the MPC is .8, the government spending multiplier is

(a) 1.10.
(b) 4.
(c) 5.
(d) 8.

Answer: (c)

10.86:. If the MPC is .6, the government spending multiplier is

(a) 2.5.
(b) 4.
(c) 6.
(d) 1.666.

Answer: (a)

10.87: If the government spending multiplier is 4 and government spending increases by $400 billion, output will increase by

(a) $100 billion.
(b) $400 billion.
(c) $1,600 billion.
(d) $2,000 billion.

Answer: (c)

10.88: If the government spending multiplier is 8 and government spending increases by $100 billion, output will increase by
(a) $800 billion.
(b) $700 billion.
(c) $80 billion.
(d) $2,000 billion.

Answer: (a)

The economy of Marshland can be characterized by the following equations:

$$C = 200 + .6Y_d$$
$$T = 50$$
$$G = 100$$
$$I = 70$$

Figure 10.9

Challenging
Multi
Page: 205
CT Page: 648

10.89: Refer to Figure 10.9. The equilibrium level of income in Marshland is

(a) 567.
(b) 800.
(c) 850.
(d) 910.

Answer: (c)

Challenging
Multi
Page: 205
CT Page: 648

10.90: Refer to Figure 10.9. If government spending in Marshland increases by $50, equilibrium output increases by

(a) 50.
(b) 75.
(c) 83.
(d) 125.

Answer: (d)

Challenging
Multi
Page: 205
CT Page: 648

10.91: Refer to Figure 10.10 The equilibrium level of income in Bordeaux is

(a) 4200.
(b) 4400.
(c) 4700.
(d) 5200.

Answer: (c)

The economy of Bourdeaux can be characterized by the following equations:

$$C = 200 + .8Y_d$$
$$T = 200$$
$$G = 800$$
$$I = 100$$

Figure 10.10

Challenging
Multi
Page: 205
CT Page: 648

10.92: Refer to Figure 10.10.
If government spending in Bordeaux increases by $100, equilibrium output increases by

(a) 50.
(b) 100.
(c) 500.
(d) 5000.

Answer: (c)

Easy
Single
Page: 207
CT Page: 649

10.93: Refer to Figure 10.11. When autonomous planned expenditure equals $325 billion, the equilibrium level of output is

(a) $1,150 billion.
(b) $1,300 billion.
(c) $1,567 billion.
(d) $1,700 billion.

Answer: (b)

10.94: If the government spending multiplier is 2 and government spending decreases by $100 billion, the equilibrium level of output will

(a) decrease by $200 billion.
(b) decrease by $100 billion.
(c) increase by $100 billion.
(d) increase by $200 billion.

Easy
Single
Page: 207
CT Page: 649

Answer: (a)

10.95: Refer to Figure 10.11. When autonomous planned expenditure equals $425 billion, the equilibrium level of output is

(a) $1,150 billion.
(b) $1,300 billion.
(c) $1,567 billion.
(d) $1,700 billion.

Easy
Single
Page: 207
CT Page: 649

Answer: (d)

10.96: Refer to Figure 10.11. An increase in government spending of $100 billion shifts the aggregate expenditure function from AE to AE'. This $100 billion increase in government spending causes the equilibrium level of output to increase by

(a) $133 billion.
(b) $267 billion.
(c) $400 billion.
(d) $417 billion.

Moderate
Multi
Page: 207
CT Page: 649

Answer: (c)

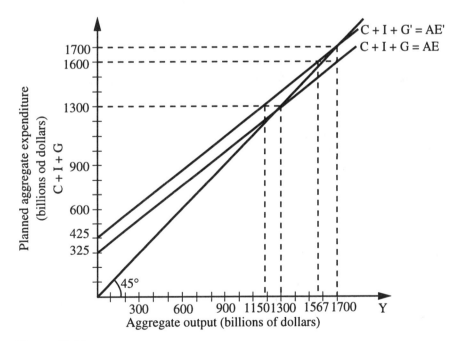

Figure 10.11

Challenging
Multi
Page: 207
CT Page: 649

10.97: Refer to Figure 10.11. An increase in government spending of $100 billion shifts the aggregate expenditure function from AE to AE'. The value of the government spending multiplier in this example is

(a) 1.33.
(b) 2.67.
(c) 4.
(d) 4.17.

Answer: (c)

Easy
Single
Page: 207
CT Page: 649

10.99: If the government spending multiplier is 4 and government spending decreases by $40 billion, the equilibrium level of output will

(a) decrease by $160 billion.
(b) decrease by $40 billion.
(c) increase by $40 billion.
(d) increase by $160 billion.

Answer: (a)

Moderate
Single
Page: 207
CT Page: 649

10.100: Government spending increases by $50 billion and the equilibrium level of output increases by $250 billion. The government spending multiplier

(a) is .5.
(b) is 2.5.
(c) is 5.
(d) cannot be determined from this information, because the MPC is not given.

Answer: (c)

Moderate
Single
Page: 207
CT Page: 649

10.101: Government spending increases by $200 billion and the equilibrium level of output increases by $1000 billion. The government spending multiplier

(a) is 5.
(b) is 2.5.
(c) cannot be determined from this information, because the MPC is not given.
(d) is .5.

Answer: (a)

Moderate
Single
Page: 207
CT Page: 649

10.102: Assume an economy is in equilibrium at an output level of $600 billion. If government spending increases by $30 billion, then at the output level of $600 billion, there is

(a) an unplanned fall in inventories.
(b) an unplanned increase in inventories.
(c) an unplanned inventory change of zero.
(d) either an unplanned increase or decrease in inventories depending on the value of the MPC.

Answer: (a)

Moderate
Single
Page: 207
CT Page: 649

10.103: Assume an economy is in equilibrium at an output level of $400 billion. If government spending increases by $50 billion, then at the output level of $400 billion, there is

(a) an unplanned increase in inventories.
(b) an unplanned inventory change of zero.
(c) either an unplanned increase or decrease in inventories depending on the value of the MPC.
(d) an unplanned fall in inventories.

Answer: (d)

10.104: A decrease in lump-sum taxes will

(a) make the consumption function flatter.
(b) make the consumption function steeper.
(c) have no effect on the slope of the consumption function.
(d) make the consumption function nonlinear.

Answer: (c)

Challenging
Multi
Page: 208
CT Page: 650

10.105: The tax multiplier is

(a) the ratio of the change in taxes to the change in the equilibrium level of output.
(b) the ratio of the change in the equilibrium level of output to the change in taxes.
(c) the difference in taxes multiplied by the change in the equilibrium level of output.
(d) the MPC multiplied by the MPS.

Answer: (b)

Easy
Definition
Page: 208
CT Page: 650

10.106: The formula for the tax multiplier is

(a) -(MPS/MPC).
(b) -(MPC/MPS).
(c) MPS/MPC.
(d) -1/MPS.

Answer: (b)

Easy
Definition
Page: 208
CT Page: 650

10.107: If the MPC is .8, the tax multiplier is

(a) -5.
(b) -4.
(c) -1.10.
(d) 10.

Answer: (b)

Easy
Single
Page: 208
CT Page: 650

10.108: If the MPC is .7, the tax multiplier is

(a) -7.
(b) -4.
(c) -2.33.
(d) -3.33.

Answer: (c)

Easy
Single
Page: 208
CT Page: 650

10.109: If the MPS is .4, the tax multiplier is

(a) -2.5.
(b) -1.67.
(c) -1.5.
(d) 67.

Answer: (c)

Easy
Single
Page: 208
CT Page: 650

Easy
Single
Page: 208
CT Page: 650

10.110: If the MPS is .9, the tax multiplier is

(a) -9.
(b) 10.
(c) -1.5.
(d) -0.9.

Answer: (a)

Moderate
Multi
Page: 208
CT Page: 650

10.111: Taxes are reduced by $200 billion and income increases by $800 billion. The value of the tax multiplier is

(a) -4.
(b) 10.
(c) .10.
(d) 4.

Answer: (a)

Moderate
Multi
Page: 208
CT Page: 650

10.112 Taxes are reduced by $200 billion and income increases by $1,000 billion. The value of the tax multiplier is

(a) -4.
(b) -5.
(c) .10.
(d) 5.

Answer: (b)

Moderate
Single
Page: 208
CT Page: 650

10.113: If the tax multiplier is -5 and taxes are reduced by $200 billion, output

(a) falls by $1,000 billion.
(b) falls by $40 billion.
(c) increases by $40 billion.
(d) increases by $1,000 billion.

Answer: (d)

Moderate
Single
Page: 208
CT Page: 650

10.114: If the tax multiplier is -3 and taxes are reduced by $100 billion, output

(a) falls by $300 billion.
(b) falls by $30 billion.
(c) increases by $300 billion.
(d) increases by $1,000 billion.

Answer: (c)

Challenging
Multi
Page: 208
CT Page: 650

10.115: Refer to Figure 10.12. If taxes are increased by $100 billion, the aggregate expenditure function shifts from AE to AE'. The tax multiplier

(a) is -4.
(b) is -3.
(c) is 4.
(d) cannot be determined because the MPC is not given.

Answer: (b)

10.116: Refer to Figure 10.12. If taxes are increased by $100 billion, the aggregate expenditure function shifts from AE to AE'. The MPC

(a) is .10.
(b) is .5.
(c) is .75.
(d) cannot be determined from the available information.

Answer: (c)

Challenging
Multi
Page: 208
CT Page: 650

10.117: If the MPC is .8 and taxes are increased by $400, then consumption _____ and saving _____.

(a) increases by $320; increases by $80
(b) increases by $320; decreases by $80
(c) decreases by $320; decreases by $80
(d) decreases by $320; increases by $80.

Answer: (c)

Moderate
Multi
Page: 208
CT Page: 650

10.118: If the MPC is .4 and taxes are increased by $200, then consumption _____ and saving _____.

(a) increases by $80; decreases by $120
(b) decreases by $80; increases by $120.
(c) increases by $80; increases by $120
(d) decreases by $80; decreases by $120

Answer: (d)

Moderate
Multi
Page: 208
CT Page: 650

10.119: If taxes are $200 billion, the equilibrium level of output is $6,000 billion. If taxes increase to $300 billion, everything else the same, the equilibrium level of output falls to $5,500 billion. The value of the tax multiplier

(a) is -5.5.
(b) is -5.
(c) is 5.
(d) cannot be determined from this information because the MPC is not given.

Answer: (b)

Moderate
Single
Page: 208
CT Page: 650

10.120: If taxes are $100 billion, the equilibrium level of output is $1,000 billion. If taxes increase to $200 billion, everything else the same, the equilibrium level of output falls to $700 billion. The value of the tax multiplier

(a) is -5.5.
(b) is 3.
(c) is -3.
(d) none of the above.

Answer: (c)

Moderate
Single
Page: 208
CT Page: 650

10.121: The value of the balanced-budget multiplier

(a) is always 0.
(b) is always 1.
(c) is always -1.
(d) depends on the value of the MPC.

Answer: (b)

Easy
Fact
Page: 209
CT Page: 652

Moderate
Single
Page: 209
T Page: 652

10.122: Which of the following statements is FALSE?

(a) As the government increases spending by $1, planned aggregate expenditure increases initially by $1.
(b) When taxes are cut, the initial increase in planned aggregate expenditure is less than the change in taxes.
(c) The final effect on the equilibrium level of income is smaller for a tax increase of $1 billion than it is for a government spending decrease of $1 billion.
(d) The balanced-budget multiplier is used whenever the increase in government spending is the same size as the decrease in taxes.

Answer: (d)

Easy
Single
Page: 209
CT Page: 652

10.123: If the government spending multiplier is 5, then the tax multiplier is

(a) is -5
(b) is -4.
(c) is 1.
(d) cannot be determined because the MPS is not given.

Answer: (b)

Easy
Single
Page: 209
CT Page: 652

10.124: If the government spending multiplier is 10, then the tax multiplier is

(a) is 9
(b) is -9.
(c) is 10.
(d) cannot be determined because the MPS is not given.

Answer: (b)

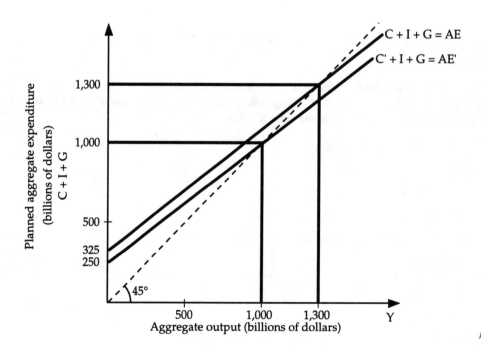

Figure 10.12

10.125: If government spending is increased by $500 and taxes are reduced by $500, equilibrium output will change by

(a) -$500.
(b) $0.
(c) $500.
(d) an amount that cannot be determined from this information.

Answer: (d)

Challenging
Multi
Page: 209
T Page: 652

10.126: If government spending is increased by $200 and taxes are reduced by $200, equilibrium output will change by

(a) -$200.
(b) $0.
(c) $200.
(d) an amount that cannot be determined from this information.

Answer: (d)

Challenging
Multi
Page: 209
T Page: 652

10.127: If government spending is increased by $700 and taxes are increased by $700, the equilibrium level of income will

(a) decrease by $700.
(b) increase by $700.
(c) not change.
(d) increase by $1,400.

Answer: (b)

Easy
Single
Page: 209
CT Page: 652

10.128: If government spending is increased by $800 and taxes are increased by $800, the equilibrium level of income will

(a) decrease by $800.
(b) increase by $800.
(c) not change.
(d) increase by $1600

Answer: (a)

Easy
Single
Page: 209
CT Page: 652

10.129: Assume that the MPC is .75. By increasing government spending by $400, equilibrium output _____ ; and by increasing taxes by $400, equilibrium output _____.

(a) increases by $1,600; decreases by $1,600.
(b) increases by $1,600; decreases by $1,200.
(c) increases by $1,200; decreases by $1,600.
(d) increases by $400; decreases by $400.

Answer: (b)

Moderate
Multi
Page: 209
CT Page: 652

10.130: Assume that the MPC is .9. By increasing government spending by $100, equilibrium output _____ ; and by increasing taxes by $100, equilibrium output _____.

(a) increases by $1,000; decreases by $1,000.
(b) increases by $900; decreases by $1,000.
(c) increases by $1,000; decreases by $900.
(d) increases by $400; decreases by $400.

Answer: (c)

Moderate
Multi
Page: 209
CT Page: 652

Moderate
Multi
Page: 209
CT Page: 652

10.131: You are hired by the Council of Economic Advisors (CEA) as an economic consultant. The Chairperson of the CEA tells you that she believes the current unemployment rate is too high. The unemployment rate can be reduced if aggregate output increases. She wants to know what policy to pursue to increase aggregate output by $300 billion. The best estimate she has for the MPC is .8. Which of the following policies should you recommend?

(a) To increase government spending by $60 billion.
(b) To increase government spending by $150 billion.
(c) To cut taxes by $60 billion.
(d) To cut taxes by $60 billion and to increase government spending by $60 billion.

Answer: (a)

Moderate
Multi
Page: 209
CT Page: 652

10.132: You are hired by the Bureau of Economic Analogies (BEA) as an economic consultant. The Chairperson of the BEA tells you that he believes the current unemployment rate is too low. The unemployment rate can be increased if aggregate output decreases. He wants to know what policy to pursue to decrease aggregate output by $100 billion. The best estimate he has for the MPC is .9. Which of the following policies should you recommend?

(a) To decrease government spending by $10 billion.
(b) To decrease government spending by $100 billion.
(c) To increase taxes by $100 billion.
(d) To cut taxes by $60 billion and to increase government spending by $60 billion.

Answer: (a)

Moderate
Multi
Page: 209
CT Page: 652

10.133: You are hired by the Council of Economic Advisors (CEA) as an economic consultant. The Chairperson of the CEA tells you that she believes the current unemployment rate is too high. The unemployment rate can be reduced if aggregate output increases. She wants to know what policy to pursue to increase aggregate output by $300 billion. The best estimate she has for the MPC is .8. Which of the following policies should you recommend?

(a) To increase government spending by $75 billion.
(b) To reduce taxes by $75 billion.
(c) To reduce taxes by $75 billion and to increase government spending by $75 billion.
(d) To reduce the budget deficit by $300 billion.

Answer: (b)

Moderate
Multi
Page: 209
CT Page: 652

10.134: You are hired by the Bureau of Economic Analogies (BEA) as an economic consultant. The Chairperson of the BEA tells you that he believes the current unemployment rate is too high. The unemployment rate can be reduced if aggregate output increases. He wants to know what policy to pursue to increase aggregate output by $500 billion. The best estimate he has for the MPC is .7. Which of the following policies should you recommend?

(a) To decrease government spending by $75 billion.
(b) To reduce taxes by $214.3 billion.
(c) To reduce taxes by $314.3 billion and to decrease government spending by $500 billion.
(d) To reduce the budget deficit by $300 billion.

Answer: (b)

10.135: You are hired by the Council of Economic Advisors (CEA) as an economic consultant. The Chairperson of the CEA tells you that she believes the current unemployment rate is too high. The unemployment rate can be reduced if aggregate output increases. She wants to know what policy to pursue to increase aggregate output by $300 billion. The best estimate she has for the MPC is .8. Which of the following policies should you recommend?

Moderate
Multi
Page: 209
CT Page: 652

(a) To increase government spending by $300 billion and reduce taxes by $300 billion.
(b) To reduce government spending by $300 billion and increase taxes by $300 billion.
(c) To increase both government spending and taxes by $300 billion.
(d) To decrease both government spending and taxes by $300 billion.

Answer: (c)

10.135: You are hired by the Bureau of Economic Analogies (BEA) as an economic consultant. The Chairperson of the BEA tells you that he believes the current unemployment rate is too high. The unemployment rate can be reduced if aggregate output increases. He wants to know what policy to pursue to increase aggregate output by $200 billion. The best estimate she has for the MPC is .8. Which of the following policies should you recommend?

Moderate
Multi
Page: 209
CT Page: 652

(a) To reduce government spending by $300 billion and reduce taxes by $300 billion.
(b) To increase both government spending and taxes by $300 billion.
(c) To increase government spending by $300 billion and reduce taxes by $300 billion.
(d) none of the above.

Answer: (d)

10.136: As the size of the MPC increases, the value of the balanced-budget multiplier

Moderate
Single
Page: 209
CT Page: 652

(a) increases.
(b) decreases.
(c) could either increase or decrease.
(d) remains constant.

Answer: (d)

10.137: Which of the following statements is FALSE?

Easy
Fact
Page: 209
CT Page: 652

(a) For a given change in taxes, the change in consumption is less than the change in taxes,
because the MPC is less than one.
(b) An increase in government spending has a direct initial effect on
planned aggregate expenditure; a tax increase does not.
(c) The positive stimulus from a government spending increase
equals the negative stimulus from a tax increase.
(d) The initial effect of a tax increase is that households cut
consumption by the MPC times the change in taxes.

Answer: (c)

10.138: Imports are _____ the circular flow and exports are _____
circular flow.

Easy
Fact
Page: 211
CT Page: 655

(a) a leakage from; a leakage from
(b) an injection into; an injection into
(c) an injection into; a leakage from
(d) a leakage from; an injection into

Answer: (d)

Easy
Fact
Page: 211
CT Page: 655

10.139: The equilibrium position for an open economy is

(a) $Y = C + I + G + (EX - IM)$.
(b) $Y = C + I + G + (IM - EX)$.
(c) $Y = C + I + G + EX + IM$.
(d) $Y = C + I + G + EX$.

Answer: (a)

Easy
Fact
Page: 211
CT Page: 655

10.140: If some domestic spending leaks into foreign markets, the multiplier effect on domestic production will

(a) be increased.
(b) be reduced.
(c) not be affected.
(d) become zero.

Answer: (b)

Easy
Fact
Page: 214
CT Page: 655

10.141: Which of the following is NOT a cause of the large federal deficit of the 1980s and 1990s?

(a) Transfer payments as a percentage of GDP have risen in the 1980s.
(b) Government purchases as a percentage of GDP have risen since 1980.
(c) Interest payments as a percentage of GDP have risen substantially since 1980.
(d) Personal income tax rates have fallen since 1981 as a result of the Economic Recovery Tax Act of 1981.

Answer: (a)

Easy
Definition
Page: 214
CT Page: 657

10.142: The total amount owed by the federal government to the public is the

(a) federal budget deficit.
(b) federal debt.
(c) net tax revenue.
(d) fiscal drag.

Answer: (b)

Easy
Definition
Page: 218
CT Page: 659

10.143: The negative effect on the economy that occurs when average tax rates increase because taxpayers have moved into higher income brackets during an expansion is

(a) fiscal drag.
(b) bracket creep.
(c) the Laffer curve.
(d) debt burden.

Answer: (a)

Moderate
Fact
Page: 218
CT Page: 659

10.144: Indexing or adjusting the tax brackets for inflation

(a) has substantially increased the amount of fiscal drag built into the system.
(b) has substantially reduced the amount of fiscal drag built into the system.
(c) means that the federal personal income tax system no longer operates as an automatic stabilizer.
(d) has substantially reduced the federal deficit.

Answer: (b)

10.145: Automatic stabilizers act to _____ government expenditures and _____ government revenues during recessions.

Easy
Fact
Page: 217
CT Page: 659

(a) increase; increase
(b) increase; decrease
(c) decrease; increase
(d) decrease; decrease

Answer: (b)

10.146: Automatic stabilizers act to _____ government expenditures and _____ government revenues during an expansionary period.

Easy
Fact
Page: 217
CT Page: 659

(a) increase; increase
(b) increase; decrease
(c) decrease; increase
(d) decrease; decrease

Answer: (c)

10.147: The presence of automatic stabilizers means that the federal deficit is _____ than it otherwise would be in a recession and _____ than it otherwise would be in an expansion.

Easy
Fact
Page: 217
CT Page: 659

(a) smaller; smaller
(b) smaller; larger
(c) larger; smaller
(d) larger; larger

Answer: (c)

10.148: During a recession, automatic stabilizers cause the federal deficit to

Easy
Fact
Page: 217
CT Page: 659

(a) decrease.
(b) increase.
(c) remain unchanged.
(d) either increase or decrease.

Answer: (b)

10.149: An example of an automatic stabilizer is

Moderate
Single
Page: 217
CT Page: 659

(a) the indexation of social security benefits to the Consumer Price Index.
(b) changing the tax laws to increase the marginal tax rates.
(c) the food stamp program.
(d) the interest the government pays on loans.

Answer: (c)

10.150: If the economy is in a recession, the full-employment deficit is _____ the actual deficit.

Easy
Fact
Page: 218
CT Page: 659

(a) larger than
(b) smaller than
(c) equal to
(d) equal to or larger than

Answer: (b)

Easy
Definition
Page: 218
CT Page: 659

10.151: The deficit that remains at full employment is the

(a) natural employment deficit.
(b) cyclical deficit.
(c) structural deficit.
(d) debt deficit.

Answer: (c)

Easy
Definition
Page: 218
CT Page: 659

10.152: The deficit that occurs because of a downturn in the business cycle is the

(a) natural employment deficit.
(b) cyclical deficit.
(c) structural deficit.
(d) actual deficit.

Answer: (b)

Moderate
Single
Page: 218
CT Page: 659

10.153: Assume that in the United States the actual deficit is $300 billion. If the United States were at full employment, the deficit would be $100 billion. The structural deficit in the United States is
(a) $100 billion.
(b) $200 billion.
(c) $300 billion.
(d) $400 billion.

Answer: (a)

Moderate
Single
Page: 218
CT Page: 659

10.154: Assume that in the United States of Bell Pepper Growers (U.S.B.P.G.) the actual deficit is $200 billion. If the U.S.B.P.G. were at full employment, the deficit would be $50 billion. The structural deficit in the United States is

(a) $100 billion.
(b) $200 billion.
(c) $50 billion.
(d) $150 billion.

Answer: (c)

Moderate
Single
Page: 218
CT Page: 659

10.155: The existence of automatic stabilizers tends to _____ the size of the cyclical deficit.
(a) reduce
(b) increase
(c) have no effect upon
(d) eliminate

Answer: (b)

Moderate
Single
Page: 222
CT Page: 663

10.156: Assume that taxes depend on income and the equation for net taxes is $T = -400 + .25Y$. If income is zero, then

(a) the government collects positive net taxes of 400.
(b) the government collects net taxes of zero.
(c) the government collects negative net taxes of 400, which means it makes transfer payments of 400.
(d) the value for net taxes cannot be determined because the value for t is not known.

Answer: (c)

10.157: If taxes are a function of income, then the AE function is

(a) flatter than if taxes are a lump-sum amount.
(b) steeper than if taxes are a lump-sum amount.
(c) vertical.
(d) downward sloping.

Answer: (a)

Moderate
Single
Page: 223
CT Page: 663

10.158: Assume that taxes depend on income. The MPC is .8 and t is .25. The government spending multiplier is

(a) 1.67.
(b) 2.5.
(c) 5.
(d) 10.

Answer: (b)

Moderate
Single
Page: 223
CT Page: 664

10.159: Assume that taxes depend on income. The MPC is .9 and t is .3. The government spending multiplier is

(a) 10.
(b) 2.7.
(c) 1.17.
(d) 1.42.

Answer: (b)

Moderate
Single
Page: 223
CT Page: 664

10.160: Assume that taxes depend on income. The MPC is .5 and t is .2. If government spending increases by $10 billion, the equilibrium level of output will increase by

(a) $16.7 billion
(b) $25 billion.
(c) $50 billion.
(d) $100 billion.

Answer: (a)

Moderate
Single
Page: 223
CT Page: 664

10.161: Assume that taxes depend on income. The MPC is .8 and t is .4. If government spending increases by $100 billion, the equilibrium level of output will increase by

(a) $16.7 billion
(b) $215.9 billion.
(c) $57.5 billion.
(d) $192.31 billion.

Answer: (d)

Moderate
Single
Page: 223
CT Page: 664

10.162: If taxes depend on income and the MPC is .8 and t is .5, the tax multiplier is

(a) -1.6.
(b) -1.3.
(c) 75.
(d) 67.

Answer: (b)

Challenging
Single
Page: 223
CT Page: 664

Challenging
Multi
Page: 223
CT Page: 664

10.163: Assume that taxes depend on income and the MPC is .8 and t is .5. An increase in taxes of $10 billion will decrease equilibrium income by

(a) $16 billion.
(b) $13.3 billion.
(c) $7.5 billion.
(d) $6.7 billion.

Answer: (b)

Moderate
Fact
Page: 223
CT Page: 664

10.164: If taxes depend on income, then the magnitude of the government spending multiplier_____ it would be if taxes were a lump-sum amount.

(a) could be either larger than or smaller than
(b) is larger than
(c) is equal to what
(d) is smaller than

Answer: (d)

Moderate
Fact
Page: 223
CT Page: 664

10.165: If taxes depend on income, then the absolute value of the tax multiplier _____ it would be if taxes were a lump-sum amount.

(a) could be either larger than or smaller than
(b) is larger than
(c) is equal to what
(d) is smaller than

Answer: (d)

Moderate
Single
Page: 223
CT Page: 664

10.166: As the tax rate increases, the government spending multiplier

(a) increases.
(b) decreases.
(c) does not change.
(d) could either increase or decrease depending on the value of the MPC.

Answer: (b)

Moderate
Single
Page: 223
CT Page: 664

10.167: As the tax rate increases, the absolute value of the tax multiplier

(a) increases.
(b) decreases.
(c) does not change.
(d) could either increase or decrease depending on the value of the MPC.

Answer: (b)

TRUE/FALSE QUESTIONS

Easy
Fact
Page: 200
CT Page: 642

10.168: Disposable income excludes taxes paid by households, but includes transfer payments made to households.

Answer: True

10.169: For the economy to be in equilibrium, the following two conditions must be satisfied: G = T and S = I.

Answer: False

Easy
Fact
Page: 205
CT Page: 646

10.170: As the MPC increases, the government spending multiplier increases.

Answer: True

Easy
Fact
Page: 206
CT Page: 647

10.171: If the MPC equaled zero, the government spending multiplier would be zero.

Answer: False

Easy
Fact
Page: 206
CT Page: 647

10.172: A tax cut has no direct impact on spending.

Answer: True

Easy
Fact
Page: 207
CT Page: 647

10.173: A tax cut of $10 billion will have less effect on the economy than an increase in government spending of $10 billion.

Answer: True

Easy
Fact
Page: 208
CT Page: 651

10.174: The size of the multiplier is reduced if taxes depend on income.

Answer: True

Easy
Fact
Page: 210
CT Page: 655

10.175: The open-economy equilibrium condition is: Y = C + I + G + (IM - EX).

Answer: False

Easy
Fact
Page: 211
CT Page: 655

10.176: During recessions, automatic stabilizers work to reduce government expenditures and increase government revenues.

Answer: False

Easy
Fact
Page: 217
CT Page: 659

10.177: The cyclical deficit of the full-employment budget is zero.

Answer: True

Easy
Fact
Page: 218
CT Page: 659

SHORT ANSWER QUESTIONS

10.178: Identify the broad contrasting views regarding the role of government within the macroeconomy.

Answer: The proponents of government action argue that public policy is needed to insure long-term economic stability and growth because of the disruptions associated with cyclical fluctuations. The critics of government policy argue that it is incapable of stabilizing the economy and contributes to inflation and recession.

Moderate
Application
Page: 199
CT Page: 640

Moderate
Definition
Page: 217
CT Page: 641

10.179: Explain non-discretionary fiscal policy. What are some examples of non-discretionary fiscal policy?

Answer: Non-discretionary fiscal policy represents changes in taxes and spending that occur in response to cyclical fluctuations without congressional or executive approval. Examples include automatic changes in government spending for unemployment compensation, for public assistance programs, and the progressive nature of the income tax that alters collected tax revenues in response to cyclical fluctuations.

Moderate
Application
Page: 213
CT Page: 643

10.180: What is a budget deficit? What are ways in which the government could finance the deficit?

Answer: A budget deficit is the difference between government spending (G) and collected tax revenues (T) during a specified period of time. It is the amount of spending that exceeds collected tax revenues. The government could print additional money which might be inflationary. Also, the government could borrow from the public by selling Treasury bonds and bills which results in some portion of household saving flowing to government.

Moderate
Math
Page: 206
CT Page: 648

10.181: Determine the impact of an increase in government spending of $10 billion when the MPC is .8. Determine the impact of a decrease in government spending of $5 billion when the MPS is .25.

Answer: The government spending multiplier will be 5. Thus, the increase in government spending of $10 billion will increase aggregate output and income by $50 billion. The government spending multiplier will be 4. Thus, the decrease in government spending of $5 billion will decrease aggregate output and income by $20 billion.

Moderate
Application
Page: 208
CT Page: 651

10.182: Discuss an important difference between the spending and tax multipliers.

Answer: A change in government spending has an immediate and direct impact upon the economy's total spending and income level. In contrast, a change in taxes directly changes disposable income which then may impact upon spending and income.

Moderate
Math
Page: 208
CT Page: 651

10.183: Determine the impact of an increase in taxes of $20 billion when the MPS is .25. Determine the impact of a decrease in taxes of $10 billion when the MPC is .2.

Answer: The tax multiplier will be -3. Thus, an increase in taxes of $20 billion will decrease aggregate output and income by $60 billion. The tax multiplier will be -4. Thus, a decrease in taxes of $10 billion will increase aggregate output and income by $40 billion.

Difficult
Math
Page: 209
CT Page: 652

10.184: Determine the net impact upon the nation's economy that results from equal increases in spending and taxes of $10 billion when the MPC is .8.

Answer: With an MPC of .8, the spending multiplier is 5 and the additional spending will increase income by $50 billion. With an MPC of .8, the tax multiplier is -4 and the increase in taxes of $10 billion will decrease income by $40 billion. The net impact is an increase in aggregate output or income of $10 billion.

Difficult
Math
Page: 209
CT Page: 652

10.185: Determine the net impact upon the nation's economy that results from equal decreases in spending and taxes of $5 billion when the MPC is .75.

Answer: With an MPC of .75, the spending multiplier is 4 and the increase in spending of $5 billion will lower income by $20 billion. The value of the tax multiplier is -3 and a decrease in taxes of $5 billion will increase income by $15 billion. The net impact is a decrease in aggregate output or income of $5 billion.

10.186: Explain the importance of exports and imports to an economy.

Answer: Exports (EX) are domestically produced products that are sold abroad. They represent an injection into the nation's income stream. Imports (IM) are foreign-produced products that are consumed domestically. They are a leakage from the nation's income stream.

Moderate
Application
Page: 211
CT Page: 655

10.187: Explain why saving plus taxes must equal investment plus government spending in equilibrium.

Answer: For the economy to be in equilibrium, aggregate expenditure must equal aggregate output. Aggregate expenditure is C + I + G and aggregate output is C + S + T. Subtracting C from each side yields I + G = S + T. For the economy to be in equilibrium, the amount being withdrawn from the circular flow as saving and taxes must be exactly offset by the amount being added to the circular flow as investment and government spending.

Easy
Fact
Page: 204
CT Page: 646

10.188: You are given the following income-expenditures model for the economy of Vulcan.

C = 200 + .8Y_d
T = 50
G = 100
I = 140

(a.) What is the equilibrium level of income in Vulcan?
(b.) At the equilibrium level of income, what is the amount of consumption?
(c.) What is the value of the government spending multiplier in this economy?
(d.) If government spending increases to 150, what is the new level of equilibrium income?

Answer: (a.) The equilibrium level of income is 2,000. (b.) At the equilibrium level of output, consumption is 1,760. (c.) The government spending multiplier is 5. (d.) If government spending increases to 150, the new equilibrium level of output is 2,250.

Challenging
Multi
Page: 206
CT Page: 646

10.189: The MPC in Montavada is .75.

(a.) If taxes were reduced by $1,000 in Montavada, by how much would equilibrium output change?
(b.) If government spending were increased by $1,000 in Montavada, by how much would equilibrium output change?
(c.) Explain why a tax cut of $1,000 would have less effect on the economy of Montavada than an increase in
government spending of $1,000.

Answer: (a.) If taxes are reduced by $1,000, equilibrium output increases by $3,000. (b.) If government spending is increased by $1,000, equilibrium output increases by $4,000. (c.) The change in taxes has a smaller impact than the increase in government spending, because when taxes are cut the initial increase in aggregate expenditure is only MPC times the change in taxes. When government spending is increased, the initial increase in aggregate expenditure equals the increase in government spending.

Moderate
Single
Page: 208
CT Page: 648

Challenging
Multi
Page: 208
CT Page: 650

10.190: How do the values of the tax multiplier and the government spending multiplier change as the MPC increases? Explain why the multipliers change. If the MPC were 0, what would the government spending and tax multipliers equal? If the MPC were 1, what would the government spending and tax multipliers equal?

Answer: As the MPC increases, the value of the government spending multiplier increases and the absolute value of the tax multiplier increases. The multipliers increase as the MPC increases because for any given change in expenditures or taxes, the change in consumption increases as the MPC increases. If the MPC were 0, the tax multiplier would be -1 and the government spending multiplier would be 1. If the MPC were 1, the tax multiplier would be negative infinity and the government spending multiplier would be positive infinity.

Moderate
Single
Page: 209
CT Page: 652

10.191: Draw a graph of an economy's aggregate expenditure function. Using this graph, explain how equilibrium income is determined. Show graphically the effect on the equilibrium level of output if government spending and taxes are increased by the same amount. Explain why the balanced-budget multiplier equals 1.

Answer: If taxes and government spending are increased by the same amount, the final change in equilibrium output equals the change in government spending and taxes. Increases in government spending increase output by more than an increase in taxes reduces output. The balanced-budget multiplier is the sum of the government spending and tax multipliers. The sum of these multipliers is one.

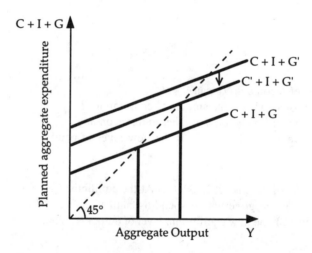

Easy
Fact
Page: 218
CT Page: 655

10.192: The federal budget is really three different budgets. Explain.

Answer: First, the federal budget is a political document that disperses favors to certain groups and places burdens on other groups. Second, it is a reflection of certain goals the government wants to achieve. Third, the budget may be an embodiment of some beliefs about how the government should manage the macroeconomy.

Easy
Single
Page: 218
CT Page: 659

10.193: Give an example of an automatic stabilizer. Explain how automatic stabilizers operate within the economy during a recession and during an expansion.

Answer: An example of an automatic stabilizer is unemployment compensation. During a recession, automatic stabilizers tend to increase the deficit by increasing government expenditures and reducing tax revenue. During an expansionary period, automatic stabilizers tend to decrease the deficit by reducing government expenditures and increasing tax revenue.

10.194: Explain why the full-employment budget is the benchmark for evaluating fiscal policy.

Easy
Fact
Page: 218
CT Page: 659

Answer: The full-employment budget is the benchmark for evaluating fiscal policy because it identifies what the budget would be like if the economy were producing at the full-employment level of output. The full-employment budget eliminates the effects of the business cycle.

10.195: Explain what is meant by the structural deficit. Explain the relationship of the structural deficit compares to the actual deficits during periods of recession and periods of expansion.

Easy
Fact
Page: 218
CT Page: 660

Answer: The structural deficit is the deficit that remains at full employment. During an expansion, the structural deficit is less than the actual deficit. During an expansion, the structural deficit is greater than the actual deficit.

10.196: If taxes are not lump-sum but depend on income, what happens to the size of the government spending and tax multipliers? Explain why the multipliers change.

Moderate
Single
Page: 223
CT Page: 665

Answer: The government spending multiplier and the absolute value of the tax multiplier decrease, if taxes are a function of income. The multipliers decrease because part of each additional increase in income is taxed away.

11 The Supply of Money and the Federal Reserve System

(Chapter 26 in Combined Text)

MULTIPLE CHOICE QUESTIONS

11.1: Money is

(a) the same as income.
(b) anything that is generally accepted as a medium of exchange.
(c) the value of all coins and currency in circulation at any time.
(d) all of the above.

Answer: (b)

Easy
Definition
Page: 226

11.2: The direct exchange of goods and services for other goods and services is

(a) barter.
(b) a fiat exchange.
(c) a legal tender exchange.
(d) a unit of account exchange.

Answer: (a)

Easy
Definition
Page 226

11.3: Mike makes excellent cheesecake and Sue is very good at changing the oil in a car. Sue agrees to change the oil in Mike's car, if he makes her a cheesecake. This is an example of

(a) legal tender.
(b) fiat money.
(c) commodity money.
(d) barter.

Answer: (d)

Easy
Single
Page: 226

11.4: Which of the following statements does NOT constitute one of the weaknesses of a barter economy?

(a) Both parties to an exchange must want what the other has.
(b) Some stores of value are difficult to transport.
(c) People are generally uninterested in exchanging goods with one another.
(d) Some stores of value are not easily divisible.

Answer: (c)

Easy
Fact
Page: 226

11.5: Mary wants to trade piano lessons for ice-skating lessons. Sarah wants to trade ice-skating lessons for piano lessons. Mary and Sarah have

(a) a double coincidence of wants.
(b) a double incidence of demand.
(c) the basis for a double fiat exchange.
(d) the basis for a liquidity exchange.

Answer: (a)

Easy
Single
Page: 226

Moderate
Single
Page: 226

11.6: The development of money as a medium of exchange has facilitated the expansion of trade because

(a) holding money increases people's wealth.
(b) holding money increases people's income.
(c) no other mediums of exchange are available.
(d) money eliminates the "double coincidence of wants" problem.

Answer: (d)

Easy
Fact
Page: 226

11.7: A medium of exchange is

(a) what sellers generally accept and buyers generally use to pay for goods and services.
(b) an asset that can be used to transport purchasing power from one period of time to another.
(c) a standard unit that provides a consistent way of quoting prices.
(d) the ability to buy something today but to defer payment to the future.

Answer: (a)

Moderate
Single
Page: 226

11.8: Dena won $10,000 at a bingo game. She deposits her $10,000 winnings into a money market fund so that she can use the money next year to pay her tuition. This is an example of money serving as

(a) a unit of account.
(b) a store of value.
(c) a medium of exchange.
(d) an investment good.

Answer: (b)

Moderate
Single
Page: 226

11.9: Kenny T. won $50,000 playing Craps at the MGMGrand in Las Vegas. He deposits his $50,000 winnings into a money market fund so that he can use the money next year to pay his gambling debts. This is an example of money serving as

(a) a store of value.
(b) an investment good.
(c) a medium of exchange.
(d) a unit of account.

Answer: (a)

Moderate
Single
Page: 226

11.10: Ashley received a federal income tax refund of $500 in May 1993. Ashley put this money in a shoebox in her closet so that she could spend it when she went on vacation in July 1993. This is an example of money serving as

(a) a unit of account.
(b) a medium of exchange.
(c) a store of value.
(d) an investment good.

Answer: (c)

Easy
Definition
Page: 226

11.11: A store of value is

(a) what sellers generally accept and buyers generally use to pay for goods and services.
(b) an asset that can be used to transport purchasing power from one period of time to another.
(c) a standard unit that provides a consistent way of quoting prices.
(d) the ability to buy something today but to defer payment to the future.

Answer: (b)

11.12: The main disadvantage of using money as a store of value is that

(a) the value of money actually falls when the prices of goods and services rise.
(b) it requires a double coincidence of wants.
(c) currency is intrinsically worthless.
(d) money is not portable.

Easy
Fact
Page: 227

Answer: (a)

11.13: The liquidity property of money is the property that makes money

(a) a good medium of exchange and a good unit of account.
(b) a good medium of exchange and a good store of value.
(c) a good store of value and a good unit of account.
(d) a good store of value and a good standard of deferred payment.

Easy
Definition
Page: 227

Answer: (b)

11.14: A unit of account is

(a) what sellers generally accept and buyers generally use to pay for goods and services.
(b) an asset that can be used to transport purchasing power from one period of time to another.
(c) a standard unit that provides a consistent way of quoting prices.
(d) the ability to buy something today but to defer payment to the future.

Easy
Definition
Page: 227

Answer: (c)

11.15: Floral Plus, a wholesale supplier of real and silk flowers, has 200 different products in inventory. Floral Plus reports its inventory is worth $400,000. This is an example of using money as

(a) a medium of exchange.
(b) a store of value.
(c) a standard of deferred payment.
(d) a unit of account.

Moderate
Single
Page: 227

Answer: (d)

11.16: The Seafood Source quotes the price of lobster at $12 a pound and the price of flounder at $4 a pound. This is an example of money serving as

(a) a unit of account.
(b) a store of value.
(c) a medium of exchange.
(d) an investment good.

Moderate
Single
Page: 227

Answer: (a)

11.17: In Israel, many apartment leases quote rents in U.S. dollars, not in Israeli shekels. The explanation for this situation is that

(a) the shekel is not accepted as a medium of exchange.
(b) the rate of inflation in Israel has been very high and variable.
(c) many landlords in Israel are U.S. citizens.
(d) the shekel is not issued in convenient denominations.

Moderate
Fact
Page:227

Answer: (b)

Easy
Definition
Page: 227

11.18: An item used as money that also has intrinsic value in some other use is

(a) fiat money.
(b) token money.
(c) commodity money.
(d) legal tender.

Answer: (c)

Easy
Single
Page:227

11.19: On the island of Sulam, chocolate chip cookies are used as money. This is an example of

(a) fiat money.
(b) commodity money.
(c) token money.
(d) legal money.

Answer: (b)

Easy
Definition
Page: 227

11.20: An item designated as money that is intrinsically worthless is

(a) fiat money.
(b) precious metals.
(c) barter items.
(d) commodity money.

Answer: (a)

Easy
Single
Page: 227

11.21: Which of the following is an example of fiat money?

(a) cigarettes
(b) an ounce of gold
(c) a one-hundred dollar bill
(d) a government bond.

Answer: (c)

Easy
Definition
Page: 227

11.22: Money that a government has required to be accepted in settlement of debts is

(a) legal tender.
(b) commodity money.
(c) barter money.
(d) currency value.

Answer: (a)

Easy
Fact
Page: 227

11.23: To ensure that paper money will be accepted, the U.S. government promises the public that

(a) it will not change currency denominations so that the paper currencies U.S. citizens have will continue to be used for exchanges.
(b) it will not change the rate at which the dollar is exchanged for other currencies.
(c) it will not print money so fast that it loses its value.
(d) the U.S. monetary system will always be backed by a precious metal.

Answer: (c)

11.24: Currency debasement occurs when

(a) the government requires that a certain form of money must be accepted in settlement of debts.
(b) the value of money falls as a result of a rapid increase in its supply.
(c) items are designated as money that are intrinsically worthless.
(d) items are used as money that also have intrinsic value in some other use.

Answer: (b)

Easy
Definition
Page: 228

11.25: Assume that in the country of Salmon, the government tripled the money supply overnight. As a result of this action, the price of a loaf of bread increased from 1 bill to 100 bills. This is an example of

(a) a change in the legal tender.
(b) a change from commodity money to fiat money.
(c) currency debasement.
(d) deflation.

Answer: (c)

Moderate
Single
Page: 228

11.26: Currency held outside banks + demand deposits + travelers checks + other checkable deposits =

(a) M1.
(b) M2.
(c) M3.
(d) L.

Answer: (a)

Easy
Definition
Page: 228

11.27: Money that can be directly used for transactions is

(a) near money.
(b) broad money.
(c) M1.
(d) M2.

Answer: (c)

Easy
Definition
Page: 228

11.28: Automatic-transfer savings accounts are

(a) included only in M1.
(b) included only in M2.
(c) included in both M1 and M2.
(d) not included in either M1 or M2.

Answer: (c)

Easy
Pact
Page: 228

11.29: Which of the following is included in M2, but not included in M1?

(a) currency held outside banks.
(b) savings accounts.
(c) automatic-transfer savings accounts.
(d) travelers checks.

Answer: (b)

Easy
Fact
Page:229

Moderate
Single
Page:229

11.30: Dana transfers $5,000 from her checking account to her savings account. This transaction will

(a) decrease both M1 and M2.
(b) decrease M1 and not change M2.
(c) not change M1 and decrease M2.
(d) increase both M1 and M2.

Answer: (b)

Moderate
Single
Page:229

11.31: Rob transfers $15,000 from his saving account to his checking account. This transaction will

(a) decrease both M1 and M2.
(b) not change M1 and decrease M2.
(c) increase both M1 and M2.
(d) increase M1 and not change M2.

Answer: (d)

Moderate
Single
Page: 229

11.32: Matthew transfers $2,000 from his money market fund to his checking account. This transaction will

(a) decrease M2 and increase M1.
(b) decrease M1 and increase M2.
(c) increase M1, but leave M2 unchanged.
(d) decrease both M1 and M2.

Answer: (c)

Moderate
Single
Page: 229

11.33: Bruce transfers $4,000 from his his checking account to his money market fund. This transaction will

(a) decrease M2 and increase M1.
(b) decrease M1 and increase M2.
(c) increase M1, but leave M2 unchanged.
(d) none of the above.

Answer: (d)

Easy
Fact
Page: 229

11.34: Che.cking account balances are included in

(a) M1 only.
(b) M2 only.
(c) neither M1 nor M2.
(d) both M1 and M2.

Answer: (d)

Easy
Fact
Page: 229

11.35: Money market accounts are included in

(a) M1 only.
(b) M2 only.
(c) neither M1 nor M2.
(d) both M1 and M2.

Answer: (b)

11.36: Currency held outside banks is included in

(a) M1 only.
(b) M2 only.
(c) both M1 and M2.
(d) neither M1 nor M2.

Answer: (c)

Easy
Fact
Page:229

11.37: Close substitutes for transactions money are known as

(a) fiat monies.
(b) token monies.
(c) commodity monies.
(d) near monies.

Answer: (d)

Easy
Definition
Page: 229

11.38: Which of the following is the best example of a near money?

(a) a dollar bill
(b) a valuable painting
(c) a money market account
(d) a negotiable order of withdrawal (NOW) account

Answer: (c)

Moderate
Single
Page: 229

11.39: The equation for M2 is

(a) M1 + Savings Accounts + Money Market Accounts + Other Near Monies.
(b) M1 + Savings Accounts + Currency Held Outside Banks + Other Near Monies.
(c) Money Market Accounts + Automatic-transfer Savings Accounts.
(d) M1− Near Monies.

Answer: (a)

Easy
Definition
Page: 229

11.40: The main advantage of using M2 instead of M1 as the measure for money is that

(a) M2 can be measured more accurately.
(b) M2 is sometimes more stable.
(c) M2 includes only readily spendable assets.
(d) M2 varies as the interest rate varies.

Answer: (b)

Easy
Fact
Page: 229

11.41: Which of the following institutions would not be considered a financial intermediary?

(a) auto insurance companies
(b) life insurance companies
(c) commercial banks
(d) pension funds

Answer: (a)

Moderate
Single
Page: 229

11.42: Net worth is

(a) assets + liabilities.
(b) assets + capital.
(c) assets − capital.
(d) assets − liabilities.

Answer: (d)

Easy
Definition
Page: 232
CT Page: 675

Moderate
Single
Page: 232

11.43: First National Bank has liabilities of $500,000 and capital of $400,000. First National Bank's assets

(a) are $100,000.
(b) are $180,000.
(c) are $900,000.
(d) cannot be determined from this information.

Answer: (c)

Moderate
Single
Page: 232

11.44: Hazard County Savings and Loan has liabilities of $200,000 and capital of $100,000. Hazard County Savings and Loan's assets

(a) are $100,000.
(b) are $180,000.
(c) are $300,000.
(d) none of the above.

Answer: (c)

Moderate
Single
Page: 232

51: First National Trust has assets of $900,000, liabilities of $600,000, and capital of $300,000. First National Trust's net worth is

(a) $0.
(b) $300,000.
(c) $600,000.
(d) $900,000.

Answer: (b)

Moderate
Single
Page: 232

11.46: Hazard County Savings and Loan has assets of $600,000, liabilities of $300,000, and capital of $300,000. Hazard County Savings and Loan's net worth is

(a) $-300,000.
(b) $300,000.
(c) $600,000.
(d) $200,000.

Answer: (b)

Easy
Definition
Page: 232

11.47: Things that a firm owns that are worth something are classified
as

(a) liabilities.
(b) deposits.
(c) assets.
(d) net worth.

Answer: (c)

Easy
Definition
Page: 233

11.48: The value of a firm to its stockholders or owners is its

(a) liabilities.
(b) deposits.
(c) assets.
(d) net worth.

Answer: (d)

11.49: The central bank of the United States is known as the

(a) Federal Reserve System.
(b) Federal Deposit Insurance Corporation.
(c) Department of the Treasury.
(d) Federal Savings and Loan Insurance Corporation.

Easy
Fact
Page: 232

Answer: (a)

11.50: A loan made by a bank is considered _____ of that bank.

(a) a liability
(b) an asset
(c) net worth
(d) capital

Easy
Fact
Page: 233

Answer: (b)

11.51: A checking deposit in a bank is considered _____ of that bank.

(a) a liability
(b) an asset
(c) net worth
(d) capital

Easy
Fact
Page: 233

Answer: (a)

11.52: Refer to Figure 11.1. The required reserve ratio is 10%. If the First Charter Bank is meeting its reserve requirement and has no excess reserves, its reserves equal

Easy
Single
Page: 233

(a) 40.
(b) 50.
(c) 80.
(d) 90.

Answer: (a)

11.53: Refer to Figure 11.1. The required reserve ratio is 10%. If the First Charter Bank is meeting its reserve requirement and has no excess reserves, its loans equal

Moderate
Multi
Page: 233

(a) 360.
(b) 400.
(c) 410.
(d) 450.

Answer: (c)

T Account for First Charter Bank			
Assets		**Liabilities**	
Reserves	_____	400	Deposits
Loans	_____	50	Net Worth
Total	_____	450	Total

Figure 11.1

T Account for First Charter Bank

Assets			Liabilities
Reserves	————	500	Deposits
Loans	————	100	Net Worth
Total	————	600	Total

Figure 11..2

Easy
Single
Page: 233

11.54: Refer to Figure 11.1. First Charter Bank's total assets

(a) are 400.
(b) are 450.
(c) are 500.
(d) cannot be determined from this information.

Answer: (b)

Easy
Single
Page: 233

11.55: Refer to Figure 11.2. The required reserve ratio is 20%. If the First Intrastate Bank is meeting its reserve requirement and has no excess reserves, its reserves equal

(a) 1000.
(b) 90.
(c) 100.
(d) 500.

Answer: (c)

Moderate
Multi
Page: 233

11.56: Refer to Figure 11.2. The required reserve ratio is 20%. If the First Intrastate Bank is meeting its reserve requirement and has no excess reserves, its loans equal

(a) 500.
(b) 400.
(c) 100.
(d) 480.

Answer: (a)

Easy
Single
Page: 233

11.57: Refer to Figure 11.2. First Intrastate Bank's total assets

(a) are 500.
(b) are 600.
(c) are 700.
(d) none of the above.

Answer: (b)

Moderate
Single
Page: 233

11.58: Refer to Figure 11.3. Second National Bank has a reserve requirement of 20%. Second National Bank is meeting its reserve requirement and has no excess reserves. Second National Bank's deposits are

(a) 200.
(b) 250.
(c) 350.
(d) 400.

Answer: (b)

T Account for Second NationalBank

Assets		Liabilities	
Reserves	50	———	Deposits
Loans	350	———	Net Worth
Total	400	———	Total

Figure 11.3

11.59: Refer to Figure 11.3. Second National Bank has a reserve requirement of 20%. Second National Bank is meeting its reserve requirement and has no excess reserves. Second National Bank's net worth

Moderate
Multi
Page: 233

(a) is 150.
(b) is 250.
(c) is 350.
(d) cannot be determined from this information.

Answer: (a)

11.60: Refer to Figure 11.2. Second National Bank has a reserve requirement of 20%. Second National Bank is meeting its reserve requirement and has no excess reserves. Second National Bank's liabilities are

Easy
Single
Page: 233

(a) 200.
(b) 250.
(c) 350.
(d) 400.

Answer: (d)

11.61: Dollar Bank has $500 million in deposits. Dollar Bank is meeting its reserve requirement and has no excess reserves. It has $125 million in reserves. Dollar Bank faces a required reserve ratio of

Easy
Single
Page: 233

(a) 1.25%.
(b) 4%.
(c) 20%.
(d) 25%.

Answer: (d)

11.62: Bank of Sim City has $200 million in deposits. Bank of Sim City is meeting its reserve requirement and has no excess reserves. It has $75 million in reserves. Bank of Sim City faces a required reserve ratio of

Easy
Single
Page: 233

(a) 1.25%.
(b) 4%.
(c) 20%.
(d) 37.5%.

Answer: (d)

Easy
Single
Page: 233

11.63: Third National Bank has $600 million in deposits. The required reserve ratio is 10%. Third National Bank must keep _____ in reserves.

(a) $6 million
(b) $60 million
(c) $100 million
(d) $160 million

Answer: (b)

Easy
Single
Page: 233

11.64: Bank of Sim City has $700 million in deposits. The required reserve ratio is 20%. Bank of Sim City must keep _____ in reserves.

(a) $70 million
(b) $700 million
(c) $140 million
(d) $160 million

Answer: (c)

Moderate
Single
Page: 234

11.65: Bank One has $100 million in reserves. Bank One is meeting its reserve requirement and has no excess reserves. The required reserve ratio is 20%. Bank One's demand deposits are

(a) $120 million.
(b) $200 million.
(c) $500 million.
(d) $600 million.

Answer: (c)

Easy
Definition
Page: 234

11.66: The difference between a bank's actual reserves and its required reserves is its

(a) excess reserves.
(b) required reserve ratio.
(c) profit margin.
(d) net worth.

Answer: (a)

Easy
Single
Page: 234

11.67: The Guaranteed Deposit Bank has actual reserves of $100 million and required reserves of $75 million. The Guaranteed Deposit Bank has excess reserves of

(a) $25 million.
(b) $75 million.
(c) $100 million.
(d) $175 million.

Answer: (a)

Easy
Single
Page: 234

11.68: Refer to Figure 11.3. If the required reserve ratio is 20%, First Charter Bank

(a) is loaned up.
(b) has too few reserves on hand.
(c) is meeting its required reserve ratio and has no excess reserves.
(d) has excess reserves of 100.

Answer: (d)

T Account for First Charter Bank			
Assets		**Liabilities**	
Reserves	300	1,000	Deposits
Loans	700		
	1,000	1,000	

Figure 11.4

11.69: Refer to Figure 11.4. First Charter Bank will be loaned up if the required reserve ratio is

(a) 3%.
(b) 7%.
(c) 30%.
(d) 33.33%.

Moderate
Multi
Page: 234

Answer: (c)

11.70: Refer to Figure 11.4 First Charter Bank could make additional loans of 200, if the required reserve ratio were

(a) 10%.
(b) 20%.
(c) 25%.
(d) 30%.

Moderate
Multi
Page: 234

Answer: (a)

11.71: Refer to Figure 11.4. First Charter Bank is the only bank in the economy and the banking system is closed. The required reserve ratio is 30%. If a new deposit of $300 is made, the bank can expand its loans up to the point where its total deposits are

(a) 1,300.
(b) 1,900.
(c) 2,000.
(d) 3,000.

Challenging
Multi
Page: 234

Answer: (c)

11.72: Dollar Bank is currently loaned up. If the required reserve ratio is lowered,

(a) Dollar Bank's net worth will increase.
(b) Dollar Bank will have excess reserves that it can lend out.
(c) Dollar Bank will still be loaned up because it did not receive any additional deposits.
(d) Dollar Bank's actual reserves will increase, but it will still be loaned up.

Moderate
Multi
Page:234

Answer: (b)

11.73: When a bank has no excess reserves, and thus can make no more loans, it is said to be

(a) bankrupt.
(b) ripe for a takeover.
(c) in receivership.
(d) loaned up.

Easy
Definition
Page: 234

Answer: (d)

Easy
Fact
Page: 234

11.74: Banks can create money

(a) only by illegally printing additional dollar bills.
(b) by paying interest to their depositors.
(c) by making loans that result in additional deposits.
(d) by offering financial services, such as money market accounts.

Answer: (c)

Easy
Definition
Page: 236

11.75: The multiple by which total deposits can increase for every dollar increase in reserves is the

(a) required reserve ratio.
(b) bank's line of credit.
(c) deposit insurance limit.
(d) money multiplier.

Answer: (d)

Moderate
Multi
Page: 236

11.76: Assume the banking system is closed. The required reserve ratio is 25%. If a new deposit of $10,000 is made, total deposits can increase by

(a) $10,000.
(b) $25,000.
(c) $40,000.
(d) $50,000.

Answer: (c)

Moderate
Multi
Page: 236

11.77: Assume the banking system is closed. The required reserve ratio is 20%. If a new deposit of $1,000 is made, loans can increase by

(a) $1,000.
(b) $4,000.
(c) $5,000.
(d) $6,000.

Answer: (b)

Easy
Single
Page: 236

11.78: The required reserve ratio is 10%. The money multiplier is

(a) .1.
(b) 1.
(c) 9.
(d) 10.

Answer: (d)

Easy
Single
Page: 236

11.79: The required reserve ratio is 20%. The money multiplier is

(a).2.
(b) .8.
(c) 5.
(d) 10.

Answer: (c)

11.80: If the money multiplier is 2, the required reserve ratio is

(a) 2%.
(b) 20%.
(c) 25%.
(d) 50%.

Answer: (d)

Moderate
Multi
Page: 236

11.81: Assume that banks become more conservative in their lending policies, and start holding some excess reserves. Compared to a situation in which banks are not holding excess reserves, the size of the money multiplier will be

(a) smaller.
(b) larger.
(c) the same.
(d) zero.

Answer: (a)

Moderate
Multi
Page: 236

11.82: As the required reserve ratio is decreased, the money multiplier

(a) decreases.
(b) increases.
(c) remains the same, as long as banks hold no excess reserves.
(d) could either increase or decrease.

Answer: (b)

Easy
Single
Page: 236

11.83: Assume that some people who receive bank loans do not deposit the full amount of the loan into a bank. This will cause the money multiplier to be _____ the money multiplier that results when all loans are deposited in banks.

(a) the same as
(b) either greater than or smaller than
(c) greater than
(d) smaller than

Answer: (d)

Moderate
Single
Page: 236

11.84: A money multiplier of 8 means that an increase in reserves of $1 could cause an increase in deposits of _____ if there were no leakage out of the system.

(a) $.80
(b) $1.00.
(c) $1.80.
(d) $8.00

Answer: (d)

Easy
Single
Page: 236

11.85: A bank has excess reserves to lend but is unable to find anyone to borrow the money. This will _____ the size of the money multiplier.

(a) reduce
(b) increase
(c) have no effect on
(d) double

Answer: (a)

Moderate
Single
Page: 236

Easy
Fact
Page: 237

11.86: In the United States, monetary policy is formally set by the

(a) Federal Open Market Committee.
(b) Council of Economic Advisors.
(c) Department of the Treasury.
(d) Office of Management and Budget.

Answer: (a)

Easy
Fact
Page: 237

11.87: Which of the following activities is not one of the responsibilities of the Federal Reserve?

(a) clearing interbank payments
(b) regulating the banking system
(c) managing exchange rates
(d) administering the federal tax code

Answer: (d)

Moderate
Fact
Page: 237

11.88: Which of the following activities is one of the responsibilities of the Federal Reserve?

(a) issuing new bonds to finance the federal budget deficit
(b) loaning money to other countries that are friendly to the United States
(c) assisting banks that are in a difficult financial position
(d) auditing the various agencies and departments of the federal government

Answer: (c)

Easy
Fact
Page: 241

11.89: Which of the following instruments is not used by the Federal Reserve to change the money supply?

(a) the federal tax code
(b) the required reserve ratio
(c) the discount rate
(d) open market operations

Answer: (a)

Moderate
Single
Page: 241

11.90: Which of the following actions by the Federal Reserve will result in a decrease in the money supply?

(a) a decrease in federal spending
(b) a decrease in the discount rate
(c) buying government securities in the open market
(d) raising the required reserve ratio

Answer: (d)

Moderate
Single
Page: 242

11.91: The Home Loan Bank has $40 million in deposits and is loaned up. The required reserve ratio is increased. The Home Loan Bank finds that

(a) it now has excess reserves to lend.
(b) it has insufficient reserves on hand.
(c) it must lower the interest rate that it charges on loans.
(d) its net worth decreases.

Answer: (b)

11.92: The banking system has deposits of $100 million and no excess reserves. The required reserve ratio is reduced from 25% to 20%. If there are no leakages from the banking system, the banking system

Challenging
Multi
Page: 242

(a) could make additional loans up to $5,000.
(b) could make additional loans up to $20,000.
(c) could make additional loans up to $25,000.
(d) could not make any additional loans because it has not received any new deposits.

Answer: (c)

11.93: The banking system has $200 million in deposits. The required reserve ratio is 20%. The Federal Reserve wants to increase deposits in the banking system to $400 million. There are no leakages from the banking system. Deposits would increase to $400 million if the reserve ratio is

Challenging
Multi
Page: 242

(a) reduced to 5%.
(b) reduced to 10%.
(c) increased to 25%.
(d) increased to 40%.

Answer: (b)

11.94: Assume that all commercial banks are loaned up. Total deposits in the banking system are $200 million. The required reserve ratio is increased from 20% to 25%. The money supply will

Challenging
Multi
Page: 242

(a) decrease by $40 million.
(b) decrease by $10 million.
(c) decrease by $5 million.
(d) not change because there was no change in deposits.

Answer: (a)

11.95: The Fed has tended not to use changes in the reserve requirement as a means of controlling the money supply because

Moderate
Fact
Page: 243

(a) only banks that are members of the Fed are subject to reserve requirements, and most banks do not belong to the Fed.
(b) a change in the reserve requirement has only a very small impact on the money supply.
(c) it takes a long time for the Congress to approve a change in the reserve requirement.
(d) it is a crude monetary policy tool since a change in the requirement does not affect banks until about two weeks after the change is implemented.

Answer: (d)

11.96: The interest rate banks pay to borrow money from the Fed is the

Easy
Definition
Page: 243

(a) federal funds rate.
(b) prime lending rate.
(c) discount rate.
(d) reserve rate.

Answer: (c)

Moderate
Single
Page: 244

11.97: Which of the following represents an action by the Federal Reserve which is designed to increase the money supply?

(a) an increase in the required reserve ratio
(b) a decrease in the discount rate
(c) a decrease in federal tax rates
(d) selling government securities in the open market

Answer: (b)

Moderate
Single
Page: 244

11.98: Which of the following represents an action by the Federal Reserve which is designed to decrease the money supply?

(a) buying government securities in the open market
(b) a decrease in the required reserve ratio
(c) a decrease in federal spending
(d) an increase in the discount rate

Answer: (d)

Easy
Fact
Page: 244

11.99: The discount rate cannot be used to control the money supply with great precision because

(a) its effects on banks' demand for reserves are uncertain.
(b) only banks that are members of the Fed can borrow from the Fed,
and most banks are not members of the Fed.
(c) a change in the discount rate will not affect a bank until two
weeks after the change is implemented.
(d) there is a maximum amount of money that banks can borrow from the Fed in any one
year.

Answer: (a)

Moderate
Multi
Page: 244

11.100: Assume that commercial banks are holding excess reserves because business firms and consumers are not willing to borrow money. A decrease in the discount rate is likely to

(a) increase the money supply because it is now cheaper for banks to borrow from the Fed.
(b) decrease the money supply because it is now cheaper for banks to borrow from the Fed instead of buying government securities.
(c) not change the money supply because banks already have excess reserves they cannot lend.
(d) decrease the money supply because it will now be more expensive for business firms and consumers to borrow money.

Answer: (c)

Moderate
Fact
Page: 245

11.101: Which of the following represents an action by the Federal Reserve which is designed to increase the money supply?

(a) an increase in the discount rate
(b) an increase in federal spending
(c) buying government securities in the open market
(d) an increase in the required reserve ratio

Answer: (c)

11.102: Which of the following represents an action by the Federal Reserve which is designed to decrease the money supply?

Moderate
Fact
Page: 245

(a) an increase in federal tax rates
(b) selling government securities in the open market
(c) a decrease in the discount rate
(d) a decrease in the required reserve ratio

Answer: (b)

11.103: The best instrument for controlling week-to-week changes in the money supply is

Easy
Fact
Page: 245

(a) the required reserve ratio.
(b) moral suasion.
(c) open market operations.
(d) the discount rate.

Answer: (c)

11.104: Which of the following statements is FALSE?

Easy
Fact
Page: 247

(a) Open market operations can be used by the Federal Reserve with some precision.
(b) Open market operations are extremely flexible.
(c) The Federal Reserve undertakes open market operations on an infrequent basis.
(d) Open market operations have a fairly predictable effect on the supply of money.

Answer: (c)

11.105: An open market purchase of securities by the Fed results in _____ in reserves and _____ in the supply of money.

Moderate
Single
Page: 247

(a) an increase; a decrease
(b) an increase; an increase
(c) a decrease; a decrease
(d) a decrease; an increase

Answer: (b)

11.106: An open market sale of securities by the Fed results in _____ in reserves and _____ in the supply of money.

Moderate
Single
Page: 247

(a) an increase; a decrease
(b) an increase; an increase
(c) a decrease; a decrease
(d) a decrease; an increase

Answer: (c)

11.107: Assume there is no leakage from the banking system and that all commercial banks are loaned up. The required reserve ratio is 25%. If the Fed buys $5 million worth of government securities from the public, the change in the money supply will be

Moderate
Multi
Page: 247

(a) −$20 million.
(b) −$12.5 million.
(c) $12.5 million.
(d) $20 million.

Answer: (d)

Moderate
Multi
Page: 247

11.108: Assume there is no leakage from the banking system and that all commercial banks are loaned up. The required reserve ratio is 20%. If the Fed sells $10 million worth of government securities to the public, the change in the money supply will be

(a) −$50 million.
(b) −$20 million.
(c) $20 million.
(d) $50 million.

Answer: (a)

Moderate
Single
Page: 247

11.109: The money supply has increased from $1 trillion to $1.1 trillion. Which of the following could have caused this increase?

(a) The Fed sold government securities to the public.
(b) Consumers who were holding money outside the banking system deposit this money to buy government securities.
(c) The Fed increased the discount rate.
(d) Commercial banks began to hold excess reserves.

Answer: (b)

Easy
Fact
Page: 248

11.110: If the Fed sets the money supply independent of the interest rate, then the money supply curve is

(a) upward sloping.
(b) downward sloping.
(c) vertical.
(d) horizontal.

Answer: (c)

TRUE/FALSE QUESTIONS

Easy
Single
Page: 226

11.111: Kate deposits 10% of her paycheck into a savings account every month. This is an example of money serving as a medium of exchange.

Answer: False

Easy
Fact
Page: 277

11.112: Fiat money is money that is intrinsically worthless.

Answer: True

Easy
Single
Page: 234

11.113: The First National Bank has $100,000 in actual reserves and its required reserves are $80,000. First National Bank, therefore, has excess reserves of $20,000.

Answer: True

Easy
Single
Page: 236

11.114: If the required reserve ratio is increased, the money multiplier increases.

Answer: False

Easy
Fact
Page: 236

11.115: The money multiplier = 1/the discount rate.

Answer: False

11.116: A money multiplier of 5 implies that the reserve requirement is 25%.

Answer: False

Easy
Single
Page: 236

11.117: An increase in the required reserve ratio will increase the rate of growth of the money supply.

Answer: False

Easy
Fact
Page: 242

11.118: A decrease in the discount rate will increase the rate of growth of the money supply.

Answer: True

Easy
Fact
Page: 242

11.119: A sale of government securities to the public by the Federal Reserve will increase the rate of growth of the money supply.

Answer: False

Easy
Fact
Page: 244

11.120: The discount rate cannot be used to control the money supply with great precision because its effects on banks' demand for reserves are uncertain.

Answer: True

Easy
Fact
Page: 244

SHORT ANSWER QUESTIONS

11.121: Explain the difference between commodity monies, fiat money, and legal tender.

Answer: Commodity monies are those tangible items that are used as monies that also have an intrinsic value in other forms of use. Examples include gold, precious stones, jewelry, cigarettes, and countless other items. Fiat or token money is intrinsically worthless and has value only because it is universally accepted as money. The dollar is intrinsically worthless and acquires value only because it is accepted in performing the functions of money. Legal tender represents money that a government declares to be accepted to perform the various functions of money. It is used to fulfill debt obligations.

Moderate
Definition
Page: 226

11.122: What is transactions money (M1)? Identify the components of transactions money.

Answer: Transactions money (M1) consists of money that can be directly used to facilitate exchange or the purchase of goods and services. Transactions money (M1) consists of currency held outside banks, checking account monies, demand deposits, travelers checks, and other checkable deposits.

Moderate
Application
Page: 228

11.123: Define a financial intermediary.

Answer: A financial intermediary is a bank or other institution that serves as a link between lenders and borrowers. They typically accept savings deposits from consumers and then lend money to consumers and businesses to finance purchases of goods and services or for investment purposes.

Moderate
Definition
Page:229

**Moderate
Application
Page: 230**

11.124: What was particularly important about the Depository Institutions Deregulation and Monetary Control Act of 1980?

Answer: This 1980 statute eliminated many of the previous restrictions that controlled the practices of financial institutions. It permitted non-commercial banks to service checking accounts, allowed non-commercial banks such as savings and loan associations to make non-residential mortgage loans, and has encouraged financial service businesses to offer a diverse variety of services.

**Moderate
Definition
Page: 234**

11.125: Explain the money creation process.

Answer: When a bank extends a loan, it is actually creating a demand deposit for the borrower upon which a new check can be written. This check writing process represents the actual creation of new money from the banking lending process.

**Moderate
Definition
Page: 236**

11.126: Discuss the monetary multiplier. Assume that the banking system's total excess reserves total $100 million and that the required reserve ratio is 20%. Calculate the money multiplier and the total potential expansion of the nation's money supply.

Answer: The money multiplier represents the multiple by which deposits can increase for every dollar increase in reserves. Thus, the entire banking system has the capacity to expand the nation's money supply by the multiple of its initial reserve balance. The money multiplier equals the reciprocal of 20% of 5. Thus, the banking system's total excess reserves could expand the nation's money supply by $500 million (5 x $10 million).

**Moderate
Application
Page: 237**

11.127: Explain the Federal Open Market Committee of the Federal Reserve System.

Answer: The Federal Open Market Committee is a group composed of seven members of the Fed's Board of Governors, the president of the New York Federal Reserve Bank, and four other bank presidents. It is responsible for establishing interest rate and money supply targets and directs the operations of the Open Market Desk.

**Moderate
Application
Page: 238**

11.128: Explain the Fed's function as a lender of last resort.

Answer: The Fed serves as a lender of last resort to private banks for two reasons. Banks that are unprofitable are not likely to borrow from other profit oriented, privately owned banks. Thus, the Fed is a source of funds since its interest is the economic well-being of the nation. In addition, the Fed has an unlimited supply of funds that can be lent to financial institutions.

**Moderate
Application
Page: 240**

11.129: Discuss the nature of the Fed's largest held asset and liability.

Answer: The Fed's largest asset consists of government securities which represent debt obligations, such as Treasury bills and bonds that have been purchased to control the nation's money supply. The largest shares of its liabilities are Federal Reserve notes, the nation's paper currency. Another large liability consists of the bank deposits held by the Fed to meet required reserve obligations.

**Moderate
Definition
Page: 244**

11.130: Explain the process of moral suasion.

Answer: Moral suasion characterizes the pressure exerted by the Federal Reserve on member banks to discourage them from borrowing heavily from the Fed.

**Moderate
Application
Page: 245**

11.131: Explain the impact of Fed open market purchases of securities upon the nation's money supply.

Answer: The Fed's purchase of government securities from banks is paid by an increase in the banks' actual reserves for the amount of the transaction. This will increase the banks' excess reserves, their lending potential, and result in an increase in the money supply.

11.132: Summarize the appropriate policy initiatives of the Fed if it seeks to pursue an expansionary monetary policy.

Moderate
Application
Page: 241

Answer: An expansionary monetary policy can be achieved if:
(a) the required reserve ratio is lowered
(b) the discount rate is lowered
(c) the Fed purchases government securities.

11.133: Summarize the appropriate policy initiatives of the Fed if it seeks to pursue a contractionary monetary policy.

Moderate
Application
Page: 241

Answer: A contractionary monetary policy can be achieved if:
(a) the required reserve ratio is increased
(b) the discount rate is increased
(c) the Fed sells government securities.

11.134: What is money? Explain the three functions that money performs. Which one is the primary function of money?

Easy
Fact
Page: 226

Answer: Money is anything that is generally accepted as a medium of exchange. Money must be able to act as a medium of exchange, a store of value, and a unit of account. For money to act as a medium of exchange, sellers must generally accept and buyers must generally use it to pay for goods and services. For money to serve as a store of value, it can be used to transport purchasing power from one period of time to another. For money to serve as a unit of account, it must function as a consistent way of quoting prices. The primary function of money is to serve as a medium of exchange.

11.135: Explain why a market structure in which money is used as a medium of exchange is more conducive to the expansion of trade and exchange than a barter system.

Moderate
Single
Page: 226

Answer: A barter system relies on a double coincidence of wants. Exchange can take place only if the individuals involved in the exchange each have something the other person wants. If money is used instead of direct exchange of goods and services, the number of exchanges that can take place increases. A system based on money eliminates the necessity of the double coincidence of wants.

11.136: Explain what will happen to the size of both M1 and M2 in each of the following situations: (a.) Jane, a millionaire, withdraws $500,000 from her money market account to buy a famous painting. (b.) Paul transfers $10,000 from his NOW account to his savings account.(c.) Sarah takes $5,000 out of her checking account to buy IBM stock.

Challenging
Multi
Page: 229

Answer: (a.) M1 stays the same and M2 decreases. (b.) M1 decreases and M2 stays the same. (c.) Both M1 and M2 decrease.

11.137: Assume there is only one bank in Maldavia—The First National Bank. The required reserve ratio is 20%. The First National Bank is loaned up. Use a balance sheet for First National Bank to show the effect of a new deposit of $200 million. Assume there is no leakage from the banking system. What is the value of the money multiplier in Maldavia? By how much does the money supply increase in Maldavia?

Moderate
Multi
Page: 234

Answer: The value of the money multiplier is 5. The money supply will increase by $1,000 million.

Assets		Liabilities	
Reserves	+200m	Deposits	+1,000m
Loans	+800m		
	+1,000m		+1,000m

Challenging
Multi
Page: 234

11.138: The required reserve ratio is 25%. Dollar Bank has $20,000 in deposits and $12,000 in reserves. Assume all other commercial banks are loaned up.

(a.) What is the value of this bank's excess reserves?
(b.) What is the value of the additional loans that can be made by the commercial banking system?
(c.) What is the money multiplier?
(d.) By how much will total deposits expand if this bank lends all its excess reserves and there is no leakage from the banking system?

Answer: (a.) Dollar Bank has $7,000 in excess reserves. (b.) The commercial banking system can make additional loans of $28,000. (c.) The money multiplier is 4. (d.) Deposits can be expanded by $28,000.

Easy
Fact
Page: 232

11.139: What is a run on a bank? What safeguards have been instituted to reduce the likelihood of a run on a bank?

Answer: A run on a bank occurs when depositors panic about the safety of their deposits and decide to withdraw all their money from their accounts. The safeguards that have been instituted to reduce the likelihood of a run on a bank arc insuring deposits through the FDIC and the Fed's functioning as the lender of last resort.

Easy
Fact
Page: 238

11.140: The Fed is responsible for controlling the money supply. Explain three other functions of the Fed.

Answer: The functions of the Fed include clearing interbank payments, regulating and supervising of commercial banks, and serving as lender of last resort.

Moderate
Single
Page: 241

11.141: Explain how each of the following policy actions by the Federal Reserve would affect the rate of growth of the money supply:

(a.) a decrease in the required reserve ratio
(b.) an increase in the discount rate
(c.) the Fed purchases government securities from the public

Answer: (a.) A decrease in the required reserve ratio will increase the rate of growth of the money supply. (b.) An increase in the discount rate will decrease the rate of growth of the money supply. (c.) A Fed purchase of government securities from the public will increase the rate of growth of the money supply.

Challenging
Multi
Page: 246

11.142: Refer to Figure 11.119. The required reserve ratio is 20%. Trace through the effects of Joe Q. Public buying $50 worth of government securities in each of these T-accounts. Assume there is no leakage from the banking system. What is the final change in the money supply?

Answer: The money supply is reduced by $250.

Moderate
Single
Page: 247

11.143: Explain why open market operations are a better tool for controlling week-to-week changes in the money supply the discount rate or the required reserve ratio.

Answer: The discount rate cannot be used to control the money supply with great precision because its effects on banks' demand for reserves are uncertain. Changes in the required reserve ratio are a crude tool. A change in reserve requirements does not affect banks for about two weeks. Open market operations are the Fed's preferred means of controlling the money supply because open market operations can be used with some precision, are flexible, and have a fairly predictable effect on the supply of money.

Federal Reserve			
Assets		**Liabilities**	
Government Securities	$400	$300	Reserves
		$100	Currency
	$400	$400	

Federal Reserve			
Assets		**Liabilities**	
Government Securities	$350	$250	Reserves
		$100	Currency
	$350	$350	

Commercial Banks			
Assets		**Liabilities**	
Reserves	$300	$1,500	Deposits
Loans	$1200		
	$1,500	$1,500	

Commercial Banks			
Assets		**Liabilities**	
Reserves	$250	$1,250	Deposits
Loans	$1000		
	$1,250	$1,250	

Joe Q. Public			
Assets		**Liabilities**	
Reserves	$100	$0	Deposits
Securities	$0	$100	Net Worth
	$100	$100	

Joe Q. Public			
Assets		**Liabilities**	
Reserves	$50	$0	Deposits
Securities	$50	$100	Net Worth
	$100	$100	

Figure 11-119a   **Figure 11-119b**

The Demand for Money, the Equilibrium Interest Rate, and Monetary Policy

(Chapter 27 in Combined Text)

MULTIPLE CHOICE QUESTIONS

12.1: The fee that a borrower pays to a lender for the use of the lender's funds is

(a) points.
(b) interest.
(c) the loan premium.
(d) the application fee.

Answer: (b)

Easy
Definition
Page: 251

12.2: A $20,000 bond that pays $1,000 a year in interest has an interest rate of

(a) 1%.
(b) 2%.
(c) 5%.
(d) 10%.

Answer: (c)

Easy
Single
Page: 251

12.3: A $10,000 bond that pays $1,000 a year in interest has an interest rate of

(a) 2%.
(b) 5%.
(c) 6%.
(d) 10%.

Answer: (d)

Easy
Single
Page: 251

12.4: The main reason that people hold money — to buy things — is referred to as the

(a) speculation motive.
(b) precautionary motive.
(c) transactions motive.
(d) profit motive.

Answer: (c)

Easy
Definition
Page: 252

12.5: When economists speak of the "demand for money," which of the following questions are they asking?

(a) How much cash do you wish you could have?
(b) How much income would you like to earn?
(c) How much wealth would you like?
(d) What proportion of your financial assets do you want to hold in noninterest bearing forms?

Answer: (d)

Easy
Single
Page: 252

Easy
Definition
Page: 252

12.6: The mismatch between the timing of money inflow and the timing of money outflow is known as the

(a) financial float.
(b) cash flow problem.
(c) nonsynchronization of income and spending.
(d) source of most business bankruptcies.

Answer: (c)

Easy
Single
Page: 252

12.7: Mary is paid on the first of every month and her rent is due on the fifteenth of every month. This is an example of the

(a) cash flow problem.
(b) nonsynchronization of income and spending.
(c) money management problem.
(d) financial float.

Answer: (b)

Moderate
Single
Page: 253

12.8: The average monthly balance in Derek's bank account is $750. Derek spends the same amount of money each day during the month and at the end of the month his account balance is $0. Derek's monthly starting balance is

(a) $750.
(b) $1500.
(c) $2250.
(d) $22,500.

Answer: (b)

Moderate
Single
Page: 253

12.9: The average monthly balance in Bill's bank account is $1000. Bill spends the same amount of money each day during the month and at the end of the month his account balance is $0. Bill's monthly starting balance is

(a) $750.
(b) $1500.
(c) $2000.
(d) $22,500.

Answer: (c)

Challenging
Multi
Page: 253

12.10: The average monthly balance in Derek's bank account is $750. Derek spends the same amount of money each day during a 30-day month and at the end of the month his account balance is $0. Derek spends his money at a constant rate of _____ per day.

(a) $25.
(b) $30.
(c) $50.
(d) $75.

Answer: (c)

Challenging
Multi
Page: 253

12.11: The average monthly balance in Bill's bank account is $1500. Bill spends the same amount of money each day during a 30-day month and at the end of the month his account balance is $0. Bill spends his money at a constant rate of _____ per day.

(a) $75.
(b) $100.
(c) $125.
(d) $150.

Answer: (b)

12.12: Ed's monthly starting balance is $3,000. Ed spends $100 per day. Initially, Ed keeps all of his income in a non-interest bearing checking account. Ed decided to change his strategy and at the beginning of each month he deposits one-third of his income into his checking account and buys two bonds with the remainder of his income. After ten days he cashes in one bond and after ten days after that he cashes in the other bond. Which of the following statements is TRUE?

Challenging
Multi
Page: 254

(a) If Ed uses either strategy, his average monthly balance is $1,500.
(b) The second strategy involves lower money management costs because Ed now earns interest on the bonds he has purchased.
(c) Ed's optimal money balance is $100.
(d) If the interest rate paid on bonds decreases, the opportunity cost of Ed's original strategy is reduced.

Answer: (d)

12.13: An increase in the interest rate will

Easy
Fact
Page: 255

(a) lower the optimal money balance.
(b) increase the optimal money balance.
(c) have no impact on the optimal money balance.
(d) either increase or decrease the optimal money balance depending upon the level of current household wealth.

Answer: (a)

12.14: Bob's optimal money balance has increased. This could have been caused by

Moderate
Single
Page: 255

(a) a reduction in the costs paid for switching from bonds to money.
(b) a decrease in the interest rate.
(c) a decrease in the inflation rate.
(d) a decrease in the price of bonds.

Answer: (b)

12.15: Tom's optimal balance has decreased. This could have been caused by

Moderate
Single
Page: 255

(a) a reduction in the costs paid for switching from bonds to money.
(b) an decrease in the interest rate.
(c) an increase in the inflation rate.
(d) an increase in the price of bonds.

Answer: (a)

12.16: In terms of the demand for money, the interest rate represents

Moderate
Fact
Page: 255

(a) the price of borrowing money.
(b) the return on money that is saved for the future.
(c) the rate at which current consumption can be exchanged for future consumption.
(d) the opportunity cost of holding money.

Answer: (d)

12..17: The interest rate paid on bonds increases from 5% to 8%. This will cause

Moderate
Single
Page: 255

(a) no change in optimal balances because checking deposits don't earn interest.
(b) optimal balances to increase because it raises the opportunity costs of holding money.
(c) optimal balances to decrease because it raises the opportunity cost of holding money.
(d) optimal balances to increase because it reduces the opportunity cost of holding money.

Answer: (c)

Easy
Fact
Page: 255

12.18: If the interest rate falls

(a) bond values remain the same, but interest payments are made more frequently.
(b) bond values rise.
(c) bond values fall.
(d) bond values could either rise or fall depending on the magnitude of the decrease in the interest rate.

Answer: (b)

Moderate
Multi
Page: 255

12.19: Jimmy bought a 5% bond a year ago for $10,000. The interest rate has increased to 10%. Jimmy wants to sell the bond. To be able to sell the bond Jimmy must charge a price of no more than

(a) $500.
(b) $1,000.
(c) $5,000.
(d) $6,000.

Answer: (c)

Moderate
Multi
Page: 255

12.20: Dirk bought a 10% bond a year ago for $30,000. The interest rate has increased to 20%. Jimmy wants to sell the bond. To be able to sell the bond Jimmy must charge a price of no more than

(a) $500.
(b) $1,000.
(c) $15,000.
(d) $20,000.

Answer: (c)

Moderate
Single
Page: 255

12.21: Nick bought an 8% bond a year ago for $5,000. He just sold the bond for $6,666. This could have been caused by

(a) a decrease in the demand for bonds.
(b) an increase in the demand for money.
(c) a decrease in interest rates.
(d) a decrease in the supply of money.

Answer: (c)

Moderate
Single
Page: 255

12.22: Nick bought an 4% bond a year ago for $10,000. He just sold the bond for $7,666. This could have been caused by

(a) a increase in interest rates.
(b) a decrease in the demand for bonds.
(c) an decrease in the demand for money.
(d) a increase in the supply of money.

Answer: (a)

Easy
Definition
Page: 255

12.23: The motive for holding money that encourages investors to hold bonds when interest rates are low, with the hope of selling them when interest rates are high, is the

(a) precautionary motive.
(b) speculation motive.
(c) transactions motive.
(d) profit motive.

Answer: (b)

12.24: The current interest rate is 6%. Karen knows that normally interest rates are 8%. What is Karen most likely to do?

(a) Hold bonds instead of cash because interest rates are likely to increase in the future and this will bring about an increase in the value of bonds.
(b) Hold cash instead of bonds because interest rates are likely to increase in the future and this will bring about an increase in the value of bonds.
(c) Hold bonds instead of cash because interest rates are likely to increase in the future and this will bring about a decrease in the value of bonds.
(d) Hold cash instead of bonds because interest rates are likely to increase in the future and this will bring about a decrease in the value of bonds.

Answer: (d)

Moderate
Single
Page: 255

12.25: Brenda expects that the interest rate will decrease in the future. Brenda should

(a) hold cash instead of bonds because as the interest rate increases, the market value of bonds will increase.
(b) hold bonds instead of cash because as the interest rate decreases, the market value of bonds will increase.
(c) hold cash instead of bonds because as the interest rate increases, the market value of bonds will decrease.
(d) hold bonds instead of cash because as the interest rate increases, the market value of bonds will decrease.

Answer: (b)

Moderate
Single
Page: 255

12.26: The opportunity cost of holding money is determined by

(a) the inflation rate.
(b) the level of aggregate output.
(c) the interest rate.
(d) the discount rate.

Answer: (c)

Easy
Fact
Page: 255

12.27: The demand for money represents the idea that there is

(a) a negative relationship between the price level and the quantity of money demanded.
(b) a negative relationship between the level of aggregate output and the quantity of money demanded.
(c) a positive relationship between the interest rate and the quantity of money demanded.
(d) a negative relationship between the interest rate and the quantity of money demanded.

Answer: (d)

Moderate
Single
Page: 258

12.28: When interest rates are higher than normal,

(a) the opportunity cost of holding cash balances is high.
(b) there is speculation motive for holding cash in lieu of bonds.
(c) the opportunity cost of holding bonds is zero.
(d) households will probably expect interest rates to rise even farther.

Answer: (a)

Moderate
Single
Page: 255

Moderate
Single
Page: 255

12.29: When interest rates are lower than normal,

(a) the opportunity cost of holding bonds is low.
(b) households will probably expect interest rates to rise in the future.
(c) the opportunity cost of holding cash balances is high.
(d) there is a speculation motive for holding a larger amount of bonds.

Answer: (b)

Easy
Fact
Page: 255

12.30: When the interest rate rises, bond values

(a) fall.
(b) rise.
(c) are unchanged because the interest rate paid on a bond is fixed.
(d) will either increase or decrease depending on the type of bond.

Answer: (a)

Moderate
Single
Page: 255

12.31: If the interest rate is lower than normal, people will hold onto

(a) bonds instead of money because as the interest rate starts to rise, the value of the bonds will increase.
(b) bonds instead of money because the opportunity cost of money is high.
(c) money instead of bonds because the brokerage fees and other costs of buying bonds are high when the interest rate is low.
(d) money instead of bonds because there is a speculation motive for holding a larger amount of money.

Answer: (d)

Easy
Single
Page: 258

12.32: Refer to Figure 12.1. The money demand curve will shift from M_1^d to M_2^d if

(a) the interest rate increases.
(b) the interest rate decreases.
(c) aggregate output increases.
(d) b and c.

Answer: (c)

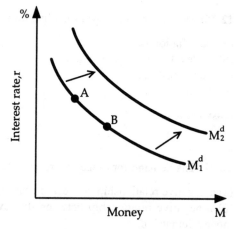

Figure 12.1

Easy
Single
Page: 259

12.33: Refer to Figure 12.1. The money demand curve will shift from M_1^d to M_2^d if

(a) the interest rate increases.
(b) the price level increases.
(c) bond values fall.
(d) aggregate income decreases.

Answer: (b)

Easy
Single
Page: 258

12.34: Refer to Figure 12.1. There will be a move from point A to point B along money demand curve M_1^d if

(a) the interest rate decreases.
(b) the price level increases.
(c) the value of bonds decreases.
(d) a and b.

Answer: (a)

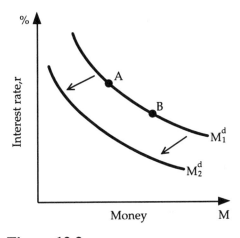

Figure 12.2

12.35: Refer to Figure 12.2. The money demand curve will shift from M_1^d to M_2^d if

(a) the interest rate decreases.
(b) the price level increases.
(c) bond values fall.
(d) aggregate income falls.

Answer: (d)

Easy
Single
Page: 258

12.36: Refer to Figure 12.2. The money demand curve will shift from M_1^d to M_2^d if

(a) the interest rate decreases.
(b) the price level decreases.
(c) aggregate income increases.
(d) the supply of money decreases.

Answer: (b)

Easy
Single
Page: 259

12.37: Which of the following events will lead to an increase in the demand for money?

(a) An increase in the level of aggregate output
(b) A decrease in the price level
(c) An increase in the interest rate
(d) An increase in the supply of money

Answer: (a)

Moderate
Single
Page: 258

12.38: Increases in the price level will

(a) increase the number of transactions and therefore increase the demand for money.
(b) increase the demand for money because the quantity of money needed for transactions will be higher.
(c) decrease the demand for money because the opportunity cost of holding money will be higher.
(d) move the economy down its money demand curve.

Answer: (b)

Moderate
Fact
Page: 259

12.39: For a given interest rate, a higher level of output means

(a) a decrease in the number of transactions and thus a lower demand for money.
(b) a decrease in the number of transactions and thus a higher demand for money.
(c) an increase in the number of transactions and thus a lower demand for money.
(d) an increase in the number of transactions and thus a higher demand for money.

Answer: (d)

Easy
Fact
Page: 258

12.40: As the average dollar amount of each transaction increases,

(a) the demand for money will decrease.
(b) the demand for money will increase.
(c) the quantity demanded of money will increase.
(d) the quantity demanded of money will decrease.

Answer: (b)

Easy
Fact
Page: 259

Moderate
Fact
Page: 259

12.41: What factor(s) is (are) assumed to be constant for a given money demand curve?

(a) only the interest rate
(b) only the level of aggregate output
(c) only the price level
(d) both the level of aggregate output and the price level

Answer: (d)

Easy
Single
Page: 261

12.42: Refer to Figure 12.3. At an interest rate of 8%, there is

(a) an excess supply of money of 250.
(b) an excess supply of money of 150.
(c) an excess demand for money of 150.
(d) an excess demand for money of 250.

Answer: (b)

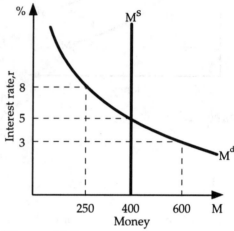

Figure 12.3

Easy
Single
Page: 261

12.43: Refer to Figure 12.3. At an interest rate of 3%, there is

(a) an excess supply of money of 200.
(b) an excess supply of money of 400.
(c) an excess demand for money of 200.
(d) an excess demand for money of 400.

Answer: (c)

Easy
Single
Page: 261

12.44: Refer to Figure 12.3. The money market will be in equilibrium at an interest rate of

(a) 0%.
(b) 3%.
(c) 5%.
(d) 8%.

Answer: (c)

Moderate
Single
Page: 261

12.45: Refer to Figure 12.3. At an interest rate of 8%, firms and households

(a) will attempt to reduce their holdings of money by buying bonds.
(b) will attempt to increase their holdings of money by selling bonds.
(c) are satisfied with the amount of money they are holding.
(d) will attempt to increase both their holdings of money and their holdings of bonds.

Answer: (a)

Moderate
Single
Page: 261

12.46: Refer to Figure 12.3. At an interest rate of 3%, firms and households

(a) will attempt to reduce their holdings of money by buying bonds.
(b) will attempt to increase their holdings of money by selling bonds.
(c) are satisfied with the amount of money they are holding.
(d) will attempt to increase both their holdings of money and their holdings of bonds.

Answer: (b)

12.47: Refer to Figure 12.3. At an interest rate of 5%, firms and households

(a) will attempt to reduce their holdings of money by buying bonds.
(b) will attempt to increase their holdings of money by selling bonds.
(c) are satisfied with the amount of money they are holding.
(d) will attempt to increase both their holdings of money and their holdings of bonds.

Easy
Single
Page: 261

Answer: (c)

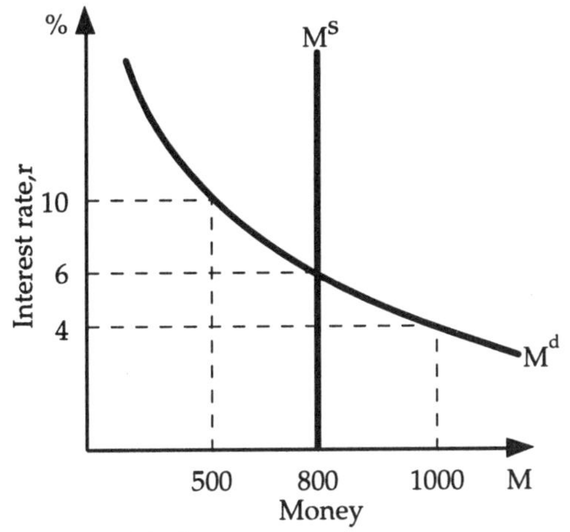

Figure 12.4

12.37: Refer to Figure 12.4. At an interest rate of 10%, there is

(a) an excess demand for money of 300.
(b) an excess supply of money of 500.
(c) an excess supply of money of 300.
(d) an excess demand for money of 500.

Easy
Single
Page: 261

Answer: (c)

12.38: Refer to Figure 12.4. At an interest rate of 4%, there is

(a) an excess supply of money of 200.
(b) an excess supply of money of 600.
(c) an excess demand for money of 600.
(d) an excess demand for money of 200.

Easy
Single
Page: 261

Answer: (d)

12.48: Refer to Figure 12.4. The money market will be in equilibrium at an interest rate of

(a) 0%.
(b) 6%.
(c) 3%.
(d) 8%.

Easy
Single
Page: 261

Answer: (b)

12.49: Refer to Figure 12.4. At an interest rate of 10%, firms and households

(a) will attempt to increase their holdings of money by selling bonds.
(b) are satisfied with the amount of money they are holding.
(c) will attempt to increase both their holdings of money and their holdings of bonds.
(d) will attempt to reduce their holdings of money by buying bonds.

Easy
Single
Page: 261

Answer: (d)

12.50: Refer to Figure 12.4. At an interest rate of 4%, firms and households

(a) are satisfied with the amount of money they are holding.
(b) will attempt to increase their holdings of money by selling bonds.
(c) will attempt to increase both their holdings of money and their holdings of bonds.
(d) will attempt to reduce their holdings of money by buying bonds.

Easy
Single
Page: 261

Answer: (b)

Easy
Single
Page: 261

12.51:.Refer to Figure 12.4. At an interest rate of 6%, firms and households

(a) are satisfied with the amount of money they are holding.
(b) will attempt to reduce their holdings of money by buying bonds.
(c) will attempt to increase their holdings of money by selling bonds.
(d) will attempt to increase both their holdings of money and their holdings of bonds.

Answer: (a)

Moderate
Fact
Page: 261

12.52: As interest rates rise,

(a) the money demand curve will shift to the right.
(b) people are discouraged from buying bonds.
(c) people are discouraged from moving out of bonds and into money.
(d) the money supply curve will shift to the right.

Answer: (c)

Moderate
Single
Page: 261

12.53 If the quantity of money demanded exceeds the quantity of money supplied, then the interest rate will

(a) change in an uncertain direction.
(b) rise.
(c) fall.
(d) remain constant.

Answer: (b)

Easy
Single
Page: 262

12.54: If the quantity of money demanded is less than the quantity of money supplied, then the interest rate will

(a) either increase or decrease, depending on the amount of excess demand.
(b) increase.
(c) decrease.
(d) not change.

Answer: (c)

Easy
Single
Page: 262

12.55: An increase in the money supply, ceteris paribus,

(a) will decrease the interest rate.
(b) will increase the interest rate.
(c) will increase the excess demand for money.
(d) will increase the demand for money.

Answer: (a)

Easy
Single
Page: 262

12.56: Refer to Figure 12.5. Assume the interest rate equals 8% and the money supply increases from M_0^S to M_1^S. If the interest rate remains at 8%,

(a) money demand will increase.
(b) money demand will decrease.
(c) there will be an excess demand for money of 100.
(d) there will be an excess supply of money of 100.

Answer: (d)

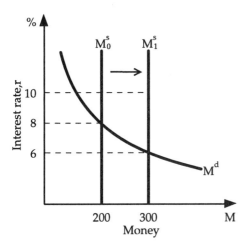

Figure 12.5

12.57: Refer to Figure 12.5. If the money supply increases from M_0^S to M_1^S,

(a) money demand must increase for the money market to return to equilibrium.
(b) the interest rate will fall to 6%.
(c) the interest rate will increase to 10%.
(d) the money market will return to equilibrium only if the money supply is decreased to its original level.

Answer: (b)

Easy
Single
Page: 262

12.58: Refer to Figure 12.5. The money supply curve will shift from M_0^S to M_1^S if

(a) the Fed increases the reserve requirement.
(b) the Fed increases the discount rate.
(c) the equilibrium level of output increases.
(d) the Fed buys U.S. government securities in the open market.

Answer: (d)

Moderate
Single
Page: 262

12.59: Refer to Figure 12.5. The money supply curve will shift from M_0^S to M_1^S if

(a) the Fed increases the reserve requirement.
(b) the Fed decreases the discount rate.
(c) the equilibrium level of output increases.
(d) the Fed sells U.S. government securities in the open market.

Answer: (b)

Moderate
Single
Page: 262

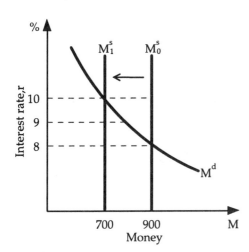

Figure 12.6

12.60: Refer to Figure 12.6. If the money supply decreases from M_0^S to M_1^S,

(a) money demand must decrease for the money market to return to equilibrium.
(b) the interest rate will increase to 9%.
(c) the interest rate will increase to 10%.
(d) the money market will return to equilibrium only if the money supply is increased to its original level.

Answer: (c)

Moderate
Single
Page: 262

12.61: Refer to Figure 12.6. The money supply curve will shift from M_0^S to M_1^S, if

(a) the Fed increases the reserve requirement.
(b) the price level increases.
(c) the equilibrium level of output decreases.
(d) the Fed buys U.S. government securities in the open market.

Answer: (a)

Easy
Fact
Page: 262

Moderate
Single
Page: 262

12.62: Refer to Figure 12.6. The money supply curve will shift from M_0^S to M_1^S, if

(a) the Fed decreases the reserve requirement.
(b) the price level increases.
(c) the equilibrium level of output decreases.
(d) the Fed sells U.S. government securities in the open market.

Answer: (d)

Moderate
Single
Page: 262

12.63: The money market is currently in equilibrium, but the Fed wants to reduce the interest rate. The Fed should pursue policies to

(a) increase the money supply.
(b) decrease the money supply.
(c) increase money demand.
(d) make the supply of money more inelastic.

Answer: (a)

Easy
Fact
Page: 262

12.64: If there is an excess supply of money, then the interest rate

(a) is below the equilibrium interest rate.
(b) is above the equilibrium interest rate.
(c) equals the equilibrium interest rate.
(d) must be equal to zero.

Answer: (b)

Challenging
Multi
Page: 263

12.65: Which of the following pairs of events will definitely lead to an increase in the equilibrium interest rate?

(a) a decrease in the level of aggregate output and a purchase of government securities by the Federal Reserve
(b) an increase in the price level and a decrease in the discount rate
(c) a decrease in the level of aggregate output and an increase in the required reserve ratio
(d) an increase in the price level and a sale of government securities by the Federal Reserve

Answer: (d)

Challenging
Multi
Page: 263

12.66: Which of the following pairs of events will definitely lead to an increase in the equilibrium interest rate?

(a) a decrease in the level of aggregate output and a decrease in the required reserve ratio
(b) an increase in the price level and an increase in the discount rate
(c) an increase in the level of aggregate output and the purchase of government securities by the Federal Reserve
(d) a decrease in the price level and the sale of government securities by the Federal Reserve

Answer: (b)

Challenging
Multi
Page: 263

12.67: An increase in the level of aggregate output and the sale of government securities by the Fed will have what effect on the equilibrium interest rate?

(a) an increase in the interest rate
(b) a decrease in the interest rate
(c) no effect on the interest rate
(d) an indeterminate effect on the interest rate

Answer: (a)

12.68: Which of the following pairs of events will definitely lead to a decrease in the equilibrium interest rate?

(a) the sale of government securities by the Federal Reserve and an increase in the price level
(b) a decrease in the discount rate and an increase in the level of aggregate output
(c) the purchase of government securities by the Federal Reserve and a decrease in the price level
(d) an increase in the required reserve ratio and a decrease in the level of aggregate output

Challenging
Multi
Page: 263

Answer: (c)

12.69: Which of the following pairs of events will definitely lead to a decrease in the equilibrium interest rate?

(a) the purchase of government securities by the Federal Reserve and a decrease in the level of aggregate output
(b) an increase in the discount rate and an increase in the price level
(c) a decrease in the required reserve ratio and an increase in the level of aggregate output
(d) the sale of government securities by the Federal Reserve and a decrease in the price level

Challenging
Multi
Page: 263

Answer: (a)

12.70: A decrease in the discount rate and a decrease in the level of aggregate output will have what effect on the equilibrium interest rate?

(a) an increase in the interest rate
(b) a decrease in the interest rate
(c) no effect on the interest rate
(d) an indeterminate effect on the interest rate

Challenging
Multi
Page: 263

Answer: (a)

12.71: Refer to Figure 12.7. The demand for money curve will shift from M_0^d to M_1^d if

(a) the Fed sells government securities on the open market.
(b) the price level decreases.
(c) if the interest rate increases.
(d) the aggregate level of output increases.

Moderate
Single
Page: 263

Answer: (d)

12.72: Refer to Figure 12.7. If the demand for money curve shifts from M_0^d to M_1^d, the equilibrium interest rate will

(a) increase from 5% to 7%.
(b) increase from 5% to 9%.
(c) increase from 7% to 9%.
(d) remain at 5%.

Easy
Single
Page: 263

Answer: (b)

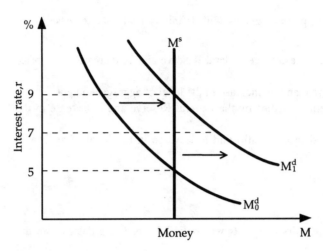

Figure 12.7

Easy
Single
Page: 263

12.73: Refer to Figure 12.7. If the demand for money curve shifts from M_0^d to M_1^d and the interest rate remains at 5%, there will be

(a) an excess demand for money.
(b) an excess supply of money.
(c) an equilibrium in the money market.
(d) an equilibrium in the bond market.

Answer: (a)

Easy
Fact
Page: 263

12.74: An increase in the level of aggregate output

(a) leads to an increase in the interest rate.
(b) leads to a decrease in the interest rate.
(c) will increase money demand, but will not affect the interest rate.
(d) will increase money supply, but will not affect the interest rate.

Answer: (a)

Easy
Fact
Page: 263

12.75: An increase in the price level

(a) leads to an increase in the   interest rate.
(b) leads to a decrease in the interest rate.
(c) will increase money demand, but will not affect the interest rate.
(d) will increase money supply, but will not affect the interest rate.

Answer: (a)

Moderate
Single
Page: 263

12.76: Refer to Figure 12.8. The demand for money curve will shift from M_0^d to M_1^d if

(a) the Fed sells government securities on the open market.
(b) the price level decreases.
(c) if the interest rate increases.
(d) the level of aggregate output increases.

Answer: (b)

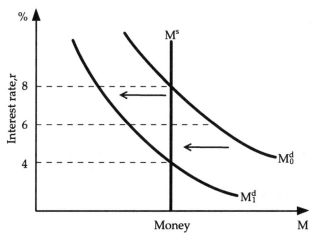

Figure 12.8

12.77: Refer to Figure 12.8. If the demand for money curve shifts from M_0^d to M_1^d, the equilibrium interest rate will

Easy
Single
Page: 263

(a) decrease from 8% to 4%.
(b) decrease from 8% to 6%.
(c) decrease from 6% to 4%.
(d) remain at 8%.

Answer: (a)

12.78: Refer to Figure 12.8. If the demand for money curve shifts from M_0^d to M_1^d and the interest rate remains at 8%, there will be

Easy
Single
Page: 263

(a) an excess demand for money.
(b) an excess supply of money.
(c) an equilibrium in the money market.
(d) an equilibrium in the bond market.

Answer: (b)

12.79: An increase in aggregate output, ceteris paribus, will cause the demand for money to _____ and the interest rate to _____.

Easy
Single
Page: 263

(a) increase; increase
(b) increase; decrease
(c) decrease; decrease
(d) decrease; increase

Answer: (a)

12.80: A decrease in the price level, ceteris paribus, will cause the demand for money to _____ and the interest rate to _____.

Easy
Single
Page: 263

(a) increase; increase
(b) increase; decrease
(c) decrease; decrease
(d) decrease; increase

Answer: (c)

Easy
Fact
Page: 263

12.81: As the number of transactions in the economy increases,

(a) the supply of money increases.
(b) the supply of money decreases.
(c) the demand for money increases.
(d) the demand for money decreases.

Answer: (c)

Moderate
Single
Page: 263

12.82: Which of the following events will lead to an increase in the equilibrium interest rate?

(a) an increase in the level of aggregate output
(b) a decrease in the required reserve ratio
(c) a decrease in the price level
(d) a purchase of government securities by the Federal Reserve

Answer: (a)

Moderate
Multi
Page: 263

12.83: Which of the following events will lead to an increase in the equilibrium interest rate?

(a) an increase in the price level
(b) a decrease in the discount rate
(c) a decrease in the level of aggregate output
(d) a purchase of government securities by the Federal Reserve

Answer: (a)

Moderate
Multi
Page: 263

12.84: Which of the following events will lead to a decrease in the equilibrium interest rate?

(a) an increase in the required reserve ratio
(b) an increase in the price level
(c) a sale of government securities by the Federal Reserve
(d) a decrease in the level of aggregate output

Answer: (d)

Moderate
Multi
Page: 263

12.85: Which of the following events will lead to a decrease in the equilibrium interest rate?

(a) a decrease in the price level
(b) an increase in the discount rate
(c) an increase in the level of aggregate output
(d) a sale of government securities by the Federal Reserve

Answer: (a)

Easy
Definition
Page: 264

12.86: When economists refer to "tight" monetary policy, they mean that the Federal Reserve is taking actions that will

(a) increase the demand for money.
(b) decrease the demand for money.
(c) expand the money supply.
(d) contract the money supply.

Answer: (d)

12.87: An example of a tight monetary policy is

(a) a decrease in the reserve requirement.
(b) the Fed selling government securities in the open market.
(c) a decrease in the discount rate.
(d) an increase in the federal funds rate.

Answer: (b)

Moderate
Single
Page: 264

12.88: An example of a tight monetary policy is

(a) an increase in the reserve requirement.
(b) the Fed buying government securities in the open market.
(c) a decrease in the prime lending rate.
(d) a decrease in the discount rate.

Answer: (a)

Moderate
Single
Page: 264

12.89: When economists refer to "easy" monetary policy, they mean that the Federal Reserve is taking actions that will

(a) increase the demand for money.
(b) decrease the demand for money.
(c) expand the money supply.
(d) contract the money supply.

Answer: (c)

Easy
Definition
Page: 264

12.90: Which of the following is an example of an easy monetary policy?

(a) an increase in the reserve requirement
(b) a decrease in the discount rate
(c) a decrease in the federal funds rate
(d) the Fed selling government securities in the open market

Answer: (b)

Moderate
Single
Page: 264

SITUATION 12.1: Arthur has two investment opportunities. He can buy a two-year security today, hold onto it for two years and then cash it in. The interest rate on the two-year security is 6%. Or Arthur can buy a one-year security today. At the end of the year he can cash in the one-year security and buy another one-year security. The interest rate on the first one-year security is 7%.

12.91: Refer to Situation 12.1. Which of the following is TRUE?

(a) The strategy of buying two one-year securities is preferable to buying the two-year security because the first one-year security has a higher interest rate than the two-year security.
(b) The strategy of buying a two-year security is preferable to buying two one-year securities because the two-year security offers more certainty than two one-year securities.
(c) Arthur should be indifferent between a two-year security and two one-year securities because the rate of return on the two types of securities is always the same.
(d) Arthur does not have enough information to determine which of the two investment strategies is preferable.

Answer: (d)

Moderate
Single
Page: 267

Moderate
Multi
Page: 267

12.92: Refer to Situation 12.1. If the expected interest rate on the second one-year security that Arthur could buy is 6%, Arthur

(a) will be indifferent between the two one-year securities and the two-year security.
(b) will prefer the two one-year securities over the two-year security.
(c) will prefer the two-year security over the two one-year securities.
(d) doesn't have enough information to decide which investment opportunity is preferable.

Answer: (b)

Moderate
Multi
Page: 267

12.93: Refer to Situation 12.1. If the expected interest rate on the second one-year security that Arthur could buy is 5%, Arthur

(a) will be indifferent between the two one-year securities and the two-year security.
(b) will prefer the two one-year securities over the two-year security.
(c) will prefer the two-year security over the two one-year securities.
(d) doesn't have enough information to decide which investment opportunity is preferable.

Answer: (a)

Moderate
Multi
Page: 267

12.94: Refer to Situation 12.1. If the expected interest rate on the second one-year security that Arthur could buy is 4%, Arthur

(a) will be indifferent between the two one-year securities and the two-year security.
(b) will prefer the two one-year securities over the two-year security.
(c) will prefer the two-year security over the two one-year securities.
(d) doesn't have enough information to decide which investment opportunity is preferable.

Answer: (c)

Moderate
Single
Page: 267

12.95: Assume the one-year interest rate on a bond is 5% and the expected one-year rate a year from now is 7%. According to the expectations theory of the term structure of interest rates, the two-year rate will be

(a) 5%.
(b) 6%.
(c) 7%.
(d) 12%.

Answer: (b)

Moderate
Single
Page: 267

12.96: Assume the current one-year interest rate on a bond is 7%, and the one-year expected rate a year from now is 9%. According to the expectations theory of the term structure of interest rates, the two-year interest rate is

(a) 7%.
(b) 8%.
(c) 9%.
(d) 16%.

Answer: (b)

12.97: The interest rate on a two-year security will continue to adjust until it is equal to

(a) half the interest rate on a one-year security.
(b) twice the interest rate on a one-year security.
(c) the average of the current one-year rate and the expected one-year rate for next year.
(d) the sum of the current one-year rate and the expected one-year rate for next year.

Answer: (c)

Moderate
Fact
Page: 287

12.98: The Fed can influence long-term interest rates by

(a) influencing the current one-year rate.
(b) affecting people's expectations of future short-term rates.
(c) influencing the demand for money in the short run.
(d) a and b.

Answer: (d)

Easy
Fact
Page: 267

12.99: Government securities that mature in less than a year are called

(a) Treasury bills.
(b) government bonds.
(c) Federal Reserve bonds.
(d) Federal funds bonds.

Answer: (a)

Easy
Definition
Page: 268

12.100: What is the most widely followed short-term interest rate?

(a) the federal funds rate
(b) the three-month Treasury bill rate
(c) the commercial paper rate
(d) the government bond rate

Answer: (b)

Easy
Fact
Page: 268

12.101: Government securities with terms of more than one year are called

(a) Treasury bills.
(b) government bonds.
(c) capital bills.
(d) federal funds bonds.

Answer: (b)

Easy
Definition
Page: 268

12.102: The interest rate that banks are charged when they borrow reserves from other banks is the

(a) commercial paper rate.
(b) AAA corporate bond rate.
(c) federal funds rate.
(d) prime rate.

Answer: (c)

Easy
Definition
Page: 268

Easy
Fact
Page: 268

12.103: The federal funds rate is a

(a) one-day rate.
(b) one-week rate.
(c) one-month rate.
(d) one-year rate.

Answer: (a)

Easy
Fact
Page: 268

12.104: The rate that the Fed controls most closely through its open market operations is the

(a) prime rate.
(b) government bonds rate.
(c) commercial paper rate.
(d) federal funds rate.

Answer: (d)

Easy
Definition
Page: 268

12.105: The rate that the least risky firms pay on bonds that they issue is the

(a) prime rate.
(b) commercial paper rate.
(c) triple-A corporate bond rate.
(d) federal funds rate.

Answer: (c)

Challenging
Multi
Page: 269

12.106: Refer to Figure 12.9. If it costs $3 each time a bond is sold, the optimal average money holdings are

(a) $600.
(b) $400.
(c) $300.
(d) $200.

Answer: (d)

Number of Switches	Average Money Holdings	Average Bond Holdings	Interest Earned
0	$1,200	$ 0	$ 0
1	$ 600	$ 600	$30
2	$ 400	$ 800	$40
3	$ 300	$ 900	$45
4	$ 200	$1,000	$50

Figure 12.9

12.107: Refer to Figure 12.9. If it costs $6 each time a bond is sold, the optimal average money holdings are

(a) $600.
(b) $400.
(c) $300.
(d) $200.

Answer: (b)

Challenging
Multi
Page: 269

12.108: Refer to Figure 12.9. The interest rate paid on bonds

(a) is 2%.
(b) is 3%.
(c) is 5%.
(d) cannot be determined from this information.

Answer: (c)

Moderate
Single
Page: 269

TRUE/FALSE QUESTIONS

12.109: The mismatch between the timing of money inflow to the household and the timing of money outflow for household expenses is known as the nonsynchronization of income and spending.

Answer: True

Easy
Fact
Page: 252

12.110: Less switching from bonds to money means less interest revenue lost, but higher money management costs.

Answer: False

Easy
Fact
Page: 254

12.111: The optimal money balance will increase as the interest rate rises, ceteris paribus.

Answer: False

Easy
Fact
Page: 255

12.112: When interest rates fall, bond values rise.

Answer: True

Easy
Fact
Page: 256

12.113: Investors may wish to hold bonds when interest rates are low with the hope of selling them when interest rates increase.

Answer: False

Easy
Fact
Page: 256

12.114: An increase in the price level will lead to a decrease in the demand for money.

Answer: False

Easy
Fact
Page: 259

12.115: An excess supply of money drives interest rates down.

Answer: True

Easy
Fact
Page: 262

12.116: If the Federal Reserve wants interest rates to increase, it will take actions to reduce the money supply.

Answer: True

Easy
Fact
Page: 262

Easy
Fact
Page: 262

12.117: A purchase of government securities by the Federal Reserve will put upward pressure on the equilibrium interest rate.

Answer: False

Easy
Single
Page: 263

12.118: An increase in the demand for money, combined with an "easy" monetary policy on the part of the Federal Reserve, will have an uncertain effect on the equilibrium interest rate.

Answer: True

SHORT ANSWER QUESTIONS

Moderate
Definition
Page: 252

12.119: What is the nonsynchronization of income and spending?

Answer: The nonsynchronization of income and spending relates to the mismatch between the timing of money inflows to the household and the outflow of money to meet household expenses. That is, a typical household may receive their income once or twice a month while they incur daily expenses and financial obligations.

Moderate
Fact
Page: 256

12.120: What is the relationship between interest rates or yields on bonds and their price or market value?

Answer: There is an inverse relationship between changes in bond prices and their yield or interest rate. When prices rise, the interest rate decreases, and when prices fall, the interest rate increases.

Moderate
Fact
Page: 259

12.121: Summarize the determinants of the demand for money.

Answer: The demand for money depends upon:
      (1) the rate of interest
      (2) the dollar volume of transactions
          (a) aggregate output
          (b) the prices of goods and services.

Moderate
Definition
Page: 268

12.122: What is the federal funds rate? What is the commercial paper rate? What is the prime rate of interest?

Answer: The federal funds rate is the rate of interest banks charge each other when borrowing reserves. The commercial paper rate is the interest that large businesses pay lenders when borrowing short-term funds. The prime rate of interest is the rate that banks charge their larger low-risk corporate borrowers.

Easy
Definition
Page: 256

12.123: Explain the transaction and speculation motives for holding money.

Answer: The transaction motive for holding money is the main reason why people hold money — to buy things. The speculation motive for holding money is as follows when interest rates are lower than normal, people may expect them to increase in the future thus bringing about a decline in the value of bonds. People hold money speculating that the price of bonds will fall in the future and that they can then sell them at a profit.

12.124: Explain the trade-off between holding bonds and holding money. Why don't people keep all their assets in the forms that are the easiest to use for making transactions?

Easy
Single
Page: 255

Answer: The opportunity cost of holding money is forgone interest. The opportunity cost of holding bonds is that bonds cannot be used for exchange. A bond must be converted to cash before it can be used to make transactions. This conversion involves both monetary and time costs. People don't keep all of their assets in cash because cash earns no interest and there is a nonsynchronization of income and spending. People don't need to spend all their income when it is received, so they are able to purchase interest-bearing bonds with some of their cash.

12.125: Draw a demand curve for money. Explain the two factors that could cause an increase in the demand for money.

Moderate
Single
Page: 259

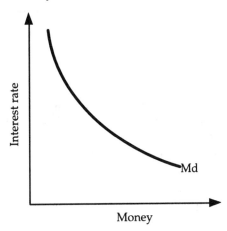

Answer: Money demand will increase if there is an increase in the price level or an increase in aggregate output.

12.126: Use a graph to illustrate the effect an expansionary fiscal policy will have on the money market. What happens to the interest rate? What impact will this have on the effectiveness of fiscal policy?

Honors
Multi
Page: 263

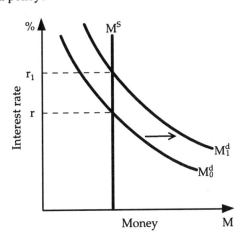

Answer: An expansionary fiscal policy will increase the demand for money and increase the interest rate. If investment is sensitive to the interest rate, an increase in the interest rate may cause investment to fall. If consumption is sensitive to the interest rate, an increase in the interest rate may cause consumption to fall. Fiscal policy will not be as effective if investment and consumption are sensitive to the interest rate.

Moderate
Single
Page: 262

12.127: Draw a graph of a money demand curve and a money supply curve. On the graph, indicate the equilibrium interest rate. Also indicate the new equilibrium interest rate if the Fed increases the money supply.

Answer: If the Fed increases the money supply, the interest rate will fall.

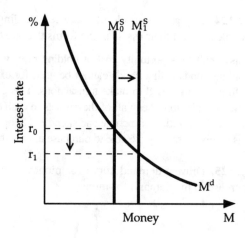

Challenging
Multi
Page: 263

12.128: Illustrate each of the following situations using supply and demand curves for money. In each case explain what happens to the equilibrium interest rate. (a) Aggregate output increases. (b) The Fed sells government securities in the open market during a recession. (c) During a period of rapid growth, the Fed reduces the reserve requirement.

Answer: (a) The interest rate increases. (b) The change in the equilibrium interest rate is indeterminate. (c) The change in the equilibrium interest rate is indeterminate.

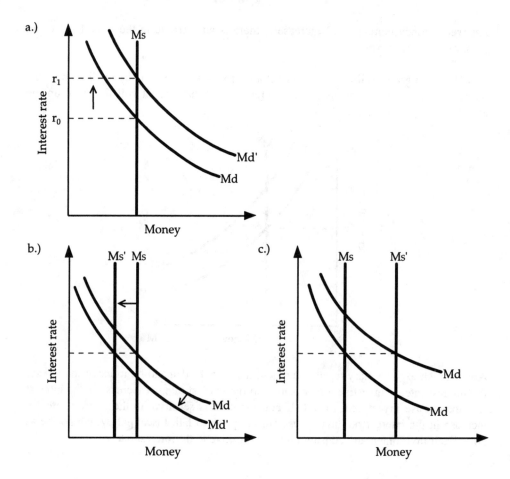

12.129: What do economists mean when they say that there is an "excess supply of money" in the economy? Illustrate this situation graphically. If there is an excess supply of money, what happens to the interest rate? How does the change in the interest rate influence the trade-off between holding money and holding bonds?

Moderate
Single
Page: 262

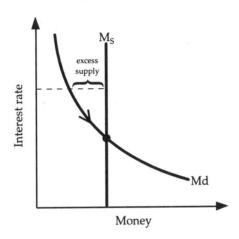

Answer: An excess supply of money means that the quantity of money supplied exceeds the quantity of money demanded. An excess supply of money occurs when the interest rate is above the equilibrium interest rate. The interest rate should fall until quantity of money demanded equals quantity of money supplied. As the interest rate falls, the opportunity cost of holding money is reduced and money becomes more attractive. The lower interest rate will increase the price of bonds and bonds will become less attractive.

12.130: (a) Explain how the Federal Reserve might carry out a "tight" monetary policy.(b) Explain how the Federal Reserve might carry out an "easy" monetary policy.(c) How would each of the policies affect the equilibrium interest rate?

Moderate
Fact
Page: 264

Answer: (a) A tight monetary policy means that the Fed is seeking to reduce the growth rate of the money supply. The Fed can implement a tight monetary policy by increasing the required reserve ratio, increasing the discount rate, or selling government bonds in the open market. (b) An easy monetary policy means that the Fed is trying to increase the growth rate of the money supply. The Fed can implement an easy monetary policy by decreasing the required reserve ratio, decreasing the discount rate, or buying government bonds in the open market. (c) A tight monetary policy will cause the interest rate to increase and an easy monetary policy will cause the interest rate to decrease.

12.131: Joe has two investment opportunities. He can buy a two-year security today, hold onto it for two years, and then cash it in. The interest rate on the two-year security is 8%. Or Joe can buy a one-year security today. At the end of the year he can cash in the one-year security and buy another one-year security. The interest rate on the first one-year security is 7%. Explain under what circumstances it would be preferable for Joe to: (a) buy the two-year security. (b) buy the two one-year securities. (c) Under what circumstance would Joe be indifferent between the two-year security and the two one-year securities?

Challenging
Multi
Page: 267

Answer: (a) It would be preferable for Joe to buy the two-year security if the expected rate of return on the two one-year securities is less than the rate of return on the two-year security. If the expected interest rate on the second one-year security is less than 9%, then the expected rate of return on the two one-year securities is less than 8% and Joe would prefer the two-year security. (b) It would be preferable for Joe to buy the two one-year securities if the expected rate of return on the two one-year securities is greater than the rate of return on the two-year security. If the expected interest rate on the second one-year security is greater than 9%, then the expected rate of return on the two one-year securities is greater than 8% and Joe would prefer the two one-year securities. (c) Joe will be indifferent between the two-year security and the two one-year securities if the expected rate of return on the two one-year securities is the same as the return on the two-year security. The two rates of return will be equal if the expected interest rate on the second one-year security is 9%.

Challenging
Multi
Page: 269

12.132: Mary earns a monthly income of $3,000. She spends the entire amount each month at the rate of $100 a day. (Assume there are 30 days in the month.) The interest rate paid on bonds is 5% per month. It costs $10 every time Mary sells a bond. (a) Describe briefly how Mary should go about deciding how much money to hold. (b) Mary can switch from bonds to cash up to a maximum of three times. How many times should Mary switch from bonds to cash? (c) What is Mary's optimal balance?

Answer: (a) Mary should determine how much money to hold by calculating the net profit from different levels of money holdings. If she holds more money in bonds, interest payments increase, but switching costs also increase. (b) Mary should switch from bonds to cash three times. (c) Mary's optimal money balance is $750.

13 Money, the Interest Rate, and National Income: Analysis and Policy

(Chapter 28 in Combined Text)

MULTIPLE CHOICE QUESTIONS

13.1: The market in which the equilibrium level of aggregate output is determined is the

(a) labor market.
(b) goods market.
(c) money market.
(d) bond market.

Answer: (b)

Easy
Definition
Page: 273

13.2: The market in which the equilibrium level of the interest rate is determined is the

(a) labor market.
(b) goods market.
(c) money market.
(d) bond market.

Answer: (c)

Easy
Definition
Page: 273

13.3: If output increases and the interest rate remains constant, there will be

(a) a decrease in the quantity of money demanded.
(b) an increase in the quantity of money demanded.
(c) a decrease in the quantity of money supplied.
(d) an increase in the quantity of money supplied.

Answer: (b)

Easy
Fact
Page: 274

13.4: The two links between the goods market and the money are

(a) income and the interest rate.
(b) the interest rate and the unemployment rate.
(c) income and the inflation rate.
(d) the inflation rate and the unemployment rate.

Answer: (a)

Easy
Fact
Page: 274

13.5: Which of the following statements is FALSE?

(a) Income, which is determined in the money market, has an important influence on the demand for money in the goods market.
(b) The interest rate, which is determined in the money market, has important effects on planned investment in the goods market.
(c) When the interest rate falls, planned investment rises.
(d) When the interest rate rises, planned investment falls.

Answer: (a)

Easy
Fact
Page: 274

Easy
Fact
Page: 274

13.6: Which of the following statements is CORRECT?

(a) When the interest rate rises, it becomes more expensive to borrow, and fewer investment projects are likely to be undertaken.
(b) When the interest rate rises, it becomes more expensive to borrow, and more investment projects are likely to be undertaken.
(c) When the interest rate rises, it becomes less costly to borrow, and more investment projects are likely to be undertaken.
(d) When the interest rate rises, it becomes less costly to borrow, and fewer investment projects are likely to be undertaken.

Answer: (a)

Easy
Single
Page: 275

13.7: Refer to Figure 13.1. If planned investment increases as the interest rate falls, the planned investment schedule will be represented by Panel

(a) A.
(b) B.
(c) C.
(d) D.

Answer: (d)

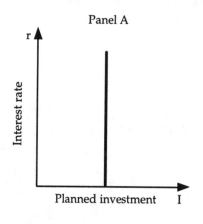

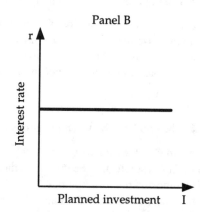

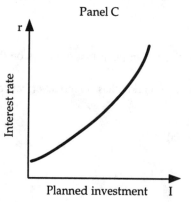

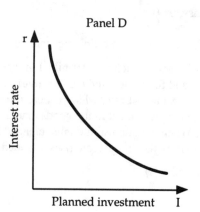

Figure 13.1

13.8: Refer to Figure 13.1. If the economy's planned investment schedule was represented by Panel _____, the crowding—out effect would be zero.

(a) A
(b) B
(c) C
(d) D

Answer: (a)

Easy
Single
Page: 279

13.9: A decrease in the interest rate will cause the

(a) long-run aggregate supply curve to shift out.
(b) aggregate expenditure curve to shift down.
(c) aggregate expenditure curve to shift up.
(d) investment demand curve to shift to the right.

Answer: (c)

Easy
Fact
Page: 275

13.10: Refer to Figure 13.2. Which of the following statements is TRUE?

(a) $r_0 = r_1 = r_2$.
(b) $r_0 > r_1 > r_2$.
(c) $r_0 < r_1 < r_2$.
(d) $r_0 < r_1 > r_2$.

Answer: (b)

Moderate
Single
Page: 276

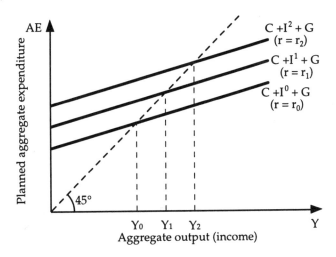

Figure 13.2

13.11: As the interest rate increases,

(a) planned investment decreases, but aggregate expenditure remains constant.
(b) planned investment increases, but aggregate expenditure remains constant.
(c) planned investment decreases and aggregate expenditure decreases.
(d) planned investment increases and aggregate expenditure increases.

Answer: (c)

Easy
Single
Page: 276

Easy
Fact
Page: 276

13.12: As the interest rate increases ,

(a) planned investment decreases, aggregate expenditure decreases, and the equilibrium level of output falls.
(b) planned investment increases, aggregate expenditure increases, and the equilibrium level of output increases.
(c) planned investment decreases, aggregate expenditure increases, and the equilibrium level of output increase.
(d) planned investment increases, aggregate expenditure decreases, and the equilibrium level of output falls.

Answer: (a)

Moderate
Single
Page: 276

13.13: The equilibrium level of output in the United States will fall if

(a) the price level falls.
(b) the interest rate increases.
(c) the money supply increases.
(d) the demand for money decreases.

Answer: (b)

Easy
Fact
Page: 274

13.14: The interest rate

(a) is determined in the money market and has no influence on the goods market.
(b) is determined in the goods market and has no influence on the money market.
(c) is determined in the money market and influences the level of planned investment and thus the goods market.
(d) is determined in the goods market and influences the level of planned investment and thus the money market.

Answer: (c)

Easy
Single
Page: 277

13.15: Refer to Figure 13.3. The equilibrium interest rate is

(a) 0%.
(b) 4%.
(c) 6%.
(d) 12%.

Answer: (c)

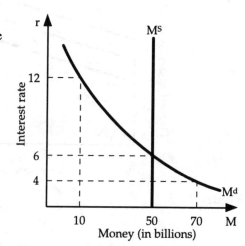

Figure 13.3

Easy
Single
Page: 277

13.16: Refer to Figure 13.3. If the interest rate is 12%, there is

(a) an excess supply of money.
(b) an excess demand for money.
(c) an equilibrium in the money market.
(d) disequilibrium in the money market, but equilibrium in the goods market.

Answer: (a)

13.17: Refer to Figure 13.3. If the interest rate is 12%,

(a) people will shift their assets out of interest-bearing bonds and into money and the interest rate will fall.
(b) people will shift their funds into interest-bearing bonds and the interest rate will fall.
(c) people want to hold more money than is being supplied, so the money supply will increase and the interest rate will not change.
(d) people want to hold less money than is being supplied, so the money supply will decrease and the interest rate will not change.

Answer: (b)

Moderate
Single
Page: 277

13.18: Refer to Figure 13.3. If the interest rate is 4%, there is

(a) an excess supply of money.
(b) an excess demand for money.
(c) an equilibrium in the money market.
(d) disequilibrium in the money market, but equilibrium in the goods market.

Answer: (b)

Easy
Single
Page: 277

13.19: Refer to Figure 13.3. If the interest rate is 4%,

(a) people will shift their assets out of interest-bearing bonds and into money and the interest rate will increase.
(b) people will shift their funds into interest-bearing bonds and the interest rate will increase.
(c) people want to hold less money than is being supplied, so the money supply will decrease and the interest rate will not change.
(d) people want to hold more money than is being supplied, so the money supply will increase and the interest rate will not change.

Answer: (a)

Moderate
Single
Page: 277

13.20: Refer to Figure 13.3. Which of the following statements is TRUE?

(a) The demand for money depends only on income.
(b) Even if the demand for money changes, the interest rate will remain constant.
(c) The money supply is independent of the interest rate.
(d) Given that the money supply curve is a vertical line, changes in the money market will not affect the goods market.

Answer: (c)

Easy
Fact
Page: 277

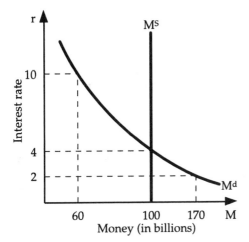

13.21: Refer to Figure 13.4. The equilibrium interest rate is

(a) 0%.
(b) 2%.
(c) 4%.
(d) 10%.

Answer: (c)

Easy
Single
Page: 277

Figure 13.4

Easy
Single
Page: 277

13.22: Refer to Figure 13.4. If the interest rate is 10%, there is

(a) an excess demand for money.
(b) an equilibrium in the money market.
(c) equilibrium in the money market, but disequilibrium in the goods market.
(d) an excess supply of money.

Answer: (d)

Moderate
Single
Page: 277

13.23: Refer to Figure 13.4. If the interest rate is 10%,

(a) people will shift their assets out of interest-bearing bonds and into money and the interest rate will fall.
(b) people want to hold more money than is being supplied, so the money supply will increase and the interest rate will not change.
(c) people will shift their funds into interest-bearing bonds and the interest rate will fall.
(d) people want to hold less money than is being supplied, so the money supply will decrease and the interest rate will not change.

Answer: (c)

Easy
Single
Page: 277

13.24: Refer to Figure 13.4. If the interest rate is 2%, there is

(a) an excess supply of goods.
(b) an excess demand of money.
(c) an excess demand for goods.
(d) disequilibrium in the money market, but equilibrium in the goods market.

Answer: (b)

Moderate
Single
Page: 277

13.25: Refer to Figure 13.4. If the interest rate is 2%,

(a) people will shift their funds into of interest-bearing bonds and the interest rate will increase.
(b) people want to hold less money than is being supplied, so the money supply will decrease and the interest rate will decrease.
(c) people want to hold more money than is being supplied, so the money supply will increase and the interest rate will not change.
(d) people will shift their assets out of interest-bearing bonds and into money and the interest rate will increase.

Answer: (d)

Easy
Single
Page: 277

13.26: Refer to Figure 13.4. Which of the following statements is TRUE?

(a) The money supply is independent of the interest rate.
(b) The demand for money depends only on the weather.
(c) Even if the demand for money changes, the interest rate will remain constant.
(d) Given that the money supply curve is a vertical line, changes in the money market will not affect the goods market, and vice-versa.

Answer: (a)

Easy
Fact
Page: 277

13.27: If the amount of money demanded by households and firms is less than the amount in circulation as determined by the Fed,

(a) the money supply will decrease.
(b) the money supply will increase.
(c) the interest rate will increase.
(d) the interest rate will decrease.

Answer: (d)

13.28: If the amount of money demanded by households and firms is greater than the amount in circulation as determined by the Fed,

(a) the money supply will decrease.
(b) the money supply will increase.
(c) the interest rate will increase.
(d) the interest rate will decrease.

Answer: (c)

Easy
Fact
Page: 277

13.29: Which of the following statements is FALSE?

(a) Changes in aggregate output, which take place in the goods market, shift the money-demand curve and cause changes in the interest rate.
(b) The equilibrium level of the interest rate is determined exclusively in the money market, and is not affected by changes in the goods market.
(c) With a given quantity of money supplied, higher levels of aggregate output will lead to higher equilibrium levels of the interest rate.
(d) Lower levels of aggregate output will lead to lower equilibrium levels of the interest rate.

Answer: (b)

Easy
Fact
Page: 278

13.30: An increase in aggregate output causes the demand for money to _____ and the interest rate to _____.

(a) increase; increase
(b) increase; decrease
(c) decrease; decrease
(d) decrease; increase

Answer: (a)

Easy
Fact
Page: 278

13.31: A decrease in aggregate output causes the demand for money to _____ and the interest rate to _____.

(a) increase; increase
(b) increase; decrease
(c) decrease; decrease
(d) decrease; increase

Answer: (c)

Easy
Fact
Page: 278

13.32: An increase in government spending or a reduction in net taxes aimed at increasing aggregate output is referred to as

(a) contractionary fiscal policy.
(b) expansionary fiscal policy.
(c) expansionary monetary policy.
(d) contractionary monetary policy.

Answer: (b)

Easy
Definition
Page: 278

13.33: Which of the following is an example of an expansionary fiscal policy?

(a) the Fed selling government securities in the open market
(b) the federal government increasing the marginal tax rate on incomes above $200,000
(c) the federal government increasing the amount of money spent on public health programs.
(d) the federal government reducing pollution standards to allow firms to produce more output.

Answer: (c)

Easy
Single
Page: 278

Moderate
Single
Page: 278

13.34: Which of the following actions is an example of expansionary fiscal policy?

(a) an increase in defense spending
(b) a purchase of government securities in the open market
(c) a reduction in the discount rate
(d) elimination of certain income tax deductions

Answer: (a)

Moderate
Single
Page: 278

13.35: Which of the following actions is an example of expansionary fiscal policy?

(a) a decrease in welfare payments
(b) a purchase of government securities in the open market
(c) a decrease in the required reserve ratio
(d) a decrease in the corporate profits tax rates

Answer: (d)

Easy
Definition
Page: 280

13.36: An increase in the money supply aimed at increasing aggregate output is referred to as

(a) contractionary fiscal policy.
(b) expansionary fiscal policy.
(c) expansionary monetary policy.
(d) contractionary monetary policy.

Answer: (c)

Easy
Single
Page: 286

13.37: An example of an expansionary monetary policy is

(a) an increase in the required reserve ratio.
(b) an increase in the discount rate.
(c) a reduction in the taxes banks pay on their profits.
(d) the Fed buying government securities in the open market.

Answer: (d)

Easy
Single
Page: 286

13.38: An example of an expansionary monetary policy is

(a) a decrease in the required reserve ratio.
(b) the Fed selling bonds in the open market.
(c) an increase in the required reserve ratio.
(d) a law placing a ceiling the maximum interest rate that banks can pay to depositors.

Answer: (a)

Easy
Fact
Page: 278

13.39: The intended goal of expansionary fiscal and monetary policy is

(a) an increase in interest rates.
(b) an increase in the price level.
(c) the equalization of the distribution of income.
(d) an increase in the level of aggregate output.

Answer: (d)

13.40: Refer to Figure 13.5. Planned investment would decrease from $15 million to $10 million if

Moderate
Multi
Page: 280

(a) the government increases government expenditures.
(b) the Fed increases the money supply.
(c) the government reduces government expenditures.
(d) the government increases net taxes.

Answer: (a)

13.41: Refer to Figure 13.5. Planned investment would decrease from $18 million to $15 million if

Moderate
Multi
Page: 280

(a) the government reduces government expenditures.
(b) the Fed buys bonds in the open market.
(c) the government reduces net taxes.
(d) firms expect their sales to decrease in the future.

Answer: (c)

13.42: Refer to Figure 13.5. Planned investment would increase from $10 million to $15 million if

Moderate
Single
Page: 328

(a) the government increases government spending.
(b) the government reduces net taxes.
(c) the Fed sells bonds in the open market.
(d) the Fed reduces the required reserve ratio.

Answer: (d)

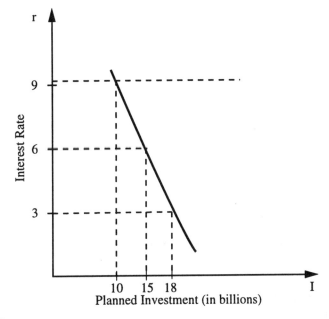

Figure 13.5

Moderate
Single
Page: 283

13.43: Refer to Figure 13.5. Planned investment would increase from $10 million to $15 million if

(a) the government increases net taxes.
(b) the government increases government spending.
(c) the Fed sells bonds in the open market.
(d) both b and c.

Answer: (a)

Moderate
Single
Page: 283

13.44: Refer to Figure 13.5. Planned investment would decrease from $18 million to $15 million if

(a) the government reduces government spending.
(b) the Fed sells bonds in the open market.
(c) the government increases net taxes.
(d) b and c.

Answer: (b)

Easy
Fact
Page: 280

13.45: If the government increases government spending,

(a) only the goods market will be affected.
(b) only the money market will be affected.
(c) both the goods market and the money market will be affected.
(d) neither the goods market nor the money market will be affected.

Answer: (c)

Moderate
Single
Page: 280

13.46: If the government reduces net taxes which of the following chain of events will occur?

(a) Aggregate output increases, the demand for money decreases, the interest rate decreases, planned investment spending increases, and aggregate output increases.
(b) Aggregate output decreases, the demand for money increases, the interest rate increases, planned investment decreases, and aggregate output decreases.
(c) Aggregate output decreases, the demand for money decreases, the interest rate decreases, planned investment increases, and aggregate output increases.
(d) Aggregate output increases, the demand for money increases, the interest rate increases, planned investment decreases, and aggregate output decreases.

Answer: (d)

Easy
Definition
Page: 279

13.47: The tendency for increases in government spending to cause reductions in private investment spending is

(a) fiscal drag.
(b) the crowding-out effect.
(c) Ricardian equivalence.
(d) bracket creep.

Answer: (b)

Moderate
Single
Page: 280

13.48: In the absence of an increase in the money supply, an increase in government spending will lead to a reduction in planned investment spending as a result of

(a) an increase in aggregate output.
(b) an increase in the price level.
(c) an increase in the interest rate.
(d) an increase in the tax rate.

Answer: (c)

13.49: If planned investment decreases as the interest rate increases, the size of the government spending multiplier will be

(a) smaller than the government spending multiplier that would result if planned investment were independent of the interest rate.
(b) larger than the government spending multiplier that would result if planned investment were independent of the interest rate.
(c) the same as the government spending multiplier that would result if planned investment were independent of the interest rate.
(d) zero.

Easy
Single
Page: 280

Answer: (a)

13.50: If planned investment decreases as the interest rate increases, the absolute value of the tax multiplier will be

(a) smaller than the absolute value of the tax multiplier that would result if planned investment were independent of the interest rate.
(b) larger than the absolute value of the tax multiplier that would result if planned investment were independent of the interest rate.
(c) the same as the absolute value of the tax multiplier that would result if planned investment were independent of the interest rate.
(d) zero.

Moderate
Single
Page: 280

Answer: (a)

13.51: Refer to Figure 13.6. The crowding-out effect is represented by the movement from

(a) C+I+G to C+I'+G'.
(b) C+I+G to C+I+G'.
(c) C+I+G' to C+I+G.
(d) C+I+G' to C+I'+G'.

Easy
Single
Page: 279

Answer: (d)

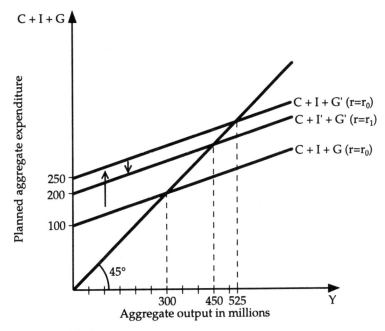

Figure 13.6

Challenging
Multi
Page: 279

13.52: Refer to Figure 13.6. If investment does not depend on the interest rate, the government spending multiplier

(a) is 1.5.
(b) is 2.1.
(c) is 3.
(d) cannot be determined from the information available.

Answer: (a)

Challenging
Multi
Page: 279

13.53: Refer to Figure 13.6. If investment does depend on the interest rate, the government spending multiplier

(a) is .67.
(b) is 1.
(c) is 1.5.
(d) cannot be determined from the information available.

Answer: (b)

Challenging
Multi
Page: 282

13.54: If the Fed increases the money supply at the same time the federal government increases government spending, the severity of the crowding-out effect

(a) will not be affected.
(b) will be increased.
(c) will be reduced.
(d) could either increase or decrease depending on the sensitivity of planned investment to the interest rate.

Answer: (c)

Moderate
Single
Page: 282

13.54: The severity of the crowding-out effect will be reduced if

(a) the Fed increases the money supply at the same time the federal government increases government spending.
(b) the Fed decreases the money supply at the same time the federal government increases government spending.
(c) the Fed does not change the money supply when the government increases government spending.
(d) business firms become pessimistic about the future.

Answer: (a)

Moderate
Multi
Page: 282

13.55: If the Fed decreased the money supply at the same time the federal government increases government spending, the crowding-out effect

(a) will not be affected.
(b) will be increased.
(c) will be reduced.
(d) could either increase or decrease depending on the sensitivity of planned investment to the interest rate.

Answer: (b)

13.56: If planned investment becomes more sensitive to interest rate changes, the crowding-out effect will

Moderate
Single
Page: 279

(a) fall to zero.
(b) not be affected.
(c) be reduced.
(d) be increased.

Answer: (d)

13.57: The size of the "crowding-out" effect depends on several things, including

Easy
Fact
Page: 279

(a) the sensitivity of planned investment spending to changes in the interest rate.
(b) the composition of the federal budget.
(c) the structure of the personal income tax code.
(d) the size of the government spending multiplier.

Answer: (a)

13.58: If planned investment does not fall when the interest rate rises, there will be

Moderate
Single
Page: 279

(a) no crowding-out effect.
(b) a substantial crowding-out effect.
(c) a slight crowding-out effect.
(d) a complete crowding-out effect.

Answer: (a)

13.59: As the size of the crowding-out effect increases, the government spending multiplier

Moderate
Single
Page: 279

(a) will increase.
(b) will decrease.
(c) will remain unchanged, but the investment multiplier will increase.
(d) will either increase or decrease, depending upon the size of the marginal propensity to consume.

Answer: (b)

13.60: The government increases spending while the Fed increases the money supply so that the interest rate will remain unchanged. In this situation, there will be

Moderate
Single
Page: 282

(a) complete crowding-out.
(b) substantial, but less than complete, crowding-out.
(c) slight crowding-out.
(d) no crowding-out.

Answer: (d)

13.61: An increase in government spending will

Moderate
Single
Page: 280

(a) have no effect on the interest rate, because the money supply has not been changed.
(b) decrease the interest rate, because income in the economy has risen.
(c) decrease the interest rate, because government spending will partially replace investment.
(d) increase the interest rate, because the demand for money will increase.

Answer: (d)

Easy
Fact
Page: 280

13.62: The chain of events that results from an expansionary monetary policy is

(a) aggregate output increases, the demand for money increases, the interest rate increases, planned investment decreases, and aggregate output falls.
(b) money supply increases, the interest rate decreases, planned investment increases, aggregate output increases, and money demand increases.
(c) money demand increases, the interest rate decreases, planned investment increases, aggregate output increases, and money demand increases.
(d) money supply increases, the interest rate increases, planned investment increases, aggregate output increases, and money demand increases.

Answer: (b)

Moderate
Fact
Page: 280

13.63: If the amount that firms plan to invest does not vary with the interest rate, then as the money supply is increased, the level of aggregate output will

(a) increase.
(b) decrease.
(c) remain constant.
(d) either increase or decrease, depending on the amount by which the money supply is increased.

Answer: (c)

Moderate
Fact
Page: 280

13.64: If firms sharply increase the number of investment projects undertaken when interest rates fall and sharply reduce the number of investment projects undertaken when interest rates increase, then

(a) expansionary fiscal policy will be very effective.
(b) contractionary fiscal policy will be very effective.
(c) expansionary monetary policy will be very effective.
(d) contractionary monetary policy will not be effective.

Answer: (c)

Moderate
Single
Page: 280

13.65: If planned investment is sensitive to the interest rate, an increase in the interest rate causes the

(a) long-run aggregate supply curve to shift out.
(b) aggregate expenditure curve to shift up.
(c) aggregate expenditure curve to shift down.
(d) investment demand schedule to shift to the right.

Answer: (c)

Moderate
Single
Page: 280

13.66: Monetary policy can be effective only if

(a) the money supply reacts to changes in the interest rate.
(b) money demand reacts to changes in the interest rate.
(c) planned investment reacts to changes in the interest rate.
(d) government spending reacts to changes in the interest rate.

Answer: (c)

13.67: Dan, a writer for a business magazine, interviewed managers at 100 large corporations. All of the managers indicated that the primary determinant of planned investment is expected sales and not the interest rate. From this information, Dan concluded that

Moderate
Multi
Page: 280

(a) expansionary fiscal policy would be very effective, but contractionary fiscal policy would not be very effective.
(b) expansionary fiscal policy would not be very effective, but contractionary fiscal policy would be effective.
(c) both expansionary and contractionary monetary policy would be very effective.
(d) neither expansionary nor contractionary monetary policy would be very effective.

Answer: (d)

13.68: Assuming that investment spending depends on the interest rate, as the supply of money is increased, the interest rate _____ and planned investment spending _____ __.

Easy
Fact
Page: 280

(a) falls; increases
(b) falls; decreases
(c) rises; decreases
(d) rises; increases

Answer: (a)

13.69: Laura is in charge of economic policy, and her major concern is that interest rates are too high.She asks you what policy she should pursue to lower interest rates. Which of the following policies would you recommend?

Moderate
Single
Page: 280

(a) an expansionary fiscal policy
(b) an expansionary monetary policy
(c) a contractionary monetary policy
(d) the demand for money should be increased

Answer: (b)

13.70: Monetary policy affects the goods market by

Moderate
Single
Page: 280

(a) changing the interest rate, which changes planned investment.
(b) directly increasing consumption, which increases aggregate output.
(c) changing money demand, which changes the interest rate and the level of planned investment.
(d) changing the level of aggregate output, which changes the level of planned expenditure.

Answer: (a)

13.71: The primary policy response of the Congress to the recessions of 1974-1975 and 1980-1982 was

Easy
Fact
Page: 282

(a) a tax cut.
(b) an increase in government spending.
(c) an increase in the rate of growth in the money supply.
(d) a reduction in interest rates.

Answer: (a)

Easy
Fact
Page: 282

13.72: Did the anti-recession policies of 1974-1975 and 1980-1982 produce a crowding-out effect?

(a) Yes, because the expansionary fiscal policies that were enacted drove up interest rates and displaced private spending.
(b) No, because the tax cuts that were enacted proved to be ineffective in bringing about an end to these recessions.
(c) No, because the demand for money fell during the expansions that followed these recessions.
(d) No, because the Federal Reserve simultaneously increased the money supply.

Answer: (d)

Challenging
Multi
Page: 282

13.73: If the investment demand curve is vertical,

(a) both monetary and fiscal policy are ineffective.
(b) both monetary and fiscal policy are effective.
(c) monetary policy is effective, but fiscal policy is ineffective.
(d) monetary policy is ineffective, but fiscal policy is effective.

Answer: (d)

Honors
Multi
Page: 282

13.74: If the federal government is reducing net taxes to stimulate the economy at the same time the Fed is selling bonds in the open market, the effectiveness of the expansionary fiscal policy will be

(a) increased, because the Fed's actions will result in lower interest rates and a reduction in the crowding-out effect.
(b) increased, because the Fed's actions will result in lower interest rates and an increase in the crowding-out effect.
(c) reduced, because the Fed's actions will result in higher interest rates and an increase in the crowding-out effect.
(d) reduced, because the Fed's actions will result in lower interest rates and an increase in the crowding-out effect.

Answer: (c)

Easy
Fact
Page: 282

13.75: If the Fed accommodates a fiscal expansion by increasing the money supply so that the interest rate does not increase, the crowding-out effect will

(a) be zero.
(b) increase.
(c) decrease, but still be positive.
(d) become infinitely large.

Answer: (a)

Moderate
Single
Page: 282

13.76: Refer to Figure 13.7. Money demand will shift from Md0 to Md1 as a result of

(a) an expansionary monetary policy.
(b) an expansionary fiscal policy.
(c) a contractionary monetary policy.
(d) a contractionary fiscal policy.

Answer: (b)

13.77: Refer to Figure 13.7. The current level of the money supply is Ms0. An expansionary fiscal policy shifts money demand from Md0 to Md1. There will be no crowding-out effect if money supply

Moderate
Single
Page: 282

(a) remains constant at Ms0.
(b) increases to Ms1.
(c) increases to Ms2.
(d) decreases by any amount.

Answer: (c)

13.78: Refer to Figure 13.7. The current level of the money supply is Ms0. An expansionary fiscal policy shifts money demand from Md0 to Md1. An expansionary monetary policy increases the money supply to Ms1. Which of the following is true?

Moderate
Single
Page: 282

(a) The increase in the money supply eliminates the crowding-out effect.
(b) The increase in the money supply increases the crowding-out effect.
(c) The size of the crowding-out effect is not influenced by an increase in the money supply.
(d) There is still a crowding-out effect, but it is smaller than it would be if there were no increase in the money supply.

Answer: (d)

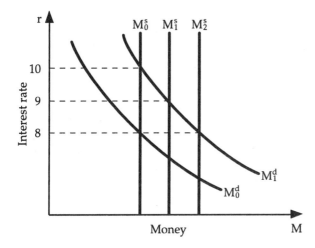

Figure 13.7

13.79: A decrease in government spending or an increase in net taxes aimed at reducing aggregate output is referred to as

Easy
Definition
Page: 283

(a) an expansionary fiscal policy.
(b) a contractionary fiscal policy.
(c) a contractionary monetary policy.
(d) an expansionary monetary policy.

Answer: (b)

13.80: An example of a contractionary fiscal policy is

Moderate
Single
Page: 283

(a) an increase in the amount of income subject to the social security payroll tax.
(b) the Fed selling government securities in the open market.
(c) the government strengthening environmental regulations, which results in a decrease in the amount of output produced by manufacturing firms
(d) the lifting of price supports for agricultural products

Answer: (a)

Moderate
Single
Page: 283

13.81: Which of the following actions is an example of a contractionary fiscal policy?

(a) an increase in the discount rate
(b) a decrease in defense spending
(c) a sale of government securities in the open market
(d) a decrease in income tax rates

Answer: (b)

Moderate
Fact
Page: 283

13.82: Which of the following sequence of events occurs in response to a contractionary fiscal policy?

(a) aggregate output decreases, causing money demand to decrease, causing the interest rate to decrease and planned investment to increase
(b) aggregate output decreases, causing money demand to increase, causing interest rates to increase and planned investment to decrease
(c) aggregate output decreases, causing planned investment to decrease, causing interest rates to decrease and money demand to decrease
(d) aggregate output decreases, causing the demand for money to increase, causing interest rates to increase and planned investment to increase

Answer: (a)

Moderate
Multi
Page: 283

13.83: Refer to Figure 13.8. After government spending is reduced, the planned aggregate expenditure function may shift up to C+I'+G' because the reduction in output will cause

(a) money supply to increase, the interest rate to decrease, and planned investment to increase.
(b) money supply to decrease, the interest rate to decrease, and planned investment to increase.
(c) money demand to decrease, the interest rate to decrease, and planned investment to increase.
(d) money demand to increase, the interest rate to decrease, and planned investment to increase.

Answer: (c)

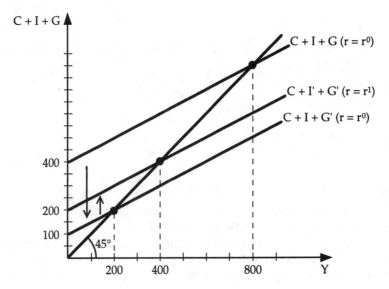

Figure 13.8

13.84: Refer to Figure 13.8. The initial aggregate expenditure function is given by   Moderate
C+I+G. A decrease in government spending shifts the aggregate expenditure function to   Multi
C+I+G'. If investment does not depend on the interest rate, the multiplier   Page: 283

(a) is .5.
(b) is 1.33.
(c) is 2.
(d) cannot be determined from the information available.

Answer: (c)

                                                                                             Challenging
                                                                                             Multi
                                                                                             Page: 283

13.85:Refer to Figure 13.8. The initial aggregate expenditure function is given by
C+I+G. A decrease in government spending shifts the aggregate expenditure function to
C+I+G'. If investment does depend on the interest rate, the multiplier

(a) is .67.
(b) is 1.33.
(c) is 2.
(d) cannot be determined from the information available.

Answer: (b)

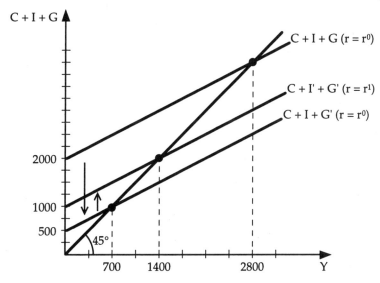

Figure 13.9

13.86: Refer to Figure 13.9. The initial aggregate expenditure function is given   Moderate
by C+I+G. A decrease in government spending shifts the aggregate expendi-   Multi
ture function to C+I+G'. If investment does not depend on the interest rate, the   Page: 283
multiplier

(a) is .5.
(b) is 1.4.
(c) is 2.
(d) none of the above.

Answer: (b)

Challenging
Multi
Page: 283

13.87: Refer to Figure 13.9. The initial aggregate expenditure function is given by C+I+G'. A increase in government spending shifts the aggregate expenditure function to C+I+G. If investment does depend on the interest rate, the multiplier

(a) is .67.
(b) is 1.2.
(c) is 5.
(d) 0.93.

Answer: (d)

Moderate
Single
Page: 283

13.88: A decrease in government spending will cause interest rates to_____ and planned investment spending to_____.

(a) fall; decrease
(b) fall; increase
(c) rise; increase
(d) rise; decrease

Answer: (b)

Moderate
Single
Page: 283

13.89: If investment depends on the interest rate, an increase in net taxes will cause aggregate output to _____ than if investment doesn't depend on the interest rate.

(a) increase by more
(b) increase by less
(c) decrease by more
(d) decrease by less

Answer: (d)

Easy
Definition
Page: 283

13.90: A decrease in the money supply aimed at decreasing aggregate output is

(a) an expansionary fiscal policy.
(b) a contractionary fiscal policy.
(c) a contractionary monetary policy.
(d) an expansionary monetary policy.

Answer: (c)

Moderate
Single
Page: 284

13.91: Which of the following is the sequence of events following a contractionary monetary policy?

(a) money demand increases, causing interest rates to increase, causing planned investment to fall and aggregate output to fall.
(b) aggregate output falls, causing the demand for money to fall, causing interest rates to rise, causing planned investment to decrease
(c) interest rates decrease, causing planned investment to decrease,
causing aggregate output to decrease, causing money demand to decrease
(d) interest rates increase, causing planned investment to decrease, causing aggregate output to decrease, causing money demand to decrease

Answer: (d)

13.92: Refer to Figure 13.10. Interest rate r1 is greater than interest rate r0. Which of the following would have caused the planned aggregate expenditure function to shift from C+I+G to C+I'+G?

Moderate
Multi
Page: 283

(a) a contractionary monetary policy
(b) a contractionary fiscal policy
(c) an increase in the cost of capital relative to labor
(d) all of the above

Answer: (a)

13.93: Which of the following actions is an example of a contractionary monetary policy?

Moderate
Single
Page: 284

(a) a reduction in federal spending on education
(b) a sale of government securities in the open market
(c) a decrease in the discount rate
(d) an increase in income tax rates

Answer: (b)

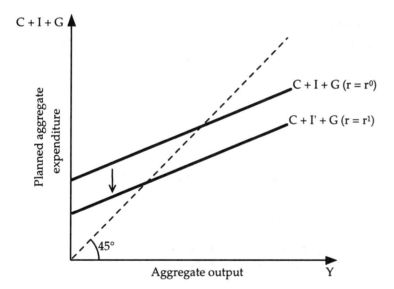

Figure 13.10

13.94: You are a member of the Council of Economic Advisors, and you are concerned that the inflation rate is too high. Which of the following policies should you recommend?

Moderate
Single
Page: 284

(a) an increase in the money supply
(b) a decrease in the money supply
(c) a decrease in income tax rates
(d) an increase in government spending

Answer: (b)

Easy
Fact
Page: 284

13.95: The Federal Reserve has pursued strong contractionary policies twice in recent years:first in 1973-74, and again in 1979-80.The Fed's purpose in following a tight monetary policy was to

(a) reduce the interest rate.
(b) reduce the level of planned investment.
(c) reduce the government deficit.
(d) slow the inflation rate.

Answer: (d)

Easy
Definition
Page: 284

13.96: The combination of monetary and fiscal policies in use at a given time is referred to as the

(a) crowding-out mix.
(b) discretionary mix.
(c) policy mix.
(d) package mix.

Answer: (c)

Moderate
Fact
Page: 284

13.97: A policy mix that consists of a contractionary fiscal policy and an expansionary monetary policy would

(a) be neutral with respect to the composition of aggregate spending
in the economy.
(b) favor investment spending over government spending.
(c) favor government spending over investment spending.
(d) lead to higher interest rates.

Answer: (b)

Moderate
Fact
Page: 284

13.98: A policy mix that consists of an expansionary fiscal policy and a contractionary monetary policy would

(a) be neutral with respect to the composition of aggregate spending
in the economy.
(b) favor investment spending over government spending.
(c) favor government spending over investment spending.
(d) lead to lower interest rates.

Answer: (c)

Moderate
Multi
Page: 284

13.99: A policy mix of contractionary fiscal policy and expansionary monetary policy would cause output to _____ and interest rates to _____.

(a) increase; decrease
(b) decrease; increase
(c) decrease; increase, decrease, or remain unchanged
(d) increase, decrease, or remain unchanged; decrease

Answer: (d)

13.100: A policy mix of an expansionary fiscal policy and an expansionary monetary policy would cause output to _____ and interest rates to _____.

Moderate
Multi
Page: 284

(a) increase; increase
(b) increase; increase, decrease, or remain unchanged
(c) increase, decrease, or remain unchanged; increase
(d) decrease; increase

Answer: (b)

13.101: The policy mix of a contractionary fiscal policy and a contractionary monetary policy would cause output to _____, and interest rates to_____.

Moderate
Multi
Page: 284

(a) decrease; increase
(b) decrease; decrease
(c) decrease;increase, decrease, or remain unchanged
(d) increase, decrease, or remain unchanged; decrease

Answer: (c)

13.102: The policy mix that would cause the interest rate to increase, and investment to decrease, but have an indeterminate effect on aggregate output, is a mix of

Challenging
Multi
Page: 284

(a) expansionary fiscal policy and expansionary monetary policy.
(b) expansionary fiscal policy and contractionary monetary policy.
(c) contractionary fiscal policy and expansionary monetary policy.
(d) contractionary fiscal policy and contractionary monetary policy.

Answer: (b)

13.103: The policy mix that would cause the interest rate to decrease, and investment to increase, but have an indeterminate effect on aggregate output, is a mix of

Challenging
Multi
Page: 284

(a) expansionary fiscal policy and expansionary monetary policy.
(b) expansionary fiscal policy and contractionary monetary policy.
(c) contractionary fiscal policy and expansionary monetary policy.
(d) contractionary fiscal policy and contractionary monetary policy.

Answer: (c)

13.104: Between the spring of 1990 and the spring of 1991, interest rates in the United States dropped by nearly two full percentage points.A possible explanation for this decrease in interest rates is

Challenging
Multi
Page: 284

(a) the demand for money increased as the economy sank into recession during the fall of 1990.
(b) the implementation of an expansionary fiscal policy.
(c) the implementation of an expansionary monetary policy by the Federal Reserve.
(d) a major increase in the size of the federal budget deficit.

Answer: (c)

13.105: During the spring of 1991, economists began to observe that lower interest rates were not having much of an effect on investment spending plans. A possible explanation for this is that

Moderate
Multi
Page: 285

(a) firms were expecting their sales to increase in the near future.
(b) the cost of capital was falling relative to the cost of labor.
(c) investment demand is very sensitive to changes in the interest rate.
(d) capital utilization rates were very low.

Answer: (d)

Moderate
Fact
Page: 285

13.106: Which of the following events will lead to a decrease in the level of planned investment?

(a) a decrease in the interest rate
(b) businesses expect their sales to decline in the future
(c) capital utilization rates increase
(d) relative to labor, capital becomes less expensive

Answer: (b)

Moderate
Fact
Page: 285

13.107: Which of the following events will lead to an increase in the level of planned investment?

(a) an increase in the interest rate
(b) businesses expect their sales to decrease in the future
(c) capital utilization rates increase
(d) relative to labor, capital becomes more expensive

Answer: (c)

Easy
Fact
Page: 288

13.108: Each point on the IS curve represents the equilibrium point in the

(a) goods market for the given interest rate.
(b) money market for the given value of aggregate output.
(c) goods market for the given level of government spending.
(d) money market for the given level of the money supply.

Answer: (a)

Easy
Fact
Page: 288

13.109: The curve that illustrates the negative relationship between the equilibrium values of aggregate output and the interest rate in the goods market is the

(a) aggregate demand curve.
(b) LM curve.
(c) IS curve.
(d) aggregate supply curve.

Answer: (c)

Easy
Fact
Page: 289

13.110: The curve that illustrates the positive relationship between the equilibrium values of aggregate output and the interest rate in the money market is the

(a) money demand curve.
(b) money supply curve.
(c) IS curve.
(d) LM curve.

Answer: (d)

Easy
Single
Page: 289

13.111: When the money supply increases,

(a) the economy moves up the LM curve.
(b) the economy moves down the LM curve.
(c) the LM curve shifts to the right.
(d) the LM curve shifts to the left.

Answer: (c)

13.112: Each point on the LM curve represents the equilibrium point in the

(a) goods market for the given interest rate.
(b) money market for the given value of aggregate output.
(c) goods market for the given level of government spending.
(d) money market for the given level of the money supply.

Easy
Fact
Page: 289

Answer: (b)

13.113: Refer to Figure 13.11. The IS curve will shift from IS1 to IS0 if

(a) government spending decreases.
(b) government spending increases.
(c) taxes decrease.
(d) consumption increases.

Moderate
Single
Page: 290

Answer: (a)

13.114: Refer to Figure 13.11. The LM curve will shift from LM0 to LM1 if

(a) the money supply increases.
(b) the money supply decreases.
(c) money demand decreases.
(d) aggregate output decreases.

Moderate
Single
Page: 290

Answer: (b)

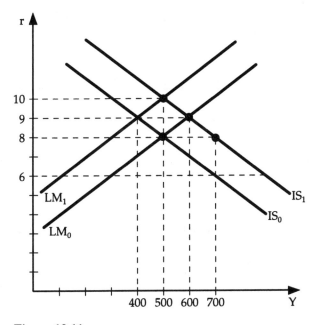

Figure 13.11

13.115: Refer to Figure 13.11. The economy is initially in equilibrium at an output level of $500 million and an interest rate of 8%. The new equilibrium would be at an output level of $600 million and an interest rate of 9% if

Moderate
Multi
Page: 290

(a) money supply decreased.
(b) money supply increased.
(c) government spending decreased.
(d) government spending increased.

Answer: (d)

Moderate
Multi
Page: 290

13.116: Refer to Figure 13.11. The economy is initially in equilibrium at an output level of $500 million and an interest rate of 8%. The new equilibrium would be at an output level of $400 million and an interest rate of 9% if

(a) money supply decreased.
(b) money supply increased.
(c) government spending decreased.
(d) government spending increased.

Answer: (a)

Challenging
Multi
Page: 290

13.117: Refer to Figure 13.11. The economy is initially in equilibrium at an output level of $500 million and an interest rate of 8%. The new equilibrium would be at an output level of $500 million and an interest rate of 10% if

(a) money supply decreased.
(b) government spending increased.
(c) government spending increased and money supply decreased.
(d) government spending decreased and money supply increased.

Answer: (c)

TRUE/FALSE QUESTIONS

Easy
Definition
Page: 278

13.118: An expansionary fiscal policy is an increase in government spending or a reduction in net taxes aimed at increasing aggregate output.

Answer: True

Easy
Fact
Page: 280

13.119: An expansionary monetary policy is an increase in the money supply aimed at increasing aggregate output.

Answer: True

Easy
Definition
Page: 278

13.120: The tendency for increases in government spending to cause reductions in private investment spending is known as the crowding-out effect.

Answer: True

Easy
Single
Page: 279

13.121: As the interest sensitivity of investment demand increases, the size of the crowding-out effect decreases.

Answer: False

Easy
Fact
Page: 279

13.122: If planned investment does not fall as the interest rate rises, there is no crowding-out effect.

Answer: True

Easy
Single
Page: 279

13.123: The more sensitive planned investment is to the interest rate, the greater the government spending multiplier will be.

Answer: False

Easy
Single
Page: 281

13.124: The more sensitive planned investment is to the interest rate, the greater the effectiveness of monetary policy.

Answer: True

13.125: If the Fed wants to reduce the inflation rate, it should buy bonds in the open market.

Answer: False

Easy
Single
Page: 284

13.126: The policy mix of an expansionary monetary policy and a contractionary fiscal policy will lead to a decrease in the interest rate.

Answer: True

Easy
Single
Page: 284

13.127: If the cost of capital increases relative to the cost of labor, planned investment will tend to decrease.

Answer: True

Easy
Fact
Page: 285

SHORT ANSWER QUESTIONS

13.128: Graphically illustrate the relationship between interest rate changes and the level of planned investment.

Answer:

Moderate
Math
Page: 275

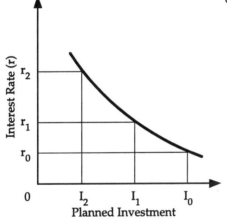

13.129: Geographically illu-strate the impact of a decrease in the interest rate upon aggregate expenditure. On your graph, illustrate the impact of an increase in the interest rate upon aggregate expenditure. Summarize the relationship among changes in the rate of interest (r), the change in planned investment spending (I), its impact upon the aggregate expenditure function (AE), and the multiple effect upon income (Y).

Moderate
Math
Page: 276

Answer:

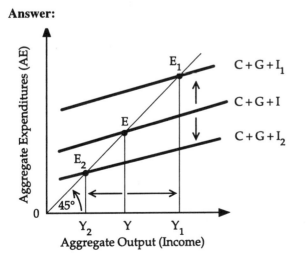

As

$$r\uparrow \Rightarrow I\downarrow \Rightarrow AE\downarrow \Rightarrow Y\downarrow$$

$$r\downarrow \Rightarrow I\uparrow \Rightarrow AE\uparrow \Rightarrow Y\uparrow$$

Moderate
Math
Page: 278

13.130: Graphically illustrate the relationship among income changes, the demand for money, and the changes in the rate of interest. Summarize the relationship among the level of income (Y), the demand for money (Md), and the rate of interest (r).

Answer: As illustrated in the figure below, an increase income will increase the demand for money and result in a rightward parallel shift in the money demand which will increase the rate of interest. A decrease in income will lessen the demand for money and result in a leftward parallel shift in the money demand which will lower the rate of interest.

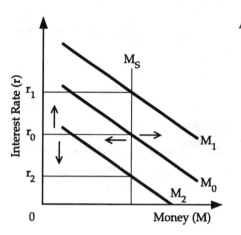

As

$$Y\uparrow \Rightarrow M_d\uparrow \Rightarrow r\uparrow$$

$$Y\downarrow \Rightarrow M_d\downarrow \Rightarrow r\downarrow$$

Difficult
Application
Page: 282

13.131: Explain the impact upon the crowding-out effect if the Federal Reserve changes the money supply when government spending increases.

Answer: The increase in government spending increases the demand for money. However, the rate of interest would not increase and result in a decrease in investment spending if the Federal Reserve increased the supply of money. An increase in the money supply would stabilize the rate of interest, not adversely change investment spending, and the multiplied impact of increased government spending upon income would be at its greatest.

Difficult
Application
Page: 278

13.132: Discuss the impact of an increase in the money supply upon the goods and money markets. What most importantly determines the effectiveness of monetary policy?

Answer: The increase in the money supply will decrease the rate of interest which will increase investment spending. As a result, production output and income will rise, which will increase the demand for money and contribute to upward pressure on the rate of interest. The effectiveness of monetary policy is most importantly dependent upon the sensitivity of investment spending to changes in the rate of interest.

Moderate
Application
Page: 283

13.133: Summarize the effects of a contractionary fiscal policy where government spending (G) and/or taxes (T) are changes upon output and income (Y), the demand for money (Md), the rate of interest (r), and investment spending (I).

Answer: A contractionary fiscal policy can be summarized as: $G\downarrow\ orT\uparrow \Rightarrow Y\downarrow \Rightarrow M_d\downarrow \Rightarrow r\downarrow \Rightarrow I\uparrow$.

Moderate
Application
Page: 284

13.134: Summarize the effects of a contractionary monetary policy where the change in the money supply (M) impacts upon the rate of interest (r), investment spending (I), output and income (Y), and the demand for money (Md).

Answer: A contractionary monetary policy can be summarized as: $M_s\downarrow \Rightarrow r\uparrow \Rightarrow I\downarrow \Rightarrow Y\downarrow \Rightarrow M_d\downarrow$.

13.135: In addition to the rate of interest, what other conditions effect the level of planned investment? Explain how these factors effect planned investment spending.

Answer: Other determinants of planned investment include:

      (a) expectations regarding business and overall economic conditions.

      (b) capital utilization rates.

      (c) relative labor and capital costs.

Planned investment will likely increase if the economy is expected to expand, when the firm's capital utilization rates are high, and if the cost of labor is high compared to the cost of capital. In contrast, planned investment will likely lessen if the economic future is bleak, if the firm's capital utilization rates are low, and if the cost of labor is low compared to the cost of capital.

13.136: What is determined in the goods market? What is determined in the money market? Explain the two links between the goods market and the money market.

Answer: The equilibrium level of output is determined in the goods market. The equilibrium interest rate is determined in the money market. The link from the goods market to the money market is changes in the level of output which will affect the demand for money and the equilibrium interest rate. The link from the money market to the goods market is changes in the interest rate, which will affect the level of planned investment and the equilibrium level of output.

13.137: Summarize the effects of an expansionary fiscal policy. Illustrate graphically the effects of an expansionary fiscal policy on the equilibrium level of output.

Answer: An expansionary fiscal policy increases the level of government spending, increases aggregate output, increases the demand for money, increases the interest rate, decreases planned investment and decreases aggregate output. The final increase in aggregate output is reduced because of the crowding-out effect.

13.138: Define the crowding-out effect. What factors can influence the extent to which crowding-out occurs when the government implements an expansionary fiscal policy?

Answer: The crowding-out effect is the tendency for increases in government spending to cause reductions in private investment spending. The two factors that influence the size of the crowding-out effect are the interest sensitivity of investment demand and whether or not the Fed accommodates the expansionary fiscal policy by increasing the money supply. The more sensitive planned investment is to the interest rate, the larger the crowding-out effect. If the Fed increases the money supply at the same time the government is increasing government spending, the amount by which the interest rate increases will be reduced and the crowding-out effect will be reduced.

Challenging
Multi
Page: 280

13.139: Explain why the effectiveness of an expansionary monetary policy in increasing aggregate output is partially dependent on the interest sensitivity of the demand for money.

Answer: As the money supply is increased, the interest rate decreases, planned investment increases, and the equilibrium level of output increases. The effectiveness of expansionary monetary policy in reducing the interest rate will depend on how much the interest rate is reduced as a result of the increase in the money supply. If the demand for money is perfectly elastic with respect to the interest rate, a change in the money supply will have no effect on the interest rate. The more inelastic the demand for money, the larger the reduction in the interest rate from a given change in the money supply. The larger the change in the interest rate, the larger the potential increase in investment and aggregate output.

Moderate
Multi
Page: 280

13.140: Assume that planned investment is independent of the interest rate. Is expansionary monetary policy as effective as expansionary fiscal policy? Explain.

Answer: No, the two policies are not equally effective. If investment is independent of the interest rate, there will be no crowding-out and expansionary fiscal policy will be an effective way to increase aggregate output. But if investment is independent of the interest rate, then expansionary monetary policy will be completely ineffective at increasing aggregate output. As the money supply increases and the interest rate falls, there will be no change in planned investment and therefore no change in aggregate output.

Challenging
Multi
Page: 284

13.141: Indicate the effect of each of the following policies on the variables: Y, C, S, r, I, Ms, and Md. (a.) The government reduces the personal income tax rates. (b.) Firms become more pessimistic about future sales. (c.) People believe that interest rates are going to fall in the future so they transfer their assets from cash to bonds.

Answer: (a.) The decrease in personal income tax rates will increase disposable income, so consumption and saving will increase. The increase in consumption will increase aggregate output, which will increase the demand for money. The increase in the demand for money will increase the interest rate. The increase in the interest rate will cause planned investment to decrease and aggregate output to decrease, and the final increase in aggregate output is less than it would have been if the interest rate did not increase. Money supply will not change. (b.) If firms become pessimistic about future sales, planned investment will decrease, aggregate output will decrease, consumption and saving will decrease, the demand for money will decrease, the interest rate will decrease, planned investment will increase, and aggregate output will increase. Money supply will not change. (c.) If people transfer assets from cash to bonds, the money supply will decrease, the interest rate will increase, planned investment will decrease, aggregate output will decrease, consumption and saving will decrease, and the demand for money will decrease, which will reduce the interest rate.

Challenging
Multi
Page: 284

13.142: Comment on the accuracy of the following statement: "A mix of expansionary fiscal policy and contractionary monetary policy will produce the same results as a mix of contractionary fiscal policy and expansionary monetary policy."

Answer: This statement is FALSE. A mix of expansionary fiscal policy and contractionary monetary policy will cause the interest rate to increase and planned investment to fall, but the effect on aggregate output and consumption is indeterminate. A mix of contractionary fiscal policy and expansionary monetary policy will the cause interest rate to fall and investment to increase, but the effect on aggregate output and consumption is indeterminate. Therefore, the same results are not produced by both policy mixes.

13.143: Between the spring of 1990 and the spring of 1991, interest rates in the United States dropped nearly two full percentage points, but this did not have much of an effect on investment spending plans. Explain how this could happen.Draw a graph of the investment demand schedule that would represent this situation. During this time period would an expansionary monetary policy have been an effective way to stimulate the economy? Explain.

Moderate
Single
Page: 280

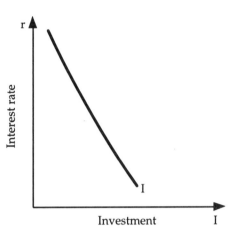

Answer: A drop in the interest rate wouldn't have an effect on the level of planned investment if investment was not sensitive to the interest rate. Investment at that time may have depended more on a firm's expectation of future sales, capital utilization rates, and the cost of capital relative to labor. An expansionary monetary policy would not have been an effective way to stimulate the economy because a reduction in the interest rate did not increase planned investment and therefore there could have been no change in aggregate output.

13.144: Would each of the following cause planned investment to increase or decrease?

(a.) owners of firms become more optimistic about their future sales
(b.) the degree of utilization of a firm's capital stock is very low
(c.) the cost of capital relative to the cost of labor increases

Moderate
Single
Page: 285

Answer: (a.) If the owners of firms become more optimistic about sales, planned investment will increase. (b.) If the degree of capital utilization is very low, planned investment will be low. (c.) If the cost of capital increases relative to the cost of labor, planned investment will fall.

13.145: What does each point on the IS curve represent? What does each point on the LM curve represent? Using the IS-LM diagram, explain how equilibrium output is determined. On the graph, illustrate the effect of an increase in the money supply. Explain how this change affects the equilibrium level of output and the interest rate.

Moderate
Multi
Page: 290

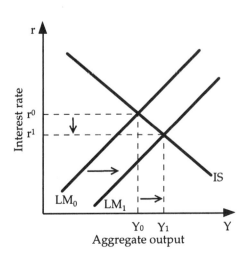

Answer: Each point on the IS curve represents the equilibrium point in the goods market for the given interest rate. Each point on the LM curve represents the equilibrium point in the money market for the given value of aggregate output. The intersection of the IS and LM curves determines the equilibrium level of aggregate output and the equilibrium interest rate. An increase in the money supply will shift the LM curve to the right. The equilibrium level of output will increase and the equilibrium interest rate will decrease.

Aggregate Demand, Aggregate Supply, and Inflation

(Chapter 29 in combined text)

MULTIPLE CHOICE QUESTIONS

14.1: Money demand is a function of all the following variables except the

(a) interest rate
(b) tax rate
(c) price level
(d) level of real income

Answer: (b)

Easy
Fact
Page: 291

14.2: If prices and wages are falling by 2% per year, we can expect

(a) the demand for money to fall by 2% per year, ceteris paribus.
(b) the demand for money to increase by 2% per year, ceteris paribus.
(c) the supply of money to increase by 2% per year, ceteris paribus.
(d) the supply of money to decrease by 2% per year, ceteris paribus.

Answer: (a)

Easy
Single
Page: 291

14.3: If prices and wages are falling by 8% per year, we can expect

(a) the supply of money to increase by 8% per year, ceteris paribus.
(b) the supply of money to decrease by 8% per year, ceteris paribus.
(c) the demand for money to increase by 8% per year, ceteris paribus.
(d) the demand for money to decrease by 8% per year, ceteris paribus.

Answer: (d)

Easy
Single
Page: 291

14.4: The aggregate demand curve is derived under the assumption that all the following variables remain unchanged except

(a) government purchases.
(b) net taxes.
(c) the price level.
(d) the money supply.

Answer: (c)

Easy
Fact
Page: 292

14.5: Assuming that the Fed takes no action to change the money supply, as the price level increases, what chain of events will occur?

(a) As the price level rises, there will be a decrease in the demand for money, leading to an excess supply of money which causes interest rates to fall and investment and aggregate output to increase.
(b) As the price level rises, there will be an increase in the demand for money, which leads to excess demand in the money market, which will cause interest rates to rise investment and aggregate output to fall.
(c) As the price level rises, there will be no change in the money market and, therefore, there will be no change in aggregate output.
(d) As the price level rises, money demand increases, but the money market will remain in equilibrium so that there will be no change in the level of aggregate output.

Answer: (b)

Moderate
Multi
Page: 292

385

Easy
Fact
Page: 293

14.6: Aggregate output will fall if

(a) the interest rate is reduced.
(b) net taxes are reduced.
(c) the money supply is increased.
(d) the price level increases.

Answer: (d)

Easy
Single
Page: 292

14.7: Refer to Figure 14.1. The money demand curve will shift from Md0 to Md1, if

(a) the price level increases.
(b) the interest rate decreases.
(c) the level of aggregate output decreases.
(d) the inflation rate increases.

Answer: (c)

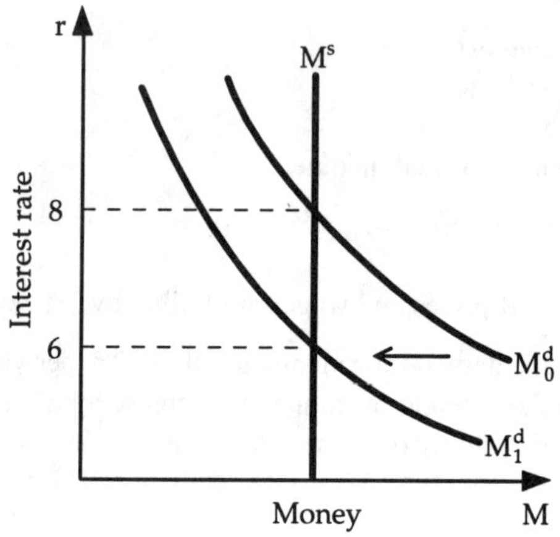

Figure 14.1

Moderate
Multi
Page: 292

14.8: Refer to Figure 14.1. If the money demand curve shifts from Md0 to Md1,

(a) planned investment will decrease and aggregate output will decrease.
(b) planned investment will decrease and aggregate output will increase.
(c) planned investment will increase and aggregate output will decrease.
(d) planned investment will increase and aggregate output will increase

Answer: (d)

Easy
Fact
Page: 293

14.9: An increase in the price level will cause the demand for money to _____ and planned aggregate expenditure to _____.

(a) decrease; decrease
(b) decrease; increase
(c) increase; increase
(d) increase; decrease

Answer: (d)

Easy
Definition
Page: 293

14.10: The curve that shows the negative relationship between aggregate output and the price level is known as the

(a) aggregate demand curve.
(b) aggregate supply curve.
(c) aggregate production function.
(d) money demand curve.

Answer: (a)

Moderate
Fact
Page: 293

14.11: Each point on the aggregate demand curve is a point at which both the _____ market and the _____ market are in equilibrium.

(a) goods; labor
(b) labor; money
(c) labor; bond
(d) goods; money

Answer: (d)

14.12: Aggregate demand falls when the price level increases because the higher price level causes

Easy
Fact
Page: 294

(a) the market demand for all goods and services to decrease.
(b) the supply of money to decrease.
(c) the demand for money to rise.
(d) interest rates to fall.

Answer: (c)

14.13: Aggregate demand increases when the price level falls because the lower price level

Moderate
Single
Page: 294

(a) means that people can afford to buy more goods.
(b) causes the demand for money to fall.
(c) means that the prices of some goods fall relative to the prices of other
goods.
(d) causes the interest rate to rise.

Answer: (b)

14.14: Which of the following statements is TRUE?

Easy
Fact
Page: 293

(a) The aggregate demand curve is the sum of all market demand curves in the economy.
(b) The aggregate demand curve is a market demand curve.
(c) Each point on the aggregate demand curve corresponds to a point at which both the goods market and the money market are in equilibrium.
(d) All of the above.

Answer: (c)

14.15: A decrease in the money supply will cause planned investment to _____ and consumption to _____.

Moderate
Multi
Page: 294

(a) decrease; decrease
(b) decrease; increase
(c) increase; increase
(d) increase; decrease

Answer: (a)

14.16: The level of aggregate output demanded falls when the price level rises, because the resulting increase in the interest rate will lead to

Moderate
Single
Page: 294

(a) lower investment spending and lower consumption spending.
(b) lower investment spending and higher consumption spending.
(c) higher investment spending and lower consumption spending.
(d) higher investment spending and higher consumption spending.

Answer: (a)

14.17: If household wealth decreases,

Easy
Fact
Page: 295

(a) current consumption will be reduced, but future consumption will not be affected.
(b) current consumption will be reduced, but future consumption will increase.
(c) current consumption will not be affected, but future consumption will be reduced.
(d) both future and current consumption will be reduced.

Answer: (d)

Moderate
Fact
Page: 295

14.18: Which of the following statements is NOT one of the reasons why the level of aggregate output demanded falls when the price level rises?

(a) The higher price level causes the demand for money to rise.
(b) The higher interest rates, which indirectly result from a higher price level, reduce both investment and consumption spending.
(c) People can afford to buy fewer goods.
(d) The higher price level lowers the real value of some types of wealth.

Answer: (c)

Easy
Fact
Page: 295

14.19: One of the reasons why the level of aggregate output demanded falls when the price level rises is that

(a) people can afford to buy fewer goods.
(b) the prices of some goods rise relative to the prices of other goods.
(c) the higher price level causes the demand for money to fall.
(d) an increase in the price level lowers the real value of some types of wealth.

Answer: (d)

Easy
Definition
Page: 295

14.20: The change in consumption brought about by a change in real wealth that results from a change in the price level is the

(a) consumption effect.
(b) real balance effect.
(c) money supply effect.
(d) interest rate effect.

Answer: (b)

Easy
Fact
Page: 295

14.21: At every point along the aggregate demand curve, the level of aggregate output demanded is

(a) greater than planned aggregate expenditure.
(b) equal to planned aggregate expenditure.
(c) less than planned aggregate expenditure.
(d) unrelated to the concept of planned aggregate expenditure.

Answer: (b)

Easy
Fact
Page: 295

14.22: At every point along the aggregate demand curve,

(a) $Y = C+I+G$.
(b) $S = I$.
(c) $Y = C$.
(d) $G = T$.

Answer: (a)

Easy
Fact
Page: 296

14.23: An increase in the quantity of money supplied at a given price level causes

(a) no change in aggregate demand.
(b) a decrease in aggregate demand.
(c) an increase in aggregate demand.
(d) an increase in aggregate supply.

Answer: (c)

14.24: A decrease in the quantity of money supplied at a given price level causes

(a) a decrease in aggregate demand.
(b) an increase in aggregate demand.
(c) no change in aggregate demand.
(d) a decrease in aggregate supply.

Answer: (a)

Easy
Fact
Page: 296

14.25: An increase in government purchases at a given price level leads to

(a) an increase in aggregate supply.
(b) a decrease in aggregate demand.
(c) no change in aggregate demand.
(d) an increase in aggregate demand.

Answer: (d)

Easy
Fact
Page: 296

14.26: The aggregate demand curve would shift to the right if

(a) government spending were increased.
(b) net taxes were increased.
(c) the money supply were decreased.
(d) the cost of energy were to increase.

Answer: (a)

Easy
Single
Page: 296

14.27: A decrease in net taxes at a given price level leads to

(a) no change in aggregate demand.
(b) a decrease in aggregate demand.
(c) an increase in aggregate demand.
(d) a decrease in aggregate supply.

Answer: (c)

Easy
Fact
Page: 296

14.28: The aggregate demand curve would shift to the left if

(a) government spending were increased.
(b) net taxes were increased.
(c) the money supply were increased.
(d) the interest rate decreased.

Answer: (b)

Easy
Fact
Page: 296

14.29: Which of the following policies will lead to an increase in aggregate demand?

(a) a decrease in government purchases
(b) an increase in net taxes
(c) an increase in the money supply
(d) an increase in the demand for money

Answer: (c)

Easy
Moderate
Page: 296

14.30: Refer to Figure 14.2. The aggregate demand curve would shift from AD₁ to AD₂ if ,

(a) the price level increased.
(b) the money supply were increased.
(c) net taxes were increased.
(d) the demand for money increased.

Answer: (b)

Moderate
Single
Page: 296

Moderate
Single
Page: 296

14.31: Refer to Figure 14.2. The aggregate demand curve would shift from AD₁ to AD₂ if

(a) the price level increased.
(b) the money supply were decreased.
(c) net taxes were decreased.
(d) the demand for money increased.

Answer: (c)

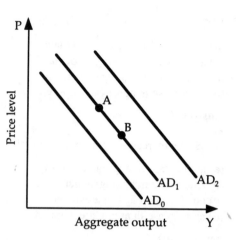

Figure 14.2

Moderate
Single
Page: 296

14.32: Refer to Figure 14.2. The aggregate demand curve would shift from AD₁ to AD₀ if

(a) the price level decreased.
(b) the money supply was increased.
(c) net taxes were decreased.
(d) government spending were decreased.

Answer: (d)

Moderate
Single
Page: 296

14.33: Refer to Figure 14.2. The aggregate demand curve would shift from AD₁ to AD₀ if

(a) the Fed sold bonds in the open market.
(b) the demand for money decreased.
(c) government spending were increased.
(d) net taxes were decreased.

Answer: (a)

Easy
Fact
Page: 296

14.34: Refer to Figure 14.2. The economy would move from point A to B along aggregate demand curve AD₁ if

(a) the demand for money increased.
(b) the supply of money were increased.
(c) the price level fell.
(d) both b and c.

Answer: (c)

Easy
Fact
Page: 296

14.35: A contractionary monetary policy will shift the

(a) aggregate demand curve to the left.
(b) aggregate demand curve to the right.
(c) aggregate supply curve to the left.
(d) aggregate supply curve to the right.

Answer: (a)

Easy
Definition
Page: 297

14.36: The graph that shows the relationship between the aggregate quantity of output supplied by all the firms in an economy and the overall price level is

(a) the aggregate demand curve.
(b) the aggregate production function.
(c) the production possibilities frontier.
(d) the aggregate supply curve.

Answer: (d)

14.37: The aggregate supply curve cannot be the sum of the supply curves of all the individual firms in the economy because

(a) it is unrealistic to believe that costs are constant for
individual firms if the overall price level is increasing.
(b) the output of some firms are the inputs of other firms.
(c) some firms actually set prices instead of just responding to
prices determined in the market.
(d) all of the above.

Answer: (d)

14.38: The aggregate supply curve

(a) is the sum of the individual supply curves in the economy.
(b) is a market supply curve.
(c) embodies the same logic that lies behind an individual firm's supply curve.
(d) is none of the above.

Answer: (d)

14.39: In the short run, the aggregate supply curve is

(a) fairly flat at very low levels of output and vertical at
capacity.
(b) vertical at low levels of output and fairly flat at capacity.
(c) is a straight upward sloping line with a constant slope.
(d) is horizontal over all levels of output.

Answer: (a)

14.40: Refer to Figure 14.3. Between the output levels of $400 million and $900 million, the relationship between the price level and output is

(a) positive.
(b) negative.
(c) constant.
(d) indeterminate.

Answer: (a)

14.41: Refer to Figure 14.3. The Batavian economy reaches capacity at

(a) $400 million.
(b) $650 million.
(c) $900 million.
(d) an output level that is indeterminate from this information because aggregate demand
is not given.

Answer: (c)

14.42: Refer to Figure 14.3. At aggregate output levels below $400 million, the Batavian economy is most likely experiencing

(a) a recession.
(b) a boom.
(c) excess supply in all markets.
(d) rapid increases in the growth rate of the money supply.

Answer: (a)

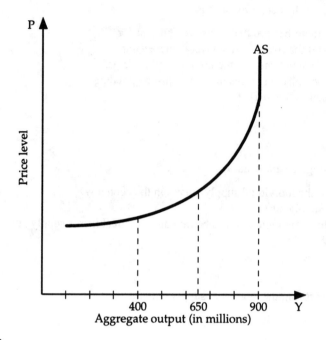

Figure 14.3

Easy
Single
Page: 299

14.43: Refer to Figure 14.4. Between the output levels of $200 million and $800 million, the relationship between the price level and output is

(a) negative.
(b) constant.
(c) positive.
(d) there is no relationship between the price level and output.

Answer: (c)

Easy
Single
Page: 299

14.44: Refer to Figure 14.4. The Cascadian economy reaches capacity at

(a) $200 million.
(b) $500 million.
(c) $800 million.
(d) an output level that is indeterminate from this information because aggregate demand is not given.

Answer: (c)

Easy
Single
Page: 299

14.45: Refer to Figure 14.4. At aggregate output levels below $200 million, the Cascadian economy is most likely experiencing

(a) a boom.
(b) excess supply in all markets.
(c) a recession.
(d) rapid increases in the population growth rate.

Answer: (c)

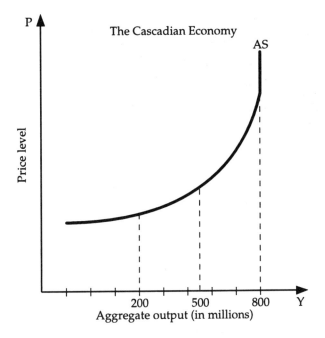

Figure 14.4

14.46: As the economy nears full capacity, the short-run aggregate supply curve

(a) becomes flatter.
(b) becomes steeper.
(c) shifts to the right.
(d) shifts to the left.

Moderate
Single
Page: 299

Answer: (b)

14.47: If input prices respond very quickly to changes in the overall price level, the short-run aggregate supply curve will be

(a) very steep.
(b) very flat.
(c) downward sloping.
(d) U-shaped.

Moderate
Single
Page: 299

Answer: (a)

14.48: Even if firms are not holding excess labor and capital, the economy may be operating below its capacity if there is

(a) seasonal unemployment.
(b) frictional unemployment.
(c) structural unemployment.
(d) cyclical unemployment.

Easy
Fact
Page: 299

Answer: (d)

Moderate
Fact
Page: 300

14.49: An increase in aggregate demand when the economy is operating at low levels of output is likely to result in

(a) an increase in the overall price level but little or no increase in output.
(b) an increase in output but little or no increase in the overall price level.
(c) an increase in both output and the overall price level.
(d) little or no increase in either output or the overall price level.

Answer: (b)

Easy
Fact
Page: 300

14.50: The aggregate supply curve is likely to be fairly flat at low levels of aggregate output because

(a) interest rates are very low and therefore investment will be increasing.
(b) aggregate demand is low.
(c) at low levels of output, the additional cost of producing more output is likely to be small.
(d) prices and wages are below their equilibrium levels.

Answer: (c)

Moderate
Fact
Page: 300

14.51: An increase in aggregate demand when the economy is operating at high levels of output is likely to result in

(a) a large increase in both output and the overall price level.
(b) an increase in output but little or no increase in the overall price level.
(c) an increase in the overall price level but little or no increase in output.
(d) little or no increase in either output or the overall price level.

Answer: (c)

Moderate
Fact
Page: 300

14.52: An increase in aggregate demand when the economy is operating at full capacity is likely to result in

(a) an increase in the overall price level but no increase in output.
(b) an increase in output but no increase in the overall price level.
(c) an increase in both output and the overall price level.
(d) no increase in either output or the overall price level.

Answer: (a)

Easy
Fact
Page: 300

14.53: The aggregate supply curve is likely to be nearly vertical for output levels close to capacity because

(a) interest rates are very high and therefore investment will be decreasing.
(b) aggregate demand is high.
(c) at output levels close to capacity the additional cost of producing more output is likely to be very high.
(d) prices and wages are above their equilibrium levels.

Answer: (c)

14.54: When the economy is producing at full capacity, the aggregate supply curve becomes

Easy
Fact
Page: 300

(a) horizontal.
(b) downward sloping.
(c) upward sloping.
(d) vertical.

Answer: (d)

14.55: If input prices changed at exactly the same rate as output prices, the aggregate supply curve would be

Easy
Fact
Page: 300

(a) horizontal.
(b) upward sloping.
(c) vertical.
(d) downward sloping.

Answer: (c)

14.56: For the aggregate supply curve to slope upward in the short run,

Moderate
Fact
Page: 300

(a) input price changes must lag behind output price changes.
(b) input price changes must move ahead of output price changes.
(c) input prices must adjust immediately to output prices.
(d) price level changes must be fully anticipated.

Answer: (a)

14.57: If the percentage of employees whose wages rise automatically with increases in the price level increases, the aggregate supply curve will become

Challenging
Multi
Page: 301

(a) steeper.
(b) flatter.
(c) horizontal.
(d) vertical.

Answer: (a)

14.58: Coal is used as a source of energy in many manufacturing processes. Assume a long strike by coal miners reduced the supply of coal and increased the price of coal. This would cause

Moderate
Single
Page: 301

(a) the short-run aggregate supply curve to shift to the right.
(b) the short-run aggregate supply curve to shift to the left.
(c) the short-run aggregate supply curve to become flatter.
(d) the short-run aggregate supply curve to become nearly vertical at all levels of output.

Answer: (b)

14.59: If the United States were to pass legislation that would make it easier for people to emigrate to the United States, this would cause

Moderate
Single
Page: 302

(a) the short-run aggregate supply curve to shift to the right.
(b) the short-run aggregate supply curve to shift to the left.
(c) the short-run aggregate supply curve to become flatter.
(d) the short-run aggregate supply curve to become nearly vertical at all levels of output.

Answer: (a)

Moderate
Single
Page: 302

14.60: When Clinton ran for office in 1992, he promised to increase investment in the economy's infrastructure. If he is successful in getting legislation passed to increase investment in the economy's infrastructure, this would cause

(a) the short-run aggregate supply curve to shift to the right.
(b) the short-run aggregate supply curve to shift to the left.
(c) the short-run aggregate supply curve to become flatter.
(d) the short-run aggregate supply curve to become nearly vertical at all levels of output.

Answer: (a)

Moderate
Single
Page: 302

14.61: Which of the following would cause the short-run aggregate supply curve to shift to the right?

(a) higher energy prices
(b) an increase in taxes
(c) increases in government regulation
(d) retired workers reentering the labor force

Answer: (d)

Moderate
Single
Page: 303

14.62: Refer to Figure 14.5. The flooding in the Midwest during the summer of 1993 destroyed a large portion of the agricultural crop in the United States. This caused

(a) the short-run aggregate supply curve to shift from AS_1 to AS_2.
(b) the short-run aggregate supply curve to shift from AS_1 to AS_0.
(c) the economy to move from point B to point A along AS_1.
(d) the economy to move from point C to point B along AS_1.

Answer: (a)

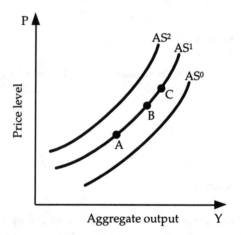

Figure 14.5

Easy
Single
Page: 303

14.63: Refer to Figure 14.5. An increase in aggregate supply is represented by

(a) a movement from point B to point A along AS_1.
(b) a movement from point B to point A along AS_1.
(c) a shift from AS_1 to AS_2.
(d) a shift from AS_1 to AS_0.

Answer: (d)

Moderate
Single
Page: 303

14.64: Refer to Figure 14.5. During the 1980s, many firms in the United States were not investing in new capital. This would have caused

(a) the short-run aggregate supply curve to shift from AS_1 to AS_0.
(b) the short-run aggregate supply curve to shift from AS_1 to AS_2.
(c) the economy to move from point B to point A along AS_1.
(d) the economy to move from point C to point B along AS_1.

Answer: (b)

14.65: Refer to Figure 14.5. A decrease in aggregate supply is represented by

(a) a movement from point B to point A along AS1.
(b) a movement from point B to point A along AS1.
(c) a shift from AS1 to AS2.
(d) a shift from AS1 to AS0.

Easy
Single
Page: 303

Answer: (c)

14.66: Refer to Figure 14.6. The immigration influx into the United States in the early part of the twentieth century caused the number of workers to increase. This caused

(a) the short-run aggregate supply curve to shift from AS2 to AS1.
(b) the economy to move from point B to point A along AS1.
(c) the economy to move from point C to point B along AS1.
(d) the short-run aggregate supply curve to shift from AS0 to AS1.

Moderate
Single
Page: 303

Answer: (d)

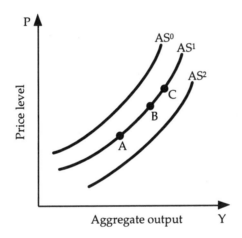

Figure 14.6

14.67: Refer to Figure 14.6. An increase in aggregate supply is represented by

(a) a movement from point B to point A along AS1.
(b) a movement from point C to point B along AS1.
(c) a shift from AS1 to AS2.
(d) a shift from AS1 to AS0.

Easy
Single
Page: 303

Answer: (c)

14.68: Refer to Figure 14.6. During the 1990s, many firms in the United States were investing in new capital. This would have caused

(a) the short-run aggregate supply curve to shift from AS1 to AS2.
(b) the economy to move from point B to point A along AS1.
(c) the economy to move from point C to point B along AS1.
(d) the short-run aggregate supply curve to shift from AS1 to AS0.

Moderate
Single
Page: 303

Answer: (a)

Easy
Single
Page: 303

14.69: Refer to Figure 14.6. A decrease in aggregate supply is represented by

(a) a shift from AS1 to AS0.
(b) a movement from point B to point A along AS1.
(c) a movement from point B to point C along AS1.
(d) a shift from AS1 to AS2.

Answer: (a)

Easy
Fact
Page: 303

14.70: The rationale underlying policies to deregulate the economy is that these policies would shift the

(a) the short-run aggregate supply curve to the right.
(b) the short-run aggregate supply curve to the left.
(c) aggregate demand curve to the left.
(d) aggregate demand curve to the right.

Answer: (a)

Moderate
Multi
Page: 303

14.71: Refer to Figure 14.7. Batavia is in equilibrium at price level P_0 and output level Y_0. If the price of oil increases in Batavia, the new equilibrium price will be _____ P_0 and the new equilibrium level of output will be _____ Y_0.

(a) greater than; greater than
(b) greater than; less than
(c) less than; less than
(d) less than; greater than

Answer: (b)

The AD/AS curves for Batavia

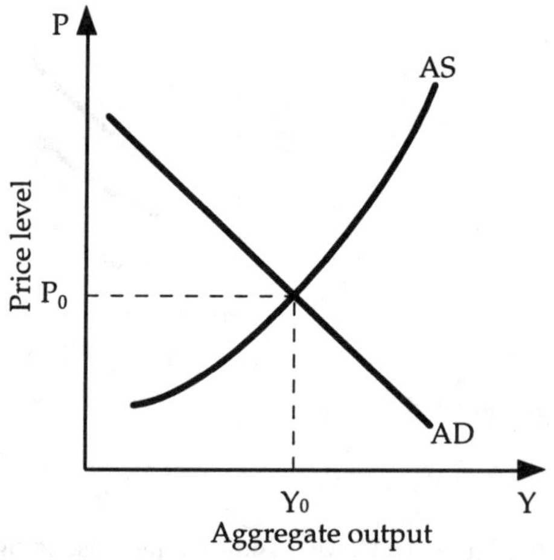

Figure 14.7

Moderate
Multi
Page: 303

14.72: Refer to Figure 14.7. Batavia is in equilibrium at price level P_0 and output level Y_0. If the money supply is increased in Batavia, the new equilibrium price will be _____ P_0 and the new equilibrium level of output will be _____ Y_0.

(a) greater than; greater than
(b) greater than; less than
(c) less than; less than
(d) less than; greater than

Answer: (a)

Moderate
Multi
Page: 303

14.73: Refer to Figure 14.7. Batavia is in equilibrium at price level P_0 and output level Y_0. If the size of the labor force increases in Batavia, the new equilibrium price will be _____ P_0 and the new equilibrium level of output will be _____ Y_0.

(a) greater than; greater than
(b) greater than; less than
(c) less than; less than
(d) less than; greater than

Answer: (d)

14.74: Refer to Figure 14.7. Batavia is in equilibrium at price level P$_0$ and output level Y$_0$. If government spending is reduced in Batavia, the new equilibrium price will be _____ P$_0$ and the new equilibrium level of output will be _____ Y$_0$.

Moderate
Multi
Page: 303

(a) greater than; greater than
(b) greater than; less than
(c) less than; less than
(d) less than; greater than

Answer: (c)

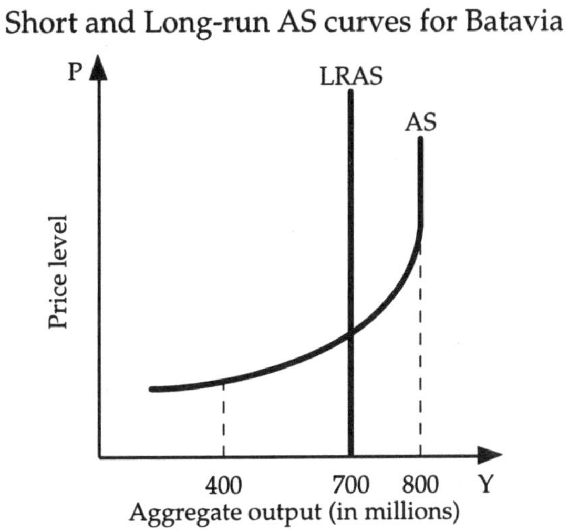

Short and Long-run AS curves for Batavia

Figure 14.8

14.75: Refer to Figure 14.8. Which of the following statements characterizes an output level of $800 billion?

Moderate
Single
Page: 305

(a) It is sustainable over the long run without inflation.
(b) It is achievable only in the long run.
(c) It is attainable in the short run but it is associated with increases in the price level.
(d) It can be achieved only if investment is independent of the interest rate.

Answer: (c)

14.76: Refer to Figure 14.8. Batavia's potential output

Moderate
Single
Page: 305

(a) is $400 million.
(b) is $700 million.
(c) is $800 million.
(d) cannot be determined from this information because aggregate demand is not given.

Answer: (b)

14.77: Refer to Figure 14.8. The level of aggregate output that can be sustained in the long run without inflation in Batavia

Moderate
Single
Page: 305

(a) is $400 million.
(b) is $700 million.
(c) is $800 million.
(d) cannot be determined from this information because aggregate demand is not given.

Answer: (b)

14.78: The level of aggregate output that can be sustained in the long run without inflation is known as

Easy
Definition
Page: 304

(a) nominal output.
(b) real output.
(c) money output.
(d) potential output.

Answer: (d)

Moderate
Multi
Page: 305

14.79: If the level of aggregate output in an economy is significantly less than its potential output, then an expansionary economic policy will result in

(a) a small increase in equilibrium output and a large increase in the equilibrium price level.
(b) a large increase in equilibrium output and a small increase in the equilibrium price level.
(c) large increases in both equilibrium output and the equilibrium price level.
(d) small increases in both equilibrium output and the equilibrium price level.

Answer: (b)

Moderate
Multi
Page: 305

14.80: If a decrease in net taxes in the United States resulted in a very small increase in aggregate output and a very large increase in the price level, then the U.S. economy must have been

(a) on the very steep part of the short-run aggregate supply curve.
(b) on the very flat part of the short-run aggregate supply curve.
(c) on the very steep part of the short-run aggregate demand curve.
(d) on the very flat part of the short-run aggregate demand curve.

Answer: (a)

Moderate
Multi
Page: 306

14.81: If a decrease in the U.S. money supply resulted in a very small change in the price level and a very large change in aggregate output,

(a) then in the U.S. economy investment demand must not be sensitive to the interest rate.
(b) then the U.S. economy must have been on the very steep part of its short-run aggregate supply curve.
(c) then the U.S. economy must have been on the very flat part of its short-run aggregate supply curve.
(d) then the U.S. aggregate demand curve must be very steep.

Answer: (c)

Easy
Fact
Page: 305

14.82: An increase in government spending will completely crowd out investment if

(a) money supply is increased at the same time.
(b) money demand is not sensitive to the interest rate.
(c) the economy is operating well below capacity.
(d) the economy is operating at capacity.

Answer: (d)

Easy
Fact
Page: 308

14.83: If the aggregate supply curve is vertical in the long run, then

(a) fiscal policy but not monetary policy has an effect on aggregate output in the long run.
(b) monetary policy but not fiscal policy has an effect on aggregate output in the long run.
(c) contractionary policies but not expansionary policies have an effect on aggregate output in the long run.
(d) neither monetary nor fiscal policy has any effect on aggregate output in the long run.

Answer: (d)

14.84: If the long-run aggregate supply curve is vertical, fiscal and monetary policies affect

Easy
Fact
Page: 308

(a) both the price level and the level of aggregate output in the long run.
(b) neither the price level nor the level of aggregate output in the long run.
(c) only the price level in the long run.
(d) only the level of aggregate output in the long run.

Answer: (c)

14.85: If the long-run aggregate supply curve is vertical, the multiplier effect of a change in net taxes on aggregate output in the long run

Easy
Fact
Page: 308

(a) is infinitely large.
(b) is zero.
(c) is one.
(d) depends on the price level.

Answer: (b)

14.86: An increase in the overall price level is

Easy
Definition
Page: 308

(a) stagflation.
(b) a recession.
(c) inflation.
(d) a price index.

Answer: (c)

14.87: Refer to Figure 14.9. Demand-pull inflation occurs if

Easy
Single
Page: 308

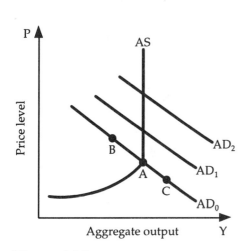

Figure 14.9

(a) aggregate demand shifts from AD_1 to AD_0.
(b) aggregate demand shifts from AD_1 to AD_2.
(c) the economy moves from point A to point B on aggregate demand curve AD_0.
(d) the economy moves from point A to point C on aggregate demand curve AD_0.

Answer: (b)

14.88: Refer to Figure 14.9. Assume the economy is initially in equilibrium at point A. The government reduces net taxes and the aggregate demand curve shifts to AD_1. The aggregate demand curve will shift out to AD_2 if

Moderate
Fact
Page: 310

(a) the Fed expands the supply of money to keep the interest rate constant.
(b) the Fed decreases the supply of money to increase the interest rate.
(c) the Fed keeps the supply of money constant to decrease the interest rate.
(d) the government reduces government spending to try to balance its budget.

Answer: (a)

Moderate
Single
Page: 310

14.89: If the economy is operating at potential GDP, an increase in the money supply will lead to

(a) stagflation.
(b) a sustained inflation.
(c) demand-pull inflation.
(d) cost-push inflation.

Answer: (c)

Moderate
Single
Page: 310

14.90: Inflation that causes an increase in the price level and a reduction in output is

(a) demand-pull inflation.
(b) cost-push inflation.
(c) fully-anticipated inflation.
(d) hyperinflation.

Answer: (b)

Easy
Definition
Page: 310

14.91: A situation that occurs when output is falling at the same time that prices are rising is

(a) a sustained inflation.
(b) demand-pull inflation.
(c) a hyperinflation.
(d) stagflation.

Answer: (d)

Easy
Single
Page: 310

14.92: Refer to Figure 14.10. Cost-push inflation occurs if

(a) the economy moves from point A to point B on aggregate supply curve AS_1.
(b) the economy moves from point A to point C on the aggregate supply curve AS_1.
(c) the aggregate supply curve shifts from AS_1 to AS_0.
(d) the aggregate supply curve shifts from AS_1 to AS_2.

Answer: (d)

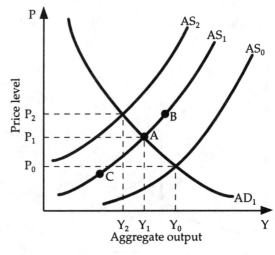

Figure 14.10

Moderate
Single
Page: 311

14.93: Refer to Figure 14.10. Assume the economy is at point A. Higher oil prices shift the aggregate supply curve to AS_2. If the government decides to counter the effects of higher oil prices by increasing government spending, then the price level will be _____ than P_2 and output will be _____ than Y_2.

(a) greater; greater
(b) greater; less
(c) less; less
(d) less; greater

Answer: (a)

14.94: Refer to Figure 14.10. Assume the economy is at point A. Higher oil prices shift the aggregate supply curve to AS2. If the government decides to counter the effects of higher oil prices by increasing net taxes, then the price level will be _____ than P2 and output will be _____ than Y2.

Moderate
Single
Page: 311

(a) greater; greater
(b) greater; less
(c) less; less
(d) less; greater

Answer: (c)

14.95: Refer to Figure 14.10. Assume the economy is currently at point A on aggregate supply curve AS1. An increase in inflationary expectations that causes firms to increase their prices

Moderate
Single
Page: 311

(a) shifts the aggregate supply curve to AS0.
(b) shifts the aggregate supply curve to AS2.
(c) moves the economy to point C on aggregate supply curve AS1.
(d) moves the economy to point B on aggregate supply curve AS1.

Answer: (b)

14.96: A cost shock, that increased costs, with no change in monetary or fiscal policy would

Easy
Fact
Page: 310

(a) shift the aggregate supply curve to the right, increase output, and reduce the price level.
(b) shift the aggregate supply curve to the left, lower output, and raise the price level.
(c) shift the aggregate demand curve to the left, increase output, and raise the price level.
(d) shift the aggregate demand curve to the right, lower output, and decrease the price level.

Answer: (b)

14.97: If the government responds to a cost shock, that increased costs, by using expansionary fiscal policy, then

Moderate
Fact
Page: 311

(a) the level of output falls even more than it would have without the policy action.
(b) the economy moves back to the output and price levels that existed before the cost shock.
(c) the price level increases even more than it would have without the policy action.
(d) both output and the price level fall even more than they would have without the policy action.

Answer: (c)

14.98: An earthquake destroyed 50% of the Maldavian manufacturing base. The Maldavian government decided to use a contractionary fiscal policy to counter the effects of the earthquake on the economy. The use of the contractionary fiscal policy would have caused

Challenging
Multi
Page: 311

(a) both the price level and output level to be lower than what they would have been without the policy action.
(b) both the price level and the output level to be higher than they would have been without the policy action.
(c) the price level to be lower and the output level to be higher than they would have been without the policy action.
(d) the price level to be higher and the output level to be lower than they would have been without the policy action.

Answer: (a)

Challenging
Multi
Page: 311

14.99: An earthquake destroyed 50% of the Trembleland manufacturing base. The Trembleland government decided to use a contractionary fiscal policy to counter the effects of the earthquake on the economy. The use of the contractionary fiscal policy would have caused

(a) both the price level and the output level to be higher than they would have been without the policy action.
(b) both the price level and the output level to be lower than what they would have been without the policy action.
(c) the price level to be lower and the output level to be higher than they would have been without the policy action.
(d) Because the earthquake destroyed 50% of the manufacturing base fiscal policy will have no effect on prices or output.

Answer: (b)

Easy
Fact
Page: 311

14.100: An increase in inflationary expectations that causes firms to increase their prices shifts the

(a) aggregate demand curve to the right.
(b) aggregate demand curve to the left.
(c) aggregate supply curve to the right.
(d) aggregate supply curve to the left.

Answer: (d)

Moderate
Single
Page: 311

14.101: A decrease in inflationary expectations that causes firms to decrease their prices shifts the

(a) aggregate demand curve to the right.
(b) aggregate demand curve to the left.
(c) aggregate supply curve to the right.
(d) aggregate supply curve to the left.

Answer: (c)

Easy
Single
Page: 312

14.102: During the fall of 1993, prices were increasing by 1% an hour in Bosnia. This is an example of

(a) an expectations inflation.
(b) hyperinflation.
(c) sustained inflation.
(d) monetary inflation.

Answer: (b)

Easy
Single
Page: 312

14.103: During the early 1980's, prices were increasing by approximately 2,000% a year in Argentina. This is an example of

(a) an expectations inflation.
(b) monetary inflation.
(c) hyperinflation.
(d) sustained inflation.

Answer: (c)

14.104: Economists generally agree that for a sustained inflation to occur,

(a) the government must accommodate it by increasing government spending.
(b) the government must accommodate it by decreasing taxes.
(c) the Federal Reserve must accommodate it by increasing the money supply.
(d) the Federal Reserve must accommodate it by decreasing the money supply.

Easy
Fact
Page: 312

Answer: (c)

14.105: For the Fed to keep the interest rate unchanged as the government increases spending, the Fed must continue to

(a) decrease the money supply.
(b) increase the money supply.
(c) decrease the demand for money.
(d) increase the demand for money.

Moderate
Single
Page: 312

Answer: (b)

14.106: If the Fed tries to keep the interest rate constant when the economy is operating on the steep part of the AS curve, _____ will occur.

(a) a recession
(b) a depression
(c) a hyperinflation
(d) stagflation

Easy
Fact
Page: 312

Answer: (c)

14.107: According to the "simple" Keynesian view, the aggregate supply curve is

(a) vertical until it reaches full capacity and then becomes horizontal.
(b) horizontal until it reaches full capacity and then becomes vertical.
(c) upward sloping over all levels of output.
(d) downward sloping over all levels of output.

Moderate
Fact
Page: 308

Answer: (b)

14.108: According to the "simple" Keynesian view, if the economy is below capacity, an expansionary policy will

(a) increase output, but not the price level.
(b) increase the price level, but not output.
(c) increase both the price level and output.
(d) increase neither the price level nor output.

Moderate
Single
Page: 308

Answer: (a)

14.109: If an economy is experiencing an inflationary gap,

(a) planned aggregate expenditure is increasing.
(b) planned aggregate expenditure is less than capacity output.
(c) planned aggregate expenditure equals capacity output.
(d) planned aggregate expenditure is greater than capacity output.

Moderate
Single
Page: 308

Answer: (d)

Moderate
Single
Page: 308

14.110: According to the "simple" Keynesian view, if the economy is at full capacity, an increase in aggregate demand will cause

(a) both output and the price level to rise in the short run.
(b) the level of output to rise, but no change in the price level will occur in the short run.
(c) the price level to increase, but no change in output will occur in the short run.
(d) output to fall and the price level to increase in the short run.

Answer: (c)

TRUE/FALSE QUESTIONS

Easy
Single
Page: 293

14.111: Each pair of values of the price level (P) and aggregate output (Y) on the aggregate demand curve corresponds to a point at which both the goods market and the money market are in equilibrium.

Answer: True

Easy
Fact
Page: 294

14.112: The reason that the amount of aggregate output demanded falls when the price level rises is that people can afford to buy fewer goods.

Answer: False

Easy
Fact
Page: 294

14.113: A higher interest rate reduces both planned investment and consumption spending.

Answer: True

Easy
Fact
Page: 295

14.114: An increase in the price level lowers the real value of all types of wealth.

Answer: False

Easy
Fact
Page: 296

14.115: An increase in the demand for money will shift the aggregate demand curve to the right.

Answer: False

Easy
Fact
Page: 300

14.116: If input prices changed at exactly the same rate as output prices, the aggregate supply curve would be vertical.

Answer: True

Easy
Fact
Page: 302

14.117: An investment in the economy's infrastructure will shift the short-run aggregate supply curve to the right.

Answer: True

Easy
Fact
Page: 300

14.118: If an economy is on the steep portion of its short-run aggregate supply curve, a contractionary economic policy would result in a small decrease in equilibrium output and a large decrease in the equilibrium price level.

Answer: True

Easy
Fact
Page: 304

14.119: If the aggregate supply curve is vertical in the long run, then both monetary policy and fiscal policy can have an effect on aggregate output in the long run.

Answer: False

14.120: Most economists would disagree with the contention that for a sustained inflation to occur, the Federal Reserve must accommodate it with a monetary expansion.

Answer: False

SHORT ANSWER QUESTIONS

14.121: Define the aggregate demand curve. Explain the impact of an increase in the price level on the level of aggregate output.

Easy
Definition
Page: 293

Answer: The aggregate demand curve represents the total demand for goods and services in the economy at a given point in time. An increase in the price level increases the demand for money, which results in an increase in the rate of interest and a decrease in investment spending. The decrease in overall investment spending contributes to a decrease in equilibrium output (income) with increased unemployment.

14.122: Graphically illustrate the impact of the increase in the price level upon equilibrium output.

Moderate
Math
Page: 292

Answer: The impact of an increase in the price level upon aggregate output and income is illustrated in the figure below. The increased price level has a multiplied contractionary impact upon the economy.

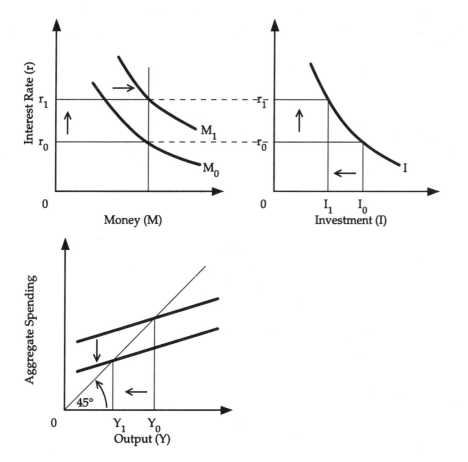

Moderate
Application
Page: 294

14.123: Explain the consumption link. Summarize the consumption link with regard to a decrease in the price level.

Answer: A change in the price level impacts upon the demand for money which then changes the rate of interest. The change in the rate of interest inversely effects both planned investment and consumption spending. This change in consumption results in a change in output and income and illustrates another link between the money and goods markets. The consumption link with regard to a decrease in the price level would be:
$$P\downarrow \Rightarrow M_d\downarrow \Rightarrow r\downarrow \Rightarrow C\uparrow \Rightarrow Y\uparrow$$

Moderate
Application
Page: 295

14.124: Explain the real wealth effect upon aggregate demand. Summarize the real wealth effort with regard to an increase in the price level.

Answer: The real wealth effect measures the impact of a price change upon the real value of wealth and its subsequent effect upon consumption and output. An increase in the price level will lower the real value of wealth which will result in less consumption spending. This will contribute to less production and an overall decrease in output and income.

Difficult
Application
Page: 296

14.125: Summarize the impact of fiscal and monetary policies upon the aggregate demand function.

Answer: Expansionary Monetary Policy: An increase in Ms will shift AD to the right.

Expansionary Fiscal Policy: An increase in G and/or a decrease in T will shift AD to the right.

Contractionary Monetary Policy: A decrease in Ms will shift AD to the left.

Contractionary Fiscal Policy: A decrease in G and/or an increase in T will shift AD to the left.

Moderate
Math
Page: 299

14.126: Graphically illustrate and explain the aggregate supply (AS) curve.

Answer: An aggregate supply curve is illustrated in the figure below. It relates the relationship between aggregate output and prices.

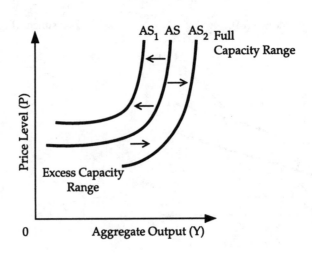

14.127: Discuss why the aggregate supply function is relatively flat within the low ranges of aggregate output. Discuss why the aggregate supply function is relatively vertical within the ranges of high aggregate output.

Moderate
Application
Page: 300

Answer: The relatively flat portion of the aggregate supply function is associated with excess or unused productive capacity. As a result, increases in aggregate demand will contribute to production increases but very limited changes in price. It is the range of excess capacity. The vertical portion of the aggregate supply function is associated with full utilization of capacity and high levels of output. As a result, increases in aggregate demand will contribute to limited output gains and sharp increases in the price level. It is the range of full capacity utilization.

14.128: Indicate the effects of cost shocks upon the aggregate supply (AS) function.

Moderate
Application
Page: 301

Answer: An increase in costs will result in a leftward parallel shift in the AS curve, and a decrease in costs will be exhibited as a rightward parallel shift in the AS curve. A leftward shift means that prices are higher at all levels of output and a rightward shift means that prices are lower at all levels of output.

14.129: Explain what equilibrium price means with regard to the macroeconomic conditions within the economy.

Moderate
Definition
Page: 304

Answer: Each point on the AD curve means that the goods and money markets are in equilibrium. Each point on the AS curve represents price and output relationships within the economy. The equilibrium price (P0) and the aggregate output (Y0) correspond to equilibrium in the goods and money markets and to a set of price and output relationships.

14.130: What is the likely impact of expansionary policies when the economy is operating at excess capacity on the flat, horizontal portion of the AS curve? Graphically illustrate this policy effect.

Moderate
Application
Page: 306

Answer: Expansionary policies, such as an increase in the money supply, decrease in taxes, or increase in government spending, within this range of the AS curve will result in substantial output and income gains with little or no impact upon the price level. In the figure below, the increase in aggregate demand from AD0 to AD1 results in significant increases in the aggregate output and income and only slight price increases. This is because of the excess or under-utilized productive capacity that exists within this output range.

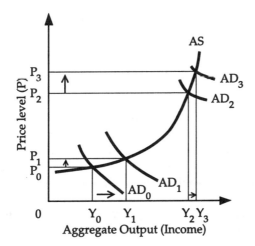

Moderate
Application
Page: 306

14.131: What is the likely impact of expansionary policies when the economy is operating at full capacity on the vertical portion of the AS curve? Graphically illustrate this policy effect.

Answer: Expansionary policies within this range of the AS curve will result in negligible or no aggregate output increases and accelerated increases in prices. In the figure provided for the solution to Question 36 above, the increase in aggregate demand from AD2 to AD3 results in very limited increases in aggregate output and income and significant increases in prices. This is the full capacity range of productive capacity.

Moderate
Application
Page: 308

14.132: What is the general economic view regarding whether the AS curve is vertical in the long run?

Answer: The "new classical" economics assumes that prices and wages are flexible and adjust quickly to changing conditions. This is consistent with the existence of a vertical AS curve in both the short and long run. The simple Keynesian view would dispute this contention and question a completely vertical AS curve in the long run. Thus, it advances the need for appropriate government policies.

Moderate
Definition
Page: 311

14.133: How do expectations impact upon inflation?

Answer: Expectations can have a significant impact upon pricing decisions and inflation. A business may decide to increase its prices because it expects its competitors to increase price. Consumers may spend more now in anticipation of a future event or condition. This may increase current prices and contribute to inflation.

Moderate
Single
Page: 294

14.134: An economy's aggregate demand curve is derived by horizontally summing the market demand curves for all the products consumed in the economy. Do you agree with this statement? Explain your answer.

Answer: An economy's aggregate demand curve is not derived by horizontally summing the market demand curves for all the products consumed in the economy. The logic that explains why a simple demand curve slopes downward fails to explain why the aggregate demand curve also has a negative slope. Aggregate demand falls when the price level rises because the higher price level causes the demand for money to rise. As the demand for money increases, the interest rate increases and planned investment and consumption fall.

Easy
Fact
Page: 297

14.135: Explain why the AS curve cannot be the sum of the supply curves of all the individual firms in the economy.

Answer: An individual firm's supply curve shows what would happen to a firm's output if the price of its output changes with no corresponding changes in costs. But if the overall price level is increasing, it is unrealistic to assume that costs are constant for individual firms. Therefore, the AS curve cannot be the sum of the supply curves of the individual firms in the economy. The outputs of some firms are the inputs of other firms, so if output prices are increasing there will be an increase in at least some input prices. It is also unrealistic to assume that wage rates will remain constant as the overall price level is increasing. Another reason why the AS curve cannot be the sum of the supply curves of the individual firms in the economy: imperfectly competitive firms don't have supply curves.

14.136: Explain why the shape of the aggregate supply curve is dependent upon the speed with which wage rates and other costs adjust to changes in the price level.

Moderate
Single
Page: 300

Answer: If input prices changed at exactly the same rate as output prices, the AS curve would be vertical. If all input and output prices were changing at the same rate, no firm would find it advantageous to change its output level. But if input prices change more slowly than output prices, it will be advantageous to a firm to produce more output as the output price increases. This would allow the firm to increase its profit because revenues would be increasing by more than costs.

14.137: Using aggregate supply and aggregate demand curves, indicate what impact each of the following would have on the price level and on the equilibrium level of aggregate output in the short run. (a.) The Fed buys bonds in the open market. (b.) The economy is far below capacity and the government increases government spending. (c.) The floods in the Midwest in the 1993 destroyed a large portion of the United States' agricultural crops.

Moderate
Multi
Page: 305

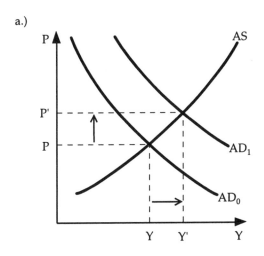

Answer: (a.) Aggregate demand will increase and the price level and the equilibrium level of output will increase. (b.) Aggregate demand will increase, the price level will increase by a small amount, and the equilibrium level of output will increase by a large amount. (c.) Aggregate supply decreased, the price level increased, and the equilibrium level of output fell.

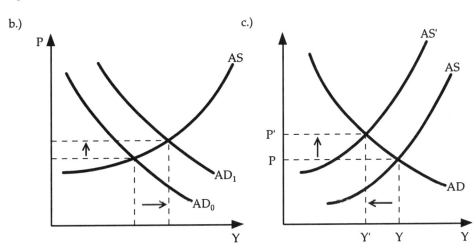

14.138: Explain why increases in long-run aggregate supply are the only means to achieve sustained increases in aggregate output.

Challenging
Multi
Page: 304

Answer: Output can exceed potential GDP in the short run, but only if output prices are increasing faster than input prices. Eventually there will be upward pressure on input prices and this will constrain growth. Increases in output in the long run can be sustained only if potential GDP is increasing.

Moderate
Multi
Page: 300

14.139: Assume that in the long run input prices fully adjust to changes in output prices. Use a diagram to indicate the effect of an expansionary fiscal policy on the price level and equilibrium level of output in the long run.

Answer: The long-run aggregate supply curve will be vertical. An expansionary fiscal policy will increase the price level but not change the equilibrium level of output in the long run.

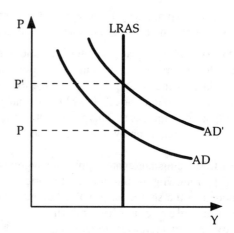

Moderate
Single
Page: 310

14.140: Define cost-push inflation. Using an AS/AD diagram, illustrate how cost-push inflation affects the level of aggregate output and the price level in the economy. Suppose that the government uses expansionary fiscal policy to counter the effects of the cost-push inflation. Indicate on the diagram the impact of this policy on the price level and level of aggregate output.

Answer: Cost-push inflation is inflation caused by an increase in costs. Cost-push inflation leads to an increase in the price level and a reduction in the level of aggregate output. If the government uses expansionary fiscal policy to counter the effects of cost-push inflation, aggregate output will increase and the price level will again increase.

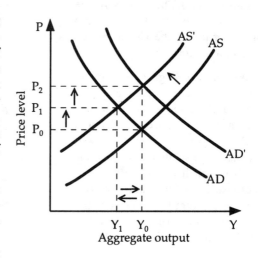

Challenging
Multi
Page: 310

14.141: In 1993 there was a severe drought in Maldavia. As a result of the drought, approximately two-thirds of the country's agricultural crops were destroyed. Using an AS/AD diagram, indicate what effect this drought would have on the overall price level and the equilibrium level of output. The Maldavian government is considering a number of policies to counter the effects of the drought on the economy. For each of the following policies, draw a graph that indicates the effects of the drought and then indicate how the policy would affect the overall price level and level of equilibrium aggregate output in Maldavia. (a.) The government is considering reducing net taxes. (b.) The monetary authority in Maldavia is considering a one-time increase in the money supply. (c.) The government is considering reducing public investment in agriculture and not spending that money on any other projects.

Answer: The drought would cause the aggregate supply curve to shift to the left. This would increase the overall price level and reduce the equilibrium level of output. (a.) A reduction in net taxes would increase both the overall price level and the equilibrium level of aggregate output. (b.) An increase in the money supply will increase aggregate demand. This will increase the overall price level and the level of aggregate output. (c.) A reduction of public investment in agriculture will cause both aggregate demand and aggregate supply to decrease. Output will fall farther than if there were no policy action, but the price level will be reduced.

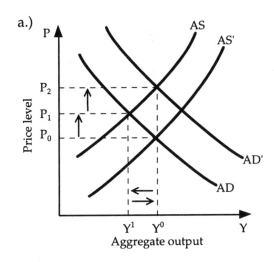

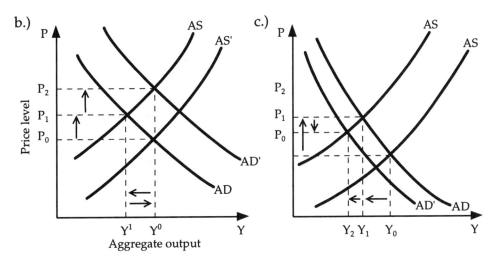

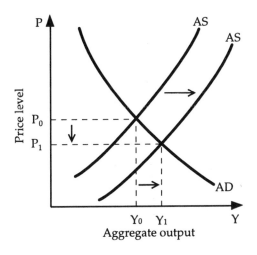

14.142: Will a decrease in inflationary expectations affect aggregate supply or aggregate demand? Explain why it affects the one you chose. Using an AS/AD diagram, illustrate how a decrease in inflationary expectations affects the output level and the price level in the economy. Explain why these changes occur.

Honors
Multi
Page: 311

Answer: A decrease in inflationary expectations will shift the aggregate supply curve to the right. If prices have been falling or if the rate of inflation has been slowing, people will come to expect this trend to continue. Firms may decrease their prices because input prices are falling. The price level will fall and the equilibrium level of aggregate output will increase.

Moderate
Multi
Page: 312

14.143: Explain why a sustained inflation must be a purely monetary phenomenon cannot exist without the cooperation of the Federal Reserve.

Answer: An expansionary monetary or fiscal policy will increase aggregate demand, the equilibrium level of output, and the demand for money. As the demand for money increases with no change in the money supply, the interest rate will increase and there will be some crowding out of investment. If the Fed decides to keep interest rates constant by increasing the money supply, aggregate demand will increase again, with a higher price level resulting. The price level will continue to rise only if the Fed continues to increase the money supply so as to keep the interest rate constant.

15 The Labor Market, Unemployment, and Inflation

(Chapter 30 in Combined Text)

MULTIPLE CHOICE QUESTIONS

15.1: In August of 1993 the number of people unemployed in the United States, was 9,000,000 and the number of people in the labor force was approximately 128,000,000. The U.S. unemployment rate for August 1993 was

Moderate
Single
Page: 317

(a) 6.5%
(b) 7%.
(c) 7.4%.
(d) 14%.

Answer: (b)

15.2: In August of 1995 the number of people unemployed in the Cascadia, was 6,000,000 and the number of people in the labor force was approximately 125,000,000. The Cascadian unemployment rate for August 1995 was

Moderate
Single
Page: 317

(a) 4.8%.
(b) 5%.
(c) 6.3%.
(d) 10%.

Answer: (a)

15.3: Refer to Figure 15.1. If the demand for labor increases from D to D', classical economists would argue that

Moderate
Single
Page: 317

(a) the wage rate will rise to $12 and there will be no unemployment.
(b) the wage will remain at $10 and there will be persistent unemployment.
(c) the supply of labor will rise until equilibrium is reestablished at a wage of $10 and an employment level of 150 million.
(d) the wage rate will rise to $12 and there will be 50 million workers unemployed.

Answer: (a)

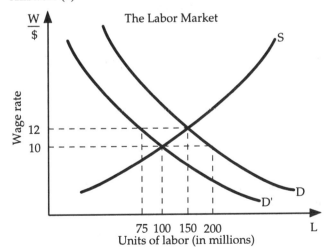

Figure 15.1

415

Moderate
Single
Page: 317

15.4: Refer to Figure 15.1. If the demand for labor decreases from D to D', and workers are not willing to work for a wage lower than $12 and continue searching for jobs paying $12, there will be

(a) no unemployment because workers are not willing to accept jobs paying less than $12 an hour.
(b) unemployment of 20 million.
(c) unemployment of 75 million.
(d) unemployment of 100 million.

Answer: (c)

Moderate
Single
Page: 317

15.5: Refer to Figure 15.1. Suppose there is an decrease in the fertility rate and this causes some men and women to place a lower value on their time spent in nonmarket activities. This will cause

(a) the labor supply curve to shift to the left of S.
(b) the labor supply curve to shift to the right of S.
(c) the labor demand curve to shift from D to D'.
(d) the labor demand curve to shift from D' to D.

Answer: (b)

Moderate
Single
Page: 317

15.6: Refer to Figure 15.1. If the demand for labor falls from D to D', and wages are sticky on the downward side, there will be unemployment of _____ million.

(a) 75
(b) 100
(c) 150
(d) none of the above

Answer: (a)

Moderate
Single
Page: 317

15.7: Refer to Figure 15.1. The demand for labor falls from D to D'. If firms enter into social, or implicit, contracts with workers not to cut wages, then the wage rate will remain at $12 and

(a) employment will fall to 75 million.
(b) employment will fall to 100 million.
(c) employment will remain at 150 million.
(d) labor supply will decrease to restore the market to equilibrium.

Answer: (a)

Easy
Definition
Page: 317

15.8: The portion of unemployment that is due to the normal working of the labor market is

(a) structural unemployment.
(b) frictional unemployment.
(c) cyclical unemployment.
(d) seasonal unemployment.

Answer: (b)

Easy
Definition
Page: 317

15.9: The portion of unemployment that is due to changes in the economy that result in a significant loss of jobs in certain industries is

(a) cyclical unemployment.
(b) seasonal unemployment.
(c) structural unemployment.
(d) frictional unemployment.

Answer: (c)

15.10: The increase in unemployment that occurs during recessions and depressions is

Easy
Definition
Page: 318

(a) cyclical unemployment.
(b) seasonal unemployment.
(c) frictional unemployment.
(d) structural unemployment.

Answer: (a)

15.11: Which of the following situations would be an example of cyclical unemployment?

Moderate
Single
Page: 318

(a) A woman reenters the labor force now that all her children are enrolled in school.
(b) A teacher loses his job as his school converts to computer-assisted, self-paced instruction that does not require as many classroom teachers.
(c) An assembly-line worker in a pie factory is laid off every January because pie sales usually decline sharply after the holiday season.
(d) An assembly-line worker in an automobile factory is laid off because a reduction in aggregate income led to a big decline in the demand for new cars.

Answer: (d)

15.12: A decline in the demand for labor

Moderate
Single
Page: 318

(a) means that unemployment will necessarily rise.
(b) means that unemployment will necessarily fall.
(c) does not necessarily mean that unemployment will rise.
(d) does not necessarily mean that employment will fall.

Answer: (c)

15.13: Refer to Figure 15.2. If the demand for labor falls from D to D', classical economists would argue that

Moderate
Single
Page: 318

(a) the wage will remain at $8 and there will be persistent unemployment.
(b) the supply of labor will fall until equilibrium is reestablished at a wage of $8 and an employment level of 150 million.
(c) the wage rate will fall to $7 and there will be no unemployment.
(d) the wage rate will fall to $7 and there will be 45 million workers unemployed.

Answer: (c)

15.14: Refer to Figure 15.2. If the demand for labor falls from D to D', and workers are not willing to work for a wage lower than $8 and continue searching for jobs paying $8, there will be

Moderate
Multi
Page: 319

(a) no unemployment because workers are not willing to accept jobs paying less than $8 an hour.
(b) unemployment of 20 million.
(c) unemployment of 30 million.
(d) unemployment of 50 million.

Answer: (d)

15.15: Refer to Figure 15.2. Suppose there is an increase in the fertility rate and this causes some men and women to place a higher value on their time spent in nonmarket activities. This will cause

Moderate
Multi
Page: 319

(a) the labor supply curve to shift to the left of S.
(b) the labor supply curve to shift to the right of S.
(c) the labor demand curve to shift from D to D'.
(d) the labor demand curve to shift from D' to D.

Answer: (a)

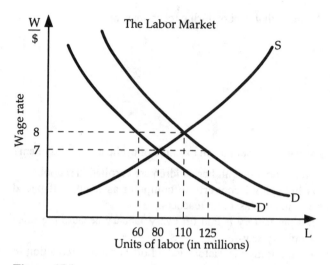

Figure 15.2

Moderate
Single
Page: 321

15.16: Refer to Figure 15.2. If the demand for labor falls from D to D', and wages are sticky on the downward side, there will be unemployment of _____ million.

(a) 20
(b) 30
(c) 45
(d) 50

Answer: (d)

Moderate
Single
Page: 321

15.17: Refer to Figure 15.2. The demand for labor falls from D to D'. If firms enter into social, or implicit, contracts with workers not to cut wages, then the wage rate will remain at $8 and

(a) employment will remain at 110 million.
(b) employment will fall to 80 million.
(c) employment will fall to 60 million.
(d) labor supply will decrease to restore the market to equilibrium.

Answer: (c)

Moderate
Single
Page: 318

15.18: A change occurs so that the value individuals place on their time in nonmarket activities decreases. The

(a) labor demand curve will shift to the right.
(b) labor demand curve will shift to the left.
(c) labor supply curve will shift to the left.
(d) labor supply curve will shift to the right.

Answer: (d)

Easy
Single
Page: 318

15.19: Susan is not employed. The value Susan places on her leisure time is $12 an hour. Susan looks for a job and all the offers she has are for less than $12 an hour. Susan should supply

(a) 0 hours in the labor market.
(b) between 0 and 40 hours per week in the labor market.
(c) exactly 40 hours per week in the labor market.
(d) more than 40 hours per week in the labor market.

Answer: (a)

15.20: Alec is not employed. The value Alec places on his leisure time is $20 an hour. Alec looks for a job and all the offers he has are for less than $20 an hour. Alec should supply

Easy
Single
Page: 318

(a) 0 hours in the labor market.
(b) between 0 and 20 hours per week in the labor market.
(c) between 20 and 40 hours per week in the labor market.
(d) exactly 40 hours per week in the labor market.

Answer: (a)

15.21: Glenna is currently not employed. She places a value of $10 an hour on her time in nonmarket activities. If Glenna is offered a job paying $15 an hour,

Moderate
Single
Page: 318

(a) she should supply 0 hours in the labor market and allocate all of her time to nonmarket activities.
(b) she should supply a positive number of hours in the labor market and to nonmarket activities.
(c) she should supply a positive number of hours in the labor market and allocate no time to nonmarket activities.
(d) she is indifferent between supplying hours to the labor market and using her time in nonmarket activities.

Answer: (b)

15.22: Barney is currently not employed. He places a value of $4.50 an hour on his time in nonmarket activities. If Barney is offered a job paying $5 an hour,

Moderate
Single
Page: 318

(a) he should supply 0 hours in the labor market since Barney couldn't survive earning $5 an hour.
(b) he should supply a positive number of hours in the labor market and allocate no time to nonmarket activities.
(c) he is indifferent between supplying hours to the labor market and using his time in nonmarket activities.
(d) he should supply a positive number of hours in the labor market and to nonmarket activities.

Answer: (d)

15.23: If a household member is not in the labor force, it is because he or she has decided that the value of his or her time is

Moderate
Single
Page: 318

(a) more valuable in nonmarket activities.
(b) more valuable in market activities.
(c) less valuable in nonmarket activities.
(d) equally valuable in both market and nonmarket activities.

Answer: (a)

15.24: A new policy is implemented that guarantees every adult an annual income of $15,000 whether they work or not. This will most likely shift the

Moderate
Single
Page: 318

(a) labor demand curve to the right.
(b) labor demand curve to the left.
(c) labor supply curve to the right.
(d) labor supply curve to the left.

Answer: (d)

Moderate
Single
Page: 318

15.25: The government raises the marginal income tax rates so that after-tax wages are reduced. This most likely will shift the labor

(a) supply curve to the right.
(b) supply curve to the left.
(c) demand curve to the right.
(d) demand curve to the left.

Answer: (b)

Easy
Single
Page: 319

15.26: According to classical economists, how will the economy respond to an increase in the demand for output? As the demand for output increases,

(a) output prices will rise, the demand for labor will decrease, the wage rate will fall, and unemployment will result.
(b) output prices will rise, the demand for labor will increase, the wage rate will not change, and there will be an excess demand for labor.
(c) output prices will rise, the demand for labor will increase, the wage rate will rise, and more workers will be drawn into the labor market.
(d) output prices will fall, the demand for labor will increase, the wage rate will rise, and more workers will be drawn into the labor market.

Answer: (c)

Easy
Fact
Page: 319

15.27: One of the tenets of the classical view of the labor market is that the wage adjustments that are necessary to clear the labor market occur

(a) very infrequently.
(b) slowly.
(c) instantly.
(d) quickly.

Answer: (d)

Moderate
Single
Page: 319

15.28: Which of the following statements is FALSE?

(a) According to classical economists, the people who are not working are those who have chosen not to work at the market wage.
(b) Classical economists believe that the labor market will achieve the optimal result if left to its own devices, and there is nothing the government can do to make things better.
(c) Classical economists saw the workings of the labor market as optimal from the standpoint of both individual households and firms and from the standpoint of society.
(d) The classical view of the labor market is consistent with a horizontal AS curve.

Answer: (d)

Easy
Fact
Page: 319

15.29: The classical view of the labor market is basically consistent with the assumption of _____ aggregate supply curve.

(a) a horizontal (or almost horizontal)
(b) a vertical (or almost vertical)
(c) an upward-sloping
(d) a downward-sloping

Answer: (b)

15.30: Those who hold the classical view of the labor market are likely to believe that

(a) monetary and fiscal policy have a substantial effect on output and employment in both the short run and the long run.
(b) monetary and fiscal policy have some effect on output and employment in both the short run and the long run.
(c) monetary and fiscal policy have little or no effect on output and employment in both the short run and the long run.
(d) monetary and fiscal policy have some effect on output and employment in the short run, but not in the long run.

Answer: (c)

Moderate
Fact
Page: 320

15.31: Those who hold the classical view of the labor market are likely to believe that

(a) monetary, but not fiscal policy will have an effect on output and employment.
(b) fiscal but not monetary policy will have an effect on output and employment.
(c) both monetary and fiscal policy will have an effect on output and employment.
(d) neither monetary nor fiscal policy will have an effect on output and employment.

Answer: (d)

Easy
Fact
Page: 320

15.32: Assume that the percentage of the labor force covered by labor contracts that set wages for a predetermined period of time decreases. This will tend to   .

(a) decrease the effectiveness of both monetary and fiscal policy.
(b) decrease the effectiveness of both monetary and fiscal policy.
(c) increase the effectiveness of fiscal policy, but decrease the effectiveness of monetary policy.
(d) have no impact on the effectiveness of either monetary or fiscal policy.

Answer: (a)

Challenging
Multi
Page: 320

15.33: According to the classical economists, those who are not working

(a) are unable to find a job at the current wage rate.
(b) are too productive to be hired at the current wage.
(c) have chosen not to work at the market wage.
(d) have given up looking for a job, but would accept a job at the current wage if one were offered to them.

Answer: (c)

Easy
Fact
Page: 320

15.34: Classical economists argue that the unemployment rate

(a) is a very accurate indicator of whether the labor market is working properly, because to be considered unemployed a person must actively seek work.
(b) is a very accurate indicator of whether the labor market is working properly because it includes those that are structurally, frictionally, and cyclically unemployed.
(c) is not a very accurate indicator of whether the labor market is working properly since many people who are classified as unemployed have chosen not to accept jobs at the wages offered.
(d) is not a very accurate indicator of whether the labor market is working properly because those who have given up looking for work are not counted as unemployed.

Answer: (c)

Moderate
Fact
Page: 320

Moderate
Single
Page: 320

15.35: What definition of unemployment would you expect classical economists to use?

(a) Anyone who is actively seeking work.
(b) Anyone who is willing to work at the current market wage, but has not yet been able to find employment.
(c) Anyone who is willing to work if the market wage increases.
(d) Anyone who is currently not working.

Answer: (b)

Easy
Fact
Page: 321

5.36: If wages are "sticky," then as the demand for labor decreases the wage rate will stick at its original level

(a) and there will be an excess supply of labor.
(b) and there will be an excess demand for labor.
(c) but the quantity of labor supplied will fall so that equilibrium is restored in the labor market.
(d) but the quantity of labor demanded will fall so that equilibrium is restored in the labor market.

Answer: (a)

Challenging
Multi
Page: 321

15.37: During the recession of 1990-1991, the demand for longshoremen fell. The wage rate paid to longshoremen did not fall during the recession because of union-negotiated contracts. As a result of this, there was a significant amount of measured unemployment among longshoremen. A classical economist would argue that

(a) this is proof that labor markets are not efficient.
(b) these longshoremen should not be counted as unemployed, because they are not willing to work for lower wages.
(c) the unemployment resulted from an increase in the supply of labor in response to the relatively high wage rate paid to longshoremen.
(d) these longshoremen should be counted as unemployed, because they cannot find employment at the union-negotiated wage.

Answer: (b)

Moderate
Single
Page: 322

15.38: An assembly-line worker in an automobile factory loses his job as a result of a sharp decline in new car sales associated with the latest recession. Employment is available in other lines of work at a lower wage. The assembly-line worker is not willing to accept a job at a lower wage. An advocate of the classical view of the labor market would conclude that this worker

(a) is seasonally unemployed.
(b) is structurally unemployed.
(c) has chosen to be unemployed.
(d) is frictionally unemployed.

Answer: (c)

Moderate
Single
Page: 322

15.39: Aaron loses his job as a dry-wall construction worker as a a result of a sharp decline in new dry-wall installations associated with the latest recession. Employment is available in other lines of work at a lower wage. Aaron is not willing to accept a job at a lower wage. An advocate of the classical view of the labor market would conclude that Aaron

(a) has chosen to be unemployed.
(b) is seasonally unemployed.
(c) is structurally unemployed.
(d) is frictionally unemployed.

Answer: (a)

15.40: Advocates of the classical view of the labor market would maintain that unemployment results from

(a) voluntary decisions on the part of those who are out of work.
(b) unspoken agreements between workers and firms that firms will not cut wages.
(c) the unwillingness of workers to accept a wage cut, unless they know that all other workers are receiving similar cuts.
(d) the incentives that firms have to hold wages above the market clearing rate.

Moderate
Single
Page: 322

Answer: (a)

15.41: An unspoken agreement between workers and firms that the firm will not cut wages is known as

(a) a relative-wage contract.
(b) an explicit contract.
(c) an implicit or social contract.
(d) employment-at-will.

Easy
Definition
Page: 322

Answer: (c)

15.42: The social contract explanation for the existence of downwardly sticky wages focuses on

(a) employment contracts that stipulate workers' wages, usually for a period of one to three years.
(b) the contention that workers in one industry may be unwilling to accept a wage cut, unless they know that workers in other industries are receiving similar cuts.
(c) the incentive that firms have to hold wages above the market clearing rate.
(d) unspoken agreements between workers and firms that firms will not cut wages.

Easy
Fact
Page: 322

Answer: (d)

15.43: Cool Air, a major manufacturer of air conditioners, saw the demand for its product drop by 25%. Even though the demand for its product decreased, Cool Air did not cut the wages of its nonunionized workers. This is an example of

(a) employment-at-will.
(b) a relative-wage contract.
(c) an explicit contract not to cut wages
(d) an implicit or social contract not to cut wages.

Moderate
Single
Page: 321

Answer: (d)

15.44: Enz of The World, a major manufacturer of tools, saw the demand for its product drop by 25%. Even though the demand for its product decreased, Enz of The World did not cut the wages of its non-unionized workers. This is an example of

(a) an implicit or social contract not to cut wages.
(b) employment-at-will.
(c) poor management.
(d) an explicit contract not to cut wages

Moderate
Single
Page: 321

Answer: (a)

15.45: Suppose that steelworkers are laid off during a recession because of an unspoken agreement between steelworkers and steel producers that wages will not be reduced. This example is consistent with the

(a) relative-wage explanation of unemployment.
(b) social contract explanation of unemployment.
(c) explicit contract explanation of unemployment.
(d) efficiency wage explanation of unemployment.

Moderate
Single
Page: 322

Answer: (b)

Easy
Fact
Page: 322

15.46: A firm may violate the "social contract" and cut nominal wages if it is faced with

(a) increasing capital costs.
(b) higher corporate income taxes.
(c) increasing labor productivity.
(d) increasing foreign competition.

Answer: (d)

Easy
Fact
Page: 322

15.47: The relative-wage explanation for the existence of downwardly sticky wages emphasizes

(a) unspoken agreements between workers and firms that firms will not cut wages.
(b) the contention that workers in one industry may be unwilling to accept a wage cut, unless they know that workers in other industries are receiving similar cuts.
(c) employment contracts that stipulate workers' wages, usually for a period of one to three years.
(d) the incentive that firms may have to hold wages above the market clearing rate.

Answer: (b)

Easy
Definition
Page: 322

15.48: According to the relative-wage explanation of unemployment, workers will be willing to accept wage cuts only if

(a) they know that unemployment is increasing in other industries.
(b) they can be convinced that they are overpaid relative to workers doing similar jobs at other firms.
(c) they know that workers in other firms are receiving similar cuts.
(d) the economy is in a prolonged recession.

Answer: (c)

Moderate
Single
Page: 322

15.49: Construction workers are laid off during a recession because they are unwilling to accept a wage cut, unless they know that workers in other industries are receiving similar cuts. This example is consistent with the

(a) social contract explanation of unemployment.
(b) explicit contract explanation of unemployment.
(c) relative-wage explanation of unemployment.
(d) efficiency wage explanation of unemployment.

Answer: (c)

Moderate
Single
Page: 322

15.50: The percentage of workers whose wages are set by explicit contracts falls. This should

(a) make it more difficult for the labor market to reach an equilibrium after a change in the demand for labor.
(b) make it easier for the labor market to reach an equilibrium after a change in the demand for labor.
(c) have no impact on the movement of the labor market toward equilibrium after a change in the demand for labor.
(d) cause the labor market to always be at an equilibrium, even if there is a change in the demand for labor.

Answer: (b)

15.51: Even though explicit contracts may lead to layoffs during recessions, explicit contracts may still be efficient because such contracts

Easy
Fact
Page: 322

(a) minimize negotiation costs.
(b) minimize unemployment effects.
(c) guarantee that only the least productive workers will be laid off.
(d) will equitably spread the layoffs among junior and senior workers.

Answer: (a)

15.52: Suppose that loggers are laid off during a recession because their wages have been locked into place by a three-year contract. This example is consistent with the

Moderate
Single
Page: 322

(a) social contract explanation of unemployment.
(b) relative-wage explanation of unemployment.
(c) efficiency wage explanation of unemployment.
(d) explicit contract explanation of unemployment.

Answer: (d)

15.53: In 1992, the members of a 9 to 5 union had an average seniority level of fifteen years. During 1993, many of the union members retired and the average seniority level declined to five years. Which of the following changes may take place in the next contract?

Moderate
Single
Page: 323

(a) The union negotiates a contract that guarantees that its wage rate relative to workers in other industries will remain constant regardless of potential employment losses. (Assume that junior workers are the first to be laid off.)
(b) The union negotiates a contract that guarantees that its wage rate will remain constant regardless of the potential employment losses. (Assume that junior workers are the first to be laid off.)
(c) The union negotiates a contract that calls for fixed employment levels rather than a fixed wage rate. (Assume that junior workers are the first to be laid off.)
(d) The union negotiates a contract that calls for layoffs to be implemented so that the last hired is the first fired.

Answer: (c)

15.54: Workers may sign contracts that in effect call for layoffs instead of wage cuts because of the problem of monitoring information. What is meant by the monitoring of information?

Moderate
Fact
Page: 323

(a) It is difficult for workers to know if the reduction in their wage rate is comparable to the wage reductions accepted by other workers.
(b) It is difficult for workers to know what the inflation rate actually is.
(c) Workers are not able to monitor the changes that are taking place in the macroeconomy.
(d) Workers are not willing to accept pay cuts unless firms have cut prices in response to lower demand, and it is difficult to determine whether or not prices have been cut.

Answer: (d)

15.55: Which of the following arguments is NOT offered to explain the existence of "sticky" wages?

Easy
Fact
Page: 323

(a) the social contract explanation
(b) the classical explanation of the labor market
(c) the relative-wage explanation
(d) the explicit contract explanation

Answer: (b)

Easy
Single
Page: 322

15.56: In the United States, social security retirement benefits automatically increase as the inflation rate increases. This automatic adjustment in benefits is an example of

(a) a cost-of-living adjustment.
(b) the relative-income hypothesis.
(c) the social contract theory.
(d) an expansionary fiscal policy.

Answer: (a)

Easy
Definition
Page: 322

15.57: Suppose that the productivity of workers increases with the wage rate. As a result, firms elect to hold wages above the market clearing rate. This example is consistent with the

(a) efficiency wage explanation of unemployment.
(b) social contract explanation of unemployment.
(c) explicit contract explanation of unemployment.
(d) relative-wage explanation of unemployment.

Answer: (a)

Moderate
Single
Page: 322

15.58: Refer to Figure 15.3. Assume that the productivity of workers increases as the wage rate increases. This efficiency wage

(a) would be below $10.
(b) would equal $10.
(c) would be above $10.
(d) could either be above or below $10.

Answer: (c)

Moderate
Single
Page: 323

15.59: Refer to Figure 15.3. If this firm pays the efficient wage of $11,

(a) the firm's demand for labor will increase until $11 is also the equilibrium wage.
(b) the supply of labor will decrease until $11 is also the equilibrium wage.
(c) there will be an excess supply of labor of 2,000.
(d) there will be an excess supply of labor of 3,000.

Answer: (d)

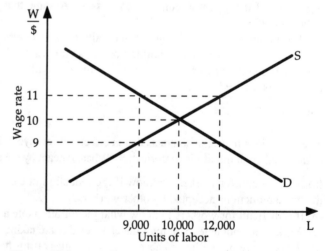

Figure 15.3

Easy
Fact
Page: 322

15.60: Efficiency wage theory suggests that firms may hold wages above the market clearing rate because

(a) it is required by law that they do so.
(b) unspoken agreements between workers and firms are in place.
(c) they believe that the productivity of workers increases with the wage rate.
(d) long-term contracts fix wage rates for a period of one to three years.

Answer: (c)

15.61: If productivity increases as wages increase and firms pay a wage above the market clearing wage, then

Moderate
Fact
Page: 322

(a) these firms will go out of business in the long run because they will not be able to compete with firms paying lower wages.
(b) these firms will have lower profit levels than their competitors.
(c) these firms will face an excess demand for labor and will be able to hire the best workers in the market.
(d) a potential benefit these firms may receive is a reduction in employee turnover.

Answer: (d)

15.62: A firm may benefit by paying workers more than the market clearing wage because the higher wages may lead to

Easy
Fact
Page: 323

(a) lower worker turnover.
(b) improved worker morale.
(c) reduced shirking of work.
(d) all of the above.

Answer: (d)

15.63: If firms have incomplete information and set wages above the market clearing level,

Easy
Fact
Page: 323

(a) wage rates will quickly fall to the market clearing level, because firms will realize there is a surplus of labor.
(b) it may take considerable time before the wage rate equals the market clearing level, because of the complexity of the labor market.
(c) the government will intervene and set the wage rate equal to the market clearing level.
(d) the supply of labor will fall until the current wage equals the market clearing wage.

Answer: (b)

15.64: If firms set wage rates on the basis of imperfect or incomplete information,

Moderate
Single
Page: 323

(a) wages that are above the market clearing level and a higher unemployment rate.
(b) wages that are above the market clearing level and a lower unemployment rate.
(c) wages that are below the market clearing level and a higher unemployment rate.
(d) wages that are below the market clearing level but no change in the unemployment rate.

Answer: (a)

15.65: Minimum wage laws contribute to a higher unemployment rate by

Moderate
Single
Page: 323

(a) pushing wages below the market clearing level in all labor markets.
(b) pushing wages below the market clearing level in some labor markets.
(c) raising wages above the market clearing level in all labor markets.
(d) raising wages above the market clearing level in some labor markets.

Answer: (d)

15.66: Many economists claim that the minimum wage law contributes to a

Easy
Fact
Page: 323

(a) lower unemployment rate among teenage workers.
(b) lower unemployment rate among adult workers.
(c) higher unemployment rate among teenage workers.
(d) higher unemployment rate among retired workers who want to return to work.

Answer: (c)

Moderate
Single
Page: 323

15.67: Refer to Figure 15.4. A minimum wage of $4.25

(a) will lead to unemployment of 10.
(b) will lead to unemployment of 20.
(c) will lead to unemployment of 30.
(d) will have no effect because the minimum wage is set above the equilibrium wage and for a minimum wage to have any effect on the labor market it must be below the equilibrium wage.

Answer: (c)

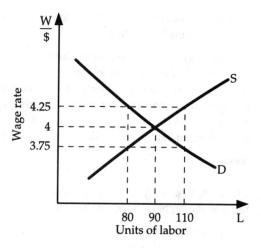

Figure 15.4

Challenging
Multi
Page: 323

15.68: Refer to Figure 15.4. A minimum wage of $3.75

(a) will lead to an excess demand for labor of 10.
(b) will lead to an excess demand for labor of 20.
(c) will lead to an excess demand for labor of 30.
(d) will have no effect because the minimum wage is set below the equilibrium wage and for a minimum wage to have any effect on the labor market it must be above the equilibrium wage.

Answer: (d)

Easy
Fact
Page: 323

15.69: The unemployment rate falls if

(a) the demand for labor falls.
(b) aggregate output increases.
(c) the supply of labor increases.
(d) firms begin to pay an efficient wage.

Answer: (b)

Easy
Single
Page: 324

15.70: What sequence of events results from an increase in aggregate demand?

(a) The price level falls, inventories decline, firms respond by increasing output and employment.
(b) The price level falls, inventories increase, firms respond by reducing output and employment.
(c) The price level rises, inventories decline, firms respond by increasing output and employment.
(d) The price level rises, inventories increase, firms respond by increasing output and employment.

Answer: (c)

15.71: What sequence of events results from a decrease in aggregate demand?

(a) The price level falls, inventories decline, firms respond by increasing output and employment.
(b) The price level falls, inventories increase, firms respond by reducing output and employment.
(c) The price level rises, inventories decline, firms respond by increasing output and employment.
(d) The price level rises, inventories increase, firms respond by increasing output and employment.

Easy
Single
Page: 324

Answer: (b)

15.72: Refer to Figure 15.5. The hypothesized relationship between the price level and the unemployment rate is represented in Panel

Easy
Single
Page: 325

(a) A.
(b) B.
(c) C.
(d) D.

Answer: (a)

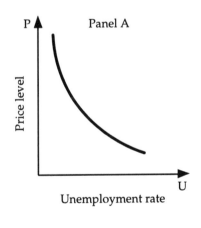
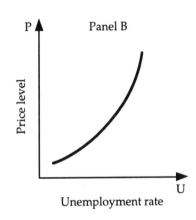

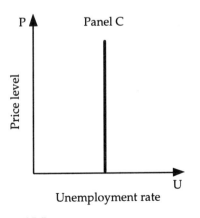
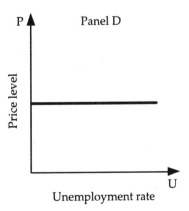

Figure 15.5

Moderate
Single
Page: 325

15.73: As the unemployment rate declines in response to the economy moving closer and closer to capacity output, the aggregate price level

(a) falls at an increasing rate.
(b) falls at a declining rate.
(c) rises at an increasing rate.
(d) rises at a declining rate.

Answer: (c)

Moderate
Single
Page: 325

15.74: In the Batavian economy unemployment has been falling, but the price level has increased by very little. The most likely explanation for this is that

(a) the Batavian economy is very close to capacity and is operating on the steep portion of its AS curve.
(b) the Batavian economy is well below capacity and is operating on the flat portion of its AS curve.
(c) the monetary authority in Batavia has been reducing the money supply to keep interest rates high.
(d) all wages in the Batavian economy are set by explicit contracts that last for a minimum of a year.

Answer: (b)

Easy
Definition
Page: 325

15.75: The percentage change in the price level is the

(a) inflation rate.
(b) unemployment rate.
(c) average price level.
(d) price rate.

Answer: (a)

Easy
Fact
Page: 325

15.76: The Phillips curve indicates that there is a

(a) positive relationship between the inflation rate and the employment rate.
(b) negative relationship between the inflation rate and the unemployment rate.
(c) positive relationship between labor supply and the inflation rate.
(d) negative relationship between the inflation rate and labor demand.

Answer: (b)

Easy
Definition
Page: 325

15.77: The Phillips curve is a graph showing the relationship between

(a) the price level and the unemployment rate.
(b) the level of aggregate output and the price level.
(c) the inflation rate and the unemployment rate.
(d) the inflation rate and the level of aggregate demand.

Answer: (c)

Easy
Single
Page: 326

15.78: Refer to Figure 15.6. The Phillips curve is represented in Panel

(a) A.
(b) B.
(c) C.
(d) D.

Answer: (b)

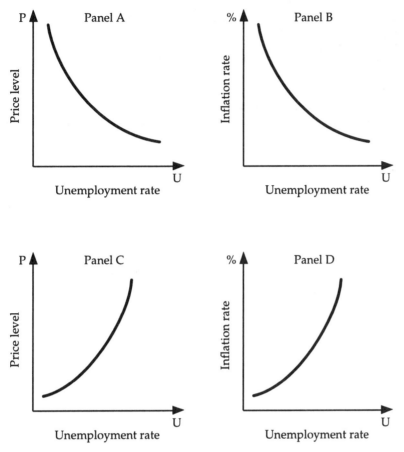

Figure 15.6

15.79: If input price prices adjusted very rapidly to output prices, as classical economists argue, the Phillips curve would be

Challenging
Multi
Page: 331

(a) upward sloping.
(b) downward sloping.
(c) horizontal or nearly horizontal.
(d) vertical or nearly vertical.

Answer: (d)

15.80: The view of the Phillips Curve, that prevailed in the 1960s implied that policies that

Easy
Fact
Page: 326

(a) lower the unemployment rate will also tend to lower the inflation rate.
(b) lower the inflation rate will also tend to lower the unemployment rate.
(c) raise the inflation rate will also tend to raise the unemployment rate.
(d) lower the unemployment rate will also tend to raise the inflation rate.

Answer: (d)

Easy
Fact
Page: 327

15.81: In the 1960s, discussions of economic policy revolved around the Phillips curve. The role of the policy maker, it was thought, was to choose a point on the curve. In political terms, this meant that

(a) conservatives usually argued for choosing a point with a lower rate of unemployment and were willing to accept a higher inflation rate.
(b) conservatives usually argued for choosing a point with a lower rate of inflation and were willing to accept a higher unemployment rate.
(c) liberals usually argued for accepting more unemployment to keep inflation at very low levels.
(d) both conservatives and liberals sought the best of both worlds - low inflation and low unemployment at the same time.

Answer: (b)

Easy
Fact
Page: 327

15.82: Doubts about the nature and the existence of the Phillips curve arose in the 1970s when the economy experienced

(a) simultaneously high rates of inflation and unemployment.
(b) simultaneously low rates of inflation and unemployment.
(c) a high rate of unemployment, along with a low rate of inflation.
(d) a high rate of inflation, along with a low rate of unemployment.

Answer: (a)

Easy
Fact
Page: 327

15.83: According to the Phillips curve, if policy makers want to reduce the unemployment rate, they must accept

(a) a lower inflation rate.
(b) a higher inflation rate.
(c) a reduction in aggregate demand.
(d) a reduction in aggregate supply.

Answer: (b)

Challenging
Multi
Page: 328

15.84: Refer to Figure 15.7. The economy is currently at point A. Increases in aggregate demand with no change in aggregate supply will move the economy from point A to point

(a) E.
(b) B.
(c) C.
(d) D.

Answer: (d)

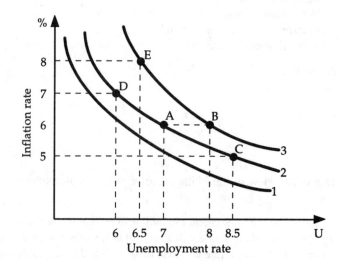

Figure 15.7

15.85: Refer to Figure 15.7. The economy is currently at point A along Phillips curve 2. Decreases in aggregate supply with no change in aggregate demand will

Moderate
Single
Page: 328

(a) shift the Phillips curve to Phillips curve 1.
(b) shift the Phillips curve to Phillips curve 3.
(c) move the economy to a point like D.
(d) will move the economy to a point like C.

Answer: (b)

15.86: Refer to Figure 15.7. The economy is currently at point A. Decreases in the level of government spending with no changes in aggregate supply will move the economy from point A to point

Challenging
Multi
Page: 328

(a) E.
(b) B.
(c) C.
(d) D.

Answer: (c)

15.87: Refer to Figure 15.7. The economy is currently at point A along Phillips curve 1. Increases in energy prices with no changes in aggregate demand, will

Challenging
Multi
Page: 328

(a) shift the Phillips curve to Phillips curve 1.
(b) shift the Phillips curve to Phillips curve 3.
(c) move the economy to a point like D.
(d) will move the economy to a point like C.

Answer: (b)

15.88: Refer to Figure 15.7. The economy is currently at point A. If net taxes are decreased and there is no change in aggregate supply, the economy will move from point A to point

Challenging
Multi
Page: 328

(a) E.
(b) B.
(c) C.
(d) D.

Answer: (d)

15.89: Refer to Figure 15.7. The economy is currently at point A. A movement to point E is consistent with

Moderate
Multi
Page: 328

(a) a decrease in aggregate demand and no change in aggregate supply.
(b) no change in aggregate demand and a decrease in aggregate supply.
(c) an increase in aggregate demand and a no change in aggregate supply.
(d) no change in aggregate demand and an increase in aggregate supply.

Answer: (b)

15.90: Refer to Figure 15.7. The economy is currently at point A. A movement to point C is consistent with

Moderate
Multi
Page: 328

(a) a decrease in aggregate demand and no change in aggregate supply.
(b) no change in aggregate demand and a decrease in aggregate supply.
(c) an increase in aggregate demand and a no change in aggregate supply.
(d) no change in aggregate demand and an increase in aggregate supply.

Answer: (a)

Moderate
Multi
Page: 328

15.91: Refer to Figure 15.7. The economy is currently at point A. A movement to point E is consistent with

(a) a decrease in aggregate demand and no change in aggregate supply.
(b) no change in aggregate demand and a decrease in aggregate supply.
(c) an increase in inflationary expectations.
(d) a decrease in inflationary expectations.

Answer: (c)

Moderate
Single
Page: 328

15.92: Refer to Figure 15.7. The economy is currently at point A. If inflationary expectations increase,

(a) the economy will move to point D.
(b) the economy will move to point C.
(c) the Phillips curve will shift to Phillips curve 1.
(d) the Phillips curve will shift to Phillips curve 3.

Answer: (d)

Moderate
Single
Page: 328

15.93: Refer to Figure 15.7. The economy is currently at point A. If inflationary expectations decrease,

(a) the economy will move to point D.
(b) the economy will move to point C.
(c) the Phillips curve will shift to Phillips curve 1.
(d) the Phillips curve will shift to Phillips curve 3.

Answer: (c)

Moderate
Single
Page: 328

15.94: If aggregate supply decreases and aggregate demand remains unchanged,

(a) there will be a positive relationship between the price level and the level of aggregate output.
(b) there will be a negative relationship between the price level and the level of aggregate output.
(c) there will be no systematic relationship between the price level and the level of aggregate output.
(d) the price level will remain unchanged, but aggregate output will decrease.

Answer: (b)

Moderate
Single
Page: 328

15.95: The economy experiences both inflation and unemployment when

(a) aggregate demand decreases and aggregate supply increases.
(b) aggregate demand increases and aggregate supply decreases.
(c) aggregate demand decreases and aggregate supply remains unchanged.
(d) aggregate supply decreases and aggregate demand remains unchanged.

Answer: (d)

Moderate
Single
Page: 328

15.96: There is no systematic relationship between the price level and the level of aggregate output when

(a) neither aggregate demand nor aggregate supply is changing.
(b) aggregate demand is changing, but aggregate supply is not.
(c) aggregate supply is changing, but aggregate demand is not.
(d) both aggregate supply and aggregate demand are changing simultaneously.

Answer: (d)

15.97: If the AD curve shifts from year to year, but the AS curve does not, then the Phillips curve will be

Moderate
Single
Page: 328

(a) downward sloping.
(b) upward sloping.
(c) horizontal.
(d) vertical in both the long run and the short run.

Answer: (a)

15.98: If the AS curve shifts from year to year, but the AD curve does not, then the Phillips curve would show

Challenging
Single
Page: 328

(a) a negative relationship between the inflation and unemployment rates.
(b) a positive relationship between the inflation and unemployment rates.
(c) no particular relationship between the inflation and unemployment rates.
(d) a constant trade-off between the inflation and unemployment rates.

Answer: (b)

15.99: If inflationary expectations increase, the Phillips curve will

Easy
Fact
Page: 329

(a) shift to the right.
(b) shift to the left.
(c) become vertical.
(d) become upward sloping.

Answer: (a)

15.100: The United States began to pull out of a recession in the spring of 1991. Unemployment fell, but inflation did not increase. What was the most likely cause of this?

Challenging
Multi
Page: 328

(a) aggregate demand was increasing but aggregate supply was decreasing.
(b) both aggregate demand and aggregate supply were decreasing.
(c) aggregate supply was increasing at a faster rate than aggregate demand.
(d) aggregate demand was increasing at a faster rate than aggregate supply.

Answer: (c)

15.101: In the long run, the Phillips curve will be vertical at the natural rate of unemployment if

Easy
Fact
Page: 330

(a) the long-run aggregate demand curve is vertical at potential GDP.
(b) the long-run aggregate demand curve is horizontal at the natural
rate of inflation.
(c) the long-run supply curve is horizontal at the natural rate of
inflation.
(d) the long-run aggregate supply curve is vertical at potential GDP.

Answer: (d)

15.102: If the Phillips curve is vertical in the long run, then

Easy
Fact
Page: 330

(a) there is a trade-off between inflation and unemployment in the long run.
(b) there is no trade-off between inflation and unemployment in the long run.
(c) the unemployment rate will be zero in the long run.
(d) the inflation rate will always be zero in the long run.

Answer: (b)

Challenging Multi
Page: 330

15.103: If input price changes lag behind output price changes in both the long run and the short run, then

(a) the short-run Phillips curve will be downward sloping, but the long-run Phillips curve will be vertical.
(b) the short-run Phillips curve will be vertical, but the long-run Phillips curve will be downward sloping.
(c) both the short-and long-run Phillips curves will be vertical.
(d) both the short-and long-run Phillips curves will be downward sloping.

Answer: (d)

Moderate
Multi
Page: 331

15.104: Refer to Figure 15.8. If the economy is operating at potential GDP, the frictional unemployment rate is 3% and the structural unemployment rate is 2%. The long-run Phillips curve will be

(a) the same as the vertical axis.
(b) equal to LRPC1.
(c) equal to LRPC2.
(d) equal to LRPC3.

Answer: (d)

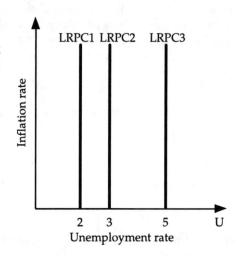

Figure 15.8

Easy
Definition.
Page: 331

15.105: Potential GDP is the level of aggregate output

(a) that can be produced at a zero unemployment rate.
(b) that can be sustained in the long run without inflation.
(c) that can be sustained in the long run, if the inflation rate is zero.
(d) that can be produced if structural unemployment is zero.

Answer: (b)

Easy
Definition
Page: 331

15.106: The natural rate of unemployment is generally thought to be the sum of

(a) frictional unemployment and cyclical unemployment.
(b) cyclical unemployment and structural unemployment.
(c) frictional unemployment and structural unemployment.
(d) frictional unemployment and seasonal unemployment.

Answer: (c)

Easy
Fact
Page: 331

15.107: Economists who argue that the AS curve is vertical in the long run at potential GDP also argue that the Phillips curve in the long run is

(a) horizontal at the natural rate of inflation.
(b) upward sloping.
(c) downward sloping.
(d) vertical at the natural rate of unemployment.

Answer: (d)

15.108: The measured unemployment rate can be pushed below the natural rate, but

(a) only in the long run, and only if the price level is constant.
(b) only in the long run, and not without inflation.
(c) only in the short run, and not without inflation.
(d) only in the short run, and only if the price level is constant.

Answer: (c)

Easy
Fact
Page: 330

15.109: Which of the following statements is FALSE?

(a) Even if the natural rate of unemployment is fixed in the long run, if a cost shock drives the level of unemployment above the natural rate, policy can play a role in reducing unemployment.
(b) There is a trade-off between inflation and unemployment, but other factors besides unemployment affect inflation.
(c) There is a limit to how low the unemployment rate can be pushed without setting off a round of inflation.
(d) Those who believe that the AS curve is vertical in the long run believe that the Phillips curve is vertical in the long run.

Answer: (a)

Moderate
Single
Page: 332

TRUE/FALSE QUESTIONS

15.110: If a household member is not in the labor force, it is because he or she has decided his or her time is more valuable in nonmarket activities.

Answer: True

Easy
Fact
Page: 318

15.111: Those who believe that the wage rate adjusts quickly to clear the labor market are likely to believe that the aggregate supply curve is positively sloped, and that monetary and fiscal policy have a substantial effect on output and employment.

Answer: False

Easy
Single
Page: 319

15.112: The classical view of the labor market holds that, at equilibrium, the people who are not working are those who have chosen not to work at the market wage.

Answer: True

Easy
Fact
Page: 319

15.113: It takes very little time for market clearing wages to be reestablished after they have been disturbed from an equilibrium position.

Answer: False

Easy
Fact
Page: 319

15.114: If the minimum wage is set below the market clearing wage, wages will be "sticky" in the downward direction.

Answer: False

Easy
Single
Page: 321

15.115: As the unemployment rate declines in response to the economy moving closer and closer to capacity output, the aggregate price level rises, but at a decreasing rate.

Answer: False

Easy
Single
Page: 325

15.116: The Phillips curve suggests that if we want to lower the inflation rate, we must accept a higher unemployment rate in return.

Answer: True

Easy
Fact
Page: 327

Easy
Single
Page: 328

15.117: Increases in aggregate supply with no change in aggregate demand move the economy down along its Phillips curve.

Answer: False

Easy
Single
Page: 328

15.118: An increase in inflationary expectations shifts the economy's Phillips curve to the left.

Answer: False

Easy
Fact
Page: 331

15.119: In the long run, if input prices fully adjust to output price changes, then the long-run Phillips curve is vertical at the natural rate of unemployment.

Answer: True

SHORT ANSWER QUESTIONS

Easy
Definition
Page: 317

15.120: Differentiate between frictional unemployment, structural unemployment, and cyclical unemployment.

Answer: Frictional unemployment represents short-term unemployment that results from job changes or the search of recent graduates for long-term, career-oriented employment. Structural unemployment represents long-term labor displacement that results from a lack of necessary skills or educational requirements. Individuals must be retrained to meet new employment requirements. Cyclical unemployment is a measure of job losses that result from cyclical downturns in the economy. During a recessionary period, businesses typically lay off employees until sales and production needs increase during expansionary periods.

Moderate
Math
Page: 319

15.121: Graphically illustrate an increase in the labor supply curve and explain its impact upon the equilibrium wage rate and quantities. Graphically illustrate an increase in the labor demand curve and explain its impact upon the equilibrium wage rate and quantities.

Answer: In the figure below, the supply of labor has increased as illustrated by the shift in the supply curve from S0 to S1 . The increase in labor supply lowers the equilibrium wage rate from W* to W1 which results in greater quantities supplied and demanded to L1.
In the figure below, the demand for labor has increased as illustrated by the shift in the demand curve from D0 to D1 . This results in an increase in the equilibrium wage rate to W1 and additional quantities demanded and supplied to L1 .

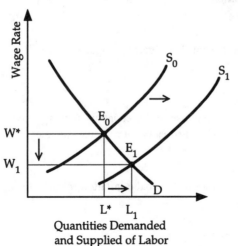

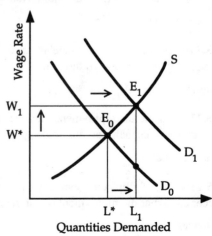

15.122: According to the Classical economists, will the entire labor force be fully employed at any and all wage rates? Do Classical economists recommend government intervention in the labor market?

Moderate
Application
Page: 318

Answer: Classical economists believe that the labor market always clears. At the equilibrium wage rate, everyone who wants a job will have one. Some laborers will elect not to work at lower wage rates and make themselves available only as the wage rate increases. Thus, they are voluntarily unemployed. At the equilibrium wage rate, those workers who are not employed have voluntarily elected not to work at that wage. The Classical economists recommend that the labor market operate freely without any government intervention. The market wage rate will automatically respond to changes in demand and supply and gravitate to a new equilibrium level where the quantity demanded and quantity supplied will be equal.

15.123: Graphically illustrate and describe the principle of sticky wages. What are some causes of inflexible or sticky wages?

Moderate
Math
Page: 321

Answer: The principle of sticky wages is illustrated in the figure below. Assume the initial equilibrium market wage was W0 and quantities demanded and supplied were L0 . If the demand for labor declined from D0 to D1 and the wage rate remains stuck at W0 , then quantities supplied (L0) would exceed quantities demanded (L2). This excess level of quantities supplied is a measure of unemployment.

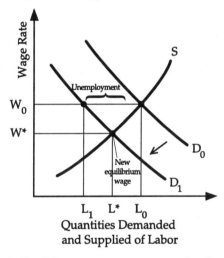

Quantities Demanded
and Supplied of Labor

Inflexible wage rates are a result of social or implicit contracts and explicit union-management contract agreements.

15.124: Explain the relative-wage explanation of unemployment.

Easy
Definition
Page: 322

Answer: The relative wage explanation of unemployment suggests that laborers are concerned about their wages relative to the wages of other workers in other firms and industries and may be unwilling to accept wage cuts unless other workers are receiving similar cuts.

15.125: Explain how incomplete or imperfect market information may contribute to unemployment.

Moderate
Application
Page: 323

Answer: Incomplete or imperfectly communicated information between labor and management may result in unemployment in this way. A firm may want to lower its product costs by lowering wages and labor costs when its sales decrease. This would permit it to lower product price and restore sales. However, labor would resist the wage cut which may require the business to lay off workers as a means of lowering its costs because they may not believe that the firm will actually lower the price.

**Moderate
Application
Page: 323**

15.126: Explain how the minimum wage laws may cause unemployment. What age group is most adversely effected by the minimum wage law?

Answer: If the established minimum wage is higher than the market clearing equilibrium wage, there will be an excess of labor supplied and unemployment will result. Young, new workers into the labor markets tend to be most adversely effected by the minimum wage laws. Their lack of job-related experience and education or training means that businesses can't afford to pay them the mandated minimum wage since their productivity does not match the wage rate.

**Easy
Definition
Page: 325**

15.127: Define the Phillips Curve. Graphically illustrate the relationship between the inflation rate and the unemployment rate.

Answer: The Phillips Curve illustrates the relationship between the inflation rate and the unemployment rate. The inverse relationship between the unemployment rate and the rate of inflation (percentage change in price) is illustrated below.

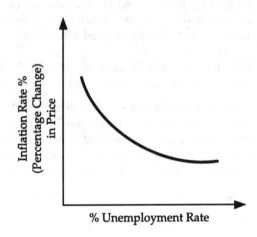

**Moderate
Application
Page: 329**

15.128: Explain how expectations can be self-fulfilling in contributing to inflation.

Answer: If inflation is expected to be high in the future, negotiated union wages are likely to be higher than if inflation were expected to be low. Wage induced inflation is thus driven by expectations of future price inflation. Thus, price expectations that affect wage negotiations eventually affect prices themselves.

**Easy
Fact
Page: 319**

15.129: Explain why a decline in the demand for labor does not necessarily mean that unemployment will rise. Under what conditions would you expect a decline in the demand for labor to lead to an increase in unemployment?

Answer: If the wage rate is flexible, a decline in the demand for labor should cause a decrease in the wage rate. The wage rate would continue to decline until the quantity of labor demanded equals the quantity of labor supplied. If wages are not flexible, then a decline in the demand for labor could lead to unemployment. Wages may not be flexible in the downward direction if there are implicit or explicit contracts not to cut wages, if workers will accept wage cuts only if they are convinced that other workers are taking wage cuts, or if wages are set by minimum wage laws.

**Moderate
Single
Page: 318**

15.130: Explain how the value that people place on the time they spend on nonmarket activities affects their decisions with respect to participation in the labor force.

Answer: If a person places a higher value on his or her time in nonmarket activities than the wage he or she is offered in the labor market, the person would choose not to supply any hours to the labor market. As the value that people place on their time in nonmarket activities changes, the labor supply also changes.

15.131: Classical economists argue that when the labor market is in equilibrium, those people who are not working are those who have CHOSEN not to work at that market wage. Why might an individual choose not to work at the market wage? Do you agree with the classical view of the labor market? Why or why not?

Moderate
Single
Page: 319

Answer: An individual may choose not to work because the value he or she places on his or her time in nonmarket activities is greater than the wage rate he or she could earn. Answers to the second part will vary.

15.132: What explanations do those economists who hold the classical view of the labor market offer for the existence of unemployment?

Moderate
Single
Page: 321

Answer: Classical economists argue that unemployment results from wages being sticky. The explanations for sticky wages include the relative-wage explanation and explicit contracts. Wages may also be held above the equilibrium wage because of efficiency wages, imperfect information, or minimum wages.

15.133: Explain the efficiency wage theory. Why would a firm be willing to pay an efficient wage?

Easy
Fact
Page: 322

Answer: The efficiency wage theory states that productivity increases as wages increase, so firms may be willing to pay above the market clearing wage. The benefits the firm may receive include lower turnover, improved morale, and less shirking.

15.134: The Phillips curve indicates that there is a stable trade-off between inflation and unemployment. Do you agree with this statement? Explain.

Moderate
Multi
Page: 327

Answer: There is a trade-off between inflation and unemployment if the Phillips curve is stable. If, however, the economy experiences cost shocks or changes in inflationary expectations, the Phillips curve is not stable and there is not a stable trade-off between inflation and unemployment.

15.135: The relationship between the inflation rate and the unemployment rate was stable during the 1960s. Why was it stable? The relationship between the inflation rate and the unemployment rate was not stable during the 1970s and 1980s. Why wasn't it stable?

Easy
Fact
Page: 327

Answer: The relationship was stable in the 60s because aggregate demand was changing, but aggregate supply was not. In the 70s and 80s, the relationship was not stable because aggregate supply was changing at the same time as aggregate demand, so both inflation and unemployment were increasing simultaneously.

15.136: For each of the following indicate if there would be a positive relationship, a negative relationship, or no systematic relationship between the unemployment and inflation rates. (a.) The government increases government spending. (b.) At the same time the government is increasing the money supply the prices of imports are increasing. (c.) The price of energy is falling.

Challenging
Multi
Page: 328

Answer: (a.) negative relationship (b.) no systematic relationship (c.) positive relationship

15.137: Explain how inflationary expectations affect the Phillips curve. How do expectations of inflation affect the trade-off between inflation and unemployment?

Easy
Fact
Page: 329

Answer: If inflationary ex-pectations increase, the Phillips curve will shift to the right. This worsens the trade-off between inflation and unemployment.

Moderate
Single
Page: 331

15.138: Draw a graph of a long-run Phillips curve. What does this graph imply about the long-run trade-off between inflation and unemployment? What does this graph imply about the effectiveness of monetary and fiscal policy in the long run?

Answer: There is no trade-off in the long run. In the long run neither monetary nor fiscal policy will be effective in changing the level of output. In the long run these policies can influence only the inflation rate.

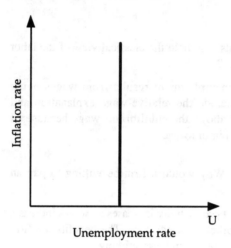

16
Deficit Reduction, Stabilization Policy, and Macro Issues Abroad

(Chapter 31 in Combined Text)

MULTIPLE CHOICE QUESTIONS

16.1: The legislative intent of the Gramm-Rudman-Hollings Act was to

(a) increase defense-related expenditures.
(b) increase federal interstate highway expenditures.
(c) reduce the federal deficit by a set amount each year.
(d) decrease personal and corporate taxes.

Answer: (c)

Moderate
Multi
Page: 337

16.2: The Gramm-Rudman-Hollings Act sought to

(a) reduce the federal deficit by 36 billion each year between 1987 and 1991.
(b) increase the level of federal government spending by 20% over two years.
(c) reduce taxes by 30% over three years.
(d) reduce the nation's balance-of-payments deficit by 5% over 10 years.

Answer: (a)

Moderate
Multi
Page: 338

16.3: Under the original Gramm-Rudman-Hollings Act, a congressional enacted budget deficit that was larger than the targeted amount would

(a) result in automatic tax cuts.
(b) result in automatic spending increases.
(c) result in both automatic tax cuts and spending increases.
(d) result in automatic spending cuts.

Answer: (d)

Moderate
Multi
Page: 338

16.4: The U.S. Supreme Court declared that part of the Gramm-Rudman-Hollings Act was illegal and that

(a) taxes had to be decreased each year.
(b) expenditures would have to increase by 5% each year.
(c) taxes had to be decreased and expenditures increased proportionally.
(d) the mandated automatic spending cuts had to be approved by the Congress.

Answer: (d)

Moderate
Multi
Page: 338

16.5: The Omnibus Budget Reconciliation Act of 1993

(a) mandated increases of $205 billion in government spending through 1998.
(b) mandated decreases in taxes of $105 billion through 1998.
(c) authorized an additional $250 billion in defense spending for 1994.
(d) sought to reduce the federal deficit of $504.8 billion by 1998.

Answer: (d)

Easy
Fact
Page: 338

**Moderate
Multi
Page: 338**

16.6: The deficit reduction projections contained in the 1993 Omnibus Budget Reconciliation Act were to be achieved through

(a) decreases in government spending of $504.8 billion.
(b) increases in taxes of $504.8 billion.
(c) increases in exports of $504.8 billion.
(d) federal spending cuts of $254.7 billion and tax increases of $250.1 billion.

Answer: (d)

**Moderate
Single
Page: 338**

16.7: The recommended tax increases proposed under the Omnibus Budget Reconciliation Act of 1993 were to be levied upon

(a) high income taxpayers.
(b) middle income taxpayers.
(c) all income level taxpayers.
(d) low income taxpayers.

Answer: (a)

**Moderate
Multi
Page: 338**

16.8: The Republican Party congressional victories in 1994 and its "Contract with America" called for

(a) increases in government spending and taxes.
(b) increases in spending and decreases in taxes.
(c) decreases in spending and increases in taxes.
(d) decreases in spending, taxes, and the federal deficit.

Answer: (d)

**Moderate
Multi
Page: 338**

16.9: The Republican Party's "Contract with America" recommends

(a) tax increases.
(b) spending increases on social programs.
(c) a cyclically balanced budget.
(d) a balanced budget amendment.

Answer: (d)

**Moderate
Multi
Page: 339**

16.10: The government spending multiplier measures the

(a) multiple change in GDP and income that results from an increase or decrease in government spending.
(b) proportional change in imports that results from a change in government spending.
(c) multiple change in GDP and income that results from a change in taxes.
(d) proportional change in imports that result from a change in taxes.

Answer: (a)

**Moderate
Multi
Page: 339**

16.11: If the government spending multiplier were 1.4, a $1 billion decrease in government spending would lower GDP by

(a) $10.4 billion after one year.
(b) $100.4 billion after two years
(c) $1.4 billion after one year.
(d) $2.9 billion after one year.

Answer: (c)

16.12: The government tax multiplier measures the

(a) multiple change in imports when taxes change.
(b) multiple change in exports when taxes change.
(c) multiple change in spending when taxes change.
(d) multiple change in GDP and income that results from an increase or decrease in government taxes.

Answer: (d)

16.13: The amount by which government spending must be decreased to achieve a specified deficit target is dependent upon the value of

(a) tariff levels on certain imported products.
(b) foreign tariff levels on exports.
(c) foreign portfolio investment.
(d) the government expenditures multiplier value.

Answer: (d)

16.14: The amount by which government taxes must be increased to achieve a specified deficit target is dependent upon the value of

(a) tariff levels on certain imported products.
(b) foreign tariff levels on exports.
(c) foreign portfolio investment.
(d) the government tax multiplier value.

Answer: (d)

16.15: A recession and decrease in the nation's GDP will result in

(a) an increase in personal and corporate taxes.
(b) a decrease in government spending on transfer payments for unemployment compensation.
(c) an increase in the nation's imports.
(d) a decrease in personal and corporate taxes and increases in government transfer payments.

Answer: (d)

16.16: An increase in government spending and a decrease in taxes will cause the

(a) deficit to decrease.
(b) deficit to increase.
(c) deficit to remain unchanged.
(d) deficit to decrease slightly.

Answer: (b)

16.17: A decrease in government spending and an increase in taxes will cause the

(a) deficit to decrease.
(b) deficit to remain unchanged.
(c) deficit to increase.
(d) deficit to increase slightly.

Answer: (a)

Challenging
Multi
Page: 339

16.18: If the numerical value of the government spending multiplier is greater than the numerical value of the tax multiplier, then equal increases in spending and taxes will

(a) decrease GDP.
(b) not change GDP.
(c) increase GDP.
(d) decrease GDP slightly.

Answer: (c)

Challenging
Multi
Page: 339

16.19: If the numerical value of the government spending multiplier is greater than the numerical value of the tax multiplier, then equal decreases in spending and taxes will

(a) decrease GDP.
(b) increase GDP.
(c) increase GDP slightly.
(d) not change GDP.

Answer: (a)

Moderate
Multi
Page: 339

16.20: The deficit tends to increase when

(a) GDP decreases.
(b) GDP increases rapidly.
(c) GDP increases slightly.
(d) GDP remains unchanged.

Answer: (a)

Moderate
Multi
Page: 339

16.21: The deficit tends to decrease when

(a) GDP decreases slightly.
(b) GDP decreases rapidly.
(c) GDP increases.
(d) GDP remains unchanged.

Answer: (c)

Easy
Definition
Page: 339

16.22: The deficit response index (DRI) measures the amount by which the deficit changes with a

(a) change in imports.
(b) change in exports.
(c) one dollar change in GDP.
(d) change in foreign investment.

Answer: (c)

Moderate
Fact
Page: 339

16.23: If the deficit response index (DRI) is –.22, it means that a $1 billion decrease in GDP will increase the deficit by

(a) $.88 billion.
(b) $2.2 billion.
(c) $.22 billion.
(d) $8.6 billion.

Answer: (c)

16.24: Assume that government spending decreased by $10 billion to meet a deficit reduction target. If the expenditure multiplier is 2, then GDP will decrease by $20 billion. If the deficit response index (DRI) is 3, this decrease in GDP will increase the deficit by

Challenging
Multi
Page: 339

(a) $10 billion.
(b) $6 billion.
(c) $12 billion.
(d) $2 billion.

Answer: (b)

16.25: If the deficit response index (DRI) is 4, an increase in GDP of $100 billion should

Moderate
Multi
Page: 339

(a) increase the deficit by $20 billion.
(b) decrease the deficit by $40 billion.
(c) decrease the deficit by $4 billion.
(d) increase the deficit by $4 billion.

Answer: (b)

16.26: If the deficit response index (DRI) is 5, a decrease in GDP of $50 billion should

Moderate
Multi
Page: 339

(a) increase the deficit by $25 billion.
(b) increase the deficit by $50 billion.
(c) decrease the deficit by $10 billion.
(d) decrease the deficit by $50 billion.

Answer: (a)

16.27: A negative demand shock is something that

Moderate
Multi
Page: 340

(a) increases the nation's exports.
(b) increases investment and consumer spending.
(c) decreases investment and consumer spending.
(d) increases overall taxes.

Answer: (c)

16.28: Automatic stabilizers represent tax revenue and spending initiatives in the federal budget that

Moderate
Multi
Page: 340

(a) automatically change in response to congressional action.
(b) automatically change in response to changes in the economy.
(c) automatically change in response to the President's actions.
(d) automatically change in response to foreign trade flows.

Answer: (b)

16.29: Examples of automatic stabilizers within the economy include

Moderate
Multi
Page: 340

(a) tariffs on imports.
(b) a tax cut approved by Congress.
(c) defense spending changes.
(d) changes in spending for unemployment compensation and the progressive nature of the federal income tax.

Answer: (d)

Challenging
Multi
Page: 340

16.30: The potential decrease in GDP caused by negative demand shocks is

(a) increased somewhat by the growth of the deficit.
(b) decreased somewhat by the growth of the deficit.
(c) unchanged by the growth of the deficit.
(d) increased significantly by the growth of the deficit.

Answer: (b)

Moderate
Multi
Page: 341

16.31: An increase in taxes and decrease in government spending during a recessional period are examples of

(a) automatic stabilizer policies.
(b) multi-lateral trade policies.
(c) automatic de-stabilizer policies.
(d) import and export tariff issues.

Answer: (c)

Moderate
Multi
Page: 341

16.32: Automatic de-stabilizing policies would tend to

(a) negate inflation and stimulate expansion.
(b) reinforce inflationary pressures and deepen recessionary conditions.
(c) promote the nation's exports.
(d) decrease the nation's imports.

Answer: (b)

Moderate
Multi
Page: 341

16.33: The enacted Gramm-Rudman-Hollings Act would tend to have an

(a) automatic stabilizing impact upon the economy.
(b) automatic de-stabilizing impact upon the economy.
(c) overall neutral impact upon the economy.
(d) overall positive impact upon the economy during any stage of a business cycle.

Answer: (b)

Moderate
Multi
Page: 341

16.34: During periods of negative demand shocks, deficit target reductions such as those mandated in the Gramm-Rudman-Hollings Act would tend to

(a) stimulate the economy and increase employment.
(b) stimulate the nation's imports.
(c) result in additional recessional declines in employment and income.
(d) stimulate defense spending.

Answer: (c)

Moderate
Multi
Page: 341

16.35: Two very important policy objectives of the Federal Reserve are

(a) high levels of output and low rates of inflation.
(b) high levels of output and inflation.
(c) low inflation and levels of output.
(d) increased imports.

Answer: (a)

16.36: Stagflation is an economic condition characterized by

(a) high inflation and low unemployment.
(b) low inflation and low unemployment.
(c) high inflation and high unemployment.
(d) low inflation and high unemployment.

Answer: (c)

Easy
Definition
Page: 341

16.37: The Federal Reserve is likely to increase the money supply during

(a) periods of excessive expansion with high inflation.
(b) periods of moderate expansion with high inflation.
(c) periods of low output and low inflation.
(d) periods of excessive expansion and moderate inflation.

Answer: (c)

Moderate
Multi
Page: 342

16.38: The Federal Reserve is likely to decrease the money supply during

(a) periods of low output and low inflation.
(b) periods of high output and moderate inflation.
(c) periods of moderate output and low inflation.
(d) periods of high output and high rates of inflation.

Answer: (d)

Moderate
Multi
Page: 342

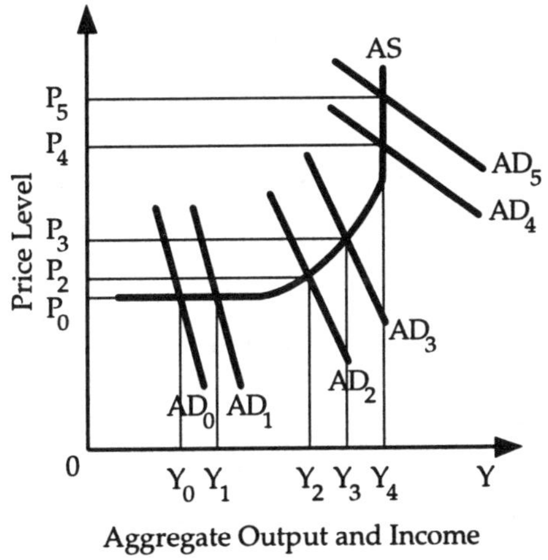

Figure 16.1

(a) the increased income levels of Y_2 to Y_3.
(b) the increased income levels of Y_0 to Y_1.
(c) the decreased income levels of Y_1 to Y_0.
(d) the decreased income levels of Y_3 to Y_2.

Answer: (a)

16.41: In FIG.16.1, an increase in the money supply would not likely change prices at

(a) the increased income levels of Y_0 to Y_1.
(b) the increased income levels of Y_2 to Y_3.
(c) the increased income level at Y_4.
(d) the increased income level of Y_1 to Y_3.

Answer: (a)

Moderate
Multi
Page: 342

16.39: In FIG 16.1, an increase in the money supply would be most inflationary at

(a) the increased income levels of Y_2 to Y_3.
(b) the increased income levels of Y_3 to Y_1.
(c) the maximum output level of Y_4.
(d) the increased income levels of Y_1 to Y_2.

Answer: (c)

Moderate
Multi
Page: 342

16.40: In FIG 16.1, an increase in the money supply would be moderately inflationary at

Moderate
Multi
Page: 342

Challenging
Multi
Page: 342

16.42: The Federal Reserve's policy to "lean against the wind" means that

(a) open market operations are used to raise interest rates during periods of economic growth.
(b) changes in reserve requirements are used to negate excessive growth.
(c) the discount rate is changed to increase inflation.
(d) open market operations are used to decrease interest rates during periods of economic growth.

Answer: (a)

Moderate
Multi
Page: 342

16.43: The Federal Reserve's policy to "lean against the wind" means that

(a) interest rates are increased as the economy contracts.
(b) reserve requirements are increased as the economy contracts.
(c) interest rates are decreased gradually as the economy contracts.
(d) reserve requirements are increased significantly during an economic slowdown.

Answer: (c)

Moderate
Fact
Page: 343

16.44: The Federal Reserve's behavior during the 1990-1991 recession is a clear example of its tendency to

(a) "lean against the wind".
(b) always decrease required reserves.
(c) always increase required reserves.
(d) always increase and decrease required reserves.

Answer: (a)

Moderate
Definition
Page: 345

16.45: Stabilization policy represents the use of monetary and fiscal policy to

(a) expand the economy at the expense of inflation.
(b) limit economic growth over the long run.
(c) limit inflation and contract economic growth.
(d) smooth out fluctuations in output and employment and keep prices as stable as possible.

Answer: (d)

Easy
Definition
Page: 345

16.46: Time lags which often erode effectiveness of monetary and fiscal policy measures represent

(a) delays in the response of the economy to stabilization policy.
(b) the foreign response to price changes.
(c) the change in export and import prices.
(d) the change in exchange rates.

Answer: (a)

Easy
Definition
Page: 347

16.47: The recognition lag of stabilization policy represents

(a) the time that is necessary to put the desired policy into effect.
(b) the time that it takes for policy makers to recognize the existence of a boom or bust.
(c) the time that it takes for the economy to adjust to the new conditions after a new policy is introduced.
(d) the time needed for the Federal Reserve Board to meet.

Answer: (b)

16.48: The implementation policy of stabilization policy represents

Easy
Definition
Page: 347

(a) the time that is needed for policy makers to recognize the need to do something.
(b) the time needed for the economy to adjust to new conditions after new policies are introduced.
(c) the time needed for the Federal Reserve to meet.
(d) the time that is necessary to put the desired policy into effect once economists and policy makers recognize the need.

Answer: (d)

16.49: The implementation lag for monetary policy is generally

Moderate
Multi
Page: 348

(a) much longer than it is for fiscal policy.
(b) the same as it is for fiscal policy.
(c) much shorter than it is for fiscal policy.
(d) unrelated to Federal Reserve action.

Answer: (c)

16.50: The response lag of stabilization policy represents

Easy
Definition
Page: 348

(a) the time that it takes for the economy to adjust to the new conditions after a new policy has been implemented.
(b) the time that is necessary to put the desired policy into effect.
(c) the time that it takes for policy makers to recognize the existence of a boom or bust.
(d) the time needed for Congress to enact a tax cut.

Answer: (a)

16.51: The response lag in fiscal policy represents

Challenging
Multi
Page: 348

(a) the time needed for the consumers and businesses who benefit from changes in government spending or taxes to change their spending.
(b) the time needed to change unemployment compensation payments.
(c) the time needed to change tax laws.
(d) the time needed to change defense spending.

Answer: (a)

16.52: In general, how long does it take for the full effects of fiscal policy changes to be felt within the economy?

Moderate
Multi
Page: 349

(a) 5 years
(b) 10 years
(c) 1 month
(d) 1 year

Answer: (d)

16.53: In general, the cyclical changes within the Japanese economy between 1980 and 1993 have been

Moderate
Multi
Page: 353

(a) very severe compared to the United States.
(b) very mild compared to the United States.
(c) equal to the United States.
(d) the worst of any industrialized nation.

Answer: (b)

Moderate
Single
Page: 354

16.54: While employment conditions have varied among the European nations, a general characteristic of all the European nations between 1980 and 1993 has been the

(a) relatively low rates of unemployment.
(b) extremely high rates of employment.
(c) fairly high rates of unemployment.
(d) uncontrollable levels of inflation.

Answer: (c)

Moderate
Multi
Page: 340

16.55: For spending cuts of a certain amount to reduce the deficit by the same amount, the government

(a) tax multiplier must be 2.
(b) spending multiplier must be 2.
(c) spending multiplier must be zero.
(d) tax multiplier must be 3.

Answer: (c)

Easy
Single
Page: 339

16.56: The federal deficit tends to rise when

(a) GDP increases.
(b) GDP decreases.
(c) GDP remains unchanged.
(d) exports increase.

Answer: (b)

Easy
Single
Page: 339

16.57: The federal deficit tends to fall when

(a) GDP increases.
(b) GDP decreases.
(c) GDP remains unchanged.
(d) exports decrease.

Answer: (a)

Moderate
Multi
Page: 354

16.58: One explanation for the general pattern of relatively high levels of unemployment throughout Europe during 1980 to 1993 is that

(a) governments' monetary policies were not expansionary enough.
(b) governments' tax policies were too expansionary.
(c) governments' spending policies were too expansionary.
(d) exports were increasing at too rapid a rate.

Answer: (a)

Moderate
Multi
Page: 346

16.59: Milton Friedman's criticism of stabilization policy being compared to "the Fool in the Shower" means that government

(a) is stimulating or contracting the economy at the appropriate times.
(b) is stimulating or contracting the economy at the wrong times.
(c) is excessively stimulating or contracting the economy at any time.
(d) is not sufficiently stimulating or contracting the economy at any time.

Answer: (b)

16.60: The implementation lag for fiscal policy tends to be much longer than for monetary policy because it requires

(a) changes in required reserves.
(b) changes in open market operations.
(c) changes in congressional-approved spending and tax programs.
(d) changes in exports and imports.

Answer: (c)

Moderate
Multi
Page: 348

16.61: The implementation lag for monetary policy tends to be much shorter than for fiscal policy because it requires

(a) Congressional changes in spending and taxes.
(b) changes in exports and imports.
(c) changes in state funding rebates.
(d) rather immediate changes in open market operations.

Answer: (d)

Moderate
Multi
Page: 348

16.62: During periods of excessive expansionary growth characterized by strong inflationary pressures, the Federal Reserve will likely

(a) increase the money supply to increase interest rates.
(b) increase the money supply to decrease interest rates.
(c) decrease the money supply to increase interest rates.
(d) decrease the money supply to decrease interest rates.

Answer: (c)

Easy
Single
Page: 342

16.63: During periods of recessionary decline, the Federal Reserve will likely

(a) decrease the money supply to increase interest rates.
(b) increase the money supply to decrease interest rates.
(c) increase the money supply to increase interest rates.
(d) decrease the money supply to decrease interest rates.

Answer: (b)

Easy
Single
Page: 342

16.64: A measure of how the government deficit changes in response to a change in the nation's GDP is called

(a) a recognition lag.
(b) a response lag.
(c) a deficit response index.
(d) a policy lag.

Answer: (c)

Easy
Definition
Page: 339

16.65: The increase in government spending had a multiple expanded effect upon GDP income of $100 billion. If the deficit response index is 15, this means that

(a) the deficit will increase by $55 billion.
(b) the deficit will decrease by $85 billion.
(c) the deficit will decrease by $15 billion.
(d) the deficit will increase by $15 billion.

Answer: (d)

Easy
Single
Page: 339

Challenging
Multi
Page: 340

16.66: If the Federal Reserve sought to offset the effects of a decrease in government spending by increasing the money supply, lowering interest rates, and stimulating investment spending to equal the spending cut, the net numerical multiplier effect upon the economy would be

(a) 2.
(b) 1.
(c) 0.
(d) 10.

Answer: (c)

Easy
Definition
Page: 340

16.67: A decrease in consumer or investment spending is called a

(a) negative demand shock.
(b) automatic stabilizer.
(c) non-automatic stabilizer.
(d) budget stimulant.

Answer: (a)

Moderate
Multi
Page: 340

16.68: The economic impact of automatic stabilizers during expansionary periods is to

(a) moderate expansionary growth.
(b) accelerate expansionary growth.
(c) have no impact upon expansionary growth.
(d) increase exports.

Answer: (a)

Moderate
Multi
Page: 340

16.69: The economic impact of automatic stabilizers during inflationary periods is to

(a) accelerate inflationary pressures.
(b) moderate inflationary pressures.
(c) have no impact upon inflation.
(d) increase exports.

Answer: (b)

Easy
Definition
Page: 341

16.70: An economic condition characterized by high unemployment and excessive inflation is called

(a) expansionary growth.
(b) recessionary downturn.
(c) stagflation.
(d) depression.

Answer: (c)

Easy
Multi
Page: 342

16.71: During periods of stagflation, an increase in the money supply will

(a) decrease prices.
(b) decrease output.
(c) increase exports.
(d) increase prices.

Answer: (d)

16.72: During periods of stagflation, decreases in the money supply will

(a) lower inflation and the level of output.
(b) increase inflation and the level of output.
(c) increase inflation and lower the level of output.
(d) increase exports.

Answer: (a)

Easy
Multi
Page: 342

16.73: A policy initiative by the Federal Reserve to use open market operations to raise interest rates gradually in an effort to prevent the economy from expanding too rapidly is called

(a) an easy money policy.
(b) stagflation policy.
(c) to "lean against the wind".
(d) an expansionary policy.

Answer: (c)

Moderate
Multi
Page: 342

16.74: A policy initiative by the Federal Reserve to use open market operations to lower interest rates gradually in an effort to lessen or stop a cyclical contraction is often called

(a) a tight money policy.
(b) an anti-inflation policy.
(c) an export oriented policy.
(d) to "lean against the wind".

Answer: (d)

Moderate
Multi
Page: 342

16.75: The critics of stabilization policy such as Milton Friedman argue that monetary policy is comparable to "the Fool in the Shower." This means that

(a) policy initiatives are often de-stabilizing because of time lags.
(b) policy initiatives are perfect in maintaining the economy.
(c) policy initiatives are perfectly timed.
(d) policy initiatives always impact at the proper time in stabilizing the economy.

Answer: (a)

Moderate
Multi
Page: 346

16.76: When stock prices rise,

(a) household wealth and consumption both fall.
(b) household wealth and consumption both rise.
(c) household wealth rises, but household consumption falls.
(d) household wealth falls, but household consumption rises.

Answer: (b)

Easy
Fact
Page: 349

16.77: When stock prices fall,

(a) household wealth and consumption both rise.
(b) household wealth rises, but household consumption falls.
(c) household wealth and consumption both fall.
(d) household wealth falls, but household consumption rises.

Answer: (c)

Easy
Fact
Page: 350

<table>
<tr><td>Easy
Fact
Page: 350</td><td>

16.78: On one day - October 19, 1987 - the value of stocks fell nearly $700 billion. This event corresponded to a

(a) large decrease in household wealth.
(b) small decrease in household wealth.
(c) large increase in household wealth.
(d) small increase in household wealth.

Answer: (a)

</td></tr>
<tr><td>Easy
Fact
Page: 350</td><td>

16.79: It has been estimated that households adjust their consumption by about _____ of their decrease in wealth each year.

(a) 1%
(b) 5%
(c) 25%
(d) 100%

Answer: (b)

</td></tr>
<tr><td>Challenging
Multi
Page: 350</td><td>

16.80: Assume that households adjust their consumption by about 5% of their decrease in wealth. Also assume that the multiplier is 1.5. A $100 billion decrease in wealth will cause GDP to decrease by

(a) $5 billion.
(b) $7.5 billion.
(c) $66.67 billion.
(d) $150 billion.

Answer: (b)

</td></tr>
<tr><td>Easy
Fact
Page: 350</td><td>

16.81: If you buy a bond from a firm, you are

(a) borrowing money from the firm.
(b) a partial owner of the firm and have a claim on the firm's profits.
(c) lending money to the firm.
(d) trading future consumption for current consumption.

Answer: (c)

</td></tr>
<tr><td>Easy
Definition
Page: 350</td><td>

16.82: The payment on a bond is known as the

(a) maturity payment.
(b) dividend payment.
(c) yield.
(d) coupon.

Answer: (d)

</td></tr>
<tr><td>Moderate
Single
Page: 350</td><td>

16.83: If you buy a $2,000, 10%, 10-year bond from ABC Company, you will receive

(a) $200 a year for nine years, and in the tenth year you will receive $2,000.
(b) $200 a year for nine years, and in the tenth year you will receive a payment of $2,200.
(c) $2,200 the first year, and $200 every year for the next nine years.
(d) $200 each year until you have been repaid your initial expenditure of $2,000.

Answer: (b)

</td></tr>
</table>

16.84: When interest rates rise, bond prices

(a) remain constant, because the annual interest payment on a bond does not change with fluctuations in the interest rate.
(b) fall, because a person would be willing to buy the bond only at less than its face value.
(c) rise, because an individual would be willing to buy the bond at more than its face value.
(d) rise, because the interest payments made on the bond increase as the interest rates increase.

Answer: (b)

Moderate
Fact
Page: 350

16.85: When interest rates increase, bond holders

(a) enjoy a capital gain.
(b) are unaffected, because the coupon payment on a bond is independent of interest rate changes.
(c) suffer a capital loss.
(d) suffer a loss in current income, but no change in wealth.

Answer: (c)

Easy
Fact
Page: 350

16.86: If interest rates fall, bond prices _____ and bond holders _____.

(a) fall; suffer a capital loss
(b) fall; experience a capital gain
(c) rise; suffer a capital loss
(d) rise; experience a capital gain

Answer: (d)

Moderate
Single
Page: 350

16.87: If a bond is listed at "7 1/5 04", that the bond pays a coupon of _____ per $100 of face value and matures in _____.

(a) $7.50; 1994
(b) $7.50; 2004
(c) $7.20; 2004
(d) $7.20; 1994

Answer: (c)

Moderate
Multi
Page: 351

16.88: A bond pays a coupon of $9.25 per $100 of face value, but the current yield is 10%. This means that the current price of the bond

(a) must be higher than its face value.
(b) must be lower than its face value.
(c) must equal its face value, because the coupon rate will remain constant at 9 1/4 even though the yield is now 10%.
(d) is either higher or lower than its face value, depending upon the demand for bonds.

Answer: (b)

Moderate
Single
Page: 351

16.89: When a corporation issues new shares of stock,

(a) it adds to its debt.
(b) it brings in additional owners of the firm.
(c) it adds more debt and brings in additional owners to the firm.
(d) it increases its liabilities and reduces its assets.

Answer: (b)

Easy
Fact
Page: 352

Easy
Fact
Page: 352

16.90: Which of the following statements is correct?

(a) Both stocks and bonds promise a fixed annual payment.
(b) A stock, but not a bond, promises a fixed annual payment.
(c) A bond, but not a stock, promises a fixed annual payment.
(d) Neither a bond nor a stock promises a fixed annual payment.

Answer: (c)

Easy
Definition
Page: 352

16.91: On the stock page, the column titled "yield percent" is found by taking the dividend as a percentage of the stock's

(a) highest price during the year.
(b) lowest price during the year.
(c) average price during the year.
(d) closing price for the day.

Answer: (d)

Easy
Definition
Page: 352

16.92: The price-earning ratio of a stock is the ratio of the price of a share of stock to

(a) the company's total earnings per share.
(b) the dividends the company pays.
(c) the company's retained earnings.
(d) the company's after-tax profits.

Answer: (a)

Moderate
Single
Page: 352

16.93: The price of a share of stock in Nashbar Bike is $25 and the earnings per share are $10. The price-earnings ratio for Nashbar Bike is

(a) .4.
(b) .6.
(c) 1.67.
(d) 2.5.

Answer: (d)

TRUE/FALSE QUESTIONS

Easy
Definition
Page: 337

16.94: The annual federal budget deficit represents the difference between the level of government expenditures and the lesser level of tax revenues.

Answer: True

Easy
Definition
Page: 337

16.95: The nation's total federal debt represents the total of all accumulated deficits minus surpluses over time.

Answer: True

Easy
Fact
Page: 337

16.96: The legislative intent of the Gramm-Rudman-Hollings Act was to increase the nation's spending on defense.

Answer: False

16.97: The Omnibus Budget Reconciliation Act of 1993 sought to sharply increase government spending for health care reform and reduce taxes.

Answer: False

Easy
Fact
Page: 338

16.98: The Republican Party's "Contract with America" recommends spending increases on social programs and sizable tax increases for higher incomes.

Answer: False

Easy
Fact
Page: 338

16.99: The budget deficit tends to increase when GDP decreases as a result of the impact of the automatic stabilizers and the need for expansionary government initiatives.

Answer: True

Easy
Fact
Page: 340

16.100: The deficit response index (DRI) measures the change in the budget deficit in response to changes in the nation's GDP.

Answer: True

Easy
Definition
Page: 339

16.101: A negative demand shock increases consumer and investment spending and tends to lessen the budget deficit.

Answer: False

Moderate
Multi
Page: 340

16.102: The Federal Reserve is likely to increase the money supply during periods of low output and low inflation to stimulate economic growth.

Answer: True

Moderate
Multi
Page: 342

16.103: As interest rates fall, bond prices will fall and bondholders will have a capital loss.

Answer: False

Moderate
Application
Page: 350

16.104: When interest rates rise, bond prices fall.

Answer: True

Easy
Fact
Page: 848

SHORT ANSWER QUESTIONS

16.105: Explain the "balanced-budget amendment" that is an integral part of the Republican Party's contract with America. Why are many economists who favor deficit reduction opposed to the balanced-budget amendment? Describe a condition in which a mandated balanced budget would be harmful to the nation's economic health

Moderate
Application
Page: 338

Answer: The "balanced-budget amendment" that has been introduced by the Republican Party's Contract with America is a deficit reduction measure. It would require that the annual government expenditures and taxes be equal so that budget deficits would be eliminated. Opponents of the balanced-budget amendment are concerned that it may seriously weaken the ability of government to implement appropriate macroeconomic policies. A balanced-budget requirement would negate the ability of the national government to pursue expansionary macroeconomic policies during a recession. Government would not be able to stimulate the economy with increased spending or reduced taxes.

Difficult
Math
Page: 339

16.106: Assume that government spending is reduced by $10 billion, the value of the expenditure multiplier is 2, and the DRI is -.25. What is the net effect of the spending decrease upon the deficit?7

Answer: The expenditure multiplier of 2 means that the decrease in government spending of $10 billion will decrease GDP by $20 billion. The $20 billion decrease in GDP will increase the deficit by $5 billion (20 x -2.5). Thus, the net effect of the spending cut is to lower the deficit by $5 billion (10 billion - 5 billion = 5 billion).

Moderate
Application
Page: 339

16.107: What would be the Federal Reserve's expansionary response to offset the effects of a decrease in government spending?

Answer: The Federal Reserve would offset the effect of a decrease in government spending by expanding the nation's money supply. This would tend to lower interest rates which would stimulate increases in private business investment spending.

Moderate
Application
Page: 342

16.108: Explain the Federal Reserve's policy that is often called : to "lean against the wind".

Answer: The "lean against the wind" policy means that the Federal Reserve uses open market operations to raise interest rates gradually to prevent the economy from expanding too rapidly. Conversely, the Fed lowers interest rates gradually over a contraction to lessen the recessionary slide.

Moderate
Application
Page: 347

16.109: Explain the nature of the implementation lag for fiscal policy.

Answer: Discretionary fiscal policy measures most often require cooperative support from both the executive and legislative branches of government. Issues regarding government spending and taxes are often endlessly debated, reviewed, and changed, which leads to lengthy policy delays. The response lag for fiscal policy is most critically dependent upon the government spending and tax multipliers. Changes in taxes may not stimulate immediate changes in consumer spending, and government spending changes may not have an immediate multiplier effect if the income from additional spending is held in idle balances.

Moderate
Application
Page: 348

16.110: What is the most important determinant of the response lag for monetary policy?

Answer: Monetary policy impacts upon interest rates which then affect consumer and business investment spending. The response lag is most dependent upon the time that elapses before consumers and businesses react to the change in interest rates. The response lag will be very long if consumers and businesses fail to alter their spending as interest rates change.

Moderate
Application
Page: 354

16.111: Explain some of the reasons that have been suggested for persistent high unemployment in Europe in recent years.

Answer: It has been suggested that the persistent high rates of unemployment in Europe have resulted from: generous social welfare benefits, union-imposed high wages, technological labor displacement, and a lack of aggressive expansionary government policies.

Moderate
Multi
Page: 340

16.112: Explain automatic stabilizers and their impact upon the economy.

Answer: Automatic stabilizers represent automatic and non-discretionary changes in government spending and tax revenue receipts that seek to be counter-cyclical. Thus, they result in higher government spending and lower taxes during a recession, and lower government spending and higher taxes during a rapid expansionary period.

16.113: Illustrate examples of the counter-cyclical effects of the automatic stabilizers.

Moderate
Multi
Page: 340

Answer: Government spending for needed public assistance for unemployment compensation are examples of automatic spending changes. Government spending for unemployment compensation increases during a recession as unemployment rises, and decreases during an expansionary period when unemployment declines.

Also, the progressive income tax increases tax obligations of consumers as incomes rise during economic expansion, and decreases tax obligations as incomes decline during recessionary periods. They tend to moderate the recessionary decline in spending and the excessive spending of rapid expansion.

16.114: Under what economic conditions could the deficit reduction targets of the Gramm-Rudman-Hollings Act be de-stabilizing?

Moderate
Multi
Page: 341

Answer: The deficit reduction targets of the Gramm-Rudman-Hollings Act mandated decreases in government spending and increases in taxes, regardless of economic conditions. Efforts to reduce the deficit during a recession would further accelerate the recessionary downturn and contribute to decreases in GDP income and employment.

16.115: Explain the important policy objectives of Federal Reserve monetary policies.

Moderate
Multi
Page: 341

Answer: The Federal Reserve strives to evolve and implement monetary policies that will provide for sustained and non-inflationary economic growth. These policies are based upon the relationship between changes in the money supply, the inverse impact upon interest rates, and the resulting effects upon consumer and business investment spending.

16.116: Explain the relationship between changes in the money supply, interest rates, spending, and prices.

Moderate
Multi
Page: 342

Answer: Changes in the money supply inversely impact upon interest rates. If the Federal Reserve seeks to pursue an anti-inflationary policy, it would decrease the money supply which will increase interest rates. Higher interest rates will decrease consumer and business investment spending, which in turn will moderate aggregate spending and the inflationary pressure. To pursue an expansionary policy, the Federal Reserve would expand the money supply which will lower interest rates and stimulate additional consumer and business investment spending. The increase in aggregate demand will stimulate the economy.

16.117: Explain stagflation and the policy dilemma it presents.

Moderate
Multi
Page: 342

Answer: Stagflation is a condition characterized by high levels of inflation and unemployment. Thus, if the Federal Reserve pursues an expansionary policy to eliminate unemployment, the increased spending will further accelerate inflation. Equally, if the Federal Reserve seeks to pursue an anti-inflationary policy, the lessened spending will further accentuate the recessionary conditions of unemployment.

16.118: Explain stabilization policy.

Moderate
Multi
Page: 345

Answer: Stabilization policy involves the use of both monetary and fiscal policy measures to maintain sustainable long-term non-inflationary economic growth. To expand the economy, stabilization policies would consist of coordinated efforts to increase aggregate spending through increases in the money supply and increased government spending and lower taxes. To negate inflation, stabilization policies would consist of coordinated efforts to decrease aggregate spending through decreases in the money supply and decreased government spending and higher taxes.

Moderate
Multi
Page: 347

16.119: Identify the time lags that are associated with stabilization policies.

Answer: Effective stabilization policies are subject to various time lags that can seriously weaken its objective of achieving non-inflationary and sustained economic growth. The recognition lag is the elapsed time for policy makers to realize the need to do something. The implementation lag is the time needed to implement the policies and the response lag is the time between the introduction of the policy measures and their impact.

Difficult
Definition
Page: 352

16.120: Explain the differences between a stock and a bond.

Answer: A stock represents ownership and gives the owner the right to have some degree of input in the management of the company. A bondholder, however, has no say in a firm's management. As well, owning stocks does not promise a fixed payment at the end of some period, like holding bonds does. In fact the returns on stocks, unlike bonds, are extremely variable and can fluctuate depending on the performance of the company.

Easy
Definition
Page: 350

16.121: Define and describe the characteristics of a bond. Explain the relationship between interest rates and the price of a bond.

Answer: A bond is a financial instrument that a firm can issue in exchange for cash. Bonds are issued with a face value, generally in denominations of $1000, that represents the amount the buyer agrees to loan the bond issuer. Bonds also have a maturity date, on which the firm promises to pay back the funds that were lent out. Lastly, there is a fixed payment of a specified amount generally paid annually to the bondholder. This fixed payment is called a coupon and is determined using the prevailing interest rate at the time the bond is issued. The bond price and interest rates move in opposite directions. Thus, if interest rates climb, the price of bonds will fall. The price of the bond would need to fall because no one would willingly buy the bond if it cost more than other investments that yield the same amount in the future.

Easy
Definition
Page: 350

16.122: Suppose you are interested in helping the Carson City Transit Authority support a new bond issue for extension of the existing highway network. In order to undertake this project they are issuing $5,000, 10%, 10-year bonds. If you decide to buy the bond, what will your annual interest payment be? How much will the transit authority owe you in the tenth year? After ten years, what will be the return on your $5,000 initial investment? If the interest rate went up to 12%, what would happen to the price of the bond?

Answer: $5,000 * .10 = $500. Your annual interest is $500. In the tenth year, they will owe you your original $5,000 plus 10% or $500, for a total of $5,500. After ten years you will have made $500 a year for nine years, plus $5500 in the tenth year. Thus, $5500 + $4500 = $10,000. If you subtract out your initial investment of $5000, you will have made $5000 on the bond investment. As interest rates increase, the price of bonds must fall in order to remain competitive with other investments. For example, if the interest rate went up to 12% the price of the bond would fall to $4545.45.

Easy
Math
Page: 350

16.123: Many financial experts believe the market is due for a correction in the upcoming year. Assume that this occurs in February 1999 and the value of stocks declines by $500 billion. Answer the following questions concerning this market correction. Assume all stocks are held by households and that they change their consumption patterns by 6% of any decline in wealth. In general, what happens to consumption? After the value of stocks has fallen, how much will GDP change if the multiplier is 3?

Answer: When the stock market falls, generally consumption declines because the wealth of all households is affected. $500 * .06 = $30. With a $500 billion decline in wealth, households will decrease consumption by $30 billion. A $30 billion change in consumption will cause GDP to fall by $90 billion or $30 * 3 = $90.

16.124: A $1.00 decrease in wealth leads roughly to a $.05 decrease in consumption spending per year. The multiplier for the economy is approximately 1.4. If there is a $500 billion decrease in the value of stocks, what will be the change in aggregate output? How will your answer change if the multiplier increases to 1.6?

Challenging
Multi
Page: 350

Answer: If the multiplier is 1.4, a $500 billion decrease in wealth will lead to a $35 billion decrease in aggregate output. If the multiplier is 1.6, a $500 billion decrease in wealth will lead to a $40 billion decrease in aggregate output.

17 Household and Firm Behavior in the Macroeconomy

(Chapter 32 in Combined Text)

17.1: The proportion of income households spend on consumption is known as the

(a) marginal propensity to consume.
(b) average propensity to consume.
(c) household spending multiplier.
(d) average standard of living.

Easy
Definition
Page: 358

Answer: (b)

17.2: Natalie earns $40,000 and spends $30,000. Natalie's APC is

(a) .25.
(b) .75.
(c) 1.33.
(d) 4.

Easy
Single
Page: 358

Answer: (b)

17.3: Aaron earns $90,000 and spends $20,000. Aaron's APC is

(a) .25.
(b) .75.
(c) .22.
(d) 4.

Easy
Single
Page: 358

Answer: (c)

17.4: David's APC is .8 and he earns $60,000. David spends

(a) $30,000.
(b) $48,000.
(c) $75,000.
(d) an amount that cannot be determined from this information.

Moderate
Single
Page: 358

Answer: (b)

17.5: Bruce's APC is .9 and he earns $20,000. Bruce spends

(a) $18,000.
(b) $20,000.
(c) $25,000.
(d) an amount that cannot be determined from this information.

Moderate
Single
Page: 358

Answer: (a)

17.6: According to Keynes, as income rises, the APC

(a) falls.
(b) rises.
(c) remains constant.
(d) first rises, then falls.

Easy
Fact
Page: 358

Answer: (a)

465

Easy
Definition
Page: 358

17.7: A theory of household consumption that assumes households make consumption decisions based on their expectations of lifetime income is known as the

(a) interest income theory of consumption.
(b) classical theory of consumption.
(c) life-cycle theory of consumption.
(d) Keynesian theory of consumption.

Answer: (c)

Easy
Fact
Page: 358

17.8: People tend to

(a) consume less than they earn during their prime working years.
(b) consume more than they earn during their prime working years.
(c) consume less than they earn during their early and later working years.
(d) always consume less than they earn.

Answer: (a)

Easy
Fact
Page: 359

17.9: Households are said to have negative wealth when

(a) the market value of their assets is zero.
(b) the value of their assets is greater than the debts they owe.
(c) the value of their assets is equal to the debts they owe.
(d) the value of their assets is less than the debts they owe.

Answer: (d)

Easy
Fact
Page: 359

17.10: Households are said to have positive wealth when

(a) the market value of their assets is greater than zero.
(b) the value of their assets is greater than the debts they owe.
(c) the value of their assets is less than the debts they owe.
(d) the value of their assets is equal to the debts they owe.

Answer: (b)

Moderate
Single
Page: 359

17.11: Refer to Figure 17.1. Ann's APC is highest between points

(a) OA and AB.
(b) AB and BC.
(c) OA and CD.
(d) BC and CD.

Answer: (c)

Moderate
Single
Page: 359

17.12: Refer to Figure 17.1. Ann's APC is low between points

(a) OA and AB.
(b) AB and BC.
(c) OA and CD.
(d) BC and CD.

Answer: (b)

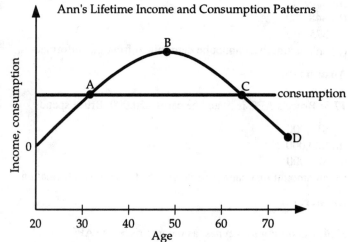

Figure 17.1

17.13: Refer to Figure 17.1. Ann is borrowing over the range

(a) OA.
(b) AB.
(c) BC.
(d) CD.

Answer: (a)

Easy
Single
Page: 359

17.14: Refer to Figure 17.1. Ann is spending accumulated savings over the range

(a) OA.
(b) AB.
(c) BC.
(d) CD.

Answer: (d)

Easy
Single
Page: 359

17.15: The key difference between the Keynesian theory of consumption and the life-cycle theory is that

(a) the Keynesian theory suggests that consumption and saving decisions are likely to be based on expectations of future income alone.
(b) the life-cycle theory suggests that consumption and saving decisions are likely to be based on current income alone.
(c) the life-cycle theory suggests that consumption and saving decisions are likely to be based on both current income and expectations of future income.
(d) the Keynesian theory suggests that consumption and saving decisions are likely to be based on pre-tax income alone.

Answer: (c)

Moderate
Fact
Page: 359

17.16: The average level of one's expected future income stream is

(a) permanent income.
(b) disposable income.
(c) gross income.
(d) taxable income.

Answer: (a)

Easy
Definition
Page: 359

17.17: The life-cycle theory of consumption can be summarized by saying that consumption decisions are based

(a) only on current income.
(b) on permanent income rather than current income.
(c) on current income rather than permanent income.
(d) on an individual's highest expected annual income.

Answer: (b)

Easy
Fact
Page: 359

17.18: Which of the following statements is true?

(a) Households make consumption decisions first, followed by labor supply decisions.
(b) Households make labor supply decisions first, followed by consumption decisions.
(c) There is no connection between a household's labor supply and consumption decisions.
(d) Households make consumption and labor supply decisions simultaneously.

Answer: (d)

Easy
Fact
Page: 360

Easy
Fact
Page: 360

17.19: The key variable that determines how a household responds to the trade-off between the goods and services that wage income will buy and nonmarket activities is the

(a) price of market goods and services.
(b) wage rate.
(c) value placed on nonmarket production.
(d) value placed on market-produced goods.

Answer: (b)

Moderate
Fact
Page: 360

17.20: An increase in the wage rate means that the opportunity cost of

(a) leisure is lower.
(b) nonmarket production is lower.
(c) nonmarket production is higher.
(d) market-produced goods is higher.

Answer: (c)

Moderate
Single
Page: 360

17.21: The opportunity cost of leisure will fall if

(a) the wage rate increases.
(b) the wage rate decreases.
(c) nonlabor income increases.
(d) nonlabor income decreases.

Answer: (b)

Moderate
Fact
Page: 360

17.22: The substitution effect of a wage rate decrease should lead to

(a) an increase in the quantity of labor supplied and a decrease in leisure.
(b) an increase in the quantity of labor supplied and an increase in leisure.
(c) a decrease in quantity of labor supplied and an increase in leisure.
(d) a decrease in the quantity of labor supplied and a decrease in leisure.

Answer: (c)

Moderate
Fact
Page: 360

17.23: The substitution effect of a wage rate increase should lead to

(a) an increase in the quantity of labor supplied and a decrease in leisure.
(b) an increase in the quantity of labor supplied and an increase in leisure.
(c) a decrease in quantity of labor supplied and an increase in leisure.
(d) a decrease in the quantity of labor supplied and a decrease in leisure.

Answer: (a)

Moderate
Fact
Page: 360

17.24: The income effect of a wage rate decrease should lead to

(a) an increase in the quantity of labor supplied and a decrease in leisure.
(b) an increase in the quantity of labor supplied and an increase in leisure.
(c) a decrease in quantity of labor supplied and an increase in leisure.
(d) a decrease in the quantity of labor supplied and a decrease in leisure.

Answer: (a)

Moderate
Fact
Page: 360

17.25: The income effect of a wage rate increase should lead to

(a) an increase in the quantity of labor supplied and a decrease in leisure.
(b) an increase in the quantity of labor supplied and an increase in leisure.
(c) a decrease in quantity of labor supplied and an increase in leisure.
(d) a decrease in the quantity of labor supplied and a decrease in leisure.

Answer: (c)

17.26: A combination of the income and substitution effects of a wage increase leaves us with

Moderate
Fact
Page: 360

(a) an increase in the amount of labor supplied.
(b) a decrease in the amount of labor supplied.
(c) no change in the amount of labor supplied.
(d) an ambiguous result with respect to the amount of labor supplied.

Answer: (d)

17.27: Paul got a raise from $10 an hour to $11 an hour. As a result of the wage increase, Paul desires to work more hours and take fewer hours of leisure. For Paul

Moderate
Multi
Page: 360

(a) the income effect dominates the substitution effect.
(b) the substitution effect dominates the income effect.
(c) the substitution effect must equal the income effect.
(d) the substitution effect must be zero.

Answer: (b)

17.28: Derrick got a raise from $5 an hour to $7 an hour. As a result of the wage increase, Derrick desires to work more hours and take less hours of leisure. For Derrick

Moderate
Multi
Page: 360

(a) the income effect dominates the substitution effect.
(b) the substitution effect dominates the income effect.
(c) the substitution effect must equal the income effect.
(d) the substitution effect must be zero.

Answer: (b)

17.29: Yvette's hourly wage rate was reduced from $18 to $16. As a result of the wage decrease, Yvette desires to work more hours and take fewer hours of leisure. For Yvette

Challenging
Multi
Page: 360

(a) the income effect must be zero.
(b) the substitution effect dominates the income effect.
(c) the substitution effect must equal the income effect.
(d) the income effect dominates the substitution effect.

Answer: (d)

17.30: Empirical evidence with respect to the labor supply decision suggests that

Moderate
Fact
Page: 360

(a) the income effect seems to dominate for most people, which means that the aggregate labor supply responds negatively to an increase in the wage rate.
(b) the income effect seems to dominate for most people, which means that the aggregate labor supply responds positively to an increase in the wage rate.
(c) the substitution effect seems to dominate for most people, which means that the aggregate labor supply responds negatively to an increase in the wage rate.
(d) the substitution effect seems to dominate for most people, which means that the aggregate labor supply responds positively to an increase in the wage rate.

Answer: (d)

Easy
Fact
Page: 361

17.31: If the wage rate rises, then consumption

(a) rises because the income and substitution effects are working in opposite directions to change consumption.
(b) falls because the income and substitution effects are both working in the same direction to decrease consumption.
(c) rises because the income and substitution effects are both working in the same direction to increase consumption.
(d) falls because the income and substitution effects are working in opposite directions to change consumption.

Answer: (c)

Easy
Definition
Page: 360

17.32: The wage rate in current dollars is the

(a) real wage rate.
(b) deflated wage rate.
(c) nominal wage rate.
(d) life-cycle wage.

Answer: (c)

Easy
Definition
Page: 360

17.33: The wage rate that is adjusted for changes in the price level over time, is the

(a) real wage rate.
(b) nominal wage rate.
(c) expected future wage rate.
(d) money wage rate.

Answer: (a)

Easy
Single
Page: 361

17.34: Jim's nominal wage increased by 10% and the prices of goods that Jim buys increased by 15%. Jim's real wage has

(a) increased.
(b) decreased.
(c) remained constant.
(d) changed by 5% but the direction of the change is ambiguous.

Answer: (b)

Moderate
Multi
Page: 360

17.35: Pam's nominal wage is $20 and the price index is 2. Pam's real wage is

(a) $2.
(b) $10.
(c) $30.
(d) $40.

Answer: (b)

Moderate
Multi
Page: 360

17.36: John's nominal wage is $10 and the price index is 5. John's real wage is

(a) $2.
(b) $10.
(c) $30.
(d) $40.

Answer: (a)

17.37: When households make their current consumption and labor supply decisions, they look at

(a) only the current nominal wage rate.
(b) only the current real wage rate.
(c) both the current nominal wage rate and the expected future nominal wage rate.
(d) both the current real wage rate and the expected future real wage rate.

Answer: (d)

Easy
Fact
Page: 361

17.38: Holding everything else constant, the more wealth a household has,

(a) the less it will consume, both now and in the future.
(b) the more it will consume now, but the less it will consume in the future.
(c) the less it will consume now, but the more it will consume in the future.
(d) the more it will consume, both now and in the future.

Answer: (d)

Easy
Fact
Page: 361

17.39: Holding everything else constant, the less wealth a household has,

(a) the less it will consume, both now and in the future.
(b) the more it will consume now, but the less it will consume in the future.
(c) the less it will consume now, but the more it will consume in the future.
(d) the more it will consume, both now and in the future.

Answer: (a)

Easy
Fact
Page: 361

17.40: Any income that is received from sources other than working (for example, inheritance, interest, dividends, and transfer payments) is known as

(a) capital gains.
(b) nonlabor income.
(c) unearned income.
(d) windfall income.

Answer: (b)

Easy
Definition
Page: 361

17.41: An unexpected increase in nonlabor income will have _____ effect on a household's consumption.

(a) an uncertain
(b) no
(c) a positive
(d) a negative

Answer: (c)

Easy
Fact
Page: 361

17.42: An unexpected decrease in nonlabor income will have _____ effect on a household's consumption.

(a) an uncertain
(b) a negative
(c) a positive
(d) no

Answer: (b)

Easy
Fact
Page: 361

Easy
Fact
Page: 362

17.43: An unexpected increase in wealth or nonlabor income leads to

(a) an uncertain effect on labor supply.
(b) an increase in labor supply.
(c) a decrease in labor supply.
(d) a zero effect on labor supply.

Answer: (c)

Moderate
Single
Page: 362

17.44: Anthony has decided to reduce the number of hours he works. Which of the following could have led to that decision?

(a) an increase in his nonlabor income.
(b) a decrease in his nonlabor income.
(c) an increase in the wage rate if the substitution effect dominates the income effect.
(d) either a or c.

Answer: (a)

Moderate
Single
Page: 362

17.45: Shirley has decided to increase the number of hours she works. Which of the following could have led to that decision?

(a) an increase in her nonlabor income.
(b) a decrease in her nonlabor income.
(c) an decrease in the wage rate if the substitution effect dominates the income effect.
(d) either b or c.

Answer: (b)

Moderate
Single
Page: 362

17.46: Shawn has decided to decrease the number of hours she works. Which of the following could have led to that decision?

(a) a decrease in her nonlabor income.
(b) an increase in her nonlabor income.
(c) a decrease in the wage rate if the income effect dominates the substitution effect.
(d) either b or c.

Answer: (b)

Easy
Fact
Page: 362

17.47: One major source of fluctuations in the wealth of the household sector is the

(a) import market.
(b) labor market.
(c) money market.
(d) stock market.

Answer: (d)

Easy
Fact
Page: 362

17.48: An increase in the interest rate

(a) increases the opportunity cost of future consumption, but has no effect on the opportunity cost of present consumption.
(b) decreases the opportunity cost of future consumption, but has no effect on the opportunity cost of present consumption.
(c) lowers the opportunity cost of present consumption.
(d) reduces the opportunity cost of future consumption.

Answer: (d)

17.49: The substitution effect of a decrease in the interest rate has

Moderate
Single
Page: 362

(a) no effect on either current or future consumption.
(b) a negative effect on current consumption.
(c) a positive effect on current consumption.
(d) a negative effect on current consumption and a positive effect on future consumption.

Answer: (c)

17.50: For households with positive wealth, the income effect of a decrease in the interest rate has

Moderate
Single
Page: 362

(a) no effect on either current or future consumption.
(b) a negative effect on current consumption.
(c) a positive effect on current consumption.
(d) a positive effect on current consumption and a positive effect on future consumption.

Answer: (b)

17.51: Assume that households have positive wealth. Which of the following explains how the income effect of an interest rate increase affects consumption?

Moderate
Single
Page: 362

(a) As the interest rate increases, the opportunity cost of current consumption falls, and therefore current consumption increases.
(b) As the interest rate increases, nonlabor income increases and current consumption increases.
(c) As the interest rate increases, expected future income increases and future consumption increases.
(d) As the interest rate increases, permanent income increases and future consumption increases.

Answer: (b)

17.52: According to the substitution effect, when interest rates fall households substitute away from

Moderate
Single
Page: 362

(a) future consumption toward current consumption because of the increase in the relative price of future consumption.
(b) current consumption toward future consumption because of the decrease in the relative price of future consumption.
(c) future consumption toward current consumption because of the decrease in the relative price of future consumption.
(d) current consumption toward future consumption because of the increase in the relative price of future consumption.

Answer: (a)

17.53: According to the substitution effect, when interest rates rise households substitute away from

Moderate
Single
Page: 362

(a) future consumption toward current consumption because of the increase in the relative price of future consumption.
(b) future consumption toward current consumption because of the decrease in the relative price of future consumption.
(c) current consumption toward future consumption because of the decrease in the relative price of future consumption.
(d) current consumption toward future consumption because of the increase in the relative price of future consumption.

Answer: (c)

Challenging
Multi
Page: 362

17.54: At the beginning of 1994, Tony planned to buy a new CD player, television set, and car by borrowing money. Tony already owes $20,000 on other loans. He also planned to buy new clothing and sports equipment out of current income. An increase in interest rates, during 1994, will most likely

(a) cause Tony to decide to borrow less money, but not change what he planned to spend on goods purchased with current income.
(b) cause Tony to decide to borrow less money and to spend less on goods purchased with current income.
(c) cause Tony to decide to borrow more money, but not change what he planned to spend on goods purchased with current income.
(d) cause Tony to decide to borrow more money and to spend more on goods purchased with current income.

Answer: (b)

Moderate
Single
Page: 362

17.55: Assume that Brenda has positive wealth. As the interest rate increased, Brenda reduced her current consumption. For Brenda,

(a) the substitution effect of an interest rate increase outweighs the income effect
(b) the income effect of an interest rate decrease outweighs the substitution effect.
(c) the substitution effect of an interest rate increase must be zero.
(d) the income effect of an interest rate decrease must equal the substitution effect.

Answer: (a)

Easy
Fact
Page: 362

17.56: If an individual is a debtor,

(a) the substitution effect of an interest rate increase is zero.
(b) the income effect of an interest rate increase is zero.
(c) the income and substitution effects of an increase in the interest rate work in opposite directions.
(d) the income and substitution effects of an increase in the interest rate work in the same direction.

Answer: (d)

Moderate
Single
Page: 362

17.57: If an individual is a debtor, an increase in the interest rate

(a) increases current consumption.
(b) decreases current consumption.
(c) has no effect on current consumption.
(d) will either increase or decrease current consumption depending on the size of the income and substitution effects.

Answer: (b)

Moderate
Multi
Page: 362

17.58: Which of the following explains why monetary policy may be less effective today than in the past?

(a) The magnitude of the substitution effect of an interest rate decrease has been increasing so that as the money supply is expanded and interest rates fall, the increase in present consumption is larger than it used to be.
(b) The magnitude of the substitution effect of an interest rate decrease has been decreasing so that as the money supply is expanded and interest rates fall, the increase in present consumption is smaller than it used to be.

(c) The magnitude of the income effect of an interest rate decrease has been increasing so that as the money supply is expanded and interest rates fall, the decrease in present consumption is larger than it used to be.

(d) The magnitude of the income effect of an interest rate decrease has been decreasing so that as the money supply is expanded and interest rates fall, the decrease in present consumption is smaller than it used to be.

Answer: (c)

17.59: Assume that the substitution effect dominates. When the government raises tax rates, after-tax real wage rates

Moderate
Multi
Page: 363

(a) fall, consumption decreases, and labor supply decreases.
(b) fall, consumption decreases, and labor supply increases.
(c) rise, consumption increases, and labor supply increases.
(d) fall, consumption increases, and labor supply decreases.

Answer: (a)

17.60: Assume that the substitution effect dominates. When the government lowers tax rates, after-tax real wage rates

Moderate
Multi
Page: 363

(a) fall, consumption decreases, and labor supply decreases.
(b) rise, consumption decreases, and labor supply increases.
(c) rise, consumption increases, and labor supply increases.
(d) rise, consumption increases, and labor supply decreases.

Answer: (c)

17.61: Assume that the substitution effect dominates the income effect. An increase in both consumption and labor supply would result from

Moderate
Single
Page: 363

(a) an increase in transfer payments.
(b) a decrease in transfer payments.
(c) an increase in tax rates.
(d) a decrease in tax rates.

Answer: (d)

17.62: An increase in transfer payments will result in

Moderate
Multi
Page: 363

(a) a decrease in both consumption and labor supply.
(b) a decrease in consumption and an increase in labor supply.
(c) an increase in consumption and a decrease in labor supply.
(d) an increase in both consumption and labor supply.

Answer: (c)

17.63: A decrease in transfer payments will result in

Moderate
Multi
Page: 363

(a) an increase in consumption and a decrease in labor supply.
(b) an increase in both consumption and labor supply.
(c) a decrease in both consumption and labor supply.
(d) a decrease in consumption and an increase in labor supply.

Answer: (d)

Moderate
Single
Page: 363

17.64: An increase in consumption and a decrease in labor supply would result from

(a) an increase in transfer payments.
(b) a decrease in transfer payments.
(c) an increase in tax rates.
(d) a decrease in tax rates.

Answer: (a)

Moderate
Fact
Page: 363

17.65: Which of the following statements is true?

(a) Changes in tax rates that are expected to be temporary have a greater effect on current consumption and labor supply than those that are expected to be permanent.
(b) Changes in tax rates that are expected to be permanent have a greater effect on current consumption, but a smaller effect on labor supply, than those that are expected to be temporary.
(c) Changes in tax rates that are expected to be permanent have a greater effect on labor supply, but a smaller effect on current consumption, than those that are expected to be temporary.
(d) Changes in tax rates that are expected to be permanent have a greater effect on current consumption and labor supply than those that are expected to be temporary.

Answer: (d)

Easy
Fact
Page: 364

17.66: Which of the following factors is NOT one of the determinants of a household's budget constraint?

(a) income
(b) consumer's preferences
(c) wealth
(d) prices

Answer: (b)

Easy
Definition
Page: 364

17.67: The amount a household would like to work within a given period at the current wage rate if it could find the work is the

(a) constrained supply of labor.
(b) classical supply of labor.
(c) unconstrained supply of labor.
(d) Keynesian supply of labor.

Answer: (c)

Easy
Definition
Page: 364

17.68: The amount a household actually works in a given period at the current wage rate is the

(a) constrained supply of labor.
(b) unconstrained supply of labor.
(c) classical supply of labor.
(d) Keynesian supply of labor.

Answer: (a)

Moderate
Single
Page: 364

17.69: A person's labor supply will equal his or her unconstrained supply of labor if

(a) the economy is operating below full employment.
(b) the economy is operating at full employment.
(c) the person is employed.
(d) both b and c.

Answer: (b)

17.70: A household may have

(a) no control over its constrained supply of labor, but does have control over its consumption.
(b) control over its constrained supply of labor, but has no control over its consumption.
(c) control over both its constrained supply of labor and its consumption.
(d) no control over either its constrained supply of labor or its consumption.

Easy
Fact
Page: 364

Answer: (a)

17.71: Keynesian theory is considered to pertain to periods of

(a) more-than-full employment.
(b) full employment.
(c) either more-than-full employment or full employment.
(d) less-than-full employment.

Easy
Fact
Page: 365

Answer: (d)

17.72: Income is directly determined by firms' hiring decisions if

(a) households are unconstrained in their labor supply decisions.
(b) households are constrained in their labor supply decisions.
(c) the economy is at full employment.
(d) either a or c.

Easy
Fact
Page: 365

Answer: (b)

17.73: Which of the following is a way in which a firm can add to its capital stock?

(a) expanding its labor force
(b) purchasing raw materials
(c) plant and equipment investment
(d) unplanned inventory disinvestment

Easy
Fact
Page: 369

Answer: (c)

17.74: Purchases by firms of additional machines, factories, or buildings within a given period is

(a) plant and equipment investment.
(b) unplanned inventory investment.
(c) planned inventory investment.
(d) investment in human capital.

Easy
Definition
Page: 369

Answer: (a)

17.75: Which of the following is a way that a firm can add to its capital stock?

(a) purchasing of raw materials
(b) expanding its labor force
(c) switching to new sources of energy
(d) inventory investment

Easy
Fact
Page: 369

Answer: (d)

17.76: A labor-intensive technology is a technique of production that

(a) relies entirely on human effort; no capital is employed.
(b) uses a large amount of labor relative to capital.
(c) uses a large amount of capital relative to labor.
(d) requires employees to work at a very rapid pace.

Easy
Definition
Page: 369

Answer: (b)

Easy
Definition
Page: 370

17.77: A capital-intensive technology is a technique of production that

(a) relies entirely on physical inputs; no human labor is required.
(b) uses a large amount of labor relative to capital.
(c) uses a large amount of capital relative to labor.
(d) is used only in cases where few skilled workers are available.

Answer: (c)

Easy
Single
Page: 370

17.78: Assume that in Montega the price of labor has doubled and the price of capital has remained constant. Firms in Montega

(a) may shift to more labor-intensive technologies because the increase in labor costs must have been caused by an increase in the productivity of labor.
(b) may shift to a more capital-intensive technology because of the increase in labor costs relative to capital costs.
(c) have no incentive to change production technologies unless the demand for their products changes.
(d) have no incentive to change production technologies because there has been no change in tax incentives.

Answer: (b)

Easy
Fact
Page: 370

17.79: The relative impact of an expansion of output on employment depends on

(a) both the wage rate and the cost of capital.
(b) the wage rate.
(c) the cost of capital.
(d) the overall price level.

Answer: (a)

Easy
Fact
Page: 370

17.80: The relative impact of an expansion of output on investment demand depends on

(a) the wage rate.
(b) the cost of capital.
(c) the overall price level.
(d) both the wage rate and the cost of capital.

Answer: (d)

Easy
Single
Page: 370

17.81: When a labor-intensive technology is used, an expansion is likely to

(a) substantially increase the demand for both labor and capital.
(b) increase the demand for labor and decrease the demand for capital.
(c) increase the demand for labor while increasing the demand for capital only modestly.
(d) substantially increase the demand for capital while increasing the demand for labor only modestly.

Answer: (c)

Easy
Fact
Page: 370

17.82: When forming their expectations, firms gather information about all the following factors EXCEPT

(a) the projected demand for their specific line of products.
(b) the historical supply of their competitors' line of products.
(c) the future plans of their competitors.
(d) the overall health of the macroeconomy.

Answer: (b)

17.83: The phrase that was coined by John Maynard Keynes to describe the feelings of investors was the _____ of entrepreneurs.

(a) optimism
(b) pessimism
(c) animal spirits
(d) karma

Answer: (c)

Easy
Definition
Page: 370

17.84: The tendency for investment to increase when aggregate output increases and decrease when aggregate output decreases is known as the _____ effect.

(a) accelerator
(b) multiplier
(c) cyclical
(d) disequilibrium

Answer: (a)

Easy
Definition
Page: 371

17.85: Refer to Figure 17.2. The interest rate is 7%. Which of the following is a possible explanation for why investment is higher along I2 than I1?

Moderate
Single
Page: 371

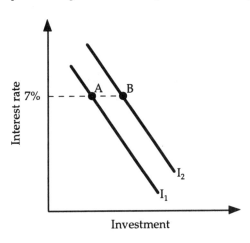

(a) Investment demand curve I2 must correspond to a low level of output.
(b) Investment demand curve I2 must correspond to a lower inflation rate.
(c) Investment demand curve I2 corresponds to more optimistic expectations on the part of business firms than investment demand curve I1.
(d) Investment demand curve I1 corresponds to more optimistic expectations on the part of business firms than investment demand curve I2.

Answer: (c)

Figure 17.2

17.86: If output is growing rapidly, then at any given level of the interest rate, expectations are likely to be more

Moderate
Single
Page: 371

(a) pessimistic, and planned investment is likely to be lower than when output is growing slowly or falling.
(b) pessimistic, and planned investment is likely to be higher than when output is growing slowly or falling.
(c) optimistic, and planned investment is likely to be lower than when output is growing slowly or falling.
(d) optimistic, and planned investment is likely to be higher than when output is growing slowly or falling.

Answer: (d)

Moderate
Single
Page: 371

17.87: If output is growing slowly or falling, then at any given level of the interest rate, expectations are likely to be more

(a) pessimistic, and planned investment is likely to be higher than when output is growing rapidly.
(b) pessimistic, and planned investment is likely to be lower than when output is growing rapidly.
(c) optimistic, and planned investment is likely to be higher than when output is growing rapidly.
(d) optimistic, and planned investment is likely to be lower than when output is growing rapidly.

Answer: (b)

Moderate
Single
Page: 371

17.88: Historically, the long-term growth rate in the United States has been about a 3% increase in real GDP per year. Economists forecast that for the growth rate both 1994 and 1995 is likely to be 5%. Which of the following would you expect to occur?

(a) Firms will believe that these high growth rates will not be maintained and will reduce investment, which will cause aggregate output to fall.
(b) Firms will become more optimistic about the future and will increase investment which will cause aggregate output to increase.
(c) Firms will begin to worry about rising input prices and will begin to hoard capital and labor.
(d) Firms will not change their investment plans until after 1995, when they have determined whether or not the growth rate was actually 5%.

Answer: (b)

Challenging
Multi
Page: 371

17.89: In spite of a decrease in its sales, a firm may elect to keep excess labor and capital on hand when

(a) the firm expects that the decrease in sales will last indefinitely.
(b) interest rates are relatively low.
(c) the adjustment costs associated with its new level of production are less than the cost savings associated with a smaller work force and capital stock.
(d) the adjustment costs associated with its new level of production are greater than the cost savings associated with a smaller work force and capital stock.

Answer: (d)

Easy
Fact
Page: 372

17.90: The more excess capital and labor a firm already has,

(a) the less likely it is to invest in new capital and hire new workers in the future.
(b) the less likely it is to invest in new capital, but the more likely it is to hire new workers in the future.
(c) the more likely it is to invest in new capital, but the less likely it is to hire new workers in the future.
(d) the more likely it is to invest in new capital and hire new workers in the future.

Answer: (a)

Challenging
Multi
Page: 372

17.91: The amount firms pay into the unemployment compensation fund depends on how many of its workers it lays off during the year. The more workers it lays off during the year, the more the firm has to pay into the unemployment compensation fund. If this rule was changed so that the unemployment compensation program was funded through a tax on employees instead of a tax on employers, which of the following would occur?

(a) Adjustment costs would increase and firms would be more likely to hold excess labor.

(b) Adjustment costs would increase and firms would be less likely to hold excess labor.

(c) Adjustment costs would decrease and firms would be more likely to hold excess labor.

(d) Adjustment costs would decrease and firms would be less likely to hold excess labor.

Answer: (d)

17.92: The unemployment rate does not tend to fall as soon as the economy pulls out of a recession. Which of the following best explains this?

(a) Firms are not able to find qualified workers to fill the job vacancies.

(b) Firms' optimism about the state of the economy increased prior to the economy pulling out of the recession, so firms increased their employment earlier.

(c) Firms are holding excess labor, so as the economy pulls out of the recession, firms do not need to hire new workers immediately.

(d) During recessionary periods, firms switch to more capital-intensive production techniques, so they do not need to increase employment as the economy pulls out of the recession.

Answer: (c)

Challenging
Multi
Page: 372

17.93: The cost to recruit and train new workers is an example of

(a) an excess labor cost.
(b) an adjustment cost.
(c) an accelerator cost.
(d) a capital cost.

Answer: (b)

Easy
Fact
Page: 371

17.94: Which of the following relationships is correct?

(a) Stock of Inventories (End of Period) = Stock of Inventories (Beginning of Period) - Production + Sales

(b) Stock of Inventories (End of Period) = Stock of Inventories (Beginning of Period) - Production - Sales

(c) Stock of Inventories (End of Period) = Stock of Inventories (Beginning of Period) + Production + Sales

(d) Stock of Inventories (End of Period) = Stock of Inventories (Beginning of Period) + Production - Sales

Answer: (d)

Easy
Definition
Page: 372

17.95: At the beginning of 1994, the Smile Greeting Card Company has 8,000 greeting cards in stock. During 1994, the company produces 100,000 greeting cards and sells 95,000 greeting cards. The Smile Greeting Card Company's stock of inventory at the end of 1994 is _____ greeting cards.

(a) 3,000
(b) 5,000
(c) 8,000
(d) 13,000

Answer: (d)

Easy
Single
Page: 372

Easy
Definition
Page: 372

17.96: The desired level of inventories is the level at which the extra cost (in lost sales) from lowering inventories by a small amount is

(a) greater than the gain (in interest revenue and decreased storage costs).
(b) just equal to the gain (in interest revenue and decreased storage costs).
(c) less than the gain (in interest revenue and decreased storage costs).
(d) zero.

Answer: (b)

Moderate
Single
Page: 372

17.97: The Unique Toy Company rents space by the square foot in a warehouse to store its inventory. The owner of the warehouse just doubled the rent he charges the Unique Toy Company. Everything else equal, the rent increase is likely to _____ Unique's optimal level of inventory.

(a) not change
(b) increase
(c) decrease
(d) reduce to zero

Answer: (c)

Easy
Fact
Page: 373

17.98: An unexpected increase in inventories has

(a) no effect on future production.
(b) a positive effect on future production.
(c) a negative effect on future production.
(d) a negative effect on current production.

Answer: (c)

Easy
Fact
Page: 373

17.99: An unexpected decrease in inventories has

(a) a positive effect on future production.
(b) a negative effect on future production.
(c) no effect on future production.
(d) a positive effect on current production.

Answer: (a)

Moderate
Single
Page: 373

17.100: If a firm's sales turn out to be less than expected, inventories will be

(a) lower than expected, and there will be more production in the future.
(b) lower than expected, and there will be less production in the future.
(c) higher than expected, and there will be more production in the future.
(d) higher than expected, and there will be less production in the future.

Answer: (d)

Moderate
Single
Page: 373

17.101: If a firm's sales turn out to be more than expected, inventories will be

(a) higher than expected, and there will be less production in the future.
(b) lower than expected, and there will be more production in the future.
(c) higher than expected, and there will be more production in the future.
(d) lower than expected, and there will be less production in the future.

Answer: (b)

17.102: Which of the following statements is true?

(a) Production and sales will fluctuate by the same amount and in the same direction over time.
(b) Production will not fluctuate over time, but a firm's sales will fluctuate over time.
(c) Production will fluctuate somewhat over time, but not as much as sales fluctuate over time.
(d) Production and sales will both fluctuate by the same amount over time, but in different directions.

Answer: (c)

Moderate
Fact
Page: 373

17.103: Due to an increase in the birth rate, the Solid Wood Furniture Company expects an increase in the sale of its cribs over the next few years. The Solid Wood Furniture Company will most likely

(a) keep current production constant, but plan to increase production in the future.
(b) increase current production.
(c) decrease current production so that it can increase production in the future.
(d) not change its current investment plans, but plan to increase investment in the future.

Answer: (b)

Moderate
Single
Page: 373

17.104: Which of the following statements is true?

(a) Plant and equipment investment is the most volatile component of GDP.
(b) Housing investment fluctuates more than plant and equipment investment.
(c) Investment increases when GDP decreases and investment decreases when GDP increases.
(d) Inventory investment is the most stable component of GDP.

Answer: (b)

Easy
Fact
Page: 374

17.105: On average the inventory/sales ratio has been declining since 1982. This suggests that

(a) the costs of holding inventory have been falling.
(b) firms are holding less excess capital and labor.
(c) aggregate output has been falling.
(d) firms are becoming more efficient in their management of inventory stocks.

Answer: (d)

Easy
Fact
Page: 375

17.106: If a tax cut is expected to be temporary rather than permanent, it will have

(a) more of an effect on household behavior.
(b) less of an effect on household behavior.
(c) no effect on household behavior.
(d) the same effect on household behavior.

Answer: (b)

Easy
Fact
Page: 359

Easy
Fact
Page: 359

17.107: Some economists believe that the saving rate in the United States is low partly because of the Social Security system. Which of the following statements provides a logical rationale for this argument?

(a) If workers expect to receive Social Security benefits, they may decrease their personal saving for retirement and consume less today.
(b) If workers expect to receive Social Security benefits, they may increase their personal saving for retirement and consume more today.
(c) If workers expect to receive Social Security benefits, they may increase their personal saving for retirement and consume less today.
(d) If workers expect to receive Social Security benefits, they may decrease their personal saving for retirement and consume more today.

Answer: (d)

Easy
Fact
Page: 359

17.108: A tax cut that is expected to be permanent will have more of an effect on household behavior than a tax cut that is expected to be temporary. Because

(a) a temporary tax cut will influence only permanent income, but a permanent tax cut will influence only current income.
(b) a permanent tax cut will have more of an impact on a household's permanent income than a temporary tax cut will.
(c) households are not easily convinced that a temporary tax cut has been made, but they are easily convinced that a permanent tax cut has been made.
(d) temporary tax cuts have a much longer time lag than permanent tax cuts do.

Answer: (b)

Moderate
Single
Page: 362

17.109: If the U.S. social security system were eliminated, what would happen to private saving?

(a) Private saving would decrease, because the elimination of the social security tax would be an increase in income, and as income increases consumption increases.
(b) Private saving would not change, because the social security system has no impact on private saving.
(c) Private saving would increase, because the social security system acts as a substitute for private saving.
(d) Private saving would not change, because companies would offer their employees company pension plans to replace social security.

Answer: (c)

Moderate
Single
Page: 363

17.110: Let us consider two different proposals for tax reduction. The first proposal, a "refundable" income tax credit, would cut everyone's taxes by $1,000, regardless of their income. The second proposal is a reduction in income tax rates that would initially increase disposable income by the same amount as the tax credit. Why would we expect these two proposals to have differing effects on consumption spending, and ultimately on output?

(a) The reduced tax rate produces an income effect, but the tax credit does not.
(b) The reduced tax rate produces a substitution effect away from leisure, but the tax credit does not.
(c) The tax credit produces a substitution effect away from leisure, but the reduced tax rate does not.
(d) The tax credit produces an income effect, but the reduced tax rate does not.

Answer: (b)

17.111: A reduction in tax rates will lead to an increase in labor supply if

Moderate
Single
Page: 363

(a) the substitution effect is larger than the income effect.
(b) the substitution effect is smaller than the income effect.
(c) the substitution effect equals the income effect.
(d) the substitution effect is zero.

Answer: (a)

17.112: A tax refund will cause

Easy
Fact
Page: 363

(a) labor supply to increase or decrease depending on the relative magnitudes of the income and substitution effects.
(b) an unambiguous increase in labor supply.
(c) an unambiguous decrease in labor supply.
(d) no change in labor supply.

Answer: (c)

17.113: A reduction in tax rates produces _____, while a lump-sum tax credit produces _____.

Moderate
Fact
Page: 363

(a) both an income and substitution effect; only an income effect
(b) only an income effect; both an income and substitution effect
(c) only a substitution effect; both an income and substitution effect
(d) both an income and substitution effect; only a substitution effect

Answer: (a)

17.114: If a policy maker wants to change taxes to encourage individuals to increase their labor supply, the policy maker should

Moderate
Single
Page: 363

(a) reduce taxes by a lump-sum amount.
(b) reduce the tax rates that individuals pay.
(c) increase taxes by a lump sum.
(d) increase the tax rates that individuals pay.

Answer: (b)

17.115: Which of the following is NOT a transfer payment?

Easy
Fact
Page: 363

(a) Social Security payments
(b) welfare benefits
(c) dividends
(d) unemployment compensation

Answer: (c)

17.116: Cash payments made by the government directly to households are

Easy
Definition
Page: 363

(a) dividends.
(b) national income payments.
(c) compensating differential payments.
(d) transfer payments.

Answer: (d)

Easy
Fact
Page: 362

17.117: An increase in nonlabor income leads to _____consumption and _____ in labor supply.

(a) a decrease; a decrease
(b) a decrease; an increase
(c) an increase; a decrease
(d) an increase; an increase

Answer: (c)

Easy
Fact
Page: 362

17.118: Which of the following is TRUE of a change in nonlabor income?

(a) There is no substitution effect because a change in nonlabor income does not change the trade-off between work and leisure.
(b) There is no income effect because a change in nonlabor income does not change the trade-off between work and leisure.
(c) There is no substitution effect because a change in nonlabor income does not change a household's permanent income.
(d) There is no income effect because a change in nonlabor income does not change a household's permanent income.

Answer: (a)

Easy
Definition
Page: 361

17.119: The portion of a corporation's profits that the firm pays out each period to shareholders is known as

(a) dividends.
(b) capital gains.
(c) interest.
(d) retained earnings.

Answer: (a)

Easy
Fact
Page: 362

17.120: An increase in dividend payments will

(a) have no effect on labor supply.
(b) lead to an increase in labor supply.
(c) lead to a decrease in labor supply.
(d) either lead to an increase or decrease in labor supply depending on the relative magnitude of the income and substitution effects.

Answer: (c)

Honors
Fact
Page: 362

17.121: Which of the following is TRUE of a change in dividend payments?

(a) There is no substitution effect because a change in dividend payments does not change the trade-off between work and leisure.
(b) There is no income effect because a change in dividend payments does not change the trade-off between work and leisure.
(c) There is no substitution effect because a change in dividend payments does not change a household's permanent income.
(d) There is no income effect because a change in dividend payments does not change a household's permanent income.

Answer: (a)

17.122: The government reduces the corporate profits tax. As a result, corporate profits increase. This will

(a) have no effect on households.
(b) increase the nonlabor income of households causing consumption to increase and labor supply to decrease.
(c) increase the nonlabor income of households, causing consumption to increase and labor supply to increase.
(d) increase the nonlabor income of households, causing consumption to increase and labor supply to increase or decrease depending on the relative magnitude of the income and substitution effects.

Answer: (b)

17.123: The government increases the corporate profits tax. As a result, corporate profits decrease. This will

(a) have no effect on households.
(b) decrease the nonlabor income of households causing consumption to decrease and labor supply to decrease.
(c) decrease the nonlabor income of households causing consumption to decrease and labor supply to increase.
(d) decrease the nonlabor income of households causing consumption to decrease and labor supply to decrease or increase depending on the relative magnitude of the income and substitution effects.

Answer: (c)

17.124: If the substitution effect is greater than the income effect, an increase in interest rates will

(a) reduce saving and stimulate consumption spending by households.
(b) reduce both saving and consumption spending by households.
(c) stimulate both saving and consumption spending by households.
(d) stimulate saving and reduce consumption spending by households.

Answer: (d)

17.125: Assume households have positive wealth. If the income effect is greater than the substitution effect, a decrease in interest rates will

(a) increase saving and decrease consumption spending by households.
(b) decrease saving and increase consumption spending by households.
(c) decrease both saving and consumption spending by households.
(d) increase both saving and consumption spending by households.

Answer: (a)

17.126: Assume households have positive wealth. If the income effect is greater than the substitution effect, an increase in interest rates will

(a) increase saving and decrease consumption spending by households.
(b) decrease saving and increase consumption spending by households.
(c) decrease both saving and consumption spending by households.
(d) increase both saving and consumption spending by households.

Answer: (b)

Moderate
Single
Page: 362

17.127: If the substitution effect is greater than the income effect, a decrease in interest rates will

(a) increase saving and decrease consumption spending by households.
(b) decrease saving and increase consumption spending by households.
(c) decrease both saving and consumption spending by households.
(d) increase both saving and consumption spending by households.

Answer: (b)

Easy
Fact
Page: 362

17.128: Monetary policy is less effective than it was in the past because

(a) investment has become less sensitive to interest rate changes.
(b) the substitution effect of an interest rate change on consumption has increased.
(c) the income effect of an interest rate change on consumption has increased.
(d) the government deficit has decreased.

Answer: (c)

Easy
Fact
Page: 368

17.129: The two channels through which monetary policy can influence behavior in the goods market are

(a) investment and government spending.
(b) investment and consumption.
(c) government spending and consumption.
(d) taxation and investment.

Answer: (b)

Easy
Fact
Page: 371

17.130: If firms believe that a downturn in sales and output is temporary and that increased output will be needed in the future, they may choose to

(a) fire all their workers.
(b) reassign their workers to different jobs.
(c) close a plant permanently.
(d) sell off the plant.

Answer: (b)

Easy
Fact
Page: 372

17.131: At low levels of output, the economy can expand with little or no increase in the overall price level because

(a) at low levels of output the aggregate supply curve is negatively sloped.
(b) people will be expecting the price level to fall.
(c) there is excess supply so prices are kept low.
(d) firms likely hold excess labor and capital, and production can be increased without causing input prices to increase.

Answer: (d)

Moderate
Single
Page: 379

17.132: Firms believe that the current economic downturn will be long-lasting and have decided to hold very little excess labor. The government reports that the unemployment rate is 12.5%. The government has decided to stimulate the economy by increasing government spending. In this situation the multiplier is likely to be

(a) negative.
(b) zero.
(c) small.
(d) large.

Answer: (d)

17.133: Firms report that their workers are working 6 hours of overtime per week. The government reports that the unemployment rate is 3.5%. In this situation, the multiplier is likely to be

Moderate
Single
Page: 379

(a) negative.
(b) small.
(c) large.
(d) infinitely large.

Answer: (b)

17.134: As the economy approaches full employment, the size of the multiplier will

Easy
Fact
Page: 379

(a) remain unchanged.
(b) become negative.
(c) become larger.
(d) become smaller.

Answer: (d)

17.135: The government spending multiplier is likely to be smaller during periods of

Easy
Fact
Page: 379

(a) high output and high unemployment.
(b) high output and low unemployment.
(c) low output and low unemployment.
(d) low output and high unemployment.

Answer: (b)

17.136: The government spending multiplier is likely to be larger during periods of

Easy
Fact
Page: 379

(a) low output and high unemployment.
(b) low output and low unemployment.
(c) high output and low unemployment.
(d) high output and high unemployment.

Answer: (a)

17.137: Provided that firms have sufficient capital and labor to support an output increase, monetary and fiscal policy are likely to be the most effective when

Moderate
Fact
Page: 379

(a) prices and inventory stocks are both high.
(b) output and inventory stocks are both high.
(c) output is low and inventory stocks are low.
(d) output is low and inventory stocks are high.

Answer: (c)

17.138: If inventory stocks are high,

Easy
Fact
Page: 379

(a) monetary policy will be effective, but fiscal policy will be ineffective.
(b) fiscal policy will be effective, but monetary policy will be ineffective.
(c) monetary and fiscal policy will be very effective.
(d) neither monetary nor fiscal policy will be effective.

Answer: (d)

Easy
Fact
Page: 379

17.139: If inventory stocks are low and firms have enough capital and labor to support an output increase,

(a) monetary policy will be effective, but fiscal policy will be ineffective.
(b) fiscal policy will be effective, but monetary policy will be ineffective.
(c) monetary and fiscal policy will be very effective.
(d) neither monetary nor fiscal policy will be effective.

Answer: (c)

Moderate
Fact
Page: 379

17.140: There is an increase in aggregate demand, and firms do not have sufficient capital and labor to support an output increase. In this case, inventory stocks will

(a) continue to fall, and there will be a large increase in the price level.
(b) continue to increase, and there will be a large increase in the price level.
(c) continue to fall, and the price level will fall.
(d) remain unchanged, and the price level will remain unchanged.

Answer: (a)

Moderate
Single
Page: 379

17.141: If the economy is on the steep part of the AS curve, the multiplier will be

(a) larger than it would be if the economy were on the flat portion of the AS curve.
(b) smaller than it would be if the economy were on the flat portion of the AS curve.
(c) constant regardless of where the economy is on the AS curve.
(d) infinite (as compared to zero) if the economy is on the flat portion of the AS curve.

Answer: (b)

Easy
Definition
Page: 376

17.142: The amount of output produced by an average worker in one hour is

(a) a production quota.
(b) labor productivity.
(c) the marginal product of labor.
(d) the marginal revenue product of labor.

Answer: (b)

Easy
Fact
Page: 376

17.143: Productivity tends to

(a) rise during contractions.
(b) rise during expansions.
(c) fall during expansions.
(d) rise throughout the business cycle.

Answer: (b)

Easy
Fact
Page: 376

17.144: Productivity tends to

(a) fall during contractions.
(b) fall during expansions.
(c) rise during contractions.
(d) rise throughout the business cycle.

Answer: (a)

17.145: Joe's Lawn Service employs hires workers. Each worker works eight hours per day. The five workers are able to mow 40 lawns per day. The labor productivity is therefore _____ lawn(s) per person/hour.

Easy
Single
Page: 376

(a) 1
(b) 5
(c) 8
(d) 10

Answer: (a)

17.146: A firm is holding excess labor. This will

Moderate
Single
Page: 376

(a) increase the productivity of capital.
(b) decrease the productivity of capital.
(c) increase labor productivity.
(d) reduce labor productivity.

Answer: (d)

17.147: Refer to Figure 17.3. This figure suggests that

Moderate
Multi
Page: 377

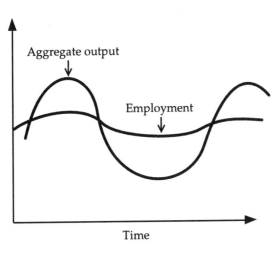

Figure 17.3

(a) employment does not fluctuate as much as output over the business cycle, which leads to high productivity during periods of low output and low productivity during periods of high output.
(b) output does not fluctuate as much as employment over the business cycle, which leads to high productivity during periods of high output and low productivity during periods of low output.
(c) output does not fluctuate as much as employment over the business cycle, which leads to high productivity during periods of low output and low productivity during periods of high output.
(d) employment does not fluctuate as much as output over the business cycle, which leads to high productivity during periods of high output and low productivity during periods of low output.

Answer: (d)

17.148: During economic expansions,

Moderate
Fact
Page: 377

(a) employment rises by a higher percentage than output, and the ratio of output to workers falls.
(b) output rises by a larger percentage than employment, and the ratio of output to workers rises.
(c) employment rises by a larger percentage than output, and the ratio of output to workers rises.
(d) output rises by a larger percentage than employment, and the ratio of output to workers falls.

Answer: (b)

Moderate
Fact
Page: 377

17.149: During economic downswings,

(a) employment falls faster than output, and the ratio of output to workers rises.
(b) employment falls faster than output, and the ratio of output to workers falls.
(c) output falls faster than employment, and the ratio of output to workers falls.
(d) output falls faster than employment, and the ratio of output to workers rises.

Answer: (c)

Easy
Fact
Page: 377

17.150: When the economy is in a slump, labor productivity tends to fall because firms have

(a) excess capital.
(b) excess labor.
(c) too little capital.
(d) too little labor.

Answer: (b)

Moderate
Fact
Page: 377

17.151: Which of the following statements is TRUE?

(a) The long-run potential of the economy declines as output per worker falls during a recession.
(b) The long-run potential of the economy increases as output per worker rises during an expansion.
(c) The long-run potential of the economy increases as output per worker rises during an expansion, but the long-run potential of the economy doesn't change as output per worker falls during a recession.
(d) Changes in output per worker over the business cycle have nothing to do with the long-run potential of the economy.

Answer: (d)

Easy
Fact
Page: 377

17.152: Okun's Law states that the unemployment rate decreases about

(a) one percentage point for every 3% increase in GDP.
(b) three percentage points for every 1% increase in GDP.
(c) one percentage point for every 1% increase in GDP.
(d) one percentage point for every 2% increase in GDP.

Answer: (a)

Easy
Single
Page: 377

17.153: According to Okun's Law, if GDP increased by 6%, the unemployment rate would decrease by

(a) one percentage point.
(b) two percentage points.
(c) three percentage points.
(d) six percentage points.

Answer: (b)

Easy
Single
Page: 377

17.154: If Okun's Law holds true, then a 9% increase in GDP would lead to a _____ percentage point decrease in the unemployment rate.

(a) 1
(b) 2
(c) 3
(d) 6

Answer: (c)

17.155: Although the relationship between output and the unemployment rate is not as simple as Okun's Law represents it to be, it is true that

(a) a 1% increase in output tends to correspond to a greater than 1% decrease in the unemployment rate.
(b) a 1% increase in output tends to correspond to a less than 1% decrease in the unemployment rate.
(c) a 1% increase in output tends to correspond to a 1% decrease in the unemployment rate.
(d) a 1% increase in output will have no effect on the unemployment rate.

Answer: (b)

17.156: Okun's Law has

(a) been proven to be completely incorrect - there isn't a negative relationship between GDP and the unemployment rate.
(b) proven to be correct over time in that as GDP increases by 3%, there has been a one percentage point decline in unemployment.
(c) not turned out to be a law - the relationship between changes in GDP and the unemployment rate is more complex than Okun's Law indicates.
(d) been proven false, because there is a positive relationship between changes in GDP and the unemployment rate.

Answer: (c)

17.157: Which of the following is NOT one of the "slippages" between changes in output and changes in the unemployment rate?

(a) The labor force increases when output increases.
(b) The percentage increase in the number of jobs is less than the percentage increase in output.
(c) As the size of the labor force increases, the interest rate increases, and therefore output falls.
(d) The change in the number of jobs and the change in the number of people employed are not equal.

Answer: (c)

17.158: An increase in output will cause the unemployment rate to fall by a large percentage if

(a) firms are holding excess labor.
(b) firms aren't holding excess labor.
(c) firms have their workers work more overtime.
(d) firms hire workers who were already employed by other firms to work for them part-time.

Answer: (b)

Moderate
Single
Page: 378

17.159: When output increases by 1%, the number of jobs does not tend to rise by 1% in the short run. Which of the following statements represents one of the reasons why this is true?

(a) A firm is likely to meet some of the increase in output by increasing the number of hours worked per job.
(b) A firm is likely to meet some of the increase in output by decreasing the number of hours worked per job.
(c) Firms are likely to meet some of the increase in output by reducing labor productivity.
(d) Firms are likely to meet part of the increase in output by eliminating any excess labor they may have.

Answer: (a)

Easy
Single
Page: 378

17.160: When output increases by 1%, the unemployment rate does not tend to fall by 1% in the short run because

(a) a firm is likely to meet some of the increase in output by increasing the number of hours worked per job.
(b) the number of people who become employed is less than the number of new jobs created.
(c) as output increases, the size of the labor force increases.
(d) all of the above.

Answer: (d)

Easy
Fact
Page: 378

17.161: People who have two jobs,

(a) are counted twice in both the job data and the persons-employed data.
(b) are counted twice in the job data, but only once in the persons-employed data.
(c) are counted once in the job data, but twice in the persons-employed data.
(d) are counted once in both the job data and the persons-employed data.

Answer: (b)

Easy
Fact
Page: 378

17.162: The slippage between output and the unemployment rate occurs because the unemployment rate is calculated from data on

(a) the number of jobs.
(b) the number of people who do not want to work.
(c) the number of people employed.
(d) the civilian adult population.

Answer: (c)

Easy
Fact
Page: 378

17.163: The unemployment rate is

(a) one minus the employment rate.
(b) one plus the employment rate.
(c) the difference between the number of people in the labor force and the number of people employed.
(d) the ratio of the labor force to the number of people unemployed.

Answer: (a)

17.164: The employment rate is the ratio of

(a) the number of people unemployed to the number of people employed.
(b) the number of people unemployed to the number of people in the labor force.
(c) the number of people in the labor force to the number of people employed.
(d) the number of people employed to the number of people in the labor force.

Answer: (d)

Easy
Fact
Page: 378

17.165: Which of the following is NOT one of the "slippages" between changes in output and changes in the unemployment rate?

(a) the relationship between the change in output and the change in the number of jobs in the economy
(b) the relationship between the change in the number of jobs in the economy and the change in the number of people employed
(c) the relationship between the change in output and the amount of structural unemployment in the economy
(d) the response of the labor force to an increase in output

Answer: (c)

Moderate
Single
Page: 378

17.166: The decline in the measured unemployment rate that results when people who want to work, but who cannot find work, drop out of the ranks of the unemployed and the labor force is the

(a) discouraged-worker effect.
(b) leisure-preference effect.
(c) surplus labor effect.
(d) disguised unemployment effect.

Answer: (a)

Easy
Fact
Page: 378

17.167: If discouraged workers were counted as unemployed, then as output increased the unemployment rate would

(a) not change at all.
(b) fall by more than is the case if discouraged workers are not counted as unemployed.
(c) fall by less than is the case if discouraged workers are not counted as unemployed.
(d) increase by less than is the case if discouraged workers are not counted as unemployed.

Answer: (b)

Challenging
Multi
Page: 378

17.168: The measured unemployment rate does not fall as much as one might expect when output increases because as the economy expands,

(a) more people leave the labor force.
(b) firms want to hire additional workers.
(c) more people find jobs.
(d) more people enter the labor force.

Answer: (d)

Easy
Fact
Page: 378

Easy
Fact
Page: 378

17.169: As the economy expands the labor force _____ and as the economy contracts, the labor force _____.

(a) increases; decreases
(b) increases; increases
(c) decreases; decreases
(d) decreases; increases

Answer: (a)

Easy
Fact
Page: 378

17.170: In general, the relationship between output and unemployment

(a) has been quite stable over the long run.
(b) is a simple one, as represented by Okun's Law.
(c) has been completely unpredictable over time.
(d) depends on the state of the economy at the time of the output change.

Answer: (d)

Moderate
Fact
Page: 378

17.171: Which of the following is NOT one of the reasons why the actual size of the multiplier is smaller than its simplified version would suggest?

(a) the presence of automatic stabilizers
(b) the effects of interest rate changes
(c) the fact that the United States exports a very small percentage of what it consumes
(d) the response of the price level

Answer: (c)

Moderate
Fact
Page: 379

17.172: If the economy has automatic stabilizers built in, the multiplier will

(a) be smaller than it would have been in the absence of automatic stabilizers.
(b) be larger than it would have been in the absence of automatic stabilizers.
(c) be zero.
(d) be infinitely larger than it would have been in the absence of automatic stabilizers.

Answer: (a)

Moderate
Fact
Page: 379

17.173: Which of the following statements is TRUE?

(a) Increases in the interest rate crowd out both consumption and investment spending, and this reduces the size of the multiplier.
(b) Increases in the interest rate crowd out both consumption and investment spending, and this increases the size of the multiplier.
(c) Increases in the interest rate have no effect on the size of the multiplier because higher interest rates cause consumption to increase, which offsets the crowding out of investment.
(d) Increases in the interest rate cause the size of the multiplier to be smaller if the economy is on the flat portion of the AS curve and to be larger if the economy is on the steep portion of the AS curve.

Answer: (a)

17.174: Which of the following would lead to an increase in the value of the multiplier?

(a) The economy is in a downturn, but because firms do not expect the downturn to last for long they decide to hold onto excess capital and labor.
(b) Due to changes in the structure of the economy, the economy's short-run AS curve becomes much steeper.
(c) The government reduces tariffs on imported goods, and this increases the amount that is imported into the country.
(d) At the beginning of an expansion, firms find that their inventory levels are very low.

Answer: (d)

Challenging
Multi
Page: 379

17.175: Which of the following would lead to an increase in the value of the multiplier?

(a) The economy is in a downturn, but because firms do not expect the downturn to last for long they decide to hold onto excess capital and labor.
(b) Due to changes in the structure of the economy, the economy's short-run AS curve becomes much steeper.
(c) The government increases tariffs on imported goods, and this decreases the amount that is imported into the country.
(d) At the beginning of an expansion, firms find that their inventory levels are very high.

Answer: (c)

Challenging
Multi
Page: 379

17.176: Which of the following statements is TRUE?

(a) The multiplier effects for policy changes that are perceived to be temporary are smaller than those for policy changes that are perceived to be permanent.
(b) The multiplier effects for policy changes that are perceived to be temporary are larger than those for policy changes that are perceived to be permanent.
(c) The multiplier effects for policy changes that are perceived to be temporary are the same as those for policy changes that are perceived to be permanent.
(d) There is no relationship between the size of the multiplier effect and whether policy changes are perceived to be temporary or permanent.

Answer: (a)

Easy
Fact
Page: 379

17.177: Suppose that the value of the multiplier has decreased in recent years. Which of the following could have caused this?

(a) Consumption has become less sensitive to changes in the interest rate.
(b) The costs of inventory storage have risen.
(c) Changes in the way the unemployment compensation fund is financed have made it more expensive for firms to lay off workers.
(d) "Buy America" campaigns launched by many unions have succeeded in reducing the demand for imported goods.

Answer: (c)

Challenging
Multi
Page: 379

17.178: Suppose that the value of the multiplier has increased in recent years. Which of the following could have caused this?

(a) Consumption has become more sensitive to changes in the interest rate.
(b) The costs of inventory storage have fallen.
(c) Changes in the way the unemployment compensation fund is financed have made it more expensive for firms to lay off workers.
(d) "Buy America" campaigns launched by many unions have succeeded in reducing the demand for imported goods.

Answer: (d)

Challenging
Multi
Page: 379

Moderate
Single
Page: 379

17.179: If it becomes more expensive for firms to hold excess capital and labor, the multiplier will

(a) decrease.
(b) increase.
(c) remain unchanged.
(d) either increase or decrease depending on the value of the MPC.

Answer: (b)

Moderate
Single
Page: 379

17.180: Firms have inventories that they can draw down to meet an increase in demand. This will

(a) have no effect on the multiplier, because the MPC remains unchanged.
(b) increase the size of the multiplier, because firms will be able to respond more quickly to a change in demand.
(c) decrease the size of the multiplier, because output will not immediately respond to changes in demand.
(d) either increase or decrease the multiplier, depending on the size of the MPC.

Answer: (c)

Challenging
Multi
Page: 379

17.181: Suppose that input prices respond very quickly to output price. This will

(a) reduce the value of the multiplier.
(b) increase the value of the multiplier.
(c) have no effect on the value of the multiplier.
(d) either increase or decrease the value of the multiplier depending on the value of the MPC.

Answer: (a)

Moderate
Single
Page: 379

17.182: Suppose that in the United States people begin to spend a smaller fraction of their income on imports. This would cause the multiplier to

(a) decrease.
(b) increase.
(c) remain unchanged.
(d) either increase or decrease depending on the value of the MPC.

Answer: (b)

Easy
Fact
Page: 379

17.183: In practice, the size of the multiplier is about

(a) 1.
(b) 1.4.
(c) 2.5.
(d) 3.

Answer: (b)

Easy
Fact
Page: 379

17.184: The multiplier reaches its peak about _____ months after a spending increase began.

(a) three
(b) six to nine
(c) nine to twelve
(d) twelve to fifteen

Answer: (c)

TRUE/FALSE QUESTIONS

17.185: The key difference between the Keynesian theory of consumption and the life-cycle theory is that the life-cycle theory suggests that consumption and saving decisions are likely to be based not just on current income, but on expectations of future income as well.

Easy
Fact
Page: 359

Answer: True

17.186: Households look at expected future wage rates, as well as the current wage rate, in making their current consumption and labor supply decisions.

Easy
Fact
Page: 361

Answer: True

17.187: Jennifer just won the state lottery. This will likely have a positive effect on her labor supply.

Easy
Single
Page: 361

Answer: False

17.188: An unexpected decrease in wealth or nonlabor income leads to a decrease in the labor supply.

Easy
Fact
Page: 361

Answer: False

17.189: If the substitution effect dominates, an increase in transfer payments will have a positive effect on both consumption and labor supply.

Easy
Fact
Page: 363

Answer: False

17.190: A household's unconstrained and constrained supply of labor will generally be equal if there is full employment.

Easy
Fact
Page: 364

Answer: True

17.191: According to the accelerator effect, there is a tendency for investment to increase when aggregate output increases, thus accelerating the growth of output.

Easy
Fact
Page: 371

Answer: True

17.192: The more excess capital a firm has, the less likely it is to invest in new capital in the future.

Easy
Fact
Page: 371

Answer: True

17.193: The optimal level of inventories is the level at which the extra cost (in lost sales) from lowering inventories by a small amount is just equal to the gain (in interest revenue and decreased storage costs).

Easy
Fact
Page: 372

Answer: True

17.194: An unexpected increase in inventories has a positive effect on future production.

Easy
Fact
Page: 373

Answer: False

17.195: If the substitution effect is larger than the income effect, a decrease in tax rates will lead to an increase in the labor supply.

Difficult
Application
Page: 363

Answer: True

Easy
Application
Page: 359

17.196: A permanent tax cut of 10% would cause an increase in consumption, an increase in output, an increase in the price level, and a decrease in unemployment equally as much as a temporary tax cut would.

Answer: False

Moderate
Application
Page: 376

17.197: The long-run potential of the economy declines as productivity declines in a recession.

Answer: False

Easy
Fact
Page: 362

17.198: Any increase in nonlabor income unambiguously leads to an increase in consumption and a decrease in labor supply.

Answer: True

Easy
Fact
Page: 362

17.199: An increase in corporate profits will increase consumption and increase labor supply.

Answer: False

Easy
Fact
Page: 373

17.200: Output is likely to respond more to sales increases in high-output periods than in low-output periods, provided that firms have enough capital and labor to support the output increase.

Answer: True

Easy
Fact
Page: 377

17.201: Productivity fluctuates over the business cycle, tending to fall during expansions and rise during contractions.

Answer: False

Easy
Fact
Page: 378

17.202: Recent research and data have shown that the relationship between output and unemployment is as stable as Okun's Law predicts.

Answer: False

Easy
Fact
Page: 379

17.203: The presence of automatic stabilizers increases the size of the multiplier.

Answer: False

Easy
Fact
Page: 379

17.204: The fact that the United States imports a good deal of what it consumes makes the multiplier larger than it would be if the U.S. economy were closed to trade.

Answer: False

SHORT ANSWER QUESTIONS

Easy
Definition
Page: 358

17.205: Define the average propensity to consume (APC). What portions of income tend to be spent by lower and higher income households? How does this affect a household's APC?

Answer: The average propensity to consume (APC) is the ratio or proportion of income spent at any level of income.

$$APC = \frac{C}{Y}$$

A larger portion of total income (higher APC) tends to be spent by low income consumers and a lower portion of total income (lower APC) tends to be spent by higher income consumers.

17.206: Define the substitution effect of a wage rate change. Define the income effect of a wage rate change. Discuss the impact of a wage rate increase upon the consumption decision of households.

Easy
Definition
Page: 360

Answer: The substitution effect of wage rate changes measures the rate at which an individual trades off wage rate changes, the motivation to work and earn income, and the need for leisure time. An increase in wages results in an increase in the quantity of labor supplied and less leisure. A lower wage rate increases leisure time at the expense of labor supplied. The income effect measures how a change in the person's wage rate alters their purchasing power and purchases of goods and services versus the pursuit of leisure time. An increase in the wage rate results in both the income and substitution effects working in the same direction to increase consumption. There is a positive income effect which results in increased consumption and a substitution effect that would additionally result in increased work and less leisure. In sum, consumption increases when the wage rate increases.

17.207: What is the usual and expected relationship between changes in wealth and the labor supply?

Moderate
Application
Page: 361

Answer: In general, there would tend to be an inverse relationship between a person's and household's wealth and changes in the labor supply. An unexpected increase in wealth or nonlabor income tends to result in a decrease in labor supply.

17.208: Explain the substitution effect with regard to the impact of interest rate changes on consumption. Explain the income effect with regard to the impact of interest rate changes on consumption.

Moderate
Application
Page: 362

Answer: The interest rate substitution effect relates to the opportunity cost of present or future consumption in response to interest rate changes. The income effect of interest rate changes relates to the effect of interest rate changes upon nonlabor income and its impact upon consumption. Increases in interest rates result in greater nonlabor income which should discourage immediate, rather than future, consumption.

17.209: Explain how a decrease in taxes and increase in transfer payments effect consumption and labor supply payments.

Moderate
Application
Page: 363

Answer: A decrease in taxes increases disposable income which will increase consumption. Also, an increase in transfer payments means that nonlabor income has increased which will increase consumption. The decrease in taxes will increase the labor supply, while the higher transfer payments will decrease the labor supply.

17.210: Explain the life-cycle theory of consumption. How does it differ from the Keynesian theory of consumption?

Moderate
Fact
Page: 358

Answer: According to the life-cycle theory of consumption, households make lifetime consumption decisions based on their expectations of lifetime income. Individuals are likely to borrow during their early years, save during their prime working years, and live off accumulated savings during their later years. According to the Keynesian theory of consumption, the main determinant of consumption is current income.

Moderate
Multi
Page: 359

17.211: Using the life-cycle theory of consumption, explain each of the following: (a.) Mary and Tom both earn $15,000. Mary spends $30,000 a year and Tom spends $14,000 a year. Mary is working on her MBA degree and Tom, a high school dropout, works as a window washer. (b.) Paul's current income has not changed, but he becomes pessimistic about the economy and worries about losing his job. As a result, he reduces his current consumption.

Answer: (a.) Mary's permanent income is higher than Tom's, so Mary's current and future consumption will be higher than Tom's. (b.) Paul's expectation of future income is reduced. This reduces his permanent income and causes him to reduce his current level of consumption.

Easy
Fact
Page: 360

17.212: Households make consumption and labor supply decisions simultaneously. Explain why.

Answer: Consumption cannot be considered separately from labor supply because an individual earns the income that makes consumption possible by working. To be able to spend a certain amount on consumption, an individual must have a sufficient income. Thus the amount an individual plans to spend will influence his or her decision about the number of hours to work.

Moderate
Multi
Page: 362

17.213: Rick has net assets of $50,000. How will an increase in the interest rate affect Rick's consumption? How will your answer change if Rick's fortunes change and his net assets fall to -$10,000?

Answer: If Rick's net assets are $50,000, an increase in the interest rate will have an ambiguous effect on his consumption. The substitution effect will cause Rick to reduce his consumption, because he will substitute away from current consumption toward future consumption. An increase in the interest rate increases the price of current consumption relative to future consumption. The income effect will cause Rick's current consumption to increase because his current wealth has increased. If Rick becomes a debtor, the increase in the interest rate will not have an ambiguous effect, but will cause Rick's consumption to fall. The substitution effect raises the price of current consumption relative to future consumption, so current consumption will be reduced. Higher interest rates now mean higher interest payments, so Rick's income is reduced, which causes his consumption to fall.

Easy
Fact
Page: 364

17.214: Explain the difference between the unconstrained supply of labor and the constrained supply of labor. Why doesn't a household have control over its constrained supply of labor?

Answer: A household's unconstrained supply of labor is the amount it would like to work within a given period at the current wage rate if it could find the work. A household's constrained supply of labor is the amount it actually works in a given period at the current wage rate. A household doesn't have control over its constrained supply of labor because the amount of labor the household supplies is imposed on it by the workings of the economy.

Moderate
Multi
Page: 365

17.215: Explain what impact each of the following is likely to have on consumption. (a.) stock prices fall. (b.) The government announces that in 1994 and only in 1994 every family will have to pay an additional lump-sum tax of $100. (c.) Most economic forecasts indicate that the growth rate will slow down considerably over the next decade.

Answer: (a.) If stock prices fall, household wealth is decreased and consumption should fall. (b.) A one-time lump-sum tax should not have much effect on consumption because it will not change a household's permanent income. (c.) A forecast of lower growth rates should cause people to expect lower incomes in the future and to reduce their current consumption.

17.216: Explain the accelerator effect.

Easy
Definition
Page: 371

Answer: According to the accelerator effect, there is a tendency for investment to increase when aggregate output increases and a tendency for investment to decrease when aggregate output decreases. As investment increases, the growth in output is accelerated. As investment decreases, the decline in output is accelerated.

17.217: What did Keynes mean by the phrase "animal spirits of entrepreneurs"? Why do these "spirits" make investment a volatile component of GDP?

Easy
Fact
Page: 370

Answer: Animal spirits of entrepreneurs refers to the feelings of entrepreneurs and the fact that investment decisions are often made on the basis of a firm's optimism or pessimism about the state of the economy. Expectations are subject to uncertainty, which makes investment volatile.

17.218: Explain why the presence of significant adjustment costs might induce a firm to hold excess labor. Would you expect adjustments costs to be high or low in a firm whose workers' skills are very specific to the firm? Explain.

Moderate
Single
Page: 371

Answer: If adjustment costs are high, it may be more costly to lay off workers than to retain them. A firm whose workers' have skills very specific to the firm is likely to have high adjustment costs. If the firm has to hire new workers when production increases, it will incur great expense to train these new workers.

17.219: What is the optimal level of inventories? What are the costs of holding inventories? What are the benefits of holding inventories? How will an increase in interest rates affect the optimal level of inventories?

Moderate
Single
Page: 372

Answer: The optimal level of inventories is the level of inventory at which the extra cost from lowering inventories by a small amount is just equal to the extra gain. The cost of holding inventories is the cost of storage and the interest revenue that is lost on the income tied up in inventories. The benefit of holding inventories is the ability to meet an unforeseen increase in demand. An increase in the interest rate would reduce the optimal level of inventory because it would increase the cost of holding inventory.

18.220: Define and explain the difference between the income and substitution effects in relation to changes in taxes.

Difficult
Definition
Page: 352

Answer: Assume that the government passes a tax cut. This makes households better off than they were before. The income effect leads workers to consume more leisure time, thus to work less. However, the substitution effect leads workers to want to work more. Note: This would not be true if the government passed a lump sum tax reduction because this tax cut does not realize the same trade-offs between work and leisure.

18.221: Explain the discouraged worker effect and how it relates to changes in output.

Easy
Application
Page: 378

Answer: The discouraged worker effect is the decline in the measured unemployment rate that results when people who want to work but cannot find work grow discouraged and stop looking for work, thus dropping out of the ranks of the unemployed and the labor force. When output begins to increase in the economy, job prospects improve and some people begin looking for work again. When they do, they are back in the labor force so the labor force increases. Thus, as output increases, discouraged workers begin moving back into the labor force and the labor force increases as well.

Easy
Application
Page: 377

18.222: Define and explain Okun's Law. Assume the economy in 1995 grew 4%. Based on Okun's Law, how would the unemployment rate be affected? Is Okun's Law really a law? Is it true all of the time?

Answer: This is the theory developed by Arthur Okun that the unemployment rate decreases about one percent for every 3% increase in GDP. According to Okun's law, if GDP grew 4%, then unemployment would fall 1.33%. No, Okun's Law has turned out not really to be a law after all. This relationship between output and unemployment has turned out not to be very stable. The economy is far too complex for there to be such simple and predictable relationships as Okun's Law indicates.

Honors
Single
Page: 363

18.223: Explain why a reduction in tax rates will have a different effect on household labor supply decisions than a lump-sum tax rebate that initially raises disposable income by the same amount.

Answer: A reduction in tax rates has both an income effect and a substitution effect. The income effect would cause labor supply to decrease, but the substitution effect would cause labor supply to increase. The impact of a reduction in tax rates is ambiguous. The impact of a lump-sum tax rebate is not ambiguous. A lump-sum tax rebate has only an income effect, which causes labor supply to fall.

Challenging
Multi
Page: 379

18.224: For each of the following, indicate the likely effects on consumer spending, labor supply, planned aggregate investment, the overall price level, aggregate output, and employment. (a.) The economy is operating at capacity and the Fed contracts the money supply. (b.) The economy is operating well below capacity and the government increases the level of welfare payments and changes the eligibility rules to make more people eligible for welfare. (c.) The economy is in a mild recession and the government enacts a permanent change in the tax code that will increase corporate profits.

Answer: (a.) If the economy is operating at capacity and the Fed reduces the money supply, interest rates will increase. This will cause consumer spending either to increase or decrease depending on the income and substitution effects. Planned aggregate investment will decrease, which will decrease aggregate demand, causing the price level to rise. Because the economy is on the steep portion of the AS curve, there will be very little change in aggregate output or employment. (b.) An increase in transfer payments will increase consumption and decrease labor supply in those households eligible for the transfer payments. This increase in consumption will increase aggregate demand, and because the economy is well below capacity, aggregate output will increase with little or no increase in the price level. The increase in output should increase employment if firms are not holding excess labor. The increase in output should also increase investment if firms are not holding excess capital. (c.) If the economy is in a mild recession and a permanent change in the tax code increases corporate profits, consumption should increase and labor supply should decrease. The increase in consumption will increase aggregate demand, causing aggregate output and the overall price level to increase. The increase in output should increase employment if firms are not holding excess labor. The increase in output should also increase investment if firms are not holding excess capital.

Moderate
Single
Page: 376

18.225: Productivity tends to rise during periods of high output and fall during periods of low output. Explain why this is TRUE. Are productivity figures a good way to diagnose the health of the economy over the short run? Why or why not?

Answer: Productivity is measured as output per worker hour. During periods of low output, firms tend to hold excess labor. This tends to reduce productivity because output is falling, but employment does not fall as much as productivity does. During periods of high output, productivity will tend to rise because output will be increasing and employment will initially remain constant. Productivity figures are not a good way to diagnose the health of the economy because business cycles distort the meaning of the productivity measurements. Productivity will change as the amount of excess labor held by the firm changes. A change in productivity in the short run does not actually mean that the productivity of workers has changed.

18.226: A 1% increase in output tends to correspond to a less-than-1% decrease in the unemployment rate. What are the three "slippages" that occur between changes in output and changes in the unemployment rate?

Moderate
Fact
Page: 378

Answer: The first slippage is between the change in output and the change in the number of jobs in the economy. When output increases by 1%, the number of jobs increases by less than 1%. The second slippage is between the change in the number of jobs and the change in the number of people employed. If a person has two jobs, that person is counted only once in the persons-employed data. If some new jobs are filled by people who already have jobs, there will be no change in the unemployment rate. The third slippage is between the response of the labor force to an increase in output. As output increases, the size of the labor force increases. Discouraged workers reenter the labor force as the economy expands, and this means that the measured unemployment rate does not fall as much as it would have if the discouraged workers had not reentered the labor force.

18.227: Is it possible that the aggregate output in the economy could be increasing at the same time that unemployment is increasing? Why or why not?

Moderate
Single
Page: 378

Answer: It is possible for aggregate output in the economy to be increasing at the same time that unemployment is increasing. This could be caused by discouraged workers reentering the labor force once the economy starts to expand. If discouraged workers are reentering at a faster rate than unemployed people are finding jobs, the unemployment rate will rise. An increasing unemployment rate may also be caused by firms switching from labor-intensive to capital-intensive production techniques.

18.228: Explain why each of the following reduces the size of the multiplier.

(a.) automatic stabilizers
(b.) an increase in the interest rate
(c.) the existence of excess capital and excess labor
(d.) imported goods

Moderate
Multi
Page: 379

Answer: (a.). When the economy expands, automatic stabilizers cause an increase in the amount of taxes collected. As tax collections increase, income falls and consumption falls. Thus, automatic stabilizers reduce the effectiveness of an expansionary policy. (b.) As interest rates increase, investment is crowded out, causing aggregate demand to fall and aggregate output to increase by less than it would have if investment had not been crowded out. Higher interest rates may also reduce consumption, which will also reduce the effectiveness of an expansionary policy. (c.) If firms are holding excess capital and labor, then they will not increase employment and investment as the economy starts to expand, and the effectiveness of expansionary policy will be reduced. (d.) Expenditures on imported goods represent a leakage. Money that is spent on imported goods is not passed on to domestic business firms, but goes outside the country. This reduces the size of the multiplier.

Challenging
Multi
Page: 379

18.229: The government wants to enact policies that will lead to an increase in the size of the multiplier. Suggest two policies that the government could implement to accomplish this goal. Why do you think the policies you have suggested have not been implemented?

Answer: Two policies would be

(1.) the elimination of automatic stabilizers and (2.) increased restrictions on imports. These policies have most likely not be implemented because of the negative consequences that would result. The elimination of automatic stabilizers would make the effects of expansions and contractions worse. Imposing stricter controls on imports may lead to retaliation by trading partners.

18 Debates in Macroeconomics: Monetarism, New Classical Theory, and Supply-Side Economics

(Chapter 33 in Combined Text)

MULTIPLE CHOICE QUESTIONS

18.1: In recent years, the term "Keynesian" has been used to refer to economists

(a) who oppose government intervention in the macroeconomy.
(b) who advocate active government intervention in the macroeconomy.
(c) who argue that "supply management" should be at the heart of macroeconomic policy.
(d) who believe that firms, on average, set market-clearing wages and prices.

Answer: (b)

Easy
Fact
Page: 386

18.2: In recent years, two major schools of thought have developed that are decidedly against government intervention in the macroeconomy. One of those schools is known as

(a) post-Keynesian economics.
(b) Marxism.
(c) monetarism.
(d) institutionalism.

Answer: (c)

Easy
Fact
Page: 386

18.3: Which of the following schools of economic thought is not decidedly opposed to government intervention in the macroeconomy?

(a) Keynesian
(b) monetarism
(c) new classical
(d) rational expectations

Answer: (a)

Easy
Fact
Page: 386

18.4: Tod, an economist, argues that the government should always use expansionary fiscal policy to move the economy out of a recession. Tod should be classified as a

(a) monetarist.
(b) Keynesian.
(c) supply-side economist.
(d) new classical economist

Answer: (b)

Easy
Single
Page: 386

18.5: The ratio of nominal GDP to the stock of money is the

(a) money multiplier.
(b) GDP deflator.
(c) real GDP.
(d) velocity of money.

Answer: (d)

Easy
Definition
Page: 386

507

Easy
Definition
Page: 386

18.6: The number of times a dollar bill changes hands on average during the course of a year is the

(a) velocity of money.
(b) inflation rate.
(c) price level of money.
(d) average money supply.

Answer: (a)

Easy
Definition
Page: 386

18.7: The income velocity of money is the ratio of

(a) real GDP to the stock of money.
(b) nominal GDP to the stock of money.
(c) the overall price level to the stock of money.
(d) nominal GDP to the overall price level.

Answer: (b)

Easy
Single
Page: 386

18.8: If nominal GDP is $900 billion and the money supply is $300 billion, the velocity of money is

(a) .33.
(b) 1.5.
(c) 2.
(d) 3.

Answer: (d)

Moderate
Single
Page: 386

18.9: The velocity of money is 4. If nominal GDP is $1,200 billion then the stock of money

(a) is $300 billion.
(b) is $400 billion.
(c) is $4,800 billion.
(d) cannot be determined from this information.

Answer: (a)

Moderate
Single
Page: 386

18.10: The velocity of money is 2. If the money stock is $500 billion, then nominal GDP

(a) is $250 billion.
(b) is $750 billion.
(c) $1,000 billion.
(d) cannot be determined from this information.

Answer: (c)

Easy
Fact
Page: 387

18.11: The identity MV = PY can be given economic content by a simple assumption that

(a) real output always (or almost always) expands at a constant rate.
(b) the money supply always (or almost always) expands at a constant rate.
(c) the velocity of money is constant (or virtually constant).
(d) the velocity of money always (or almost always) expands at a constant rate.

Answer: (c)

18.12: The quantity theory of money implies that a given percentage change in the money supply will cause

Moderate
Fact
Page: 387

(a) an equal percentage change in nominal GDP.
(b) a smaller percentage change in nominal GDP.
(c) a larger percentage change in nominal GDP.
(d) an equal percentage change in real GDP.

Answer: (a)

18.13: According to the quantity theory of money if the money supply is increased by 20%, then nominal GDP

Moderate
Fact
Page: 387

(a) increases by 20%.
(b) decreases by 20%.
(c) remains constant.
(d) decreases by less than 20%.

Answer: (a)

18.14: According to the quantity theory of money, nominal GDP will triple if the money supply is

Moderate
Single
Page: 387

(a) reduced by one-third.
(b) reduced three fold.
(c) increased by one-third.
(d) tripled.

Answer: (d)

18.15: The quantity theory of money can be written as

Easy
Fact
Page: 387

(a) $M/V = PY$.
(b) $MV = PY$.
(c) $MV = P/Y$.
(d) $MP = VP$.

Answer: (b)

18.16: According to the quantity theory of money, if velocity is constant then nominal GDP cannot increase unless

Easy
Fact
Page: 387

(a) the price level increases.
(b) the interest rate increases.
(c) the capital stock increases.
(d) the money supply increases.

Answer: (d)

18.17: Velocity is not constant if

Easy
Fact
Page: 387

(a) the demand for money depends on the interest rate.
(b) the supply of money depends on the interest rate.
(c) the price level increases as aggregate output increases.
(d) the money supply does not depend on the interest rate.

Answer: (a)

Moderate
Single
Page: 387

18.18: If the demand for money depends on the interest rate, velocity is

(a) not constant, and the quantity theory of money does hold.
(b) constant, and the quantity theory of money does not hold.
(c) not constant, and the quantity theory of money does not hold.
(d) constant, and the quantity theory of money does hold.

Answer: (c)

Moderate
Single
Page: 387

18.19: If the demand for money does not depend on the interest rate, velocity

(a) may very well be constant, and the quantity theory of money does hold.
(b) may very well be constant, and the quantity theory of money does not hold.
(c) is not constant, and the quantity theory of money does hold.
(d) is not constant, and the quantity theory of money does not hold.

Answer: (a)

Moderate
Single
Page: 389

18.20: If the demand for money depends on the interest rate, then a 10% increase in the money supply will increase

(a) nominal GDP by 10%.
(b) nominal GDP by less than 10%.
(c) nominal GDP by more than 10%.
(d) real GDP by 10%.

Answer: (b)

Honors
Multi
Page: 388

18.21: Assume that the demand for money depends on the interest rate. An increase in the money supply will cause

(a) the interest rate to increase, the quantity demanded of money to decrease, and the velocity of money to decrease.
(b) the interest rate to increase, the quantity demanded of money to decrease, and the velocity of money to increase.
(c) the interest rate to decrease, the quantity demanded of money to decrease, and the velocity of money to increase.
(d) the interest rate to decrease, the quantity demanded of money to increase, and the velocity of money to decrease.

Answer: (d)

Moderate
Single
Page: 388

18.22: If the demand for money depends on the interest rate, then as the supply of money is reduced the velocity of money

(a) either increases or decreases depending upon how much the money supply was reduced.
(b) remains constant.
(c) decreases.
(d) increases.

Answer: (d)

18.23: If the demand for money depends on the interest rate, then as the money supply is increased the velocity of money

Moderate
Single
Page: 388

(a) increases.
(b) decreases.
(c) remains constant.
(d) either increases or decreases, depending upon the amount by which the money supply was increased.

Answer: (b)

18.24: Which of the following statements is NOT consistent with the quantity theory of money?

Moderate
Single
Page: 388

(a) The velocity of money can be affected by how frequently workers are paid.
(b) Velocity should change with changes in the interest rate.
(c) The velocity of money should be affected by the manner in which the banking system clears transactions between banks.
(d) The velocity of money should be affected by the development of new financial instruments, such as interest-bearing checking accounts.

Answer: (b)

18.25: Velocity will be constant if the demand for money with respect to the interest rate is

Challenging
Single
Page: 388

(a) unitarily elastic.
(b) perfectly elastic.
(c) perfectly inelastic.
(d) elastic, but not perfectly elastic.

Answer: (c)

18.26: Which of the following statements is FALSE?

Moderate
Single
Page: 388

(a) The velocity of money can be affected by institutional arrangements, such as how often people are paid and how the banking system clears transactions between banks.
(b) If the demand for money depends on the interest rate, then the velocity of money is not constant.
(c) If the velocity of money is constant, then nominal GDP cannot change unless the money supply changes.
(d) The quantity theory of money is valid only if the demand for money depends on the interest rate.

Answer: (d)

18.27: Empirical evidence suggests that

Easy
Fact
Page: 388

(a) the velocity of money is independent of the interest rate.
(b) the velocity of money has been constant over time.
(c) since 1960 the long-term trend has been an increase in the velocity of money.
(d) on average, since 1960 the velocity of money has not changed in any consistent manner.

Answer: (c)

Challenging
Multi
Page: 388

18.28: Assume the velocity of money is calculated by using M1 to measure the supply of money. Now suppose banking regulations are changed so that banks can now pay higher interest rates on money market accounts. This will cause

(a) no change in the velocity of money.
(b) the velocity of money to decrease.
(c) the velocity of money to increase.
(d) the velocity of money to change, but the direction of the change is ambiguous.

Answer: (c)

Easy
Fact
Page: 389

18.29: It is difficult to determine if the velocity of money is constant over time, because

(a) there has been very little fluctuation in the money supply over time.
(b) whether velocity is constant or not may depend on how the money supply is measured.
(c) it is difficult to measure the value of nominal GDP over time.
(d) it is difficult to measure the demand for money over time.

Answer: (b)

Easy
Fact
Page: 389

18.30: It is difficult to test whether the velocity of money is constant over time, because

(a) there has been very little variation in the money supply over time.
(b) there is only one definition of the money supply.
(c) there may be a time lag between a change in the money supply and its effects on nominal GDP.
(d) it is difficult to measure the value of nominal GDP over time.

Answer: (c)

Easy
Fact
Page: 389

18.31: One of the main insights of monetarism is that

(a) velocity is unstable and subject to wide fluctuations.
(b) the government can effectively manage aggregate demand by using its spending and taxing powers.
(c) sustained inflation is a purely monetary phenomenon.
(d) inflation can continue indefinitely without the cooperation of the Federal Reserve.

Answer: (c)

Moderate
Single
Page: 389

18.32: Assume that the velocity of money is constant and that the economy is on the vertical portion of the aggregate supply curve. An increase in the money supply will cause

(a) an increase in aggregate output, but no change in the price level.
(b) an increase in the price level, but no change in aggregate output.
(c) an increase in both the price level and aggregate output.
(d) no change in either the price level or aggregate output.

Answer: (b)

Easy
Fact
Page: 390

18.33: Inflation cannot continue indefinitely without

(a) increases in the money supply.
(b) increases in aggregate output.
(c) increases in investment.
(d) increases in the interest rate.

Answer: (a)

18.34: The leading spokesman for monetarism over the last few decades
has been

Easy
Fact
Page: 390

(a) Milton Friedman.
(b) John Kenneth Galbraith.
(c) Robert E. Lucas.
(d) Paul Samuelson.

Answer: (a)

18.35: Monetarists advocate

Easy
Fact
Page: 390

(a) an activist stabilization policy.
(b) a policy of steady and slow money growth.
(c) expanding the money supply during recessions, and slowing the growth of the money
supply during expansions.
(d) the view that the government should attempt to "πmanage" the economy.

Answer: (b)

18.36: Monetarists argue that the money supply should

Easy
Fact
Page: 390

(a) grow at a rate greater than the average growth of real output.
(b) grow at a rate slower than the average growth of real output.
(c) grow at a rate equal to the average growth of real output.
(d) be held constant over the business cycle.

Answer: (c)

18.37: If the average growth rate of real output is 3%, then monetarists would argue that

Easy
Single
Page: 390

(a) the money supply should be increased by 3% per year.
(b) the money supply should be increased by 6% per year.
(c) the money supply should be increased by 1.5% per year.
(d) government spending should be increased by 3% per year.

Answer: (a)

18.38: Which of the following statements is TRUE?

Moderate
Fact
Page: 390

(a) Keynesians no longer advocate the application of coordinated monetary and fiscal
policy to reduce instability in the economy.
(b) All Keynesians advocate an activist federal government.
(c) Keynesians argue that only money matters in terms of fighting inflation and
unemployment.
(d) The notion that monetary and fiscal expansions and contractions can "fine tune" the
economy is gone forever.

Answer: (d)

18.39: New classical theories were an attempt to explain

Easy
Fact
Page: 390

(a) how unemployment could have persisted for so long during the Great Depression.
(b) the increase in the growth rate of real output in the 1950s.
(c) why policy changes that are perceived as permanent have more of an impact on a
person's behavior than policy changes that are viewed as temporary.
(d) the stagflation of the 1970s.

Answer: (d)

Easy
Fact
Page: 392

18.40: Traditional macroeconomic models assume that people's expectations of inflation

(a) are determined by looking at all the relevant information and forecasting the future inflation rate.
(b) are set by assuming a continuation of present inflation.
(c) will be zero in the future.
(d) are set by merely guessing what the future inflation rate will be.

Answer: (b)

Easy
Fact
Page: 392

18.41: Which of the following statements would a new classical macroeconomist agree with?

(a) The expectations that individuals have about the future are irrelevant to macroeconomic analysis.
(b) People actively seek to forecast the future.
(c) People generally assume that the future will be like the past.
(d) Traditional macroeconomic models incorporate a realistic view of the way in which people form their expectations.

Answer: (b)

Easy
Fact
Page: 391

18.42: The problem with the traditional macroeconomic treatment of expectations of inflation is that

(a) the way people formulate expectations in that model assumes that individuals are highly sophisticated in their economic thinking.
(b) the model assumes that individuals will merely guess at what the inflation rate will be.
(c) in the model people always assume that inflation will be zero.
(d) the model is not consistent with the microeconomic assumption that individuals are rational, forward-looking people.

Answer: (d)

Easy
Definition
Page: 392

18.43: The hypothesis that people know the "true model" of the economy and that they use this model to form their expectations of the future is the

(a) rational-expectations hypothesis.
(b) adaptive-expectations hypothesis.
(c) passive-expectations hypothesis.
(d) lagged-expectations hypothesis.

Answer: (a)

Easy
Definition
Page: 392

18.44: According to the rational-expectations hypothesis,

(a) people assume that the current inflation rate will continue into the future.
(b) if people incorrectly anticipate the inflation rate, they adjust their expectations of inflation by some fraction of the difference between their original forecast and the actual inflation rate.
(c) people form expectations of inflation only if the benefits of doing so exceed the costs of not forming expectations.
(d) people know the true model that generates inflation and use this model to forecast future inflation rates.

Answer: (d)

18.45: The rational-expectations hypothesis suggests that the forecasts that people make concerning future inflation rates

Moderate
Fact
Page: 392

(a) are always correct.
(b) consistently overestimate the actual rate of inflation in the future.
(c) consistently underestimate the actual rate of inflation in the future.
(d) are correct on average, but are subject to errors that are distributed randomly.

Answer: (d)

18.46: The rational-expectations hypothesis suggests that errors in forecasting future inflation rates are due to

Easy
Fact
Page: 392

(a) the fact that people assume that the current inflation rate will continue into the future.
(b) random, unpredictable events.
(c) the fact that people consistently underestimate future inflation.
(d) the fact that people consistently overestimate future inflation.

Answer: (b)

18.47: People are said to have rational expectations if they

Easy
Fact
Page: 392

(a) assume that this year's inflation rate will be the same as last year's inflation rate.
(b) assume that this year's inflation rate will be equal to the average inflation rate over the past 10 years.
(c) merely guess at the inflation rate.
(d) use all available information in forming their expectations.

Answer: (d)

18.48: If firms have rational expectations and if they set prices and wages on this basis, then prices and wages

Easy
Fact
Page: 392

(a) will always be at market-clearing levels.
(b) will always be above market-clearing levels.
(c) will, on average, be set at market-clearing levels.
(d) will never be set at market-clearing levels.

Answer: (c)

18.49: If firms have rational expectations and if they set prices and wages on this basis, then on average

Moderate
Fact
Page: 392

(a) prices and wages will be set at levels that do not clear the goods and labor markets.
(b) prices will be set at levels that ensure equilibrium in the goods market, but wages will be set at levels that do not clear the labor market.
(c) prices and wages will be set at levels that ensure equilibrium in the goods and labor markets.
(d) wages will be set at levels that ensure equilibrium in the labor market, but prices will be set at levels that do not clear the goods market.

Answer: (c)

18.50: When expectations are rational, disequilibrium in any market

Moderate
Fact
Page: 392

(a) is only a temporary phenomenon resulting from random, unpredictable shocks.
(b) is a permanent condition resulting from institutional rigidities in the economy.
(c) is only a temporary phenomenon resulting from the tendency for prices to adjust downward quickly but upward slowly.
(d) is a permanent condition resulting from random, unpredictable shocks.

Answer: (a)

Challenging
Multi
Page: 393

18.51: If expectations are rational, the multiplier would be

(a) negative.
(b) zero.
(c) infinitely large.
(d) larger than its currently estimated value of 1.4.

Answer: (b)

Moderate
Fact
Page: 393

18.52: According to the rational expectations hypothesis, the existence of unemployment is due to

(a) imperfect information.
(b) a deficient level of aggregate demand.
(c) downwardly rigid wages.
(d) unpredictable shocks.

Answer: (d)

Moderate
Fact
Page: 393

18.53: According to the rational-expectations hypothesis,

(a) there is a need for government stabilization policies, and unemployment is a problem that the government should worry about.
(b) there is no need for government stabilization policies, and unemployment is not a problem that the government needs to worry about.
(c) there is no need for government stabilization policies, but unemployment is a problem that the government needs to worry about.
(d) there is a need for government stabilization policies, but unemployment is not a problem that the government needs to worry
about.

Answer: (b)

Easy
Definition
Page: 393

18.54: The function that embodies the idea that output depends on the difference between the actual price level and the expected price level is known as the

(a) aggregate supply function.
(b) aggregate production function.
(c) Lucas supply function.
(d) production possibilities frontier.

Answer: (c)

Easy
Fact
Page: 393

18.55: According to the Lucas supply function, real output depends on the difference between the

(a) actual level of output and the full-employment level of output.
(b) actual price level and the expected price level.
(c) actual unemployment rate and the full-employment rate of unemployment.
(d) current price level and last period's price level.

Answer: (b)

Easy
Definition
Page: 393

18.56: In the Lucas supply function, the price surprise is

(a) the actual price level minus the expected price level.
(b) the actual inflation rate minus the expected inflation rate.
(c) the expected price level minus the actual price level.
(d) the expected rate of inflation minus the actual rate of inflation.

Answer: (a)

18.57: The Lucas supply function can be represented by:

(a) $Y = f(P_e - P)$.
(b) $Y = f(P - P_e)$.
(c) $Y = f(P/P_e)$.
(d) $Y = f(P_e / P)$.

Easy
Fact
Page: 393

Answer: (b)

18.58: An assumption underlying the Lucas supply function is that people and firms are

(a) specialists in consumption, but generalists in production.
(b) generalists in both production and consumption.
(c) specialists in both production and consumption.
(d) specialists in production, but generalists in consumption.

Easy
Fact
Page: 393

Answer: (d)

18.59: The assumption that underlies the Lucas supply function implies

(a) people know much more about the prices of the things they buy than they do about the prices of the things they sell.
(b) people know much more about the prices of the things they sell than they do about the prices of the things they buy.
(c) people have extensive knowledge about both the prices of the things they sell and the prices of the things they buy.
(d) people have little knowledge about the prices of the things they sell or about the prices of the things they buy.

Easy
Fact
Page: 393

Answer: (b)

18.60: According to the Lucas supply function, if the average price level turns out to be higher than a firm expected, then the firm

(a) correctly perceives that its price has risen relative to other prices, which leads it to produce more output.
(b) incorrectly perceives that its price has fallen relative to other prices, which leads it to produce less output.
(c) incorrectly perceives that its price has risen relative to other prices, which leads it to produce more output.
(d) correctly perceives that its price has fallen relative to other prices, which leads it to produce less output.

Moderate
Single
Page: 393

Answer: (c)

18.61: According to the Lucas supply function, if the average price level turns out to be lower than the firm expected, then the firm

(a) incorrectly perceives that its price has fallen relative to other prices, which leads it to produce less output.
(b) correctly perceives that its price has fallen relative to other prices, which leads it to produce less output.
(c) incorrectly perceives that its price has risen relative to other prices, which leads it to produce more output.
(d) correctly perceives that its price has risen relative to other prices, which leads it to produce more output.

Moderate
Single
Page: 393

Answer: (a)

Moderate
Multi
Page: 393

18.62: Assume the substitution effect dominates the income effect. If there is a positive price surprise, workers believe that their real wage

(a) has fallen and they will supply more labor.
(b) has fallen and they will supply less labor.
(c) has risen and they will supply more labor.
(d) has risen and they will supply less labor.

Answer: (c)

Challenging
Multi
Page: 393

18.63: Assume that the substitution effect dominates the income effect. When workers experience a negative price surprise, they

(a) correctly perceive that their real wage rate has fallen, which leads them to work fewer hours.
(b) incorrectly perceive that their real wage rate has fallen, which leads them to work fewer hours.
(c) correctly perceive that their real wage rate has risen, which leads them to work more hours.
(d) incorrectly perceive that their real wage rate has risen, which leads them to work more hours.

Answer: (b)

Moderate
Fact
Page: 393

18.64: According to the Lucas supply function, if workers experience a positive price surprise, they will work more hours. This conclusion is based on the assumption that

(a) there is no substitution effect from a positive price surprise.
(b) there is no income effect from a positive price surprise.
(c) the substitution effect dominates the income effect.
(d) the income effect dominates the substitution effect.

Answer: (c)

Easy
Fact
Page: 393

18.65: According to the Lucas supply function, the amount of output produced is not related to the price level, if

(a) people's expectations of the price level are on target.
(b) people's expectations of the price level are higher than the actual price level.
(c) people's expectations of the price level are lower than the actual price level.
(d) people's expectations of the price level are either higher or lower than the actual price level.

Answer: (a)

Moderate
Single
Page: 393

18.66: According to the Lucas supply function, the economy will produce more output when

(a) prices are exactly equal to the expected level.
(b) wages are below the expected level.
(c) prices are unexpectedly lower than when prices are at their expected level.
(d) prices are unexpectedly higher than when prices are at their
expected level.

Answer: (d)

18.67: The Lucas supply function in combination with the assumption that expectations are rational implies that announced policy changes

(a) will have no effect on the actual price level.
(b) will have no effect on the expected price level.
(c) will have no effect on real output.
(d) will have no effect on nominal output.

Easy
Fact
Page: 394

Answer: (c)

18.68: According to the Lucas supply function, if people's expectations are on target, then the amount of output they produce

(a) is not related to the price level.
(b) is directly related to the price level.
(c) will always be below potential GDP.
(d) will always be above potential GDP.

Moderate
Fact
Page: 394

Answer: (a)

18.69: The Lucas supply function in combination with the assumption that expectations are rational implies that

(a) an anticipated monetary policy change will have no effect on real output, but an anticipated fiscal policy change will have an effect on real output.
(b) an anticipated monetary policy change will have an effect on real output, but an anticipated fiscal policy change will not have an effect on real output.
(c) both anticipated monetary and fiscal policy changes will affect real output.
(d) neither anticipated monetary policy changes nor anticipated fiscal policy changes will have an effect on real output.

Moderate
Fact
Page: 394

Answer: (d)

18.70: The Lucas supply function, in combination with the assumption that expectations are rational, implies that

(a) anticipated policy changes have a significant effect on real output.
(b) unanticipated policy changes have no effect on real output.
(c) anticipated policy changes have no effect on real output.
(d) the effect that policy changes have on real output is the same, regardless of whether those changes are anticipated or not.

Moderate
Fact
Page: 394

Answer: (c)

18.71: According to the Lucas supply function in combination with the assumption that expectations are rational, change in government policy can affect real output only if

(a) the policy change is a surprise.
(b) the policy change is correctly anticipated by the public.
(c) the policy change is a mix of both fiscal and monetary policy changes.
(d) expansionary policy changes are made.

Easy
Fact
Page: 394

Answer: (a)

18.72: The Lucas supply function, in combination with the assumption that expectations are rational, implies that an announced change in monetary policy affects

(a) the actual price level, but not the expected price level.
(b) both the actual price level and the expected price level.
(c) the expected price level, but not the actual price level.
(d) neither the actual price level nor the expected price level.

Easy
Fact
Page: 394

Answer: (b)

Moderate
Fact
Page: 394

18.73: The Lucas supply function, in combination with the assumption that expectations are rational, implies that an announced monetary policy change will lead to

(a) a positive price surprise.
(b) a negative price surprise.
(c) no price surprise.
(d) a positive price surprise for expansionary monetary policy, and a negative price surprise for contractionary monetary policy.

Answer: (c)

Moderate
Single
Page: 394

18.74: The Lucas supply function, in combination with the assumption that expectations are rational, implies that an announced monetary policy change will

(a) increase output, but never decrease output.
(b) decrease output, but never increase output.
(c) either increase or decrease output, depending on the type of monetary policychange.
(d) not change output.

Answer: (d)

Easy
Fact
Page: 394

18.75: The Lucas supply function implies that if people have rational expectations,

(a) known policy changes can produce no price surprises, and thus no increases in real output.
(b) unknown policy changes can produce no price surprises, and thus no increases in real output.
(c) known policy changes can produce price surprises, and thus increases in real output.
(d) known policy changes are impossible.

Answer: (a)

Easy
Fact
Page: 394

18.76: Rational-expectations theory, combined with the Lucas supply function, proposes

(a) an extensive role for government policy in the economy.
(b) a very small role for government policy in the economy.
(c) no role for government policy in the economy.
(d) a role for fiscal policy, but not monetary policy, in the economy.

Answer: (b)

Easy
Fact
Page: 394

18.77: The Lucas supply model, in combination with the assumption that expectations are rational, leads to the conclusion that

(a) expansionary policies, but not contractionary policies, can have an impact on real output.
(b) contractionary policies, but not expansionary policies, can have an impact on real output.
(c) only unanticipated policy changes can have an impact on output.
(d) neither anticipated nor unanticipated policy changes can have an impact on output.

Answer: (c)\

Moderate
Single
Page: 394

18.78: The argument in favor of rational expectations is that

(a) people will continue to acquire information as long as the marginal benefit of that information is positive.
(b) individuals have a very good idea of what to expect from the government in terms of monetary policy but not fiscal policy.
(c) it is costless for individuals and firms to form rational expectations.
(d) if expectations were not rational, there would be unexploited profit opportunities available.

Answer: (d)

18.79: The primary argument against the rational-expectations assumption is that

(a) the costs of formulating rational expectations are very low.
(b) it requires households and firms to know too much.
(c) it assumes that unexploited opportunities for profit persist in the economy.
(d) people expect certain outcomes from the government's policy actions.

Easy
Fact
Page: 394

Answer: (b)

18.80: The key question regarding the new classical macroeconomics is how realistic is the assumption

(a) that markets do not clear quickly.
(b) that fiscal policy affects aggregate demand.
(c) of rational expectations.
(d) that monetary policy affects aggregate demand.

Easy
Fact
Page: 394

Answer: (c)

18.81: Which of the following statements is TRUE?

(a) It may be unreasonable to expect people to form rational expectations because the gain from forming rational expectations may be less than the cost of doing so.
(b) The formation of rational expectations is completely consistent with the profit-maximizing assumption of microeconomics.
(c) It is realistic to assume that firms will form rational expectations, but it is not reasonable to assume that households will form rational expectations.
(d) The assumption that people form rational expectations has been proven by empirical analysis.

Easy
Fact
Page: 394

Answer: (a)

18.82: A group of economists argue that the real problem with the economy is high rates of taxation and heavy regulation that reduce the incentives to work, save, and invest. These economists are

(a) rational-expectations economists.
(b) new classical economists.
(c) supply-side economists.
(d) neo-Keynesian economists.

Easy
Definition
Page: 396

Answer: (c)

18.83: According to the advocates of supply-side economics, the real problem with the U.S. economy in the 1970s was that

(a) high rates of taxation and heavy regulation had reduced the incentives to work, and invest.
(b) the level of aggregate demand was too high, which led to a high rate of inflation.
(c) the level of aggregate demand was too low, which led to a high rate of unemployment.
(d) the federal budget deficit was too high, which led to the crowding out of private investment.

Moderate
Fact
Page: 396

Answer: (a)

18.84: According to supply-side economics, the government needs to focus on policies to

(a) stimulate demand.
(b) decrease demand.
(c) stimulate supply.
(d) decrease supply.

Easy
Fact
Page: 396

Answer: (c)

Moderate
Single
Page: 396

18.85: Which of the following would be considered a supply-side policy?

(a) an increase in the minimum wage that would cause consumer spending to increase
(b) an increase in government spending that would lead to increased aggregate demand
(c) investment tax credits for businesses to encourage investment
(d) restrictions placed on the amount that can be imported into the United States

Answer: (c)

Easy
Definition
Page: 396

18.86: The curve that assumes that there is some tax rate beyond which the supply response is large enough to lead to a decrease in tax revenue for further increases in the tax rate is the

(a) aggregate supply curve.
(b) Lucas supply curve.
(c) aggregate production function.
(d) Laffer curve.

Answer: (d)

Easy
Single
Page: 396

18.87: According to supply-side economists, if taxes are cut so that people have an increased incentive to work and businesses have an increased incentive to invest

(a) aggregate supply will increase, aggregate output will increase, and the price level will increase.
(b) aggregate supply will increase, aggregate output will increase, and the price level will decrease.
(c) both aggregate supply and demand will increase, aggregate output will increase, and the price level will increase.
(d) aggregate supply will increase, aggregate demand will decrease, aggregate output will increase, and the price level will decrease.

Answer: (b)

Challenging
Multi
Page: 396

18.88: According to supply-side economists, as tax rates are reduced, labor supply should increase. This implies that

(a) the income effect of a wage change is greater than the substitution effect of a wage change.
(b) the substitution effect of a wage change is greater than the income effect of a wage change.
(c) there is no income effect when tax rates are changed.
(d) there is no substitution effect when tax rates are changed.

Answer: (b)

Easy
Single
Page: 396

18.89: Refer to Figure 18.1. A cut in tax rates will increase tax revenue if the economy is at point

(a) A.
(b) B.
(c) C.
(d) O.

Answer: (c)

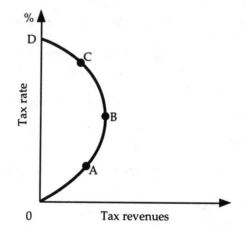

Figure 18.1

18.90: Refer to Figure 18.1. According to supply-side followers of the Laffer curve, the economy is at a point such as _____ on the Laffer Curve.

Easy
Single
Page: 396

(a) A
(b) B
(c) C
(d) D

Answer: (c)

18.91: According to the Laffer curve, if the economy is on the positively sloped section of the curve, then

Easy
Single
Page: 397

(a) an increase in the tax rate will increase tax revenue.
(b) a decrease in the tax rate will increase tax revenue.
(c) both an increase and a decrease in tax rates will increase tax revenue.
(d) both an increase and a decrease in tax rates will decrease tax revenues.

Answer: (a)

18.92: According to the Laffer curve, as tax rates increase, tax revenues

Easy
Fact
Page: 396

(a) rise continuously.
(b) decrease continuously.
(c) initially decrease and then increase.
(d) initially increase and then decrease.

Answer: (d)

18.93: According to the Laffer curve, a cut in tax rates

Moderate
Multi
Page: 397

(a) will always increase tax revenue.
(b) will always decrease tax revenues.
(c) will increase tax revenues if the economy is on the positively sloped portion of the Laffer curve, and reduce tax revenues if the economy is on the negatively sloped portion of the Laffer curve.
(d) will decrease tax revenues if the economy is on the positively sloped portion of the Laffer curve, and increase tax revenues if the economy is on the negatively sloped portion of the Laffer curve.

Answer: (d)

18.94: Proponents of supply-side policies argue that a reduction in tax rates will

Moderate
Single
Page: 397

(a) reduce both the amount of taxable income and tax revenues.
(b) increase the amount of taxable income, but reduce tax revenues.
(c) increase both the amount of taxable income and tax revenues.
(d) increase the amount of taxable income, but will not change the amount of tax revenues.

Answer: (c)

18.95: The Economic Recovery Tax Act of 1981 allowed firms to depreciate their capital at a very rapid rate for tax purposes. This

Easy
Fact
Page: 397

(a) increased the tax liability of firms and discouraged them from investing.
(b) increased the tax liability of firms and encouraged them to invest
(c) decreased tax liability and encouraged investment.
(d) decreased tax liability and discouraged investment.

Answer: (c)

Challenging
Multi
Page: 397

18.96: The implicit assumption behind the Economic Recovery Tax Act of 1981, which cut the individual income tax rate by 25% over three years, was that

(a) the economy was on the positively sloped portion of the Laffer curve.
(b) the economy was on the negatively sloped portion of the Laffer curve.
(c) tax rate reductions will stimulate demand in the economy and move the economy to full employment.
(d) tax rate reductions will decrease supply in the economy and therefore choke off the high rate of inflation that the economy was experiencing.

Answer: (b)

Easy
Fact
Page: 397

18.97: The Economic Recovery Tax Act of 1981 cut corporate taxes in a way that was designed to

(a) encourage firms to hire more workers.
(b) encourage firms to use fewer nonrenewable resources.
(c) stimulate capital investment.
(d) reduce corporate profits.

Answer: (c)

Easy
Fact
Page: 397

18.98: Supporters of supply-side economics claim that Reagan's tax policies were quite successful in stimulating the economy because

(a) almost immediately after the tax cuts, the economy expanded and the recession of 1980-1982 came to an end.
(b) inflation rates fell sharply from the high rates of 1980 and 1981.
(c) throughout most of the 1980s, federal receipts continued to rise even though tax rates had been cut.
(d) all of the above.

Answer: (d)

Moderate
Fact
Page: 397

18.99: Critics of supply-side economics agree that shortly after the Reagan tax cuts were put into place, the economy began to expand. These critics, though, argue that the expansion did not result from the supply-side policies, but rather from

(a) the self-correcting nature of the economy.
(b) the fact that the Federal Reserve dramatically increased the money supply at the same time that the tax cuts became effective.
(c) the increases in government spending that occurred at the same time the tax cuts became effective.
(d) a very large increase in the demand for U.S. exports at the same time that U.S. imports fell dramatically.

Answer: (b)

Moderate
Fact
Page: 399

18.100: Which of the following is NOT one of the reasons why it is difficult to empirically test alternative macroeconomic models against one another?

(a) Macroeconomic models cannot be expressed in mathematical terms.
(b) Macroeconomic models differ in ways that are hard to standardize for.
(c) The rational-expectations assumption is difficult to test.
(d) The amount of data available is fairly small.

Answer: (a)

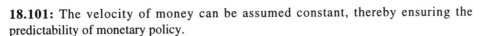
TRUE/FALSE QUESTIONS

18.101: The velocity of money can be assumed constant, thereby ensuring the predictability of monetary policy.

Answer: False

Moderate
Application
Page: 388

18.102: When comparing Keynesians and Monetarists, it can be argued that Monetarists, like Keynesians, are activists about the government's ability to successfully manage the economy.

Answer: False

Easy
Definition
Page: 390

18.103: A rational-expectations theorist argues for increased government involvement in the economy to ensure stable price and employment growth.

Answer: False

Easy
Definition
Page: 392

18.104: The Economic Recovery Act of 1981 was a supply-side economic policy aimed at reducing taxes and encouraging investment.

Answer: True

Easy
Definition
Page: 387

18.105: Velocity is constant if the demand for money depends on the interest rate.

Answer: False

Easy
Fact
Page: 387

18.106: If the velocity of money is constant, then an increase in the money supply will lead to an equal percentage increasein nominal GDP.

Answer: True

Easy
Fact
Page: 388

18.107: Sustained inflation is a purely monetary phenomenon, even if velocity is not constant over time.

Answer: True

Easy
Fact
Page: 389

18.108: Most monetarists advocate an activist monetary stabilization policy.

Answer: False

Easy
Fact
Page: 390

18.109: Traditional macroeconomic models have generally assumed that people form their expectations of future inflation by assuming a continuation of present inflation.

Answer: True

Easy
Fact
Page: 391

18.110: The rational-expectations hypothesis implies that there is no need for government stabilization policies.

Answer: True

Easy
Fact
Page: 393

18.111: When expectations are rational and there are institutional rigidities, disequilibrium exists only temporarily as a result of random, unpredictable shocks.

Answer: True

Easy
Fact
Page: 393

Easy
Fact
Page: 393

18.112: The Lucas supply function suggests that as long as people's expectations are on target, the amount of output they produce is not related to the price level.

Answer: True

Easy
Fact
Page: 396

18.113: The Laffer curve suggests that increasing the tax rate always results in additional tax revenue.

Answer: False

Easy
Fact
Page: 399

18.114: One of the problems with empirical tests of alternative macroeconomic models is that the amount of data available to test the various theories is fairly small.

Answer: True

SHORT ANSWER QUESTIONS

Easy
Definition
Page: 390

18.115: Explain the key concepts of Keynesian economics. Why do Keynesians still support monetary and fiscal policy intervention even though it is clearly not capable of perfectly "fine tuning" the economy? Define and explain the basic equations of Keynesians and Monetarists. Hint: aggregate expenditures.

Answer: Keynes was really the first to emphasize aggregate demand and the connection between the money and goods markets. Keynes also emphasized the problem of "sticky" or downwardly inflexible wages. Keynesian economics is often associated with active government intervention into the economy. Because most Keynesians recognize that stabilization policies, while not perfect, can help prevent even larger economic problems. For example, without the tax cuts and money supply expansion in 1975 and 1982 the recessions in those years could have been much worse. Keynesians are associated with the equation GDP = C + I + G + X - N, while Monetarists are associated with the quantity theory of money, MV = PQ. Keynesians focus on the coordination of monetary and fiscal policies to manipulate one or all of the variables in the aggregate expenditure function. Monetarists, basically, argue that monetary policy, or changes in the money supply, is the primary determinant of GDP.

Moderate
Application
Page: 387

18.116: Explain how the following statements relate to the velocity of money. Assume a constant money supply.

A. Businesses around the country decide to pay workers only once a month in order to reduce paperwork and improve efficiency.

B. Banks around the country begin using a new check clearing system that allows checks to clear much faster than they did previously.

C. Credit card companies and banks announce a huge promotion to increase the use of credit cards for most, if not all, purchases. This includes food, utility bills, and most other necessities.

Answer: A. Velocity would fall. This would cause money to change hands fewer times, on average, in a year. When workers are paid only once a month say from twice a month, this is one less time a month that workers are out there buying things with their paychecks. Thus, money, on average, changes hands fewer times in a year.

B. Velocity would increase. This would cause money to change hands more, on average, in a year. When checks clear more quickly, this allows money to circulate in the economy more rapidly. Thus, velocity would increase.

C. Velocity would increase. This would cause money to change hands more times, on average, in a year. This situation is similar to the check-clearing example in Part B. With more uses for credit cards for basic necessity items, the more rapidly money is exchanged through the economy.

18.117: In 1994 the velocity of money = 3 and the Money Supply = $700 billion. Based on this information answer the following questions. Assume 1994 is the base year.

A. What are the values of nominal and real GDP for 1994?

B. If the money supply increases 10% in 1995, what is the effect on nominal GDP?

C. Using the same data from Part B, if the velocity of money also changes from 3 to 2, now what is the effect on GDP?

Easy
Math
Page: 387

Answer:

A. M * V = GDP (nominal), thus $700 * 3 = $2100 billion.
   If 1994 is your base year then both nominal and real GDP are $2100 billion.

B. $700 * .10 = 70, thus a 10% increase in the Ms = $770.
   Nominal GDP is now $770 * 3 = $2310 billion in 1995.

C. Nominal GDP is now $770 * 2 = $1540 billion.

18.118: Use the quantity theory of money to answer the following questions. We know that for 1994 this small nation had the following economic data:
Ms = $200 billion, P = 3, and V = 2. (Assume output = income and GDP = P * Q.)
A. What is Income for 1994? What is real GDP?

Moderate
Math
Page: 387

B. By how much would the money supply need to change if Income were $400 billion?

C. If annual GDP growth is 5%, by how much will the Ms need to change in 1995? (Use the GDP figure from Part A.).

Answer: A. M * V = P * Y, $200 * 2 = 3 * Y, thus Y = $400/3, Y = $133.33 billion
            Income (Output) = $133.33 billion, while nominal GDP = P * Q.
            Thus, 3 * $133.33 = $399.99 billion.

B. M * 2 = $400 * 3, or M = $1200/2, so M = $600 billion. The money supply would need to change by $400 billion if income were $400 billion.

C. $399.99 * .05 = 20. Thus, GDP would grow by $20 billion in 1995 to a new level of $418.99 billion. With a velocity of 2, the money supply would need to increase by $10 billion. M * 2 = $418.99, M = $418.99/2, or $210 billion is the new money supply.

18.119: Define the rational-expectations hypothesis.Explain the following statement. A rational-expectations theorist argues that all markets, on average, will settle at equilibrium levels.

Easy
Definition
Page: 392

Answer: This is the hypothesis that people know the "true model" of the economy and that they use this model to form their expectations of the future. If all firms have rational expectations and use all available information to set prices and wages on this basis, then all prices and wages should, on average, be at market-clearing levels. When a firm has rational expectations, it knows the demand curve for its output and the supply curve of labor that it faces; therefore, they should be in equilibrium, except for temporary shocks to the economy.

Moderate
Math
Page: 393

18.120: Evaluate the following situations, given a Lucas supply function where $Y = 200 + 75(P-Pe)$, the current price level is 2, and the expected price level is 2.

A. What happens to output when sudden oil shortages cause the price to increase from 2 to 2.5?

B. The Federal Reserve was expected to enact a new policy that would have increased the price level from 2 to 2.4, but due to unexpected increases the price level increased to 2.8. With these changes, what is the effect on output?

C. The news media found unreported information that inflation would increase considerably under a recent fiscal policy package. What is the effect on output if the media reports to the public that, with this fiscal policy approach, inflation is expected to increase to a level of 3?

Answer: A. $Y = 200 + 75(2-2.5)$. $Y = \$162.5$ billion. Output therefore falls from $200 billion to \$162.5 billion due to the price surprise from the temporary shock to the economy.

B. $Y = 200 + 75(2.4-2.8)$. $Y = \$170$ billion. With this price surprise output falls from $200 billion to \$170 billion.

C. $Y = 200 + 75(3-3)$. $Y = \$200$ billion. There is no price surprise because the news media found out and reported the expected increase ahead of time. Thus, with no price surprise the actual price level and the expected price level are the same, thus output remains at $200 billion.

Difficult
Math
Page: 396

18.121: Using aggregate demand and supply analysis, graphically illustrate what supply-side economists mean by stimulating the economy. How does this compare to the traditional Keynesian approach? Explain using graphs.

Answer:

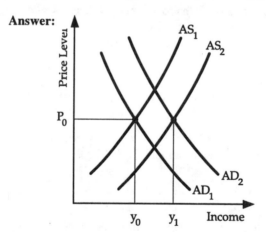

Supply Side: When taxes fall, people work more and harder. Also, businesses invest more. This leads to an increase in AS, to AS2. In addition, as AS increases, AD1 is pulled up to AD2 as there is now more money to spend in the economy.

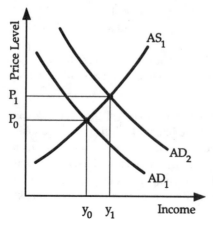

Keynesian: This approach utilizes fiscal policy tools to adjust AD. Thus, by increasing government spending or decreasing taxes, the government can stimulate AD from AD1 to AD2. This, however, pushes prices up to P1.

18.122: Define the velocity of money. If the demand for money depends on the interest rate, will velocity be constant?Why or why not?

Answer: The velocity of money is the number of times a dollar bill changes hands, on average, during the course of a year. If the demand for money depends on the interest rate, the velocity of money will not be constant. As the money supply is increased, the interest rate will fall and the quantity demanded of money will increase. This will decrease the velocity of money because there is more money held per dollar of income.

18.123: What is the equation for the quantity theory of money? (a.) If the velocity of moneyis constant and the economy is at capacity, what impact will an increase in the money supply have? (b.) If the velocity of money is constant and the economy is operating below capacity, what impact will an increase in the money supply have?

Answer: The quantity theory of money is written as MV = PY. (a.) If velocity is constant and the economy is at capacity, an increase in the money supply will only increase the price level. (b.) If the velocity of money is constant and the economy is operating below capacity, an increase in the money supply will increase nominal GDP by the same percentage.

18.124: Most monetarists argue against an activist monetary policy. Explain why. Explain the type of monetary policy that monetarists do advocate.

Answer: Monetarists argue against an activist monetary policy because they are skeptical about the government's ability to manage the macroeconomy. They argue that because of the time lags, activist policies tend to destabilize rather than stabilize the economy. Monetarists advocate that the money supply be increased at a rate equal to the average growth of real output

18.125: What assumption is made in traditional macroeconomic models about how expectations are formed? Explain the shortcomings of this assumption.

Answer: Traditional macroeconomic models assume that people form their expectations of future inflation by assuming a continuation of present inflation. The problem with this traditional treatment of expectation formation is that it is not consistent with the assumptions of microeconomics. It assumes that people ignore information that would allow them to make better forecasts, even though there are costs to being wrong.

18.126: Assume that households and firms have rational expectations. The current unemployment rate is 7%, which is above the full-employment rate of unemployment. Explain how this can happen. Would you expect this unemployment rate to persist for long? Why or why not?

Answer: The unemployment rate can temporarily be above the full-employment rate of unemployment if there has been some type of random, unpredictable shock. This will be only a temporary phenomenon because firms, on average, set market-clearing wages and prices. Thus, unemployment will not persist for long.

18.127: According to the Lucas supply function, how will workers react to a positive price surprise? (Assume that the substitution effect is greater than the income effect.)

Answer: If there is a positive price surprise, workers will be fooled into thinking their real wage has risen. As a result, workers will supply more hours and output will increase. Workers will realize, though, that their real wage has not really increased and labor supply and output will return to their former levels.

Challenging
Multi
Page: 394

18.128: Assume that the rational-expectations theory is a realistic assumption of how people and firms set their expectations. Indicate the effect of each of the followingon the price level and aggregate output. (a.) The Fed announces that it will increase the supply of money. (b.) The government unexpectedly increases government spending.

Answer: (a.) If the increase in the money supply is expected, people will expect the price level to increase. Therefore, there will be no price surprise and no change in the level of output. (b.) If the government unexpectedly increases government spending, there will be a positive price surprise and firms will incorrectly believe that the price of their output has risen relative to other prices, and will therefore increase production. Workers will incorrectly believe that their real wage rates have risen and will increase their supply of labor which also leads to an increase in output. Workers and firms will realize that they were wrong and that all prices have risen, and output will fall to its original level.

Moderate
Fact
Page: 394

18.129: Explain the primary argument against the rational-expectations hypothesis. Explain why it is difficult to test whether or not the assumption of rational expectations is valid.

Answer: The primary argument against the rational-expectations hypothesis is that it requires households and firms to know too much. Rational expectations requires that households and firms know the true model of how the economy operates. The gain from knowing the true model may not be worth the costs. It is difficult to empirically test whether or not the assumption of rational expectations is valid because to test the assumption one must know the true model. A test of rational expectations is a joint test that (1) expectations are formed rationally and (2) that the model being used is the true model. If the empirical test leads us to reject the hypothesis that people form their expectations rationally, it may be that the model is not the true one rather than that expectations are not rational.

Moderate
Single
Page: 397

18.130: What is the basic principle behind supply-side economics? After supply-side policies were implemented in 1981, the economy pulled out of the 1980 recession and entered an expansionary period. How would a supply-side economist explain the success of these policies? Show do critics of supply-side policies explain the recovery from the recession?

Answer: According to supply-side economists, the real problem with the economy is that high rates of taxation and heavy regulation have reduced incentives to work, to save, and to invest. They argue that what is needed is better incentives to stimulate supply. A supply-sider would argue that the tax cuts of 1981 increased the incentives to work and to invest. As a result, aggregate supply increased which increased output and reduced the inflation rate. Critics of supply-side policies argue that the inflation rate fell not because of the reduction in tax rates, but because the economy was in a recession. They also argue that the economy pulled out of the recession because the tax cuts had a large demand-side effect that increased aggregate output.The other reason that the economy pulled out of the recession was the increase in the money supply between 1981 and 1983.

19 Economic Growth and Productivity

(Chapter 35 in Combined Text)

19.1: Economic growth is defined as an increase in

(a) economic welfare.
(b) real output.
(c) household consumption.
(d) personal satisfaction.

Answer: (b)

Easy
Definition
Page: 405

19.2: An increase in real output is known as

(a) economic growth.
(b) technological change.
(c) inflation.
(d) social progress.

Answer: (a)

Easy
Definition
Page: 405

19.3: The period of rapid and sustained increase in real output per capita that began in the Western World with the Industrial Revolution is known as the period of

(a) social progress.
(b) technological change.
(c) modern economic growth.
(d) creative destruction.

Answer: (c)

Easy
Definition
Page: 405

19.4: Graphically, economic growth can be represented by

(a) a leftward shift in the aggregate supply curve.
(b) a leftward shift in the aggregate demand curve.
(c) a rightward shift in the production possibilities frontier.
(d) a rightward shift in the aggregate demand curve.

Answer: (c)

Easy
Fact
Page: 406

19.5: Economic growth is the process of

(a) producing fewer agricultural products and more industrial products.
(b) urbanization.
(c) expanding the production possibilities frontier.
(d) all of the above.

Answer: (c)

Easy
Fact
Page: 406

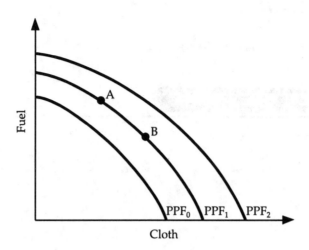

Figure 19.1

Easy
Single
Page: 406

19.6: Refer to Figure 19.1. Economic growth is represented by

(a) the movement from point A to point B along ppf_1.
(b) the movement from point B to point A along ppf_1.
(c) a shift in the production possibilities frontier from ppf_1 to ppf_0.
(d) a shift in the production possibilities frontier from ppf_1 to ppf_2.

Answer: (d)

Easy
Fact
Page: 407

19.7: Economic growth in an industrial society results from

(a) technological change.
(b) innovation.
(c) capital production.
(d) all of the above.

Answer: (d)

Moderate
Single
Page: 407

19.8: Which of the following CANNOT cause an increase in GDP?

(a) an increase in environmental regulations
(b) an increase in labor
(c) an increase in capital
(d) an increase in productivity

Answer: (a)

Moderate
Single
Page: 407

19.9: If nominal GDP is $400 billion and the money supply is $100 billion, the velocity of money is

(a) .33.
(b) .25.
(c) 4.
(d) 5.

Answer: (c)

19.10: Economic growth allows a society to consume

(a) more goods per person.
(b) a higher quality of goods.
(c) a wider variety of goods.
(d) all of the above.

Easy
Fact
Page: 407

Answer: (d)

19.11: The velocity of money is 8. If nominal GDP is $16,000 billion then the stock of money

(a) is $8 billion.
(b) is $128,000 billion.
(c) is $2,000 billion.
(d) none of the above.

Easy
Fact
Page: 407

Answer: (c)

19.12: For economic growth to increase living standards,

(a) society must discover ways of using available resources more efficiently.
(b) the rate of growth must exceed the rate of population increase.
(c) the choices available to consumers must increase.
(d) society must acquire more resources.

Easy
Fact
Page: 407

Answer: (b)

19.13: The velocity of money is 3. If the money stock is $250 billion, then nominal GDP

(a) is $250 billion.
(b) is $750 billion.
(c) is $83.33 billion.
(d) cannot be determined from this information.

Easy
Fact
Page: 407

Answer: (b)

19.14: The strict definition of economic growth that requires economic growth to increase living standards is

(a) an increase in capital accumulation per capita.
(b) an increase in nominal GDP per capita.
(c) an increase in real GDP per capita.
(d) an increase in investment per capita.

Easy
Definition
Page: 407

Answer: (c)

19.15: In Maldavia, real GDP increased by 5% and the population increased by 6% in 1994. In 1994, Maldavia experienced

(a) economic growth, but not an increase in living standards.
(b) economic growth and an increase in living standards.
(c) no economic growth, but an increase in living standards.
(d) an economic decline.

Moderate
Single
Page: 407

Answer: (a)

Moderate
Single
Page: 407

19.16: In Seneca, real GDP increased by 4% and the population increased by 3% in 1994. In 1994, Seneca experienced

(a) economic growth, but not an increase in living standards.
(b) economic growth and an increase in living standards.
(c) no economic growth, but an increase in living standards.
(d) an economic decline.

Answer: (b)

Moderate
Single
Page: 407

19.17: According to the quantity theory of money if the money supply is increased by 10%, then nominal GDP

(a) decreases by 10%.
(b) increases by 10%.
(c) remains constant.
(d) cannot be determined from this information since velocity is not known.

Answer: (b)

Easy
Definition
Page: 407

19.18: The mathematical representation of the technological relationship between inputs and national output is known as the

(a) aggregate production function.
(b) production possibilities frontier.
(c) aggregate supply function.
(d) input-output table.

Answer: (a)

Easy
Definition
Page: 407

19.19: The aggregate production function is the mathematical representation of the technological relationship between

(a) inputs and national output.
(b) national income and national output.
(c) fiscal and monetary policy changes and national output.
(d) the rate of capital accumulation and national output.

Answer: (a)

Challenging
Single
Page: 407

19.20: The aggregate production function is $Y = 2K^{.5}L^{.5}$. If there are 100 units of capital and 144 units of labor, aggregate output is

(a) 120 units.
(b) 170 units.
(c) 240 units.
(d) 244 units.

Answer: (c)

19.21: The aggregate production function is Y = 3KL. If there are 30 units of capital and 50 units of labor, aggregate output is

Moderate
Single
Page: 407

(a) 83 units.
(b) 450 units.
(c) 1500 units.
(d) 4500 units.

Answer: (d)

19.22: In an aggregate production function, changes in national output are explained by changes in the amount of

Moderate
Fact
Page: 407

(a) raw materials and the amount of energy.
(b) labor and the amount of energy.
(c) raw materials and the amount of capital.
(d) labor, the amount of capital, and all other inputs.

Answer: (d)

19.23: Which of the following will NOT cause an increase in real GDP?

Easy
Fact
Page: 408

(a) an increase in the labor supply
(b) an increase in the price level
(c) an increase in physical or human capital
(d) an increase in the productivity of capital or labor.

Answer: (b)

19.24: When there are 90 units of labor and 45 units of capital, the productivity of labor is 3. When there are 100 units of labor and 45 units of capital, the productivity of labor is 2.8. This is an example of

Moderate
Single
Page: 408

(a) a reduction in the growth rate.
(b) a decrease in living standards.
(c) diminishing returns.
(d) a leftward shift of the ppf.

Answer: (c)

19.25: If the capital stock remains fixed while the supply of labor increases, it is likely that

Moderate
Fact
Page: 408

(a) the new labor will be more productive than the old labor.
(b) output per capita will rise.
(c) the productivity of labor will not change.
(d) the new labor will be less productive than the old labor.

Answer: (d)

Easy
Fact
Page: 408

19.26: Thomas Malthus and David Ricardo, who lived in England during the nineteenth century, were concerned that the fixed supply of_____would ultimately lead to diminishing returns.

(a) labor
(b) land
(c) capital
(d) energy

Answer: (b)

Easy
Fact
Page: 408

19.27: Thomas Malthus and David Ricardo believed that to increase agricultural output, people would be forced to

(a) farm more productive land, in which case the returns to successive increases in population would increase.
(b) farm less productive land, in which case the returns to successive increases in population would increase.
(c) farm less productive land, in which case the returns to successive increases in population would diminish.
(d) farm more productive land, in which case the returns to successive increases in population would diminish.

Answer: (c)

Easy
Fact
Page: 408

19.28: Thomas Malthus and David Ricardo believed that to increase agricultural output, people would be forced to

(a) farm land more intensively, in which case the returns to successive increases in population would diminish.
(b) farm land less intensively, in which case the returns to successive increases in population would increase.
(c) farm land more intensively, in which case the returns to successive increases in population would increase.
(d) farm land less intensively, in which case the returns to successive increases in population would diminish.

Answer: (a)

Easy
Fact
Page: 408

19.29: Both Malthus and Ricardo failed to account for the effect of _____ on agricultural production.

(a) diminishing returns
(b) increasing returns
(c) capital depreciation
(d) technological change

Answer: (d)

Easy
Fact
Page: 408

19.30: Diminishing returns can occur if a nation's stock of capital

(a) grows more rapidly than its work force.
(b) grows more slowly than its work force.
(c) grows at the same rate as its work force.
(d) grows while the size of its work force remains constant.

Answer: (b)

19.31: New entrants into the labor force do not displace other workers if

(a) the price level is falling.
(b) real wages are increasing rapidly enough.
(c) the economy and the capital stock are expanding rapidly enough.
(d) the productivity of labor is increasing.

Easy
Fact
Page: 409

Answer: (c)

19.32: An increase in the capital stock

(a) can increase output, even if it is not accompanied by an increase in the labor force.
(b) provides valuable services directly, but not indirectly.
(c) can increase output, but only if it is accompanied by an increase in the labor force.
(d) cannot increase output, even if it is accompanied by an increase in the labor force.

Moderate
Fact
Page: 409

Answer: (a)

19.33: A decrease in the capital-labor ratio of an economy

(a) decreases the productivity of capital.
(b) decreases the productivity of labor.
(c) decreases the productivity of both capital and labor.
(d) may either increase or decrease the productivity of labor.

Moderate
Single
Page: 409

Answer: (b)

19.34: Capital that is used in production

(a) reduces the productivity of labor.
(b) enhances the productivity of labor.
(c) has no effect on the productivity of labor.
(d) has an uncertain effect on the productivity of labor.

Easy
Fact
Page: 409

Answer: (b)

19.35: Which of the following statements is TRUE?

(a) Investment in private capital is a source of economic growth, but investment in public capital is not.
(b) Investment in public capital is a source of economic growth, but investment in private capital is not.
(c) Investment in both private and public capital is conducive to economic growth and higher productivity.
(d) Neither investment in private nor public capital has any effect on economic growth and productivity.

Moderate
Fact
Page: 409

Answer: (c)

19.36: Which of the following is TRUE?

(a) Both capital and labor are subject to diminishing returns.
(b) Only capital is subject to diminishing returns.
(c) Only labor is subject to diminishing returns.
(d) Neither capital nor labor are subject to diminishing returns.

Easy
Fact
Page: 410

Answer: (a)

Easy
Fact
Page: 410

19.37: An important source of increasing productivity is

(a) an increase in the ratio of capital to labor.
(b) an increase in the ratio of labor to capital.
(c) a decrease in the ratio of capital to labor.
(d) faster growth in the labor force than in the capital stock.

Answer: (a)

Easy
Fact
Page: 410

19.38: If the capital-labor ratio of an economy increases,

(a) output increases.
(b) output will increase only if there is also an improvement in technology.
(c) output decreases because of diminishing marginal returns.
(d) output per person must decrease.

Answer: (a)

Easy
Fact
Page: 410

19.39: In all economies experiencing modern economic growth,

(a) labor expands at a more rapid pace than capital.
(b) capital expands at a more rapid pace than labor.
(c) capital and labor expand at a constant rate.
(d) capital expands, but labor remains constant.

Answer: (b)

Moderate
Single
Page: 412

19.40: Which of the following is an investment in infrastructure?

(a) Southstar Steel has two office buildings separated by one-half mile. The company lays a fiber optic cable between the buildings to take advantage of new technology.
(b) The federal government makes it easier for college students to obtain loans and this increases the number of students attending college.
(c) The city of Robesonia builds a new sewage treatment plant.
(d) Residents of a suburban housing development hire a private security force because they have been concerned about crime.

Answer: (c)

Easy
Fact
Page: 412

19.41: Increased investments in infrastructure or public capital would

(a) cause a decrease in the growth rate, because they would require areduction in private investment.
(b) have no impact on growth, because they do not affect the private sector.
(c) most likely increase growth.
(d) increase growth in a developing country, but have no impact on growth in a developed country.

Answer: (c)

Easy
Fact
Page: 411

19.42: An increase in human capital

(a) increases the productivity of labor.
(b) decreases the productivity of labor.
(c) increases the productivity of labor only if there is a corresponding technological change.
(d) increases the capital-labor ratio.

Answer: (a)

19.43: Which of the following is NOT an investment in human capital?

(a) Local governments begin providing free hepatitis vaccinations to any resident who wants one.
(b) The Precision Tool Company teaches all its workers how to repair all the machines in the factory.
(c) Older workers return to school to update their skills.
(d) The Ferris Advertising Agency replaces its secretary's typewriters with personal computes.

Moderate Single Page: 411

Answer: (d)

19.44: Which of the following is not an investment in human capital?

(a) An individual decides to enroll in a vocational training program.
(b) A firm engages in on-the-job training.
(c) The government expands its programs to improve health care.
(d) The government increases the level of unemployment benefits.

Moderate Single Page: 411

Answer: (d)

19.45: Which of the following does NOT necessarily increase the productivity of labor?

(a) increases in education
(b) a higher capital-labor ratio
(c) growth in output
(d) technological change

Easy Fact Page: 411

Answer: (c)

19.46: Growth that cannot be explained by increases in the quantity of inputs can be explained only

(a) as an illusion.
(b) by an increase in the productivity of those inputs.
(c) as a temporary phenomenon.
(d) through an increase in imports.

Easy Fact Page: 411

Answer: (b)

19.47: An advance in knowledge is referred to as an

(a) external economy of scale.
(b) innovation.
(c) invention.
(d) internal economy of scale.

Easy Definition Page: 411

Answer: (c)

19.48: The use of new knowledge to produce a new product, or to produce an existing product more efficiently, is an

(a) invention.
(b) external economy of scale.
(c) innovation.
(d) internal economy of scale.

Easy Definition Page: 411

Answer: (c)

Moderate
Single
Page: 411

19.49: A firm used to produce a product using three units of labor and one unit of capital. The firm discovers, though, that it can produce more output at a lower cost if it combines two units of labor with two units of capital. This is an example of

(a) an innovation.
(b) an invention.
(c) increasing returns.
(d) economic growth.

Answer: (a)

Moderate
Single
Page: 411

19.50: A rescarcher discovered the adhesive that allows a piece of paper to be stuck to a surface temporarily and then removed many years before a use was found for this adhesive. Which of the following is TRUE?

(a) The discovery represents an invention and the finding of a use for the adhesive represents an innovation.
(b) The discovery represents an innovation and the finding of a use for the adhesive represents an invention.
(c) This is an example of an invention only.
(d) This is an example of an innovation only.

Answer: (a)

Easy
Single
Page: 411

19.51: The productivity of an input is not affected by

(a) technological change.
(b) advances in knowledge.
(c) economies of scale.
(d) diminishing returns.

Answer: (d)

Easy
Fact
Page: 411

19.52: Improvements in managerial knowledge are an example of

(a) a labor-saving innovation.
(b) a capital-saving innovation.
(c) a way to increase the productivity of inputs.
(d) an internal economy of scale.

Answer: (c)

Moderate
Single
Page: 413

19.53: Relaxed trucking regulations increase the maximum weight a tractor-trailer combination can haul, from 40 tons to 60 tons. This change in regulations reduces the transportation costs per ton and is

(a) capital-saving only.
(b) labor-saving only.
(c) both capital-saving and labor-saving.
(d) an external diseconomy of scale.

Answer: (c)

Easy
Fact
Page: 413

19.54: The introduction of robotics is an example of

(a) a labor-saving innovation.
(b) a capital-saving innovation.
(c) an external economy of scale.
(d) an external diseconomy of scale.

Answer: (a)

19.55: An accounting firm purchased two computers and found that two workers using the computers could do the same work it used to take four workers to do. This introduction of computers is an example of

Moderate
Single
Page: 413

(a) a labor-saving innovation.
(b) a capital-saving innovation.
(c) both capital and labor-saving innovation.
(d) neither a capital nor a labor-saving innovation.

Answer: (a)

19.56: Improved production management doubles the number of air conditioners that can be produced. This managerial innovation is

Moderate
Single
Page: 413

(a) capital-saving.
(b) labor-saving.
(c) both capital-saving and labor-saving.
(d) an external economy of scale.

Answer: (c)

19.57: Cost savings that result from increases in the size of industries but not individual firms are

Easy
Definition
Page: 413

(a) external economies of scale.
(b) internal economies of scale.
(c) capital-saving innovations.
(d) labor-saving innovations.

Answer: (a)

19.58: Which of the following is an example of an external economy of scale?

Moderate
Single
Page: 413

(a) As a shirt manufacturer buys more cotton cloth, the cloth supplier reduces the price per yard of cloth.
(b) A moving company buys computers for its office staff and as a result can reduce its office staff by 10%.
(c) As more firms hired computer programmers, more schools began training computer programmers and firms were able to spend less money on training employees to be computer programmers.
(d) The U.S. government eliminates restrictions on hiring non-U.S. citizens.

Answer: (c)

19.59: Which of the following would be an external economy of scale?

Moderate
Single
Page: 413

(a) As a firm increases the amount of a raw material it uses, the firm is able to negotiate a quantity discount with its supplier.
(b) Firms have found more efficient ways to manage their inventories by using the concept of just- in-time delivery.
(c) The government provides investment tax credits that reduce the cost of acquiring capital.
(d) The number of manufacturing firms located in an industrial park increases. As a result, a trucking company moves into the park to serve the manufacturing firms and this reduces the cost of transporting goods into and out of the industrial park.

Answer: (d)

Challenging
Multi
Page: 413

19.60: If there are constant returns to scale, a 5% increase in inputs should increase output by 5%.But if as a result of increasing inputs by 5% output increased by 7%, then

(a) all 7% of the increase in output resulted from the increase in inputs.
(b) all 7% of the increase in output must have resulted from an increase in factor productivity.
(c) 2% of the increase in output resulted from the increase in inputs, and 5% of the increase in output resulted from an increase in factor productivity.
(d) 5% of the increase in output resulted from the increase in inputs, and 2% of the increase in output resulted from an increase in factor productivity.

Answer: (d)

Easy
Fact
Page: 413

19.61: Which of the following factors would NOT contribute to an increase in measured factor productivity?

(a) an advance in managerial knowledge
(b) the introduction of robotics
(c) an increase in expenditures on research and development
(d) the imposition of additional environmental regulations

Answer: (d)

Easy
Fact
Page: 413

19.62: Which of the following factors would NOT contribute to an increase in measured factor productivity?

(a) improved inventory management techniques
(b) improved personnel management techniques
(c) a severe drought in the farm belt
(d) the introduction of new job-training programs

Answer: (c)

Easy
Fact
Page: 413

19.63: Increased environmental regulation is likely to

(a) decrease measured productivity and decrease output.
(b) increase measured productivity and increase output.
(c) have no effect on either productivity or output.
(d) increase measured productivity, but decrease output.

Answer: (a)

Easy
Fact
Page: 413

19.64: Which of the following statements is FALSE?

(a) Increasing environmental regulations diverted capital and labor from the production of measured output and thus reduced productivity.
(b) Even though stricter environmental regulations may have reduced output, this negative effect is offset by the gain in the improved environmental quality.
(c) Environmental regulations have imposed only costs on society. No benefits have been gained.
(d) Over time stricter environmental regulations may actually cause productivity to be higher than it would be in the absence of these regulations, if these regulations lead to a healthier labor force.

Answer: (c)

19.65: Over the long term, real output in the United States has been growing annually at about

Easy
Fact
Page: 414

(a) 1%.
(b) 3%.
(c) 5%.
(d) 7%.

Answer: (b)

19.66: If real output increased by 5% and during the same period the population increased by 3%, real GDP per capita grew at a rate of

Moderate
Single
Page: 414

(a) .6%.
(b) 1.67%.
(c) 2%.
(d) 8%.

Answer: (c)

19.67: According to Edward Denison, about what proportion of U.S. growth in output over the entire period from 1929 to 1982 has come from increases in factors of production?

Easy
Fact
Page: 415

(a) one-fourth
(b) one-third
(c) one-half
(d) two-thirds

Answer: (c)

19.68: According to Edward Denison, about what proportion of U.S. growth in output over the entire period from 1929 to 1982 has come from increases in productivity?

Easy
Fact
Page: 415

(a) one-third
(b) one-half
(c) two-thirds
(d) three-fourths

Answer: (b)

19.69: According to Edward Denison, about _____ of the U.S. growth in output over the entire period from 1929 to 1982 has come from increases in factors of production and about _____ has come from increases in productivity.

Easy
Fact
Page: 415

(a) one-fourth; three fourths
(b) one-third; two-thirds
(c) two-thirds; one-third
(d) one-half; one-half

Answer: (d)

Easy
Fact
Page: 415

19.70: According to Edward Denison, what was the single most important factor contributing to the increase in the productivity of inputs between 1929 and 1983?

(a) growth of knowledge
(b) technological change
(c) economies of scale
(d) capital-saving innovations

Answer: (a)

Easy
Fact
Page: 416

19.71: Between 1950 and 1990,

(a) real GDP increased, but population increased at a faster rate so real GDP per capita fell.
(b) real GDP increased at a faster rate than population so real GDP per capita increased.
(c) real GDP fell and population increased, so real per capita GDP fell.
(d) real GDP fell at a faster rate than the decrease in the population, so real GDP per capita increased.

Answer: (b)

Easy
Fact
Page: 414

19.72: The most remarkable growth performance since 1975 has taken place in

(a) Japan.
(b) China.
(c) Germany.
(d) Eastern Europe.

Answer: (b)

Easy
Fact
Page: 416

19.73: Which of the following was NOT one of the likely causes of the productivity problem in the 1970s?

(a) a slowdown in investment spending
(b) reduced research and development spending
(c) a reduction in government regulation
(d) low saving rates

Answer: (c)

Easy
Fact
Page: 416

19.74: Which of the following was NOT one of the likely causes of the productivity problem in the 1970s?

(a) the increase in energy prices in the 1970s
(b) a slowdown in investment spending
(c) an increase in government regulation
(d) high saving rates

Answer: (d)

Easy
Fact
Page: 416

19.75: Which of the following was one of the likely causes of the productivity problem of the 1970s?

(a) rapid growth in investment spending
(b) a reduction in government regulation
(c) an increase in research and development spending
(d) low saving rates

Answer: (d)

19.76: Higher energy prices in the 1970s reduced labor productivity because

Moderate
Fact
Page: 416

(a) energy and capital are substitute inputs.
(b) the rise in energy prices tended to push firms away from labor-intensive measures and toward more capital-intensive techniques.
(c) a great deal of investment went into transforming the existing capital stock into more energy-efficient forms.
(d) labor productivity has been lower when used with more capital-intensive techniques.

Answer: (c)

19.77: The productivity problem of the 1970s referred to the fact that

Easy
Fact
Page: 416

(a) the overall growth rate in the United States during that period was significantly below the long-run average growth rate in the United States.
(b) net investment was negative during that period.
(c) measured output per employed worker had dropped by a substantial amount during that period.
(d) there had been a decline in real per capita GDP during that period.

Answer: (c)

19.78: Why should U.S. citizens be concerned about a low national saving rate?

Moderate
Fact
Page: 418

(a) Because the saving rate in the United States is much lower than that of its most important trading partners.
(b) If individuals saved more, the size of the multiplier would increase and fiscal policy would become more effective.
(c) Savings are used to finance investments, and a low saving rate limits the rate of capital accumulation.
(d) Because the U.S. saving rate used to be the highest of all developed countries, and now it is the lowest.

Answer: (c)

19.79: Some economists claim that the social security system in the United States is biased against saving. Their argument is that

Easy
Fact
Page: 418

(a) the social security system reduces the incentive for people to save by providing guaranteed retirement incomes.
(b) private pension plans are better managed than the social security funds, and are used for more productive investments.
(c) the social security system discourages people from making risky, but profitable, investments.
(d) social security taxes are used to finance only investments in public infrastructure, and are not available for business investment.

Answer: (a)

19.80: Public subsidization of research and development has been justified on the grounds that

Easy
Fact
Page: 418

(a) there are no private returns to research and development.
(b) basic research cannot be undertaken by private firms.
(c) only large corporations have the financial resources to undertake research and development.
(d) social returns to research and development exceed the private returns.

Answer: (d)

Moderate
Fact
Page: 419

19.81: Those who argue that research and development spending, especially on basic research, should be subsidized by the public sector believe that

(a) the rate of return on investments in research and development is very high.
(b) private spending is insufficient to finance investments in research and development.
(c) the social returns from research and development are high compared with the social returns from other public investment projects.
(d) the benefits from research and development cannot be adequately captured by those undertaking the research.

Answer: (d)

Easy
Fact
Page: 418

19.82: Which of the following policies has NOT been suggested as a means of increasing the rate of economic growth in the United States?

(a) lowering the savings rate
(b) reducing government regulation
(c) increasing research and development spending
(d) enactment of an industrial policy

Answer: (a)

Easy
Fact
Page: 417

19.83: Which of the following policies has been suggested as a means of increasing the rate of economic growth in the United States?

(a) reducing the savings rate
(b) reducing expenditures on research and development
(c) improving the quality of education
(d) increasing the degree of government regulation in the economy

Answer: (c)

Moderate
Single
Page: 419

19.84: To determine the merits of environmental regulation by the government, the question that should be asked is:

(a) Do the regulations stand in the way of industrial progress?
(b) Are the costs of environmental regulation outweighed by the added benefits of research and development spending that results from the regulation?
(c) Has the value of the improved environment and safety been worth it?
(d) Have the regulations improved the standard of living for all members of the society?

Answer: (c)

Easy
Definition
Page: 419

19.85: Government involvement in the allocation of capital across manufacturing sectors is

(a) supply management.
(b) regulatory policy.
(c) industrial policy.
(d) balanced growth policy.

Answer: (c)

Easy
Definition
Page: 419

19.86: The public policy of "targeting" industries for special and rapid investment is

(a) international trade policy.
(b) industrial policy.
(c) fiscal policy.
(d) growth policy.

Answer: (b)

19.87: Which of the following is an example of an industrial policy?

(a) An increase in the federal subsidization of higher education that reduces tuition costs and enables more people to attend college.
(b) An increase in the age at which people are eligible for full social security retirement benefits.
(c) An investment tax credit that is available to all firms.
(d) A subsidy to agricultural producers that makes it easier for them to export their products.

Moderate
Single
Page: 419

Answer: (d)

19.88: Critics of industrial policy argue that the government should not be involved in the allocation of capital across manufacturing sectors because

(a) the Japanese government is already practicing industrial policy, and because of its experience, it is much better at it than the United States. would be.
(b) the government does not have enough information on the profitability and riskiness of industrial investments to make the correct decisions.
(c) the United States is losing out in international competition.
(d) investments are always risky and the U.S. government cannot afford to bear the risk.

Moderate
Fact
Page: 419

Answer: (b)

19.89: Those who favor industrial policy argue that

(a) the government is the best judge of how risky investments are because it has more information than firms.
(b) the government should help finance investment in the private sector because it has such easy access to funds.
(c) it is an effective way to reduce the government deficit.
(d) because other countries follow this practice, the United States must also use industrial policy so as not to lose out in international competition.

Easy
Fact
Page: 419

Answer: (d)

19.90: One of the reasons why politicians are often reluctant to enact pro-growth economic policies is that

(a) their costs are incurred in the short run, while their benefits are received in the long run.
(b) their costs are incurred in the long run, while their benefits are received in the short run.
(c) both their costs and benefits occur in the short run.
(d) both their costs and benefits occur in the long run.

Moderate
Fact
Page: 420

Answer: (a)

19.91: Advocates of economic growth argue that

(a) you can have progress without growth, but not the other way around.
(b) you can have growth without progress, but not the other way around.
(c) growth and progress have nothing to do with one another.
(d) growth is synonymous with progress.

Easy
Fact
Page: 420

Answer: (d)

Easy
Fact
Page: 420

19.92: The proponents of growth argue that growth

(a) gives us more freedom.
(b) saves time.
(c) improves the standard of living.
(d) all of the above.

Answer: (d)

Easy
Fact
Page: 421

19.93: For developing countries, the only hope for an improvement in the standard of living in the long run is

(a) redistributing income in more equitably.
(b) economic growth.
(c) the use of industrial policy.
(d) establishment of markets for them to sell their natural resources.

Answer: (b)

Easy
Fact
Page: 421

19.94: Which of the following arguments is NOT made by opponents of economic growth?

(a) Growth has positive effects on the quality of life.
(b) Growth encourages the creation of artificial needs.
(c) Growth means the rapid depletion of a finite quantity of resources.
(d) Growth requires and reinforces an unfair distribution of income.

Answer: (a)

Moderate
Fact
Page: 421

19.95: Those who argue against unchecked economic growth argue that

(a) welfare and happiness depend on more than the material goods and services included in real GDP.
(b) the present generation consumes too many resources at the cost of the welfare of future generations.
(c) real output per person matters, but that how the output is distributed among consumers also matters.
(d) all of the above.

Answer: (d)

Moderate
Fact
Page: 423

19.96: Which of the following statements is true?

(a) Growth benefits all groups of society equally.
(b) Growth will always lead to an improvement in the quality of life, because consumers will have more goods available to consume.
(c) Proponents of growth argue that we do not need to be concerned about the depletion of natural resources because the supply of natural resources is not limited.
(d) If the distribution of income were less equally distributed, the economy would grow more quickly because the rich save more, and this would lead to greater capital accumulation.

Answer: (d)

Easy
Fact
Page: 423

19.97: Which of the following arguments is advanced by opponents of economic growth?

(a) Growth has positive effects on the quality of life.
(b) Growth encourages the creation of artificial needs.
(c) Growth promotes the conservation of resources.
(d) Growth reduces the degree of inequality in the distribution of income.

Answer: (b)

19.98: Which of the following arguments is NOT made by opponents of economic growth?

(a) Growth has negative effects on the quality of life.
(b) Growth encourages the creation of artificial needs.
(c) Growth encourages the conservation of resources.
(d) Growth requires and reinforces an unfair distribution of income.

Easy
Fact
Page: 423

Answer: (c)

19.99: According to predictions made by the Club of Rome in 1972, the collapse of the world economy will occur because of

(a) the world's limited capacity to produce food.
(b) the ever increasing birth rate in developed countries.
(c) the depletion of nonrenewable resources.
(d) low saving rates and, therefore, low rates of capital accumulation.

Easy
Fact
Page: 423

Answer: (c)

19.100: A weakness in the Club of Rome's study entitled The Limits to Growth is that

(a) it assumed the rate of population growth would slow.
(b) it did not account for changes in technological knowledge.
(c) it assumed a constant demand for products.
(d) it assumed a declining investment rate.

Moderate
Fact
Page: 423

Answer: (b)

19.101: An argument against growth is that growth leads to the depletion of resources. Which of the following offers an explanation of why depletion is not likely to happen?

(a) As resources become scarce, the price of the resources will go up and the quantity of those resources demanded will fall.
(b) An increase in a resource price, this provides an incentive for firms to find alternative resources to use.
(c) As resources become scarce, governments are likely to impose very strict controls on how those resources can be used.
(d) both a and b.

Moderate
Single
Page: 423

Answer: (d)

19.102: Critics of growth claim that the real beneficiaries of growth are

(a) the rich.
(b) the politicians.
(c) owners of corporations.
(d) retired individuals.

Easy
Fact
Page: 423

Answer: (a)

19.103: An optimal growth policy should

(a) maximize growth in real GDP.
(b) limit the growth of real GDP to the rate ofpopulation growth, so that real output per person stays constant.
(c) limit growth of real GDP to the level at which the added benefits of growth equal the added costs of growth.
(d) limit growth of real GDP to the level at which growth does not damage the environment or increase the level of income inequality.

Challenging
Multi
Page: 424

Answer: (c)

Moderate
Single
Page: 419

19.104: Which of the following would be an example of an implicit industrial policy in the United States?

(a) A law that requires the U.S. automobile industry to meet certain safety standards for passenger cars.
(b) A law requiring toys that are imported into the United States to meet the same consumer product safety standards as products produced in the United States.
(c) The imposition of a quota restricting the amount of cotton that can be imported into the United States.
(d) A law requiring that all automobiles meet certain emission standards by 1994.

Answer: (c)

TRUE/FALSE QUESTIONS

Easy
Definition
Page: 411

19.105: A decrease in the amount of product produced by each unit of labor will cause GDP to increase, and thereby raise living standards.

Answer: False

Moderate
Application
Page: 409

19.106: An increase in capital must always be accompanied by an increase in the labor force if output is to increase.

Answer: False

Easy
Application
Page: 408

19.107: The U.S. economy has adapted well to the substantial increase in the labor force from 1947 to present.

Answer: True

Moderate
Definition
Page: 411

19.108: Invention and innovation are the two key components of productivity increases.

Answer: True

Difficult
Application
Page: 423

19.109: Economic growth always leads to a more equitable distribution of income.

Answer: False

Easy
Fact
Page: 407

19.110: The aggregate production function implies that there are only two ways to generate an increase in GDP: through an increase in labor or an increase in capital.

Answer: False

Easy
Fact
Page: 409

19.111: As long as the economy and the capital stock are expanding rapidly enough, new entrants into the labor force do not displace existing workers.

Answer: True

Easy
Fact
Page: 411

19.112: Growth that cannot be explained by increases in the quantity of inputs can be explained only by increases in the productivity of those inputs.

Answer: True

Easy
Fact
Page: 413

19.113: External economies of scale are cost savings that result from increases in the size of industries.

Answer: True

19.114: Edward Denison has estimated that growth of knowledge was the single most important factor contributing to increases in the productivity of inputs from 1929 to 1982.

Answer: True

19.115: The rate of growth in investment spending increased during the 1970s, thus countering the decade's trend toward slower productivity growth.

Answer: False

19.116: Policies to improve the quality of American education are desirable for their own sake, but they have little, if any, relationship to the rate of economic growth.

Answer: False

19.117: Industrial policy refers to government involvement in the allocation of capital across manufacturing sectors.

Answer: True

19.118: Economic growth makes it possible to improve conditions for the less fortunate in society.

Answer: True

19.119: Opponents of economic growth maintain that growth means the rapid depletion of a finite quantity of resources.

Answer: True

SHORT ANSWER QUESTIONS

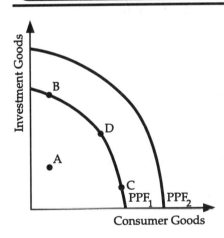

19.120: Answer the following questions by analyzing the production possibilities frontier below.

A. Explain what is happening in the economy at point A. How can the economy move to a point on PPF1?

B. Why will producing investment goods today cause different results for the future of the economy than focusing more on consumer goods today?

C. How would any nation move to higher and higher production possibilities frontiers? For example, moving from PPF1 to PPF2.

Answer: A. At a point like A the economy is in a recession. To get out of the recession and move to a point on the production possibilities frontier would require either expansionary fiscal or monetary policy. (It is also possible to do this by using resources more efficiently.)

B. A strategy that favors investment goods over consumer goods will lead to a much faster shift in the PPF. A strategy that favors consumption over investment will lead to a higher standard of living, but a slower rate of growth.

C. In order to move to a higher production possibilities frontier a nation must achieve economic growth or, in other words, more output of all goods and services. In our example, to move from PPF1 to PPF2 this country would have to be able to produce more of both investment and consumer goods. An example of this might occur if there were technological changes that allowed the nation to produce more goods.

Moderate
Math
Page: 408

19.117: Given the following production information answer the next set of questions.

Year	L	K	Y	Labor Productivity
1	5	5	20	
2	6	5	22	
3	7	5	23	

A. Calculate labor productivity for all three years.

B. Explain whether labor productivity is increasing or decreasing and why.

C. What theory explains the trend exhibited in this production table?

Answer: A. Labor productivity is calculated by taking Y/L. In Year 1 Y/L = 20/5 = 4, in year 2 Y/L = 22/6 = 3.66, and in year 3 Y/L = 23/7 = 3.29.

B. Labor productivity is falling because labor is increasing, while the capital stock is remaining constant. Because the capital stock is constant, new labor is not as productive as old labor and, therefore, productivity will fall and there will be a lower standard of living.

C. This idea is called the theory of diminishing returns.

Easy
Math
Page: 408

19.118: Answer the following set of questions, given the production schedules for the computer chip industry and the clothing industry.

Computer Chips

Year	L	K	Y	Output Growth	Labor Productivity
1	100	300	450		
2	105	330	475		
3	109	365	502		
4	113	410	532		

Clothing

Year	L	K	Y	Output Growth	Labor Productivity
1	100	50	200		
2	110	52	210		
3	125	55	220		
4	143	58.5	230		

A. Calculate the labor productivity in the computer chip industry for years 1-4.

B. Calculate the labor productivity in the clothing industry for years 1-4.

C. Compute the growth rate for both industries for years 1-4.

D. Compare the productivity and growth of the computer chip industry and the clothing industry. Explain the differences.

Answer: A. Labor productivity is calculated by taking Y/L. Thus, in year 1 Y/L = 4.5, in year 2 Y/L = 4.52, in year 3 Y/L = 4.6, and in year 4 Y/L = 4.7.

B. Labor productivity is calculated by taking Y/L. Thus, in year 1 Y/L = 2, in year 2 Y/L = 1.91, in year 3 Y/L = 1.76, and in year 4 Y/L = 1.6.

C. The growth rates in the computer chip industry are as follows: year 1-2: 5.5%, year 2-3: 5.6%, and year 3-4: 5.9%. The growth rates in the clothing industry are as follows: year 1-2: 5%, year 2-3: 4.7%, and year 3-4: 4.5%.

D. In the computer chip industry both output and capital are increasing faster than labor, so productivity and output growth are growing. Output growth in the computer chip industry is growing, while output growth is falling in the clothing industry. In the clothing industry labor is growing faster than capital and output and, therefore, output growth and productivity are declining.

19.121: Describe public capital's, or infrastructure's, importance to our economy. How does it assist in the achievement of productivity and growth?

Difficult
Application
Page: 410

Answer: Infrastructure, or public capital, refers to all roads, bridges, police and fire stations, sewage plants, etc. All of these facilities help improve our standard of living. Infrastructure can be a factor in improving productivity and growth. For example, a safe and efficient transportation network makes it less expensive to transport goods and easier for people to get to and from work. Clean water and clean air improve the health of the population, which translates into higher productivity. As a result, infrastructure can make it easier for the nation to be more productive and, therefore, achieve economic growth.

19.122: What is human capital and what is its role in productivity?

Easy
Definition
Page: 411

Answer: Human capital includes all of the skills and knowledge that people have acquired over the years through education and training. Improvements in human capital, like more education, allow people to be more productive.

19.123: Explain some of the reasons given for the productivity decline in the United States in the 1970s.

Moderate
Application
Page: 416

Answer: Answers will vary. Some of the reasons given for the low rate of productivity in the 1970s are the low savings rate in the United States, increased environmental and government regulation on businesses, the lack of research and development, and that high energy costs in the `70s diverted investment resources away from other investment projects.

19.124: Discuss some of the controversy over immigration into the United States. From an economic growth standpoint, why is this so controversial?

Moderate
Application
Page: 409

Answer: Answers will vary. Some critics argue that too many immigrants hinder economic growth because they come here and use many government services, while contributing little, if any, back in. However, many immigrants are hard-working and skilled. They are human capital that can be used to increase productivity. As well, many immigrants are motivated to succeed, which adds to their ability to be productive.

19.125: Explain the three different ways an increase in GDP can come about.

Easy
Fact
Page: 407

Answer: An increase in GDP can come about in three ways: (1) through an increase in labor, (b) through an increase in physical or human capital, or (3) through an increase in the amount of product produced by each unit of capital or labor.

19.126: Explain the difference between an invention and an innovation. Provide an example of an invention and an innovation.

Moderate
Single
Page: 411

Answer: An invention is an advance in knowledge. An innovation is the use of new knowledge to produce a new product or to produce an existing product more efficiently. An innovation requires finding a use for new knowledge. Examples will vary.

19.127: The output per worker at the XYZ Manufacturing Company has increased. What factors could have caused this increase?

Easy
Fact
Page: 411

Answer: This increase could have been caused by an increase in the capital stock or an increase in human capital. The productivity of labor could also have increased if a result of a technological change, other advances in knowledge, or economies of scale.

Easy
Fact
Page: 415

19.128: According to the work done by Edward Denison, how much of the U.S. growth in output from 1929 to 1982 has come from increases in factors of production?How much of the U.S. growth in output has come from increases in factor productivity?What factors have caused
the increases in factor productivity?

Answer: Edward Dennison found that about half of the U.S. growth in output has come from increases in factors of production and the other half has come from increases in factor productivity. Factor productivity has increased because of the growth of knowledge.

Moderate
Single
Page: 418

19.129: Presidential candidates in the 1992 election argued that it was necessary to reduce the government deficit to increase the growth rate in the United States. Explain.

Answer: High government deficits cause interest rates to increase. As the interest rate increases, investment falls. A reduction in investment reduces the growth rate in the economy. To stimulate growth investment must increase, and to increase investment the interest rate must be reduced.

Moderate
Single
Page: 418

19.130: Explain how each of the following is related to the rates of productivity and economic growth in an economy:

(a.) the level of investment spending
(b.) the extent of government regulation
(c.) the level of spending on research and development
(d.) the saving rate

Answer: (a.) and (c.) Investment and spending on research and development increase productivity and economic growth. (b.) Regulation may improve efficiency and therefore increase productivity and growth. But if the costs imposed by regulations are greater than the benefits, productivity and growth will be reduced. (d.) As the saving rate increases, there is more money available for investment and therefore productivity and economic growth could increase.

Challenging
Multi
Page: 416

19.131: You have just been appointed to a special Presidential Task Force on Economic Growth. You are responsible for proposing three policies that the government can enact to increase the growth rate. What policies would you recommend and why?

Answer: Answers will vary.

Moderate
Single
Page: 419

19.132: Define industrial policy. What are the arguments for and against industrial policy in the United States. Based on these arguments, do you feel that the government should pursue an industrial policy? Explain your answer in detail.

Answer: Industrial policy is government involvement in the allocation of capital across manufacturing sectors. Industrial policy targets some industries for special subsidies and rapid investment. The argument in favor of industrial policy is that other countries use industrial policy and this puts the United States at a disadvantage in international competition. Critics of industrial policy argue that the best people to judge the appropriateness of investment in a particular industry are the firms in that industry. Answers to the last part will vary.

19.133: Explain the arguments for economic growth.

Easy
Fact
Page: 420

Answer: The arguments for economic growth are that growth is progress, growth leads to an improvement in the quality of life, growth increases consumer choice, growth leads to an improvement in the quality of goods, and growth makes it possible to improve conditions for the poor.

19.134: What are the arguments against growth?

Easy
Fact
Page: 421

Answer: The arguments against growth are that growth reduces the quality of life, for growth to continue firms must create wants, growth will lead to a rapid depletion of resources, and growth requires that resources be distributed unfairly.

(Chapter 35 in Combined Text)

20 International Trade, Comparative Advantage, and Protectionism

MULTIPLE CHOICE QUESTIONS

20.1: We refer to the situation when a country exports more than it imports as

(a) an expansion.
(b) a trade deficit.
(c) a trade surplus.
(d) a recession.

Answer: (c)

Easy
Definition
Page: 428

20.2: The situation when a country imports more than it exports is

(a) an expansion.
(b) a trade deficit.
(c) a trade surplus.
(d) a recession.

Answer: (b)

Easy
Definition
Page: 428

20.3: The value of a Montega's exports is $10 billion and this country imports goods and services worth $15 billion. This country has a

(a) $5 billion trade deficit.
(b) $5 billion trade surplus.
(c) $25 billion trade deficit.
(d) $25 billion trade surplus.

Answer: (a)

Easy
Single
Page: 428

20.4: The tariffs, subsidies, and restrictions enacted by the British Parliament in the early nineteenth century to discourage imports and encourage exports of grain were the

(a) Corn Laws.
(b) Wheat Laws.
(c) Barley Laws.
(d) Grain Laws.

Answer: (a)

Easy
Fact
Page: 428

20.5: The purpose of the Corn Laws was to

(a) encourage imports and discourage exports, and thus keep the price of food low.
(b) discourage imports and encourage exports, and thus keep the price of food high.
(c) discourage both imports and exports in order to promote economic self-sufficiency in Britain.
(d) encourage both exports and imports in order to integrate the British economy with the rest of Europe.

Answer: (b)

Easy
Fact
Page: 428

557

Easy
Definition
Page: 429

20.6: David Ricardo's theory that specialization and free trade will benefit all trading partners is known as the theory of

(a) absolute advantage.
(b) mutual advantage.
(c) comparative advantage.
(d) unilateral advantage.

Answer: (c)

Easy
Definition
Page: 429

20.7: Country A would have an absolute advantage over Country B in the production of corn, if

(a) Country A uses fewer resources to produce corn than Country B does.
(b) corn can be produced at lower cost in terms of other goods than it could be in Country B.
(c) the demand for corn is higher in Country A than in Country B.
(d) corn sells for a higher price in Country A than in Country B.

Answer: (a)

Easy
Definition
Page: 429

20.8: The advantage in the production of a product enjoyed by one country over another when it uses fewer resources to produce that product than the other country does is

(a) a relative advantage.
(b) a comparative advantage.
(c) an absolute advantage.
(d) a productive advantage.

Answer: (c)

Easy
Fact
Page: 429

20.9: According to the theory of comparative advantage, specialization will benefit all trading partners,

(a) even those that may be absolutely less efficient producers.
(b) except those that may be absolutely less efficient producers.
(c) except those that may be relatively more efficient producers.
(d) except those that may be relatively less efficient producers.

Answer: (a)

Easy
Single
Page: 429

20.10: Sweaters are produced using wool and labor. In Montega, a sweater can be produced with 3 skeins of wool and 3 hours of labor time. In Xena, a sweater can be produced with 3 skeins of wool and 2 hours of labor time. Which of the following is TRUE?

(a) Xena has both a comparative and an absolute advantage in the production of sweaters.
(b) Montega has both a comparative and an absolute advantage in the production of sweaters.
(c) Xena has an absolute advantage in the production of sweaters, but from this information it cannot be determined if Xena has a comparative advantage in the production of sweaters.
(d) Montega has an absolute advantage in the production of sweaters, but from this information it cannot be determined if Montega has a comparative advantage in the production of sweaters.

Answer: (c)

20.11: Country A has a comparative advantage over Country B in the production of wheat, if

(a) Country A can produce wheat at a lower monetary cost than Country B can.
(b) Country A can produce wheat using fewer resources than Country B can.
(c) Country A can produce wheat at a lower cost in terms of other goods than Country B can.
(d) the demand for wheat is higher in Country A than in Country B.

Answer: (c)

20.12: A country enjoys a comparative advantage in the production of a good if

(a) it uses fewer resources to produce that product than the other country does.
(b) that good can be produced at a lower cost in terms of other goods.
(c) that good can be produced at a lower monetary cost.
(d) it uses more resources to produce that product than the other country does.

Answer: (b)

20.13: When one country can produce a product at a lower cost in terms of other goods, that country is said to have

(a) a comparative advantage.
(b) an absolute advantage.
(c) a productive advantage.
(d) an unfair advantage.

Answer: (a)

20.14: Suppose that two countries, Argentina and Chile, are each engaged in the production of two goods—wheat and copper. If Argentina has an absolute advantage in the production of wheat and Chile has an absolute advantage in the production of copper, then

(a) there is no basis for trade between the two countries.
(b) Argentina should specialize in the production of copper and Chile should specialize in the production of wheat.
(c) both countries should engage in the production of both goods.
(d) Argentina should specialize in the production of wheat and Chile should specialize in the production of copper.

Answer: (d)

20.15: If Argentina has an absolute advantage in the production of wheat and Chile has an absolute advantage in the production of copper, then

(a) neither country has anything to gain from specialization and trade.
(b) it is reasonable to expect that specialization and trade will benefit both countries.
(c) it is reasonable to expect that specialization will benefit both countries, but trade will not.
(d) it is reasonable to expect that trade will benefit both countries, but specialization will not.

Answer: (b)

Moderate
Single
Page: 429

20.16: If Argentina has an absolute advantage in the production of wheat and Chile has an absolute advantage in the production of copper, then trade

(a) does not permit either country to move out beyond its previous resource and productivity constraints.
(b) enables both countries to move out beyond their previous resource constraints, but not their productivity constraints.
(c) enables both countries to move out beyond their previous resource and productivity constraints.
(d) enables both countries to move out beyond their previous productivity constraints, but not their resource constraints.

Answer: (c)

Moderate
Single
Page: 429

20.17: The aggregate production function is $Y = 5K^{0.5}L^{0.5}$. If there are 400 units of capital and 100 units of labor, aggregate output is

(a) 120 units.
(b) 500 units.
(c) 50,000 units.
(d) 1,000 units.

Answer: (d)

Challenging
Multi
Page: 431

20.18: Suppose that Argentina and Chile are both engaged in the production of copper and wheat, and that Argentina has an absolute advantage in the production of both goods. If Chile has a lower opportunity cost for producing copper, then

(a) Chile has a comparative advantage in wheat production, but there will be no gains from specialization and trade.
(b) Argentina still has a comparative advantage in the production of both goods.
(c) Chile has a comparative advantage in the production of copper, but it is outweighed by Argentina's absolute advantage in wheat production.
(d) Chile has a comparative advantage in the production of copper, and specialization and trade between the two countries can be mutually beneficial.

Answer: (d)

Challenging
Multi
Page: 431

20.19: The aggregate production function is $Y = 7KL$. If there are 10 units of capital and 20 units of labor, aggregate output is

(a) 83 units.
(b) 30 units.
(c) 1400 units.
(d) 4500 units.

Answer: (c)

Challenging
Multi
Page: 431

20.20: Suppose that Argentina and Chile are both engaged in the production of copper and wheat, and that Argentina has an absolute advantage in the production of both goods. If Chile has a comparative advantage in the production of copper, then Chile

(a) has a lower opportunity cost for producing copper, but specialization is not feasible because Argentina has a lower monetary cost of copper production.
(b) has a lower opportunity cost for copper, which means that it should specialize in production of copper and engage in trade.
(c) has a higher opportunity cost for copper, which means it should specialize in the production of wheat and engage in trade.
(d) should continue to produce copper, but only for domestic consumption, because trade is not a viable option.

Answer: (b)

	U.S.	Mexico
Apples	1000 bushels	300 bushels
Oranges	200 bushels	1200 bushels

Figure 20.1.

20.21: Refer to Figure 20.1. In the United States. the opportunity cost of 1 bushel of oranges is _____ of apples.

(a) 1/5 bushel
(b) 2 bushels
(c) 3.3 bushels
(d) 5 bushels

Answer: (d)

Moderate
Single
Page: 431

20.22: Refer to Figure 20.1. In Mexico the opportunity cost of 1 bushel of oranges is _____ of apples.

(a) 1/4 bushel
(b) 1/3 bushel
(c) 4 bushels
(d) 6 bushels

Answer: (a)

Moderate
Single
Page: 431

20.23: When there are 100 units of labor and 36 units of capital, the productivity of labor is 3. When there are 120 units of labor and 36 units of capital, the productivity of labor is 4. This is an example of

(a) a increase in the growth rate.
(b) increasing returns.
(c) a decrease in living standards.
(d) a leftward shift of the ppf.

Answer: (b)

Moderate
Single
Page: 431

20.24: Refer to Figure 20.1. Mexico has an absolute advantage in the production of

(a) apples.
(b) oranges.
(c) both apples and oranges.
(d) neither apples nor oranges.

Answer: (b)

Moderate
Single
Page: 431

20.25: Refer to Figure 20.1. Mexico has a comparative advantage in the production of

(a) apples.
(b) oranges.
(c) both apples and oranges.
(d) neither apples nor oranges.

Answer: (b)

Moderate
Single
Page: 431

Moderate
Single
Page: 431

20.26: Refer to Figure 20.1. The United States has a comparative advantage in the production of

(a) apples.
(b) oranges.
(c) both apples and oranges.
(d) neither apples nor oranges.

Answer: (a)

Moderate
Single
Page: 429

20.27: Refer to Figure 20.1. The United States has an absolute advantage in the production of

(a) apples.
(b) oranges.
(c) both apples and oranges.
(d) neither apples nor oranges.

Answer: (a)

Moderate
Multi
Page: 431

20.28: Refer to Figure 20.1. The United States has _____ and Mexico has _____.

(a) an absolute but not a comparative advantage in the production of apples; an absolute but not a comparative advantage in the production of oranges
(b) a comparative but not an absolute advantage in the production of apples; a comparative but not an absolute advantage in the production of oranges
(c) an absolute advantage in the production of apples, but a comparative advantage in the production of oranges; an absolute advantage in the production of oranges, but a comparative advantage in the production of apples
(d) both an absolute and a comparative advantage in the production of apples; an absolute and a comparative advantage in the production of oranges

Answer: (d)

Moderate
Single
Page: 432

20.29: Refer to Figure 20.1. Which of the following statements is TRUE?

(a) Since the United States can produce more apples than Mexico and Mexico can produce more oranges than the United States both countries are better off if they do not trade.
(b) Both the United States and Mexico would be better off if each country specialized in the production of the product for which they had the lower opportunity cost and then traded with each other.
(c) If the United States and Mexico decide to trade then the maximum amount of oranges available would be 1400 bushels and the maximum amount of apples available would be 1300 bushels.
(d) both b and c.

Answer: (b)

Moderate
Multi
Page: 434

20.30: Refer to Figure 20.1. For both countries to benefit from trade, the terms of trade must be between _____ apples to oranges.

(a) 1/5 : 1 and 1/4 : 1
(b) 4 : 1 and 5 : 1
(c) 1 : 4 and 1 : 5
(d) 1 : 1/5 and 1 : 4

Answer: (d)

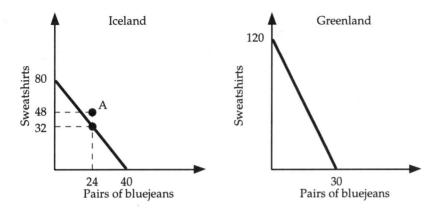

Figure 20.2.

20.31: Refer to Figure 20.2. The opportunity cost of a pair of bluejeans is

(a) 1/2 a sweatshirt in Iceland.
(b) 2 sweatshirts in Iceland.
(c) 1/4 sweatshirt in Greenland .
(d) 1 1/3 sweatshirts in Greenland.

Moderate
Single
Page: 434

Answer: (b)

20.32: Refer to Figure 20.2. The opportunity cost of a pair of bluejeans in Greenland is
_____ sweatshirt(s).

(a) 1/4
(b) 1/2
(c) 2
(d) 4

Moderate
Single
Page: 434

Answer: (d)

20.33: Refer to Figure 20.2. Which of the following statements is TRUE?

(a) Iceland has an absolute advantage in the production of sweatshirts, but a comparative advantage in the production of bluejeans.
(b) Iceland has a comparative advantage in the production of bluejeans, but an absolute advantage in the production of sweatshirts.
(c) Iceland has both a comparative and an absolute advantage in the production of bluejeans.
(d) Iceland has neither an absolute nor a comparative advantage in the production of either good.

Moderate
Multi
Page: 534

Answer: (c)

20.34: Refer to Figure 20.2. Which of the following statements is TRUE?

(a) Greenland has an absolute advantage in the production of sweatshirts, but a comparative advantage in the production of bluejeans.
(b) Greenland has a comparative advantage in the production of bluejeans, but an absolute advantage in the production of sweatshirts.
(c) Greenland has both a comparative and an absolute advantage in the production of sweatshirts.
(d) Greenland has neither an absolute nor a comparative advantage in the production of either good.

Moderate
Multi
Page: 534

Answer: (c)

Challenging
Multi
Page: 534

20.35: Refer to Figure 20.2. Both Iceland and Greenland will benefit when the terms of trade are set between _____ and _____ bluejeans to sweatshirts.

(a) 2 : 1; 4 : 1
(b) 1 : 1; 2 : 1
(c) 1 : 2; 1 : 4
(d) 1/2 : 1; 4 : 1

Answer: (c)

Honors
Multi
Page: 534

20.36: Refer to Figure 20.2. If after specialization and trade Iceland is consuming at point A, then

(a) consumption in Greenland is 88 sweatshirts and 6 pairs of bluejeans.
(b) consumption in Greenland is 72 sweatshirts and 16 pairs of bluejeans.
(c) consumption in Greenland is 32 sweatshirts and 6 pairs of bluejeans.
(d) it cannot be determined from this information how many pairs of bluejeans nor how many sweatshirts are being consumed in Greenland.

Answer: (b)

Challenging
Multi
Page: 434

20.37: Refer to Figure 20.2. If after specialization and trade Iceland is consuming at point A, the terms of trade are

(a) 2 : 1 sweatshirts to bluejeans.
(b) 2 : 3 sweatshirts to bluejeans
(c) 3 : 1 sweatshirts to bluejeans.
(d) 3 : 4 sweatshirts to bluejeans.

Answer: (c)

Moderate
Multi
Page: 434

20.38: Refer to Figure 20.2. Only Greenland will benefit from trade if the terms of trade are set at _____ bluejeans to sweatshirts.

(a) 1 : 4
(b) 1 : 2
(c) 1 : 5
(d) 1 : 6

Answer: (b)

Moderate
Multi
Page: 434

20.39: Refer to Figure 20.2. Only Iceland will benefit from trade if the terms of trade are set at _____ bluejeans to sweatshirts.

(a) 1 : 4
(b) 1 : 2
(c) 4 : 1
(d) 2 : 1

Answer: (a)

Easy
Fact
Page: 432

20.40: The main advantage of trade between two countries is that

(a) both countries move out beyond their previous resource and productivity constraints.
(b) employment in both countries will increase.
(c) trade makes both countries more self-sufficient.
(d) trade will lead to a more equitable distribution of income in both countries.

Answer: (a)

20.41: According to comparative advantage, trade between two countries

(a) allows each of the trading countries to use its resources most efficiently.
(b) guarantees that consumption levels will be equal in the two countries.
(c) will benefit all the industries in each of the countries.
(d) maximizes the amount of inputs that are used in the production of all products.

Answer: (a)

Easy
Fact
Page: 433

20.42: When countries specialize in producing those goods in which they have a comparative advantage, they

(a) maximize their combined output and allocate their resources more efficiently.
(b) maximize their combined output, but they do not necessarily allocate their resources more efficiently.
(c) allocate their resources more efficiently, but they do not necessarily maximize their combined output.
(d) do not necessarily maximize their combined output, and they also do not necessarily allocate their resources more efficiently.

Answer: (a)

Easy
Fact
Page: 433

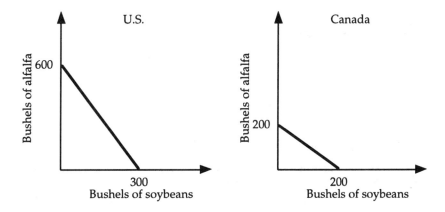

Figure 20.3

20.43: Refer to Figure 20.3. Which of the following statements is TRUE?

(a) The United States has both an absolute advantage and a comparative advantage in the production of soybeans and alfalfa.
(b) The United States has an absolute advantage in the production of soybeans and alfalfa, but a comparative advantage only in the production of soybeans.
(c) The United States has an absolute advantage in the production of soybeans and alfalfa, but a comparative advantage only in the production of alfalfa.
(d) The United States has a comparative advantage in the production of both soybeans and alfalfa, but an absolute advantage only in the production of soybeans.

Answer: (c)

Moderate
Multi
Page: 432

Moderate
Multi
Page: 432

20.44: Refer to Figure 20.3. Which of the following statements is TRUE?

(a) Only Canada can benefit from trade because the United States has an absolute advantage in the production of both soybeans and alfalfa.
(b) Trade will benefit both countries because the United States has a comparative advantage in the production of soybeans and Canada has a comparative advantage in the production of alfalfa.
(c) Trade will benefit both countries because the United States has a comparative advantage in the production of alfalfa and Canada has a comparative advantage in the production of soybeans.
(d) Trade will benefit neither country because the United States has an absolute advantage in the production of both soybeans and alfalfa, but Canada has a comparative advantage in the production of both soybeans and alfalfa.

Answer: (c)

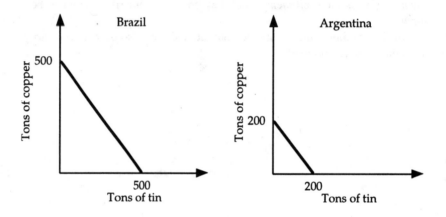

Figure 20.4

Challenging
Multi
Page: 432

20.45: Refer to Figure 20.4. Which of the following statements is TRUE?

(a) Trade will not take place between these two countries because Brazil has an absolute advantage in the production of both copper and tin.
(b) Trade will take place between these two countries because Brazil has an absolute advantage in the production of both copper and tin.
(c) Trade will not take place because Argentina has lower opportunity costs than Brazil in the production of both goods.
(d) Trade will not take place because the opportunity costs of producing tin and copper are the same in both countries.

Answer: (d)

Easy
Fact
Page: 434

20.46: The ratio at which a country can trade domestic products for imported products is the

(a) exchange rate.
(b) balance of payments.
(c) customs duty.
(d) terms of trade.

Answer: (d)

20.47: Assume that Outland specializes in producing rollerblades and Inland specializes in producing surfboards. After trade Outland exports 500 pairs of rollerblades and imports 100 surfboards. The terms of trade

Moderate
Single
Page: 434

(a) are 1 : 5 rollerblades to surfboards.
(b) are 5 : 1 rollerblades to surfboards.
(c) are 1/5 : 1 rollerblades to surfboards.
(d) cannot be determined from this information.

Answer: (b)

20.48: When trade is free, patterns of trade and trade flows result from

Easy
Fact
Page: 434

(a) the collective decisions of a few importers and exporters, as well as the governments of the countries in which they reside.
(b) the independent decisions of thousands of importers and exporters, as well as millions of private households and firms.
(c) the collective decisions of a few importers and exporters, as well as millions of private households and firms.
(d) the independent decisions of thousands of importers and exporters, as well as the governments of the countries in which they reside.

Answer: (b)

20.49: If you are traveling in Mexico and you purchase a meal that costs 1,000 pesos and the current exchange rate is 200 pesos to the dollar, then the price of the meal in U.S. currency is

Moderate
Single
Page: 435

(a) $.50.
(b) $2.
(c) $5.
(d) $20.

Answer: (c)

20.50: Suppose a U.S. dollar exchanges for 2 German deutsche marks (DM). Each DM is worth

Moderate
Single
Page: 435

(a) $.50.
(b) $1.
(c) $2.
(d) $4.

Answer: (a)

20.51: If the price of a car in the United States is $20,000, and the exchange rate between the dollar and the British pound rises from $1.50 to $1.75 per pound, then the price of the American car in Britain will

Moderate
Single
Page: 436

(a) fall.
(b) rise.
(c) remain the same.
(d) be irrelevant, because the British government will impose restrictions on imports from the United States.

Answer: (a)

Moderate
Fact
Page: 435

20.52: For any pair of countries, there is

(a) one single exchange rate that will lead automatically to both countries realizing the gains from specialization and comparative advantage.
(b) one single exchange rate that will lead indirectly to one country realizing the gains from specialization and comparative advantage, but not the other country.
(c) a range of exchange rates that can lead indirectly to one country realizing the gains from specialization and comparative advantage, but not the other country.
(d) a range of exchange rates that can lead automatically to both countries realizing the gains from specialization and comparative advantage.

Answer: (d)

	United States	**Germany**
Corn	$ 3	6 DM
Wheat	$ 4	10 DM

Figure 20.5

Challenging
Multi
Page: 436

20.53: Refer to Figure 20.5. If the exchange rate is $1 = 1 DM, then

(a) the United States will import both corn and wheat.
(b) Germany will import both corn and wheat.
(c) the United States will import wheat and Germany will import corn.
(d) the United States will import corn and Germany will import wheat.

Answer: (b)

Challenging
Multi
Page: 436

20.54: Refer to Figure 20.5. If the exchange rate is $1 = 3 DM, then

(a) the United States will import both corn and wheat.
(b) Germany will import both corn and wheat.
(c) the United States will import wheat and Germany will import corn.
(d) the United States will import corn and Germany will import wheat.

Answer: (a)

Challenging
Multi
Page: 436

20.55: Refer to Figure 20.5. If the exchange rate is $1 = 2 DM, then

(a) the United States will import both corn and wheat.
(b) Germany will import both corn and wheat.
(c) the United States will import corn and Germany will import wheat.
(d) Germany will import wheat.

Answer: (d)

Honors
Multi
Page: 436

20.56: Refer to Figure 20.5. Trade will flow in both directions between countries only if the price of DM is between

(a) $.40 and $.50.
(b) $2.00 and $2.50.
(c) $.60 and $.75.
(d) $1.33 and $1.67.

Answer: (a)

20.57: If the exchange rate between the United States and Japan changes from $1 = 100 yen to $1 = 150 yen, then, ceteris paribus, the price of American goods in Japan

Moderate
Single
Page: 436

(a) will increase.
(b) will decrease.
(c) will remain the same.
(d) could either increase or decrease.

Answer: (a)

20.58: If the exchange rate between the United States and Japan changes from $1 = 100 yen to $1 = 150 yen, then, ceteris paribus, the price of Japanese goods in the United States

Moderate
Single
Page: 436

(a) will increase.
(b) will decrease.
(c) will remain the same.
(d) could either increase or decrease.

Answer: (b)

20.59: If two countries engage in trade with one another, what determines which country will gain the most from trade?

Moderate
Fact
Page: 435

(a) the exchange rate
(b) comparative advantage
(c) absolute advantage
(d) all of the above

Answer: (a)

20.60: Suppose that the United States and Italy both produce wine and shoes. In the United States, wine sells for $10 a bottle and shoes sell for $40 a pair. In Italy, wine sells for 12,000 lira a bottle and shoes sell for 18,000 lira a pair. If the current exchange rate is 1,000 lira to the dollar, then

Challenging
Multi
Page: 436

(a) Italy will import both shoes and wine from the United States.
(b) the United States will import both shoes and wine from Italy.
(c) the United States will import wine from Italy and Italy will import shoes from the United States.
(d) the United States will import shoes from Italy and Italy will import wine from the United States.

Answer: (d)

20.61: Suppose that the United States and Italy both produce wine and shoes. In the United States, wine sells for $10 a bottle and shoes sell for $40 a pair. In Italy, wine sells for 15,000 lira a bottle and shoes sell for 20,000 lira a pair. Given this information, trade will flow in both directions if the price of a dollar is between

Honors
Multi
Page: 436

(a) 500 and 1,500 lira.
(b) 1,500 and 3,750 lira.
(c) 1,500 and 2,000 lira.
(d) 2,000 and 3,750 lira.

Answer: (a)

Easy
Definition
Page: 437

20.62: The quantity and quality of labor, land, and natural resources of a country are its

(a) capital stock.
(b) productive capacity.
(c) economic potential.
(d) factor endowments.

Answer: (d)

Easy
Definition
Page: 437

20.63: The theory that states that a country has a comparative advantage in the production of a product if that country is relatively well endowed with inputs used intensively in the production of that product is the

(a) Ricardo-Malthus theorem.
(b) Heckscher-Ohlin theorem.
(c) Lucas-Laffer theorem.
(d) Friedman-Samuelson theorem.

Answer: (b)

Easy
Fact
Page: 437

20.64: A significant portion of actual world trade patterns results from

(a) the industrial policies of governments.
(b) the different tastes and preferences of people in different countries.
(c) different factor endowments between countries.
(d) different sizes of the countries.

Answer: (c)

Moderate
Single
Page: 438

20.65: An example of an acquired comparative advantage is

(a) the United States producing more agricultural products than other countries because land is more abundant in the United States than in other countries.
(b) the United States purchasing coconuts from other countries, because they cannot be produced in the United States.
(c) United States companies selling to other countries chemical products that cannot be sold in the United States.
(d) United States consumers buying television sets produced in Japan because Japanese companies have a reputation for producing a higher quality TV than those produced in the United States.

Answer: (d)

Moderate
Single
Page: 438

20.66: If real output increased by 10% and during the same period the population increased by 15%, real GDP per capita grew at a rate of

(a) 5%.
(b) 10%.
(c) 15%.
(d) -5%.

Answer: (d)

20.67: An example of acquired comparative advantage is

(a) that some U.S. consumers prefer German cars over American cars because German cars have a reputation for being very safe.
(b) the United States imports coffee beans because coffee beans cannot be grown in the United States.
(c) China specializes in the production of labor-intensive goods because of the amount of labor available in the country relative to capital.
(d) the U.S. government provides a subsidy to firms that are trying to increase their exports to other countries.

Moderate
Single
Page: 438

Answer: (a)

20.68: Which of the following phenomena cannot be explained by the simple comparative advantage theory?

(a) A country imports and exports the same goods.
(b) A country with a lot of skilled labor tends to export highly technical goods.
(c) A country tends to export the goods that it can produce at a lower opportunity cost.
(d) A country that does not have much farmland tends to import agricultural goods.

Challenging
Single
Page: 438

Answer: (a)

20.69: The Heckscher-Ohlin theorem looks to _____ to explain trade flows.

(a) acquired comparative advantage
(b) the existence of trade barriers
(c) relative factor endowments
(d) the differences in preferences among consumers

Easy
Fact
Page: 438

Answer: (c)

20.70: Which of the following is NOT a valid explanation for the existence of international trade?

(a) Some economies of scale that are available when producing for a domestic market may not be available when producing for a world market.
(b) The existence of acquired comparative advantage.
(c) The existence of natural comparative advantage.
(d) Industries may differentiate their products in order to please the wide variety of tastes that exist worldwide.

Moderate
Fact
Page: 438

Answer: (a)

20.71: A tariff is

(a) a limit on the quantity of a good that can be imported into a country.
(b) the difference between the price a product sells for in the country it is produced in and the price it is sold for in another country.
(c) a government payment made to domestic firms to encourage exports.
(d) a tax on imports.

Easy
Definition
Page: 439

Answer: (d)

Easy
Definition
Page: 439

20.72: Government payments made to domestic firms in order to encourage exports are called

(a) tariffs.
(b) bribes.
(c) subsidies.
(d) quotas.

Answer: (c)

Easy
Single
Page: 439

20.73: It costs a computer manufacturer $2,000 to produce a personal computer. This manufacturer sells these computers abroad for $1,800. This is an example of

(a) a negative tariff.
(b) dumping.
(c) export subsidy.
(d) a trade-related economy of scale.

Answer: (b)

Moderate
Multi
Page: 442

20.74: If the United States increases the tariff on imported tuna steaks, this will

(a) reduce the number of tuna steaks imported into the United States and reduce production of tuna steaks in the United States.
(b) increase the number of tuna steaks imported in the United States and increase the production of tuna steaks in the United States.
(c) reduce the number of tuna steaks imported in the United States and increase the production of tuna steaks in the United States.
(d) increase the number of tuna steaks imported in the United States and reduce the production of tuna steaks in the United States.

Answer: (c)

Easy
Single
Page: 439

20.75: The United States placed a limit on the amount of steel that can be imported into the United States. This is an example of

(a) a tariff.
(b) a quota.
(c) an export subsidy.
(d) dumping.

Answer: (b)

Moderate
Single
Page: 439

20.76: A quota imposed on textiles imported into the United States would

(a) reduce U.S. imports of textiles and reduce U.S. production of textiles.
(b) increase U.S. imports of textiles and reduce U.S. production of textiles.
(c) reduce U.S. imports of textiles and increase U.S. production of textiles.
(d) increase U.S. imports of textiles and increase U.S. production of textiles.

Answer: (c)

20.77: Which of the following statements is FALSE?

(a) If the United States imposes a tariff on Japanese car imports, the price of cars in the United States is likely to increase.
(b) If the United States imposes a quota on Japanese car imports, the price of cars in the United States is likely to increase.
(c) If Japan imposes a "voluntary export restraint" on car exports to the United States, the price of cars in the United States is likely to increase.
(d) If Japan imposes a subsidy on car exports to the United States, the price of cars in the United States is likely to increase.

Moderate
Single
Page: 439

Answer: (d)

20.78: The U.S. tariff law which set off an international trade war in the 1930s was the

(a) Taft-Hartley Tariff.
(b) Smoot-Hawley tariff.
(c) Bentsen-Gephardt tariff.
(d) Landrum-Griffin tariff.

Easy
Fact
Page: 439

Answer: (b)

20.79: The international agreement signed by the United States and 22 other countries in 1947 to promote the liberalization of foreign trade is known by its initials as

(a) SALT.
(b) START.
(c) GATT.
(d) IMF.

Easy
Fact
Page: 439

Answer: (c)

20.80: Every president who has held office since the General Agreement on Tariffs and Trade was signed has

(a) argued for free-trade policies, yet each one has used his powers to protect various sectors of the economy.
(b) argued that certain domestic industries deserve protection, yet each one has been reluctant to use his powers to protect individual sectors of the economy.
(c) argued for free-trade policies, but only Eisenhower and Reagan successfully resisted all calls for protection from various sectors of the economy.
(d) argued for free-trade policies, but only Kennedy and Carter successfully resisted all calls for protection from various sectors of the economy.

Easy
Fact
Page: 440

Answer: (a)

20.81: Over time, the general movement in the United States has been toward

(a) higher tariffs and stricter import quotas.
(b) managed trade.
(c) complete elimination of tariffs, import quotas, and export subsidies.
(d) freer trade.

Easy
Fact
Page: 440

Answer: (d)

Easy
Fact
Page: 440

20.82: If a nation has most-favored-nation status conferred upon it, then exports from that country

(a) will be priced higher than products exported from countries without most-favored-nation status.
(b) are exempt from all safety regulations.
(c) are sold below cost.
(d) are taxed at the lowest negotiated tariff rates.

Answer: (d)

Easy
Definition
Page: 440

20.83: Economic integration

(a) occurs when countries develop an acquired comparative advantage that makes their industries more competitive in international markets.
(b) occurs when two or more nations join to form a free-trade zone.
(c) occurs when countries are granted most-favored-nation status.
(d) occurs when one country voluntarily agrees to reduce its exports to another country.

Answer: (b)

Moderate
Multi
Page: 440

20.84: The U.S. - Canadian Free-Trade Agreement, that will remove all barriers to trade including tariffs and quotas between the United States and Canada by 1998, should have which of the following effects?

(a) The price of Canadian goods sold in the United States will increase.
(b) The price of U.S. goods sold in Canada will increase.
(c) The amount that the United States exports to Canada and the amount that the United States imports from Canada should increase.
(d) All of the above.

Answer: (c)

Easy
Definition
Page: 440

20.85: In 1991, what group of countries began the process of forming the largest free-trade zone in the world?

(a) the United States, Canada, and Mexico
(b) the North Atlantic Treaty Organization
(c) the European Community
(d) the Organization of Petroleum Exporting Countries

Answer: (c)

Moderate
Single
Page: 440

20.86: Which of the following can be considered a free-trade zone?

(a) the United States
(b) countries which are members of GATT
(c) all English-speaking nations
(d) the industrialized OECD nations

Answer: (a)

Moderate
Fact
Page: 442

20.87: The case for free trade is based on the

(a) theory of comparative advantage.
(b) theory of absolute advantage.
(c) argument for a diversified economy.
(d) theory of balanced growth.

Answer: (a)

20.88: Which of the following statements is NOT true?

(a) Trade is beneficial because it allows more efficient production.
(b) Trade is beneficial because it allows consumers to buy goods at cheaper prices.
(c) Trade is beneficial because it allows all domestic industries to increase production.
(d) Trade is beneficial because it allows consumption beyond the production possibility frontier.

Easy
Fact
Page: 442

Answer: (c)

20.89: A tariff imposed on imported shoes will cause the domestic price of shoes to _____ and the domestic production of shoes to _____.

Easy
Multi
Page: 443

(a) increase; increase
(b) increase; decrease
(c) decrease; increase
(d) decrease; decrease

Answer: (a)

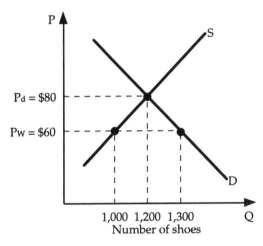

Figure 20.6.

20.90: Refer to Figure 20.6. The domestic price of shoes is $80. After trade the price of a pair of shoes is $60. After trade this country will import

Moderate
Single
Page: 443

(a) 100 pairs of shoes.
(b) 200 pairs of shoes.
(c) 300 pairs of shoes.
(d) 1,300 pairs of shoes.

Answer: (c)

20.91: Refer to Figure 20.6. The domestic price of shoes is $80. After trade the price of a pair of shoes is $60. Now domestic production costs fall so that the equilibrium domestic price of a pair of shoes is $70. This would cause

Challenging
Multi
Page: 443

(a) the number of pairs of shoes imported into this country to increase.
(b) the number of pairs of shoes imported into this country to decrease.
(c) the number of pairs of shoes exported from this country to increase.
(d) the number of pairs of shoes exported from this country to decrease.

Answer: (b)

20.92: Refer to Figure 20.6. The domestic price of shoes is $80. After trade the price of a pair of shoes is $60. If shoes are a normal good and income in this country rises, then we would expect

Challenging
Multi
Page: 443

(a) the number of pairs of shoes imported into this country to increase.
(b) the number of pairs of shoes imported into this country to decrease.
(c) the number of pairs of shoes exported from this country to increase.
(d) the number of pairs of shoes exported from this country to decrease.

Answer: (a)

Moderate
Single
Page: 443

20.93: Refer to Figure 20.7. The domestic price of a leather wallet is $20. With free trade the price of a leather wallet is $10 and after the tariff is imposed the price is $15. If there is free trade, this country will import _____ leather wallets.

(a) 50
(b) 100
(c) 200
(d) 300

Answer: (c)

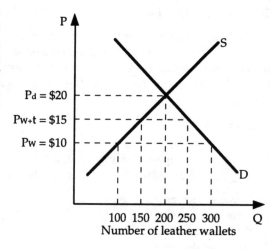

Figure 20.7.

Moderate
Single
Page: 443

20.94: Refer to Figure 20.7. The domestic price of a leather wallet is $20. With free trade the price of a leather wallet is $10 and after the tariff is imposed the price is $15. After the tariff is imposed, this country will import _____ leather wallets.

(a) 50
(b) 100
(c) 150
(d) 200

Answer: (b)

Moderate
Single
Page: 443

20.95: Refer to Figure 20.7. The domestic price of a leather wallet is $20. With free trade the price of a leather wallet is $10 and after the tariff is imposed the price is $15. After the tariff is imposed, tariff revenue in this country will be

(a) $50.
(b) $250.
(c) $500.
(d) $750.

Answer: (c)

Moderate
Multi
Page: 443

20.96: Refer to Figure 20.7. The domestic price of a leather wallet is $20. With free trade the price of a leather wallet is $10 and after the tariff is imposed the price is $15. After the tariff is imposed,

(a) domestic production and consumption will increase by 50 wallets, and domestic consumption will increase by 50 wallets.
(b) domestic production will increase by 150 wallets and domestic consumption will decrease by 250 wallets.
(c) domestic production will increase by 100 wallets and domestic consumption will decrease by 100 wallets.
(d) domestic production will increase by 50 wallets and domestic consumption will decrease by 50 wallets.

Answer: (d)

20.97: Refer to Figure 20.7. The domestic price of a leather wallet is $20. With free trade the price of a leather wallet is $10 and after the tariff is imposed the price is $15. If the tariff is raised so that it now equals $10, tariff revenue in this country will be

Challenging
Multi
Page: 443

(a) $0.
(b) $1,000.
(c) $2,000.
(d) $3,000.

Answer: (a)

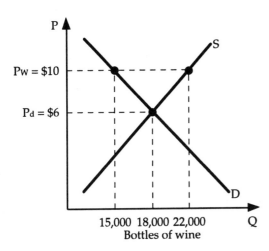

Figure 20.8

20.98: Refer to Figure 20.8. The domestic price of a bottle of wine is $6 and the world price of a bottle of wine is $10. If there is free trade, this country will

Challenging
Multi
Page: 443

(a) import 4,000 bottles of wine.
(b) import 7,000 bottles of wine.
(c) export 4,000 bottles of wine.
(d) export 7,000 bottles of wine.

Answer: (d)

20.99: Refer to Figure 20.8. The domestic price of a bottle of wine is $6 and the world price for a bottle of wine is $10. If this country's production costs increase so that the domestic price of wine is now $8 and there is still free trade, then this country's

Challenging
Multi
Page: 443

(a) imports of wine will increase.
(b) imports of wine will decrease.
(c) exports of wine will increase.
(d) exports of wine will decrease.

Answer: (d)

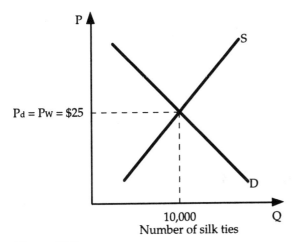

Figure 20.9

20.100: Refer to Figure 20.9. The domestic and world price of silk ties in this country is $25. If there is free trade, this country will

Challenging
Single
Page: 443

(a) import 10,000 silk ties.
(b) export 10,000 silk ties.
(c) import 5,000 silk ties and export 5,000 silk ties.
(d) neither import nor export silk ties.

Answer: (d)

Challenging
Multi
Page: 443

20.101: Refer to Figure 20.9. If the demand for silk ties in this country increases and the world price stays constant at $25 then, this country will

(a) increase its imports of silk ties.
(b) decrease its imports of silk ties.
(c) increase its exports of silk ties.
(d) decrease its exports of silk ties.

Answer: (a)

Moderate
Single
Page: 445

20.102: Which of the following statements is FALSE?

(a) The argument that U.S. industries need to be protected from foreign competition because wages in foreign countries are lower than wages in the United States is false because trade flows according to comparative and not absolute advantage.
(b) The main argument for protection against foreign competition is that it costs Americans their jobs.
(c) In the United States new industries are much more likely to seek protection from foreign competition than established industries because new industries need time to develop a comparative advantage.
(d) Trade protection may be necessary when a country's currency is overvalued and therefore buys more foreign currency than it should.

Answer: (c)

Moderate
Single
Page: 444

20.103: The owners of steel companies have argued that they need to be protected from foreign competition because the wages paid to workers in foreign countries are significantly lower than the wages paid to U.S. steel workers. What is the best economic response to this argument?

(a) Wages reflect productivity and if U.S. steel workers are more productive than workers in foreign countries then the U.S. steel industry should still be able to compete internationally.
(b) Even though U.S. workers earn more than workers in foreign countries, the United States would still have an absolute advantage in the production of steel and should therefore be able to compete internationally.
(c) It is essential to protect the steel industry so that there are no additional job losses in this industry.
(d) The steel industry should be protected from foreign competition because low foreign wages are an unfair barrier to trade.

Answer: (a)

Moderate
Fact
Page: 446

20.104: The vast majority of economists would contend that

(a) foreign trade and full employment are mutually exclusive goals.
(b) foreign trade can be pursued, but full employment is an unattainable goal.
(c) foreign trade and full employment can be pursued simultaneously.
(d) full employment can be pursued, but foreign trade is an undesirable activity.

Answer: (c)

TRUE/FALSE QUESTIONS

Moderate
Definition
Page: 435

20.105: In general, for any two countries, there are many exchange rates that will lead to gains from trade, based on comparative advantage.

Answer: True

20.106: If the exchange rate between the United States and France changes from $1 = 5FF to $1 = 9FF then, holding everything else constant, the price of U.S. goods in France will increase.

Difficult
Application
Page: 436

Answer: True

20.107: If France increases subsidies to its wheat farmers, U.S. farmers will increase the price of their wheat in order to compete.

Moderate
Application
Page: 439

Answer: False

20.108: It is a valid argument that industries need to be protected from foreign competition because foreign wages are substantially lower than wages paid to U.S. workers.

Difficult
Application
Page: 444

Answer: False

20.109: A country is said to enjoy an absolute advantage over another country in the production of a product if it uses fewer resources to produce that product than the other country does.

Easy
Definition
Page: 429

Answer: True

20.110: A country enjoys a comparative advantage in the production of a good if that good can be produced at a lower cost in terms of other goods.

Easy
Definition
Page: 429

Answer: True

20.111: For any pair of nations and goods, if each country has an absolute advantage in the production of one product, it is reasonable to expect that specialization and trade will benefit both countries.

Easy
Fact
Page: 429

Answer: True

20.112: For any pair of countries, there is only one single exchange rate that can lead automatically to both countries realizing the gains from specialization and comparative advantage.

Easy
Fact
Page: 435

Answer: False

20.113: Within the range of exchange rates that permits specialization and trade to take place, the exchange rate will determine which country gains the most from trade.

Easy
Fact
Page: 435

Answer: True

20.114: If exchange rates end up in the right ranges, the free market will drive each country to shift resources into those sectors in which it enjoys a comparative advantage.

Easy
Fact
Page: 436

Answer: True

20.115: Only those products in which a country has an absolute advantage will be competitive in world markets.

Easy
Fact
Page: 437

Answer: False

20.116: Tariffs, subsidies, and quotas do not alter the gains of comparative advantage.

Easy
Fact
Page: 438

Answer: False

20.117: Trade barriers prevent a nation from reaping the benefits of specialization, push it to adopt relatively inefficient production techniques, and force consumers to pay higher prices for protected products than they would otherwise pay.

Easy
Fact
Page: 442

Answer: True

Easy
Fact
Page: 444

20.118: The main argument for protectionist policies is that foreign competition costs Americans their jobs.

Answer: True

SHORT ANSWER QUESTIONS

Easy
Definition
Page: 428

20.119: Define trade deficit and trade surplus. Does the United States have a deficit or surplus? What has been the trend in the United States?

Answer: A trade deficit occurs when a country imports more than it exports. A trade surplus occurs when a country exports more than it imports. The United States has been running a trade deficit since the mid-1970s, with it becoming very serious in the late 1980s. In 1994, it again climbed to late-1980s levels.

20.120: Define and explain the difference between tariffs and quotas.

Answer: A tariff is a tax on imports and a quota is a limit on the quantity of imports.

	Corn (bushels)	Timber (board-feet)
U.S.	10	5
Canada	4	10

Figure 20.10

Easy
Definition
Page: 439

20.121: Refer to Figure 20.10. Answer parts a through d based on the information in this table. Assume each nation has 500 acres of land for production.

a. Which nation has a comparative advantage in the production of corn? In the production of timber? Explain your answers.
b. Draw the production possibility frontier for each nation.
c. Would these nations be better off by trading with each other? Explain.

Answer: (a) The U.S. has a comparative advantage in the production of corn because the opportunity cost of producing corn (1C=0.5T) is less than that of Canada (1C=2.5T). Canada has a comparative advantage in the production of timber because the opportunity cost of producing timber (1T=0.4T) is less than that of the U.S. (1T=2C). (b)

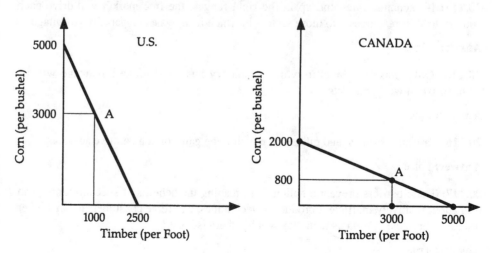

(c) Yes, they would be better off trading with each other than going at it alone. The United States should specialize in corn and Canada in timber. By doing this, each nation can increase their consumption potential and get more of both products than if they had not traded.

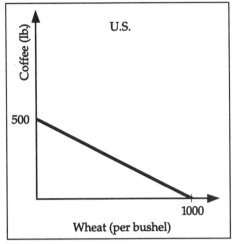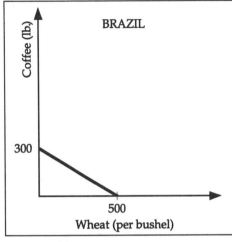

Figure 20.11

20.122:. Answer parts A through E based on the information Figure 20.11. Assume that both nations have the same amount of land in production.

Easy
Application
Page: 432

A Who has the absolute advantage in the production of coffee? In the production of wheat?
B. What are the opportunity costs of producing coffee in the United States, in Brazil?
C. What are the opportunity costs of producing wheat in the United States, in Brazil?
D. Which nation has the comparative advantage in coffee production? In wheat production?
E. In terms of wheat, where will the terms of trade lie?

Answer: (A) The United States sacrifices 2 bushels of wheat for every pound of coffee produced. Brazil sacrifices 1.67 bushels of wheat for every pound of coffee produced. (B) The United States has the absolute advantage in the production of coffee and wheat. (C) The United States sacrifices 1/2 pound of coffee for every bushel of wheat produced. Brazil sacrifices .6 pounds of coffee for every bushel of wheat produced. (D) Brazil has a lower opportunity cost in coffee production and thus, has the comparative advantage. The United States has the comparative advantage in wheat production because they have the lower opportunity cost with wheat. (E) These nations should trade based on their comparative advantage. Brazil should specialize in coffee and the United States should specialize in wheat. The terms of trade will lie between United States 1 wheat = .5 coffee and Brazil 1 wheat = .6 coffee, thus an acceptable terms of trade would be something like 1 wheat = .55 coffee.

20.123: Consider the following situation: In Japan it costs an electronics manufacturer $1,000 to produce a state-of-the-art stereo system. Because of industrial policies followed by the Japanese government, Japanese electronics manufacturers are able to sell this same stereo in the U.S. for $800. What practice are the Japanese manufacturers engaging in? What will happen to the price of goods made by U.S. electronics manufacturers? Explain. Who benefits and who loses in a trading situation like this? Are these practices acceptable in the United States? Explain.

Easy
Application
Page: 432

Answer: This practice is called dumping. In order to compete with lower priced Japanese goods, U.S. manufacturers will have to lower their prices as well, even if costs do not justify this. Answers will vary. The obvious winners are the Japanese manufacturers who make inroads into the U.S. market by selling products less than cost, but are protected from losses because of industrial policy at home. The U.S. consumers win because of lower prices on stereos. (However, if the Japanese drive U.S. manufacturers out of business, the consumer may not be better off in the long-run because there will be fewer stereo producers in the market and the Japanese can then increase their prices without fear of competition.) The U.S. manufacturers are obvious losers because they are, basically, forced to sell their stereos below cost in order to compete with the Japanese. Dumping goods is illegal in the United States, according to the Sherman Antitrust Act of 1890, which prohibits predatory pricing.

Easy
Application
Page: 443

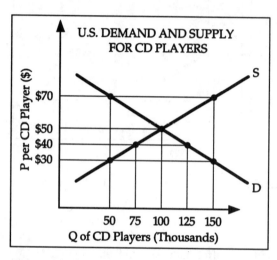

Figure 20.12

20.124: Refer to Figure 20.12. Answer parts a through e based on this figure. Assume that the world price for CD players in $30.

a. In autarky, what is the equilibrium price and quantity of CD players manufactured in the United States?

b. With free trade, how many CD players are produced in the United States? How many CD players are imported into the United States?

c. Suppose Congress places a $10 tariffs in each imported CD player. With the tariff, how many CD players are procued in the United States and how many are imported?

d. How much government revenue does the tariff generate?

e. Explain who the winners and losers are in a tariff situation like this one.

Answer: (a) P=$50, Q=100, (b) Produced=50, Imports=100, (c) Produced=75, Imports=50, (d) $500, (e) The winners are the domestic producer and the U.S. government. The former gets increased production from the tariff and the latter gets increased tax.

Easy
Definition
Page: 439

20.125: Explain which tariff law caused great international turmoil in the early part of this century.

Answer: The Smoot-Hawley tariff of the 1930s set the highest tariffs in U.S. history, with an average tariff rate of 60%. It set off an international trade war and caused a decline in trade that is often considered a cause of the worldwide depression of the 1930s.

Moderate
Definition
Page: 440

20.126: Are the U.S.-Canadian Free Trade Agreement and the North American Free Trade Agreement the same? Explain.

Answer: No. The U.S.-Canadian Free-Trade Agreement is a free trade agreement between the United States and Canada designed to eliminate all barriers to trade between the two countries by 1998. On the other hand, the North American Free Trade Agreement is one signed by Mexico, Canada, and the United States in which all three nations agreed to establish a North American free trade zone. NAFTA took effect on January 1, 1994.

20.127: Describe some of the goals of economic integration for the former European Community, now called the European Union.

Difficult
Application
Page: 440

Answer: Answers will vary. The Maastricht Treaty called for the end of border controls, an end to all tariffs, a common currency, and the coordination of member nation's monetary and political issues.

20.128: Distinguish between the concepts of comparative advantage and absolute advantage.

Easy
Definition
Page: 429

Answer: A country enjoys an absolute advantage over another country in the production of a product if it uses fewer resources to produce a product than another other country does. A country enjoys a comparative advantage in the production of a product if that product can be produced at a lower cost in terms of other products than it can be produced for in another country.

	Beans	Corn
Inland	2 bushels	4 bushels
Outland	4 bushels	2 bushels

Figure 20.13

20.129: Refer to Figure 20.13. Answer parts a through h based on the information in this table.

Challenging
Multi
Page: 432

a. Draw the production possibility frontier for each country if each country has 200 acres of land.
b. Which country has the absolute advantage in the production of beans?
c. Which country has the absolute advantage in the production of corn?
d. Which country has the comparative advantage in the production of beans? In that country, what is the opportunity cost of producing a bushel of beans?
e. Which country has the comparative advantage in the production of corn? In that country, what is the opportunity cost of producing a bushel of corn?
f. Explain why these two countries can benefit from trade.
g. What terms of trade would benefit only Inland?
h. What terms of trade would benefit only Outland?

Answer: (a)

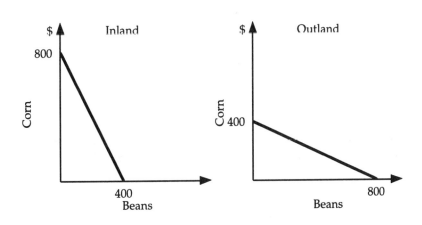

(b) Outland has the absolute advantage in the production of beans. (c) Inland has the absolute advantage in the production of corn. (d) Outland has the comparative advantage in the production of beans. Outland's opportunity cost of producing a bushel of bean is 1/2 bushel of corn. (e) Inland has the comparative advantage in the production of corn. Inland's opportunity cost of producing corn is 1/2 bushel of beans. (f) These two countries can benefit from trade because each country has a comparative advantage in the production of one of the goods. (g) The terms of trade that would only benefit Inland are 1 : 2 corn to beans. (h) The terms of trade that would benefit only Outland are 2 : 1 corn to beans.

Moderate
Single
Page: 432

20.130: Explain how specialization and trade benefit all trading partners, even those that may be inefficient producers in an absolute sense.

Answer: Trade allows countries to specialize in the production of the good for which they have a comparative advantage. Thus trade maximizes the combined output of countries and allows countries to allocate their resources more efficiently.

Challenging
Single
Page: 435

20.131: How do exchange rates facilitate the realization of the gains from specialization and comparative advantage?

Answer: If exchange rates end up in the right range, free trade will drive each country to shift resources into those sectors in which it enjoys a comparative advantage.

Challenging
Single
Page: 443

20.132: If the intellectual case for free trade, based on specialization and comparative advantage, is so powerful, then why are protectionist policies so attractive to politicians in the United States?

Answer: Protectionist policies are attractive to politicians because many people believe that protectionist policies will increase employment in the United States. Protectionist policies also appeal to politicians if it appears that other countries are not playing "fair."

Easy
Fact
Page: 437

20.133: Explain the Heckscher-Ohlin theorem.

Answer: The Heckscher-Ohlin theorem looks to relevant factor endowments to explain comparative advantage and trade flows. According to the theorem, a country has a comparative advantage in the production of a product if that country is relatively well endowed with the inputs that are used intensively in the production of the product.

Moderate
Fact
Page: 438

20.134: Comparative advantage is not the only reason why countries trade. Explain two other reasons why countries trade.

Answer: Another explanation for trade is that a consumer may prefer an imported product over a domestic product because of the characteristics of the imported product — such as design, safety, or service. It may also be the case that trade allows industries to fully take advantage of economies of scale that would not be available in the absence of trade.

20.135: A politician has proposed that the U.S. government give U.S. automobile manufacturers export subsidies to enable U.S. automobile manufacturers to export more cars. What impact is this policy likely to have on the price of cars in the United States and on the world price of cars? Why? What impact will this policy have on the allocation of resources? Why? Would you support such a policy? Explain your answer.

Challenging
Multi
Page: 439

Answer: The impact on the price on domestic cars is unknown. If the automobile industry does not reduce sales to the domestic market and only increases sales to foreign markets, the domestic price would be unchanged. If, however, the industry merely shifts products from the domestic market to international markets, the domestic price of cars would increase. The impact on the world price of cars also depends on whether or not total production of cars increases or not. If total production does not increase and cars are merely shifted from the domestic market into the international market, the world price of cars would not change. If total production of cars increases, the world price of cars would decrease. If this causes total production of cars to increase, more resources would be allocated to the automobile industry. Answers will vary as to whether the policy is supported.

20.136: Define tariff. Use a graph to illustrate the effects of a tariff on the country that imposes the tariff. Specifically, explain what will happen to the amount imported into the country, the price of the good, and the quantity demanded and the quantity supplied of the good in the country. Compare the effects of a tariff and a quota.

Moderate
Single
Page: 443

Answer: A tariff is a tax on an imported good. According to the graph, a tariff will reduce imports, increase domestic production, and reduce domestic consumption. A quota will also cause imports to fall, domestic production to increase, and domestic consumption to decrease. A quota, however, raises no revenue.

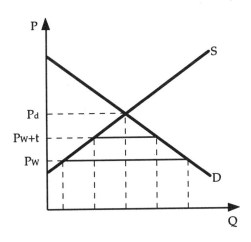

20.137: Explain three of the arguments that are made to justify trade barriers such as tariffs and quotas.

Moderate
Fact
Page: 444

Answer: Trade barriers are justified on the basis of (a) the need to protect industries that are vital to national defense (b) the need to protect infant industries from competition until they can develop a comparative advantage (c) the fact that trade barriers protect U.S. jobs (d) the fact that some countries engage in unfair trade practices (e) the fact that American industries cannot compete because U.S. wages are so much higher than wages in other countries and (f) the fact that they provides protection during temporary currency overvaluations.

21 Open-Economy Macroeconomics: The Balance of Payments and Exchange Rates

(Chapter 36 in Combined Text)

MULTIPLE CHOICE QUESTIONS

21.1: The price of one country's currency in terms of another country's currency is the

(a) balance of trade.
(b) terms of trade.
(c) exchange rate.
(d) currency valuation.

Easy
Definition
Page: 450

Answer: (c)

21.2: The agreements that were reached at the Bretton Woods conference in 1944 established a system

(a) in which the values of currencies were fixed in terms of a specific number of ounces of gold, which in turn determined their values in international trading.
(b) of floating exchange rates determined by the supply and demand of one nation's currency relative to the currency of other nations.
(c) that prohibited governments from intervening in the foreign exchange markets.
(d) of essentially fixed exchange rates under which each country agreed to intervene in the foreign exchange market when necessary to maintain the agreed-upon value of its currency.

Easy
Fact
Page: 450

Answer: (d)

21.3: In the early part of the twentieth century, nearly all currencies

(a) were held together by a system of fixed exchange rates in which the value of those currencies was set in relation to the British pound.
(b) were backed by gold.
(c) were held together by a system of fixed exchange rates in which the value of those currencies was set in relation to the U.S. dollar.
(d) were held together by a system of flexible exchange rates in which the value of those currencies fluctuated in response to the relative supply of and demand for them.

Easy
Fact
Page:450

Answer: (b)

21.4: In 1971, most countries, including the United States,

(a) returned to the gold standard.
(b) adopted a new system of fixed exchange rates.
(c) gave up trying to fix exchange rates formally and began allowing them to be determined essentially by supply and demand.
(d) adopted a single, internationally-accepted currency whose use is limited to international transactions.

Easy
Fact
Page: 450

Answer: (c)

Easy
Single
Page: 450

21.5: Under a system of floating exchange rates, if the quantity of dollars demanded exceeds the quantity of dollars supplied,

(a) the price of a dollar will increase.
(b) the price of a dollar will decrease.
(c) the price of a dollar will not change.
(d) the government will always increase the supply of money to eliminate this excess demand.

Answer: (a)

Easy
Single
Page: 450

21.6: Under a system of floating exchange rates, if the quantity of dollars demanded is less than the quantity of dollars supplied,

(a) the price of a dollar will increase.
(b) the price of a dollar will decrease.
(c) the price of a dollar will not change.
(d) the government will always decrease the supply of money to eliminate the excess supply.

Answer: (b)

Easy
Definition
Page: 451

21.7: All currencies other than the domestic currency of a given country are referred to as

(a) hard currency.
(b) foreign exchange.
(c) reserve currencies.
(d) near monies.

Answer: (b)

Easy
Definition
Page: 451

21.8: The record of a country's transactions in goods, services, and assets with the rest of the world is its

(a) current account.
(b) balance of trade.
(c) capital account.
(d) balance of payments.

Answer: (d)

Easy
Definition
Page: 451

21.9: Any transaction that brings in foreign exchange for a country is a

(a) credit item in that country's balance of trade.
(b) debit item in that country's balance of payments.
(c) credit item in that country's balance of payments.
(d) debit item in that country's balance of trade.

Answer: (c)

Easy
Definition
Page: 451

21.10: Any transaction that causes a country to lose foreign exchange is a

(a) debit item in that country's balance of payments.
(b) credit item in that country's balance of payments.
(c) debit item in that country's balance of trade.
(d) credit item in that country's balance of trade.

Answer: (a)

21.11: Which of the following would be a credit item in the U.S. balance of payments?

(a) a U.S. citizen travels to England for a two-week vacation
(b) a U.S. firm hires a non-U.S. citizen
(c) a U.S. company sells computer software to a company in Spain
(d) the U.S. government lends Russia money

Moderate
Single
Page: 451

Answer: (c)

21.12: The difference between a country's merchandise exports and its merchandise imports is the

(a) balance of payments.
(b) balance of trade.
(c) current account.
(d) capital account.

Easy
Fact
Page: 451

Answer: (b)

21.13: When a country's exports of goods are less than its imports of goods in a given period, it has a

(a) trade deficit.
(b) a positive trade balance.
(c) a trade surplus.
(d) a zero balance of trade.

Easy
Definition
Page: 452

Answer: (a)

21.14: The balance of payments is divided into two major accounts, the

(a) current account and the trade account.
(b) trade account and the capital account.
(c) current account and the reserve account.
(d) current account and the capital account.

Easy
Fact
Page: 451

Answer: (d)

21.15: Which of the following is an item in the U.S. current account?

(a) The change in private U.S. assets abroad.
(b) The change in foreign private assets in the United States.
(c) Net investment income.
(d) The change in foreign government assets in the United States.

Easy
Single
Page: 451

Answer: (c)

21.16: A German citizen buys a U.S. bond. This transaction will be entered as

(a) a credit in the U.S. current account.
(b) a debit in the U.S. current account.
(c) a credit in the U.S. capital account.
(d) a debit in the U.S. capital account.

Moderate
Single
Page: 453

Answer: (c)

21.17: A U.S. firm builds a factory in Brazil. This transaction will be entered as

(a) a credit in the U.S. current account.
(b) a debit in the U.S. current account.
(c) a credit in the U.S. capital account.
(d) a debit in the U.S. capital account.

Moderate
Single
Page: 453

Answer: (d)

Moderate
Single
Page: 453

21.18: A U.S. citizen buys stock in a Japanese company. This will be entered as a

(a) credit in the U.S. current account.
(b) debit in the U.S. current account.
(c) credit in the U.S. capital account.
(d) debit in the U.S. capital account.

Answer: (d)

Easy
Fact
Page: 452

21.19: Which of the following is an item in the U.S. capital account?

(a) The change in private U.S. assets abroad.
(b) Net export of services.
(c) Net investment income.
(d) Net transfer payments.

Answer: (a)

Easy
Fact
Page: 454

21.20: Which of the following statements is correct?

(a) The overall sum of all the entries in the balance of payments must be zero.
(b) If the current account is in deficit, then the capital account must also be in deficit.
(c) If the current account is in surplus, then the capital account must also be in surplus.
(d) The overall sum of all the entries in the balance of payments must be positive.

Answer: (a)

Easy
Fact
Page: 454

21.21: Which of the following statements is TRUE?

(a) A country runs a capital account deficit if it imports more than it exports.
(b) A country runs a current account surplus if it sells more of its assets abroad than it buys abroad.
(c) The overall sum of all the entries in the balance of payments must be positive.
(d) If the current account is in surplus, the capital account must be in deficit.

Answer: (d)

Easy
Definition
Page: 454

21.22: The difference between the balance on current account and the balance on capital account is the

(a) balance of payments.
(b) statistical discrepancy.
(c) balance of trade.
(d) trade deficit.

Answer: (b)

Easy
Fact
Page: 454

21.23: When foreign assets in the United States increase,

(a) the United States is reducing its debt to the rest of the world.
(b) the United States is increasing its stock of assets.
(c) the United States is increasing its debt to the rest of the world.
(d) foreign debts to the United States also increase.

Answer: (c)

21.24: When foreign assets in the United States decrease,

(a) the United States is reducing its debt to the rest of the world.
(b) the United States is increasing its debt to the rest of the world.
(c) foreign debts to the United States also decrease.
(d) the United States is reducing its stock of assets.

Easy
Fact
Page: 454

Answer: (a)

21.25: When the United States acquires assets abroad, it is in essence

(a) borrowing money, and foreign debts to the United States decrease.
(b) borrowing money, and foreign debts to the United States increase.
(c) lending money, and foreign debts to the United States decrease.
(d) lending money, and foreign debts to the United States increase.

Easy
Fact
Page: 454

Answer: (d)

21.26: Until the mid-1980s the United States consistently ran

(a) current account deficits and capital account surpluses.
(b) current account surpluses and capital account deficits.
(c) deficits in both the current account and the capital account.
(d) surpluses in both the current account and the capital account.

Easy
Fact
Page: 454

Answer: (b)

21.27: When income rises, imports tend to

(a) stay the same.
(b) fall.
(c) rise.
(d) behave in an unpredictable manner.

Easy
Fact
Page: 455

Answer: (c)

21.28: Planned aggregate expenditure in an open economy equals:

(a) C + I + G + IM.
(b) C + I + G + EX.
(c) C + I + G + EX - IM.
(d) C + I + G + IM - EX.

Easy
Fact
Page: 455

Answer: (c)

21.29: The change in imports caused by a $1 change in income is the marginal propensity

(a) to consume.
(b) to save.
(c) to spend.
(d) to import.

Easy
Definition
Page: 456

Answer: (d)

21.30: If the MPM is .1, then a $2,000 increase in income will

(a) increase imports by $20.
(b) increase imports by $200.
(c) increase exports by $20.
(d) increase exports by $200.

Moderate
Single
Page: 456

Answer: (b)

Moderate
Single
Page: 456

21.31: Income increased by $1,000 and imports increased by $250. The MPM

(a) is .25.
(b) is .75.
(c) is 4.
(d) cannot be determined from this information.

Answer: (a)

Moderate
Single
Page: 456

21.32: If the marginal propensity to import is .10 and income increases by $1,000, then spending on imports will

(a) increase by $100.
(b) decrease by $100.
(c) increase by $90.
(d) decrease by $90.

Answer: (a)

Easy
Fact
Page: 455

21.33: Algebraically, the relationship between imports and income can be written as

(a) IM = Y/m.
(b) Y = mIM.
(c) IM = mY.
(d) IM = m/Y.

Answer: (c)

Easy
Fact
Page: 456

21.34: The level of U.S. exports depends directly on

(a) the level of income in the United States.
(b) the level of income in other countries.
(c) the size of the spending multiplier in the United States.
(d) the size of the spending multiplier in other countries.

Answer: (b)

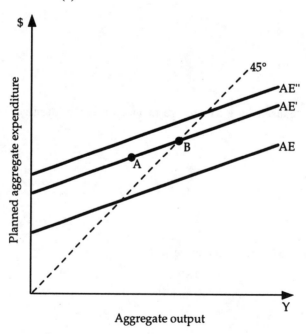

Figure 22.1

21.35: Refer to Figure 21.1. Everything else constant, an increase in imports will cause

(a) a movement from point A to point B along aggregate expenditure line AE.
(b) a movement from point B to point A along aggregate expenditure line AE.
(c) a shift from AE' to AE.
(d) a shift from AE' to AE".

Answer: (c)

Moderate
Single
Page: 456

21.36: Refer to Figure 21.1. Everything else constant, an increase in exports will cause

(a) a movement from point A to point B along aggregate expenditure line AE.
(b) a movement from point B to point A along aggregate expenditure line AE.
(c) a shift from AE' to AE.
(d) a shift from AE' to AE".

Answer: (d)

Moderate
Single
Page: 456

21.37: If the MPC is .8 and the MPM is .1, the open economy multiplier is

(a) 1.11.
(b) 1.25.
(c) 3.33.
(d) 10.

Answer: (c)

Moderate
Single
Page: 457

21.38: If the MPC is .6 and the MPM is .2, the open economy multiplier is

(a) 1.25.
(b) 1.67.
(c) 2.5.
(d) 4.

Answer: (b)

Moderate
Single
Page: 457

21.39: If the MPC is .8 and the MPM is .15, the marginal propensity to consume domestic goods is

(a) .2.
(b) .65.
(c) .85.
(d) .95.

Answer: (b)

Moderate
Single
Page: 457

21.40: The open economy multiplier will increase if

(a) the MPC decreases.
(b) the MPM decreases.
(c) either the MPM or the MPC decreases.
(d) the MPM increases.

Answer: (b)

Moderate
Single
Page: 457

Challenging
Multi
Page: 457

21.41: If an economy's MPC is .8 and the MPM is .2, then an increase in government spending of $1,000 will increase income by

(a) $1,250.
(b) $1,667.
(c) $2,000.
(d) $2,500.

Answer: (d)

Challenging
Multi
Page: 457

21.42: If an economy's MPC is .7 and the MPM is .2, then an increase in government spending of $2,000 will increase income by

(a) $2,222.
(b) $4,000.
(c) $6,667.
(d) $20,000.

Answer: (b)

Easy
Definition
Page: 457

21.43: The open economy multiplier is:

(a) 1/[1 - MPC - MPM].
(b) 1/[1 - (MPC - MPM)].
(c) 1/[1 - (MPM - MPC)].
(d) MPM/[1 - (MPC - MPM)].

Answer: (b)

Easy
Fact
Page: 457

21.44: The marginal propensity to consume domestic goods is the

(a) MPC - MPS.
(b) MPC + MPM.
(c) MPC - MPM.
(d) MPC + MPS.

Answer: (c)

Easy
Fact
Page: 457

21.45: The effect of a sustained increase in government spending (or investment) on income

(a) is larger in an open economy than in a closed economy.
(b) is the same regardless of whether the economy is open or closed.
(c) is smaller in an open economy than in a closed economy.
(d) could be larger or smaller in an open economy than in a closed economy.

Answer: (c)

Moderate
Single
Page: 457

21.46: When government spending or investment increases in an open economy,

(a) some of the extra consumption spending that results is on foreign products and not on domestically produced goods and services.
(b) all of the extra consumption spending that results is on foreign products; none of it is on domestically produced goods and services.
(c) none of the extra consumption spending that results is on foreign products; all of it is on domestically produced goods and services.
(d) consumption rises, but income does not.

Answer: (a)

21.47: Which of the following statements is true?

(a) The smaller a nation's marginal propensity to import, the smaller the open-economy multiplier.
(b) The larger a nation's marginal propensity to consume, the smaller the open-economy multiplier.
(c) The larger a nation's marginal propensity to export, the smaller the open-economy multiplier.
(d) The larger a nation's marginal propensity to import, the smaller the open-economy multiplier.

Moderate
Single
Page: 457

Answer: (d)

21.48: Which of the following is/are likely to affect the demand for imports?

(a) The relative prices of domestically produced and foreign-produced goods.
(b) The after-tax real wage.
(c) Interest rates.
(d) All of the above.

Easy
Fact
Page: 458

Answer: (d)

21.49: Which of the following will lead most directly to an increase in U.S. exports?

(a) an increase in U.S. government spending that increases aggregate demand.
(b) an increase in the income level of the countries with which the United States trades.
(c) U.S. prices increase relative to prices in the rest of the world.
(d) foreign governments implement contractionary monetary policies.

Moderate
Single
Page: 458

Answer: (b)

21.50: The tendency for an increase in the economic activity of one country to lead to a worldwide increase in economic activity is the

(a) trade feedback effect.
(b) trickle-down effect.
(c) multiplier effect.
(d) spontaneous growth effect.

Easy
Definition
Page: 458

Answer: (a)

21.51: An increased growth rate in China has increased the Chinese demand for U.S.-made steel. China increases its imports of U.S.-made steel by $2 million. U.S. net exports will

(a) increase by $2 million.
(b) increase by more than $2 million.
(c) increase by less than $2 million.
(d) increase by $2 million or more.

Moderate
Single
Page: 459

Answer: (c)

21.52: Assume that a $1.00 increase in exports increases GDP by $2.00, and a $1.00 increase in income increases import spending by $0.15. In this case, a $500 million increase in exports will increase net exports by

(a) $150 million.
(b) $350 million.
(c) $500 million.
(d) $650 million.

Challenging
Multi
Page: 459

Answer: (b)

Easy
Fact
Page: 459

21.53: The trade feedback effect illustrates the fact that

(a) an increase in U.S. economic activity leads to a decrease in the economic activity of other countries.
(b) imports affect exports and exports affect imports.
(c) imports and exports are unrelated to one another.
(d) U.S. imports depress the imports of other countries.

Answer: (b)

Easy
Single
Page: 459

21.54: Economic activity decreases in Western Europe, and this causes economic activity to decrease in the United States. This is an example of

(a) the price feedback effect.
(b) the import feedback effect.
(c) the export feedback effect.
(d) the trade feedback effect.

Answer: (d)

Moderate
Fact
Page: 459

21.55: The trade feedback effect includes all of the following steps except:

(a) an increase in U.S. economic activity stimulates U.S. imports.
(b) an increase in foreign imports stimulates U.S. exports.
(c) an increase in U.S. exports stimulates U.S. economic activity.
(d) an increase in foreign income stimulates U.S. imports.

Answer: (d)

Easy
Single
Page: 459

21.56: If exchange rates are fixed, then a decrease in Canada's export prices causes

(a) U.S. import prices to fall.
(b) U.S. import prices to rise.
(c) Canadian import prices to fall.
(d) Canadian import prices to rise.

Answer: (a)

Moderate
Single
Page: 459

21.57: The inflation rate in the United States is low relative to the inflation rates in other countries. This causes

(a) U.S. import prices to fall.
(b) U.S. imports to increase.
(c) U.S. export prices to fall.
(d) U.S. export prices to rise.

Answer: (c)

Easy
Single
Page: 459

21.58: If the inflation rate abroad is low,

(a) U.S. exports will increase
(b) U.S. import prices are likely to fall.
(c) U.S. import prices are likely to rise.
(d) U.S. export prices are likely to fall.

Answer: (b)

21.59: A country's export prices tend to move fairly closely with the

(a) general price level in that country.
(b) general price level in the countries with which it trades.
(c) worldwide price of gold.
(d) average worldwide inflation rate.

Answer: (a)

Easy
Fact
Page: 459

21.60: U.S. exports tend to decrease when

(a) economic activity abroad is decreasing.
(b) foreign GDPs are rising at a slow rate.
(c) U.S. prices are low relative to those in the rest of the world.
(d) the inflation rate in the United States is lower than the inflation rates in other countries.

Answer: (a)

Moderate
Single
Page: 459

21.61: When the prices of a country's imports increase, the prices of domestic goods may increase. This occurs because

(a) an increase in the prices of imported inputs will cause aggregate supply to increase.
(b) an increase in the prices of imported inputs will cause aggregate demand to decrease.
(c) if import prices rise relative to domestic prices, households will tend to substitute imports for domestically produced goods and services.
(d) if import prices rise relative to domestic prices, households will tend to substitute domestically produced goods and services for imports.

Answer: (d)

Moderate
Fact
Page: 459

21.62: Suppose that an increase in the price level of one country drives up prices in other countries. This, in turn, increases the price level in the first country. This process is the

(a) price feedback effect.
(b) trade feedback effect.
(c) J-curve effect.
(d) balance of trade effect.

Answer: (a)

Easy
Definition
Page: 460

21.63: The price feedback effect includes all of the following except

(a) leftward shifts of the aggregate supply curve and rightward shifts of the aggregate demand curve causing an increase in the overall domestic price level.
(b) an increase in the price of imported inputs shifting a country's aggregate supply curve to the left.
(c) when households increase their demand for domestically produced goods, exporting firms must lower their prices to sell their goods.
(d) if import prices rise relative to domestic prices, households will tend to substitute domestically produced goods for imports.

Answer: (c)

Easy
Fact
Page: 460

21.64: Exchange rates that are determined by the unregulated forces of supply and demand are

(a) fixed exchange rates.
(b) floating exchange rates.
(c) managed exchange rates.
(d) pegged exchange rates.

Answer: (b)

Easy
Definition
Page: 460

Easy
Fact
Page: 461

21.65: The most common reason for exchanging one currency for another is

(a) to purchase stocks and bonds in another country.
(b) to engage in fixed capital investment in another country.
(c) to purchase goods produced in another country.
(d) to engage in currency speculation.

Answer: (c)

Easy
Single
Page: 461

21.66: Which of the following will NOT generate a demand for dollars?

(a) British citizens want to import U.S. goods and services.
(b) British citizens travel in the United States.
(c) U.S. firms want to invest in England.
(d) British citizens buy U.S. bonds.

Answer: (c)

Moderate
Fact
Page: 462

21.67: The demand for dollars in the foreign exchange market is downward sloping because when the price of a dollar (the exchange rate)
falls,

(a) Americans demand more foreign goods because these goods have become less expensive.
(b) Americans demand fewer foreign goods because these goods have become more expensive.
(c) foreigners demand more U.S. products because these products have become less expensive.
(d) foreigners demand fewer U.S. goods because these goods have become more expensive.

Answer: (c)

Moderate
Single
Page: 463

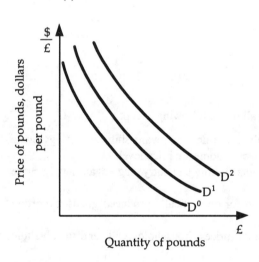

Figure 22.2

21.68: Refer to Figure 21.2. Which of the following will shift the demand for pounds from D_1 to D_0?

(a) Income in the United States decreases.
(b) The inflation rate increases in the United States relative to the inflation rate in England.
(c) U.S. companies decide to increase their investment in England.
(d) More U.S. citizens decide to travel to England.

Answer: (a)

Moderate
Single
Page: 463

21.69: Refer to Figure 21.2. Which of the following will shift the demand for pounds from D_1 to D_2?

(a) Income in the United States decreases.
(b) The inflation rate in England falls relative to the inflation rate in the United States.
(c) More British citizens travel to the United States.
(d) More British companies decide to invest in the United States.

Answer: (b)

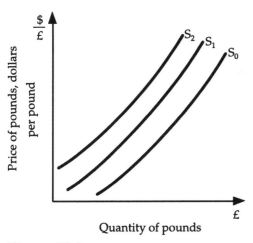

Figure 22.3

21.70: Refer to Figure 21.3. Which of the following will shift the supply of pounds from S_1 to S_0?

Moderate
Single
Page: 463

(a) Fewer British firms want to invest in the United States.
(b) The price of U.S. bonds increases relative to the price of British bonds.
(c) More British citizens travel to the United States.
(d) The inflation rate in the United States increases relative to the inflation rate in England.

Answer: (c)

21.71: Refer to Figure 21.3. Which of the following will shift the supply of pounds from S_1 to S_2?

Moderate
Single
Page: 463

(a) Fewer British firms want to invest in the United States.
(b) The price of U.S. bonds decreases relative to the price of British bonds.
(c) More British citizens travel to the United States.
(d) The inflation rate in the United States decreases relative to the inflation rate in England.

Answer: (a)

21.72: If the inflation rate falls in the United States relative to the inflation rate in England, this will cause

Challenging
Multi
Page: 465

(a) an increase in the demand for pounds and an increase in the supply of pounds.
(b) a decrease in the demand for pounds and an increase in the supply of pounds.
(c) an increase in the demand for pounds and a decrease in the supply of pounds.
(d) a decrease in the demand for pounds and a decrease in the supply of pounds.

Answer: (b)

21.73: Income increase in the United States. This will cause

Moderate
Single
Page: 465

(a) an increase in the supply of pounds.
(b) a decrease in the supply of pounds.
(c) an increase in the demand for pounds.
(d) a decrease in the demand for pounds.

Answer: (c)

21.74: The supply of dollars in the foreign exchange market is likely to be upward sloping because as the price of a dollar (the exchange rate) falls,

Challenging
Fact
Page: 462

(a) Americans demand more foreign goods because these goods have become less expensive to American consumers.
(b) Americans demand fewer foreign goods because these goods have become more expensive to American consumers.
(c) foreigners demand more American goods because these goods have become less expensive to foreign consumers.
(d) foreigners demand more foreign goods because these goods have become more expensive to foreign consumers.

Answer: (b)

Moderate
Single
Page: 462

21.75: If more U.S. citizens travel to France this year, then the demand for

(a) dollars will increase and the supply of dollars will decrease.
(b) francs will increase and the supply of dollars will increase.
(c) dollars will increase and the supply of francs will increase.
(d) francs will increase and the supply of francs will increase.

Answer: (b)

Moderate
Single
Page: 462

21.76: More Japanese companies start to invest in the United States. This will lead to

(a) a decrease in the demand for dollars and an increase in the demand for yen.
(b) an increase in the supply of dollars and a decrease in the demand for yen.
(c) an increase in the demand for dollars and an increase in the supply of yen.
(d) an increase in the demand for dollars and a decrease in the supply of yen.

Answer: (c)

Easy
Definition
Page: 463

21.77: The fall in value of one currency relative to another is

(a) a depreciation of a currency.
(b) an appreciation of a currency.
(c) a strengthening of a currency.
(d) a floating of the currency.

Answer: (a)

Easy
Definition
Page: 463

21.78: The rise in value of one currency relative to another is

(a) a depreciation of the currency.
(b) a weakening of the currency.
(c) a debasement of the currency.
(d) an appreciation of the currency.

Answer: (d)

Easy
Single
Page: 463

21.79: Under a system of floating exchange rates, an excess demand for a particular currency will lead to

(a) a depreciation of that currency.
(b) a long-term shortage of that currency.
(c) an appreciation of that currency.
(d) a long-term surplus of that currency.

Answer: (c)

Easy
Single
Page: 463

21.80: Under a system of floating exchange rates, an excess supply of a currency will lead to

(a) a depreciation of that currency.
(b) an appreciation of that currency.
(c) a long-term surplus of that currency.
(d) a long-term shortage of that currency.

Answer: (a)

21.81: The _____ states that if the costs of transportation are small, the price of the same good in different countries should be roughly the same.

(a) price feedback effect
(b) trade feedback effect
(c) balance of trade effect
(d) law of one price

Answer: (d)

Easy
Definition
Page: 464

21.82: The theory of international exchange that holds that exchange rates are set so that the price of similar goods in different countries is the same is the

(a) price feedback theory.
(b) purchasing-power-parity theory.
(c) trade feedback theory.
(d) J-curve theory.

Answer: (b)

Easy
Definition
Page: 464

21.83: Suppose that the price of a television set is $100 in the United States and 800 yen in Japan. If the current exchange rate is 10 yen to the dollar, then purchasing-power-parity theory would predict that in the long run

(a) China will begin to import television sets from the United States.
(b) the exchange value of the yen will depreciate.
(c) the exchange value of the yen will appreciate.
(d) the exchange value of the dollar will appreciate.

Answer: (c)

Challenging
Multi
Page: 464

21.84: Under a system of floating exchange rates, there is a general tendency for

(a) the currencies of relatively high-inflation countries to depreciate.
(b) the currencies of relatively high-inflation countries to appreciate.
(c) the currencies of relatively low-inflation countries to depreciate.
(d) exchange rates to be insensitive to the differential rates of inflation between countries.

Answer: (a)

Easy
Fact
Page: 465

21.85: If a nation's interest rates are relatively low compared to those of other countries, then the exchange value of its currency will tend to

(a) depreciate under a system of floating exchange rates.
(b) depreciate under a system of fixed exchange rates.
(c) appreciate under a system of fixed exchange rates.
(d) appreciate under a system of floating exchange rates.

Answer: (a)

Moderate
Single
Page: 465

Moderate
Multi
Page: 465

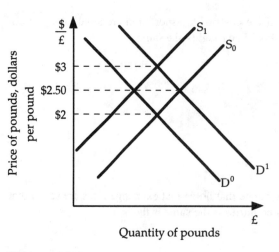

Figure 22.4

21.86: Refer to Figure 21.4. The exchange rate is currently $2 per pound. An increase in the price level in the United States relative to the price level in England will

(a) not affect the exchange rate.
(b) increase the exchange rate to $2.50.
(c) increase the exchange rate to $3.00.
(d) reduce the exchange rate below $2.00.

Answer: (c)

Moderate
Single
Page: 465

21.87: Refer to Figure 21.4. The exchange rate is currently $2 per pound. Assume that the demand for the pound increases to D_1 and the exchange rate remains constant. This means that

(a) there will be an excess demand for pounds and the pound is undervalued.
(b) there will be an excess demand for pounds and the pound is overvalued.
(c) there will be an excess supply of pounds and the pound is undervalued.
(d) there will be an excess supply of pounds and the pound is overvalued.

Answer: (a)

Moderate
Multi
Page: 465

21.88: Refer to Figure 21.4. If the demand for pounds increases from D_0 to D_1, and supply remains unchanged at S_0, then

(a) both the dollar and the pound will appreciate.
(b) both the dollar and the pound will depreciate.
(c) the dollar will appreciate and the pound will depreciate.
(d) the dollar will depreciate and the pound will appreciate.

Answer: (d)

Moderate
Multi
Page: 465

21.89: Refer to Figure 21.4. If the supply of pounds increases from S_1 to S_0, and demand remains unchanged at D_0, then

(a) both the dollar and the pound will appreciate.
(b) both the dollar and the pound will depreciate.
(c) the dollar will appreciate and the pound will depreciate.
(d) the dollar will depreciate and the pound will appreciate.

Answer: (c)

Moderate
Single
Page: 467

21.90: An increase in U.S. interest rates relative to other countries' interest rates will

(a) decrease the supply of dollars and leave the demand for dollars unaffected.
(b) decrease the demand for dollars and leave the supply of dollars unaffected.
(c) decrease the supply of dollars and increase the demand for dollars.
(d) increase the supply of dollars and decrease the demand for dollars.

Answer: (c)

21.91: A depreciation of a country's currency is likely to

(a) decrease its GDP.
(b) increase its GDP.
(c) leave GDP unaffected because it will cause an equal change in imports and exports.
(d) increase consumption, but decrease investment so that GDP remains unchanged.

Answer: (b)

Easy
Fact
Page: 468

21.92: The J-curve effect refers to the observation that

(a) GDP usually decreases before it increases after a currency depreciation.
(b) GDP usually decreases before it increases after a currency appreciation.
(c) the trade balance usually gets worse before it improves after a currency appreciation.
(d) the trade balance usually gets worse before it improves after a currency depreciation.

Answer: (d)

Easy
Fact
Page: 468

21.93: The J-curve effect suggests that the depreciation of a nation's currency may

(a) increase its exports and decrease its imports.
(b) increase its imports and decrease its exports.
(c) have an ambiguous effect on its balance of trade.
(d) lead to economic ruin.

Answer: (c)

Easy
Fact
Page: 470

21.94: Why does the depreciation of a country's currency tend to increase its price level?

(a) A currency depreciation makes imported inputs more expensive.
(b) A currency depreciation makes a country's products less competitive in world markets, so exports fall.
(c) Domestic buyers tend to substitute imports for domestic products.
(d) A currency depreciation makes imported inputs less expensive.

Answer: (a)

Moderate
Single
Page: 470

21.95: A currency depreciation is more likely to improve a country's balance of trade if the demand for that country's exports is _____ and the demand for that country's imports is_____.

(a) elastic; inelastic
(b) inelastic; elastic
(c) elastic; elastic
(d) inelastic; inelastic

Answer: (c)

Moderate
Single
Page: 470

21.96: The openness of the economy and flexible exchange rates

(a) increase the effectiveness of both expansionary and contractionary monetary policies.
(b) reduce the effectiveness of both expansionary and contractionary monetary policies.
(c) increase the effectiveness of a contractionary monetary policy, but reduce the effectiveness of an expansionary monetary policy.
(d) increase the effectiveness of an expansionary monetary policy, but reduce the effectiveness of a contractionary monetary policy.

Answer: (a)

Moderate
Single
Page: 471

Moderate
Single
Page: 471

21.97: The openness of the economy and flexible exchange rates

(a) increase the effectiveness of both expansionary and contractionary fiscal policy.
(b) reduce the effectiveness of both expansionary and contractionary fiscal policy.
(c) increase the effectiveness of contractionary fiscal policy, but reduce the effectiveness of expansionary fiscal policy.
(d) increase the effectiveness of expansionary fiscal policy, but reduce the effectiveness of contractionary fiscal policy.

Answer: (b)

Moderate
Fact
Page: 471

21.98: If the Fed reduces the money supply to reduce inflation, a floating exchange rate will aid the Fed in fighting inflation because

(a) as the money supply is decreased, the interest rate will increase, and the price of U.S. exports will fall and the price of U.S. imports will rise.
(b) as the money supply is decreased, the interest rate will increase, and the price of U.S. exports will rise and the price of U.S. imports will fall.
(c) as the money supply is decreased, the interest rate will increase, and the price of both U.S. exports and U.S. imports will rise.
(d) as the money supply is decreased, the interest rate will increase, and the price of U.S. exports and U.S. imports will fall.

Answer: (b)

Moderate
Single
Page: 471

21.99: Expansionary monetary policy

(a) tends to lead to an appreciation of a nation's currency.
(b) usually has no effect on a currency's exchange value.
(c) tends to lead to a depreciation of the currencies of other nations.
(d) tends to lead to a depreciation of a nation's currency.

Answer: (d)

Moderate
Fact
Page: 471

21.100: A fiscal expansion in the United States

(a) tends to depreciate the dollar.
(b) tends to appreciate the dollar.
(c) does not affect the price of the dollar.
(d) has no predictable effect on the price of the dollar.

Answer: (b)

TRUE/FALSE QUESTIONS

Easy
Definition
Page: 450

21.101: The current international monetary system is based on a gold standard.

Answer: False

Difficult
Application
Page: 457

21.102: An open-economy multiplier will be larger, the larger a nation's marginal propensity to import is.

Answer: False

Easy
Application
Page: 459

21.103: It could be argued that the Great Depression in the United States and the worldwide depression of the 1930s can, at least in part, be explained by the trade feedback effect. Explain.

Answer: True

21.104: The 1993 price level in Germany was relatively lower than the price level in the United States. Thus, a U.S. manufacturing facility looking to buy steel for its plant would most likely buy steel at home in the United States.

Answer: False

Moderate
Application
Page: 459

21.105: An increase in the interest rate in France, relative to the interest rates in other countries, will decrease the supply of Francs and decrease the demand for Francs.

Answer: False

Difficult
Application
Page: 466

21.106: The record of a country's transactions in goods, services, and assets with the rest of the world is its balance of trade.

Answer: False

Easy
Fact
Page: 451

21.107: The overall sum of all the entries in the balance of payments must be zero.

Answer: True

Easy
Fact
Page: 453

21.108: If the current account is in deficit, there must also be a deficit in the capital account.

Answer: False

Easy
Fact
Page: 454

21.109: When the United States acquires assets abroad, it is in essence borrowing money, and foreign debts to the United States decrease.

Answer: False

Easy
Fact
Page: 454

21.110: The effect of a sustained increase in government spending or investment on aggregate output is larger in an open economy than in a closed economy.

Answer: False

Easy
Fact
Page: 457

21.111: Export prices of other countries affect U.S. import prices.

Answer: True

Easy
Fact
Page: 459

21.112: An excess supply of pounds will cause an appreciation of the pound.

Answer: False

Easy
Fact
Page: 463

21.113: The law of one price states that if the costs of transportation are small, then the price of the same good in different countries should be roughly the same.

Answer: True

Easy
Definition
Page: 464

21.114: Purchasing-power-parity theory holds that exchange rates are set so that the price of similar goods in different countries reflects the relative interest rates in those countries.

Answer: False

Easy
Fact
Page: 464

21.115: Floating exchange rates improve the effectiveness of a contractionary monetary policy.

Answer: True

Easy
Fact
Page: 470

SHORT ANSWER QUESTIONS

Moderate
Definition
Page: 451

21.116: Define a nation's balance of payments. Explain the major accounts of a country's balance of payments and explain their relationship.

Answer: A nation's balance of payments is the record of a country's transactions in goods, services, and assets with the rest of the world; it is also the record of a country's sources and uses of foreign exchange. Simply, in the balance of payments any transaction that brings in foreign exchange is a credit and any transaction where a nation loses foreign exchange is a debit. The two major accounts in the balance of payments are the current account and the capital account. The current account is subdivided into merchandise imports and exports, exports and imports of services, and income received and paid on investments. The capital account is subdivided into change in private U.S. assets abroad, change in foreign private assets, change in U.S. government assets abroad, and change in foreign government assets in the United States.

Moderate
Application
Page: 451

21.117: In the following series of questions explain how the situations affect the United States' balance of payments.

A. A U.S. defense contractor sells its consulting services to a company in France for two
B. Your investment club decides to buy 100 shares of a promising Korean automobile manufacturer.

C. A consortium of European investors decides to build a large manufacturing facility in Montana.

Answer: A. This would bring foreign exchange into the country, thus there would be a credit on the balance of payments. This would be a credit on the U.S. current account.

B. This is a debit on the U.S. capital account. Here, U.S. dollars are leaving the country to buy a foreign stock-this would be a debit to the overall balance of payments.

C. This transaction will be a credit on the U.S. current account, as this will bring in new investment (foreign exchange) from overseas investors.

Easy
Math
Page: 455

21.118: If in 1993 the MPM = .15 and there was a $5000 increase in income, would import spending change? By how much?

Answer: $5000 * .15 = $750. Yes, import spending increases by $750.

Difficult
Math
Page: 456

21.119: Answer the questions below using the following information about the economy of Tumania. Hint: don't forget about taxes!

C = 100 + .8(Yd)
I = 100
G = 75
T = 60
EX = 50
IM = 40 + .15(Yd)

A. Determine the equilibrium level of GDP.

B. What is the government budget deficit?

C. At this level of equilibrium is there a trade deficit or surplus? What is the amount of deficit or surplus?

D. What is the open-economy multiplier in this economy?

E. If government spending increases by 15, what happens to equilibrium GDP? Does the balance of trade situation change when government spending increases?

F. The country of Tumania experiences a 5% appreciation of its currency. Assume that for every 1% increase in its currency's value, imports increase by 6 units and exports fall by 3 units. How does this currency appreciation affect GDP?

Answer: A. Equilibrium GDP = $702.86.

B. The government budget deficit is $15.

C. There is a trade deficit of $86.43.

D. The open-economy multiplier is 2.86.

E. Equilibrium GDP changes by $42.9 if government spending changes by 15. The trade deficit will increase by $6.44.

F. 5% * 6 = a 30 unit increase in imports. 5% * 3 = a 15 unit decrease in exports. Equilibrium GDP changes from $702.86 to $574.29, a change of $128.57 due to the appreciation of its currency.

21.120: Define the price feedback effect. Graphically illustrate how the price feedback effect causes the domestic aggregate supply and demand curves to shift.

Easy
Definition
Page: 460

Answer: The price feedback effect is the process by which a domestic price increase in one country can "feed back" on itself through export and import prices. An increase in the price level in one country can drive up prices in other countries, which then increases the price level in the first country.

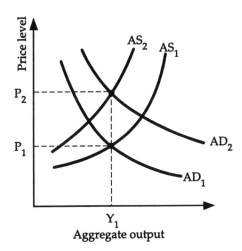

When the price feedback effect occurs, there is an increase in the price of imported inputs which causes AS to shift to the left, and if import prices increase relative to domestic prices, households will substitute domestically-produced goods for imports. With a leftward shift of AS and a rightward shift of AD, there is an increase in the overall price level.

21.121: According to purchasing-power-parity theory, in the long run what would happen to the exchange rate if the price of a computer in the U.S. = $1000, the price of a computer in Italy = 2,000,000 lira, and the current exchange rate was $1.00 = 1,000 lira?

Difficult
Application
Page: 464

Answer: The purchasing-power-parity theory holds that in the long run the exchange value of the dollar would appreciate so that the price of computers is the same in both countries.

Easy
Fact
Page: 454

21.122: Explain why there must be a surplus in a country's capital account if the country is running a deficit in its current account.

Answer: The overall balance of payments must be zero, so if there is a surplus in the capital account there must be a deficit in the current account.

Easy
Fact
Page: 457

21.123: Explain why the size of the government spending multiplier is smaller in an open economy than in a closed economy.

Answer: The government spending multiplier is smaller in an open economy because part of the increase in income is spent on foreign products and not on domestically produced goods.

Challenging
Multi
Page: 456

21.124: You are given the following information about an economy:C = 200 + .75Yd; I = 50; G = 100, EX = 25; IM = .15Yd; and T = 60.

a. What is the equilibrium level of income? b. At the equilibrium level of income is the economy running a trade deficit or trade surplus? What is the amount of the trade deficit or surplus? c. What is the open-economy multiplier? d. If government spending increases by 100, what will be the change in income? What is the new equilibrium level of income? e. At the new equilibrium level of income, what is the level of imports and exports?

Answer: (a.) The equilibrium level of income is 847.5. (b.) At the equilibrium level of income there is a trade deficit of 93.125. (c.) The open-economy multiplier is 2.5. (d.) An increase in government spending of 100 increases output by $250. The new level of income is 1097.5. (e.) Exports are still 25. Imports are 155.625.

Easy
Fact
Page: 458

21.125: Explain the trade feedback effect.

Answer: As the economic activity of one country rises and its imports increase, other countries will be exporting more. As these countries export more, their income rises and their imports increase. This increases the country's exports, and the feedback process continues.

Moderate
Single
Page: 458

21.126: Why is it in the best interest of the United States when its trading partners' levels of economic activity increase?

Answer: If there is an increase in the economic activity of the United States's trading partners, then according to the trade feedback effect economic activity in the United States will also increase.

Challenging
Multi
Page: 463

21.127: Identify whether each of the following would lead to an appreciation or depreciation of the dollar. In each case, explain why the currency either appreciates or depreciates. (a.) U.S. citizens switch from buying stock in British companies to buying stock in U.S. companies. (b.) The inflation rate in the United States increases relative to the inflation rate in England. (c.) The money supply is increased in the United States. (d.) Income in the United States increases.

Answer: (a.) This causes the supply of dollars to decrease and the value of the dollar to appreciate. (b.) An increase in the inflation rate in the United States relative to England causes the demand for dollars to decrease and the supply of dollars to increase. This leads to a depreciation of the dollar. (c.) An increase in the money supply leads to lower interest rates, which reduces the demand for dollars and increases the supply of dollars. This leads to a depreciation of the dollar. (d.) When income in the United States increases, the supply of dollars increases. This leads to a depreciation of the dollar.

21.128: Explain the law of one price.

Easy
Fact
Page: 464

Answer: According to the law of one price, if the costs of transportation are small, the price of the same good in different countries should be roughly the same. If transportation costs are small and prices were not equal, profit opportunities would persist. It will pay someone to buy the product where it is cheap and sell it where it is expensive. This will continue to happen until the prices are roughly equal.

21.129: Explain the J-curve effect.

Easy
Fact
Page: 468

Answer: According to the J curve, the balance of trade gets worse before it gets better following a currency depreciation. A currency depreciation stimulates exports and cuts back imports, but it also increases the dollar price of imports. Initially the negative effect from the import price increase dominates. Then the positive effect begins to dominate and the increase in exports dominates the increase in the price of imports.

21.130: Explain why the depreciation of a country's currency tends to increase its price level.

Easy
Fact
Page: 470

Answer: A depreciation of a country's currency tends to increase its price level because it increases the price of imported inputs. A currency depreciation stimulates exports, which increases aggregate demand, which also increases the price level.

21.131: Explain the effect of U.S. expansionary monetary policy on the U.S. economy if exchange rates are flexible. How would the effectiveness of an expansionary monetary policy change if exchange rates were fixed?

Moderate
Single
Page: 470

Answer: An expansionary monetary policy reduces the interest rate. The lower interest rate makes U.S. investments less attractive to foreigners and reduces the demand for dollars. This leads to a depreciation in the value of the dollar. The lower value of the dollar stimulates exports and reduces imports. This leads to a further expansion in aggregate demand and the multiplier actually increases. If the exchange rate is fixed, an increase in the money supply could not change the exchange rate and therefore there would be no added stimulus to the economy in the form of an increase in net exports.

22 Economic Growth in Developing Nations

MULTIPLE CHOICE QUESTIONS

22.1: Most developing countries

(a) have meaningful personal income taxes and effective tax policies.
(b) have meaningful personal income taxes, but do not have effective tax policies.
(c) have effective tax policies, but do not have meaningful personal income taxes.
(d) have neither meaningful personal income taxes nor effective tax policies.

Answer: (d)

Moderate
Fact
Page: 520

22.2: The industrialized nations of the West are often referred to as the

(a) First World.
(b) Second World.
(c) Third World.
(d) Fourth World.

Answer: (a)

Easy
Fact
Page: 520

22.3: The formerly socialist nations of Eastern Europe used to be referred to as the

(a) First World.
(b) Second World.
(c) Third World.
(d) Fourth World.

Answer: (b)

Easy
Fact
Page: 520

22.4: The term Fourth World has been coined to describe

(a) the republics of the former Soviet Union.
(b) the newly industrialized countries, like Korea.
(c) countries that have fallen far behind the economic advances of the rest of the world.
(d) countries that still have a communist government, like Cuba.

Answer: (c)

Easy
Definition
Page: 520

22.5: Which of the following is NOT a characteristic that is associated with developed countries?

(a) a high per capita GNP
(b) low infant mortality rates
(c) high life expectancy
(d) an income distribution that is very close to being equal

Answer: (d)

Moderate
Single
Page: 521

Moderate
Single
Page: 521

22.6: Characteristics of economic development include all of the following except

(a) improvements in basic education.
(b) an increase in the standard of living
(c) a decrease in the percentage of the labor force in urban areas.
(d) an increase in life expectancy.

Answer: (c)

Easy
Fact
Page: 521

22.7: Which of the following characteristics is generally representative of developed countries, relative to developing nations?

(a) a higher level of per capita GNP
(b) a shorter life expectancy
(c) a higher rate of infant mortality
(d) a smaller percentage of children enrolled in school

Answer: (a)

Easy
Fact
Page: 521

22.8: Which of the following characteristics is generally representative of developing countries, relative to developed countries?

(a) a smaller percentage of the labor force in urban areas
(b) a lower infant mortality rate
(c) a greater degree of equality in the income distribution
(d) a lower rate of illiteracy

Answer: (a)

Easy
Fact
Page: 521

22.9: Which of the following characteristics is generally representative of developing countries relative to developed countries?

(a) a greater degree of equality in the income distribution
(b) a larger percentage of the labor force in urban areas
(c) a lower infant mortality rate
(d) low productivity in the agricultural sector

Answer: (d)

Moderate
Single
Page: 521

22.10: Which of the following statements is FALSE?

(a) Low productivity in the agricultural sector in developing countries means that farm output per person is barely sufficient to feed a farmer's own family.
(b) Income tends to be more equally distributed in developing countries than in developed countries.
(c) The percentage of the labor force employed in urban areas is greater in developed nations than in developing nations.
(d) Developed nations account for only about one-quarter of the world's population, but they consume about three-quarters of the world's output.

Answer: (b)

Easy
Fact
Page: 522

22.11: In the distribution of world income, the richest one fifth of the world's population earns about _____ of the world income.

(a) 40%
(b) 65%
(c) 79%
(d) 88%

Answer: (c)

22.12: In the distribution of world income, the poorest one fifth of the world's population earns about _____ of the world income.

Easy
Fact
Page: 522

(a) .5%
(b) 2%
(c) 5%
(d) 12%

Answer: (a)

22.13: While the developed nations account for only about one quarter of the world's population, they are estimated to consume what proportion of the world's output?

Easy
Fact
Page: 521

(a) one-quarter
(b) one-half
(c) two-thirds
(d) three-quarters

Answer: (d)

22.14: While the developing nations account for about three-fourths of the world's people, they are estimated to receive what percentage of the world's income?

Easy
Fact
Page: 521

(a) one-fourth
(b) one-third
(c) two-fifths
(d) one-half

Answer: (a)

22.15: Recent studies suggest that _____ of the population of the developing nations have annual incomes insufficient to provide for adequate nutrition.

Easy
Fact
Page: 521

(a) 10%
(b) 25%
(c) 40%
(d) 75%

Answer: (c)

22.16: In recent years the degree of economic development has actually declined in about 36 countries. Which of the following is a possible explanations for why these countries have regressed?

Easy
Fact
Page: 521

(a) Development in these countries has been stopped because of an international environment that is hostile to growth.
(b) These countries have reached their physical limits to growth.
(c) Policies in these countries have led to governments supplanting rather than supporting markets.
(d) all of the above

Answer: (c)

22.17: Which of the following factors has been suggested as an explanation for the lack of economic growth in many poor nations?

Easy
Fact
Page: 522

(a) insufficient capital formation
(b) the supply of human resources is too high
(c) an adequate level of social overhead capital
(d) a lack of dependence on the already developed nations

Answer: (a)

Easy
Single
Page: 522

22.18: The lack of capital in developing nations causes

(a) labor productivity to remain low.
(b) the savings rate to be too high.
(c) output to be low in the present but high in the future.
(d) consumption rates to be too high.

Answer: (a)

Moderate
Single
Page: 522

22.19: An economy is not able to develop because of a lack of capital. Which of the following strategies would you suggest this economy pursue?

(a) Lower interest rates.
(b) Impose quotas on how much capital can be imported from other countries to reduce dependency on foreign capital.
(c) Increase the political stability of the economy.
(d) Nationalize private enterprises because the government sector is not motivated by profit maximization.

Answer: (c)

Moderate
Single
Page: 524

22.20: A developing economy is considering restricting the amount of money its citizens can invest abroad. What might the purpose of this restriction be?

(a) To reduce the dependency of the economy on developed economies.
(b) To increase capital formation by forcing its citizens to invest in their own country.
(c) To reduce the nation's trade deficit so that interest rates will be reduced and capital formation will increase.
(d) To increase the degree of equality in the income distribution.

Answer: (b)

Easy
Definition
Page: 524

22.21: The idea that suggests that poverty is self-perpetuating because poor nations are unable to save and invest enough to accumulate the capital stock that would help them grow is

(a) the dependency theory.
(b) the vicious-circle-of-poverty hypothesis.
(c) neo-colonialism.
(d) the under-consumptionist hypothesis.

Answer: (b)

Easy
Fact
Page: 524

22.22: If the vicious-circle-of-poverty hypothesis were true, then

(a) all economies would develop at the same rate.
(b) no nation could ever achieve economic development.
(c) no nation would ever fail to reach the highest level of economic development.
(d) poverty would not be self-perpetuating.

Answer: (b)

22.23: If the vicious-circle-of-poverty hypothesis is false, then

(a) all economies must develop at the same rate.
(b) the lack of capital in developing nations is the best single explanation why a country is not developing.
(c) even developing nations have some surplus that is available for investment and capital formation.
(d) no nation could ever achieve economic development.

Answer: (c)

Moderate
Single
Page: 524

22.24: Which of the following statements is TRUE?

(a) Poverty alone can explain capital shortages, and poverty is necessarily self-perpetuating.
(b) Poverty alone cannot explain capital shortages, but poverty is necessarily self-perpetuating.
(c) Poverty alone cannot explain capital shortages, nor is poverty necessarily self-perpetuating.
(d) Poverty alone can explain capital shortages, but poverty is not necessarily self-perpetuating.

Answer: (c)

Easy
Fact
Page: 524

22.25: In a developing economy, scarcity of capital may be a result of all of the following factors except

(a) an absolute scarcity of income available for capital accumulation.
(b) a lack of incentives for citizens to save and invest productively.
(c) the inherent riskiness and uncertainty that surround a developing nation's economy and its political system.
(d) the imposition of certain public policies, such as price ceilings and import controls.

Answer: (a)

Challenging
Single
Page: 524

22.26: Which of the following statements is TRUE?

(a) The availability of capital is a necessary and sufficient condition for economic growth.
(b) The availability of capital is neither a necessary nor a sufficient condition for economic growth.
(c) The availability of capital is a sufficient, but not a necessary, condition for economic growth.
(d) The availability of capital is a necessary, but not a sufficient, condition for economic growth.

Answer: (d)

Moderate
Fact
Page: 524

22.27: Which of the following is NOT an example of human capital investment in a developing country?

(a) programs to improve nutrition and health
(b) the migration of educated persons to the developed world
(c) on-the-job training
(d) development of basic literacy skills

Answer: (b)

Moderate
Single
Page: 524

Easy
Definition
Page: 525

22.28: The tendency for talented people from developing countries to become educated in a developed country and remain there after graduation has become known as the

(a) free-rider problem.
(b) neo-colonialist effect.
(c) brain drain.
(d) dependency effect.

Answer: (c)

Moderate
Single
Page: 525

22.-29: Which of the following would be an example of the phenomena referred to as the "brain drain"?

(a) A student from a developing country trains to be an engineer in the United States. After her training she returns to her country, but she is unable to find a job as an engineer.
(b) A wealthy individual in a developing country invests his money in the United States.
(c) A developing country decides to increase spending on public health programs and reduce spending on education.
(d) A physician trained in a developing country moves to a developed country to practice medicine.

Answer: (d)

Easy
Fact
Page: 525

22.30: Which of the following factors has NOT been suggested as an explanation for the lack of economic growth in many poor nations?

(a) insufficient capital formation
(b) a shortage of human resources
(c) an overabundance of social overhead capital
(d) the constraints imposed by dependency on the already-developed nations

Answer: (c)

Easy
Definition
Page: 525

22.31: Basic infrastructure projects such as roads, power generation, and irrigation systems are referred to as

(a) social overhead capital.
(b) fixed capital.
(c) human capital.
(d) the means of production.

Answer: (a)

Moderate
Single
Page: 525

22.32: One reason why investment in social overhead capital cannot successfully be undertaken by the private sector is the

(a) free-rider problem.
(b) dependency problem.
(c) central planning problem.
(d) neo-colonialism problem.

Answer: (a)

22.33: A developing country increases spending on projects such as the installation of a railroad system connecting rural areas with urban areas to facilitate the exchange of goods and services between these two areas. Which of the following statements is TRUE?

Moderate
Single
Page: 525

(a) This economy should not devote resources to these types of projects until there is a surplus of private capital in the economy.
(b) This type of investment is most appropriately undertaken by the private sector, because private firms will benefit the most from this type of investment.
(c) This type of investment is likely to make the economy worse off, because it will increase the probability of a brain drain.
(d) This type of investment in social overhead capital may be necessary to facilitate private investment and economic development.

Answer: (d)

22.34: Development strategy involves trade-offs between

Easy
Fact
Page: 526

(a) agriculture and industry.
(b) export promotion and import substitution.
(c) central planning and free markets.
(d) all of the above.

Answer: (d)

22.35: As an economy develops,

Easy
Fact
Page: 526

(a) a larger share of its GDP is devoted to both agriculture and the service sector.
(b) a larger share of its GDP is devoted to both manufacturing and agriculture.
(c) a smaller share of its GDP is devoted to both services and agriculture.
(d) a larger share of its GDP is devoted to services and a smaller share is devoted to agriculture.

Answer: (d)

22.36: Experience over the last three decades has suggested that in order for economic development to occur, it is necessary for an economy to

Easy
Fact
Page: 526

(a) promote industrial development over agriculture.
(b) stress agricultural development over industrial development.
(c) use a balanced strategy that promotes both agricultural and industrial development.
(d) stress the importation of agricultural products and the export of manufactured goods.

Answer: (c)

22.37: Strategies for development that stress agricultural projects over industrialization have numerous benefits. One of those benefits is

Easy
Fact
Page: 526

(a) that agricultural production is capital intensive.
(b) that the export prices for agricultural products tend to be very high and stable.
(c) that the benefits from agricultural projects are concentrated mainly in urban areas because urban dwellers will now have more food available.
(d) that agricultural projects usually have very low import requirements.

Answer: (d)

Easy
Fact
Page: 526

22.38: The Chinese refer to a development strategy as "walking on two legs." To which development strategy does this expression refer?

(a) maintaining a balance between agriculture and industry
(b) stressing import substitution and export promotion
(c) combining the use of central planning and free markets
(d) targeting the development of new products that can be used by both its own citizens as well as foreigners

Answer: (a)

Easy
Definition
Page: 527

22.39: An industrial trade strategy that favors developing local industries that can manufacture goods to replace imports is referred to as

(a) export promotion.
(b) unbalanced growth.
(c) industrial promotion.
(d) import substitution.

Answer: (d)

Moderate
Single
Page: 527

22.40: A developing country provides a subsidy to domestic firms producing automobiles so that the country no longer has to rely on automobiles from developed countries. This strategy is an example of

(a) an export promotion.
(b) an export subsidy.
(c) an import substitution.
(d) an import promotion.

Answer: (c)

Easy
Fact
Page: 527

22.41: Most economists believe that import-substitution policies have

(a) failed almost everywhere they have been tried.
(b) succeeded in some countries and have failed in others.
(c) generally been successful.
(d) been more successful than export-promotion strategies.

Answer: (a)

Moderate
Fact
Page: 527

22.42: Many developing countries instituted import-substitution policies because

(a) the ratio of export to import prices seemed to be increasing over the long-run.
(b) the ratio of export to import prices seemed to be on a long-run decline.
(c) the prices of the goods they imported were falling.
(d) the prices of the goods they exported were increasing.

Answer: (b)

Easy
Fact
Page: 527

22.43: Which of the following is NOT a characteristic of import-substitution policies?

(a) Import-substitution policies often encouraged capital-intensive production.
(b) Import-substitution policies encourage the use of high tariffs.
(c) Import-substitution policies have led to substantial job creation.
(d) Import-substitution policies have led to higher production costs.

Answer: (c)

22.44: In the past, import-substitution policies have led to

(a) a reduction in production costs because the output of domestic industries increased.
(b) substitution of lower-cost domestic inputs for higher-cost imported inputs.
(c) an increased ability for the country's exported products to compete in world markets.
(d) increased inefficiencies in the allocation of resources.

Answer: (d)

Moderate
Fact
Page: 527

22.45: A trade strategy designed to encourage sales abroad is referred to as

(a) import substitution.
(b) export promotion.
(c) unbalanced growth.
(d) industrial promotion.

Answer: (b)

Easy
Definition
Page: 527

22.46: A developing nation provides subsidies to firms that are producing products that will be sold to other nations. This is an example of

(a) import substitution.
(b) an import promotion.
(c) an export promotion.
(d) an adjustment in the balance of payments.

Answer: (c)

Easy
Single
Page: 527

22.47: A developing nation pursues a strategy that reduces the value of its currency relative to other currencies. This is an example of

(a) import substitution.
(b) an import promotion.
(c) an export promotion.
(d) an adjustment in the balance of trade.

Answer: (c)

Challenging
Multi
Page: 528

22.48: Which of the following is usually NOT a characteristic of export promotion policies?

(a) a favorable exchange rate to permit exports to compete with products manufactured in other countries
(b) manufacturing oriented toward foreign customers
(c) inward-looking industrial policies
(d) subsidies to exporting industries

Answer: (c)

Easy
Fact
Page: 528

22.49: Which of the following statements is TRUE?

(a) The United States has always discouraged central planning for developing countries.
(b) The Soviet Union, with its central planning system, had never experienced rapid growth and this discouraged other developing countries from using central planning.
(c) Central planning is desirable in developing countries because in these countries human resources are scarce and the political situation is unstable.
(d) Central planning was advocated in developing countries because in these countries many commodity and asset markets were imperfect and underdeveloped.

Answer: (d)

Easy
Fact
Page: 528

Moderate
Fact
Page: 528

22.50: Which of the following statements is TRUE?

(a) In the 1950s and 1960s, free-market development strategies commanded wide support.
(b) The United States has always opposed central planning in the developing nations.
(c) The failure of many free-market approaches has brought increasing calls for more government intervention and less market orientation in developing economies.
(d) Many developing countries have learned that central planning is technically difficult, highly politicized, and a nightmare to administer.

Answer: (d)

Moderate
Single
Page: 528

22.-51: Which of the following is an example of a market-oriented reform?

(a) the elimination of price controls on domestic goods.
(b) an increase in import restraints.
(c) reducing the value of the domestic currency in terms of foreign currencies below the equilibrium level.
(d) nationalizing private capital.

Answer: (a)

Easy
Single
Page: 528

22.52: Which of the following is NOT a market-oriented reform?

(a) privatization of state-run enterprises
(b) elimination of labor unions
(c) elimination of price controls
(d) reduction in import restraints

Answer: (b)

Easy
Fact
Page: 528

22.53: The international organization that exists for the purpose of stabilizing international exchange rates and lending money to countries that have problems financing their international transactions is _____.

(a) the United Nations
(b) the World Bank
(c) the International Monetary Fund
(d) the New International Economic Order

Answer: (c)

Easy
Fact
Page: 528

22.54: The international organization that exists for the purpose of **lending** money to individual countries for projects that promote economic development is _____.

(a) the World Bank
(b) the United Nations
(c) the International Monetary Fund
(d) the New International Economic Order

Answer: (a)

Easy
Fact
Page: 529

22.55: Which of the following statements is CORRECT?

(a) Economic growth and economic development are mutually exclusive.
(b) Economic growth does not guarantee economic development.
(c) Economic growth does guarantee economic development.
(d) Economic growth and economic development are synonymous with one another.

Answer: (b)

22.56: The realization that in many developing countries the benefits from increases in GDP trickled down to only a small minority of the population led to the call for new development strategies that would directly address the problem of poverty. An example of one of these new development strategies is a policy to

(a) favor agricultural development over industrial development.
(b) encourage direct foreign investment in high-tech industries.
(c) have all natural resources controlled by the state.
(d) increase the amount imported into the country and decrease the amount exported from the country.

Answer: (a)

22.57: The development strategy that encourages agricultural development over industrial development was devised as a reaction to

(a) the realization that developing countries cannot compete in the international markets for industrial products.
(b) the realization that in many developing countries the benefits from increases in GDP trickled down to only a small minority of the population.
(c) the realization that development strategies that encouraged industrialization increased the developing country's dependence on developed countries.
(d) the realization that development strategies that emphasized industrial development would lead to lower interest rates and thus make the wealthy in the developing country worse off.

Answer: (b)

22.58: Which of the following is an example of a successful development strategy for a developing country?

(a) Encourage the production of high-tech manufactured goods, such as automobiles, using the most capital-intensive production technologies so that developing countries can catch up to developed countries.
(b) Encourage the use of domestic inputs as much as possible, regardless of how expensive they are, so that the input and intermediate goods industries will grow. As the input and intermediate goods industries grow, the manufacturing industries will grow also.
(c) Reduce the amount of government intervention in price setting and institute a balanced emphasis on agricultural and industrial production.
(d) Concentrate on the manufacturing industries at the expense of all other sectors of the economy because manufacturing is the source of all economic growth. Once the manufacturing sector is established, benefits will trickle down to the rest of the society.

Answer: (c)

22.59: A review of development experiences shows that the most effective way of achieving rapid and politically sustainable improvements in the quality of life for the poor has been through a two-part strategy. The two elements of the strategy are

(a) improvement in the country's social overhead capital and policies to attract investment from companies in developed countries.
(b) to encourage exports and to discourage imports.
(c) to pursue strategies that ensure productive use of labor and the widespread provision of basic social services.
(d) central planning and state ownership of all resources.

Answer: (c)

Easy
Fact
Page: 530

22.60: Which of the following is NOT one of the common economic issues facing most developing nations?

(a) rapid population growth
(b) food shortages
(c) foreign debt
(d) labor shortages

Answer: (d)

Easy
Fact
Page: 531

22.61: Thomas Malthus, 200 years ago, predicted the increasing impoverishment of the world's people because he believed that

(a) populations grew rapidly and the capital stock grew slowly.
(b) the rate of population growth decreased over time, but the food supplies would decrease at an even faster rate.
(c) the supply of finite resources in the world could not continue to support increases in the demand for goods and services by the world's population.
(d) the absolute size of the population increase each year gets larger and larger, but food supplies grow much more slowly because of the diminishing marginal productivity of land.

Answer: (d)

Moderate
Single
Page: 531

22.62: Which of the following is NOT a possible consequence of rapid population growth in a developing country?

(a) low saving rates
(b) limitations on the country's ability to invest in human capital
(c) a change in the age composition of the population, as the number of adults grows relative to the number of children
(d) reduced investment

Answer: (c)

Easy
Fact
Page: 531

22.63: Rapid population growth

(a) increases labor productivity.
(b) improves the standard of living in developing countries.
(c) increases saving rates because individuals have more children to provide for.
(d) limits the ability of the government to improve human capital through programs such as infant nutrition.

Answer: (d)

Easy
Fact
Page: 531

22.64: Currently, populations are growing at rates of _____ to _____ per year throughout the developing world.

(a) .5% to 1%.
(b) 1.5% to 4%.
(c) 5% to 8%.
(d) 7.5% to 10%

Answer: (b)

22.65: Which of the following statements is FALSE?

(a) Rapid population growth may limit investment and thus restrain increases in labor productivity and income.
(b) Rapid population growth increases the number of dependent children relative to the number of productive adults.
(c) Rapid population growth may slow the current rate of economic development, but it will increase the rate of economic growth in the future.
(d) Rapid population growth makes it difficult to improve human capital.

Moderate
Single
Page: 531

Answer: (c)

22.66: The difference between the birth rate and the death rate is the

(a) fertility rate.
(b) natural rate of population increase.
(c) mortality rate.
(d) dependency rate.

Easy
Definition
Page: 532

Answer: (b)

22.67: If the birth rate is 5% and the death rate is 8%, the natural rate of population increase is

(a) -3%.
(b) 625%.
(c) 1.6%.
(d) 3%.

Easy
Single
Page: 532

Answer: (a)

22.68: If a country's natural rate of population increase is positive, then

(a) the country's death rate is negative.
(b) the country's birth rate is negative.
(c) the country's death rate is greater than the country's birth rate.
(d) the country's death rate is less than the country's birth rate.

Easy
Single
Page: 532

Answer: (d)

22.69: For a country to have a zero rate of population increase,

(a) the birth rate must be zero.
(b) the death rate must exceed the birth rate.
(c) the death rate must equal the birth rate.
(d) the death rate must be less than the birth rate.

Easy
Single
Page: 532

Answer: (c)

22.70: If the mortality rate remains constant, but the fertility rate increases, the natural rate of population increase will

(a) decrease.
(b) increase.
(c) remain constant.
(d) either increase or decrease depending on the amount by which the fertility rate increases.

Easy
Single
Page: 532

Answer: (b)

Easy
Fact
Page: 532

22.71: Historically, low rates of population growth were maintained because of

(a) low fertility rates.
(b) high mortality rates.
(c) migration out of developing countries.
(d) government restrictions on the number of children families can have.

Answer: (b)

Easy
Fact
Page: 532

22.72: Historically, initial increases in the rate of population growth have occurred when the

(a) mortality rate declined.
(b) death rate rose.
(c) fertility rate declined.
(d) birth rate rose.

Answer: (a)

Easy
Fact
Page: 532

22.73: Which of the following is NOT a reason why people in developing countries want large families?

(a) In developing nations, the tax laws provide incentives for having many children.
(b) In developing nations, children are important sources of farm labor.
(c) In developing nations, children provide a vital source of income for parents who are too old to support themselves.
(d) In developing nations, high infant mortality rates encourage families to have a large number of children to insure that a sufficient number will survive into adulthood.

Answer: (a)

Easy
Fact
Page: 532

22.74: Which of the following statements is TRUE?

(a) Family-size decisions are not influenced by economic incentives, nor by cultural and religious values.
(b) Family-size decisions are influenced by cultural and religious values, but not by economic incentives.
(c) Family-size decisions are influenced by economic incentives, but not by cultural and religious values.
(d) Family-size decisions are influenced by cultural and religious values, as well as by economic incentives.

Answer: (d)

Easy
Fact
Page: 533

22.75: In general, rising incomes appear to

(a) have no affect on fertility rates.
(b) increase fertility rates.
(c) decrease fertility rates.
(d) have no predictable effect on fertility rates.

Answer: (c)

22.76: In developing countries an individual family may find that having many children is a rational strategy for economic survival, but when many families decide to have a large number of children society as a whole is harmed. This is an example of the

(a) fallacy of composition.
(b) fallacy of division.
(c) the post hoc, ergo propter hoc fallacy.
(d) ceteris paribus fallacy.

Answer: (a)

22.77: Food shortages in developing countries

(a) are entirely the result of acts of nature.
(b) are largely due to misguided agricultural policies on the part of policymakers in developing countries.
(c) are entirely the result of human action.
(d) are due to the selfishness of people in developed countries.

Answer: (b)

22.78: Which of the following statements is FALSE?

(a) The primary reason for the food shortage in some developing countries is that not enough food can be produced worldwide to feed everyone because of the limits imposed by nature.
(b) Agricultural production in sub-Saharan Africa today is lower than it was 20 years ago.
(c) In many countries people are malnourished not because there is not enough food but because there are inadequate food-distribution methods.
(d) Countries with food shortages often have farm policies which discourage agricultural production.

Answer: (a)

22.79: The channels through which the governments of some developing countries buy domestic farm output and then sell it to urban residents at government-controlled prices are

(a) central planning agencies.
(b) ministries of agriculture.
(c) produce-marketing boards.
(d) industrial policy boards.

Answer: (c)

22.80: A nation's produce-marketing board keeps the price of rice below the equilibrium price. This will cause the nation's

(a) rice consumption to fall.
(b) rice production to fall.
(c) imports of rice to fall.
(d) exports of rice to increase.

Answer: (b)

Moderate
Fact
Page: 534

22.81: Governments in developing countries often set artificially low food prices in order to

(a) encourage agricultural production.
(b) reduce imports of farm commodities.
(c) eliminate black markets for agricultural products.
(d) maintain political support among urban residents.

Answer: (d)

Moderate
Fact
Page: 534

22.82: The actions of produce-marketing boards usually help _____ and hurt _____.

(a) farmers; export-oriented businesses
(b) farmers; urban residents
(c) urban residents; farmers
(d) urban residents; export-oriented businesses

Answer: (c)

Moderate
Fact
Page: 534

22.83: The policies of produce-marketing boards in developing countries have led to

(a) increases in farm output and therefore increases in exports of food.
(b) reductions in farm output and therefore increases in the imports of food products.
(c) an excess supply of food and therefore a decrease in the price of food.
(d) an increase in the demand for food and therefore an increase in the income of farmers.

Answer: (b)

Easy
Definition
Page: 534

22.84: The agricultural breakthroughs of modern science, such as the development of new, high-yield crop varieties, is the

(a) Green Revolution.
(b) greenhouse effect.
(c) global warming trend.
(d) Grain Revolution.

Answer: (a)

Easy
Fact
Page: 534

22.85: Low agricultural productivity in developing countries results from

(a) shortages of inputs, including land.
(b) migration from rural areas to urban areas.
(c) a lack of demand for food products.
(d) an overinvestment in farm equipment.

Answer: (a)

Moderate
Fact
Page: 535

22.86: The Green Revolution has failed to solve the food shortage problem because

(a) peasant farmers in developing countries are reluctant to adopt new farming techniques.
(b) high interest rates make investing in the new techniques unprofitable.
(c) the cultivation of the new seeds takes many complementary inputs that farmers in developing countries do not have.
(d) all of the above.

Answer: (d)

22.87: The policy that has been the most successful in increasing agricultural output in developing countries is

Easy
Fact
Page: 535

(a) import substitution.
(b) produce-marketing boards.
(c) land reform.
(d) export promotion.

Answer: (c)

22.88: One of the primary reasons why land reform has been successful in increasing agricultural output is that land reform

Easy
Fact
Page: 535

(a) allows the farmers to set the prices for their agricultural products.
(b) makes farmers owners of the land instead of tenants and owner-farmers are more productive than tenant farmers.
(c) enables farmers to escape the problem of diminishing returns.
(d) requircs that farmers invest in new and more productive agricultural technologies.

Answer: (b)

22.89: In the 1980s, the prospect of loan defaults by the Third World threatened

Easy
Fact
Page: 535

(a) only the people who lived in the Third World.
(b) the financial stability of a few banks in developed countries that had made the loans.
(c) the political stability of Third World governments, but it had no impact on the economic development of these countries.
(d) the entire international financial system and transformed the debt crisis into a global problem.

Answer: (d)

22.90: The roots of the current Third World debt crisis

Easy
Fact
Page: 535

(a) are in the period of colonialization.
(b) go back as far as the early 1900s.
(c) go back only as far as the early 1950s.
(d) go back only as far as the early 1970s.

Answer: (d)

22.91: In the early 1970s, banks became willing to lend substantial sums of money to developing countries because

Moderate
Fact
Page: 535

(a) funds were in abundant supply as a result of the infusion of petrodollars into the international banking system.
(b) interest rates after allowing for inflation were at their highest rates eve. So this made risky loans profitable.
(c) the international banking system was trying to encourage developing countries to abandon central planning in favor of market economies.
(d) there was a large decrease in the demand for loans in developed countries.

Answer: (a)

Easy
Definition
Page: 536

22.92: An agreement between banks and borrowers through which a new schedule of repayments of the debt is negotiated is

(a) a stabilization program.
(b) an austerity program.
(c) a debt rescheduling.
(d) a debt service agreement.

Answer: (c)

Easy
Definition
Page: 536

22.93: An agreement between a borrower country and the International Monetary Fund in which the country agrees to revamp its economic policies to provide incentives for higher export earnings and lower imports is a

(a) program for growth.
(b) debt service agreement.
(c) debt rescheduling agreement.
(d) stabilization program.

Answer: (d)

Challenging
Fact
Page: 536

22.94: Which of the following statements is FALSE?

(a) The countries that grabbed the most attention during the debt crisis were NOT the poorest of the developing countries.
(b) The debt crisis was a problem of developed countries as much as it was a problem of the developing countries.
(c) Debt service ratios of countries involved in the debt crisis approached 100% in the 1980s.
(d) Because there is no collateral for international loans, the developing nation debtors had nothing to lose by defaulting on their loans.

Answer: (d)

TRUE/FALSE QUESTIONS

Easy
Definition
Page: 525

22.95: Investment in social overhead capital refers to investment in areas like health, education, sanitation, and nutrition.

Answer: False

Difficult
Application
Page: 527

22.96: The following situation is an example of an import substitution strategy. Costa Rica has a comparative advantage in the production of coffee and, as a result, the Costa Rican government grants incentives to coffee planters to improve their performance in the international marketplace.

Answer: False

Easy
Application
Page: 533

22.97: In general, as a nation's income increases, fertility rates fall.

Answer: True

Moderate
Definition
Page: 530

22.98: The United States provides the most development assistance per capita of any developed nation.

Answer: False

22.99: Food shortages and famines are largely attributable to acts of nature like floods, droughts, etc.

Answer: False

Easy
Definition
Page: 533

22.100: Income distribution in developing countries is often so skewed that the richest households of very poor nations surpass the living standards of many high-income families in the developed economies.

Answer: True

Easy
Fact
Page: 521

22.101: In a developing economy, scarcity of capital may have more to do with a lack of incentives for citizens to save and invest productively than with any absolute scarcity of income available for capital accumulation.

Answer: True

Easy
Fact
Page: 523

22.102: Human capital shortages are NOT a barrier to economic growth in developing countries.

Answer: False

Easy
Fact
Page: 524

22.103: A frequently cited barrier to economic development is the apparent shortage of entrepreneurial activity in developing nations.

Answer: True

Easy
Fact
Page: 524

22.104: Most economists believe that import-substitution strategies have been quite successful around the world.

Answer: False

Easy
Fact
Page: 527

22.105: Policies designed to promote import substitution often encouraged labor-intensive production methods, which encouraged the creation of jobs.

Answer: False

Easy
Fact
Page: 527

22.106: Economic growth guarantees economic development.

Answer: False

Easy
Fact
Page: 529

22.107: Developing countries often pursue agricultural policies that discourage farm production.

Answer: True

Easy
Fact
Page: 534

22.108: Economic theories of population growth suggest that fertility decisions made by poor families should be viewed as uninformed and uncontrolled.

Answer: False

Easy
Fact
Page: 533

22.109: Governments in many developing countries often maintain artificially low food prices because the direct political influence of the relatively large rural population outweighs the influence of the relatively small urban population.

Answer: False

Easy
Fact
Page: 534

...

SHORT ANSWER QUESTIONS

Easy
Definition
Page: 520

22.110: Define the following four references and name a country that you argue would fall into each category.
A. First World
B. Second World
C. Third World
D. Fourth World

Answer: A. The industrialized nations of the West are often referred to as First World. The United States and most European nations fit into this category.
B. The formerly socialist nations of Eastern Europe used to be referred to as Second World. These countries included the former Soviet Union, Poland, Hungary, the former Czechoslovakia, and others.
C. The term Third World has been the term that refers to all other nations other than the developed, industrialized nations or the socialist nations of the past. As a result, this term included nations along a vast spectrum of economic growth and development. Thus, countries like Argentina and Korea were grouped in with sub-Saharan African nations. Thus, a new term, Fourth World, has been developed. This term divided nations even further to represent their level of economic advance.
D. The newly developed term Fourth World refers to countries that have fallen far behind the economic advances of the rest of the world. The countries that fall under this heading are in much of sub-Saharan Africa and some of Southern Asia.

Easy
Application
Page: 522

22.111: You are an economist for a developing country in Africa who has a serious lack of capital formation and who also has been plagued with wars and political instability over the past several years. What policy recommendations would you make?

Answer: Answers will vary. The main policy recommendation for this nation would be to ensure political stability. Without government and political stability, the country would not be able to attract any investment because of the risks.

Moderate
Definition
Page: 526

22.112: What development approach have the Chinese favored? Has practical experience backed this strategy up?

Answer: The Chinese refer to their development strategy as "walking on two legs" and this refers to their balanced investment approach between the agricultural and investment sectors of the economy. Experience over the past thirty years indicates that a balance between an agricultural approach and an investment approach is the most effective development strategy.

Difficult
Definition
Page: 527

22.113: Historically, why did the import-substitution strategy become popular among developing nations?

Answer: This strategy gained popularity throughout the 1950s because, at this time, most developing nations exported agricultural and mineral products-goods that often faced very unstable international market conditions. Moreover, the terms of trade for these nations seemed to be headed on a long-term decline. When a country experiences a decline in its terms of trade, its imports of manufactured goods become relatively more expensive in its domestic market, while its exports of primary goods become less expensive in the world market. As a result of these conditions, by the 1950s import-substitutions policies started gaining prominence.

22.114: What are the International Monetary Fund and the World Bank? Explain their roles.

Easy
Definition
Page: 528

Answer: The International Monetary Fund is an international organization whose primary goals are to stabilize international exchange rates and to lend money to countries that have problems financing their international transactions. The World Bank is an international agency that lends money to individual countries for projects that promote economic development.

22.115: Explain how rapid population growth can hinder labor productivity.

Moderate
Application
Page: 531

Answer: Rapid population growth stretches all of a nation's resources to its limits. As a result, when a nation is growing too quickly, its ability to save and invest is greatly hindered. It is through savings and investment (including human capital investment) that a nation improves the ability of labor to be productive. In order for labor to be productive, there needs to be a certain level of capital investment to aid and ensure productivity. Thus, when savings and investment are reduced due to rapid population growth, the ability of labor to improve productivity is also reduced.

22.116: Outline Mexico's debt and currency problems throughout the 1990s.

Difficult
Application
Page: 536

Answer: In 1982, Mexico had an external debt of $113 billion. However, after the approval of the North American Free Trade Agreement there was great optimism about the future for Mexico. However, as the peso's value began to climb throughout 1993 and early 1994, many investors became nervous about the possible decline of the peso. The peso did collapse in early 1995 and the Mexican government came close to defaulting on its external debt obligations. A $37 billion loan guarantee from the United States and the International Monetary Fund has temporarily restored faith and saved Mexico from default.

22.117: What are the common characteristics of developing countries?

Easy
Fact
Page: 520

Answer: Common characteristics of developing countries are: low per capita income, high fertility rates, high infant mortality rates, low levels of adult literacy, and a small percentage of the labor force in urban areas.

22.118: Define the vicious-circle-of-poverty hypothesis. Is this hypothesis true? Explain your answer.

Moderate
Single
Page: 524

Answer: The vicious-circle-of-poverty hypothesis argues that poor countries cannot escape from poverty because they cannot afford to save in order to make investments. This hypothesis is not true. If it were, no country could ever experience economic development.

22.119: Explain how each of the following limits the economic growth of developing nations:

Easy
Fact
Page: 522

a. Insufficient capital formation
b. A shortage of human resources
c. A lack of social overhead capital

Answer: (a) If there is insufficient capital formation, then capital stock does not grow and output in the future will be reduced. A lack of capital also reduces the productivity of labor. (b) A shortage of human resources may be a barrier to growth because this reduces productivity. Also, foreign companies will not invest in countries that do not have a trained labor force. (c) A lack of social overhead capital makes countries less able to attract private investment. A lack of social overhead capital also increases the difficulty of transporting food throughout the country, which worsens the food shortage.

Moderate
Single
Page: 527

22.120: Define import substitution. Evaluate the success of import substitution strategies in developing countries.

Answer: Import substitution is an industrial strategy that favors developing local industries that can manufacture goods to replace imports. Most economists would argue that import substitution has not been successful. Import substitution policies tend to create inefficiency. Industries that are inefficient are protected from foreign competition. Import substitution policies often encourage capital-intensive production techniques and therefore create relatively few jobs while encouraging the use of expensive domestic products.

Moderate
Single
Page: 528

22.121 Is the developing world moving toward centralized planning or free markets? Justify your answer.

Answer: In recent years the developing world has been moving more toward free markets. The failure of central planning in many developing countries led these countries to abandon planning efforts. Central planning is being replaced with market-oriented reforms such as privatization of state-run enterprises and the elimination of price controls.

Easy
Fact
Page: 529

22.122: Explain why growth is not necessarily synonymous with development.

Answer: Growth is not necessarily synonymous with development because it may be difficult to transform growing output into economic benefits that reach most of a nation's people. Growth measures changes in income, while development measures the increase in the well-being of a nation's citizens.

Challenging
Single
Page: 532

22.123: Critically evaluate the following statement:"People in developing countries are not poor because they have large families. Rather, they have large families because they are poor."

Answer: Children in developing countries may be viewed as an investment good. Children are needed to help contribute to the current economic well-being of the family by providing labor services. Parents also rely on children to help support them when they can no longer support themselves.

Moderate
Single
Page: 534

22.124: Explain how the agricultural policies of many developing countries have contributed to the problem of food shortages in those countries. Why do these governments enact such policies in the first place?

Answer: Government policies designed to keep the prices of agricultural products low had the impact of reducing agricultural production. Countries then had to increase their imports of food. These policies were often pursued so that food could be sold at low prices to urban residents. Urban residents have more political clout than those individuals located in rural areas.

Moderate
Single
Page: 534

22.125: Define the Green Revolution. Why hasn't the Green Revolution solved the world's food shortage problem?

Answer: The Green Revolution is the agricultural breakthroughs of modern science, such as the development of new, high-yield crop varieties. The Green Revolution has not solved the world's food shortage problem because new seeds are expensive and the new techniques of growing the seeds require expensive inputs such as fertilizers and irrigation.

22.126: Explain the evolution of the Third World debt crisis.

Moderate
Single
Page: 535

Answer: The Third World debt crisis has evolved since the 1970s. During the 1970s banks had large sums of petrodollars to lend. Many developing countries had been experiencing rapid growth and banks believed that these countries provided for profitable investment. When oil prices increased many of these developing nations found themselves paying more for imports but receiving less revenue from exports. These countries then had no export revenues to pay their loans and their debt mounted. Further tight money policies of the 1980s increased to debt obligations of the countires as the result of higher interest rates.

(Chapter 38 in Combined Text)

23 Economies in Transition and Alternative Economic Systems

MULTIPLE CHOICE QUESTIONS

23.1: The term "cold war" characterized

(a) The rivalry between the United States and former Soviet Union between the end of World War II and the mid-1980s.
(b) the rivalry between France and England in the 18th century.
(c) the rivalry between Spain and France during the 16th century.
(d) the rivalry between Russia and England in the 19th century.

Answer: (a)

Easy
Definition
Page: 541

23.2: The forty year rivalry between the United States and former Soviet Union between the end of World War II and the 1980s was called

(a) The endless war.
(b) The warm war
(c) The cold war
(d) The battle of all wars.

Answer: (c)

Easy
Definition
Page: 541

23.3: By the end of 1991, the former Soviet Union had dissolved into

(a) 2 independent states.
(b) 5 independent states.
(c) 32 independent states.
(d) 15 independent states.

Answer: (d)

Easy
Fact
Page: 541

23.4: Ten of the fifteen independent states that emerged from the former Soviet Union formed

(a) Commonwealth of Soviet Nations.
(b) the United Soviet Union.
(c) Commonwealth Independent States.
(d) the Communist League.

Answer: (c)

Easy
Fact
Page: 541

23.5: The economic system of the former Soviet Union was representative of

(a) market-based capitalism.
(b) centrally planned socialism.
(c) central based capitalism.
(d) market-oriented socialism.

Answer: (b)

Easy
Definition
Page: 541

Moderate
Multi
Page: 542

23.6: The independent states of the former Soviet Union are struggling to make the transition to

(a) market-based capitalism.
(b) communism.
(c) centrally planned socialism.
(d) autocratic planned communism.

Answer: (a)

Moderate
Multi
Page: 542

23.7: As a result of foreign investment, privatization, and entrepreneurship, the private sector of the Polish economy by 1992 accounted for

(a) 2% of total output.
(b) 80% of total output.
(c) 90% of total output.
(d) 30% of total output.

Answer: (d)

Easy
Definition
Page: 542

23.8: A political system in which ultimate power rests with the people, who make governmental decisions through voting is called

(a) dictatorship.
(b) democracy.
(c) monarchy.
(d) Fascism.

Answer: (b)

Easy
Definition
Page: 543

23.9: A political system in which political power is concentrated either in a small elite or a single person is called

(a) democracy.
(b) dictatorship.
(c) socialist democracy.
(d) cooperative socialism.

Answer: (b)

Easy
Definition
Page: 543

23.10: An economy in which most capital is owned by the government rather than private citizens is a

(a) capitalist economy.
(b) communist economy.
(c) socialist economy.
(d) dictatorship.

Answer: (c)

Easy
Definition
Page: 544

23.11: An economy in which most capital is privately owned is a

(a) capitalist economy.
(b) communist economy.
(c) socialist economy.
(d) dictatorship.

Answer: (a)

23.12: An economic system in which the people control the means of production directly, without the intervention of government is

Easy
Definition
Page: 544

(a) a socialist economy.
(b) a capitalist economy.
(c) a dictatorship.
(d) communism.

Answer: (d)

23.13: In the world envisioned by communists, the state would

Moderate
Multi
Page: 544

(a) wither away and society would plan the economy in much the same way that a collective would.
(b) become more dominant in economic planning.
(c) become more dominant in production and distribution decisions.
(d) become very dictatorial.

Answer: (a)

23.14: What percentage of total agricultural production in the former Soviet Union was produced on private plots and sold in a large "second economy."

Easy
Fact
Page: 544

(a) three-fourths
(b) three-fifths
(c) one-half
(d) one-fourth

Answer: (d)

23.15: The United States and Japan are examples of countries with essentially capitalist economic systems and are essentially

Easy
Fact
Page: 544

(a) autocratic political institutions
(b) ruled by monarchy.
(c) democratic political institutions.
(d) communist political ideologies.

Answer: (c)

23.-16: Great Britain and France are examples of political democracies that have supported strong

Easy
Fact
Page: 544

(a) communist institutions.
(b) socialist institutions.
(c) Dictatorial institutions.
(d) federal institutions

Answer: (b)

23.17: In conforming to Friedrich Hayek's thesis that certain types of political and economic systems are most compatible, it is clear that the essence and heart of both the market system and democracy is

Moderate
Multi
Page: 544

(a) communism.
(b) strong government controls.
(c) individual freedoms.
(d) strong central government planning.

Answer: (c)

Challenging
Multi
Page: 545

23.18: Critics of Friedrich Hayek's thesis argue that social reform and active government involvement in the economy are the only ways to present a totalitarian state because free and unregulated markets lead to

(a) increased economic equalities for all.
(b) an even and fair distribution of wealth within the nation.
(c) inequalities and economic power for the few.
(d) greater opportunities for all.

Answer: (c)

Easy
Definition
Page: 545

23.19: An economic system that combines government ownership with market allocation is called

(a) a centrally planned economy.
(b) a totalitarian economy.
(c) a cooperative socialist economy.
(d) a market-socialist economy.

Answer: (d)

Easy
Fact
Page: 545

23.20: A so-called market-socialist economy characterized

(a) the former Soviet Union.
(b) the former Yugoslavia.
(c) the former East Germany.
(d) the former Poland.

Answer: (b)

Moderate
Multi
Page: 545

23.21: In the former Soviet Union, production and distribution decisions were rigidly directed by

(a) the decisions of buyers and sellers.
(b) the functioning market system.
(c) targets specified in one- or five-year plans.
(d) decisions of consumers and businesses.

Answer: (c)

Moderate
Single
Page: 543

23.22: The private sector of the Polish economy now accounts for

(a) one-third of the economy's total production.
(b) four-fifths of the economy's total production.
(c) two-thirds of the economy's total production.
(d) one-fourth of the economy's total production.

Answer: (c)

Moderate
Multi
Page: 543

23.23: The rapid growth of the private sector within the Polish economy has been partly the result of

(a) "spontaneous privatization" initiated by managers of state owned enterprises.
(b) government nationalization plans.
(c) government purchases of production assets.
(d) government controls over labor unions.

Answer: (a)

23.24: The rapid growth of the private sector within the Polish economy has been partly the result of

Moderate
Multi
Page: 543

(a) "spontaneous privatization" initiated by managers of state owned enterprises.
(b) government nationalization plans.
(c) government purchases of production assets.
(d) government controls over labor unions.

Answer: (b)

23.25: Until recently, about one-third of the world's population lived in countries whose economies were based on a

Moderate
Multi
Page: 545

(a) capitalist philosophy.
(b) market-oriented philosophy.
(c) socialist and communist philosophy.
(d) democratic philosophy.

Answer: (c)

23.26: The Marxian labor theory of value specifies that the value of a product depends upon

Moderate
Definition
Page: 546

(a) market demand.
(b) market supply.
(c) market demand and supply.
(d) the amount of labor required to produce it.

Answer: (d)

23.27: Marxian economic analysis concludes that the capitalist system is

Moderate
Multi
Page: 547

(a) a commendable example to the world.
(b) destined to provide increased economic growth.
(c) responsible for long-term economic prosperity.
(d) is morally wrong and doomed to ultimate failure.

Answer: (d)

23.28: According to Marxian analysis, capital is

Moderate
Multi
Page: 546

(a) not capable of contributing to value.
(b) the physical embodiment of past labor which is then embodied in the final product.
(c) a useless resource in production.
(d) a useless resource in the distribution of final output.

Answer: (b)

23.29: The means of production in Marxian analysis represents

Easy
Definition
Page: 546

(a) the land and capital resources.
(b) the distribution of final output.
(c) market demand.
(d) market supply.

Answer: (a)

Moderate
Multi
Page: 546

23.30: According to Marxian analysis, the value of labor power represents

(a) market demand and supply.
(b) government controls over production.
(c) government controls over distribution.
(d) the wage rate, dependent on the amount of clothing, shelter, basic education, medical care, etc., that is needed to produce and sustain labor power.

Answer: (d)

Moderate
Multi
Page: 546

23.31: According to Marxian analysis,

(a) capitalists pay a wage that is just enough (subsistence level) for laborers to live on.
(b) wages will approximate a laborer's productivity.
(c) wages will be based upon market demand and supply.
(d) wages paid to laborers will exceed their productivity.

Answer: (b)

Moderate
Definition
Page: 546

23.32: According to Marxian analysis, the profit that a capitalist earns by paying workers less than the value of what they produce is called

(a) labor value.
(b) constant capital.
(c) surplus value.
(d) market value.

Answer: (c)

Moderate
Multi
Page: 547

23.33: According to Marxian analysis, profit is a measure of

(a) market forces.
(b) the capitalists' contributions to production.
(c) market price.
(d) value created by workers but expropriated by capitalists because they own and control the means of production.

Answer: (d)

Moderate
Multi
Page: 547

23.34: Marxian analysis referred to the ratio of surplus value to the value of labor power as

(a) wages.
(b) market prices.
(c) the rate of exploitation.
(d) the modes of production.

Answer: (c)

Easy
Fact
Page: 547

23.35: In contrast to Marxian analysis, neoclassical economics views

(a) both capital and labor as productive resources.
(b) only capital as a productive resource.
(c) only labor as a productive resource.
(d) only land as a product resource.

Answer: (a)

23.36: Neoclassical economics views profits as

(a) a legitimate return to capital.
(b) unproductive payments to capitalists.
(c) unproductive payments to laborers.
(d) determined by government.

Answer: (a)

Moderate
Multi
Page: 547

23.37: Marxian believed that the

(a) level of worker exploitation would lessen as profit rate declined.
(b) level of worker exploitation would increase as the rate of profit decreased.
(c) workers' economic conditions would improve over time.
(d) rate of profit would increase over time.

Answer: (b)

Moderate
Multi
Page: 547

23.-38: Ultimately, Marxian believed that the capitalist system

(a) would enjoy long run prosperity.
(b) would result in increased economic gains for workers and capitalists.
(c) would result in a worker revolt and the overthrow of capitalism.
(d) would adopt new market guidelines.

Answer: (c)

Moderate
Multi
Page: 547

23.39: Marxian believed that an economic system was defined by

(a) the social relations of production.
(b) the market system.
(c) the forces of demand.
(d) the forces of supply.

Answer: (a)

Moderate
Definition
Page: 547

23.-40: Marxian believed that capitalism would be replaced by

(a) feudalism.
(b) anarchy.
(c) socialism.
(d) a dictatorship.

Answer: (c)

Moderate
Fact
Page: 547

23.41: Marxian believed that socialism would be ultimately replaced by

(a) capitalism.
(b) feudalism.
(c) a dictatorship.
(d) communism.

Answer: (d)

Moderate
Fact
Page: 547

Challenging
Multi
Page: 547

23.42: Marxian strongly endorsed active unions among workers to

(a) push wages down and profits up.
(b) push wages and profits up.
(c) push wages up above subsistence and transfer surplus value back to workers.
(d) eliminate the need for factories.

Answer: (c)

Moderate
Multi
Page: 547

23.43: Marxian used the term "emiserization" to mean

(a) that workers would prosper under capitalism.
(b) that capitalists would increase wages.
(c) the increased worker exploitation and misery for the capitalist system.
(d) the rapid rate of economic growth under capitalism.

Answer: (c)

Moderate
Multi
Page: 547

23.44: The central theme of Marxian's arguments is that

(a) the entire population will prosper under capitalism.
(b) under capitalism, workers will prosper and capitalists are doomed to lower incomes.
(c) government will prosper under capitalism through increased controls
(d) private ownership and profit are unfair and unethical.

Answer: (d)

Moderate
Multi
Page: 548

23.45: The New Economic Policy of the Soviets between 1921 and 1928 was characterized by

(a) government ownership of all resources.
(b) government ownership of all production.
(c) government nationalization of all economic activity.
(d) decentralization and an increased use of the market process.

Answer: (d)

Moderate
Multi
Page: 548

23.46: The elimination of private land ownership, money, private trade, and wage differentials among workers characterized

(a) the period between 1775 and 1790 in the former Soviet Union.
(b) the Bolshevik Revolution in the Soviet Union in 1917.
(c) the former Soviet Union during the period from 1810 to 1812.
(d) the former Soviet Union in 1800.

Answer: (b)

Moderate
Multi
Page: 548

23.47: The economic policies of the Soviet Union from 1928 into the 1980s emphasized

(a) centralized planning, rapid industrialization, and collective agriculture.
(b) a capitalist market economy.
(c) the private ownership of all resources.
(d) market-demanded prices and wages.

Answer: (a)

23.48: Recent privatization initiatives in Russia have resulted in the private sector accounting for

Moderate
Fact
Page: 549

(a) 2% of 1995 personal income.
(b) 15% of 1995 personal income.
(c) 60% of 1995 personal income.
(d) 92% of 1995 personal income.

Answer: (c)

23.49: Russia's new "economic constitution", established in 1995, introduced

Moderate
Fact
Page: 549

(a) new laws to establish property rights and government initiatives to stimulate economic activity.
(b) new centralized planning structures.
(c) wage, price, and profit controls.
(d) more central government controls over production and distribution.

Answer: (a)

23.50: The Soviet leader that initiated striking reforms that led to his receiving the Nobel Peace Prize in 1990 for ending the Cold War was

Easy
Fact
Page: 550

(a) Alexei Kosygin.
(b) Nikita Krushchev.
(c) Joseph Stalin.
(d) Mikhail Gorbachev.

Answer: (d)

23.51: One of Mikhail Gorbachev's reforms that led to the almost completely open discussion of virtually every aspect of political and economic reform in the Soviet Union was called

Moderate
Fact
Page: 550

(a) glasnost.
(b) liberalization.
(c) economic reform.
(d) perestroika.

Answer: (a)

23.52: One of Mikhail Gorbachev's reforms that led to the establishment of new economic structures was called

Moderate
Fact
Page: 550

(a) glasnost.
(b) liberalization.
(c) economic planning.
(d) perestroika.

Answer: (d)

23.53: One of the most radical of the 1987 Gorbachev reforms was that

Moderate
Multi
Page: 550

(a) prices and wages were totally controlled by government.
(b) all production decisions were made by government.
(c) all distribution decisions were made by government.
(d) job security was reduced, workers could be severed, and unproductive enterprises shut down.

Answer: (d)

Moderate
Fact
Page: 551 **23.54**: Boris Yeltsin, the current President of the Russian Republic, is committed to

(a) nationalizing the economy.
(b) government controls over all production and distribution.
(c) de-regulating prices, privatizing public enterprises, and stabilizing the macroeconomy.
(d) rigid wage and price controls.

Answer: (c)

Moderate
Multi
Page: 552 **23.55**: The Russian transition to a market economy required macroeconomic stabilization and the need to

(a) increase the domestic money supply to expand prices.
(b) decrease the domestic money to negate serious inflationary pressures.
(c) regulate all wages.
(d) regulate all interest rates.

Answer: (b)

Moderate
Multi
Page: 551 **23.56**: The Russian transition to a market economy required

(a) increased central planning.
(b) controls over prices.
(c) controls over wages.
(d) the de-regulation of prices and the market determination of all prices for both consumer and capital goods.

Answer: (d)

Moderate
Multi
Page: 551 **23.57**: The Russian transition to a market economy required

(a) controls over prices.
(b) central planning over all production.
(c) controls over wages and interest rates.
(d) increased liberalized trade and the removal of trade barriers.

Answer: (d)

Moderate
Multi
Page: 553 **23.58**: The so-called tragedy of commons relates to the idea that

(a) collective ownership may not provide the proper private incentives for efficiency because individuals do not bear the full costs of their own decisions, but enjoy the full benefits.
(b) all wages, prices, and interest rates are controlled by government.
(c) central planning sets all production targets.
(d) central planning sets all distribution targets.

Answer: (a)

Moderate
Multi
Page: 553 **23.59**: The Russian transition to a market economy required

(a) controls over prices.
(b) controls planning overall production.
(c) controls over wages and interest rates.
(d) market-supporting institutions such as a developed banking system, functional financial markets, a code of commercial law, and developed processes for insurability of business activities.

Answer: (d)

23.60: In a centrally-planned economy,

(a) the labor market does not function freely and there is essentially no such thing as unemployment.
(b) wages tend to be exceptionally high for low skill jobs and low for high skill jobs.
(c) unemployment has always been very widespread.
(d) laborers have remained unemployed because of technology displacement.

Answer: (a)

Moderate
Multi
Page: 554

23.61: Within a fully employed, centrally-planned economy that provides basic housing, food, and clothing at very affordable levels for all,

(a) there is a real need for government social welfare programs.
(b) there is no need for unemployment insurance, welfare, or other social programs.
(c) there is a need for government to permit market-determined prices.
(d) there is a need for government to permit market-determined wages.

Answer: (b)

Moderate
Multi
Page: 554

23.62: The Russian transition to a market economy with free labor markets and uncontrolled prices means that

(a) unemployment and higher prices are inevitable.
(b) full employment and low prices can be maintained.
(c) wages will still be determined by government.
(d) prices will still be controlled by government.

Answer: (a)

Moderate
Multi
Page: 554

23.63: The transition to a market-oriented economy characterized by rising unemployment and higher prices suggests that

(a) government must continue to centrally plan all resource allocations to production.
(b) government must continue to centrally plan the distribution of all output into consumption.
(c) government must set wages, prices, and interest rates.
(d) a social safety net must be established to include unemployment compensation, and food, clothing, and housing subsidies for those in need.

Answer: (d)

Moderate
Multi
Page: 554

23.64: Most authorities agree that the transition to a market economy can be achieved

(a) without external financial and technical assistance.
(b) only with external financial and technical assistance.
(c) only with forceful central planning by the government.
(d) only with government controls on wages and prices.

Answer: (b)

Moderate
Multi
Page: 554

23.65: The transition from socialism to market capitalism by the shock therapy approach suggests that

(a) the transition be gradual with sequential changes in government controls, etc.
(b) government always centrally plan the economy.
(c) the transition proceed immediately and impact all economic variables at once.
(d) government always control wages, prices, and interest rates.

Answer: (c)

Moderate
Definition
Page: 555

Moderate
Multi
Page: 555

23.66: The immediate and total de-regulation of prices, liberalization of trade, privatization, development of financial institutions, and a social safety net represent

(a) the gradualism transition approach from socialism to a market economy.
(b) the shock therapy transition approach from socialism to a market economy.
(c) a cooperative socialist model.
(d) an authoritarian socialist model.

Answer: (b)

Moderate
Multi
Page: 555

23.67: Advocates of a gradualism transition approach from socialism to a market economy recommend

(a) an immediate and total change in all economic conditions.
(b) continued government controls over wages forever.
(c) moderate changes starting with the development of market institutions, the gradual decontrol of prices, and the privatization of only the cost efficient firms.
(d) continued government controls over prices forever.

Answer: (c)

Moderate
Multi
Page: 555

23.68: China's economic system can be described as

(a) strongly capitalistic.
(b) exclusively market-oriented.
(c) communist with private enterprise permitted and encouraged.
(d) exclusively socialistic.

Answer: (c)

Easy
Fact
Page: 555

23.69: The population of China represents

(a) one out of every 100 people in the world.
(b) one out of every 5 people in the world.
(c) one out of every 20 people in the world.
(d) one out of every 50 people in the world.

Answer: (b)

Easy
Single
Page: 556

23.70: The early structure of the Chinese economic system was built on the

(a) market-oriented model.
(b) socialist model of Western Europe.
(c) Soviet-Stalinist model.
(d) cooperative socialist model.

Answer: (c)

Moderate
Multi
Page: 556

23.71: The Chinese five-year plan from 1953 to 1957 focused on

(a) developing consumer goods industries.
(b) developing capital-intensive industries.
(c) the equal development of consumer and capital goods industries.
(d) developing market capitalist incentives.

Answer: (b)

23.72: The Chinese economic strategy developed and implemented in 1958 was called

(a) the surplus value theory.
(b) the great march.
(c) the national grand plan.
(d) the Great Leap Forward.

Answer: (d)

Moderate
Fact
Page: 556

23.73: The Chinese economic strategy incorporated in the Great Leap Forward emphasized

(a) the shift from small-scale, labor-intensive to large-scale, capital-intensive industries.
(b) the shift from large-scale, capital-intensive to small-scale, labor-intensive industries.
(c) the introduction of the profit motive for all industries.
(d) the introduction of market-determined wages and prices.

Answer: (b)

Moderate
Multi
Page: 556

23.74: The Chinese economic strategy incorporated in the Great Leap Forward emphasized

(a) the reduction of material incentives and the introduction of the motivating power of revolutionary ideology and inspiration.
(b) the use of the profit motive.
(c) the use of market-determined prices.
(d) the shift from small-scale to large-scale industry.

Answer: (a)

Moderate
Multi
Page: 556

23.75: The Chinese Great Proletarian Cultural Revolution between 1966 and 1976 was characterized by

(a) a massive market-oriented reform.
(b) the introduction of free enterprise incentives.
(c) the introduction of direct central planning over all economic transactions.
(d) a period of ideological parity in which material incentives and reforms were denounced.

Answer: (d)

Moderate
Multi
Page: 556

23.76: The government reforms introduced in Chinese manufacturing in 1976 were intended to

(a) extend government controls over all prices.
(b) extend government controls over all wages.
(c) increase the role of the producing unit, increase individual profit incentives for the producing unit, and lessen the role of state central planners.
(d) return the economy to a rigid authoritarian communist state.

Answer: (c)

Challenging
Multi
Page: 556

23.77: In late 1988, the Chinese government implemented

(a) an austerity program that included strict price controls, reduced state investment, and reduced imports.
(b) more investment and market reforms.
(c) more freer market-determined wages and interest rates.
(d) an expansion of the money supply.

Answer: (a)

Challenging
Multi
Page: 557

Moderate
Multi
Page: 557

23.78: The Chinese economy during the period between 1991 and 1995 has been characterized by

(a) sharp reduced growth with increased government controls over the economy.
(b) more efforts by the government to centrally plan the economy and set all prices and wages.
(c) rapid industrial growth with increased growth of private enterprise and the introduction of a stock market.
(d) government efforts to stop the movement towards a market system.

Answer: (c)

Easy
Multi
Page: 559

23.79: The "Japanese economic miracle" refers to

(a) the limited rates of industrial growth during the past 50 years.
(b) the limited increase in the nation's exports since the end of World War II.
(c) the remarkable rate of sustained industrialization and economic growth since World War II.
(d) the small level of manufacturing productivity.

Answer: (c)

Easy
Fact
Page: 559

23.80: Since 1950, per capita GNP in Japan has grown from less than 20% of U.S. GNP to over

(a) 100%.
(b) 40%.
(c) 30%.
(d) 70%.

Answer: (d)

Easy
Fact
Page: 559

23.81: Structurally, the Japanese economy is an example of

(a) an authoritarian socialism model.
(b) a communism.
(c) a free-market capitalist model.
(d) a centrally-planned model.

Answer: (c)

Moderate
Multi
Page: 559

23.82: Among the various contributors to Japan's economic success, the single most important factor has been the nation's

(a) rate of investment.
(b) import purchases of durable consumer goods.
(c) import purchases of non-durable consumer goods.
(d) production of defense-related products.

Answer: (a)

Moderate
Multi
Page: 558

23.83: Most of Japan's domestic investment has been financed by

(a) foreign capital.
(b) government purchases of debt instruments.
(c) government sale of debt instruments.
(d) domestic savings.

Answer: (d)

23.84: An additional important contributor to Japan's economic success has been the

(a) import purchases of non-durable consumer goods.
(b) quality of the Japanese labor force.
(c) production of defense-related products.
(d) import purchases of durable consumer goods.

Moderate
Multi
Page: 559

Answer: (b)

23.85: An important contributor to Japan's economic success has been the

(a) import purchases of non-durable consumer goods.
(b) production of defense-related products.
(c) adopted use of the most advanced industrial technologies in manufacturing industries.
(d) import purchases of durable consumer goods.

Moderate
Multi
Page: 559

Answer: (c)

23.86: The agency of the Japanese government responsible for industrial policy is called

(a) Agency for Development.
(b) Ministry of Trade and Industry.
(c) Department of Commerce.
(d) Agency for Industrial Growth.

Easy
Fact
Page: 560

Answer: (b)

23.87: The Japanese government's Ministry of Trade and Industry has

(a) introduced centralized economic planning to control production.
(b) introduced centralized economic planning to control distribution.
(c) used tariffs and import quotas to protect and subsidize several key domestic industries.
(d) imposed controls on domestic prices, wages, and interest rates.

Easy
Multi
Page: 560

Answer: (c)

23.88: The Japanese government's Ministry of Trade and Industry

(a) is actively involved in a partnership with domestic businesses and significantly determines orderly reductions in capacity and the fate of businesses.
(b) introduced centralized economic planning to control production.
(c) introduced centralized economic planning to control distribution.
(d) imposed controls on domestic prices, wages, and interest rates.

Easy
Fact
Page: 560

Answer: (a)

23.89: Some observers have referred to the Japanese economy of the 1980s as a "bubble economy." This implies that

(a) Japan has experienced sustained and uninterrupted economic growth.
(b) the recession lag from 1980 to 1990 has been followed by sustained growth to the present.
(c) the accelerated growth and inflated financial valves of the 1980s were shaken by the collapse of the stock market in 1992 and the decrease in real GDP.
(d) Japan has experienced a recession from 1980 to 1995.

Moderate
Multi
Page: 560

Answer: (c)

Moderate
Single
Page: 560

23.90: An appreciated or more expansive Japanese yen would tend to

(a) increase Japan's exports and imports.
(b) decrease Japan's exports and imports.
(c) increase exports and lower imports.
(d) decrease Japanese exports and increase imports.

Answer: (d)

Moderate
Multi
Page: 556

23.91: The sweeping reforms of Deng Xiaoping resulted in a reorganization of the Chinese economy

(a) from central planning towards open-market operations and incentives.
(b) from free enterprise towards central planning.
(c) from market capitalism towards central planning.
(d) from market capitalism towards authoritarian socialism.

Answer: (a)

Moderate
Multi
Page: 547

23.92: The Marxian prophesy regarding the inevitable collapse of capitalism was due to

(a) the shortcomings of excess government controls.
(b) the inability of workers to organize.
(c) the excess use of central planning by government.
(d) the falling rates of profits, increasing worker exploitation, and overall economic misery.

Answer: (d)

Easy
Definition
Page: 542

23.93: A democracy is a system of government in which the ultimate power rests with

(a) the dominant businesses.
(b) the select few powerful political figures.
(c) the people who direct the nation through the voting process.
(d) the dominant select corporate and civic leaders.

Answer (c)

Easy
Definition
Page: 543

23.94: A dictatorship is a political system in which ultimate power is

(a) in the hands of all the people.
(b) in the hands of only corporations.
(c) concentrated in a small elite few or a single person.
(d) determined by the voting process.

Answer: (c)

Easy
Fact
Page: 542

23.95: Among the nations of Central Europe including Hungary, Poland, the Czech Republic, Bulgaria, and Romania, the nation that has achieved the greatest level of sustained growth in the transition to the market process has been

(a) Hungary.
(b) Poland.
(c) Romania.
(d) Bulgaria.

Answer: (b)

23.96: The nations that most represent socialist centrally planned economies with concentrated political power in a single party are

(a) Poland and Japan.
(b) England and Germany.
(c) Japan and China.
(d) China and North Korea.

Moderate
Fact
Page: 544

Answer: (d)

23.97: Examples of politically democratic nations that support certain strongsocialist institutions are

(a) Great Britain and Sweden.
(b) China and Japan.
(c) North Korea and Japan.
(d) China and France.

Easy
Fact
Page: 544

Answer: (a)

23.98: The *Wall Street Journal* has recently reported that 95% of the new entrepreneurial businesses in Poland are

(a) large-sized businesses.
(b) very small "mom and pop" proprietorships.
(c) huge foreign conglomerates.
(d) medium-sized foreign businesses.

Easy
Fact
Page: 543

Answer: (b)

23.99: An economy that combines government ownership with market allocation is called

(a) free-enterprise capitalism.
(b) authoritarian socialism.
(c) communism.
(d) a market-socialist economy.

Easy
Definition
Page: 545

Answer: (d)

23.100: While capitalists view profits as an earned return to capital, Marxian viewed profits as

(a) a just return to property owners.
(b) a reasonable return to businesses.
(c) value created by labor and unjustly expropriated by non-productive capitalists.
(d) a just return to landowners.

Moderate
Multi
Page: 547

Answer: (c)

TRUE/FALSE QUESTIONS

23.101: The forty-year rivalry between the United States and former Soviet Union between the end of World War II and the 1980s was called the "Cold War."

Easy
Definition
Page: 541

Answer: True

Easy
Definition
Page: 541

23.102: The economic system of the former Soviet Union was representative of centrally-planned socialism.

Answer: True

Easy
Definition
Page: 544

23.103: An economy in which most capital is owned by the government rather than private citizens is called market capitalism.

Answer: False

Easy
Definition
Page: 545

23.104: An economic system that combines government ownership with private ownership and market determination of resource allocations and product distribution is called a market-socialist economy.

Answer: True

Easy
Definition
Page: 546

23.105: The Marxian labor theory of value specifies that the value of a product depends upon the cost of all resources used in its production.

Answer: False

Moderate
Definition
Page: 546

23.106: According to Marxian analysis, capital is the physical embodiment of past labor which is incorporated in the final product.

Answer: True

Easy
Definition
Page: 547

23.107: According to Marxian analysis, profit is a measure of the capitalists' contributions to the production process.

Answer: False

Moderate
Multi
Page: 548

23.108: The economic policies of the former Soviet Union from 1928 to the 1980s emphasized centralized planning, rapid industrialization, and collective agriculture.

Answer: True

Moderate
Multi
Page: 555

23.109: The transition from socialism to market capitalism by the so-called shock therapy approach suggests that the transition proceed immediately and impact upon all economic variables at once.

Answer: True

Easy
Definition
Page: 559

23.110: Structurally, the Japanese economy is an example of a free market capitalist model.

Answer: True

SHORT ANSWER QUESTIONS

Easy
Definition
Page: 541

23.111: What is meant by the term "Cold War"? What characterized the Cold War? In general, what were the striking economic differences between the two nations in the Cold War?

Answer: The term "Cold War" refers to the bitter rivalry between the former Soviet Union and the United States between the end of World War II and the mid 1980s. The Cold War was characterized by a struggle between two nations who held fundamentally different political and economic ideologies. The fundamental economic differences between the two nations were the market-oriented capitalist system of the United States and the authoritative, centrally planned economy of the Soviet Union.

23.112: Identify some of the noted reasons why Poland has succeeded in its transition to the market system.

Moderate
Application
Page: 543

Answer: Poland's relative success in making the transition (from socialism to capitalism) has been the result of: the large number of small businesses that have been established, the flow of foreign direct investment into the economy, and the successful privatization of formerly state-owned businesses.

23.113: What was Austrian economist Friedreich Hayek's argument regarding repressive government? What are some of the arguments against Friedreich Hayek's thesis?

Moderate
Application
Page: 544

Answer: Friedreich Hayek's argued that a socialist economy and increased government intervention would lead to personal serfdom. He felt that personal and economic freedoms are inseparable and that the capitalist market system was most compatible with personal freedoms. Critics argue that strong government reforms and economic involvement are needed to prevent the rise of a totalitarian state. They believe that unregulated capitalism will lead to economic and political inequalities.

23.114: What is the central theme of Marxian analysis? Explain Marx's labor theory of value. How does Marx account for the use of capital resource in production? What is surplus value and why is it important in the Marxian prophecy regarding the future of capitalism?

Easy
Definition
Page: 545

Answer: Marx argues that the capitalist economic system is morally wrong because of its inherent exploitive tendencies and that it will inevitably fail. According to Marx, the value of a product depended exclusively upon the amount of labor embodied in its production. Products represent the physical embodiment of the labor needed to produce them. Marx considered capital to be the physical embodiment of past labor that was used to produce products. Thus, the capital resource contributes value by passing the past embodied labor to the final product. To Marx, surplus value represents the profits earned by the capitalist by paying workers less than the value of what they produce. Profit is value that is created by workers, but is unjustly "expropriated" by capitalists who own the means of production. It is not a reward for any productive activity; it is extracted by virtue of ownership. As a result, Marx prophesied that the workers would ultimately revolt and overthrow the market system.

23.115: Explain the most important difference between market capitalism and socialism.

Easy
Definition
Page: 544

Answer: A capitalist economic system is characterized by the private ownership of resources and the reliance upon the market to allocate resources into production and distribute finished output into consumption. Thus, product prices, wages, and other economic variables are market determined. In contrast, socialism relies upon various degrees of government ownership and controls of the productive resources. Centralized planning displaces the market mechanism in the allocation of resources into production and distribution of finished output into consumption.

23.116: Discuss Marxian's major criticisms of the market capitalist economic system.

Moderate
Multi
Page: 546

Answer: Marxian stated that the private ownership and control of resources by the capitalists would inevitably result in the exploitation of workers to ensure greater business surplus value or profits. Thus, he prophesied the increased miseration of workers, falling profits for capitalists, and an eventual worker revolt and revolution.

Moderate
Definition
Page: 546

23.117: Define Marxian labor theory of value.

Answer: The labor theory of value specifies that the value of a product depends upon the amount of labor embodied in the product's production. Only labor power is value-creating and capital is value-adding when it represents the physical embodiment of past labor which is then represented in the final product.

Easy
Definition
Page: 546

23.118: Discuss the Marxian theory of surplus value.

Answer: Marxian assumed that workers were paid a minimum subsistence wage under the capitalist economic system. However, during the full work day, workers would generate a level of output which embodied their labor value which exceeded their wages received. The difference between the value of what they produced and what they received was called surplus value. The capitalists consider it to be earned profit, but Marxian viewed it as the measure of exploitation under the capitalist system.

Moderate
Multi
Page: 548

23.119: Explain the difference between the economic policies of the former Soviet Union between 1928 and the 1980s and the transition in Russia today.

Answer: The economic policies between 1928 and the 1980s of the former Soviet Union emphasized centralized planning to displace the market process, rapid industrialization, and collective agriculture. For the most part, private ownership of resources was abolished and government planning determined all production and distribution decisions. Presently, Russia is committed to the policies of privatization and the transition to a market economy with widespread private ownership of resources.

Moderate
Multi
Page: 550

23.120: Define glasnost and perestroika and explain their impact upon contemporary Russia.

Answer: Glasnost represents reforms that led to the completely open discussion of political and economic issues in the former Soviet Union under the leadership of Mikhail Gorbachev. Perestroika represents new economic reforms and structures that led to reduced job security and the closing of cost inefficient state-owned and operated businesses.

Moderate
Multi
Page: 551

23.121: Identify the requirements that are necessary for Russia to proceed on the path towards a market-oriented economy.

Answer: To proceed successfully in its transition to a market capitalist economy system, Russia must be able to: stabilize its economy and reduce domestic inflation, permit the market determination of all product prices, reduce trade barriers to encourage greater multilateral trade, and develop supportive financial, insurance, and banking institutions that promote and foster private investment.

Moderate
Multi
Page: 555

23.122: In facilitating the transition from a centrally-planned to a market-oriented economy, explain the difference between the "shock therapy" versus "gradualism" approach.

Answer: The proponents of the "shock therapy" approach argue that the transition be aggressive, quick, direct, and simultaneously impact all economic variables. In contrast, the "gradualism" approach recommends moderate and sequential changes over time starting with the development of market institutions, the gradual decontrol of prices, and the limited privatization of only the most cost-efficient state-owned and operated businesses.

23.123: Describe the changes that have occurred in the Chinese economy during the past several decades.

Moderate
Multi
Page: 565

Answer: The early structure of the Chinese economic system was built on the Soviet-Stalinist model of forceful strong government controls and central economic planning. Between 1953 and 1957, the Chinese five-year plan focused on developing capital-intensive industries. In 1958, a new economic strategy, called the Great Leap Forward, was introduced which emphasized a shift from large-scale, capital-intensive industries to small-scale, labor-intensive industries and the elimination of material incentives. More recently, reforms have increasingly emphasized selective privatization, increased profit opportunities, and the continued introduction of free enterprise initiatives.

23.124: Describe the Japanese economy and the noted contributions to the nation's industrialization since the end of World War II.

Moderate
Multi
Page: 569

Answer: The Japanese economy is an example of free-market capitalism with a unique relationship between private enterprise and government. Japan has experienced an unprecedented rate of overall economic growth since the end of World War II which is a result of several conditions. Among them is the rate of domestic savings and an extremely high rate of domestic investment. In addition, other important reasons for rapid industrialization have included: the quality of the Japanese labor force, the successful development and adaptation of advanced technologies, and the policies of the Ministry of Trade and Industry to protect and support domestic industries in their export initiatives.